Law School Publications

Administrative Law Anthology
Thomas O. Sargentich

Administrative Law: Cases and Materials
Daniel J. Gifford

An Admiralty Law Anthology
Robert M. Jarvis

Alternative Dispute Resolution: Strategies for Law and Business
E. Wendy Trachte-Huber and Stephen K. Huber

American Legal Systems: A Resource and Reference Guide
Toni M. Fine

Analytic Jurisprudence Anthology
Anthony D'Amato

An Antitrust Anthology
Andrew I. Gavil

Appellate Advocacy: Principles and Practice, Second Edition
Ursula Bentele and Eve Cary

Basic Accounting Principles for Lawyers: With Present Value and Expected Value
C. Steven Bradford and Gary A. Ames

A Capital Punishment Anthology (and Electronic Caselaw Appendix)
Victor L. Streib

Cases and Problems in Criminal Law, Third Edition
Myron Moskovitz

The Citation Workbook: How to Beat the Citation Blues, Second Edition
Maria L. Ciampi, Rivka Widerman, and Vicki Lutz

Civil Procedure Anthology
David I. Levine, Donald L. Doernberg, and Melissa L. Nelken

Civil Procedure: Cases, Materials, and Questions, Second Edition
Richard D. Freer and Wendy Collins Perdue

Clinical Anthology: Readings for Live-Client Clinics
Alex J. Hurder, Frank S. Bloch, Susan L. Brooks, and Susan L. Kay

Commercial Transactions Series: Problems and Materials
Louis F. Del Duca, Egon Guttman, Alphonse M. Squillante, Fred H. Miller, Linda Rusch, and
  Peter Winship
> Vol. 1: Secured Transactions Under the UCC
> Vol. 2: Sales Under the UCC and the CISG
> Vol. 3: Negotiable Instruments Under the UCC and the CIBN

Communications Law: Media, Entertainment, and Regulation
Donald E. Lively, Allen S. Hammond, Blake D. Morant, and Russell L. Weaver

A Conflict-of-Laws Anthology
Gene R. Shreve

Constitutional Conflicts, Parts I & II
Derrick A. Bell, Jr.

A Constitutional Law Anthology, Second Edition
Michael J. Glennon, Donald E. Lively, Phoebe A. Haddon, Dorothy E. Roberts,
  and Russell L. Weaver

Constitutional Law: Cases, History, and Dialogues
Donald E. Lively, Phoebe A. Haddon, Dorothy E. Roberts, and Russell L. Weaver

The Constitutional Law of the European Union
James D. Dinnage and John F. Murphy

The Constitutional Law of the European Union: Documentary Supplement
James D. Dinnage and John F. Murphy

Constitutional Torts
Sheldon H. Nahmod, Michael L. Wells, and Thomas A. Eaton

A Contracts Anthology, Second Edition
Peter Linzer

Contracts: Contemporary Cases, Comments, and Problems
Michael L. Closen, Richard M. Perlmutter, and Jeffrey D. Wittenberg

Contract Law and Practice: Cases and Materials
Gerald E. Berendt, Michael L. Closen, Doris Estelle Long, Marie A. Monahan, Robert J. Nye, and John H. Scheid

A Corporate Law Anthology
Franklin A. Gevurtz

Corporate and White Collar Crime: An Anthology
Leonard Orland

A Criminal Law Anthology
Arnold H. Loewy

Criminal Law: Cases and Materials
Arnold H. Loewy

A Criminal Procedure Anthology
Silas J. Wasserstrom and Christie L. Snyder

Criminal Procedure: Arrest and Investigation
Arnold H. Loewy and Arthur B. LaFrance

Criminal Procedure: Trial and Sentencing
Arthur B. LaFrance and Arnold H. Loewy

Economic Regulation: Cases and Materials
Richard J. Pierce, Jr.

Elements of Law
Eva H. Hanks, Michael E. Herz, and Steven S. Nemerson

Ending It: Dispute Resolution in America
  Descriptions, Examples, Cases and Questions
Susan M. Leeson and Bryan M. Johnston

An Environmental Law Anthology
Robert L. Fischman, Maxine I. Lipeles, and Mark S. Squillace

Environmental Law Series
Jackson B. Battle, Robert L. Fischman, Maxine I. Lipeles, and Mark S. Squillace
      Vol. 1: Environmental Decisionmaking: NEPA and the Endangered Species Act,
            Second Edition
      Vol. 2: Water Pollution, Second Edition
      Vol. 3: Air Pollution, Second Edition
      Vol. 4: Hazardous Waste, Third Edition

Environmental Protection and Justice
  Readings and Commentary on Environmental Law and Practice
Kenneth A. Manaster

European Union Law Anthology
Karen V. Kole and Anthony D'Amato

An Evidence Anthology
Edward J. Imwinkelried and Glen Weissenberger

Federal Antitrust Law: Cases and Materials
Daniel J. Gifford and Leo J. Raskind

Federal Evidence Courtroom Manual
Glen Weissenberger

Federal Income Tax Anthology
Paul L. Caron, Karen C. Burke, and Grayson M.P. McCouch

Federal Rules of Civil Procedure, 1997-98 Edition
Publisher's Staff

Federal Rules of Evidence Rules, Legislative History, Commentary and Authority 1997-98 Edition
Glen Weissenberger

Federal Rules of Evidence Handbook, 1997-98 Edition
Publisher's Staff

Federal Wealth Transfer Tax Anthology
Paul L. Caron, Grayson M.P. McCouch, Karen C. Burke

First Amendment Anthology
Donald E. Lively, Dorothy E. Roberts, and Russell L. Weaver

International Environmental Law Anthology
Anthony D'Amato and Kirsten Engel

International Human Rights: Law, Policy, and Process, Second Edition
Frank C. Newman and David Weissbrodt

Selected International Human Rights Instruments and Bibliography For Research on International Human Rights Law, Second Edition
Frank C. Newman and David Weissbrodt

International Intellectual Property Anthology
Anthony D'Amato and Doris Estelle Long

International Law Anthology
Anthony D'Amato

International Law Coursebook
Anthony D'Amato

Introduction to the Study of Law: Cases and Materials
John Makdisi

Judicial Externships: The Clinic Inside the Courthouse
Rebecca A. Cochran

Justice and the Legal System: A Coursebook
Anthony D'Amato and Arthur J. Jacobson

A Land Use Anthology
Jon W. Bruce

Law and Economics Anthology
Kenneth G. Dau-Schmidt and Thomas S. Ulen

The Law of Disability Discrimination
Ruth Colker

ADA Handbook: Statutes, Regulations and Related Materials
Publisher's Staff

The Law of Modern Payment Systems and Notes, Second Edition
Fred H. Miller and Alvin C. Harrell

Lawyers and Fundamental Moral Responsibility
Daniel R. Coquillette

Microeconomic Predicates to Law and Economics
Mark Seidenfeld

Patients, Psychiatrists and Lawyers: Law and the Mental Health System, Second Edition
Raymond L. Spring, Roy B. Lacoursiere, and Glen Weissenberger

Preventive Law: Materials on a Non Adversarial Legal Process
Robert M. Hardaway

Principles of Evidence, Third Edition
Irving Younger, Michael Goldsmith, and David A. Sonenshein

Problems and Simulations in Evidence, Second Edition
Thomas F. Guernsey

A Products Liability Anthology
Anita Bernstein

Professional Responsibility Anthology
Thomas B. Metzloff

A Property Anthology, Second Edition
Richard H. Chused

Public Choice and Public Law: Readings and Commentary
Maxwell L. Stearns

The Regulation of Banking
   Cases and Materials on Depository Institutions and Their Regulators
Michael P. Malloy

Science in Evidence
D.H. Kaye

A Section 1983 Civil Rights Anthology
Sheldon H. Nahmod

Sports Law: Cases and Materials, Third Edition
Ray L. Yasser, James R. McCurdy, and C. Peter Goplerud

A Torts Anthology
Lawrence C. Levine, Julie A. Davies, and Edward J. Kionka

Trial Practice
Lawrence A. Dubin and Thomas F. Guernsey

Unincorporated Business Entities
Larry E. Ribstein

FORTHCOMING PUBLICATIONS

A Copyright Law Anthology: The Technology Frontier
Richard H. Chused

Environmental Law: Air Pollution, Third Edition
Mark S. Squillace and David R. Wooley

International Civil Procedure Anthology
David S. Clark and Anthony D'Amato

International Taxation: Cases, Materials, and Problems
Philip F. Postlewaite

Natural Resources: Cases and Materials
Barlow Burke, Jr.

Readings in Criminal Law
Russell L. Weaver, John M. Burkoff, Catherine Hancock, Alan Reed, and Peter Seago

FEDERAL WEALTH TRANSFER TAX ANTHOLOGY

FEDERAL WEALTH TRANSFER TAX ANTHOLOGY

PAUL L. CARON

Charles Hartsock Professor of Law
University of Cincinnati
College of Law

GRAYSON M.P. MCCOUCH

Professor of Law
University of Miami
School of Law

KAREN C. BURKE

Professor of Law
University of Minnesota
Law School

ANDERSON PUBLISHING CO.
CINCINNATI, OHIO

FEDERAL WEALTH TRANSFER TAX ANTHOLOGY
PAUL L. CARON, GRAYSON M.P. MCCOUCH, AND KAREN C. BURKE

© 1998 by Anderson Publishing Co.

Anderson Publishing Co.
2035 Reading Road / Cincinnati, Ohio 45202
800-582-7295 / e-mail andpubco@aol.com / Fax 513-562-5430
World Wide Web http://www.andersonpublishing.com

ISBN: 0-87084-280-3

DEDICATION

To Brian and Brian at Crossroads,
Minnie and Hanni

TABLE OF CONTENTS

PREFACE

This *Anthology* is designed to be used both as a source of supplemental readings in the estate and gift tax course and as a primary text in tax policy seminars. We hope the *Anthology* will enrich the estate and gift tax course by giving students the opportunity to explore in greater depth many of the subjects traditionally covered in that course (Parts II-VI), as well as to consider issues that often receive only cursory attention in the standard casebooks (Parts I, VII, and VIII). We believe that the issues discussed in Parts I (*Historical, Economic, and Reform Perspectives*), VII (*Integration*), and VIII (*Alternative Tax Systems*) are particularly suited for advanced study in tax policy seminars.

In preparing this *Anthology*, we have been impressed by the breadth and diversity of contemporary wealth transfer tax scholarship. In selecting the materials included in this book, we have tried to emphasize the classic writing in the field while at the same time including a sampling of recent tax scholarship. We urge users of this *Anthology* to forward to us comments and suggestions on matters of substance, style, and coverage in anticipation of subsequent editions.

We are grateful for the help we received from people at our respective law schools in the preparation of this *Anthology*. William McKee and Molly Mickley provided excellent research assistance. Sue Ann Campbell, Nora de la Garza, Cheryl DelVecchio, Mercy Hernandez, Joanne Manees, Connie Miller, and David Zopfi-Jordan provided enormous technical assistance in converting the original sources into the excerpts reprinted here. We also received financial assistance for this project from the faculty research funds at our respective institutions.

Paul L. Caron
University of Cincinnati
College of Law

Grayson M.P. McCouch
University of Miami
School of Law

Karen C. Burke
University of Minnesota
Law School

September, 1997

PART I:

INTRODUCTION TO THE
FEDERAL WEALTH TRANSFER TAXES

Although the three federal wealth transfer taxes (estate tax, gift tax, and genera-tion-skipping transfer tax) make only a modest contribution to federal tax revenues, they affect increasing numbers of affluent and wealthy Americans and have come to the forefront of public policy debates in recent years. This *Anthology* provides a grounding in some of the major theoretical debates that have animated the federal wealth transfer taxes since their enactment. Part One begins with a historical perspective on the federal wealth transfer taxes, and then explores some economic and reform issues surrounding these taxes as well as the persistent role of state law in this area.

A.   A Historical Perspective

This Subpart examines the historical forces that have shaped the federal wealth transfer taxes. Louis Eisenstein recounts the early history of the estate tax, and C. Low-ell Harriss discusses the origins of the gift tax. David M. Hudson continues the his-torical thread through the fundamental changes ushered in by the Tax Reform Act of 1976 and the Economic Recovery Tax Act of 1981. Edward A. Zelinsky offers another perspective on these historical trends, and the Staff of the Joint Committee on Taxa-tion provides current wealth transfer tax data and projections for the future. William S. Blatt argues that participants in the wealth transfer tax debate ignore the impact of public discourse on the shape of the taxes.

Louis Eisenstein, *The Rise and Decline of the Estate Tax*, 11 TAX L. REV. 223 (1956)*

Death taxes are ancient taxes. They were known to the Egyptians, as well as the Romans and Greeks. Even the complaints against them have a venerable pedigree. Pliny the Younger provides as good an example as any. He is among the earliest critics who have left us summaries of their complaints. Pliny eloquently argued that a tax on the shares of direct heirs "was an 'unnatural' tax, augmenting the grief and sorrow of the bereaved." Almost two thousand years

---

later the same argument was still being heard. For in 1898 Senator Allen forcefully inquired whether it was right "to stand with the widow and the children at the grave side of a dead father to collect a tax," and then he sympathetically referred to the widow "in weeds" and the children "in tears."

In criticism, too, the fashions change. Now the complaints are more sensitive to the laws of economics than to the distress of the survivors. Instead of picturesque allusions to weeds and tears, there are grave observations on such formidable subjects as savings, investments, and incentives. Many voices are heard, and all speak with assurance and authority. The words may vary, but the message seems always the same. We are solemnly informed, with a suitable air of gloom and despair, that our economic system is doomed unless the estate tax is entirely repealed or severely curtailed. We are dramatically reminded, so that we are properly alarmed, that Karl Marx was inclined to favor an estate tax. Here, also, the principle of guilt by association is complacently applied. This approach is less poignant than Pliny's but probably more effective. * * *

It is easy to assume, as too many do, that if there is so much smoke, there must surely be a fire. Whether all this consternation is justified I leave to others to say. I shall try to be modestly helpful in a less emotional area. The critics of the estate tax usually build on the premise that it functions with relentless and monotonous efficiency. It is the grim guillotine of wealth. I shall therefore examine the accuracy of this assumption. Is the premise as firm as the dismay which it seems to inspire? Obviously, in order to decide how well the estate tax is doing, we must first decide what it is supposed to do. And so my inquiry divides at once into two questions: first, what are the objectives which have been assigned to the estate tax; and second, how well does the tax achieve its ends? The answers which emerge should shed some relevant light on the fearful prophesies which the tax periodically provokes. Perhaps they may also suggest a change in our way of thinking about the tax.

I. A FRAGMENT OF HISTORY

If we guide ourselves by prevailing notions, the estate tax is animated by a single purpose—the confiscation of excessive accumulations of wealth. * * *

Evidently the estate tax is not regarded as a levy designed to produce revenue. This view of the tax easily implies certain conclusions. As long as the tax prevents estates from "piling up" too high, it presumably does all that can be expected of it. While the tax produces a modest revenue, the revenue is inevitably incidental to its assault upon aggregates of wealth. The tax can hardly appropriate property without gathering some revenue in the process. But its performance is not to be judged by the size of its fiscal haul. Though its yield may be small, it may still be effective.

This understanding of the tax usually satisfies those who applaud it and those who deplore it. The first group can always argue that it is immaterial whether the tax produces much revenue because revenue is not the purpose of the tax; the crux of the matter is that the tax breaks down hereditary estates, and this vital task is sufficient unto itself. On the other hand, the second group is able to argue that the relatively small yield reinforces its conviction that the tax is a pernicious levy; not only does the tax level wealth, but this evil is not even excusable on the ground of revenue. Both schools are equally loyal to the same error of which neither is aware. It may come as a surprise, but death taxes in the United States were devised to produce revenue. Indeed, I suspect that a good deal of the emphasis on the social objective of the tax, as distinguished from its fiscal objective, is skillfully contrived to keep its yield as low as possible. The reasoning is simple. Why collect more revenue through the estate tax if the tax is not really expected to raise revenue in the first place?

Though skeptics say that history teaches us nothing, at the very least it may be informative here. Death taxes, no less than other taxes, derived from a desire to obtain revenue. What was true abroad was equally true here. The first federal death tax appeared shortly after the Constitution was adopted. In 1797, amid deteriorating relations with France, Congress levied a stamp duty on legacies and intestate shares of personalty. The rates were mild. * * * Shares passing to the surviving spouse and descendants were exempt. When the crisis passed, the tax disappeared. It had been imposed solely for revenue, and revenue was no longer urgent.

Federal death duties reappeared during the Civil War. * * * Again Congress was wholly inspired by the revenue required for military exigencies. If any other motive was about, it was successfully concealed. Secretary of the Treasury Chase proposed a death tax as a means of financing the war. In Congress the tax was lauded as "a large source of revenue" that would "be most conveniently collected." After the war the death duties were discarded. Though they had not evoked any "widespread objection," they succumbed to the pleasing assumption that taxes must be reduced whenever a war ends.

Within two decades the scene changed. By the close of the century a death tax movement had emerged in response to the stresses and strains of the period. The movement was tenacious and seemed ominous. It irrevocably identified death duties with the social control of hereditary wealth. * * * A federal death tax assumed messianic proportions in the minds of those who wished to strike hard and deep. * * *

The propaganda for a death tax soon acquired the invaluable virtue of respectability. In 1889 Andrew Carnegie became a traitor to his class by joining the movement. At the time of his treason Carnegie was worth about $30 million, though he "was not one of the richest Americans." "Why," he asked, "should men leave great fortunes to their children? If this is done from affection, is it not misguided affection? Observation teaches that, generally speaking, it is not well for the children that they should be so burdened." The wealthy who are wise, he declared, should hesitate to provide more than "moderate sources of income" for wife and daughters, and "very moderate allowances indeed, if any, for the sons." The "thoughtful man" would just as soon leave to his son "a curse as the almighty dollar," for "the parent who leaves his son enormous wealth generally deadens the talents and energies of the son, and tempts him to lead a less useful and less worthy life than he otherwise would." In the light of his startling analysis Carnegie welcomed the "growing disposition to tax more and more heavily large estates left at death." It was "a cheering indication of the growth of a salutary change in public opinion." "Of all forms of taxation," he wrote, a progressive death duty "seems the wisest." He found it "difficult to set bounds to the share of a rich man's estate" which the government should appropriate. But he was sure that the tax should be graduated; that it should exempt "moderate sums" to dependents; that it should rise "rapidly as the amounts swell"; and that "of the millionaire's hoard" at least 50 per cent should be taken.

Yet Congress remained steadfast. Despite the continuing pressure, it refused to level hereditary wealth. Though it taxed inheritances in 1894 and 1898, its objective was simply the collection of revenue. The tax of 1898, like the prior ventures of 1797 and the Civil War, was prompted by military spending. As in those cases, when the emergency was gone, the tax passed away.

The persistent demand for a death tax produced only one concrete result. A federal toll on inheritance was now a tolerable method of taxing the wealthy for the support of the Government. But a tax which seeks revenue from the well-to-do is no more peculiarly regulatory than a tax on the not so well-to-do. The taxes of 1894 and 1898 were at best a feeble recognition of what has come to be known as ability to pay. The rate of 1894 was a flat two per cent, while the rate of 1898 barely moved, in the case of close kin and normal beneficiaries, from .75 per cent to 2.25 per cent. These rates scarcely reflected a determined desire to lay low large aggregates of wealth. Neither tax had any soaring ambition beyond revenue. * * *

Soon the situation became worse. The death tax movement penetrated into the White House. In the spring of 1906 Theodore Roosevelt made a proposal which others found appalling. He recommended "the adoption of some such scheme as that of a progressive tax on all fortunes, beyond a certain amount, either given in life or devised or bequeathed upon death to any individual—a tax so framed as to put it out of the power of the owner of one of these enormous fortunes to hand on more than a certain amount to any one individual." The tax would "be aimed merely at the inheritance or transmission in their entirety of those fortunes swollen beyond all healthy limits." * * *

* * *

In 1907 the President saw things more clearly and hence he was more analytical. He focused upon the essential conflict between inheritance of wealth and equality of opportunity. "A heavy progressive tax upon a very large fortune," he declared, "is in no way such a tax upon thrift or industry as a like tax would be on a small fortune. No advantage comes either to the country as a whole or to the individuals inheriting the money by permitting the transmission in their entirety of the enormous fortunes which would be affected by such a tax; and as an incident to its function of revenue raising, such a tax would help to preserve a measurable equality of opportunity for the people of the generations growing to manhood." * * *

By this time the movement for an inheritance tax to regulate hereditary wealth had made appreciable headway. * * * Congress, however, refused to be seduced. In 1909 and again in 1913 it disapproved of death taxes.

In three years, as war approached, the picture changed. Once more military appropriations induced Congress to impose a death duty, and once more the Congressional motif was the collection of required revenue, not the control of hereditary wealth. * * *

* * *

At this point I should pause to generalize. Although the estate tax rates pushed upward for a fleeting period, they made no discernible attempt to level inherited wealth. The tax was initially imposed in response to the need for revenue, and the rates increased as the need increased. The purpose of Congress did not embrace the destruction of large fortunes. * * *

We are now on the threshold of the Mellon era in estate taxation. Secretary of the Treasury Mellon was firmly persuaded that the estate tax would eventually subvert the American economy. * * * As things were going, it might be "only two or three generations until private ownership of property would cease to exist." The Secretary vigorously denied that there was any "social necessity for breaking up large fortunes in this country." And so he set about to remove or reduce the estate tax before disaster overtook us. Very likely he would have succeeded but for the remarkable resistance of a few stubborn Congressmen. Though the tax was finally saved, the rates were thoroughly cut.

* * *

In 1931 a strange thing happened. Secretary Mellon revised his views on the estate tax as the Great Depression intensified the need for revenue. Torn between a dislike for deficits and a dislike for the tax, he recommended an increase in rates. * * * A new and better gift tax was also imposed.

I have come to the end of the Mellon era. Those years were a bleak period for the estate tax, and it barely survived the efforts to repeal it. The prevailing philosophy ordained that any federal estate tax, whether high or low, was a grave threat to our economic welfare. * * *

But for present purposes another development was more important. When the estate tax was finally revived at the end of this dismal period, the controlling motivation was a desire to obtain revenue and not a desire to break down estates. * * *

With the Roosevelt Administration the estate tax entered a new phase. The levelling of hereditary fortunes was formally approved as one of its objectives. * * *

In 1935 the accent on levelling became bolder. On June 19th of that year the President recommended, in addition to the estate tax, "an inheritance, succession, and legacy tax in respect to all very large amounts received by any one legatee or beneficiary." His message briefly and simply justified progressive death taxes as a means of regulating the wealth of the few for the benefit of the many. "The transmission from generation to generation of vast fortunes by will, inheritance, or gift is not consistent with the ideals and sentiments of the American people." "The desire to provide security for one's self and one's family is natural and wholesome," he declared, "but it is adequately served by a reasonable inheritance. Great accumulations of wealth can not be justified on the basis of personal and family security. In the last analysis such accumulations amount to the perpetuation of great and undesirable concentration of control in a relatively few individuals over the employment and welfare of many, many others." In short, "inherited economic power is as inconsistent with the ideals of this generation as inherited political power was inconsistent with the ideals of the generation which established our Government."

Congress did not pursue the route proposed by the President. Instead, it simply increased the rates of the estate tax. * * *

After the 1935 Act the emphasis on levelling died away. There were only two more changes in rates, and neither was stimulated by the philosophy of the President. Once again Congress was exclusively concerned with revenue for military purposes. * * *

What illumination do we derive from this hasty glance at history? The answer seems rather clear. In the quarter-century between 1916 and 1941 the estate tax passed through several stages. For our purposes they may be counted as four. The first stage ended with the 1921 Act. It was a period of rising rates followed by a relapse among the smaller estates. The governing objective was plainly revenue. The second stage was the dismal Mellon era. It began with the 1924 Act and closed with the 1932 Act. In that unfortunate period the tax was almost destroyed and then revitalized as a source of revenue. The third stage started with the 1934 Act and was continued by the 1935 Act. Under these two Acts the progression sharpened as the rates climbed from 45 per cent to 70 per cent. The dramatic emphasis was on levelling, but the continuing need for revenue in the face of deficits was also effective. The fourth stage was marked by the 1940 and 1941 Acts. The larger burdens which they imposed derived entirely from the quest for revenue.

At best, then, the social objective of the estate tax was prominent only in 1934 and 1935. Yet even in those years the deliberate destruction of "great accumulations of wealth" was more verbal than actual. * * *

* * *

Neither the 1934 Act nor the 1935 Act disturbs my conclusion that the estate tax has been primarily imposed for revenue. I am not unaware that the tax has also helped to redistribute wealth. But any progressive levy on income or wealth will have this effect. Nor do I forget that the desire to control accumulations significantly contributed to the development of the tax. Undoubtedly that objective infiltrated into its rate structure. Still the fact remains that the growth of the tax responded more to the stimulus of revenue than to eloquent exhortations for the dismantling of estates.

* * *

III. A FINAL APPRAISAL

It would be pleasant to end on a note of modest optimism. Unfortunately I am considerably restrained by my own analysis. The estate tax, I believe, is in a period of decline. Unlike its predicament in the Mellon era, the present problem is not so much sudden death as chronic illness. If the past is a guide to the future, the tax should continue to ail for some time. Very few seem to be concerned about its condition, and I see little help on the horizon. It scarcely evokes any friendly interest in Congress, apart from the hostility that it normally arouses as a capital levy which is constitutionally excusable. * * *

* * *

Yet apart from its limited base, it is hard to devise a better tax than a death tax. Estates represent ability to pay. And as they are mere windfalls to the beneficiaries, they should be taxed more heavily than any other kind of acquisition. * * *

The argument will, of course, be made that it is foolish to seek more revenue from the estate tax, since the additional yield will be relatively small. While this point is often made, it is always irrelevant. One may just as cogently contend that various income tax loopholes should be ignored because they benefit only a few and hence the revenue loss is minor. The question is not whether the estate tax will produce much more or little more when compared with other taxes. The question is whether estates constitute available sources of revenue which are insufficiently tapped. Congress should seek its revenue wherever it may appropriately find it.

The argument is too facile for another reason. Even if Congress is uninterested in obtaining more revenue, it should still enlarge the yield of the estate tax. The additional revenue would compensate for tax reductions which Congress might like to make elsewhere. * * *

The income tax brings to light another role for the estate tax. It is no secret that the income tax base is riddled with loopholes which I need not catalogue. * * *

In these circumstances, perhaps the only practical solution is a vigorously effective estate tax. Congress' immoderate generosity would cease at death, and the estate tax would serve as a delayed income tax. Death taxes have often been justified as compensatory levies on those who escape their share of the fiscal burden during life. Though this view is not without its defects, it still contains a hard core of truth. If the income tax fails to do its job, only the estate tax can assure an eventual day of reckoning.

Finally, the estate tax should be made a true leveller of wealth beyond "a reasonable inheritance" for the "security" of the decedent's family. I need not rehearse the old and familiar arguments which sustain this conclusion. It seems sufficient to say that an economic system which prides itself on equality of opportunity should level "unreasonable" estates without compunction. * * *

Obviously, a system of private enterprise presupposes disparities in wealth; and inequality of property among parents engenders inequality of opportunity among children. To that extent we are committed to less than full equivalence of opportunity. But it does not follow that inequality justifies much more inequality. In other words, large differences in wealth do not inevitably imply the same large differences in inherited wealth. For that matter, inheritance of any kind is neither a necessary nor inherent attribute of private property. It is not impossible to have individual ownership without devolution by will or intestacy. However, I am not in the least inclined to argue for the abolition of inheritance. My position is a good deal milder. In my view, inheritance exhausts its useful purpose once it provides for the comfort of the surviving spouse and prepares the offspring to live by their own exertions.

Many years ago John Stuart Mill made a proposal which we would do well to borrow and revise. The estate tax should fix a limit on "what anyone may acquire by the mere favour of others without any exercise of his faculties." If "he desires any further accession of fortune, he shall work for it." Or in Theodore Roosevelt's exuberant language, he should "show the stuff that is in him when compared with his fellows." When inheritance does much more, it gravely and inexcusably augments inequality of opportunity. It then becomes hereditary economic power, which is no more tenable than hereditary political power. As Roger Babson so succinctly put it, "I do not see why the control of ten or twenty thousand men should descend by inheritance through the death of some manufacturer, any more than the control of a city or a State should pass on to the son of a mayor or a governor." If we genuinely believe in a substantial equality of opportunity, then we should cheerfully desire an estate tax which truly levels. We cannot have one unless we also have the other.

* * *

NOTE

Have subsequent events borne out Eisenstein's view that the estate tax was in "a period of decline" and would "continue to ail for some time"? Would the argument for a "vigorously effective estate tax" be strengthened or weakened if Congress were to enact fundamental income tax reform, for example by adopting a "flat tax"? We return to the social desirability of curtailing inheritance in Subpart C, *infra*. For further discussion of the early history of the estate tax, see Barry W. Johnson & Martha Britton Eller, *Federal Taxation of Inheritance and Wealth Transfers, in* INHERITANCE AND WEALTH IN AMERICA (Robert K. Miller Jr. & Stephen J. McNamee eds., 1997).

C. Lowell Harriss, *Legislative History of Federal Gift Taxation*, 18 TAXES 531 (1940)*

The purpose of this paper is to sketch briefly the legislative history lying behind the federal taxation of gifts. * * * In the earlier period, it should be noted, Congress faced the fundamental decisions, primarily whether there were to be federal income and death taxes. Only after having made these basic decisions did Congress need [to] face problems of refinement and protection, the problems with which the gift tax is primarily associated.

FROM THE CIVIL WAR TO THE WILSON ADMINISTRATION

During the Civil War, Congress enacted both income and death taxes. * * *

The death taxes covered transfers to take effect at death. The legacy tax made no mention of any other type of *inter vivos* gifts, but an interesting provision appears in the act of 1864 taxing succession to real estate. It reads:

> That if any person shall, by deed of gift or other assurance of title, made without valuable and adequate consideration, and purporting to vest the estate

---

    *   Reproduced with permission from *CCH TAXES—The Tax Magazine* published and copyrighted by CCH INCORPORATED, 2700 Lake Crook Road, Riverwoods, IL 60015.

> either immediately or in the future, whether or not accompanied by the
> possession, convey any real estate to any person, such disposition shall be
> held and taken to confer upon the grantee a succession within the meaning of
> this act.

This wording is so broad as to constitute virtually a tax on gifts of real estate. In the brief debates no references seem to have been made to gifts or to any problem that might arise with respect to them. Peace brought quiet repeal.

A generation later the income tax of 1894 was passed; it included as subject to tax all property received by gift or inheritance. * * * The whole act, however, was declared unconstitutional without any specific statement by the Court as to whether gifts might constitutionally be taxed as "income."

When Congress was seeking revenue for the Spanish-American war, the House defeated attempts to reenact the income tax of 1894 (as a war measure), but the Senate Finance Committee added a legacy and succession tax to the House bill. The provisions followed closely those of the Civil War legacy tax act of 1864, providing that only gifts to take effect at death were to be taxed. The brief debates passed over the problem of gifts. Peace was again followed by repeal although complicated litigation regarding gifts taking effect at death kept the act in court for many years.

FROM 1913 TO 1924

Gradually, as part of the liberal movement of the first decade of the century, popular discussion of inheritance and income taxation brought results, more states passed death taxes, the income tax amendment was ratified, and a federal income tax was enacted in 1913. The original draft was silent regarding gifts, but a Senate amendment, accepted without extended debate, provided specifically that the gains on, or profit from, but not the value of, property acquired by gift were to be taxed. * * *

The first federal estate tax was enacted in 1916. * * *

* * *

FROM 1924 TO 1932

By 1924 general tax revision was again an issue. In the House Committee hearings [Representative] Ramseyer vigorously defended high death taxes, urged adoption of a gift tax, and called upon the committee to get data on the extent of "evasion" by gifts from the Treasury. * * *

[Treasury Secretary] Mellon opposed the principle of the death tax, argued that it was unconstitutional, and urged its reservation for war emergencies. He opposed the gift tax, saying,

> This tax also is a tax on capital, the proceeds of which do not go into capital,
> and, therefore, work a destruction of the total capital of the country. Any
> annual tax on gifts is susceptible of evasion by spreading the gifts over a
> period of years. It will mean practically nothing by way of revenue to the
> Government. It will be extremely difficult to detect and enforce. It has a most
> peculiar incidence, unlike any other tax that I know of, the one who gives
> pays the tax, and not the one who receives. * * *

* * *

As finally reported and passed without debate, the [1924 Act] contained a gift tax with rates ranging from 1 per cent on $50,000, 2 per cent on $50,000 to $100,000, up to 40 per cent on that part of gifts in any one year over $10,000,000. An annual exemption of $50,000 plus exemption of the first $500 of any gifts to any individual during the year was provided. * * *

In signing the law, President Coolidge said,

> The bill raises the estate tax to 40 per cent. As a concomitant is added a gift tax which is a further invasion of the rights of the citizen, both unusual in nature and of doubtful legality.

Mellon wrote, "The attention of Congress should be directed principally to the excessive surtax rates and the confiscatory estate tax rates. The gift tax is unworkable and unduly hampers legitimate business." He said that it was perhaps unconstitutional and that it illustrated the futility of trying to prevent avoidance of excessive rates without penalizing legitimate transactions. "Something is wrong with our tax policy," he concluded, "if legislation such as this is necessary to make the collection of revenue effective." * * *

* * *

* * * Two years later, after a campaign against federal gift and death taxation run by a few persons but financed by several wealthy individuals and large corporations, Congress with administration approval passed a tax bill, reducing the income tax, removing the gift tax, but, in spite of the administration, keeping the estate tax though with lower rates * * * . The contests were hard-fought. The protagonists divided along the lines of group economic interest, but they were able to identify the interests of the groups they represented with the national interest.

[FROM 1932 TO 1939]

When the depression cut the federal revenue and increased the demands on the government, the Hoover Administration reversed the Republican policy of the twenties and supported a gift tax. This was done partly on the grounds that it was necessary to protect the estate tax without much explicit attention to protecting the income tax and partly on the grounds that present revenue needs could be met in part by setting a differential between the gift tax and the estate tax which would encourage immediate gifts and thus anticipate estate tax revenue. Except for some debate on the reason for this rate differential, there was almost no consideration in Congress of the specific features of the act. The law as passed was the work of the committees and their draftsmen, not the work of the whole of Congress. There is no evidence that even important details of the bill received the studied attention of Congress. * * * In less than ten years the gift tax ceased being one of the most controversial parts of the tax system and became widely accepted as necessary. There is as yet little evidence of, and perhaps little reason for, any general public interest in the gift tax or understanding of what is involved.

NOTE

Did the early gift tax adequately "prevent evasion of the estate tax"? Does the current gift tax? Is the gift tax still "widely accepted as necessary"?

David M. Hudson, *Tax Policy and the Federal Taxation of the Transfer of Wealth*, 19 WILLAMETTE L. REV. 1 (1983)*

* * *

The United States entered World War II with estate and gift taxes firmly entrenched. It remained only for Congress to turn the spigot to increase the flow of revenue when desired. This Congress did in 1940, 1941, and 1942. When the war ended, modifications were made that reduced the revenue collected from the transfer taxes, but there was no significant effort to repeal them. From the late 1940s until 1976, a variety of amendments were adopted to fine-tune the transfer taxes, but no major modifications were made to the overall scheme to affect either their role as a source of revenue[130] or as instruments to modify the social structure.

The Tax Reform Act of 1976 brought major changes to the overall structure of the federal taxation of the transfer of wealth. One of the most significant features of the Act was the replacement of dual rate schedules with a single, unified one, accompanied by a unified credit in lieu of the previously allowable separate gift and estate tax exemptions. The new rate schedule and unified credit scheme, compared to the old estate tax provisions, would impose a slightly lower burden on taxable estates of less than $1.25 million, slightly higher on taxable estates from $1.25 to $9.5 million, and slightly lower on those in excess of $9.5 million. It was estimated that the revenue generated by the estate and gift taxes would decrease by slightly more than $4 billion over the five years through 1981 as a consequence of these changes in the law.

* * *

The other major innovation of the 1976 Act was the enactment of an entirely new tax to be imposed on certain "generation-skipping transfers" for the avowed purpose of imposing a transfer tax at least once every generation as property came to be enjoyed by successive generations. With only the estate and gift taxes in effect, it was possible to transfer property in trust, providing for a life-estate to a grandchild for example, with the remainder to great-grandchild. There would perhaps be estate or gift tax liability upon the creation of the trust, but because there was no transfer of either property or any interest in property upon the death of the grandchild, no further transfer tax would be incurred. The new tax was designed to backstop the estate and gift taxes in such a situation by imposing a transfer tax upon the death of the grandchild: a transfer tax calculated to approximate the tax that would have been incurred if the property had been transferred outright to grandchild, and upon her death, again transferred outright to the great-grandchild. The amount of tax was to be computed with the same rate schedule used for estate and gift taxes, at the marginal rate that would have been applicable if the value of the property in the trust corpus had been included in the grandchild's gross estate. Liability for payment of the tax would not be imposed on the grandchild's estate, however, but upon the trustee of the trust. Funds for payment of the tax would presumably come from trust assets.

[A more] recent legislative chapter in the history of the federal taxation of the transfer of wealth was written by Congress in the Economic Recovery Tax Act of 1981. The two major modifications made were to remove the dollar limitations of the marital deductions in both the

---

[130]   The revenue produced by the estate and gift taxes hovered around 2% of the total internal revenue receipts from 1948 through 1975, dipping down to 1.279% in 1953 and bobbing up to 2.616% in 1972. S. SURREY, W. WARREN, P. MCDANIEL & H. GUTMAN, FEDERAL WEALTH TRANSFER TAXATION 61-62 (1977).

estate and gift taxes, and to alter the incidence of the wealth transfer taxes by concurrent increases in the unified credits and decreases in maximum marginal rates.

The unlimited marital deduction was enacted to further the tax policy concept that a husband and wife is the appropriate unit to be subject to taxation, rather than the two individuals. * * *

* * *

* * * Residents of community property and common law jurisdictions are now treated equally, for the unlimited marital deductions are applicable to community property as well as separate property. The result is that there is no transfer tax consequence to the transfer of wealth within the husband/wife unit. * * *

Another subject of change in the 1981 Act, with more drastic economic and social consequences, was the incidence of the transfer taxes. * * *

The transfer tax threshold was raised by increasing the unified credit from $47,000 for transfers subject to tax in 1981 to $192,800 in 1987 and thereafter—an increase of more than 400%. The unified credit has the effect of permitting wealth to be transferred free of tax. The 1981 credit would shelter some $175,625 of transferred wealth; by 1987, the figure would rise to $600,000. * * *

The second change affecting the incidence of the transfer taxes was made to the maximum marginal rate. The 1976 Act had lowered the top marginal rate from seventy-seven percent (on a taxable estate in excess of $10 million) to seventy percent (on taxable transfers of more than $5 million). The 1981 Act reduces this to a maximum rate of fifty percent (on taxable transfers over $2.5 million) * * *

* * * During the spring of 1981, the Senate Finance Committee had considered legislation passed by the House calling for a variety of amendments to the income tax as well as the estate and gift tax provisions of the Code. On July 6, 1981, the Senate Finance Committee approved the House bill with a substitute amendment—the Economic Recovery Tax Act of 1981—accompanied by a Report of the Committee.[159] The Senate, with a Republican majority, had approved a version which included the increase in the unified credit, but did not include a provision for lowering the maximum marginal rate. Explanation for the changes to the unified credit was:

> Historically, one of the principal reasons for estate and gift taxes was to break up large concentrations of wealth. . . . However, inflation has increased the dollar value of property and, therefore, the transfer tax burdens, without increasing real wealth.
>
> The Committee believes that the unified credit should be increased to offset the effects of inflation and to provide estate and gift tax relief to smaller estates, especially those which consist of family businesses.[160]

Meanwhile, in the House (which had a Democratic majority, but was not "controlled by the Democrats"), members of the Ways and Means Committee prepared a Report to accompany legislation which not only provided for an increase in the unified credits, but also a reduction in the maximum marginal rate. The Committee Report explained the latter change as follows:

---

[159]   S. REP. No. 144, 97th Cong., 1st Sess., *reprinted in* 1981 U.S. CODE CONG. & AD. NEWS 105, 108.

[160]   *Id.* at 124, U.S. CODE CONG. & AD. NEWS at 226.

Despite the substantial increase in the unified credit and the more liberal deferred payment provisions of the committee bill, the present estate and gift tax rates could result in more estate and gift taxes on highly successful closely-held and family businesses than their owners could afford without disposing of the businesses. In order to help prevent forced sales of closely-held and family businesses from occurring in order to pay estate and gift taxes, the committee believes that the maximum rates of estate and gift taxes should be reduced from 70% to 50%. In addition, the committee believes that a maximum estate and gift tax rate of 50% is consistent with the committee's decision to reduce the maximum rate of income taxes to 50%.[162]

* * *

The inconsistent perception of one of the objectives of the transfer taxes—to break up large concentrations of wealth—and the appropriateness of a marginal rate able to accomplish that objective is one which has plagued transfer taxes through the years. In an examination of the estate and gift taxes written in 1956, it was noted that of the two primary objectives of the transfer taxes, revenue raising and wealth redistribution, the latter was prominent only in 1934 and 1935.[164] Even so, the legislation enacted in those two years was not consistent in its attack on large accumulations of wealth because the rates of progression in the tax tables tapered off so that "[a]s the hereditary fortune became larger the progressive impact became softer."[165]

The same observation is still accurate today with regard to the rate schedule as amended in 1981. * * *

The impact of the unified credit on the marginal rates should not be ignored: when the transfers that the credit shelters are considered, the progressiveness of the rate table virtually disappears. The unified credit effectively reduces to zero the rate of tax on transfers of wealth that generate a precredit tax liability within the limits of the credit. In 1987, the unified credit will reach $192,800, the amount of tax imposed at a marginal rate of thirty-seven percent on a taxable transfer of $600,000. The lowest rate of transfer tax resulting in a transfer tax liability is thus thirty-seven percent * * * . Therefore, the progression of marginal rates creeps upward by only thirteen percentage points, from thirty-seven percent to fifty percent * * *

* * *

In summary, the history of the transfer taxes in this country demonstrates their primary function has been to produce revenue; their social objective of redistributing wealth has been hortatory, at best. The newly enacted amendments, which increase the unified credits and which reduce the marginal rates, have crippled the revenue producing function. In addition, the wealth redistribution goal seems to have been abandoned with the adoption of a rate structure which reaches an absolute maximum of fifty percent.

* * *

---

[162]   H.R. Rep. No. 201, 97th Cong., lst Sess. 156 (1981).

[164]   Eisenstein, *The Rise and Decline of the Estate Tax,* 11 Tax L. Rev. 223, 237 (1956).

[165]   *Id.*

NOTE

Some commentators argued that the 1981 Act's unlimited marital deduction and increase in the unified credit foreshadowed the eventual abolition of the federal wealth transfer taxes. *See* Subpart C, *infra*. In contrast, the following excerpt argues that the 1981 amendments actually made further changes in the estate and gift taxes "less likely." Do developments in the intervening years vindicate one or the other of these views?

Edward A. Zelinsky, *The Estate and Gift Tax Changes of 1981: A Brief Essay on Historical Perspective*, 60 N.C. L. Rev. 821 (1982)*

I. INTRODUCTION

The future of federal estate and gift taxation has become the subject of intense political and academic debate in recent years. * * *

As part of the Economic Recovery Tax Act of 1981 (ERTA), the Ninety-seventh Congress made four major changes in the federal transfer taxes. First, the annual gift tax exclusion was increased from $3,000 per donee to $10,000 per donee. Second, Congress adopted an unlimited marital deduction, removing all restrictions on the amount a taxpayer may give or bequeath to a surviving spouse free of federal transfer taxes. Third, the unified credit available to each taxpayer has been scheduled for increases over a five-year period, culminating in 1987 in an effective exemption from the federal estate tax of all taxable estates valued at less than $600,000. Finally, for taxable estates over $2,500,000, the maximum estate tax rate will be reduced over a three-year period, from seventy percent to fifty percent.

To one with even a cursory knowledge of the federal estate and gift levies, these changes appear to reduce radically the scope of transfer taxation by the federal government. For many supporters of the 1981 alterations, these changes represent the first step in an effort to abolish the federal estate and gift taxes altogether.

As part of the current debate about federal transfer taxation, an important historical observation must be made about the estate and gift tax changes adopted by the Ninety-seventh Congress: in the context of the sixty-five-year history of the federal estate tax, the 1981 changes, while significant, are not without precedent. The contemporary effort to abolish federal transfer taxation properly can trace its origins to the early part of this century. Continuously since then, there have been opponents of federal estate and gift taxation. They have consistently argued, with varying degrees of success, that federal transfer taxation is unfair, that it destroys family enterprises and that it creates disincentives for savings and investment. Opponents of the federal estate and gift levies at times have occupied positions of influence in the federal government and have succeeded in mitigating the perceived harshness of the federal transfer taxes. We are now in such a phase: the estate and gift taxes are being restricted, their coverage lessened and their impact reduced.

Some opponents of the federal estate and gift taxes believe that the 1981 changes make repeal of these taxes inevitable. Some supporters of federal transfer taxation fear that this may

---

be correct. I suggest that both sides be more circumspect. The estate and gift tax changes made by the Ninety-seventh Congress are not as revolutionary as either their sponsors or their opponents would have us believe. In some respects the 1981 changes actually make further alterations of the estate and gift taxes less likely.

* * *

II. THE ANNUAL EXCLUSION

The annual gift tax exclusion allows each taxpayer to give to others relatively small amounts on a yearly basis without transfer tax consequences. There is no limit to the number of donees with respect to which a taxpayer may utilize the annual exclusion or to the number of years in which the exclusion may be used. A grandfather, for example, every year may give money qualifying for the annual exclusion to each of his grandchildren regardless of their number.

Until 1982 the exclusion permitted each taxpayer to give up to $3,000 per donee, free of all federal gift tax. The $3,000 annual exclusion, established in 1942, was designed to remove from the purview of the gift tax routine conveyances for weddings, holiday presents and other transfers "of relatively small amounts." In 1942 an exclusion of $3,000 per donee may have satisfied this purpose admirably. In that year annual board and room fees at Yale College were approximately $500. In the absence of the annual exclusion, the payment by a parent of this amount would have been a taxable gift. Thus, in its time the $3,000 exclusion guaranteed that the educational and similar payments by a typical professional family to or on behalf of its children had no gift tax implications.

If the $3,000 figure was satisfactory for this purpose in 1942, it obviously was outdated in 1981. In that year, annual board and room at Yale College cost $3,190. Technically, the payment of that amount by a parent in 1981 was a gift to the extent of $190. Expenditures for books, transportation and clothing, to continue the example, constituted [additional] gifts.

As a practical matter the Internal Revenue Service (IRS) rarely has assessed gift taxes for educational or similar routine transfers. Nevertheless, such transfers technically are gifts for purposes of the federal gift tax. The increase of the annual exclusion from $3,000 per donee to $10,000 per donee thus may be viewed as an updating of the 1942 figure to reflect current prices and living standards.

There is yet another sense in which the institution of a $10,000 annual exclusion is less revolutionary than first appears. Historically, the federal gift tax has been a junior partner of the estate tax—and a very junior partner at that. Until 1976 the gift tax rates were substantially lower than the estate tax rates. Moreover, prior to 1976 the federal estate tax rates were calculated without regard to a decedent's lifetime gifts. A wealthy individual could make gifts during his life, pay a relatively small gift tax to the federal government and thereby remove property from his estate. Thus, the gift levy, conceived as a complement to the estate tax, became a back route around the estate levy. Before 1976 lifetime gifts were a common technique for the avoidance of federal estate taxes.

In 1976 Congress strengthened the gift tax significantly. The gift tax rates were made equal to those of the federal estate tax. More important, the estate tax rates were restructured so that an individual's inter vivos transfers, to the extent not qualifying for the annual exclusion, increase the federal tax subsequently payable on his estate. The effect of the 1976 changes was to diminish substantially the taxes avoidable through lifetime transfers.

The Ninety-seventh Congress, through the increase of the annual exclusion, has restored the tax advantages of lifetime gifts to a significant extent. The estate and gift tax rates remain as adopted in 1976. However, the expansion of the annual exclusion allows a taxpayer and spouse to remove substantial amounts from their estates without incurring a federal gift tax and without increasing the estate tax ultimately due on their estates. Starting in 1982 a married couple may give $20,000 per year to each of their children, or a grandmother and grandfather may give $20,000 per year to each of their grandchildren. Over the course of several years, systematic gifts on this order can remove substantial amounts from the donor's taxable estate.

In short, the historical significance of the annual exclusion depends upon the base from which the increase is viewed. In comparison to the situation that prevailed from 1976 to 1981, the increase of the annual exclusion is indeed a significant change, restoring at least partially the tax advantages of inter vivos gifts. From the perspective of the years 1943 through 1976, the increase of the annual exclusion appears to be a return to the junior status that the gift tax enjoyed during those years and a restoration of the tax advantages of inter vivos transfers. From the perspective of 1982, the increase of the annual exclusion looks like an overdue adjustment for inflation between 1942 and 1981.

III. THE UNLIMITED MARITAL DEDUCTION

The original purpose of the estate tax marital deduction was to equalize the treatment of surviving spouses in common-law property states with the estate tax treatment of widows and widowers residing in community property jurisdictions. From this perspective the unlimited marital deduction adopted by the Ninety-seventh Congress is indeed a revolutionary development. Today, the marital deduction no longer ensures a widow in a common-law jurisdiction, the same estate tax burden as her community property counterpart. Rather, the marital deduction guarantees that neither need confront anything resembling a federal estate tax.

* * *

It must be remembered that the marital deduction does not forgive federal estate taxes: it generally postpones them until the subsequent death of the surviving spouse. A bequest or devise to a surviving spouse usually qualifies for the marital deduction only if such bequest or devise takes a form that ensures that the property bequeathed or devised will be taxed on the subsequent death of the surviving spouse.

The deferral of tax until the death of the surviving spouse is, of course, economically advantageous from the taxpayer's perspective. If the estate of the surviving spouse is in a lower estate tax bracket than the estate of the first spouse to die, the marital deduction is beneficial to the ultimate recipients of the property eligible for the marital deduction.

As a general rule, however, the marital deduction does not remove property from the purview of the federal estate tax but rather shifts taxation from the time of the first spouse's demise to the subsequent death of the surviving spouse. Insofar as the marital deduction affects the timing of taxability rather than [taxability] itself, removing limits from the deduction is less than revolutionary.

* * *

IV. THE INCREASE OF THE UNIFIED CREDIT AND THE REDUCTION OF THE ESTATE TAX RATES

The increase of the unified credit and the reduction of the maximum federal estate tax rates force us to confront the fundamental question of federal transfer taxation: how extensive ought to be the coverage and impact of the federal estate levy?

The unified credit is today the means by which Congress exempts the bulk of estates from the federal estate tax. In 1981 the unified credit ensured that only taxable estates in excess of $175,625 paid federal estate taxes. By virtue of the actions of the Ninety-seventh Congress, increases in the unified credit gradually will enlarge the size of the maximum estate exempt from federal tax: by 1987, because of the unified credit, taxable estates of less than $600,000 will pay no federal transfer taxes.

The Ninety-seventh Congress also reduced significantly the rates for estates exceeding $2,500,000. Prior to the Economic Recovery Tax Act of 1981, taxable estates over $2,500,000 were taxed at marginal rates from fifty-three percent to seventy percent. By 1985 the maximum rate will have been reduced for such estates to fifty percent.

An important preliminary observation is that we do not know the value of the 1987 unified credit in terms of 1982 dollars. If the rate of inflation is zero between now and 1987, the ultimate increase of the unified credit will exempt from federal taxation estates that are in real terms almost three and one-half times greater than the largest exempt estate in 1981. On the other hand, if inflation averages ten percent annually between now and 1987, the ultimate unified credit will immunize from the federal estate levy estates that are, in real terms, approximately twice the size of the largest exempt estate in 1981. Thus, while the scheduled increase of the unified credit is substantial, the magnitude of that increase in real terms is something that we probably will not know until 1987.

* * *

Historically, the opponents and proponents of federal estate taxation have fought over the proper coverage and rates of the tax. Each side at different times has exerted the upper hand. Those who would expand the coverage and impact of the tax have had an important but silent ally, inflation. Prior to 1977 inflation subjected to federal transfer taxation many previously-exempt estates because the rates and exemptions of the tax had not been altered between 1942 and 1976.

The history of the tax, however, is not one-sided. During the 1920s opponents of the estate tax managed to restrict its coverage to a significant degree. At one point they succeeded in abolishing the gift tax altogether. Only in 1932 did proponents of federal estate taxation establish rates of any significance.

In short, the increase of the unified credit looks different depending upon the base year from which one looks. In retrospect, 1977 was something of a high water mark. Over seven percent of all estates paid federal estate tax in that year; the coverage of the federal estate tax has never been broader. If one measures the unified credit adopted by the Ninety-seventh Congress against this standard, one indeed would conclude that the scope of the federal estate tax has been restricted significantly.

Let us suppose, however, that the relevant year for comparison is 1981, a year in which it is estimated that under three percent of all decedents' estates incurred federal estate tax liability. Against this background the unified credit adopted by the Ninety-seventh Congress appears to be a refinement of the actions of the Ninety-fourth Congress, the Congress that introduced the unified credit and thereby reduced the scope of the federal estate tax from its high point in 1977. And if the relevant year of comparison is 1935 or 1940, the increase of the unified credit by the Ninety-seventh Congress looks like a restoration of the estate tax to its historic level of coverage.

Similarly, the reduction of the maximum estate tax rate from seventy percent to fifty percent can be viewed from a number of historical perspectives. Prior to the Revenue Act of 1934, the highest federal estate tax bracket never exceeded forty-five percent; for part of this period, the maximum rates were as low as ten and twenty-five percent. Against this background a fifty percent maximum rate looks fairly high.

On the other hand, if the projected 1985 rates are measured against the 1981 rates, it appears that the impact of the estate tax has been reduced significantly by the Ninety-seventh Congress. If in 1981 a decedent left a taxable estate of ten million dollars, the resulting federal tax liability was $6,050,800 prior to the application of the unified credit. In 1985 a ten-million-dollar estate will incur $1,275,000 less in federal transfer taxes because of the reduction of the highest rates.

V. CONCLUDING OBSERVATIONS

It is too early to determine the ultimate implications of the estate and gift tax changes adopted by the Ninety-seventh Congress. The history of federal transfer taxation is a complex one, reflecting the ebb and flow of differing attitudes towards inherited wealth. It is undeniable that the opponents of the estate and gift levies have for the moment established the upper hand. It is premature, however, to conclude that the abolition of federal taxation is upon us.

American society always has been of two minds on the subject of transfer taxation. One current of thought, exemplified by the early proponents of a federal estate tax, has viewed inherited wealth as an evil to be combated by a democratic society through taxation. A contrary strain of opinion has viewed the accumulation and transmission of wealth as a necessary incentive for production and savings. From the latter perspective estate and gift taxation retards economic growth by diminishing the rewards for productive behavior.

The ebb and flow of these contradictory pulses has shaped the system of federal transfer taxation as we know it today. * * *

In a curious way the actions of the Ninety-seventh Congress may limit the incentive of future Congresses to abolish or restrict further the federal transfer taxes. Since there will be fewer taxable estates following ERTA, the potential constituency for abolition of the estate tax has been diminished in number. Because the final increase in the unified credit will not be effective until 1987, Congress has an excuse for not legislating further until then. It is not easy for Congress to pass tax legislation. With estate and gift tax relief occurring automatically over the next five years, Congress may choose to turn its attention to other matters.

Most important, the status of inherited wealth in a democratic society is a matter about which Americans traditionally have harbored fierce and contradictory attitudes. A Congressman may view constituents worth $200,000 as inappropriate candidates for the federal estate tax, as their wealth may reflect nothing more than long-term ownership of houses in major metropolitan areas. That same Congressman, however, may feel differently about taxpayers with assets of $700,000 or $7,000,000.

The opponents and proponents of the federal transfer taxes generally agree that these levies are aimed at the country's economic elite. The principal disagreements have been, and likely will remain, the definition of that elite and the effects of taxation upon it.

In short, we do not know yet the ultimate consequences of the estate and gift tax changes made by the Ninety-seventh Congress because these consequences are yet to be determined. By focusing the federal estate and gift levies upon a wealthier, more restricted economic elite, the Ninety-seventh Congress, with unintentional clarity, has defined the future of the federal transfer taxes in essentially populist terms, that is, the propriety of large inheritances in a democratic society. Until America resolves its ambivalent attitude toward inherited wealth, it will not resolve its ambivalent attitude toward federal transfer taxation.

NOTE

Is Zelinsky correct that the failure to index the annual exclusion and the unified credit for inflation may force Congress to periodically adjust these amounts? *See* Boris I. Bittker, *Federal Estate Tax Reform: Exemptions and Rates*, 57 A.B.A. J. 236 (1971) (noting arbitrariness of historical benchmarks; "we can find support for almost anything if we are willing to use anything that we find").

JOINT COMM. ON TAX'N, DESCRIPTION AND ANALYSIS OF TAX PROPOSALS RELATING TO SAVINGS AND INVESTMENT (CAPITAL GAINS, IRAS, AND ESTATE AND GIFT TAX) (JCS-5-97), 105th Cong., 1st Sess. (1997)

* * *

Background Data Relating to Estate and Gift Taxation

Estates Subject to the Estate Tax

Table 13 details the percentage of decedents subject to the estate tax for selected years since 1935. The percentage of decedents liable for the estate tax grew throughout the postwar era reaching a peak in the mid-1970s. The substantial revision to the estate tax in the mid-1970s and subsequent further modifications in 1981 reduced the percentage of decedents liable for the estate tax to less than one percent in the late 1980s. Since that time, the percentage of decedents liable for the estate tax has gradually increased.

* * *

The increasing percentage of decedents liable for estate tax in the period from 1940 through the mid-1970s and the similar increasing percentages since 1989 are the result of the interaction of three factors: a fixed nominal exemption; the effect of price inflation on asset val-

Table 13.—Number of Taxable Estate Tax Returns Filed as a Percentage of Adult Deaths, Selected Years, 1935-1995

Year	Deaths	Taxable estate tax returns filed	
		Number	Percent of deaths
1935	1,172,245	8,655	0.74
1940	1,237,186	12,907	1.04
1945	1,239,713	13,869	1.12
1950	1,304,343	17,411	1.33
1955	1,379,826	25,143	1.82
1961	1,548,665	45,439	2.93
1966	1,727,240	67,404	3.90
1970	1,796,940	93,424	5.20
1973	1,867,689	120,761	6.47
1977	1,819,107	139,115	7.65
1982	1,897,820	41,620	2.19
1983	1,945,913	35,148	1.81
1984	1,968,128	31,507	1.60
1985	2,086,440	30,518	1.46
1986	2,105,361	23,731	1.13
1987	2,123,323	21,335	1.00
1988	2,167,999	18,948	0.87
1989	2,150,466	20,856	0.97
1990	2,148,463	23,215	1.08
1991	2,169,518	24,897	1.15
1992	2,175,613	27,187	1.25
1993	2,268,553	27,506	1.21
1994	2,278,994	31,918	1.40
1995	2,312,180	31,564	1.37

ues; and real economic growth. The amount of wealth exempt from the Federal estate tax always has been expressed at a fixed nominal value. If the general price level in the economy rises from one year to the next and asset values rise to reflect this inflation, the "nominal" value of each individual's wealth will increase. With a fixed nominal exemption, annual increases in the price level will imply that more individuals will have a nominal wealth that exceeds the tax threshold. Alternatively stated, inflation diminishes the real, inflation-adjusted, value of wealth that is exempted by a nominal exemption. Thus, even if no one individual's real wealth increased, more individuals would be subject to the estate tax. This interaction between inflation and a fixed nominal exemption largely explains the pattern in Table 13. The fixed nominal exemption was increased effective for 1977 and again between 1982 and 1987. Prior to 1977 and subsequent to 1987, the exemption was unchanged while the economy experienced general price inflation.

However, even if the exemption were modified annually to reflect general price inflation, one would still expect to see the percentage of decedents liable for estate tax rise because of the third factor, real growth. If the economy is experiencing real growth per capita, it must be accumulating capital. Accumulated capital is the tax base of the estate tax. Thus, real growth can lead to more individuals having real wealth above any given fixed *real* exempt amount.

Indexing the exemption for inflation is equivalent to creating a fixed real exemption rather than a fixed nominal exemption. Had the $600,000 effective exemption created by the 1981 Act (effective for 1987) been indexed for inflation subsequent to 1987, its nominal value today would be approximately $838,000. Had the $175,625 effective exemption created by the 1976 Act (effective for 1982) been indexed for inflation subsequent to 1982, its nominal value today would be approximately $289,000.

Revenues from the Estate, Gift, and Generation Skipping Taxes

Table 14 provides summary statistics of the estate and gift tax over the past 20 years. * * *

* * *

Since 1993, estate and gift receipts have been averaging double digit rates of growth. There are four possible reasons for the rapid growth in these receipts. First, because neither the amount of wealth exempt from the estate and gift tax or the tax rates are indexed, as explained above, an increasing number of persons are becoming subject to estate and gift taxes. Second, the tremendous increase in value in the stock market over the past three years will both increase the value of estates that would have already been taxable, and increase the number of estates that will be taxable. For example, the Dow Jones Industrial Average ended 1993 at approximately 3750, and ended 1996 at approximately 6500. On average, one-third of the wealth in taxable estates consists of publicly traded stocks. Because the value of this component of wealth has nearly doubled during the past three years, one would expect brisk growth in estate tax receipts from this alone. Third, while the overall population of the United States is growing at about a 1 percent annual rate, the number of persons aged 85 and older is growing at a rate of almost 3.5 percent annually. This also should increase the number of estate tax returns filed. Finally, the unlimited marital deduction included in the 1981 Act delayed the payment of estate tax, in most cases, until the surviving spouse died. On average, spouses survive their mates by about ten years. Therefore, during the decade of the 1990s, an increase in estate tax receipts is expected as the result of first-spouse deaths during the 1980s that used the unlimited marital deduction.

Table 15 shows the Joint Committee on Taxation staff present-law estimate of revenues from the estate, gift, and generation skipping taxes for fiscal years 1997-2007. These estimates are based on the baseline forecast for estate, gift, and generation skipping taxes supplied [by]

Table 14.—Revenue from the Federal Estate, Gift, and Generation Skipping Transfer Taxes, Selected Years, 1940-1996

Year	Revenue ($ millions)	Percentage of total Federal receipts
1940	357	6.9
1945	638	1.4
1950	698	1.9
1955	924	1.4
1960	1,606	1.7
1965	2,716	2.3
1970	3,644	1.9
1975	4,611	1.7
1976	5,216	1.7
1977	7,327	2.1
1978	5,285	1.3
1979	5,411	1.2
1980	6,389	1.2
1981	6,787	1.1
1982	7,991	1.3
1983	6,053	1.0
1984	6,010	0.9
1985	6,422	0.9
1986	6,958	0.9
1987	7,493	0.9
1988	7,594	0.8
1989	8,745	0.9
1990	11,500	1.12
1991	11,138	1.06
1992	11,143	1.02
1993	12,577	1.09
1994	15,225	1.21
1995	15,087	1.12
1996	17,189	1.18

the Congressional Budget Office. Table 15 reports the Joint Committee on Taxation staff estimates of annual taxable estates and calculates the percentage of all deaths that taxable estates will represent.

* * *

Comparison of Transfer Taxation in the United States with Transfer Taxation Abroad

Among developed countries, an inheritance tax is more common than the type of estate tax that is imposed in the United States. An inheritance tax generally is imposed upon the amount of wealth the transferee or donee receives rather than on the total wealth of the transferor. That is, the funds the heir receives in a bequest determines the tax imposed. * * * Among developed countries, Australia and Canada impose neither an estate tax nor an inheritance tax.

Because the U.S. estate and gift tax exempts transfers between spouses, provides an effective additional exemption of $600,000 through the unified credit, and exempts $10,000 of gifts per year per donee, the United States may have a larger exemption (a larger zero-rate tax bracket) than many other developed countries. However, because most other countries have inheritance taxes, the total exemption depends upon the number and type of beneficiaries. While

Table 15.—Projections of Taxable Estates and Receipts from Estate, Gift, and Generation Skipping Transfer Taxes, 1997-2007

Fiscal year	Number of taxable estates	Receipts ($ billions)	Taxable estates as a percentage of all deaths
1997	37,200	19.2	1.66
1998	40,100	20.6	1.75
1999	43,100	21.9	1.86
2000	46,000	23.3	1.97
2001	49,300	24.7	[not available]
2002	43,000	26.2	[not available]
2003	56,700	27.8	[not available]
2004	61,100	29.5	[not available]
2005	65,100	31.4	2.64
2006	69,000	33.3	[not available]
2007	73,200	35.3	[not available]

the effective exemption may be larger, with the exception of transfers to spouses which are untaxed, marginal tax rates on taxable transfers in the United States generally are greater than those in other countries. This is particularly the case when comparing transfers to close relatives, who under many inheritance taxes face lower marginal tax rates than do other beneficiaries. On the other hand, the highest marginal tax may be applied at a greater level of wealth transfer than in other countries. It is often difficult to make comparisons between the U.S. estate tax and countries with inheritance taxes because the applicable marginal tax rate depends on the pattern of gifts and bequests.

* * *

Table 16 compares total revenue collected by OECD countries from estate, inheritance, and gift taxes to total tax revenue and to gross domestic product (GDP) to attempt to compare the economic significance of wealth transfer taxes in different countries. Among the OECD countries, Belgium, Denmark, France, Greece, and Japan collect more such revenue as a percentage of GDP than does the United States. Switzerland and the Netherlands collect modestly less revenue from such taxes as a percentage of GDP than does the United States. The remaining 15 countries collect substantially less revenue from such taxes as a percentage of GDP than does the United States.

* * *

The United States is a wealthy country, with higher average household wealth than most of the countries surveyed. While exemption levels are higher in the United States than most other countries, a significant amount of accumulated wealth still may be subject to estate and gift taxation as compared to the other countries. The data in Table 16 do not reveal the extent to which estate, inheritance, and gift taxes fall across different individuals within each country. In the United States, as reported in Table 13, above, of the 2.18 million deaths in 1992, only 27,187 or 1.25 percent of decedents, gave rise to any estate tax liability. Similar data were not available for the other countries in this survey.

* * *

Table 16.—Revenue from Estate, Inheritance and Gift Taxes as a Percentage of Total Tax Revenue and GDP in OECD Countries, 1992

Country	Percentage of total tax revenue	Percentage of GDP
Australia	0.000	0.000
Austria	0.182	0.079
Belgium	0.735	0.334
Canada	0.002	0.001
Denmark	0.555	0.274
Finland	0.456	0.214
France	0.929	0.405
Germany	0.253	0.100
Greece	1.039	0.421
Iceland	0.216	0.072
Ireland	0.304	0.112
Italy	0.138	0.058
Japan	2.006	0.590
Luxembourg	0.320	0.155
Netherlands	0.526	0.247
New Zealand	0.292	0.105
Norway	0.191	0.089
Portugal	0.252	0.083
Spain	0.366	0.131
Sweden	0.166	0.083
Switzerland	0.854	0.264
Turkey	0.111	0.026
United Kingdom	0.584	0.206
United States	0.907	0.267

NOTE

What explains the unpopularity of the wealth transfer taxes in light of the data showing that less than 2% of decedents over the past 15 years have been subject to the estate tax? *See* Subpart C, *infra*. One commentator offers the following conjecture:

> One reason contributing to some people's opposition rests on the belief that they would not want the government to claim a large slice of their winnings should they strike it rich. In short, they meld hope with selfishness. Another reason is ignorance. Many people do not realize how few decedents pay a substantial estate tax—only around 1% pay any federal estate tax at all—and wrongly believe that the odds of their heirs having to part with a sizable chunk of their inheritance are much higher than those odds actually are.

Eric Rakowski, *Transferring Wealth Liberally*, 51 TAX L. REV. 419, 424-25 (1996). For further data on the federal wealth transfer taxes, see Martha Britton Eller, *Federal Taxation of Wealth Transfers, 1992-1995*, STATISTICS OF INCOME 8 (Winter 1996-97).

William S. Blatt, *The American Dream in Legislation: The Role of Popular Symbols in Wealth Tax Policy*, 51 TAX L. REV. 287 (1996)*

* * *

II. THE ROLE OF PUBLIC DISCOURSE IN LEGISLATION

* * *

B. Abstract Discourses of Tax Legislation

* * *

* * * Tax theorists commonly describe legislation with one of two abstract discourses. One is policy analysis, the language used to evaluate tax proposals. The other is interest group politics, the language used to describe power. * * *

* * *

Tax policy analysis, like all policy analysis, involves choosing a goal and then selecting the best means for achieving it. Tax policy analysts acknowledge at least a half dozen different goals or criteria. Perhaps the most obvious relate to the use of the proceeds. The revenue norm focuses on the amount of funds raised or lost by a tax proposal. The benefit criterion examines what the taxpayer receives in exchange for her taxes. Fairness and economic efficiency, determined independently from expenditure, command the most attention among theorists. Analysts frequently distinguish horizontal equity, the comparison of those in the same economic class, from the more controversial vertical equity, the comparison of those in different classes. The traditional argument for redistribution among classes rests on the diminishing marginal utility of money: Each additional dollar brings less enjoyment than the last.

* * *

These goals have their shortcomings. For one, they often conflict. * * * Moreover, the norms raise intractable empirical issues. * * *

* * *

Tax theorists do not believe that policy alone accounts for legislation; they acknowledge the power of special interests. In doing so, they invoke a model of politics based on economic self interest. * * *

* * *

Diffuse and cohesive groups each produce distinct patterns of conflict and cooperation, which may be termed partisan confrontation and interest group accommodation. * * *

* * *

C. The Public Discourse of Symbols and Stories

* * * [T]he abstract descriptions of tax policy analysis and interest group politics both have gaps. These gaps can be filled by looking to pervasive cultural understandings, evident in the public discourse, by which I mean the common, everyday symbols and stories found in newspapers and congressional hearings. These understandings comprise the terrain in which policy analysis and interest group politics operate. Constructs from the public discourse define pol-

---

icy problems and frame issues around which interest groups organize. The public discourse is no more complete than the other accounts; it does, however, fill some gaps left by them.

* * *

III. IMPLICATIONS OF THE PUBLIC DISCOURSE FOR TAX THEORY

Viewing policy and politics as largely autonomous, theorists generally regard popular symbols and stories as outside their domain. There is, however, another vision, which, recognizing policy and public discourse as interlocking conversations, incorporates preferences revealed in the public discourse.

* * *

C. Identifying Goals

Tax theorists traditionally reject popular opinion as simply misguided. They attribute popular resistance to the estate tax to a widespread fantasy of "striking it rich" by winning the lottery or by inheriting from an unknown relative. Apparently, most people irrationally believe that they will someday be wealthy enough to worry about the transfer tax. Public resistance to transfer taxation, however, may be rooted not in irrational hopes but in value preferences. Regardless of their own prospects for accumulating wealth, people harbor substantial misgivings about estate taxation. The widespread appeal of the family business symbol is persuasive evidence that resistance to the estate tax is rooted largely in normative understandings. Not working in such businesses themselves, most Americans support family businesses for reasons beyond personal self interest. The family business symbol taps into deeply held values.

Extraction of specific policy goals from popular symbols requires a deeper theory of cognition than those currently employed in tax theory * * * .

The family business symbol draws upon two [cognitive] models—"business" and "family"— the story of the founder and the basic social unit. These models, in turn, suggest the importance of the goals of reward and community. Although perhaps less universal and quantifiable than existing tax policy goals, these norms feed into the larger, public discussion. Representing an honest effort to grapple with society's expressed preferences, they deserve overt consideration in tax policy analysis. * * *

1. Reward

The cognitive model "business" suggests that tax theorists should consider desert or reward, a return given for merit. Most Americans share the "American Dream," in which virtue and hard work lead to economic independence. The family business symbol persuades because it affirms this aspiration. * * *

* * *

Recognition of reward would prompt theorists to reconsider which effects of inheritance taxation are most troubling. Tax policy currently focuses on the impact on savings and, sometimes, innovation. In contrast, the public discourse shows the greatest concern for the effect on work incentives. * * *

* * *

2. Community

The cognitive model "family" suggests that tax theorists should consider community as a normative goal. Americans value community, particularly as institutionalized in the family. * * *

The community norm receives little attention in tax theory. * * *

* * *

3. Conclusion

Recognition of reward and community in policy analysis would narrow the gap between tax theory and the public discourse, thereby potentially changing both theorist and public attitudes. Acknowledgement of these goals might erode the theorist consensus for wealth taxation. Rational analysis of them might reduce the appeal of the family business symbol.

Such recognition also could alter the estate tax. Enactment of proposals directly tailored to reward and community might reduce the demand for rules accommodating the family business. Decreased reliance on this fuzzy concept would permit a closer fit between goal and rule. * * *

* * *

NOTE

Do differing public attitudes toward concentrations of wealth and family businesses help to explain the current (and future) shape of the wealth transfer taxes? Do the "symbols and stories found in newspapers and congressional hearings" provide a reliable basis for ascertaining popular values and preferences? What weight should be given to such symbols and stories in formulating tax policy? For further discussion of the role of "practices" and public opinion in formulating tax policy, see the exchange between Edward J. McCaffery and Anne L. Alstott in Part VIII, *infra. See* Edward J. McCaffery, *The Uneasy Case for Wealth Transfer Taxation*, 104 YALE L.J. 283, 288 (1994) (arguing that a consumption-without-estate tax would fit well with the "implicit spirit of our actual practices and beliefs"); Anne L. Alstott, *The Uneasy Liberal Case Against Income and Wealth Transfer Taxation: A Response to Professor McCaffery*, 51 TAX L. REV. 363, 396 (1996) (noting that "the interpreter of social practices also must be an alert critic," and warning that an "overly simple reading of current practices may elevate unthinking prejudices or narrow self-interest to the level of principles of justice").

B.   An Economic Perspective

This Subpart presents some of the economic arguments about the federal wealth transfer taxes. Roy Blough and Carl Shoup discuss the effect of the taxes on the formation of capital. Michael J. Boskin studies the economic effects of transfer taxes and suggests that their role be limited to breaking up only "extreme" concentrations of wealth. Gerald R. Jantscher examines the economic underpinnings of the twin justifications of the transfer taxes in raising revenue and promoting more equal distribution of wealth. B. Douglas Bernheim argues that the *net* tax yield to the government from the transfer taxes may be negative in light of the income tax revenues lost as a result of transactions designed to reduce or eliminate transfer tax liability. Henry J. Aaron and Alicia H. Munnell present empirical data showing that the transfer taxes have not had any discernible effect on the concentration of wealth.

ROY BLOUGH & CARL SHOUP, A REPORT ON THE FEDERAL REVENUE SYSTEM SUBMITTED TO UNDERSECRETARY OF THE TREASURY ROSWELL MAGILL (1937), *reprinted in* 70 TAX NOTES 1071 (1996)*

* * *

DEATH AND GIFT TAXES

1. The Desirability of Death Taxes

Universal Acceptance: Taxation of the transfer of property at death has been one of the most universally used tax forms in history. The purposes have included both revenue and control. The institution of inheritance is recognized to be [a] specially granted privilege allowed only because the results therefrom are believed to be socially desirable; principally perhaps because of the encouragement given to the production and accumulation of wealth. When the danger of the concentration of wealth in the hands of a few persons has been thought to outweigh the desirability of wealth accumulation, inheritance has been limited and modified, largely through taxation.

Painlessness: Death taxes constitute a relatively painless method of raising revenue. The decedent is dead so the tax cannot hurt him at the time it is imposed, although of course it may have caused sacrifices during his life that he would not otherwise have borne. Perhaps usually the legatee or beneficiary has not sacrificed to create the wealth so the tax causes him no real sacrifice, although of course a wife or son may have helped build up the estate. An inheritance is probably looked upon by most beneficiaries as an addition to capital rather than as expendable income, so that the tax has relatively little effect on the beneficiary's standard of living. The beneficiary usually has other financial sources than the inheritance although in the case of widows and minor children this statement would perhaps not be true. If the tax is anticipated, no expectations are frustrated. All taxes cause some sacrifice, but the inheritance tax causes less than others.

Economic Effects: Since death is an uncertain future event and since it removes from the scene of action the person chiefly interested, death taxation probably has less effect on the individual's activities than do other more immediately pressing taxes. A strongly urged argument is that heavy death taxes discourage the decedent from working and accumulating and thus prevent the creation of economic wealth that would otherwise be created. Against this view it is urged that because the tax will take a large part of the estate, the individual is encouraged to work harder and save more than he otherwise would in order to leave a competence to his heirs. Probably the forces of the two motives differ among individuals. However, the motives that induce most work and accumulation are likely to be found in an individual's own life rather than in his interest in his heirs, especially when the fortune becomes more than adequate to support his near kin.

The effect of the inheritance tax on the inheritor of wealth is probably to encourage work and accumulation. Much of the best mental power of the nation is wasted because its possessors do not need to work. While heavy inheritance taxes might deny some capable persons of capital needed to exercise their talents (although most inheritances appear not to be received until middle age), on the whole heavy inheritance taxes by making work necessary would probably lead to greater production and accumulation by the beneficiary than if such taxes were not imposed.

---

*   Reprinted with permission. Copyright 1996. Tax Analysts.

Perhaps the most influential argument brought against death taxation is that it destroys accumulated social capital. The argument runs that in order to pay the tax the estate must be liquidated, wholly or partially.

This liquidation is accepted as a destruction of social capital. This, however, is a fallacious view. Social capital consists of tangible wealth, which cannot be destroyed by merely selling the estate. The estate is sold to someone who buys it out of his income or out of his liquid accumulated savings; the social capital continues to exist.

A more valid contention is that death taxation slows up the formation of social capital. The purchaser of the assets of an estate buys them as an investment. He does not distinguish between such an investment and an investment in the production of new capital. Accordingly less liquid funds are available for investment in new capital than would probably be the case if inheritance taxes were not imposed.

Effects on social capital are in no way peculiar to death taxes. Highly progressive income tax rates, which also reduce the volume of funds available for investment, have a similar result. Indeed, the effects of income taxes on enterprise and accumulation are probably greater than those of death taxes. Income taxes apply to the present, the estate taxes to an uncertain and often distant future. Income taxes affect directly the rewards for enterprise; those rewards may never, and most of them probably will never, be subject to the estate tax.

The seriousness of this discouraging effect on capital growth depends on the ease with which a society may accumulate capital. In the early days of the capitalistic system the great need of new capital and the difficulty of accumulating it may have made heavy death taxes undesirable. At the present time, however, the surplus of the productive power of the country over minimum necessary consumption is so great that needed new capital can be brought into existence with little sacrifice and almost at will through the use of bank credit. Accordingly the argument against death taxes on the grounds that social capital is thereby prevented from growing is probably not a particularly significant one today. More light on this point, however, is badly needed.

Death taxes so severe as to result in a very substantial redistribution of wealth might result in the gradual decrease in the volume of social capital. The demands of the lower income groups for immediate income would shift productive activities from the replacement of capital to the supply of consumption goods for immediate use. The capitalistic system seems to require a considerable degree of inequality in order that it may have the necessary capital to operate — although the present degree of inequality is perhaps unnecessarily great. A system of death taxation that would lead to almost complete redistribution and equality of wealth would probably have a very repressive long-term effect on production.

* * *

Conclusion: The conclusion of the writers is that transfer of property at death is an especially good source of taxation, and that the desirable level of rates is limited largely by the effect on the accumulation of capital, about which little is known.

* * *

NOTE

Blough and Shoup contended in 1937 that "the argument against death taxes on the grounds that social capital is thereby prevented from growing is probably not a particularly significant one today." C. Lowell Harriss agreed in 1955: "Estate taxes were once condemned because they reduce . . . national wealth. . . . Even if it has some validity, however, the net amounts today are insignificant in an economy the size of ours." C. Lowell Harriss, *Economic Effects of Estate and Gift Taxation*, in JOINT COMMITTEE ON THE ECONOMIC REPORT, FEDERAL TAX POLICY FOR ECONOMIC GROWTH AND STABILITY 855, 863 (1955). Were these statements true when made? Are they true today?

Michael J. Boskin, *An Economist's Perspective on Estate Taxation*, in DEATH, TAXES AND FAMILY PROPERTY (Edward C. Halbach, Jr., ed., 1977)*

* * * [T]he purpose of this paper is to analyze the role of federal estate taxes in achieving a variety of potential social objectives. In so doing, we shall point out several badly mistaken popular notions concerning the distribution of wealth and the potential role of estate taxes in making it more equal. Toward this end, the first section presents a basic economic framework for analyzing wealth, its accumulation, and its transfer at death. After a brief discussion of the goals of taxation, estate taxes are introduced into the analysis and we discuss the various incentives such taxes create in the economy.

The second section analyzes in somewhat more detail the economic effects of estate taxation. In particular, we analyze the effects of estate taxation on efficiency and on several notions of equity. We conclude that both the potential role of estate taxation in equalizing the distribution of wealth is extremely limited and the desirability of doing so is called into question by the operation of a variety of types of economic behavior.

The third section of this paper concludes with a brief discussion of potential reform of federal estate taxation in the United States.

A FRAMEWORK FOR ANALYZING ESTATE TAXATION

The major goals of taxation are raising revenue (to finance government expenditures), discouraging certain activities and redistributing income or wealth. Estate taxation is not a major revenue raising device in the United States; indeed, the total annual revenue raised via estate taxation is substantially less than the amounts of some changes due to cuts or increases in individual and/or corporate income taxes. Nor has estate taxation been used in the same way as selective excise taxes or import duties to discourage the purchase of certain commodities. Its major goal has been—and continues to be—to decrease the inequality in the distribution of wealth, to thwart the concentration of economic (and with it, some argue, political) power. However, there is substantial disagreement as to the extent of inequality or concentration necessary to create a social problem; and further, there is an issue as to how effective estate taxation has been (indeed, can be) in achieving this goal. To begin to answer such questions, we must delve into the determinants of the distribution of wealth and expose several fallacies in the conventional "wisdom."

Understanding "Wealth" and its Relation to Income

We must begin with so basic a point as the definition of wealth, for it is here that much confusion and fallacy begin. The simplest definition for our purposes is the market value of assets minus liabilities. * * *

---

* * * [W]ealth is the capitalized value of an expected income stream. How strange, then, that we are constantly told that the distribution of wealth is much less equal, much more concentrated, than the distribution of income! Such a statement, our first popular fallacy, is extremely misleading at best, quite incorrect in any event. To a first approximation, the distribution of income and wealth—properly measured—must be equal! Why then has this popular folklore persisted? The basic problem stems from a confusion of total income or wealth with its components; both income and wealth come from two main sources: capital and labor. Labor income, of course, consists of earnings and fringe benefits; capital income consists of interest, dividends, and rents. As we move up the income scale, a larger and larger fraction of total income consists of capital income. Approximately three-fourths of total income consists of labor income.

Just as there are two sources of income, so there are two sources of wealth: ownership of what is usually considered wealth (stocks, bonds, housing) and of wealth embodied in the worker's knowledge and skills (e.g., from education or job training), which economists call human capital. Human capital is the capitalized value of an expected future labor income stream just as nonhuman capital is the capitalized value of an expected future capital [income] stream.

The comparison frequently made—and I cannot emphasize too much that it is an improper comparison—is between the distribution of total income (actually, total realized income, leaving out the capital gain component of capital income) and the distribution of *nonhuman* capital only. Indeed, when a comparison between the distribution of total income and total wealth is made, to a first approximation the two are equal. We must adjust this first impression to account for the fact that capital and labor income are taxed at very different rates and that human capital is much less liquid than most types of nonhuman capital. My opinion is that these adjustments do not alter the basic conclusion that *the distributions of income and wealth are approximately equal.*

* * * Before turning to the role of estate taxes in attempting to decrease inequality, we must turn from the definition of wealth to its accumulation over the life-cycle.

Wealth Accumulation

In the past two and a half decades, a new theory of saving and the accumulation of wealth has emerged. The work of many people, especially Milton Friedman and Franco Modigliani, has produced the life-cycle theory of saving and consumption. The basic point of this theory is rather simple (although its implications are quite intricate): the flow of income over an individual's lifetime is quite uneven and individuals adjust their saving behavior to smooth their consumption over the life-cycle. Thus, young individuals typically dissave for a while, save during their peak earning years and dissave during retirement. Thus, an individual's wealth varies over the life-cycle in a predictable manner. We may think of each individual (or family) deciding, at each point of time, how much to consume and how much to save or add to his wealth. Each individual also must decide how much, if anything, to pass to his or her heirs via inter vivos gifts or bequests.

This implies that the wealth of each family comes from two sources: the family's own saving and gifts or inheritances. The second popular fallacy is that most wealth is passed from generation to generation within the same extremely wealthy families. While some huge fortunes accumulated decades ago have not yet been dissipated, this popular notion is not correct. A variety of recent studies have shown that much of the wealth inequality may be explained by life-cycle saving combined with several other economic and demographic phenomena. At best, it is only the extreme upper tail of the wealth distribution which is primarily a result of several generations of inheritance. Even if we started everyone off with identical incomes, normal life-cycle behavior plus random deaths would produce a very unequal distribution of financial wealth in short order!

Once we recognize this natural life-cycle behavior, an extremely important fact follows immediately: *the size of one's estate* (and, therefore, one's heirs' inheritance) *is subject to choice!* At each stage of one's lifetime, a choice must be made as to how much to consume and, given income, to save or dissave. It is simply not correct to treat the size of the estate as a given amount unaffected by taxation. The size of the estate may be a very poor guide to lifetime wealth. * * * [E]state taxes create incentives for individuals to rethink their consumption/wealth accumulation decisions. To a more detailed examination of these incentives we now turn.

ECONOMIC EFFECTS OF ESTATE TAXATION

Consider an individual planning his estate during his lifetime. For our purposes, an individual has three potential uses of his wealth over his lifetime: (1) personal consumption; (2) inter vivos gifts; (3) bequests. Each of these acts provides some satisfaction to the individual; the latter two obviously also provide satisfaction to the recipients. What is the cost to the individual of a dollar's worth of each activity? Let us set the "price" of lifetime consumption equal to one, i.e., it costs one dollar to consume one dollar's worth of goods and services during one's lifetime.

Consider next the "price" of inter vivos gifts. * * * [W]ith a tax rate of 1/3, the price of "purchasing" a dollar's worth of consumption for one's children or friends is really $1.50.

Just as the gift tax dramatically increases the cost or price of inter vivos gifts, so the estate tax dramatically raises the price of bequests. * * * A rate of 50% implies an increase in the cost of bequests from one dollar per dollar bequeathed to two dollars!

Finally, we note that income and capital gains tax provisions interact with gift and estate taxes in affecting bequests. When income from capital is taxed heavily, the individual's return on savings, and hence incentive to save, is decreased substantially. For example, a 50% tax on income from capital (corporate income tax, personal income tax on interest or dividends, etc.) which decreased the after-tax return on saving from 10% to 5% would decrease the future value twenty-five years hence of a dollar of saving today by over seventy percent! Hence the size of his estate may be smaller than in the absence of heavy capital income (e.g., personal and corporate) taxation. The set of taxes (income, gift, estate) retards capital accumulation by inducing individuals to consume more earlier in their lifetime than they would prefer in the absence of such tax incentives.

What do we conclude from this analysis? Just as we generally believe a large increase in the price of beer will lead people to drink less beer, so the large increase in the price of bequests will lead to fewer and smaller bequests. Further, just as the increase in the price of beer will lead to an increase in the amount of wine consumed, so will the estate-tax induced increase in the price of bequests lead to an increase in *lifetime* consumption by the wealthy. Of course, the nature and full extent of the [effect] of a price increase on spending for beer or on saving for bequests will depend on the elasticity of demand, and on willingness to substitute wine or lifetime consumption. * * *

An estate tax also creates an opposite incentive with respect to saving. It is possible that the anticipation of the tax bite from an estate induces an increase in saving for bequests to restore their level in the absence of the tax, or to approximate a particular wealth transfer goal. It is unlikely that this effect (the wealth effect) offsets the price effect discussed above. * * *

* * *

While there will no doubt be cases of no effect or opposite effect, overall a substantial decrease in "expenditures" (saving) for bequests can be expected from increasing transfer taxes relative to income taxes.

Implications of Tax-Induced Behavior

These tax-induced changes in economic behavior have several important implications for the evaluation of the efficiency, equity and redistribution effects of estate taxes.

Inefficiency. An inefficiency is created in the allocation of family resources over the life-cycle. The government has changed the terms of trade among lifetime consumption, inter vivos gifts and bequests heavily in favor of lifetime consumption. Relative to the individual's own preferences, a substantial inefficiency results, because gifts and bequests are held below the optimal level in terms of true costs and values. In addition, lifetime consumption is distorted in favor of the early part of the life-cycle. Thus, saving and capital accumulation are impeded.

Furthermore, the estate and gift taxes can dramatically distort the composition of gifts and bequests. These taxes have never been applied to gifts of human capital. Gifts or bequests of stock may well be taxed; but the equivalent value in the form of college and medical school expenses is not taxed. Hence, these taxes create an incentive for wealthy individuals to give their heirs human instead of nonhuman capital, creating inefficiency by decreasing the total utility of a given level of transfer.

Inequality. While these effects on efficiency are themselves important, they are only one aspect of evaluating the desirability of transfer taxation. As mentioned above, the primary goal of the estate and gift taxes is to decrease inequality in society. Have they done so?

In light of the analysis above, we can be confident that estate taxes have accomplished the following: (1) raised a small amount of revenue; (2) decreased bequests substantially; (3) decreased capital accumulation. Have these effects decreased inequality? My conjecture is that while they may have been useful in breaking up extreme concentrations of wealth they have done very little to decrease total inequality.

* * *

Will a decrease in bequests decrease inequality? I very much doubt it. While a detailed analysis is quite complex, three major facts stand out. First, and perhaps most important, the decrease in bequests is probably matched by a substantial increase in lifetime consumption of already very wealthy individuals. Second, while inheritance patterns are not well documented, estates are generally divided among several heirs so that most of the very large fortunes we hear so much about are reduced to a fraction of their initial value in the hands of any one recipient. Third, natural regression towards the mean suggests that the heirs of self-made wealthy persons (apparently a substantial fraction of the wealthy population), in the absence of bequests, would be somewhat less well off than the wealthy decedent. These three factors suggest that estate taxes may, by increased consumption, decrease transfer of resources from, say, the highest five or ten percent of the wealth distribution to a much broader spectrum of the wealth distribution of the next generation, hardly an inequality decreasing policy.

Against these tendencies must be weighed the natural growth in real income. With about twenty-five years between generations, average *real* incomes about double from one generation to the next. Hence, children, on average, are likely to be wealthier than their parents. Since the estate tax historically, via exemptions and deductions, has been directed toward the top few percent of the estate size distribution, the arguments above continue to hold, although with less force once one nets out natural economic growth between generations.

The other major way estate taxation affects inequality is through its effect on saving and capital accumulation. While the extent of this effect is difficult to measure, its direction is clear. In our (mostly) competitive economy, wages reflect the productivity of labor. Just as a farmer is more productive when he has a tractor than when he does not, *labor is more productive when it has more capital per worker* at its disposal. Hence, a decrease in saving and capital accumulation will decrease the capital-labor ratio in the economy. This in turn decreases the productivity of labor and wage rates compared to what they would have been otherwise. Similar reasoning leads to the conclusion that the return to capital will increase as the supply of capital decreases. Hence, to the extent that estate taxation decreases saving (e.g., for bequests), it reduces the return to human capital or labor, and increases the return to nonhuman capital. This effect increases inequality.

Some Conclusions About Economic Effects

What, then, shall we conclude concerning the economic effects of estate taxes? So far as inequality is concerned, there are several conflicting forces at work, but on balance, the estate tax probably partially accomplishes the goal of limiting intergenerational transfers of extremely large fortunes. It probably also increases the lifetime consumption of the extremely wealthy of one generation at the expense of their potential heirs, the moderately wealthy of the next. It may decrease the incentive to save and therefore also decrease wages relative to the return to capital in the long-run. On balance, therefore, the estate tax has done little to increase equality in society.

What lessons may we infer concerning the *potential* efficacy of estate taxes in promoting equality? Clearly, driving up the rates in the estate tax, or decreasing the exemption, or both, would decrease bequests. The estate tax thus can be made a more effective device for decreasing intergenerational transfers of nonhuman capital. But the more it achieves in this direction, the more it will both increase the lifetime consumption of the extremely wealthy (at the expense of a less well-off group) and decrease the accumulation of capital (at the ultimate expense of future wages).

In sum, the economist's approach to estate taxation reveals a much less than persuasive case that estate taxation either has or can substantially decrease inequality in the distribution of consumption, income or wealth.

IMPLICATION FOR TAX POLICY

What does this analysis imply for the appropriate role of transfer taxes? The answer depends, in part, upon which other reforms, if any, are likely to occur simultaneously. My own opinion is that any attempt to reduce (substantially) inequality in the distribution of wealth via estate and gift taxation is doomed to failure, quite apart from the question of its costs and thus its desirability. I see a much less ambitious role for these taxes: preventing *extreme* concentrations of wealth from being passed from generation to generation.

I believe that the combination of economic growth and inflation has rendered far too large a proportion of decedents liable for estate taxes. The opprobrious economic effects of the tax increase in direct proportion to the percentage of the population potentially liable for estate taxes. I therefore believe a substantial increase in the exemption is desirable. I would attempt to tax only extremely large estates, perhaps the wealthiest 3 or 4%.

* * *

NOTE

According to data in the *1997 Joint Committee Report* excerpted in Subpart A, in 1977 when Boskin called for taxing only "the wealthiest 3 or 4%" of decedents' estates, the estate tax reached almost 8% of decedents. What would Boskin think of the current estate tax, which reaches less than 2% of decedents?

Gerald R. Jantscher, *The Aims of Death Taxation*, in DEATH, TAXES AND FAMILY PROPERTY (Edward C. Halbach, Jr., ed., 1977)*

The purpose of this paper is to examine the reasons that have been advanced for imposing a tax on transfers at death—transfers, that is, from the estates of decedents to their successors. Death taxes, whether of the estate tax or inheritance tax form or indeed of any other form, display a diversity of features, many of which are so different and apparently so inconsistent that an observer attempting to appraise proposals for change without understanding the purpose of the tax could scarcely escape utter confusion.

DEATH TAXES AS A SOURCE OF REVENUE

It is unlikely that the sovereigns who imposed the earliest death taxes puzzled for long over the purpose of the tax. They required revenue and an inheritance tax, in its primitive forms, was a convenient way of obtaining it. These authorities lacked the many alternative sources of revenue that are available to modern authorities and were often forced to rely in large part on the taxation of property transfers.

This justification for death taxation is clearly of no relevance today. The modern state has many alternatives to death and gift taxation. Indeed, in view of the small proportion of total receipts that these taxes contribute and the high cost of administering them, it is arguable that if the taxes were only imposed to raise revenue, they ought to be abolished. * * *

A more sophisticated version of the revenue argument for death taxes holds that even though these taxes may not be strictly necessary as revenue sources, they have fewer adverse effects on efficiency than, for example, the income tax. That is, the federal estate and gift taxes are a less costly way of raising nearly $5 billion of revenue than the federal income tax, if we define *cost* broadly enough to include not only administrative and compliance costs but also the effects of the tax on efficiency, investment, and so forth.

To evaluate the merits of this argument, one must analyze the effects of substituting another tax for a death tax. The effects will differ depending on what tax it is that replaces the death tax, but for convenience it is assumed here that the alternative is an increase in individual income tax rates.

Persons Who Do Not Save For Their Survivors

Consider first the effects of such a substitution on the many persons who save primarily for other reasons than to leave property to their survivors. They may save as a precaution against sudden illness or loss of work, or to provide income for their retirement years, or to enjoy nonpecuniary benefits such as pride, position, and respect that they believe are enjoyed by those who possess great wealth. Or they may be habitual savers, as incapable of refraining from accumulation as some men are of restraining their ambition. Or they may have large incomes but modest tastes and be unable to consume all that they earn.

Motives vary; but in the case of all these persons a change in death tax rates is not apt to affect economic behavior. Therefore, in considering the effect of substituting higher income tax rates for a death tax, we may concentrate on the increase in income tax rates.

Effect on Saving. If an equal-yield added tax on income were substituted for a death tax, the cost of saving would increase. Cost here is measured by foregone consumption. The addition of a few percentage points to the income tax rates means that forgoing $1 of current consumption would net savers less than before, say $1.90 after ten years instead of $2. At least

---

some persons would respond to this fall in the rate of return by reducing their saving and increasing their consumption, much as consumers respond to a selective increase in prices by curtailing their purchases of the more costly goods.

The reduction in everyone's after-tax income would also discourage saving, on the common assumption that the smaller one's income, the smaller the fraction that is saved. How large the decline in saving would be depends in part on whether the increase in rates were regressive, proportional, or progressive. Since the estate tax is commonly regarded as a progressive element in the total federal tax system, the alternative to it is probably an increase in upper bracket income tax rates. It is these rates that affect saving the most; hence saving might fall by a moderate fraction of the increase in income tax receipts.

Effect on Work Incentives. The effect of an increase in income tax rates on work incentives is less clear-cut. On the one hand it would make leisure more attractive and might therefore cause some persons to curtail their work effort. A number of marginal participants in the labor force—housewives, for example, with part-time jobs—might decide to withdraw. Other persons might seek early retirement. On the other hand, by reducing everyone's after-tax income an increase in rates might stimulate work effort. Deductive reasoning is incapable of telling us which of these opposite effects would predominate. Empirical evidence is also inconclusive, though majority opinion among informed economists favors the conclusion that small changes in income tax rates have little effect one way or the other on the supply of labor.

Persons Who Do Save For Their Survivors

Now consider the response among persons who are strongly motivated to save for their survivors. An increase in income tax rates would have the same effects on their willingness to work and to save as it would among the rest of the population. But the accompanying reduction in death tax rates would affect them differently.

Effects on Saving. Two opposite effects on saving are conceivable. Bequests would become less costly, in the sense that $1 of saving would purchase a larger after-tax estate. Some savers would respond by curtailing their consumption in order to take advantage of the new, lower cost of making bequests.

It is possible, however, that other persons would respond by curtailing their saving, on the ground that the reduction in death tax rates would make it possible to leave a bequest of a certain size to one's family from a smaller estate. * * *

Effect on Work Incentives. The effect of a reduction in death tax rates on work incentives would surely be slight. * * * [U]nless the accumulation of wealth absorbs a great deal of a person's income, he is unlikely to adjust his work effort in response to a change in death tax rates.

* * *

Conclusion

A reduction in death tax rates and increase in income tax rates that left total tax collections unchanged would be likely to have only slight effects on incentives to work, save, and invest. So far as one can tell from deductive reasoning, tempered by experience and observation, the supply of labor in the United States would hardly change. If a prediction must be ventured, it seems slightly more probable that incentives to work would decrease rather than increase, although very little. Saving would probably be affected more strongly; a shift from death taxes to income taxes might depress saving slightly. Investment demand might increase a little, provided that the monetary authorities allowed it to.

In my judgment, none of these effects argues strongly either for or against a system of death taxation. They are simply too weak. Recall that the federal estate and gift taxes now contribute somewhat less than $5 billion to annual federal revenues. Even if saving were not increased but *depressed* by a small fraction of this sum—the largest effect conceivable—it would be of little consequence in a nation in which annual net private saving averaged more than $70 billion between 1972 and 1975. If authorities decide that saving is too low, other instruments are available for increasing it.

There are sound reasons for imposing death taxes in societies like ours. What a consideration of the economic effects of these taxes reveals is that no one need be deterred from supporting such taxes by those effects.

* * *

TAXING CONCENTRATIONS OF WEALTH

In my opinion the one aim of a death tax that stands scrutiny is its redistributive or anticoncentration aim. Not that death taxes stand alone as effective instruments against concentration. In the United States the federal income tax also erodes concentrations of wealth, and a net wealth tax would too. But death taxes have a role to play. If many of the country's largest fortunes are composed in the main of inherited wealth, a properly designed, well administered, progressive tax on inheritances ought to be an effective means of leveling wealth.

Limitations On Effectiveness of the Tax

The word "leveling" should not be taken literally. The limitations upon the effectiveness of the tax must be acknowledged at once.

[Not All] Property is Inherited. Not all wealth is inherited wealth, and therefore even if all inheritances were confiscated by the state the distribution of wealth in American society would still be unequal, though presumably less unequal than it is today.

Not All Inheritance is of Property. Furthermore, not all of one's inheritance—for many persons, not even the most important part of it—is received in the form of property rights. Even if we all started "the race for success" without any wealth from our parents, our starting positions would nevertheless be different. * * *

So a perfectly equal distribution of wealth must be regarded as a will-o'-the-wisp. But a more equal distribution is certainly attainable. * * * [O]ther factors than inheritance help to explain—often suffice to explain—why some persons are wealthy and others are not; but the plain evidence of our senses tells us that the persistence of many of the largest American fortunes over several generations is chiefly due to the institution of inheritance and not to the socioeconomic background of the owners. The vast wealth of the four surviving Rockefeller brothers has little to do with the brothers' good Baptist upbringing.

More Equal Distribution of Wealth Is Desirable

I take it for granted here that a more equal distribution of wealth is desirable. Tastes differ, of course, and others may disagree. Lengthy books have been written upon this subject, some of them scholarly, more of them polemical, and there is little that I can say here that would be original. Nearly everyone would agree, however, that some limit ought to be placed on the amount of wealth that one man should control, an upper bound upon wealth inequality that should not be exceeded. Unreasonable inequality poses a particular danger to societies that prize a high degree of individual freedom * * * .

Suppose we agree that more equality is preferable to less, provided that the cost of attaining it is not excessive. In their remarks on the subject, economists quite naturally have focused on the economic costs of promoting equality: the trade-off between equality and efficiency, to borrow from the title of Arthur Okun's recent book. Death taxes receive high marks for being less burdensome than alternative instruments of redistribution, principally the income tax and a hypothetical wealth tax. Of course, they may be less burdensome but also less effective.

What is needed is something akin to a benefit-cost ratio for each of these taxes. We know too little to construct those, however, and so are forced to rely on thoughtful speculation.

Death taxes also have the merit of assailing concentrations of inherited wealth but not concentrations of "self-made" wealth, a discrimination that would be clumsy to incorporate into an income tax or net wealth tax. If an equally redistributive net wealth tax were substituted for a death tax, our society would presumably evolve toward one in which there would be more "old wealth" and less "new wealth." Is the influence of inherited wealth more pernicious than that of newly created wealth, and would the substitution therefore be undesirable? The question is usually answered affirmatively; but I wonder whether a thoughtful reconsideration would leave us quite so sure that it ought to be.

* * *

NOTE

Do you agree that a revenue-neutral reduction in the estate tax, coupled with an increase in income tax rates, would likely have "only slight effects" on incentives to work, save, and invest?

B. Douglas Bernheim, *Does the Estate Tax Raise Revenue?*, *in* 1 TAX POLICY AND THE ECONOMY (Lawrence H. Summers ed., 1987)*

* * *

* * * To measure the true revenues associated with transfer taxation, one must determine the net incremental contribution that these taxes make to total federal revenues, or, to put it another way, one must estimate the amount by which total revenues would decline if these taxes were eliminated. This figure may bear very little relation to measures of collected revenue reported by the government. In particular, many of the same estate-planning techniques that allow wealthy individuals to escape transfer taxation also have important income tax implications. Thus, elimination of transfer taxes might significantly affect income tax revenues.

In this paper, I argue that, as a consequence of behavioral responses to estate taxation, a substantial amount of capital income is taxed at lower marginal rates under the personal income tax. I emphasize two major channels through which this occurs. First, estate planners agree that perhaps the best method of avoiding estate taxes is to make substantial intra vivos gifts, and to make them as early in life as possible. Typically, wealthy individuals can do this in ways that minimize or entirely eliminate gift tax liabilities. The net effect is to transfer wealth, typically from parents to children, during a period of life in which children tend to pay lower marginal rates under the personal income tax. Although differences between marginal income tax rates alone create incentives for wealthy individuals to make intra vivos gifts, the estate tax adds to this incentive, presumably generating larger transfers. The government effectively forgoes a portion of its tax claim on incrementally transferred assets. Second, since charitable bequests are deductible from gross estate for tax purposes, the estate tax creates a substantial incentive to make such contributions. Even though one might well deem this

---

a desirable outcome, it is important to recognize that it too has important consequences for the income tax. In this case, resources are transferred from individuals with positive marginal tax rates to tax-exempt institutions. As a result, the government forgoes its entire claim on the transferred assets.

Unfortunately, it is extremely difficult to measure these effects precisely. The most important obstacle is the availability of extensive financial data on a sample drawn from the wealthiest 5 percent of the population. Although most of this information is, in principle, contained in federal personal income, estate, and gift tax returns, the IRS is reluctant to release such information for fear of violating the confidentiality of wealthy taxpayers. Even if this data became available, the measurement of intra vivos transfers (which are often well disguised) would pose severe conceptual difficulties. My strategy in this paper is to estimate true revenues on the basis of the best available evidence. Since this evidence is admittedly sketchy, it is appropriate to think of my calculations as suggestive rather than precise.

Two major conclusions emerge from this study. First, the indirect effects of estate taxation on federal personal income tax revenue are potentially of the same order of magnitude as the reported revenue collected by this tax. Thus, these reported figures may lead one quite far astray. Second, available evidence suggests that, historically, true revenues associated with estate taxation may well have been near zero, or even negative. Recent tax reforms that reduce the progressivity of federal personal income tax rates only partially vitiate this conclusion. Far from "backing up" the income tax as some have claimed, the estate tax may actually generate a rise in income tax avoidance activities sufficient to offset revenue collected through estate levies.

* * *

* * * I have emphasized that these conclusions are highly dependent on the progressivity of the personal income tax, but I have also shown that indirect revenue effects would continue to be extremely important even under the new tax reform bill. Accordingly, common planning techniques severely cripple the ability of the federal government to achieve the dual purposes of promoting equity and raising revenue through estate taxation.

Nevertheless, the existence of this tax does appear to effect a diversion of substantial resources (upward of $2 billion per year) to charity, and many may view this as sufficient justification for its retention. Furthermore, avenues for curtailing estate tax and gift tax avoidance have not yet been fully exhausted. By pursuing such avenues, the federal government might well succeed in reducing large concentrations of wealth while significantly enhancing total federal revenue. Yet in the absence of far-reaching reform, it seems unlikely that the estate tax will do much more than benefit charitable causes.

* * *

NOTE

Edward J. McCaffery characterizes Bernheim's conclusion that the estate tax may have a negative net revenue effect as "improbable." Edward J. McCaffery, *The Uneasy Case for Wealth Transfer Taxation*, 104 YALE L.J. 283, 303 (1994). At the same time, McCaffery criticizes Bernheim for ignoring the adverse effect of the transfer taxes on work and savings: "In this regard it is likely that Bernheim's analysis strongly *over*estimates the revenue gain from the estate tax; diminished productivity unequivocally costs the government tax revenue." *Id.*

Henry J. Aaron & Alicia H. Munnell, *Reassessing the Role for Wealth Transfer Taxes*, 45 NAT'L TAX J. 119 (1992)*

DEFINING AND MEASURING WEALTH

* * *

Concentration of Wealth Implied by U.S. Estate Tax Returns: 1922 to 1986

Although estate tax returns contain data on the wealth only of the deceased, they can provide wealth information about the living population through the "estate multiplier method." By multiplying the wealth of the deceased in various age-sex categories by weights equal to the reciprocal of the mortality rate for each group, one can infer total wealth holdings among these same categories.

* * *

* * * Figure 3 reports the results. It shows a marked decline in the concentration of asset holdings between 1922 and 1947. * * * The estate tax estimates indicate no systematic trend in the share of wealth held by the top 0.5 percent and 1 percent from 1947 through 1982, but suggest an abrupt and sizable increase thereafter. Broader definitions of wealth would show less concentration and more of a trend toward deconcentration.

Figure 3
Estimated Share of Net Worth Held by the Top 0.5 Percent and the Top 1 Percent of the Population

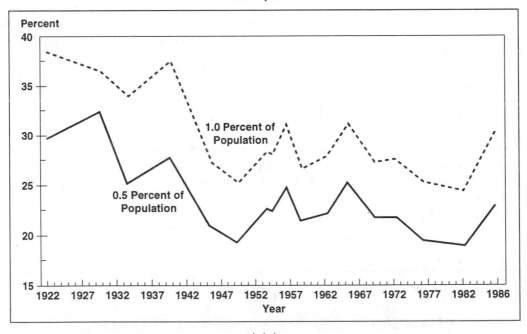

* * *

Concentration of Wealth from Survey Data: 1962 to 1986

Household surveys with reliable data on wealth holdings are available for only four years—1962, 1983, 1986, and 1989. The Federal Reserve Board initiated the process with the

---

1962 Survey of Financial Characteristics of Consumers (SFCC), which gathered detailed data on asset holdings and liabilities. Two decades later, the Fed conducted the 1983 Survey of Consumer Finances (SCF), as the first in an ongoing series of wealth surveys. Many of the participants were reinterviewed in 1986 and again in 1989, when new participants were added. Because wealth holdings are highly concentrated, these surveys over-sample households with high incomes.

* * *

Like the estate tax data, the surveys show that the concentration of wealth has remained quite stable from the 1960s to the mid 1980s, but has increased during the last half of that decade (Table 2). The wealthiest 1 percent of the U.S. population owned roughly 32 percent of [wealth] in 1962, 1983, and 1986. The 1989 survey, however, showed that their share of wealth had increased to 37 percent. * * *

Table 2
Shares of Net Worth Held by Top Wealthholders, Estimated
From Survey Data, 1962 to 1989

Percent of Population	1962	1983	1986	1989
Share of Net Worth * * *				
.5	24.8	24.3	23.9	28.8
1.0	32.2	31.5	31.7	37.1
* * *				

* * *

Overall Assessment of U.S. Wealth Distribution Data

Crude manipulations with the national balance sheets, estimates from estate tax data, and solid evidence from cross-section surveys conducted by the Federal Reserve Board all indicate that holdings of wealth in the United States are highly concentrated. Using the narrow definition, the top 1 percent of wealth holders control about 30 percent of net worth. Broader definitions reduce this value, but the holdings of the top of the distribution remain significant.

Although the estate tax data suggest a major deconcentration of wealth in the first half of the century, some researchers have suggested that this apparent trend toward equalization might simply reflect *intra*household equalization in wealth holdings between spouses, rather than reduction in the *inter*household concentration of wealth. More importantly, no trend toward deconcentration is evident in the postwar era. Rather, data on income inequality during the 1980s suggested that the concentration of wealth holdings would be likely to increase * * *. Indeed, preliminary results from the 1989 Survey of Consumer Finances indicate that a significant increase has occurred in the wealth holdings of the top 1 percent. * * *

* * *

NOTE

Other studies have reached similar conclusions. *See, e.g.*, Christopher E. Erblich, *To Bury Federal Transfer Taxes Without Further Adieu*, 24 SETON HALL L. REV. 1931, 1936-37 (1994) ("[T]he IRS studies indicate that wealth concentration is increasing, not decreasing, despite the federal transfer taxes."); Gilbert P. Verbit, *Do Estate and Gift Taxes Affect Wealth Distribution?*, 117 TR. & EST. 601, 601 (1978) ("[T]he only available data reveal no discernible redistribution or deconcentration of personally held wealth since 1949.").

C.   A Reform Perspective

This Subpart presents the views of reformers who see a continuing role for the wealth transfer taxes, as well as the views of critics who advocate repeal of the taxes. Michael J. Graetz argues for the "rejuvenation" of the estate tax to restore it as an important contributor to the progressivity of the tax system. Harry L. Gutman agrees that the wealth transfer taxes enhance progressivity and points out that they serve as a "backstop" to the income tax by taxing wealth accumulated through tax-preferred sources of income. Mark L. Ascher goes further and considers the role that a more steeply progressive tax system might play in curtailing inherited wealth. In contrast, Thomas A. Robinson issues a "ringing call to inaction" in support of a period of congressional quiescence to absorb the fundamental 1981 transfer tax changes and contends that these taxes simply are "not worth worrying about in light of other pressing national needs." Joel C. Dobris and John E. Donaldson openly call for repeal of the wealth transfer taxes.

Michael J. Graetz, *To Praise the Estate Tax, Not To Bury It*, 93 YALE L.J. 259 (1983)*

For several decades, total revenues raised by estate and gift taxes have roughly equalled those raised by excise taxes on alcohol and tobacco. Yet no law journal has ever asked me to write on alcohol or tobacco excise taxes. The law firms of America do not routinely have divisions devoted to excise tax planning. We do not hear of the suffering of widows and orphans (or even of farmers and small businesses) because of alcohol and tobacco taxes. Philosophers and economists do not routinely debate the merits of such taxes. Perhaps most significantly, increases in such excise taxes do not arouse fears that we are about to eliminate the concept of private property in this country and embrace socialism, or even communism. The estate tax, however, evokes just such responses.

---

    *   Reprinted by permission of The Yale Law Journal Company and Fred B. Rothman & Company from *The Yale Law Journal,* vol. 93, pages 256-286.

I. RECENT TRENDS IN ESTATE TAXATION

A review of the most recent history of the estate tax suggests special ironies. Just seven years ago, in 1976, after nearly thirty years of neglect, Congress adopted a series of revisions intended to make the estate and gift taxes apply on a more regular and uniform basis * * * .

* * *

Having moved toward a basically sound and well-structured wealth transfer tax system, Congress then reversed direction a few years later and moved to emasculate it. * * * [The 1980 and 1981 changes] reduce the deathtime tax base by about seventy percent and reduce the long-term revenue from taxing bequests to at most one-third of that which would have been collected if the 1976 structure had remained unchanged.

When the 1981 changes are fully phased in, the amount of appreciated property transferable at death without being subject to either income or estate taxes will have been increased tenfold since 1976, from $60,000 to $600,000. With such an exemption level, no more than $3 billion of the more than $20 billion of unrealized appreciation annually passing through estates (at 1979 levels), or only fifteen percent, will be subject to estate tax. The other eighty-five percent will escape both income and estate taxation.

* * *

II. RECENT GENERAL TRENDS IN FEDERAL TAXATION

The schizophrenic attitude of Congress toward the estate tax, manifested by the contrast between the 1976 and 1981 legislation, reflects a fundamental tension in the tax system that has dominated tax policy debates during recent years. Broadly speaking, the tension is one between a desire for structural tax reform, which would move the tax system towards greater horizontal and vertical equity, and a desire for tax provisions designed to stimulate increased savings or capital formation. This tension produces a direct conflict between the need to tax capital or the income from capital in order to achieve a progressive tax burden and the perceived need to exempt capital and capital income from tax in order to induce economic growth.

* * *

* * * [Recent tax history reveals] several trends. First, the dominant economic factor influencing tax policy today is the projection of very large current and future deficits. If spending is—as seems to be the case—not likely to be reduced further in substantial amounts, the deficit can be narrowed only by additional revenues. Economic recovery may partially close the revenue gap, but, as state and local governments are learning, increased and new taxes will undoubtedly prove necessary. This need for revenues, however, is constrained by great reluctance * * * to increase the tax burden on capital or capital income for fear of stifling economic growth. In contrast, fairness in the distribution of the tax burden seems of little political significance since it currently enjoys no meaningful constituency.

III. THE ROLE OF THE ESTATE TAX

These conditions combine to make the estate tax a very minor player indeed. Since it is a tax on savings, proposals to increase the estate tax run headlong into concerns over "capital formation." Moreover, the estate tax has very limited potential as a source of federal revenues. Although the estate tax accounted for nearly eleven percent of federal revenues at its zenith in 1936, estate and gift taxes have never produced more than two and one-half percent of total revenue since the end of the Second World War. Even if the most recent trends were reversed by returning to the pre-1976 tax-exempt level of $60,000 instead of proceeding with the phased-in increases to a $600,000 tax-exempt level, estate taxes would only be double their current total and would again produce only about two percent of total revenue. If the estate tax were increased still further to produce a post-war high of two and one-half percent of total revenue, it would generate only an additional $8 billion, an amount which would make only a very small dent in the projected federal deficits.

The limitation on potential estate tax revenues is an inherent one, not merely a product of political obstacles. Decedents annually transfer a total of about $120 billion in net assets. An average effective tax rate of twenty percent would produce total revenues of about $24 billion, approximately three times the current level. With any substantial exemption, plus exclusions for certain amounts of property passing to surviving spouses or charities, a higher average effective rate seems unrealistic. The inherent limitation on bequests as a source of revenue cannot be overcome by even a dramatic structural revision of estate and gift taxes, such as converting to an inheritance or accessions tax, or taxing gifts and bequests as income to the recipient (or, in a consumption tax world, as consumption of the donor). A tax on deathtime transfers of wealth will thus not serve as a major source of federal revenues.

So we must look elsewhere than the production of revenues if we are to justify strengthening, rather than eliminating, the estate tax. That place should be its role in the distribution of the tax burden, in particular, its role in providing an important element of progressivity in the federal tax system.

* * *

To view the estate tax, however, as contributing an important element of progressivity to the federal tax system requires shedding a myth which has come to dominate its political discussion. This myth * * * is that the proper function of the estate tax (as well as its historical role) is only to "break up large concentrations of wealth." The clear implication—indeed, the principal justification for raising the tax-exempt level of estates to $600,000—is that no estate tax should be imposed on "smaller or moderate-sized estates." In 1981, "smaller and moderate-sized estates" meant those of the wealthiest one to six percent. If the 1976 tax-exempt level of $60,000 had been maintained, the estate tax would now apply to the wealthiest ten percent of decedents. The narrowing of the estate tax base that accompanies political acceptance of this myth necessarily defeats the contribution of this tax to the progressivity of the federal tax system. The tax becomes as narrow in its intended function as it is in its contribution to the government's revenue. A strong case can then be advanced for its elimination altogether.

In fact, however, the estate tax has done very little to dilute the greatest concentrations of wealth. The portion of total wealth held by the richest one percent of wealth-holders has remained remarkably stable. * * *

* * *

The principal reason, therefore, to revise the estate tax is to rescue this mechanism for achieving progressivity, and perhaps to rescue progressivity itself, from both short- and long-term threats. * * *

* * *

V. CAPITAL FORMATION IS NOT THE TRUMP

I want now to consider what I regard as the most important objection to estate taxation, indeed to taxation of wealth or capital income in any form. This, of course, is the adverse impact of such taxes on the amount of savings and investment, that is, on capital formation.

The basic argument is quite straightforward. Our nation needs more savings if it is to enjoy economic growth. The estate tax is levied on savings, and taxing such savings will cause people to save less. The argument, of course, implicates all progressive taxation if the marginal propensity of higher-income individuals to save exceeds that of low-income individuals. Although the argument is sometimes expressed in terms of an equity-efficiency tradeoff, taxes on capital are often analyzed only in terms of their effects on economic growth and efficiency. The case for lower taxes on capital, however, is far from clear.

At the outset, one might question the alleged need for increased savings. * * * But let us put such questions aside and assume that the country needs more savings. What would that imply for the estate tax?

The estate tax is such a small revenue source that its effects on savings and investment are no doubt dwarfed by the impact of other taxes and by fiscal and monetary policies. Perhaps for this reason, the impact of the estate tax on aggregate savings has not received much explicit theoretical or empirical examination by modern economists. The modern economic literature does, however, contain observations * * * that deathtime taxes on capital, such as estate taxes, are likely to have smaller disincentive effects than lifetime income taxes.

* * *

The evidence concerning the alleged adverse economic effects of the estate tax is * * * inconclusive. Liberal economists will likely find little or no impact; conservative economists will probably discover serious deleterious effects. On balance, however, the economic evidence available to date simply fails to make a case for the elimination or reduction of estate and gift taxes on the grounds that increased savings will result. Other considerations must dominate such decisions. Persons who wish to increase the rate of capital accumulation would likely do better to focus on reducing federal deficits, stimulating business investment, and eliminating income tax incentives for inefficient investments.

VI. WHAT DOES THIS MEAN FOR THE ESTATE TAX?

So where does the foregoing leave me? First, confirmed in my view that progressive taxation complies with notions of fairness—that it is just and should not now be abandoned. Second, with the belief that a tax on bequests—an estate tax—can and should play an important role in achieving progressivity in the federal tax system; indeed, with the conviction that taxes on bequests are preferable to high tax rates on income as a means of achieving progressivity. Finally, with the view that there is no convincing evidence that the advantages of taxing bequests as a means of obtaining progressivity in taxation are overcome by the deleterious impact of estate taxes on capital formation. It is my view, therefore, that the nation's tax laws should move in the direction of the 1976 legislation, not that of the 1981 law, and that the estate tax should be rejuvenated and returned to its prior status as an important contributor to the progressivity of the tax system. But having urged this as the direction it *should* go, I cannot close without also examining where it will likely go.

There are two practical barriers to my preferred course of strengthening the role of the estate tax in the federal system. The first I have already described—namely the inherent limitation on the revenue potential of an estate tax. As I have detailed above, there simply is not enough wealth transferred annually to permit a wealth transfer tax (an estate and gift tax) to become a significant source of federal revenue. Given the current and projected levels of federal deficits, only substantial revenue sources seem likely to dominate the political agenda in the near-term. Thus, tax increases grounded predominately on distributional fairness would seem to have little chance of success.

The second practical barrier is that—for reasons which remain quite mysterious to me—taxation of bequests is extremely unpopular politically. The political obstacles take a variety of forms. It is often said that opponents of tax increases hide behind selected widows. Even with the unlimited marital deduction, when one considers estate taxation, both widows and orphans are readily at hand. The fact that most heirs of wealthy decedents are rich adults has little or no political significance.

A more important political obstacle to estate taxation lies in the objections of owners of small businesses and farms. These two groups produced the political momentum for both the 1976 and 1981 increases in the level of tax-exempt estates, and will (effectively, no doubt) resist any political efforts to reverse that trend. Although the estate tax does pose liquidity problems for some owners of small businesses and farms, their clout far outweighs their actual stake in general estate tax policies. The great bulk of assets transferred at death by people subject to the estate tax has always been composed of liquid and readily marketable assets, principally securities. Nevertheless, coherent and progressive estate tax revision seems quite unlikely unless the political obstacles posed by farmers and owners of small businesses are neutralized.

The most puzzling political obstacle to estate tax revision, however, is that the American people do not seem to like heavy taxes on bequests. George McGovern's proposal in 1972 to confiscate inheritances above a certain amount was not well received, and a recent California initiative to repeal the state's inheritance tax garnered a sixty-four percent positive vote. This was a greater majority than those in favor of a nuclear freeze or against gun registration, issues on a subsequent initiative ballot. The only convincing explanation that has occurred to me for this phenomenon lies in the optimism of the American people. In California, at least, sixty-four percent of the people must believe that they will be in the wealthiest five to ten percent when they die.

The combination of these political obstacles to the estate tax's rejuvenation and the tax's inherent limitations as a significant revenue source leads me to conclude that the estate tax seems far more likely to wither than to grow stronger. As I have suggested, this prediction makes me fear the demise of progressive taxation in the United States. * * *

* * *

NOTE

Is Graetz correct in arguing that "[t]he evidence concerning the alleged adverse economic effects of the estate tax is * * * inconclusive"? The Staff of the Joint Committee on Taxation recently observed that "it is an open question whether estate and gift taxes encourage or discourage saving and there has been no empirical analysis of this specific issue." JOINT COMM. ON TAX'N, DESCRIPTION AND ANALYSIS OF TAX PROPOSALS RELATING TO SAVINGS AND INVESTMENT (CAPITAL GAINS, IRAS, AND ESTATE AND GIFT TAX) (JCS-5-97), 105th Cong., 1st Sess. 151 (1997). The Joint Committee noted that "[b]y raising the cost, in terms of taxes, of leaving a bequest, potential transferors may be discouraged from accumulating the assets necessary to make a bequest. On the other hand, some individuals purchase additional life insurance in order to have sufficient funds to pay the estate tax without disposing of other assets in their estate." *Id.*

Graetz's analysis is not without its critics. Some argue that Graetz ignores "the possibility of inter-generational turnover in the identity of the wealthy themselves." Edward J. McCaffery, *The Uneasy Case for Wealth Transfer Taxation*, 104 YALE L.J. 283, 322 n.143 (1994). Others challenge the notion that the wealth transfer taxes significantly enhance progressivity, noting that these taxes "affect an extremely small percentage of the population and raise precious little revenue." Christopher E. Erblich, *To Bury Federal Transfer Taxes Without Further Adieu*, 24 SETON HALL L. REV. 1931,

1962 (1994). At the same time, they insist that although "the revenue *collected* from the tax is insignificant, the amount of revenue *affected* by the tax is very significant." *Id.* at 1946. Still others question the validity of progressivity as a justification for the wealth transfer taxes. *See* Jeffrey A. Schoenblum, *Tax Fairness or Unfairness? A Consideration of the Philosophical Bases for Unequal Taxation*, 12 AM. J. TAX POL'Y 221, 265-66 (1995). Are these criticisms compelling? Do they undermine Graetz's thesis?

Harry L. Gutman, *Reforming Federal Wealth Transfer Taxes After ERTA*, 69 VA. L. REV. 1183 (1983)*

* * *

I. WHY TAX WEALTH TRANSFERS?

If one were to design a tax system de novo, one would undoubtedly ask whether an excise on wealth transfers is a necessary component. Commentators have noted that a tax on wealth transfers is indistinguishable from a tax on income because in economic terms wealth is simply the capitalized present value of future income. The argument implies that if economic income were fully taxed, wealth would be fully taxed as well, making a wealth transfer tax unnecessary.

Even if this argument is correct, however, a wealth transfer tax can be justified on a number of other grounds. Suppose, for example, one believed that greater progressivity and higher marginal rates were necessary to accomplish an appropriate redistribution of income and wealth. One alternative for implementing such a goal is simply to tax income at the rates necessary to achieve the desired distribution of the tax burden. An income tax with a high maximum marginal rate, however, might have unacceptable efficiency effects of locking in invested capital and encouraging current consumption rather than saving. * * * Many economists also believe that a transfer tax has less allocative impact on investment decisions than an income tax. This is partially because individuals discount taxes that will be due at their death for purposes of current decisionmaking. Thus, several commentators have concluded that a wealth transfer tax is an appropriate supplement to the income tax in efficiently reaching a desired level of progressivity.

Other supporters of the wealth transfer tax have argued that wealth reflects an ability to pay beyond that represented by its future income stream and that a sound tax system should tax this incremental ability to pay. Still others have contended that a wealth transfer tax should exist to disperse the attributes of economic power and opportunity that are thought to accompany large accumulations of wealth. In this role, the transfer tax derives its justification from social determinations regarding the relationship of wealth to an "ideal" distribution of power and economic opportunity in society.

These justifications are intended to address the criticism that a transfer tax is not necessary to supplement a comprehensive income tax base. In reality, the current income tax base bears little resemblance to what economists would define as income and thus can hardly be described as comprehensive. * * *

* * *

That the current tax system excludes large amounts of income from the income tax base provides the most compelling reason for retaining a transfer tax. With a seriously eroded income

---

tax base, a transfer tax is needed to ensure that each taxpayer eventually bears a fair share of the tax burden. The transfer tax serves as a "backstop" to the income tax by taxing the wealth that taxpayers accumulate through tax-preferred income sources.

* * *

The most persuasive recent defenses of the transfer tax have focused precisely on its contribution to the progressivity of the tax system. The progressive effect of the transfer tax is clear in instances such as unrealized appreciation * * * . As a more general proposition, even though the transfer tax has historically applied to only a small segment of the population and has been the source of only a small percentage of total federal revenue, it is probable that these taxes have been collected almost exclusively from those who during their lifetimes had above average incomes. To the extent this observation is correct, a positive effect on progressivity results. The difficulty has been to quantify the effect.

* * *

A more accurate study would enhance empirical knowledge of the impact of the transfer tax and its relationship to the income tax. No such study, however, is necessary to understand that through the passage of ERTA, Congress has seriously eroded the transfer tax's role as a supplement to the income tax and has correlatively weakened the transfer tax's contribution to progressivity. * * *

* * *

NOTE

The Joint Committee on Taxation recently echoed Gutman's point in noting that "by serving as a 'backstop' for income that escapes income taxation, the transfer taxes may help promote overall fairness of the U.S. tax system." JOINT COMM. ON TAX'N, DESCRIPTION AND ANALYSIS OF TAX PROPOSALS RELATING TO SAVINGS AND INVESTMENT (CAPITAL GAINS, IRAS, AND ESTATE AND GIFT TAX) (JCS-5-97), 105th Cong., 1st Sess. 153 (1997). Other commentators, however, contend that "[t]he flaws of the income tax should be addressed and amended through the income tax laws, not through a dual system of taxation." Edward J. Gac & Sharen K. Brougham, *A Proposal for Restructuring the Taxation of Wealth Transfers: Tax Reform Redux?*, 5 AKRON TAX J. 75, 87 (1988).

Mark L. Ascher, *Curtailing Inherited Wealth*, 89 MICH. L. REV. 69 (1990)*

INTRODUCTION

One of the most dominant themes in American ideology is equality of opportunity. In our society, ability and willingness to work hard are supposed to make all things possible. But we know there are flaws in our ideology. Differences in native ability unquestionably exist. Similarly, some people seem to have distinctly more than their fair share of good luck. Both types

---

*   Originally published in 89 MICH. L. REV. 69 (1990).

of differences are, however, beyond our control. So we try to convince ourselves that education evens out most differences. Still, we know * * * there are vast differences in the educations parents can afford for their children. * * *

When forced to acknowledge these differences in ability, luck, and educational opportunity, we admit that we do not play on a completely level field. But because each of these differences seems beyond our control, we tend to believe the field is as level as we can make it. It is not. For no particularly good reason, we allow some players, typically those most culturally and educationally advantaged, to inherit huge amounts of wealth, unearned in any sense at all. So long as we continue to tolerate inheritance by healthy, adult children, what we as a nation actually proclaim is, "All men are created equal, except the children of the wealthy."

* * *

* * * [T]hinking about using the federal wealth transfer taxes to abolish inheritance may not be entirely futile. It may permit an entirely new type of analysis. * * * One willing, for purposes of analysis, to discard freedom of testation could start from the proposition that property rights *should* end at death. Inheritance then would be tolerated only as an exception to that general rule. This article does just that. I invite the reader to join me in speculating whether it might not make sense to use the federal wealth transfer taxes to curtail inheritance, thereby increasing equality of opportunity while raising revenue.

My proposal views inheritance as something we should tolerate only when necessary—not something we should always protect. My major premise is that all property owned at death, after payment of debts and administration expenses, should be sold and the proceeds paid to the United States government. There would be six exceptions. A marital exemption, potentially unlimited, would accrue over the life of a marriage. Thus, spouses could continue to provide for each other after death. Decedents would also be allowed to provide for dependent lineal descendants. The amount available to any given descendant would, however, depend on the descendant's age and would drop to zero at an age of presumed independence. A separate exemption would allow generous provision for disabled lineal descendants of any age. Inheritance by lineal ascendants (parents, grandparents, etc.) would be unlimited. A universal exemption would allow a moderate amount of property either to pass outside the exemptions or to augment amounts passing under them. Thus, every decedent would be able to leave something to persons of his or her choice, regardless whether another exemption was available. Up to a fixed fraction of an estate could pass to charity. In addition, to prevent circumvention by lifetime giving, the gift tax would increase substantially.

My proposal strikes directly at inheritance by healthy, adult children. * * * Children lucky enough to have been raised, acculturated, and educated by wealthy parents need not be allowed the additional good fortune of inheriting their parents' property. In this respect, we can do much better than we ever have before at equalizing opportunity. This proposal would leave "widows and orphans" essentially untouched. The disabled, grandparents, and charity would probably fare better than ever before. But inheritance by healthy, adult children would cease immediately, except to the extent of the universal exemption.

* * *

II. INHERITANCE AS A MATTER OF POLICY

A. *Society's Stake in Accumulated Wealth*

Individuals never acquire property on their own. Society plays a crucial role in every individual's acquisitive activities. Society determines the rules by which individuals acquire property. Society also educates (to one extent or another) every individual. And society enacts and enforces laws that protect individuals' enjoyment of what they acquire.

* * *

* * * The inescapable conclusion is that society has a major stake in all accumulated wealth. Given that stake, society need not continue to allow decedents nearly unlimited control over the disposition of their property after death.

B. Arguments in Favor of Curtailing Inheritance

1. Leveling the Playing Field

* * * Philosophers tend to agree that equality of opportunity is a fundamental good. It is hardly open to debate that inherited wealth contradicts equality of opportunity. * * * How society reallocates accumulated wealth at death is, therefore, a critical determinant of the degree of equality of opportunity succeeding generations will enjoy. * * *

* * *

* * * [M]y proposal attempts to distinguish those types of inequalities that are inevitable in the family context from those that are distinctly less so. * * * The fact that inequality of ability, luck, and education would continue under a system that curtailed inheritance is irrelevant. We must do what we can.

2. Deficit Reduction in a Painless and Appropriate Fashion

Another reason to curtail inheritance is the prospect of raising revenue. If $150 billion pass at death each year, curtailing inheritance has the potential to raise a substantial amount of revenue. Unfortunately, my proposal would raise nowhere near $150 billion. It contains so many generous exceptions that its very structure limits its promise. Taking those exceptions into account, my best guess is that it might raise $25-30 billion. Even so, it would raise almost four times as much as the federal wealth transfer taxes currently raise. But the exceptions are not the only limitations on the proposal's promise. Its economic effects are unknown. If it decreased incentives to work or save, its revenue yield might be lower still. All these uncertainties suggest that raising revenue is not the most important reason to implement this proposal. * * *

* * *

A tax on inheritance by healthy, adult children falls squarely on those whose only claim is by accident of birth. To them, inheritance is little more than a windfall. They, more than anyone else, truly have the ability to pay. And the extent to which a tax is based on ability to pay is widely accepted as a primary measure of a tax's fairness.

3. Protecting Elective Representative Government

In America, * * * [w]e believe all our citizens should have an equal voice in selecting their governmental representatives. We also believe all our citizens should have an equal opportunity to serve in elective office. Inheritance is inconsistent with these beliefs. Money clearly influences politicians. Similarly, because political campaigns are expensive, the wealthy have a tremendous advantage when seeking election.

* * *

* * * If we were willing to curtail inheritance, we could simultaneously eliminate one of the most blatant sources of inequality and improve the prospects for another two centuries of elective representative government in America.

4. Increasing Privatization in the Care of the Disabled and the Elderly

As the extended family vanishes, it leaves behind many victims. Elderly parents and grandparents, as well as the disabled, are often, in effect, homeless. Increasingly, the cost of supporting these individuals has fallen to the government. The government, however, often provides care for such individuals in a poor and insensitive fashion. Moreover, the cost of providing such care is an expense we as a nation seem unable to afford. A system that encourages family members to provide for the care of the elderly and disabled is, therefore, desirable. Increased privatization would ensure not only better and more sensitive care, but also reduction of the costs borne by the government.

My proposal would encourage private expenditure for the care of the elderly and disabled. It would allow a generous exemption for disabled lineal descendants. In addition, it would allow an unlimited exemption for lineal ascendants, most of whom would be elderly. * * *

No doubt the truly wealthy already take care of their elderly and disabled. Thus, curtailing inheritance might produce little privatization at that level. Those at lower wealth levels, however, do not always take care of their own. "Divestment planning," a new type of estate planning, caters to clients desiring to shift the costs of caring for elderly and disabled relatives to the government. By making it much more expensive during lifetime to give large amounts to one's children, and by limiting the amount healthy children could inherit, this proposal would achieve much greater privatization at the "near-rich" level.

* * *

C. Arguments Against Curtailing Inheritance

1. The Effect on the Economy

Several lines of argument suggest that curtailing inheritance might adversely affect the economy. The adverse economic effects most frequently mentioned fall into three categories: decreased incentives to work, increased consumption leading to decreased savings, and decreased privately held capital.

a. Incentive to work. One of the first retorts to any proposal to curtail inheritance is the assertion that such a proposal would eliminate incentives to work. According to this line of reasoning, one works in large part for the opportunity to pass something to one's children at death. People, however, work for many other reasons. First are the power and prestige that work and accumulation provide. Money makes the world go round. We work primarily to earn it. Money allows us to feed, clothe, and house ourselves. It also provides us with luxuries and amusement for our leisure. Money provides us with security. * * *

* * *

Undoubtedly it is important to ask how curtailing inheritance would affect incentives for work. But with so many other, more important incentives, it is hard to believe curtailing inheritance by healthy, adult children would have any measurable impact. * * *

* * *

b. Increased consumption and decreased savings. The second economic argument against curtailing inheritance focuses on its supposed tendency to encourage consumption. For years, estate planners have teasingly told their clients that the best estate planning was spending. If inheritance were curtailed, that advice would be truer than ever before. Anyone worried about what would happen to his or her wealth after death could consume it prior to death. If property owners generally followed such advice, curtailing inheritance would raise little revenue. More important, consumption would increase, and savings would decrease.

* * * [U]nder the current system, which itself provides strong incentives to transfer wealth during life, parents almost always keep their money. In short, the incentives to retain property dwarf the incentives to give it away.

Would this parental tendency to retain property change if inheritance were curtailed? * * * [T]he demand for the power, prestige, flexibility, and security money provides seems relatively inelastic—even in persons old enough to be worrying about what happens to their property after death. In short, the instinct for self-preservation would continue to limit spending, even if inheritance were curtailed. Curtailing inheritance might, therefore, increase consumption only slightly. * * *

* * *

c. Decrease in capital privately held. By reallocating to the government a larger portion of what is owned at death, and by subjecting lifetime transfers to higher gift taxes, this proposal would remove from the private economy a large amount of capital. This concern is, however, irrelevant to a tax providing deficit financing. * * *

* * *

8. "Wiping Out the Dream"

* * *

* * * I suggest *curtailing* inheritance, not abolishing it. A universal exemption would allow *every* decedent to bequeath a substantial amount of property. If set at $250,000, this exemption would exempt approximately 98% of the population. Thus, for the vast bulk of society, all my proposal would do is "wipe out the dream" of inheriting a purely imaginary fortune or passing a purely imaginary fortune to healthy, adult children. For the few truly wealthy, my proposal would, of course, represent a major change in the wealth transmission process. But even the truly wealthy could still pass, in addition to lifetime gifts, and in addition to other exempted amounts, $250,000 to whomever they wished. The psychological needs of 2% of the population to control more than that amount of wealth after death ought not prevail over the benefits my proposal promises.

* * *

NOTE

Are wealth distribution and equality of opportunity legitimate concerns of federal tax policy? Can they realistically be ignored in determining the structure of rates and exemptions? Do you agree with Ascher's argument that steeply progressive rates would not have a significant adverse impact on work incentives? One commentator has expressed misgivings about "practical consequences and unpredictable behavioral responses" in connection with Ascher's proposal. Jan Ellen Rein, *Misinformation and Self-Deception in Recent Long-Term Care Policy Trends*, 12 J. LAW & POL. 195, 317 (1996). Are these grounds for similar misgivings in connection with proposals to curtail the taxation of wealth transfers?

Thomas A. Robinson, *The Federal Wealth Transfer Taxes—A Requiem?*, 1 AM. J. TAX POL'Y 25 (1983)*

Many people are surprised to learn that the modern federal wealth transfer taxes were designed to raise revenue * * * . Unfortunately, despite their theoretical advantages as revenue raisers, the wealth transfer taxes have not worked well in practice. Since World War II, they have contributed less than two percent of the government's revenue, and that at the cost of encouraging inefficient property management and significant estate planning fees.

* * *

* * * I will not directly discuss the issue of whether the revenue-raising purpose of the wealth transfer taxes has been, or should have been, abandoned. I will assume it has been and shift the focus of my discussion to the alternate non-revenue arguments which have, to date, played a relatively insignificant role in shaping the taxes but which, if my assumption is correct, must now rationalize the taxes' continued existence and form.

My conclusion will be that the taxes should be retained in their post-ERTA form for two reasons: first, we need further experience with them in this form, and second, the taxes are simply not worth worrying about in light of other pressing national needs.

I. ANALYTICAL PROBLEMS WITH THE WEALTH TRANSFER TAXES

* * *

The two traditional non-revenue rationales for the wealth transfer taxes * * * are "anti-concentration" and "leveling." When these two rationales are further analyzed in terms of the benefits to be produced from the national wealth and the equality of distribution of these benefits, they are seen to be somewhat overlapping terms. * * *

II. INCREASED PRODUCTION OF BENEFITS

One of the two main goals of governmental programs, including the wealth transfer taxes, is to stimulate the flow of benefits from the nation's human and capital resources, and if possible to increase the quantum of these benefits per capita so each citizen can enjoy a better standard of living. An increased benefit stream can only come from an increased national store of invested capital. Such a store is a necessary, but not a sufficient, condition; by itself, money represents nothing more than the power to withdraw benefits from future production. At its best, invested capital should provide efficiencies of scale and an indefinite flow of benefits. * * *

Encouraging capital formation involves two quite distinct objectives: encouraging people to use their talent and energy to create stores of capital; and then encouraging people to save rather than to consume the capital so created. * * *

* * *

* * * Besides encouraging the creation and preservation of capital, governmental policy should also encourage good management of that capital. And good capital management can occur at both the macro- and micro-levels. At the macro-level, the government might want to foster competition; at the micro-level, the government might want to foster management by the most efficient and effective managers.

On the macro-level, the greatest benefits from the nation's wealth are produced by a freely competitive private sector. * * * But if this is one of the "anti-concentration" objectives

---

of the wealth transfer taxes, then it is clear the taxes cannot and do not have this effect. The action of these taxes is simply too remote. * * *

Moving to the micro-level, the policy focus is on the qualifications and motivations of the competing classes of managerial candidates: the wealth-creator, his spouse, his heirs, a professional trustee, and the government. * * *

* * *

In any case, this sort of analysis is somewhat misleading in view of the form of the post-ERTA wealth transfer taxes. More than ninety-nine percent of the country's estates will escape wealth transfer taxation entirely, and most of the capital stock of the country will pass untouched by these taxes. The wealth transfer taxes will therefore likely have only a limited effect on the macro- or micro-management of the nation's capital wealth. Moreover, much of the nation's wealth, as distinguished from its capital wealth, resides in the aggregate sum of the ability, training, motivation and organization of its people. Insofar as the wealth transfer tax system appears to level or even confiscate large blocks of inherited capital wealth, this tax system may increase the productivity of these people by increasing their perception of the system's basic fairness. Again, the lack of adequate empirical evidence precludes any complete evaluation of this claim.

III. INCREASED EQUALITY OF DISTRIBUTION

A second main objective of governmental programs is the "redistribution of purchasing power," a central rationale of the wealth transfer taxes. For equalitarians, of course, equality of distribution is the prime objective. * * *

* * *

Stating the equalitarian goal in this way initially seems to show that it does not provide a strong *non-revenue* goal for the wealth taxes. The essence of this sort of transfer is taking purchasing power from one group and distributing it to another. This would merely be a variation of the revenue goal, raising revenue for redistribution rather than for governmental services. But it does not appear to be a viable purpose of the wealth transfer taxes because they have never raised substantial revenue. On further analysis, only the redistribution of a few of the largest estates * * * , or perhaps only the appearance of redistribution, is a viable purpose of the tax. One suspects a prime "equalitarian" objective of the wealth transfer taxes is simply to inflict economic damage on the rich. * * *

* * *

V. CONCLUSION

* * *

Also clear from the history of the wealth transfer taxes is the simple fact that while the taxes are sound in theory, they have not worked well in practice. If they have been abandoned as revenue-raisers, perhaps they should now be repealed * * * since it is arguable that alternate rationales for the wealth transfer taxes have never been important. However, I suggest that the best data about these taxes are the way the taxes have been shaped by political forces, and therefore they should be retained in their present form for a time to see if there might not be some hidden function performed by the taxes as evidenced by political pressures to alter or repeal them.

And, finally, I might take a broader view. If the wealth transfer taxes only touch one percent of the estates in the country, then I suggest we devote our legislative attention to more pressing problems. * * * If this is a ringing call to inaction, so be it.

NOTE

Since 1982, the wealth transfer taxes have continued to play a prominent role in tax policy debates. What accounts for Congress's failure to turn its "legislative attention to more pressing problems"?

Joel C. Dobris, *A Brief for the Abolition of All Transfer Taxes*, 35 SYRACUSE L. REV. 1215 (1984)*

I. INTRODUCTION

Recent articles call for the reform of the estate and gift tax.[1] In a sentence, the complaint is that the tax has lost its bite. This article is a brief for the abolition of the estate and gift tax. Though not often discussed, and perhaps not likely to occur, abolition is a responsible reform proposal that deserves consideration.

II. DISCUSSION

* * *

A. Arguments in Favor of Abolishing the Transfer Tax

There are meaningful arguments in favor of abolishing all transfer taxes in our federal tax system. * * *

First, the gift and estate tax does not raise a meaningful amount of revenue and never will. Not enough property is transferred to use a transfer tax as a source of revenue, especially if the rates are not confiscatory. After the passage of the Economic Recovery Tax Act of 1981 (ERTA), this low production of revenue has been magnified. Thus, Professor Gutman states that if ERTA had been fully phased-in in 1981 that transfer tax revenue would have been only $2.54 billion. This revenue could be raised in numerous other ways, including a slight increase in the income tax rates.

Second, the current gift and estate tax arguably does not adequately vindicate any of the social policies it is supposed to. Many people believe a gift and estate tax is supposed to break up concentrations of wealth, achieve a more equitable distribution of resources, or assert the hegemony of the common people or the egalitarian nature of our society. Assuming that it is desirable to do any of this, through the tax system or otherwise, then the current gift and estate tax is not a worthwhile tool. The transfer tax does not break up concentrations of wealth. It does not function in a meaningful way to redistribute wealth in order to enhance the quality of life for persons with less wealth. Indeed, it might be said that no politically acceptable transfer tax system can obtain such a result. The tax would have to be confiscatory in order to accomplish this—a politically unacceptable result at the present time.

* * *

If the current system is not working to eliminate concentrations of wealth, that is certainly an argument for reform of the system now in place. Is it, however, an argument for abolition? I believe that it is legitimate to call for the abolition of something that is not working, and has

---

[1]   *See generally* Graetz, *To Praise the Estate Tax, Not to Bury It*, 93 YALE L.J. 259 (1983); Gutman, *Reforming Federal Wealth Transfer Taxes After ERTA*, 69 VA. L. REV. 1183 (1983) * * * .

not worked, to achieve one of its important purposes. Moreover, it is not at all clear that people want these concentrations broken up, or that a just America requires it.

The transfer tax does not accomplish another of its social purposes—the importation of progressive taxation into our tax system. * * *

It is clear that the transfer tax does not strongly contribute to progressivity. Moreover, it is unclear if we as a society are committed to progressivity in our tax system or if progressivity is an obvious social goal. It is not immediately obvious that a just America must have progressivity in its tax system. Given the failure to obtain progressivity with the current tax and the meaningful uncertainty about progressivity as a tax goal, it is quite legitimate to consider abolition insofar as progressivity is an important policy underlying the tax.

* * *

A third argument favoring abolition is that the tax is costly in many ways, both direct and indirect. The direct costs include both the cost of the constant reform of the tax and the cost of complying with the tax.

* * *

It is argued in favor of abolition that an indirect cost of transfer taxation is that a death tax discourages savings and encourages consumption, thereby interfering with capital formation via savings. * * * I am not sure I agree that a death tax interferes with capital formation. Basically, I say this because I do not believe that the estate tax plays a major role in savings or consumption decisions. * * *

Repeal might well reduce the amount of money held in trusts. This might well result in more money being invested in riskier investments, which, in turn, might result in economic growth. I am suggesting that many trusts are created only to avoid estate tax, and that trustees invest conservatively. * * *

* * *

A final argument favoring abolition is that the estate tax creates serious liquidity problems for a small, but economically important, group of decedents—owners of closely held businesses, real estate and farms. * * *

* * *

NOTE

Do you agree that there is "no politically acceptable transfer tax system" that could enhance progressivity? How would Ascher respond? At a congressional hearing called in 1981 to consider the possible repeal of the wealth transfer taxes, the chair of the Tax Section of the American Bar Association testified as follows:

> The purposes and effects of federal transfer tax laws . . . must be carefully weighed in light of long term economic, social, and political objectives, and in light of revenue needs. . . . [T]o the extent that the purposes and effects of these laws are valid, the segments of society which are to bear the burden of these transfer taxes must be determined consistent with the economic, social and political objectives to be achieved.

See Gerald P. Moran, *Estate and Gift Taxation: The Case for Repeal*, 13 TAX NOTES 339, 342 (1981). Why do you think the ABA took such an ambivalent position on the possible repeal of the wealth transfer taxes?

John E. Donaldson, *The Future of Transfer Taxation: Repeal, Restructuring and Refinement, or Replacement?*, 50 WASH. & LEE L. REV. 539 (1993)*

I. INTRODUCTION

* * * [T]he transfer tax system remains deficient in a number of ways. The adequacy of the system can be measured in terms of whether it accomplishes its objectives. Under this measure, the system, apart from raising comparatively insignificant revenue, is a failure. Its adequacy can also be measured in terms of the traditional tests of a good tax system, which employ standards of efficiency, fairness, and neutrality. Under this measure, the system also fails. * * *

* * *

II. GOALS OF THE TRANSFER TAX SYSTEM

Several goals have, from time to time, been ascribed to the transfer tax system. One that has been articulated from time to time, particularly during the 1930s, is the breaking up or reducing of concentrations of wealth. Another is that of producing revenue. More recently, the system has been "justified" for its role or potential in adding an element of progressivity to the overall federal tax system.[13] An examination of the transfer tax system in relation to these perceived goals is in order.

A. Reducing Concentrations of Wealth

However worthwhile the objective of breaking up or reducing concentrations of wealth may be, commentators generally agree that the transfer tax system has been ineffective in this regard. * * * Notwithstanding occasional expressions to the contrary, Congress has shown little interest in the role of transfer taxes in breaking up concentrations of wealth. Its actions move in the opposite direction. * * *

* * *

B. Production of Revenue

The second, and perhaps the historically more important goal of the transfer tax system, is that of producing revenue. In the mid to late 1930s, the transfer tax system was a major component of the federal tax system, producing more than six percent of total revenues and in one year, 1936, ten percent. * * * Since World War II, however, transfer tax revenues have rarely exceeded two percent of total federal tax collections and as a result of recent changes, have diminished to approximately 1.1 percent. * * *

Even if there were greater desire to use the transfer tax system as a source of revenue, it is doubtful whether such taxes could be adapted to become a major revenue source. In fact, no country, including those which have more socialistic political values, derives significant revenues from wealth transfer taxation. * * * The political factors that discourage Congress from

---

13   Michael J. Graetz, *To Praise the Estate Tax, Not to Bury It*, 93 YALE L.J. 259 (1983).

using transfer taxes to reduce concentrations of wealth also operate to discourage use of transfer taxes as sources of additional revenue.

* * *

C. Contributing to Progressivity

A third goal, or role, of transfer taxes advanced by some is that of contributing to the progressivity of the federal tax system.[38] However, that role has a more historic than continuing significance and is a function both of the progressivity of other taxes, particularly the individual income tax, in relation to the amount of transfer tax revenues, and the number of persons burdened by the tax. * * *

The existing transfer tax system simply cannot be justified by reference to its contribution to progressivity. Professor Graetz, commenting on the narrowing of the transfer tax base effected by the 1981 legislation, which was predicated on the "myth" that the proper function of the estate tax is to reduce concentrations of wealth in excess of $600,000, bemoaned that acceptance of the "myth" defeats the contribution of transfer taxes to progressivity. Professor Gutman, also a proponent of the role of transfer taxes in contributing to progressivity, refers to the 1981 legislation narrowing the transfer tax base as "emasculating" transfer taxation as an effective component of the tax system. Absent a congressional resolve to reverse the direction of the 1981 legislation and to expand the scope of transfer taxes by reducing the exemption level and increasing the effective progressivity of the transfer tax rate structure, the existing estate and gift tax system has no meaningful role as a contributor to progressivity. The prospect of such changes is remote and even proponents of the progressivity role of transfer taxation are pessimistic that restoration of such a role is politically possible.

* * *

III. FAIRNESS, EFFICIENCY, AND NEUTRALITY

* * *

A. Fairness

First, the system is not fair, from considerations of both horizontal equity and vertical equity. Horizontal equity suggests that persons transferring equal wealth within the system be taxed in the same manner. Vertical equity (progressivity) suggests that persons of greater wealth be taxed more heavily on their transfers than persons of lesser wealth. * * *

* * *

* * * [T]o a significant extent transfer taxes are "voluntary taxes," paid largely by wealthy persons who are uninformed or ill-advised, or who simply die before putting their affairs in order—all too frequent occurrences. To the extent that the tax burdens those who bear it only because of the want of effective avoidance planning, it is especially unfair. * * *

B. Efficiency

Second, the transfer tax is inefficient. This is perhaps the system's most serious shortcoming. It requires an inordinate amount of attention at the highest levels of government, especially in relation to the relative insignificance of the revenues generated. * * *

Efficiency is not properly measured by compliance costs to the government alone. The transfer tax system imposes enormous resource and opportunity costs in taxpayer compliance

---

[38]   [Graetz, *supra* note 13], at 271. *See also* Harry L. Gutman, *Reforming Federal Wealth Transfer Taxes after ERTA*, 69 Va. L. Rev. 1183, 1185 (1983) * * * .

and avoidance endeavors and in the time and energy of lawyers, accountants, trust officers, and financial planners required to understand and apply the system. * * *

* * *

C. Neutrality

In addition to the standards of fairness and efficiency used to measure the desirability of tax systems is a third, that of neutrality. A good tax system should be neutral in that it ought to be nonintrusive—it should not alter choices and behavior that would have occurred in the absence of the system. The current tax system is decidedly nonneutral and intrusive. The system encourages lifetime gifts and penalizes the failure to make them. Further, the system virtually compels use of the marital deduction in most cases involving wealthy married couples. In those instances, it thus discourages substantial outright bequests to others. Also, the system discourages heavy use of joint and survivor arrangements that might otherwise be useful and desirable probate avoidance mechanisms. * * *

D. Summary of Deficiencies

To summarize the foregoing analysis of the current transfer tax system, it fails in contributing meaningfully to breaking up concentrations of wealth or in contributing a meaningful element of progressivity to the federal tax system. The revenue that the transfer tax produces is comparatively insignificant, particularly when examined in terms of the imperfections of the system used to produce it. The system is unfair and grossly inefficient. Rather than being neutral, it is unacceptably intrusive in affecting investment decisions, donative and testamentary choices, forms of ownership, forms of dispositive arrangements, and post-transfer management of capital, and in burdening the probate process and forcing resort to expensive tax avoidance advice. The costs of compliance and related monetary and human resources consumed in the estate planning and related endeavors associated with efforts to comply with the system and avoid or reduce transfer taxes are unacceptably high in relation to revenues produced.

Some of the deficiencies involving horizontal and vertical equity within the system admit of legislative correction. Proposals for improvement[,] * * * [h]owever, * * * [are] unlikely to make the system acceptable under standards of efficiency and neutrality. If the transfer tax system was reconfigured to produce substantially increased revenues, its inefficiency and lack of neutrality would become more tolerable, particularly if value is placed on any resulting contribution to progressivity. Such reconfiguration is a political unlikelihood. Accordingly, Congress should repeal the existing estate and gift tax system.

* * *

NOTE

Much of Donaldson's critique of the wealth transfer taxes mirrors that of Graetz. Yet Donaldson calls for the repeal of the taxes while Graetz supports their revitalization and reform. What accounts for these very different prescriptions? Attacks on the taxes have continued in recent years. *See* RICHARD E. WAGNER, FEDERAL TRANSFER TAXATION: A STUDY IN SOCIAL COST (1993); William W. Beach, *The Case for Repealing the Estate Tax*, HERITAGE FOUNDATION BACKGROUNDER NO. 1091 (1996); Christopher E. Erblich, *To Bury Federal Transfer Taxes Without Further Adieu*, 24 SETON HALL L. REV. 1931 (1994).

D.   The Role of State Law

Although state law has a pervasive effect on the application of the Internal Revenue Code generally, it plays a particularly important role in the federal wealth transfer taxes. In general, state law defines the nature and extent of the property interests and rights that are included in the federal tax base. Obtaining a definitive interpretation of state law presents special problems in federal tax controversies. Michael H. Cardozo IV contends that, in light of the federal government's interest in collecting tax revenues, the Service and the federal courts should give little deference to a state court's determination of state law. Gilbert P. Verbit takes the opposite view and focuses on comity concerns in arguing that state court decisions should be given controlling effect. By contrast, in *Commissioner v. Estate of Bosch*, 387 U.S. 456 (1967), the Supreme Court announced that federal authorities need give only "proper regard" to lower state court decisions in federal tax litigation. Bernard Wolfman suggests that the Service and the federal courts should give deference only to state court decisions that are the product of an "adversarial" proceeding. Paul L. Caron argues that a better way to accommodate the revenue and comity interests is to focus on the correctness of the state court's interpretation of state law through a "bottom-up" analysis that affords the same degree of deference to a lower state court decision that it would receive on appeal in the state court system.

Michael H. Cardozo, IV, *Federal Taxes and the Radiating Potencies of State Court Decisions*, 51 YALE L.J. 783 (1942)*

* * *

It was long believed that the founding fathers provided for federal jurisdiction in cases of diversity of citizenship because they feared the prejudices of local judges in favor of their own people. Perhaps the fear was groundless, but today in tax cases the Commissioner may well fear harm from the decisions of individual state judges, although more because of the taxpayers' guile than judicial prejudice. The collection of revenue should be protected from obstruction by state court judgments procured in cases involving spurious or trumped-up issues between parties who have no fundamental difference of opinion. Proper administration of the tax structure requires that no taxpayer be allowed an advantage not available to others similarly situated, although amounts involved in particular cases may be small.

* * *

The Commissioner could not be notified of every case involving issues that might eventually arise in a federal tax matter, and the nature of the Government's interest might be obscure before the tax proceedings had been started. The tax aspects of the questions might not even appear for many years after the decision, although only in those cases brought in the best of faith would this occur. State court decisions in which the ultimate effect on tax liability was

*   Reprinted by permission of The Yale Law Journal Company and Fred B. Rothman & Company from *The Yale Law Journal,* vol. 51, pages 783-797.

not in the mind of the moving party may even redound to the Commissioner's ultimate bene-fit, as well as to the taxpayer's. The unfortunate results of other cases might be avoided by requiring a taxpayer to litigate anew every issue of law and fact in his controversy with the Commissioner, unless he gave adequate notice to the latter when the earlier proceeding was instituted. The Commissioner might then intervene to present the Government's views. How-ever, this might well prove to be but slight protection, since the position of the Government is not static, and must perforce conform to new statutes and court decisions. Furthermore, the Government's prime interest is not in arguing for one or another particular rule of state law, but in the assurance the decision shall be reached after full deliberation rather than casual pre-sentation by the advocates of only one side. The better solution to the problem would be to give all state court decisions only their proper weight. Whether or not notice were given to the Com-missioner before presentation of the question in the federal court, the earlier decision should be treated only as a precedent, not given effect equivalent to res judicata. If the prior litigation had involved only issues of fact, then the facts should be tried over again, upon the same or new evidence, as is always the situation when new parties oppose each other. If legal issues were presented, the federal judge should be as free as a state judge to decide what the law is. Thus the Commissioner could always have his say. Moreover, the federal revenue would be protected against the perfunctory actions of local courts, induced, frequently surreptitiously, by taxpay-ers who perceive that a judge is more likely to decide his way if no one on the other side has a true interest in a different result.

NOTE

Cardozo's position furthers the revenue interest by giving federal authorities broad authority to ensure the correct application of state law that bears on the federal tax result. Cardozo is right to be concerned about allowing incorrect state law rulings obtained from busy probate courts in uncontested proceedings to dictate the federal tax result. But does his approach go too far in making federal authorities the ultimate arbiters of state law?

Gilbert P. Verbit, *State Court Decisions in Federal Transfer Tax Litigation:* Bosch *Revisited*, 23 REAL PROP., PROB. & TR. J. 407 (1988)*

Decedent's will made the following bequest: "All my property shall go to my wife, with any residual after her death to my children." Decedent's personal representative deducts from the taxable estate the entire value of the decedent's property on the ground that the bequest qual-ifies for the federal estate tax marital deduction. The Commissioner of Internal Revenue dis-agrees, arguing that decedent has left his widow a life estate entitling her to all income from the property but only limited access to the principal. The deduction is disallowed because, to qualify for the marital deduction when the case arose, the bequest had to give the widow unre-stricted access to the principal while alive or, at least, a power to dispose of the principal with-out restriction at her death. After the Commissioner notifies the estate of his disallowance, the

---

personal representative petitions the local probate court to interpret an "ambiguity" in the will, seeking instructions regarding the extent of the widow's access to the corpus. The personal representative asserts that it is without significant limitation and, in resolving the "issue," the probate court applies state law. The predictable outcome, regardless of jurisdiction (and because, in the usual case, the petition is unopposed), is that the probate court will render the requested ruling that the widow possesses substantially unlimited power to invade corpus. The personal representative then takes the probate court decision to the Internal Revenue Service (IRS) and relies on it as the "correct" interpretation of the marital bequest in the will, asserting that, as interpreted by the state court, the bequest qualifies for the marital deduction. Is the Commissioner or, to put it in the usual context, is the federal court before which the question will eventually be brought, bound by the state court interpretation of the will?

* * *

Initial reliance on state law is based on the rather obvious practical reason that there exists in the jurisprudence of every state a well developed body of law surrounding the disposition of property at death. The task of raising federal revenue does not seem to require the creation of a federal law of decedents' estates or property rights to replace existing state law. The doctrinal basis for relying on state law determinations of property rights is the Rules of Decision Act, although there is some support for the view that reliance on state law is necessarily implied in the Internal Revenue Code. For whatever reason, the fact is that the federal transfer tax system rests upon state property law.

Integrating state property law into the federal transfer tax system raises the possibility of a lack of uniform impact. Differing state law interpretations of testamentary instruments can lead to different tax consequences. In the simple introductory example, state courts could legitimately interpret the gift to the widow as either a life estate or a life estate with an unlimited power to invade the principal. * * *

* * *

The general division of labor between state and federal law in tax cases does not compel an answer to the question of the weight to be given state court proceedings in subsequent federal tax litigation in a federal court. The issue is not whether state law governs the determination of an issue in a federal tax controversy. Instead, the issue is whether state court proceedings are to be accepted as binding determinations of the state issues involved.

* * *

THE *BOSCH* LITIGATION

In 1930, Herman J. Bosch established an inter vivos trust for the benefit of his wife. She was to receive the income for life and, at her death, the corpus was to be returned to the grantor or his estate. In addition to this reversion, Bosch retained the right to alter, amend or revoke the trust. In 1931, Bosch amended the trust by granting his wife a general testamentary power of appointment. Almost 20 years later, while Bosch was alive and well, his wife executed an instrument releasing her power to appoint "in favor of myself, my estate, my creditors or the creditors of my estate," her intent being to convert the general power into a nongeneral power of appointment to take advantage of the Powers of Appointment Act of 1951, which provided that the taxable estate would not include assets over which a decedent held only a nongeneral power of appointment. The effect of this transaction was to exclude the trust assets from her estate.

Bosch died in 1957 and the corpus of the trust was included in his estate under section 2038, due to his retained power to revoke the trust. His executor claimed, however, that the trust corpus, while includible under section 2038, was *deductible* from his gross estate under section 2056 (the estate tax marital deduction) because the trust provided for his surviving spouse. The difficulty with this position was that, at that time, section 2056 limited the estate tax marital deduction to trusts in which the surviving spouse enjoyed a life estate and a *general* power of appointment. By virtue of her "release" in 1951, his wife had converted the general power into a nongeneral power of appointment, thereby precluding the trust from qualifying for the marital deduction. Bosch's executor challenged the Commissioner's denial of the deduction in the Tax Court on the theory that the 1951 release was invalid. Shortly thereafter, the trustee commenced an action in the Supreme Court of New York seeking a determination of the validity of the 1951 release. The court issued a show cause order to the surviving spouse and all potential beneficiaries (persons who would take if she died without exercising her power of appointment). Briefs were filed in the case on behalf of the surviving spouse, the trustee and a guardian ad litem for a potential infant beneficiary. All three argued that the 1951 release was a "nullity,"[137] and "[n]o argument to the contrary was presented to the New York court." The court ruled that the 1951 release was a nullity.

The question for the [Supreme] Court was what weight, if any, to give this New York decision. * * *

* * *

Writing for the majority, Justice Clark reviewed what he identified as the three positions on the question that had been taken in the circuits. The first position * * * was that a state court decision was binding on the federal courts if the "question at issue was fairly presented to the state court for its independent decision. . . ." The opposite view * * * was that a federal court should only be bound "after independent examination of the state law as determined by the highest court of the State." The government urged a third position on the Court, that a state trial court adjudication is binding "only if the judgment is the result of an adversary proceeding in the state court."[160]

* * * Justice Clark turned to the legislative history of [the marital] deduction, noting that the Senate Report directed that "proper regard" should be given to state court interpretations of wills.

What did the Senate mean by "proper regard"? Justice Clark observed that "proper regard" did not mean finality and, thus, Congress did not intend that the decrees of state trial courts should be binding on the federal courts. If it had, it would have said so. Moreover, Congress "intended the marital deduction to be strictly construed and applied."[164] These two observations, plus an analogy to *Erie*, led Justice Clark to conclude that Congress intended federal courts in tax cases to be bound only by a decision of a state's highest court in the matter before it. * * *

Justices Douglas, Harlan and Fortas dissented. * * *

---

[137]   The argument was by analogy as follows: New York law was clear that a power of appointment created in a will had no legal effect before the testator died because a will is ambulatory and can be revoked at any time. Although the power of appointment was created by an inter vivos trust, it could only be exercised by her will and could have been revoked at any time by Bosch. Thus, in terms of his ability to change the power and her inability to exercise the power while either she or he was alive, the situation was the same as if the power were a power of appointment created in his will. Therefore any action on her part during her life was a nullity.

[160]   [387 U.S. 456, 463 (1967).]

[164]   [*Id.*] at 455. * * *

LOWER FEDERAL COURTS ATTEMPT TO APPLY *BOSCH*

* * *

Summary of Approaches to "Proper Regard"

* * * [F]ederal courts have taken the following attitudes towards state lower court decisions under the guise of following the rule of *Bosch*: (1) that lower state court rulings are entitled to no weight and are therefore not admissible in federal tax proceedings, (2) that lower state court decisions are relevant evidence even though the product of non-adversary proceedings, (3) that lower state court decisions are to be "followed" if they correctly applied state law, and (4) that the existence of the state court decision should be noted but the federal court will thereafter decide the case as if the state court decision did not exist.

* * *

POSSIBLE SOLUTIONS TO THE *BOSCH* PROBLEM

Wider Use of Certification of Questions
of State Law to State Supreme Courts

Certification would appear to be the implementing technique most consistent with the rule laid down in *Bosch*. It provides federal courts with definitive pronouncements on taxpayers' state-created property rights. Moreover, the pronouncement is procured at the federal court's solicitation, thus ameliorating suspicion that a state court decision was the product of an ex parte request focusing on the petitioner's tax plight.

There are, however, difficulties with using certification to implement *Bosch*. At present only 36 of the 50 states provide for certification, and many of these only allow certification from federal appellate courts, not from federal district courts. Certification procedures have heretofore been used "sparingly and selectively" because, from a federal court perspective, certification is time-consuming: the federal proceeding must be held in abeyance awaiting the state court determination of the certified questions.

Return to the Adversary Proceeding Test

Justice Harlan, dissenting in *Bosch*, thought the majority had gone too far in reducing the role of the state judiciary. He would have restored it by holding that federal courts must treat as conclusive any state court judgment that was the result of a "genuine adversary proceeding." In advocating this position, Justice Harlan was aware of the unsatisfactory experience [with this rule prior to *Bosch*.] * * * But he remained unconvinced that the rule was unworkable. * * *

* * *

The fundamental difficulty with [the adversary proceeding test] * * * is that the usual state court proceeding the federal court is asked to embrace is, by design, a non-adversary proceeding. There are no plaintiffs and defendants, as such, in a typical probate case; these are typically *in rem* proceedings. Thus, opposing parties are not easily identified. Moreover, the interests of the parties shift from issue to issue, making it difficult to separate those interests that coalesce from those that are opposed. Indeed, some disputed issues are settled by trade-off and compromise agreements that are not necessarily revealed in the record of the state proceeding. In addition to these difficulties of forcing normal probate proceedings into an adversary contest mold, the government often controls whether a proceeding will be adversary because, in many of these cases, the only potential adverse party is the IRS. By refusing to appear in a state court, which is the government's right, the Service can often preclude an adversary proceeding in the state court. In effect, then, by choosing to appear only in federal court, the United States effectively confers exclusive binding jurisdiction over questions of state property law on the federal courts. Further, unlike diversity jurisdiction, this result is not ordained by the Constitution or the Rules of Decisions Act: it comes about only because of IRS policy.

In sum, then, the adversary proceeding test, however well-defined, ousts the state courts of an effective role in many cases because the only possible adversary, the United States, refuses to appear.

The irony of a rule that directs plaintiffs to federal court as opposed to state probate court for the interpretation of wills and trusts has been lost on the Supreme Court, because the rule is in direct conflict with the "probate exception" to federal diversity jurisdiction. In broad terms, that exception states that "a federal court has no jurisdiction to probate a will or administer an estate." The exception is historic—the equity jurisdiction conferred on United States courts by the Judiciary Act of 1789 did not include probate matters. One explanation for this exception is the relative expertise of state probate judges in this area as compared to federal judges, who lack experience because they are rarely exposed to issues of trust and will interpretation. This same rationale should be applied in tax cases, because federal judges do not suddenly acquire an expertise in interpreting wills when the jurisdictional basis in the matter before them is a federal question involving taxation. The same relative lack of experiential expertise that is the basis for the probate exception to diversity jurisdiction should militate in favor of a broader acceptance of state probate court decrees in federal tax cases.

Consider All State Court Decisions Binding in Subsequent Federal Tax Proceedings

The "problem" that * * * *Bosch* attempted to resolve is the possibility (or even probability) that a state probate court judge will "improperly" interpret a testamentary instrument or state law to reach a result that will enable the petitioner to obtain an advantageous position under the federal tax laws. The effort to articulate criteria that would assist federal courts in identifying these cases has been largely unsuccessful. In frustration, the Supreme Court in *Bosch* attempted to create a bright-line test—that state court decisions will be accepted as binding in federal tax proceedings only if those decisions emanated from the highest court of the state. With regard to other state court decisions, the Supreme Court said, in effect, that our experience with state trial court and intermediate appellate court decisions has been so unsatisfactory that lower federal court judges can do whatever they want with them; that is, they should pay them "proper regard." An examination of the experience under *Bosch* indicates that this failure to provide content for the phrase "proper regard" has left the lower federal courts without a principled means for determining the weight to be given state court decisions in federal tax cases. A reexamination of two of the premises in *Bosch* (the need for a bright-line test and avoiding conspiracies to "defraud" the tax system) suggests a more promising route to that goal.

Given the multiplicity of factors involved in state probate proceedings, the search for a bright-line test seems the route most likely to lead to orderly judicial administration. Moreover, an effective test is readily at hand. In *Uterhart* [*v. United States,**] the Court accepted state trial and intermediate appellate court decisions as binding. This *Uterhart* rule should replace *Bosch* as the method of dealing with state court decisions in federal tax cases. In short, all final decisions of state courts should be accepted as binding in federal tax cases, regardless of the level of the state court or the character of the proceedings in that court.[245]

---

*   [240 U.S. 598 (1916)—Eds.]

[245]   In implementing this principle, there should be a requirement that the Internal Revenue Service be notified of any state court litigation that might affect the federal tax position in a particular case.

Adoption of such an approach would mean that federal courts must accept decisions from state court proceedings that might be characterized as pro forma, a "sham," a "stamp of approval," and similar characterizations. As noted above, these decisions allegedly result from the willingness of state court judges to distort the facts or misinterpret or misapply state law as a result of a de facto conspiracy among the court and the parties to do in the federal tax collector. This is the second premise of the *Bosch* decision that needs to be reconsidered.

One difficulty with this view of how state court judges might behave is that it is based on a most unscientific sample. Certainly some state courts have gone over the line in their efforts to aid the parties in their tax negotiations. The notable cases are those that have reached a federal court and raised the issue involved in *Bosch*. But an examination of state court reports reveals cases in which state judges decided issues against a petitioner, even when the petition was unopposed, in a way that made further litigation with the tax authorities unpromising. Many of these cases probably resulted in a compromise with the federal tax authorities so that there is no record of tax disputes that prompted the state action. Nevertheless, the existence and outcome of these decisions might indicate that, by and large, state probate court judges are not such knaves or conspirators as *Bosch* assumes them to be.

At the root of this concern about what state judges are doing is the question of why they are doing it. Are they "distorting" the facts or the law solely because they see the issue as one of the hometown crowd against Washington? Is it the case that they are amenable to the pleas and arguments of counsel and parties who are their friends, neighbors or even former colleagues? Are they, as Justice Harlan * * * suggested, simply too busy to devote much time and effort to the issues raised in the state proceeding and thus tend to approve whatever unopposed material is put before them? No reading of the cases yields a complete response to those questions. But it does reveal that many of the *Bosch*-type cases arise in the context of a mistake of law or a mistake in drafting by counsel for a decedent.

* * *

Instead of viewing the actions of state judges as participation in a "Great Treasury Raid," it is equally possible to view the situation as one in which state courts construe and reform instruments to effect the testator's intent while the IRS is attempting to capitalize on every drafting error, however slight. The case in which a taxpayer deliberately chooses to surrender a tax benefit for some non-tax reason, such as to disinherit a spouse, is rare indeed. Contemporary estate planning is often tax-driven. To the extent that is the case, a legitimate question should be considered: Why deny a tax benefit to a taxpayer who has omitted a phrase or used one word too many if the evidence is that the taxpayer intended to qualify for the tax benefit? This is particularly compelling if an error is of essentially a technical nature and the taxpayer is really the innocent victim of a drafter's error. This is not to say that the IRS should accept instruments that do not conform to the requirements of the Internal Revenue Code. But if a state court interprets an instrument to carry out the testator's intent, the IRS *ought* not to be in a position to brush aside such efforts.

This is particularly true in an era when state courts are becoming more and more active in implementing the intent of the testator. Courts appropriately consider the settlor or testator's intent the polestar for interpretation. Traditionally, intent was ascertained solely from within the four corners of the instrument and extrinsic evidence of mistake was not admissible. A developing trend, however, is to admit such extrinsic evidence if, as in the cases under consideration, intent was defeated by the action (or failure to act) of a third party; the theory is that a case of unjust enrichment is made out if a drafter's error has caused an unintended beneficiary (here the United States) to take at the expense of the intended beneficiary.

* * *

NOTE

Verbit's position furthers the comity interest by giving controlling weight to state court decisions, "regardless of the level of the state court or the character of the proceedings in that court." Verbit is right to be concerned about allowing the Service and the federal courts to ride roughshod over the application of state law by state courts. But does his approach go too far in making even lower state courts the ultimate arbiters of state law as it applies in a federal tax controversy? Is there any way to balance the revenue interest exalted by Cardozo and the comity interest exalted by Verbit?

Bernard Wolfman, Bosch, *Its Implications and Aftermath: The Effect of State Court Adjudications on Federal Tax Litigation*, 3 U. MIAMI INST. ON EST. PLAN. 2-1 (1969)*

THE *BOSCH* CASE

The United States Supreme Court's decision and opinion in *Bosch* are significant to lawyers whose practice involves estate planning. The question was whether a federal court, deciding a tax controversy in which the determination of liability turns on rights and interests created by state law, is conclusively bound by a prior state trial court adjudication respecting the property interests in question.[2] * * *

* * *

THE SUPREME COURT'S RATIONALE IN *BOSCH*

The Court's opinion, concluding that state trial court adjudications of property interests are not binding in the federal courts, has several articulated bases. * * * The * * * principal ground of decision was that the rules developed by federal courts for ascertaining state law under the mandate of *Erie Railroad Company v. Tompkins*[30] were controlling. The Court noted that in cases governed by *Erie*, the decrees of lower state courts should be attributed some weight, but they are not conclusive. Only a decision of the state's highest court binds the federal court. In the absence of such a decision, the federal court must make its own determination of state law, using the state lower court decision as only a datum. The Court was not deterred by the fact that *Erie* was intended to provide a measure of substantive uniformity in diversity cases involving a state law issue, and had not spoken to non-diversity cases involving a federal issue.

AN EVALUATION OF THE *ERIE* ANALOGY

The analogy to *Erie* formed the heart of the Court's opinion in *Bosch*. The weakness of the opinion lies in its simplistic, forcible co-opting of *Erie* doctrine.

The issue in *Bosch* arises only when it is judged that Congress intended to look to state law for definition, characterization, or determination of the property interests upon which the federal tax is to be based. "State law may control only where the federal taxing act, by express language or necessary implication, makes its own operation dependent upon state law." The

---

[2]   *See, generally*, in the pre-*Bosch* era, * * * Cardozo, *Federal Taxes and the Radiating Potencies of State Court Decisions*, 51 YALE L.J. 783 (1942) * * * .

[30]   304 U.S. 64 (1938).

decision to look to state created or protected rights in federal questions can be attributed to two prime factors: (1) the interstitial nature of federal law; and (2) the economy and logic of depending on a ready made and highly developed body of law already governing individuals.

In *Erie*, the reasons for seeking state law were entirely different. First, the federal court sitting in diversity adjudicates the rights of citizens in concurrent jurisdiction with state courts. The impact of the federal court's determination in such cases is not to fix a federally created liability, like a tax liability, but to declare the rights and liabilities traditionally, and perhaps constitutionally, left to the state's discretion to formulate. If a substantive rule were applied in diversity cases different from that applied in state courts, there would be unacceptable problems in terms of both fairness to citizens who would be required to regulate their conduct on the basis of conflicting sets of rules and the plaintiff's choice between federal and state courts on the basis of the relative attractiveness of their substantive rules of laws. These considerations prompted the Supreme Court in *Erie* to declare that in diversity cases, federal courts will sit and, like state inferior courts, determine the rights and liabilities of litigants according to the law of the relevant state as expounded by the state's highest court. The federal court would try to reach the substantive result one would expect a state court to reach if the parties had been fellow citizens litigating in their own state.

A fact of major significance that distinguishes the federal diversity environment from that in a federal tax case is simply this: In the diversity case the parties have not been before a state court for resolution of the state law question. The federal court seeks to apply the law as the state court would be expected to apply it to the parties if it had the case. In the federal tax case, the taxpayer will have been before the state court or the *Bosch* issue would not arise. * * *

The reasons which called for the *Erie* resolution in diversity cases are absent in federal tax cases. In the latter, Congress imposed tax consequences on the basis of a taxpayer's relationship to property. That relationship is often understood and accepted as a result of rules gleaned from litigation involving others. When a contest arises, however, the taxpayer's rights are determined in his own litigation. Once that litigation is concluded, his rights are determined, and that is so whether the highest state court made the determination or whether the lower court whose decision is now final was "wrong." At first blush, at least, the federal tax interest would seem to be fully satisfied if the taxpayer's rights had been so determined. Whether another taxpayer would have his rights determined differently in a case going to the state's highest court would seem irrelevant. There is no fear, as in diversity, that a taxpayer in the federal court, bound by only a state trial decision, is getting a result different than he might have gotten if he had been in a state court; by hypothesis, he has already been there.

At this point we should distinguish between two quite different situations. One is the situation with which we are *not* concerned, that is, where there is no prior state court decree fixing the specific property interest of the taxpayer in question. When the state trial court decisions are precedents only, the application of *Erie* rules for determining state law seems sensible and appropriate in their emphasis on determining state law in an unmechanical manner. This approach promotes the federal interest in having a tax system with relatively uniform impact; it strives for the ideal under which interests similar under state law are taxed similarly. Where, however, a state court has made a specific adjudication as to the taxpayer in question, the problem is both different and more complex. The majority opinion in *Bosch* did not come to grips with the relevant differences in the two situations nor with the differences in the federal policy goals sought by the rules generated in diversity cases and those in cases in which a state right lies beneath a federal question.

A BETTER RESOLUTION

If the Court had concerned itself with balancing the considerations relevant to a federal question dependent upon a state created interest, it would not have seized upon *Erie*: it would have stated a principle that stressed the nature and quality of the prior state adjudication. Where the process of prior adjudication was designed and likely to have produced a deliberate, reasoned decision under state law, there appears to be no justification for reconsideration of the merits of the final decision actually produced by the state court. If a taxpayer was involved in a genuinely adversary state court controversy involving economic stakes, independent of the federal tax considerations, there is no reason and it would be unfair to the taxpayer to disregard the result in determining tax consequences. The state determined property rights on which Congress has imposed tax consequences will have been determined in precisely the way our system of law requires their determination when asserted rights are challenged. To ignore the determination is to ignore the property right on which the tax is supposed to fall or not fall. To discuss state law in the abstract after that determination and to use the result of the abstraction to enforce tax liability is to ignore the Congressional mandate to enforce tax consequences on the basis of the taxpayer's property rights.

The situation is different, however, where there was fraud or collusion or simply a "friendly" state court suit brought in a tax planning context. There is no injustice in looking to the correct state law instead of the particular state court resolution in such a case because the nature of the proceeding does not provide assurance that the taxpayer's property rights were determined to have been derived at the time, in the way, or from the source that makes those rights relevant under the tax statute. We know only that from the effective date of the state court decree the taxpayer has rights which he wanted and that the judge was willing, absent objection, that he have them. The federal statute demands more. * * * Where the personal, substantial, and current interests of the litigants are not at stake, it is judged that the litigants will be unlikely to present their arguments in the most appealing and sharpest form. If only one side of an issue is presented, a court will not be pressed sufficiently to weigh and properly resolve conflicting considerations. * * *

Once one says * * * that a decision of a competent state court resolving a real controversy is binding on the federal courts, one says that it is to be accepted without inquiry as to its merits, although it may have been wrong. The ingredient of actual adverseness on the specific issue, however, makes it likely that the decision will be consistent with state law. In any event, state law *for the taxpayer* has been determined in the only way our system provides, and the rights determined are fixed with finality.

The majority's opinion in *Bosch* states that it will avoid much of the uncertainty that would result from the "adversary" v. "non-adversary" approach. In fact, the certainty wrought is illusory, for taxpayers who have been involved in adversary state court litigation must now face the prospect of re-litigation in federal courts which have the power and sometimes the duty to ignore the state determination in imposing tax liability, but not to change it.

* * *

CONCLUSION

Prior to *Bosch* there was undue willingness on the part of many state trial courts to rubber stamp the request of private parties for an interpretation of state law adversely affecting only the revenue interest of the federal government. In many cases it was clear that the rubber stamp would not have been applied if a private party had opposed the request. In its unrefined effort to stop the objectionable practice the Supreme Court went both too far and yet not far enough.

In concluding that state inferior court decisions are never conclusive as to "state law" in federal tax cases, taxpayers whose property interests have been adjudicated in adversary litigation run the risk of having tax consequences enforced on them on the basis of property interests different from those fixed by competent courts before whom the issue was drawn and tried. If that occurs, the Congressional purpose is frustrated.

In concluding that the decisions of a state's highest court are always conclusive, opportunities exist for a taxpayer to seek such a decision in a non-adversary setting. If he succeeds, the federal court may be imposing tax consequences on the basis of a property interest the taxpayer has, but not necessarily one which he received in the way or from the source Congress was looking to. It may be an interest not received "from the decedent," but from the enlightened self-interest of surviving heirs.

* * *

All of this suggests that the Supreme Court should reconsider the issues posed by *Bosch*. The *Erie* doctrine should be remitted to the area it serves well and not be permitted to distort federal tax adjudication. Property interests fixed by litigation conducted in the normal way, with adversary interests contending, should be the property interests on which federal tax consequences fall. State court adjudications, by the lowest or highest court, should not be accepted as determinative for federal tax purposes when the state court proceeding does not appear to have compelled the state court to resolve the issue with the full exploration and consideration of conflicting viewpoints ordinarily required in adversary proceedings.

* * *

NOTE

Wolfman uses the adversarial standard to assess "the nature and quality of the prior state adjudication." Under this approach, if the state court proceeding has the requisite degree of adversariness, it controls for federal tax purposes; if the state proceeding is insufficiently adversarial, the Service and the federal courts need not give it deference. This approach is advocated by many other commentators. *See, e.g.*, Elliott K. Braverman & Mervyn S. Gerson, *The Conclusiveness of State Court Decrees in Federal Tax Litigation*, 17 TAX L. REV. 545, 576 (1962); Jackson M. Bruce, Bosch *and Other Dilemmas: Binding the Parties and the Tax Consequences in Trust Dispute Resolution*, 18 U. MIAMI INST. ON EST. PLAN. 9-1, 9-34 (1984); David G. Sacks, *The Binding Effect of Nontax Litigation in State Courts*, 21 N.Y.U. INST. ON FED. TAX'N 277, 295 (1963); *see also* Martin L. Fried, *External Pressures on Internal Revenue: The Effect of State Court Adjudications in Tax Litigation*, 42 N.Y.U. L. REV. 647, 671 (1967) (focusing on whether parties to state court litigation were economically adverse). What factors should the Service and the Federal courts use to determine whether a state court proceeding was sufficiently adversarial? Is it possible to come up with a complete list of such factors? Would such factors necessarily constrain creative counsel for taxpayers? What would be the likely practical impact if such an adversariness standard were adopted?

Paul L. Caron, *The Role of State Court Decisions in Federal Tax Litigation:* Bosch, Erie, *and Beyond*, 71 OR. L. REV. 781 (1992)*

* * *

IV. *BOSCH*: REDEFINING THE BALANCE

* * *

A. *Supreme Court: The* Erie *Framework*

* * *

* * * [T]his Article represents the first attempt in the literature to systematically examine how the federal courts and the Service have implemented the "proper regard" standard. Although there are myriad commentaries on *Bosch,* there are no comprehensive studies on how the federal courts and the Service have applied the standard. A review of the over 900 cases and rulings citing *Bosch* reveals a quarter century of disarray caused by a misreading of the *Erie* underpinnings of the "proper regard" standard.[195]

B. *Lower Federal Courts: Giving Primacy to the Revenue Concern*

1. *Appellate Courts*

The federal courts of appeals have cited *Bosch* in 220 cases.[196] The courts of appeals have generally given primacy to the revenue concern by paying mere lip service to the "proper regard" dictate. In doing so, the courts of appeals have engaged in independent review of state law without giving *any* weight to lower state court interpretations of its own state's laws. * * *

* * *

As a result of this de novo review, the courts of appeals have concluded in over one-half (sixty-one percent) of the cases that the lower state courts had misapplied state law. Four of the circuits have reverted to a pre-*Bosch* (and pre-*Erie*) focus on the nonadversariness of a lower state court proceeding as an attempt to balance the competing concerns. * * * However, other circuits correctly have noted that *Bosch* rejected the use of nonadversariness as a balancing approach.

Thus, over a seventy-five year period, the federal courts have come full circle on the question of the effect of prior state court decisions in federal tax litigation. What began * * * as a one-sided focus on the comity concern by treating *all* state court decisions as controlling, and then became successive attempts to strike a balance between the competing revenue and comity policies through the * * * nonadversary test and the *Bosch* "proper regard" test, has been transformed by the courts of appeals into a one-sided focus on the revenue interest. This transformation also has occurred in the federal trial courts as well as in the Service.

---

*   Reprinted by permission. Copyright © 1992 by University of Oregon.

[195]   The author reviewed all of the cases and rulings that have cited *Bosch* in the 25-year period from June 5, 1967 (the date of the *Bosch* decision) through December 31, 1991. * * *

[196]   * * * The appellate court cases are examined in detail in Paul L. Caron, *The Federal Courts of Appeals' Use of State Court Decisions in Federal Tax Cases: "Proper Regard" Means "No Regard,"* [46 OKLA. L. REV. 443 (1993).]

2. Trial Courts

(a) District Courts

The federal district courts have cited *Bosch* in 363 cases. Most of the relevant district court cases give "no regard" to lower state court decisions and conduct an independent review of state law. * * *

The district courts have concluded in almost two-thirds (sixty-five percent) of the cases that the lower state courts had misapplied state law. * * *

Several district court decisions have returned to a pre-*Bosch* focus on the nonadversariness of a lower state court proceeding in trying to balance the competing concerns. * * * Other district court decisions have correctly noted that *Bosch* foreclosed the use of a nonadversary inquiry to balance the competing concerns.

(b) Tax Court

The Tax Court has cited *Bosch* in 187 cases. Like the federal courts of appeals and the federal district courts, the Tax Court has engaged in plenary review of state law and given no weight to prior lower state court decrees. * * *

As a result of this de novo review, the Tax Court has concluded in over one-half (fifty-six percent) of the cases that the lower state court had misapplied state law. Although many of these cases purported to give "due respect" to the lower state court decree, they gave virtually no weight to the state judge's application of state law. In the remaining cases, the Tax Court followed the state court's determination after its own independent review of state law.

Several Tax Court cases have also reverted to the pre-*Bosch* use of the nonadversary test. Some cases rely on nonadversariness as further justification for viewing the state law issue differently than the probate court. Other cases rely on adversariness to support adherence to the state judge's application of state law.

3. Conclusion

The application of the *Bosch* "proper regard" standard is summarized in the following chart:

TABLE 2
BOSCH IN THE FEDERAL COURTS

Court	Cases Citing *Bosch*	Tax Cases Citing *Bosch*	Tax Cases Following State Court On State Law	Tax Cases Not Following State Court On State Law
Courts of Appeals	220	74	12	19
District Courts	363	65	11	20
Tax Court	187	187	26	33
	770	326	49	72
			40%	60%

C. Internal Revenue Service: Compounding the Erie Error

The Service has cited *Bosch* in 135 revenue rulings, general counsel memoranda, technical advice memoranda, and private letter rulings. Like the lower federal courts, the Service has focused on the revenue concern by interpreting the "proper regard" standard as authority to conduct a de novo review of state law. As a result of this independent review, the Service has concluded that the lower state courts had misapplied state law in over one-half (fifty-two percent) of the rulings. The breakdown by type of ruling follows:

TABLE 3
***BOSCH* IN THE SERVICE**

Type of Ruling	Rulings Citing *Bosch*	Rulings Following State Court On State Law	Rulings Not Following State Court On State Law
Revenue Ruling	10	0	2
General Counsel Memorandum	24	1	2
Technical Advice Memorandum and Private Letter Ruling	101	10	8
	135	11	12
		48%	52%

* * *

The lower federal courts and the Service have thus used the *Bosch* "proper regard" test to give primacy to the revenue concern. This result is contrary to the *Bosch* Court's stated intention to use the *Erie* framework to balance competing revenue and comity interests. The lower federal courts and Service's departures from the *Erie* framework in reintroducing the pre-*Bosch* nonadversary test can thus be seen as attempts to inject a balance between these competing policies or, at least, to justify the result in those cases and rulings on comity grounds. * * *

* * *

VI. REVENUE V. COMITY: RESTORING THE *ERIE* BALANCE

The application of the *Bosch* "proper regard" standard by the lower federal courts and the Service has given primacy to the federal revenue interest by affording "no regard" to a probate court's application of state law. Recent commentary rejecting this approach gives primacy to the comity concern by suggesting that a probate court's application of state law should be binding on the lower federal courts and the Service.[291] This section argues that a balance should be struck between the competing revenue and comity policies.

Returning to the pre-*Bosch* focus on the nonadversariness of the probate court proceeding is one way to provide this balance. The lower federal courts and the Service have followed this approach in selected cases and rulings.[293] Under this view, as expressed by Justice Harlan in his

---

[291]   [Gilbert P.] Verbit, [*State Court Decisions in Federal Transfer Tax Litigation:* Bosch *Revisited*, 23 REAL PROP., PROB. & TR. J. 407, 457 (1988).]

[293]   * * * Several commentators have advocated this approach. *See, e.g.,* * * * Bernard Wolfman, Bosch, *Its Implications and Aftermath: The Effect of State Court Adjudications on Federal Tax Litigation*, 3 U. MIAMI INST. ON EST. PLAN. 2-1, 2-10 (1969) (footnote omitted):

The majority's opinion in *Bosch* states that it will avoid much of the uncertainty that would result from the "adversary" v. "non-adversary" approach. In fact, the certainty wrought is

Bosch dissent, the federal courts and the Service must treat a probate court's application of state law as controlling when it was the product of an adversary proceeding. Federal revenue interests are adequately served in these cases by the "considered adjudication of the relevant state law issues."[294] On the other hand, when the lower state court proceeding was nonadversary, the federal courts and the Service are free to disregard the probate court's decision and engage in an independent review of state law.

However, the nonadversary standard inadequately balances the competing revenue and comity concerns. Defining the term "nonadversary" has been difficult; lower federal courts in the pre-*Bosch* period could not agree on a set of relevant factors. Indeed, in *Bosch*, Justice Harlan refused to "define with any particularity" the weight to be given to various factors. Moreover, the nonadversary approach fundamentally is flawed because probate court proceedings by their very nature are often nonadversary. Granting controlling status to only selected probate court proceedings encourages elaborate "pillow fights" and other machinations designed to produce the perceived required degree of adversity, resulting in federal tax controversy and litigation over the nonadversary standard.

Such controversy and litigation over this collateral issue is misdirected. Why should a probate court's erroneous application of state law determine the federal tax result merely because the probate proceeding was cloaked with sufficient indicia of adversariness? Instead, deeper inquiry into the *Erie* underpinnings of *Bosch* produces an application of the "proper regard" standard which best reconciles the competing revenue and comity interests.

In the traditional *Erie* case there is no prior lower state court decision involving one of the parties. *Bosch* is invoked in these cases as authority for the proposition that a federal court is not bound by applications of state law by lower state courts in other cases *involving other parties*. The *Bosch* situation differs in requiring the determination of state law when there has been a prior lower state court decision *involving that taxpayer*. In this situation, the revenue and comity concerns offer contradictory guidance on the amount of deference required.

On the one hand, the revenue interest would require less deference, reducing the opportunity for taxpayer manipulation of state proceedings to obtain a favorable federal tax result. On the other hand, the comity concern would require more deference, reducing the chance for the federal courts and the Service to take views of state law contrary to those of the state courts. The best way to balance these competing policies is by heeding the Court's direction in *Bosch* that in applying the "proper regard" standard, federal authorities must "in effect, sit[] as a state court."

Traditional *Erie* doctrine employs a "top-down" analysis by predicting how the highest court of the state would decide the state law question. However, when the federal courts and the Service "sit as a state court" in a *Bosch* situation, they should use a "bottom-up" *Erie* analysis giving the same deference to the probate court decision as would be given to an appeal in the state court system. In the thirty-eight states that have an intermediate appellate court, federal authorities should apply the same standard of review as would be applied by that court.[302] * * *

---

illusory, for taxpayers who have been involved in adversary state court litigation must now face the prospect of re-litigation in federal courts which have the power and sometimes the duty to ignore the state determination in imposing tax liability, but not to change it.

* * *

[294]   387 U.S. at 481 (Harlan, J., dissenting).

[302]   * * * In [the 12 states without an intermediate appellate court], this approach would require that the federal courts and the Service give the same deference to the state trial court's decision as would be given on appeal by the highest court of the state. * * *

* * *

* * * In the *Bosch* situation, the federal courts and the Service should give the same deference to the lower state court decision as would be given to it on appeal in the state court system. Such an approach is necessary to prevent a result that could not have been obtained had the lower state court's decision been appealed in the state court system.

In many cases, the "bottom-up" approach will result in more deference given by the federal courts and the Service to the probate court's application of state law than currently provided through de novo review. Although the precise standard of review will depend on the state law in a given case, several general observations can be made based on the cases and rulings that have invoked *Bosch* over the past twenty-five years. Very few of these cases and rulings have presented pure questions of law where de novo review would be employed by the state appellate court. Instead, most of the cases and rulings which involve a prior probate court decision present either pure questions of fact or mixed questions of fact and law. When the probate court decree raises only factual questions, great deference is invariably given by the state appellate courts under a "clearly erroneous," "abuse of discretion" or similar standard. When the state decree raises mixed questions of law and fact, state appellate courts in many cases afford similar deference, although less deference could be given in certain situations.

In adhering to the same standard of review that would be used on appeal, the "bottom-up" approach thus gives effect to the state's view of the proper role of appellate review in its court system. This approach is particularly appropriate in the thirty-eight states with a tri-level judicial system. In these states, the "bottom-up" method satisfies the roles of error correction, law development, and "doing justice" served by the intermediate appellate court and highest state court.

* * *

The "bottom-up" approach best serves the direction in *Bosch* to "sit as a state court" by focusing on what actually would have happened had the probate court's decision been reviewed in the state court system. In virtually every case and ruling applying *Bosch* over the past twenty-five years, the taxpayer has obtained a probate court ruling on state law that would have favorable federal tax consequences for the taxpayer if followed by the federal courts and the Service. Under current practice, the federal courts and the Service treat the taxpayer's "offensive" use of the probate court decree by giving "no regard" to the probate court's application of state law. As a result, the federal courts and the Service have cavalierly held in over one-half of the cases and rulings that the probate court had misapplied state law. In contrast, the "bottom-up" approach would give teeth to the "proper regard" standard by requiring the federal courts and the Service to give the same degree of deference to the probate court decision that it would have received on appeal in the state court system.

The "bottom-up" approach accommodates both the revenue and comity concerns. Federal revenue interests are protected by permitting meaningful review of the probate court's application of state law. Comity concerns are protected by limiting federal review of the probate court's decision to the same standards that would have been applied by state courts on appeal.

In an ideal world, federal tax controversies that turn on the application of state law would have the benefit of a decision by the highest court of the state. This would render it unnecessary for the federal courts and the Service to embark on an examination of state law. However, the time and expense involved in obtaining such a definitive determination of state law may often pose a significant barrier. Moreover, federal court certification of state law issues to the highest court in the state does not provide an effective remedy in tax litigation for a variety of reasons.

* * *

The federal courts and the Service thus will continue to be confronted by state law questions in resolving federal tax controversies. Absent authoritative determinations by the state's highest court, the competing revenue and comity interests are best served by requiring the federal authorities to give "proper regard" to probate court applications of state law by applying the same standard of review as would be employed on appeal in the state court system.

CONCLUSION

* * * [T]he Court should reaffirm the use of the *Erie* framework as the best way to balance the competing revenue and comity interests. However, the Court needs to make clear that its cryptic direction in *Bosch* to give "proper regard" to lower state court decisions does not permit the federal courts and the Service to give either "no regard" (as is the current "top-down" *Erie* practice in giving primacy to the revenue concern) or "total regard" (as some commentators suggest in focusing on the comity concern) to these decisions. Instead, the Court needs to strike a balance between these competing policies by requiring that the lower federal courts and the Service employ a "bottom-up" *Erie* approach in affording the same degree of deference to a probate court's application of state law as would be given to an appeal of the decision in the state court system. This approach focuses on the central question of the correctness of the probate court's application of state law rather than on collateral issues such as the adversariness of the state court proceedings. In cases where the federal tax result turns on state law, this approach will protect federal revenue interests by allowing the federal courts and the Service to evaluate the soundness of a probate court's application of state law in a manner consistent with the comity concern by requiring the same standard of review that would be applied in the state court system.

NOTE

The appropriate degree of deference to be paid to state court adjudications in resolving federal tax litigation remains controversial. While Wolfman insists that "some degree of adversariness is essential before a federal court sitting on a tax case should be required to accept what a state court has said" (Bernard Wolfman, Bosch *Revisited*, 64 TAX NOTES 269, 269 (1994)), Caron argues that the adversariness approach is unworkable and doomed to fail because of the inherent nonadversarial nature of most probate proceedings (Paul L. Caron, Bosch *and the Allure of Adversariness*, 64 TAX NOTES 673 (1994)). Wolfman faults Caron for "ignor[ing] the fact that it is always the business of courts, particularly federal courts deciding tax cases, to look under cloaks, to see through even elaborate facades to the structure (or the lack of structure) that lies behind," and claims that Caron's approach would require that federal courts set sail on a "limitless sea." Bernard Wolfman, Bosch *and the* Erie *Blind Alley*, 64 TAX NOTES 967, 967-68 (1994). Caron acknowledges that "such substance over form considerations are endemic in many tax areas." However, he contends that his *Erie* approach is preferable to the adversarial approach "because it does not lard yet another tax area with these uncertainties," but instead encourages federal courts to focus on "the correctness of the state court's decision." Paul L. Caron, *Tax Court and Service Stake Out Positions in State Law Debate*, 71 TAX NOTES 229, 230-31 (1996).

See also Martin L. Fried, *A New Voice in the Debate Over the "Ascertainment" of State Law*, 71 TAX NOTES 543, 543 (1996) (agreeing that "the existence of what appears to be an adversarial proceeding should not control," but criticizing Caron's approach for not taking into consideration "the vicissitudes of litigation"); Judson L. Temple, *Prof. Temple Says "Bosh" to Prof. Caron's Views on* Bosch, 71 TAX NOTES 701, 701 (1996) (siding with Wolfman's view that "the legitimacy of the state court proceedings [should be] the determinative factor").

PART II:

THE GIFT TAX

From its inception, the gift tax has functioned to prevent the avoidance of estate tax by lifetime transfers. This Part examines three structural features of the gift tax that have engendered much debate since the enactment of the modern gift tax in 1932: (1) the annual exclusion; (2) disclaimers; and (3) the scope of the gift tax.

A.   The Annual Exclusion

According to the legislative history, the original function of the gift tax annual exclusion was "to obviate the necessity of keeping an account of and reporting numerous small gifts, and . . . to cover in most cases wedding and Christmas gifts and occasional gifts of relatively small amounts." S. REP. No. 665, 72d Cong., 1st Sess. 41 (1932). The annual exclusion was initially set at $5,000, then reduced in 1939 to $4,000 and again in 1942 to $3,000; in 1981, it was increased to its current level of $10,000. This Subpart first reviews several annual exclusion structural reform proposals. The Subpart then examines two specific areas that have posed particular concerns in the application of the annual exclusion—gifts to minors and *Crummey* trusts.

1. Reform Proposals

In the first excerpt, the American Law Institute recommends that a separate exclusion for "transfers for consumption" be added to the gift tax. Harry L. Gutman discusses the impact of § 2503(e) on the transfer-for-consumption issue, and advocates other reforms, including the elimination of the annual exclusion for transfers in trust. Jeffrey G. Sherman explores this latter idea in reexamining the definition of "future interests" for purposes of the annual exclusion. John G. Steinkamp offers his own "common sense" reform proposal, while Robert B. Smith draws on earlier commentary in formulating a proposal that he believes best serves the goals of the gift tax.

AMERICAN LAW INSTITUTE, FEDERAL ESTATE AND GIFT TAXATION (1969)*

* * *

There is at present a major area of common misunderstanding about the gift tax consequences of responding to the needs of various persons for help; of responding to personalized charity as distinguished from public charity. It is not generally understood by the average person that a gift tax may be payable if he provides a child with educational benefits beyond those he is legally obligated to provide, or if he pays a sick relative's doctor's bill.

The expenditure of funds by a member of a family in discharge of his legal obligations to support another member of the family does not involve a taxable gift for gift tax purposes and clearly should not. The expenditures that are deemed in discharge of a legal obligation to support another, however, are determined on the basis of local law, and local law is neither uniform nor clear on this matter. Thus, to the extent the freedom from gift tax liability is founded on the legal-obligation test, the federal gift tax is imposed on some and not on others in identical circumstances, solely because there is a difference in their geographical locations.

It is proposed that there be excluded from gift taxation various so-called "transfers for consumption," without regard to whether they in fact involve a discharge of a legal obligation to support. This will tend to eliminate the significance of differences in local law as to what constitutes a legal obligation to support another, and thus cause the transfer tax law to be applied in substantially the same way in all states.

* * *

The proposal as to transfers for consumption is applicable only to lifetime transfers. The considerations behind the proposal do not carry over significantly to deathtime dispositions. This, of course, is also true of the annual per-donee exclusion which is not available with respect to deathtime transfers.

A "transfer-for-consumption" exception may raise some difficult factual issues in borderline situations, but most situations will fall clearly on one side of the line or the other. The creation of the difficult borderline area is justified to accomplish the larger benefit of excluding typical transfers that are motivated by considerations other than the build-up of wealth in the transferee. When such a transfer occurs it should, of course, be immaterial whether payment is made on behalf of the transferee or to the transferee for the designated purposes.

With respect to the transfer-for-consumption problem the Institute adopted a resolution recommending that:

> * * * An expenditure should be excluded from transfer taxation as a lifetime transfer, under either a dual tax system or a unified tax, if the expenditure is for:
>
> (a) the benefit of any person residing in the transferor's household, or the benefit of a child of the transferor under 21 years of age, whether or not he resides in the transferor's household, provided that such expenditure does not result in such person or child acquiring property which will retain significant value after the passage of one year from the date of such expenditure; or
>
> (b) current educational, medical or dental costs of any person; or

---

(c) current costs of food, clothing and maintenance of living accommodations of any person in fact dependent on the transferor, in whole or in part, for support, provided such expenditure is reasonable in amount.

* * *

NOTE

How would the existing annual exclusion be affected by the ALI proposal? How would you determine whether a transfer for consumption would result in the donee receiving property of "significant value"? Do you agree that "[a] 'transfer-for-consumption' exception may raise some difficult factual issues in borderline situations, but most situations will fall clearly on one side or the other"? For further discussion of the ALI proposal, see Milton L. Ray, *The Transfer-for-Consumption Problem: Support and the Gift Tax*, 59 Or. L. Rev. 425 (1981).

In 1981, Congress enacted § 2503(e), which allows a gift tax exclusion for certain educational and medical payments. Should § 2503(e) be broadened to include other transfers for consumption? *See* Robert G. Popovich, *Support Your Family But Leave Out Uncle Sam: A Call for Federal Gift Tax Reform*, 55 Md. L. Rev. 343 (1996). Joseph M. Dodge has argued that "there should be an unlimited exclusion for 'support' type items (such as lodging, food, transportation, etc.) provided in kind to a person during the person's period of residency in the donor's principal place of residence." Joseph M. Dodge, *Redoing the Estate and Gift Taxes Along Easy to Value Lines*, 43 Tax L. Rev. 241, 343-44 (1988). According to Dodge, "the general idea should be to expand the [annual] exclusion to encompass all transfers which are de minimis or in the nature of consumption, support, or 'welfare,' but without regard to state law concepts." *Id.* at 344.

Harry L. Gutman, *Reforming Federal Wealth Transfer Taxes After ERTA*, 69 Va. L. Rev. 1183 (1983)*

* * *

IV. THE STRUCTURE OF A WEALTH TRANSFER TAX

* * *

B. The Tax Base

Under the normative principle, the transfer tax base is the transferor's net wealth and the tax is paid on the fair market value of wealth transferred outside the taxable unit less the fair market value of any consideration received therefor. The normative principle adopts the notion that the amount subject to tax is the net amount by which the transferor has depleted his wealth by the transfer. In general the tax is to be imposed objectively; the transferor's motivation is irrelevant.

Practical considerations, however, require that this principle be modified in a number of ways. * * *

* * * [T]ransfers for the support of those dependent upon the transferor raise problems of a practical and theoretical nature. In objective terms, the payment of medical or educational expenses of a family member and the provision of food, clothing, housing, and transportation deplete the wealth of the transferor without the receipt of offsetting consideration in money or money's worth. Yet, at least with respect to close family members, these transfers are not generally thought of as taxable gifts. Indeed, if the tax system so treated them, it is doubtful the system could be enforced. Thus, administrative convenience could provide the rationale for an exclusion for reasonable "support" expenditures made to or for the benefit of a defined category of beneficiaries. Moreover, as noted below, such an exclusion could also be justified in normative terms simply as consumption by the transferor.

Finally, one must recognize that at some point it is administratively burdensome and practically impossible to require taxpayers to account for infrequent transfers of modest amounts to any particular donee. Therefore the tax structure should contain an exclusion for inter vivos transfers of modest amounts.

In ERTA, Congress attempted to resolve these problems by enacting a new exclusion for support-type payments and increasing the present interest exclusion amount. * * *

1. The Exclusion for Tuition and Medical Expenses

Transfers to, or for the benefit of, those dependent upon the transferor have been a constant irritant in the transfer tax. Although taxable to the extent the transfers both exceed the present interest exclusion and are not encompassed by a transferor's legal support obligation with respect to the transferee, most transferors do not regard payments for such items as medical expenses, education, clothing, food, and housing of family members as taxable gifts. Consequently, transferors routinely fail to report such transfers. The Internal Revenue Service has implicitly acquiesced in this practice by failing to enforce the law in this area. This is a pragmatic decision dictated by limited audit resources, the difficulty of identifying taxpayers who have made such transfers, and the small payoff even if the transferors were identifiable.

In ERTA, Congress reacted to this problem by enacting an exclusion for tuition payments made directly to an educational institution and for unreimbursed medical expenses paid directly to a provider of medical services. The exclusion is available for a described payment made on behalf of any individual. Congress made no attempt to confine the exclusion to payments to or for the benefit of individuals closely related to the transferor.

The ERTA provision is difficult to categorize conceptually. To the extent it excludes tuition and medical expense payments that discharge a legal support obligation, it merely codifies preexisting law. To the extent it excludes payments other than those that discharge a support obligation, one could view it either as an attempt to create a "federal" support obligation for transfer tax purposes limited to tuition and medical expenses or as an attempt to define tuition and medical expense payments made on behalf of third parties as consumption by the transferor. By failing to limit the class for whose benefit excluded transfers may be made, however, the provision is too broad. There is no reason for an exclusion that extends beyond a class the transferor would normally be expected to support. Although such a class could, and perhaps should, be broader than that encompassed by most state law rules, it should not be unlimited.

By choosing to exclude certain transfers on the basis of the purpose of the transfer, Congress has taken a tentative step toward the solution of a difficult problem of administration and compliance. An exclusion confined to tuition and medical expenses is too narrow, however, if the objective is to relieve compliance problems. The 1968 American Law Institute Estate and Gift Tax Project recommended a "transfer-for-consumption" exclusion. * * *

The adoption of an exclusion along these lines would not be inconsistent with the normative principle.[173] Even though these transfers relieve the transferee of the need to expend his or her own resources for the described purposes, the types of expenditures listed may also reasonably be characterized as consumption by the transferor. * * * Finally, a broader, but carefully defined, exclusion for support-type payments would have the derivative benefit of reducing the need for a large annual exclusion for de minimis transfers.

2. The Annual Exclusion

Since 1932, the transfer tax has contained an annual exclusion, determined on a per donee basis, for gifts of "present interests" in property. The excludible amount has been altered periodically. Originally $5,000, the exclusion was $4,000 from 1939 through 1941 and $3,000 from 1942 through 1981. ERTA increased the amount to $10,000. At a $10,000 level the present interest exclusion has the potential to erode the tax base significantly. Married individuals may transfer $20,000 per year to any donee. A couple with, for example, three children and three grandchildren may transfer $120,000 per year outside the transfer tax system. * * *

As a normative matter, the transfer tax structure should treat lifetime and deathtime transfers identically. The structure, however, must recognize and accommodate the enforcement problems caused by inter vivos transfers of nominal amounts. Just as most taxpayers do not view the provision of support-type items as taxable transfers, they also simply do not think of small gifts as subject to tax. No amount of public education is likely to induce taxpayers to record and report these transfers, nor is it cost effective to attempt to collect the tax revenue resulting from these small transfers. Thus the challenge is to design an exclusion for inter vivos transfers in a form and at a level that realistically accounts for the costs associated with the enforcement of the system. This is a delicate task because an overly generous exclusion will create horizontal inequity: transfers during life would be treated more favorably than those at death. Moreover, it is generally true that only those with large amounts of wealth can afford to dispose irrevocably of assets during life. Aggressive lifetime giving tailored to the exclusion amount can significantly lower the effective tax rate on aggregate transfers and reduce the progressivity of the transfer tax system.

In constructing an appropriate present interest exclusion, several questions arise. The first question is whether gifts to trusts, or only outright transfers, should be excluded. There is no reason to exclude gifts to trusts.[181] The creation of a trust and the transfer of property to it are acts of sufficient significance that the additional act of accounting to the tax system for such transfers should not be unduly burdensome. Trustees must keep accounts of receipts and disbursements, and one could shift to the trustee the burden of reporting such transfers at little additional administrative cost.[182]

---

[173]   The ALI Recommendations, however, may need technical refinement. * * * Transfers in trust may cause particularly difficult problems. For example, suppose A transfers property in trust to pay the income to B, an adult child, for life with discretion in the trustee to distribute principal to C, a minor dependent of A, to the extent necessary to supplement C's education costs. A will obviously want an immediate exclusion for the amount transferred to the trust that is to be used by C, but how is the amount excluded to be determined? * * *

[181]   * * * If the present interest exclusion is denied to transfers in trust, it should also be denied to transfers to custodians for the benefit of minor children. This rule is necessary to assure that the tax system does not favor one form of property disposition (custodial gifts) over another (gifts in trust). * * *

[182]   * * * The exclusion could also be denied for transfers of intangible personal property, such as stocks and securities. * * *

A more important question is the determination of the dollar amount of the exclusion. This issue, however, cannot be decided in the abstract because its resolution is dependent on certain other changes in the transfer tax. For example, the exclusion level would be affected by how support-type payments, other than those for tuition and medical expenses, are treated. * * * [T]here is considerable uncertainty as to the extent to which certain payments, particularly those made by parents to or for the benefit of children, are taxable transfers. So long as this uncertainty remains, an argument can be made that the exclusion level should be sufficiently high to avoid the necessity of inquiring into the nature of all such payments. Setting a high exclusion level to deal with this problem necessarily means, however, that the same exclusion is available for transfers that would clearly be taxable absent the exclusion. In the latter circumstances, the high exemption level amounts simply to an erosion of the tax base. On the other hand, if all support-type transfers were excluded, as earlier suggested, the amount of the residual exclusion could be reduced. For this reason, the tuition and medical expense exclusion is, in theory, a promising development. In conjunction with these considerations, the level of the exclusion should be determined by a conscientious inquiry into when it is appropriate to require taxpayers to account to the system. When the question is phrased in these terms, it is obvious that there is nothing intrinsically correct about either a $3,000 or a $10,000 exclusion.

A third question is whether the exclusion level should be based on the value of each separate transfer or on all transfers to a particular donee during the reporting period. A "per transfer" exclusion is superficially appealing and simple; all transfers of, for example, $500 or less would be excluded. Such an exclusion, however, has considerable potential for abuse. Taxpayers desiring to eliminate transfer tax would be encouraged to split one large transfer into the requisite number of excluded transfers. To avoid this manipulation, one could require the aggregation of transfers to a particular donee where it could be shown that the purpose of the multiple gifts was to avoid tax. Such a rule would require taxpayers to keep records of questionable transfers even if they are not reported. Moreover, an aggregation rule in which intent must be ascertained complicates the administration of the tax system. Thus, if one is unwilling to tolerate the abuse potential of a "per transfer" exclusion, a "per donee" exclusion, which requires the same recordkeeping but dispenses with the intent inquiry, is preferable.

The final issue is what happens when the value of transfers to a donee exceeds the amount of the exclusion. When this occurs, one could make all transfers to the donee in that year immediately taxable. An alternative is to tax only the amount of the transfers that exceed the present interest exclusion. A third solution is to phase out the exclusion in some manner when it is exceeded.

Some would argue that if the exclusion level is set low enough, the system should, in the interests of administrative convenience, simply tolerate the base erosion that will occur if the exclusion is allowed even when transfers exceed the exclusion amount. The rationale for the exclusion, however, is that it is unreasonable to expect a transferor to account for aggregate gifts up to the exclusion amount. That rationale disappears once aggregate transfers exceed the exclusion amount and a return reporting all transfers is required.

This reasoning would indicate that once the exclusion level is exceeded, all transfers made during the reporting period should be taxable. That rule, however, could be viewed as too harsh because the gift that takes the taxpayer out of the exclusion for that gift and all prior gifts incurs a marginal rate in excess of one hundred percent. For example, suppose the exclusion level is set at $1,000 and A is in a marginal transfer tax bracket of thirty-seven percent. If A transfers $1,000 to B, there is no tax. If A transfers $1,001 to B, there is a tax of $370.37. The $1 gift is taxed at a rate of 37,037%. This result would indicate that the exclusion should be phased out when aggregate gifts to a donee exceed the exclusion amount. Thus, for example, the amount of the exclusion could be reduced on a dollar for dollar basis to the extent aggregate transfers exceed the excludible amount.

In summary, the existing present interest exclusion creates an unwarranted gap in the coverage of the transfer tax. Congress should revise the exclusion to meet its original purpose: alleviation of the administrative burden of accounting for numerous small gifts. Concurrently with this revision, Congress should exclude transfers to or for the benefit of a defined class of individuals for purposes generally described as support. Accounting for transfers in trust does not result in administrative burdens, however, and the base should therefore not exclude such transfers. Congress should frame the exclusion as an annual amount per donee and set the amount of the exclusion by reference to realistic appraisals of the aggregate value of incidental gifts an individual would be expected to make to a single donee in excess of excluded support-type payments. * * *

* * *

NOTE

Gutman acknowledges that the dollar amount of the exclusion "cannot be decided in the abstract" without considering other changes such as the treatment of transfers for support. If a broad exclusion for support-type transfers were allowed, coupled with a low annual exclusion for other gifts (e.g., $600), would some of Gutman's other reforms become unnecessary? For example, would it still be important to deny the annual exclusion for transfers to trusts or to custodianships?

Jeffrey G. Sherman, 'Tis a Gift to be Simple: The Need for a New Definition of "Future Interest" for Gift Tax Purposes, 55 U. Cin. L. Rev. 585 (1987)*

* * *

Section 2503(b) provides that the annual exclusion is available only for gifts "other than gifts of future interests in property;" and it has been held that the term "future interest" as used in section 2503(b) is a distinct term of federal tax art, independent of any state law definitions. * * *

The purpose of this article is * * * twofold: first, to examine how the definitions of "future interest" and "present interest" have evolved over the years * * * ; and second, to propose new definitions that are both simpler and more in keeping with Congress's original purpose in limiting the annual exclusion to gifts of present interests.

I. BACKGROUND

* * *

The principal function of the federal gift tax is to prevent or compensate for avoidance of the federal estate tax. The gift tax serves as a back-up for the estate tax by taxing * * * inter vivos transfers of property that, but for the transfer, would have been subject to the estate tax

---

*   Copyright 1987, the University of Cincinnati. Reprinted with permission from University of Cincinnati Law Review, Vol. 55, No. 3.

at the donor's death. In theory, every gift, however inconsequential, reduces the potential gross estate of the donor and may therefore be regarded as a device for avoiding federal estate taxes. But it would be burdensome to the point of ludicrousness to require a donor to file a gift tax return reporting every minor, routine gift. * * * Minor, routine gifts tend to be gifts of present interests. * * * If a gift is in the form of a future interest, it is likely to have been made as much from tax-reduction motives as from a simple desire to make the kind of gift that Congress sought to exempt through section 2503(b). Accordingly, Congress chose, rather than requiring an investigation into the motives prompting each gift of a future interest, to disqualify such gifts altogether for the annual exclusion.

* * *

* * * But exactly what is a future interest for gift tax purposes? The Internal Revenue Code contains no definition at all. The definition in the committee reports accompanying the original enactment of the annual exclusion—"any interest or estate, whether vested or contingent, limited to commence in possession or enjoyment at a future date"[26]—amounts to a mere dictionary definition and consequently offers little guidance; and the IRS regulation merely repeats almost verbatim the language of the committee reports. * * *

* * *

V. PROPOSAL FOR CHANGE

* * *

* * * I would urge that the definition of "future interest" be changed so that a gift will not qualify for the annual exclusion unless the donee receives at the instant of the gift the entire legal and equitable title to the gift property: "fee simple absolute" in the case of real property and "absolute ownership" in the case of personal property. * * *

In a sense, the proposal might be regarded as a throwback to such law as existed from 1938 to 1942, when Congress barred the annual exclusion for gifts in trust. The proposal goes further, however, in that it would also bar the annual exclusion for such nontrust gifts as legal life estates and determinable fees. * * * [T]he purpose of denying the exclusion for gifts of future interests is to limit the exclusion to the routine gifts that a donor makes for ordinary donative reasons and to bar the exclusion for gifts made for estate planning motives. * * * Thus, income interests under trusts would no longer qualify for the annual exclusion under the proposal, even if the income was to begin immediately and the right to it was unconditional. * * *

* * *

Even under the proposal, it would be desirable to retain a special rule for gifts to minors. * * * In the case of minor donees, even "casual, routine" gifts are often made to guardians or custodians, not as a way of making a testamentary kind of transfer, but as a way of assuring that the minor does in fact benefit from the gift. Under current law, an outright gift delivered to the guardian of the intended donee can qualify for the annual exclusion regardless of the guardian's power under local law to control the donee's enjoyment of the property. This rule should certainly be continued under the proposal. But under current law, gifts *in trust* for the benefit of minors may or may not qualify for the exclusion, depending upon the authority of the trustee and the interest of the beneficiary. Under the proposal as originally stated, such gifts would never qualify. It is recommended, however, that the special exception of section 2503(c) be

---

[26]   H.R. REP. No. 708, 72d Cong., 1st Sess. (1932), *reprinted in* 1939-1 C.B. (Part 2) 457, 478; S. REP. No. 665, 72d Cong., 1st Sess. (1932), *reprinted in* 1939-1 C.B. (Part 2) 496, 526.

retained so that donors could continue to make qualifying gifts to minors by means of custodians and by means of analogous trusts established simply to assure prudent management until the donee becomes an adult.

The proposal for changing the definition of "future interest" certainly would simplify the law considerably. It would render moot, for example, such confusing lines of cases as (1) those in which the availability of the exclusion may turn upon whether the assets in the trusts are income-producing; (2) those in which the trustee's discretionary powers may be too broad to assure the beneficiary a "steady flow" of income; and (3) those where a beneficiary has been given a power to demand a distribution but it is not clear whether that power may as a practical matter be exercised. The proposal would also adhere more closely than present law to the intent of Congress, since it would more truly limit the annual exclusion to routine gifts not intended to yield tax-planning benefits. * * *

* * *

NOTE

Sherman believes that it is desirable to deny the annual exclusion for all trust interests, including interests that confer an unconditional right to immediate distributions of income or corpus. Yet, unlike Gutman, he would permit gifts to custodians for the benefit of minor children and retain the exclusion for gifts to § 2503(c) trusts. Would these exceptions undermine Sherman's goal of purging the annual exclusion of complexities engendered by the definition of "present interest"?

John G. Steinkamp, *Common Sense and the Gift Tax Annual Exclusion*, 72 NEB. L. REV. 106 (1993)*

* * *

IV. ANNUAL EXCLUSION REFORM

A. The Need for Reform

* * *

Reform should accomplish two goals. The first is simplification of the annual exclusion; the law should be more certain. Taxpayers should not have to guess whether a particular transfer would qualify for the annual exclusion. Clear lines should exist over which even the most aggressive of taxpayers would not dare to step. Use of formalistic constructs by which future interests are converted into present interests in order to obtain the annual exclusion should not be possible. * * *

The second goal of reform is denial of the annual exclusion for the transfer of certain interests for which it is currently allowed. Transfers of income interests and transfers subject to lapsing demand powers (even if exercised) should not qualify for the annual exclusion. Allowing the exclusion for such transfers allows abuse of the annual exclusion. This abuse has two aspects. First, the exclusion is allowed for the transfer of future interests. Second, the annual

---

exclusion is allowed for multiple indirect transfers in excess of the annual exclusion amount
* * * in violation of the per-donee limitation. * * * Reform should shore up the future interest
and per-donee limitations of the exclusion.

B. Proposed Reform

1. The Annual Exclusion Amount

If the gift tax is to accomplish its estate tax protective function and the annual exclusion
is to provide a limited exemption for customary and occasional gifts of relatively small value,
the amount of the exclusion is important. If the exclusion is too low, gifts of relatively small
value will not be exempt and the exclusion will not accomplish its purpose. If the exclusion is
too high, transfers will be made in order to avoid the estate tax and the estate tax protective
function of the gift tax will be impaired.

* * *

The estate tax avoidance possibilities that exist through routine use of the annual exclusion
must be recognized when the amount of the exclusion is considered. The benefits of the exclusion are limited only by the taxpayer's ability and willingness to transfer property during life,
the number of individuals he desires to benefit, and the length of his life. Many donors, moreover, apparently make routine maximum use of the exclusion to transfer investment-type assets
and ignore small customary gifts, as if such customary transfers are not subject to the gift tax.

* * *

The exclusion should continue to be allowed on a per-donee basis. * * * If it is believed
that the amounts being transferred through use of the exclusion are too large, the exclusion
amount, not the per-donee nature of the exclusion, should be changed.

* * *

The $10,000 annual exclusion * * * is an appropriate amount. It affords the intended
exemption from gift taxation. While this amount permits some leakage from the transfer tax system, it will not seriously impair the estate tax protective function of the gift tax if the future interest and per-donee limitations of the exclusion are enforced. The exclusion, however, should be
indexed for inflation if it is to continue to be sufficient to exempt customary and occasional gifts
and enable taxpayers to comfortably support family members without gift tax concerns.

2. Qualifying Interests

If the gift tax is to achieve its estate tax protective function and the annual exclusion is to
provide a limited exemption for customary and occasional gifts of relatively small value, the
type of interest that qualifies for the exclusion is important. * * *

* * *

A fourth requirement should be added to the three-part annual exclusion test to provide the
desired objective test. In addition to proving that the interest transferred is a present interest,
that the donee is identifiable, and that the value of the present interest is ascertainable, the donor
should have to prove that the donee received the property outright or, if the transfer is in trust,
that the property was subject to the donee's nonlapsing demand power and that the donee was
the only trust beneficiary.

The fourth requirement arises from the manner in which customary and occasional gifts of
relatively small value are typically made; such gifts are usually made outright and not in trust.
The donee receives title to the property transferred. No one other than the donee has rights in
the gifts. A consequence of conveying title is that the donee becomes the owner of the property
for income, gift, estate, and generation-skipping transfer tax purposes.

* * *

Recognition of the fourth requirement would not preclude legitimate use of the annual exclusion within the dollar limits determined by Congress. Taxpayers could still make as many per-donee present interest gifts each calendar year as desired. The additional requirement would eliminate annual exclusion abuse by providing clear rules without adversely affecting legitimate use of the exclusion.

* * *

NOTE

As Steinkamp recognizes, leaving the amount of the annual exclusion at $10,000 and indexing it for inflation "permits some leakage from the transfer tax system." Do the other reforms proposed by Steinkamp keep this leakage to a manageable level? Should the annual exclusion be allowed for lapsing demand powers that are exercised by the donee? *See* Joseph M. Dodge, *Redoing the Estate and Gift Taxes Along Easy-to-Value Lines*, 43 TAX L. REV. 241, 344-45 (1988).

Robert B. Smith, *Should We Give Away the Annual Exclusion?*, 1 FLA. TAX REV. 361 (1993)*

* * *

V. VARIOUS APPROACHES TO MODIFICATION

A. Reasons to Retain and Modify

* * *

Taking into account the administrative need for some form of annual exclusion and the demonstrated problems with the current form, there is a preference for designing a system under which: (i) transfers for current support, which do not transfer lasting tangible wealth, are not required to be reported, even if made to persons who are not legally entitled to support; (ii) tax-free transfers that are not for current support are both limited and reported in a useful fashion; and (iii) administrative burdens on taxpayers and the government are not substantially increased. To satisfy these requirements, either "support" must be defined or its definition made unnecessary, and the ability to transfer wealth tax-free for purposes other than support should be substantially reduced.

* * *

C. Consumption Under the Transfer Tax System: A Key to the Analysis and Modification of the Tuition and Medical Care Exclusions

* * *

* * * *When Consumption for Another's Benefit Should Be Viewed as a Transfer for Transfer Tax Purposes.* — Under what circumstances, * * * if any, should consumption for the benefit of another be treated as excludible from the transfer tax system? * * * [Some factors] used

---

to determine whether consumption for the benefit of another should be treated as a transfer subject to transfer tax are: (i) the relationship of the donor and the donee (dependent minor children, residents of the household, persons who are described in section 152); (ii) the purpose of the consumption (education, medical care, dental care, food, living accommodations, etc.); (iii) the nature of the asset or assets, if any, acquired as a part of the consumption (items that will not retain a significant value one or two years after the transfer); and (iv) the amount involved * * *.

* * * [Another] factor is whether the person for whose benefit the consumption occurs is currently able, on account of the transfer inherent in the consumption, to save or make other use of some significant portion of the amount expended on the consumption. This is a key factor in determining when consumption for the benefit of another should be subject to transfer tax.

That it is a key factor can be demonstrated by considering the underlying reason for excluding from the transfer tax system any consumption for the benefit of another. The transfer tax system is designed to impose a tax on the *transfer* of wealth. While the tax due is measured on the basis of the value given up by the donor, *there must be a transfer* for the tax to apply. The basis for treating consumption for the benefit of another as not a transfer tax event is that nothing of material value exists within some short period after the expenditure occurs; it is as if no transfer occurred. Accordingly, if substance is to prevail over form, the transfer tax should not apply because the wealth is gone—consumed—not transferred. However, *if the donee is thereby enabled, at some point in time reasonably close to the time of the transfer, to accumulate or make other use of his or her own wealth because of the transfer, then there has been a lasting transfer of wealth to which the transfer tax system should apply.*

* * *

Plainly, the analysis of how likely a donee is to accumulate wealth on account of any given consumptive transfer could best be made in light of the most specific set of facts regarding the donee and the expenditure made. For example, an exclusion for education related transfers could be made more precise if each student who has other resources that could be used to pay education expenses (such as a trust established by the student's grandparent) were identified and the exclusion was denied for transfers to such students. But just as plainly, a generally applicable legal system can not deal with that degree of specifics and remain administrable when there are as many consumptive transfers as occur in the United States. * * *

D. Liberalizing the Tuition and Medical Care Exclusions

Present law provides unlimited tuition and medical care exclusions for amounts paid to the educational institution or the medical care provider. While these exclusions are helpful in protecting support-related, consumption-type transfers to persons the donor has no legal obligation to support and should be retained, they are inadequate to make certain that such transfers do not trigger the transfer tax system. The tuition exclusion falls short in failing to exclude from the transfer tax system payments for housing, books, supplies, food, clothing and transportation for students. The medical care exclusion falls short in failing to exclude nonmedical need care for the aged, such as providing for companions, paying for housing in a community for the aged where medical care is available but is not the primary reason the person resides in the community, food, clothing and transportation.

If these exclusions were expanded, the largest consumptive transfers related to another's support made by most taxpayers, including the support of adults, would be protected from transfer tax consequences. It would be unnecessary for donors to rely on the annual exclusion to protect such transfers from gift tax consequences. Accordingly, the annual exclusion could be revised without severely affecting support related transfers made to persons to whom the transferor does not have a legal duty of support.

Obviously, changing the tuition and medical care exclusions to permit additional transfers for the purposes described above could also open the door to abuses. * * *

* * *

E. Modifications of the Annual Exclusion Considered

Assuming that the changes proposed to the tuition and medical care exclusions are adopted, the annual exclusion could be modified in several direct and indirect ways. * * *

1. Reducing the Annual Exclusion Per Donee Limitation. — A simple way to limit the use of the annual exclusion to avoid transfer tax is to reduce the amount of the exclusion, as Congress did in 1939 and 1942. It could be reduced from $10,000 per donee to the amount that persons with $600,000 of wealth give on average to a single donee for birthdays, holidays, weddings, graduation and such regularly occurring events as the annual exclusion was intended to cover. For purposes of discussion, an estimate of $5,000 will be used.

* * *

Moreover, a simple reduction in the amount of the exclusion may also affect some persons who are not targets of the wealth transfer system (generally, persons with a gross estate under $600,000), but who can afford to make occasional gifts in excess of $5,000, such as an automobile, furniture or a contribution toward the purchase of a home. The excess over $5,000 would be a taxable gift. Such excess would usually use up some unified credit, but would not require any out-of-pocket payment. However, the use of credit does require the filing of a gift tax return. Nonetheless, the number of people affected should not be excessive.

2. Limiting the Amount That Can Be Transferred Under the Annual Exclusion in One Year by Any Single Donor. — Another way to limit the use of the annual exclusion to avoid transfer tax would be to place a cap on the amount that a single donor could transfer under the exclusion in any one year. For example, * * * each *donor's* transfers under the annual exclusion could be limited to $20,000 per year in the aggregate. * * *

* * *

This approach is unlikely to cause very many persons who are not targets of the wealth transfer system to file any gift tax returns they do not have to file now, since it leaves the per donee limitation at $10,000 per person. Thus, it is perhaps less likely than the straightforward reduction in the per donee limit to increase the reporting burden on those who are not targets of the system.

3. Reducing the Annual Exclusion Available Based on the Accumulated Use of Significant Amounts of Annual Exclusion. — A somewhat different type of mechanism that could be used to prevent the use of the annual exclusion to transfer large amounts of property would be to reduce the annual exclusion available to those who make frequent and substantial use of it. * * *

* * *

4. The Present Interest Requirement. * * *

* * *

The present interest requirement could be altered in at least three ways, each of which would have some impact on the use of the annual exclusion. It could be eliminated, so that gifts could qualify for the annual exclusion even if they are gifts of future interests. Second, it could be replaced with a provision under which transfers could only qualify for the annual exclusion if made outright or to a trust for one beneficiary, the terms of which force the property to be included in the beneficiary's gross estate to the extent it is not distributed to or for the benefit of that beneficiary. Third, it could be altered so that its requirements can be satisfied *only* by outright transfers.

Some guidance as to which is the appropriate approach may be provided by the legislative history underlying the present interest requirement. That history states that the present interest requirement was adopted to simplify the valuation of interests as to which the exclusion could be claimed. That is, the present interest requirement prevented any claim that the annual exclusion applied to remote or contingent future interests which are very difficult to value and the donee of which is difficult to identify.

If the primary intent behind the present interest requirement was to make valuation of the transferred interest easier, this goal could be achieved by any of the three approaches. * * *

* * *

F. Implementing the Most Effective and Administrable Modifications to Address the Problems of the Current Annual Exclusion

1. Choosing Among the Most Direct Modifications. — Of the * * * possible changes discussed above, those that would most directly affect the annual exclusion are: (i) reducing the per donee limitation in all cases (the "per donee" model); (ii) limiting the exclusion on a per donor basis (the "per donor" model); and (iii) reducing the annual exclusion based on cumulative use made thereof (the "cumulative use" model). * * *

* * *

Absent empirical data on how many taxpayers can and do utilize the annual exclusion, how many taxpayers can and do give away $600,000 (or some substantial portion thereof), the average number of donees the average donor has, and the life expectancy that donors have at the time they make such gifts, which model will actually be most effective at curtailing the use of the annual exclusion to avoid transfer taxes is not determinable with any real certainty. * * *

* * * [U]ntil such information becomes available, the choice can only be made based on judgment and experience. Based on the analysis set forth above, a combination of the per donee and the per donor models would be effective and reasonably simple to implement. * * *

* * *

2. Choosing Among the Less Direct Modifications. — Changing the present interest requirement * * * would less directly affect the annual exclusion than would the modifications discussed above. * * *

Retaining a per donee limitation * * * requires that there be a present interest requirement or some substitute for it in order to make it possible to value the amount transferred to each donee. While a per donee limit is desirable to retain, the use of meaningless withdrawal rights to create a present interest should be eliminated. Gutman would eliminate the use of withdrawal rights to create a present interest by denying the annual exclusion for transfers into trust, an approach that would also limit or make more difficult the transfer of certain types of assets under the annual exclusion. The type of assets transferred is an appropriate thing to limit in consumption type transfers, but it is not an appropriate thing to limit for the types of gifts that the annual exclusion was meant to protect. * * * [A further proposal] to require an annual exclusion gift in trust to be usable for only one beneficiary, and, to the extent not so used, to be includible in that beneficiary's gross estate, will permit a per donee limit to be retained and eliminate the use of withdrawal rights given solely to make a transfer a present interest. This approach also preserves for donors the use of trusts as vehicles to hold annual exclusion gifts. Accordingly, using a "vesting" approach to replace the present interest requirement is the most desirable alternative.

* * *

3. What These Changes Will Accomplish. — It is true that the approaches selected will not *eliminate* the problems caused by the present annual exclusion. However, * * * many of the problems will be greatly reduced and the wealth transfer opportunity that the annual exclusion now represents will be seriously limited. The amount of wealth transferable under the annual exclusion by taxpayers with many or few donees would be greatly reduced. The vertical inequity and horizontal inequity caused or contributed to by the annual exclusion will also be reduced.

* * *

NOTE

Does Smith succeed in melding previous proposals into an ideal reform package? Are there aspects of his proposal that you disagree with? Is Smith likely to have the last word on reforming the annual exclusion?

2. Gifts to Minors

Jerry A. Kasner focuses on tax issues associated with gifts to minors and discusses competing tax and nontax considerations of various planning strategies for making such gifts.

Jerry A. Kasner, *Gifts to Children and Grandchildren—With Particular Emphasis on Educational Financing*, 48 N.Y.U. INST. ON FED. TAX'N 22-1 (1990)*

* * *

V. TRANSFER TAX PROBLEMS IN PLANNING GIFTS FOR EDUCATION

A. The Retained Control Problem

Many parents or grandparents who create education funds or trusts want to retain control, as trustee or custodian. * * * For federal estate tax purposes, where the grantor retains any control over the timing or amount of distributions, or to whom distributions can be made, unless limited by ascertainable standards, the trust or custodial assets will be included in his or her taxable estate. This will be true whether or not education is covered by a legal obligation of support. Thus under no circumstances should the transferor or parent act as a custodian or trustee for the transferred property, even if the support issue can be avoided.

---

*   This material was originally published in an article entitled "Gifts to Children and Grandchildren—With Particular Emphasis on Educational Financing" by Professor Jerry Kasner, *New York University 48th Institute on Federal Taxation*, Ch. 22 (1990). © Copyright 1990 by New York University. All rights reserved.

B. Obtaining the Annual Gift Tax Exclusion

The $10,000 annual gift tax exclusion is a central planning point, particularly where the educational transfer is to be funded by periodic transfers over a number of years. With the important exception of transfers under IRC Section 2503(c), to be discussed subsequently, the annual exclusion only applies where the transferee obtains present enjoyment of the property, or in some cases, the income from the property. Direct transfers to children, or to custodians for them, will qualify for the exclusion. Where the transfer is in trust, the annual exclusion can also be obtained by giving the beneficiary a limited invasion power over the trust (a so-called *Crummey* clause).

C. Qualifying Direct Payments of Tuition for the Federal Gift Tax Exclusion

The Internal Revenue Code also exempts from federal gift tax direct tuition payments to educational institutions. The educational institution must generally meet the requirements of IRC Section 170(b)(1)(A)(ii). Under the Regulations, this unlimited exclusion is available for tuition expenses of both full and part-time students if paid directly to the qualifying educational organization providing the education.

This exclusion is severely limited. It does not extend to amounts paid for books, supplies, dormitory fees, or board. Since it covers direct payment of tuition only, it cannot be used to claim an exclusion for transfers to trusts, even if the trust required its assets be used to pay tuition. However, coupled with payments through trusts or direct gifts qualifying for the annual exclusion to cover expenses other than tuition, it can be useful.

* * *

VI. SELECTING THE VEHICLE FOR THE TRANSFER

A. Direct Transfers to Minors

Direct transfers of property or assets to minors may be considered, but is usually not practical. * * *

* * *

The direct transfer would seem most useful either for assets with deferred income, such as U.S. Savings bonds, or for gifts made when the children are over 14 or have actually started their education. * * *

B. Custodial Arrangements

Under the Uniform Gifts to Minors Act, applicable in many states, certain assets may be transferred to a custodian for a minor. Under some versions of this statute, the assets transferred are limited basically to bank accounts, securities, and life insurance policies, although this list has been expanded in many states. The property vests absolutely in the minor at the date of transfer.

The custodian has general investment power, and can apply the income or corpus of the custodial property for the minor's benefit in the custodian's discretion. The property and accumulated income must be delivered to the donee upon reaching majority, or in the event of prior death, to his or her estate.

The Internal Revenue Service has issued several rulings pertaining to the Uniform Gifts to Minors Act. The transfer to custodians under the law are completed gifts eligible for the $10,000 annual gift tax exclusion. The income from the custodial assets is taxed to the donee, unless used to discharge a support obligation of another person, in which case it is taxed to that person. Finally, if the donor appoints himself or herself as custodian, and dies before the donee attains majority, the custodial assets will be included in the donor's taxable estate.

A subsequent revised version of the law, the Uniform Transfers to Minors Act, has been adopted by several states. Transfers under it may include all types of property. A fiduciary, such as a trustee, may establish a custodianship. The investment standard is somewhat tougher [than] under the original statute. Where some states under the prior law required distribution of the custodial property to the donee at age 18, others extended this to age 21. The new law specifically permits use of age 21.

While the new law permits the expenditure of the gift property for the support of the donee, it also indicates that the use of the property for the donee will not be deemed to relieve any other person of an obligation to support the minor. Such payments are in addition to, and not in substitution for, support obligations. If education is support, does this mean that should the custodian use gift property for such a purpose, there is some right of reimbursement or recovery from parent[s] who are legally obligated to provide support? Apparently not.

The principal advantage of the custodial gift is simplicity and low cost. Where the new law is in place, there is great flexibility in selection of assets, and the ability to extend the age of distribution to 21. However, each custodial gift for each minor must be segregated, increasing administrative costs, and the custodian's powers of administration and distribution are strictly limited by law. The donor cannot control this as he or she could to at least a greater degree if a trust were used.

If the donee dies, the property will invariably pass to the parents by inheritance, and cannot be shifted to other issue. All of the property must be distributed at age 21, which many clients believe is too young. Finally, where the donee is under age 14, the Kiddie Tax will result in all income being taxed at the parents' marginal rates, which can be avoided to an extent through the use of trusts.

Beware of naming the donor, or in a community property state, either donor, as custodian, or estate tax problems will arise. If a parent is named as custodian, the power to apply the gift property for the support of the donee could constitute a general power of appointment for estate or gift tax purposes. Also avoid use of reciprocal custodians, i.e., brother and sister name each other as custodians for their own children.

* * *

* * * Section 2503(c) Trusts

A trust which permits accumulation of income will nevertheless qualify for the $10,000 annual gift tax exclusion if the trustee has the power to expend the property for the benefit of the donee until the donee attains age 21; at age 21, the donee must receive or demand receipt of the property; and if the donee dies before age 21, the property must be paid to the donee's estate, or as the donee appoints under a general testamentary power, or failing appointment, is distributed to alternative beneficiaries.

The power of the trustee to make distributions must be discretionary. Limitations restricting the trustee to payments for education should not be used. Distribution must be at age 21, although it is sufficient if the donee has an absolute right to demand distribution at that age, continuing for a reasonable time.

Because clients are frequently reluctant to authorize distribution of great wealth to a donee at age 21, the trust can be structured so that only the income and accumulated income is subject to distribution under the Section 2503(c) rules. The corpus can remain in the trust after the beneficiary attains age 21, and [be] distributed at a later date, or even shifted to other beneficiaries. The annual gift tax exclusion will then be available only for the value of the income interest to age 21 from the date of transfer to the trust, but only if the trust assets are reasonably income producing. Therefore, this alternative should not be used if the trust is funded with underproductive property, apparently including life insurance, and the trustee should not have the power to hold or acquire underproductive property.

The Section 2503(c) trust is similar to the custodial gift, but obviously more flexible. Specific administrative powers can be included, and under many state laws, separate Section 2503(c) trusts for different beneficiaries can be combined for purposes of administration. If the donee dies before the trust terminates, the trust assets can be shifted to other beneficiaries by giving the minor a general power of appointment, and providing that if it is not exercised, the trust will be distributed to such alternative beneficiaries. This avoids the problem of distribution to the estate of a minor, requiring probate administration, and in many cases resulting in distribution of the property to the parents of the decedent, who may have been the original [donors]. If the power of appointment is not exercised, the trust could be distributed to siblings of the decedent and used for their education.

From the income tax standpoint, income can be accumulated in the trust to take advantage of its 15 percent bracket and to avoid the Kiddie tax. For generation-skipping transfer tax purposes, the Section 2503(c) trust can be tailored to qualify for the $10,000 exclusion so long as it must ultimately be distributed to its single beneficiary or included in his or her taxable estate. The corpus cannot be diverted to anyone else. Finally, there should be no estate tax problems so long as the grantor, his or her spouse or parents of the beneficiary are not acting as trustees and retain no other powers over or interests in the trust. * * *

* * *

* * * The Crummey Trust

The grant of a *Crummey* invasion power to the minor beneficiary has, as a general rule, been recognized by the Internal Revenue Service as qualifying transfers to a trust for the $10,000 annual gift tax exclusion. Gifts to trust will qualify for the annual gift tax exclusion to the extent beneficiaries have an unrestricted power to invade the trust and remove assets.

One advantage of the *Crummey* trust is that it may be funded with nonproductive assets, and the trustee may have the power to accumulate income. The fact the beneficiaries are minors with no legally appointed guardian is irrelevant.

After originally agreeing that this technique is effective, the IRS has issued increasingly strict rules on its application. It has ruled that some form of notice [must be] given of any additions to the trust subject to invasion. In the case of minors, this must be to their legal or "natural" guardians, i.e., where no legal guardian is appointed, parents. The invasion period must give the beneficiary a reasonable time to exercise the right. The terms of the trust must assure that there are sufficient assets to invade during the period of invasion.

* * *

The invasion power is granted annually, generally to the extent of total additions to the trust for the year, or the amount of the available annual exclusion, whichever is less. This could be as much as $20,000 per donee where husband and wife donors split gifts. However, if the amount subject to invasion exceeds $5,000 or 5 percent of the value of the trust, whichever is greater, a failure to invade could be a taxable gift by the holder of the power if there is a possibility the assets not withdrawn could be distributed to other beneficiaries. Various solutions have been suggested to this problem. One is to provide that any amounts not withdrawn will accumulate and subsequently [be] distributed to the holder of the power, or as he or she appoints. * * * Another is to provide that the entire amount subject to invasion does not lapse each year, but only that part of it equal to the "5 or 5" limitation. The IRS may attack this annually lapsing or "hanging" power.

This form of trust provides great flexibility in funding with productive and nonproductive assets, giving the trustee total discretion in making investments and distributions, and extending the trust beyond age 21. *Crummey* clauses can be structured to permit multiple beneficiaries to invade the trust.

* * *

NOTE

Which of the vehicles discussed by Kasner offers the greatest tax and nontax advantages? For further discussion of gifts to minors, see Richard A. Atkinson, *Gifts to Minors: A Roadmap*, 42 ARK. L. REV. 567 (1989).

---

3. *Crummey* Trusts

The following excerpt criticizes the allowance of the annual exclusion for contributions to *Crummey* trusts and proposes various *Crummey* reforms. Willard H. Pedrick would eliminate *Crummey* trusts by limiting the annual exclusion to cases where the identity of the donee and the value of the gift are "accurately ascertainable."

Willard H. Pedrick, Crummey *Is Really Crummy!*, 20 ARIZ. ST. L.J. 943 (1988)*

* * *

It was early established in the administration of the Federal Gift Tax that a taxpayer could make a present interest gift to a minor notwithstanding the disabilities of minority, if the gift was (1) outright, or (2) in a trust that mandated payment of the income to the minor beneficiary. If either of these requirements were met, the Internal Revenue Service recognized the income gift as a present interest gift and allowed the taxpayer to take advantage of the gift tax exclusion. If, however, a gift in trust for a minor was made with discretion in the trustee to expend or withhold the income and principal from the minor beneficiary, the gift was a future interest not entitled to the gift tax exclusion. * * *

This doctrine presented a bit of a dilemma for taxpayers and their tax planning counsel. On the one hand, the legal disabilities of a minor beneficiary and the practical disadvantages of entrusting substantial property outright to minor beneficiaries made attractive the practice of giving the trustee discretionary control of the trust. On the other hand, the [rule], to the effect that trustee discretion to withhold benefits meant that a gift in trust to a minor was a future interest gift not eligible for the gift tax exclusion, was irksome in the extreme.

Congress responded to taxpayer distress over the apparent unavailability of the present interest exclusion from Gift Tax for discretionary trusts for minor beneficiaries. In the 1954 Revenue Code, Congress added Section 2503(c) which specifies rather precisely a road map by which gifts in trust for minor beneficiaries could qualify for the annual exclusion. But the specified conditions were (1) that the beneficiary have access to the income and the property

---

during the period of minority and (2) that all the trust property pass to the beneficiary on the beneficiary's reaching age twenty-one. The Congressional dispensation was not viewed as good enough, however, by many taxpayers and their tax planners because of a conviction held by many donors of mature years that youths becoming instant adults on reaching age twenty-one are not lightly to be entrusted with property ownership. Many property owners, recalling perhaps the follies of yesteryear, apparently believed that responsibility comes at some later stage of life such as thirty-five, forty-five or even older. Inventive counsel in due course thereupon came up with a gadget—a provision in the trust instrument that gave the minor beneficiary, however young, the right to demand in person or through a guardian (often never appointed) an amount from the trust equal to the annual exclusion.

I. THE *CRUMMEY* DOCTRINE

* * * [T]he *Crummey* rule was ushered into the world by the Ninth Circuit's announcement of a kind of Emancipation Proclamation for gifts to minors entitling such gifts to the annual exclusion, provided the minor beneficiary be given a reasonable opportunity, even though for a limited period, to withdraw the amount of the annual exclusion. At the time, hardly anyone voiced surprise, shock or outrage at the *Crummey* doctrine.

A land office business in *Crummey* trusts for minors has resulted. Astonishingly, the Treasury embraced the *Crummey* doctrine in a series of published rulings and letter rulings. It made no effort to carry the issue to the Supreme Court * * * . More recently though, in 1987 the Treasury recognized that taxpayer's counsel can try to make too much of a good thing out of the *Crummey* principle. The Treasury has now ruled that the device of enumerating a large number of potential donees as having rights of withdrawal not expected to be exercised will not entitle the donor to multiply the amount of the annual gift tax exclusion available where the several power holding donees have no vested interests in the gift property.

In the *Crummey* trust designed to exploit the now generous $10,000 per donee annual exclusion from the Gift Tax for gifts of present interest, the courts and the Treasury have plainly exalted form over substance. * * * [T]his little corner of Gift Tax law is sadly out of joint.

II. LEGISLATIVE HISTORY AND *CRUMMEY*

The *Crummey* decision makes Gift Tax consequences turn on the insertion of a withdrawal power no one expects to be exercised. Is this a defensible interpretation of the Gift Tax provisions of the Internal Revenue Code? The answer to that question calls for a brief review of the legislative history of Section 2503(b) of the Code which provides an exclusion of $10,000 for gifts "other than gifts of a future interest in property." The Committee Report makes clear that this prohibition against an exclusion for a future interest gift was a meat ax approach to the problem of ascertaining the number of beneficiaries in the case of class gifts. Unfortunately, the language chosen by Congress made critical the distinction between "future interests in property" and present interests in property. On this issue the Committee Reports provided a solid basis for the Supreme Court decisions emphasizing the right to present enjoyment and possession as constituting a gift of a present as distinguished from a gift of a future interest in property.

So it developed, naturally, that outright gifts and gifts that mandated income distribution whether to minors or to adults were recognized as present interests for Gift Tax exclusion purposes. But use of a protective device such as a trust in which a trustee would decide to distribute or withhold according to the interests of a minor beneficiary plainly would put such a gift in the category of being a "future interest." To give some relief from that plain fact of life, Congress, in the Internal Revenue Code of 1954, added Section 2503(c) which made provision for allowance of the annual exclusion for gifts to a minor in a discretionary trust but on condition that the property and the income therefrom be available during minority and distributed to the minor on his reaching age twenty-one.

It is true that the Committee Report on Section 2503(c) states that enactment of the subsection was not intended to subtract or derogate in any way from the concept of what constituted a present interest gift under Section 2503(b). But at that time and for many years before it had already been recognized both by the courts and by the Treasury that an outright gift to a minor or a Gift in Trust with a mandatory income distribution or expenditure was recognized as a present interest gift. Thus, the Committee Report merely recognized the continuing validity of those present interest gifts to minors. The question whether an illusory right of withdrawal should be enough to turn a discretionary Gift in Trust for a minor into a present interest gift is simply not addressed by the legislative history of Section 2503(c).

The question that the Court of Appeals should have faced in *Crummey* is whether Congress could possibly have intended that a right of withdrawal in an infant beneficiary, a babe in swaddling clothes, should transform a gift of a future interest into a gift of a present interest, even though plainly neither the donor, nor the tax planner, nor certainly the infant donee, ever contemplated that the right of withdrawal would be exercised.

The legislative history of Sections 2503(b) and 2503(c) does not warrant the view that a theoretical right of withdrawal in an infant beneficiary should entitle the gift to be recognized as a present interest when in fact the gift is through a discretionary trust and the protective mechanism extends to majority or beyond. Indeed, in light of the specific provision for Gifts in Trusts for the benefit of minors provided in [Section] 2503(c), conventional principles of statutory interpretation would argue that no annual exclusion should be added by a court decision on the basis of an illusory and often ephemeral right of withdrawal by an infant beneficiary. If the *Crummey* approach was sound in 1954, why did Congress need to add Section 2503(c)?

The judicial heart bled in *Crummey* when the court contemplated what it saw as unfair discrimination against gifts to minors caused by the unavailability of the annual exclusion for gifts in trust. But the annual exclusion was still available for gifts to minors in the form of outright gifts or gifts with mandated income distributions. The discrimination against gifts to minors arose only in the situation where the donee imposed a protective device between the gift and the donee's receipt.

It ought to be recognized that in substance a right of withdrawal in the infant beneficiary does not really endanger the operation of the protective device. Thus, in all probability, the beneficiary's actual possession and enjoyment of the property or the income therefrom will be long deferred, making it a future interest in property. Likewise, if such a protective device was set up for an adult beneficiary, complete with a demand right, a present interest exclusion should not be allowed if it is virtually certain that the right of withdrawal would never be exercised by the particular beneficiary. Incapacity of the beneficiary or the existence of a sub rosa agreement not to exercise a demand power also should make a gift in trust with postponed enjoyment a "future interest." In other tax planning situations the facts of life are determinative. Therefore, if the real thrust of a gift in a discretionary trust is to postpone, in fact, the donee's possession and enjoyment of the property, in the face of earlier Supreme Court decisions it is difficult to see how such a gift in trust can be characterized as anything other than a gift of a "future interest in property" when the withdrawal right is transparently a flim flam.

The decision in *Crummey* must be characterized as a blatant, shocking misinterpretation of Section 2503(b) of the Code. Not surprisingly, the court's opinion made no effort to enlist legislative history in support of its result because the legislative history summarized the above points to the opposite result.

It would be wild, indeed, to think for a moment that Congress intended to authorize the courts to create an exception in addition to [Section] 2503(c), permitting an annual exclusion through the charade of a formal withdrawal power no one expects the infant beneficiary to exercise. The notion that Congress intended to authorize an interpretation of Section 2503(b) on a revolutionary principle that form and not substance should control is simply unthinkable.

The conclusion, supported by powerful arguments, is that the decision in the *Crummey* case was wrong. The * * * Treasury strayed far from the path of virtue in its repeated endorsements of *Crummey*.

III. A LEGISLATIVE PROPOSAL, OR THREE

What is to be done? First of all, the Treasury is irretrievably stuck with its own mistake. Its endorsement of *Crummey* in repeated rulings and private letter rulings has extended over many years. The *Crummey* doctrine as announced by the Ninth Circuit and approved by the Treasury has certainly been open and notorious. During that interval Congress has enacted six Revenue Acts with estate and gift tax provisions including the comprehensive Internal Revenue Code of 1986. Throughout this period, the language of Section 2503(b) has remained unchanged. In light of the *Crummey* doctrine's extraordinary departure from the rule that substance and not form governs tax matters, the repeated Treasury endorsements of the doctrine and the repeated legislative attention to the Revenue Code without any alteration of [Section] 2503(b) all strongly suggest that in effect, the disqualification of gifts of a "future interest in property" from the per donee annual exclusion has been eliminated from the language of [Section] 2503(b) at least for gifts to minors with a power of withdrawal.

If, as submitted, the *Crummey* doctrine is now just as much the law as though it was written into Section 2503(b), is any corrective action at all called for? Corrective action by way of legislation certainly is called for. Section 2503(b) with its barnacle, the *Crummey* doctrine, is now a trap for the unwary. It stands as an anomalous rejection of the doctrine that matters of form should not affect tax consequences of particular transactions. * * * The tax law ought not to be in such a state and it certainly ought not to contain a provision that requires use of a formalistic clause of no real substance to dramatically affect the tax consequences of the gift. Congress should now seriously consider whether it would not be better to replace the parenthetical clause in Section 2503(b) denying an exclusion for the gift of a "future interest in property" with language that would more explicitly state the law as it is, in fact, now administered.

When Congress initially enacted the Federal Gift Tax in 1932, it denied the availability of the annual exclusion with respect to the gift of a "future interest in property" because of concern about the difficulty in ascertaining the actual number of donees and consequently the number of exclusions appropriate for such future interest gifts. The Congressional choice of the verbal formula for the litmus test was unfortunate. What policy difference should it make whether the donee has to wait some time to secure possession and enjoyment of the gift property? * * *

The sensible approach to the problem of handling the annual exclusion for gifts where possession and enjoyment will assuredly come to the donee in due course can be better achieved, not by denying the exclusion for gifts of future interest in property, but by limiting the availability of the exclusion to cases where the identity of the donee and the value of the gift is accurately ascertainable. * * *

Under the proposed legislative revision of Section 2503(b) a Gift Tax exclusion would be allowed in any case where the identity of the donee and the present value of the gift (up to the amount of the exclusion) can be accurately determined, with the burden of proof on the taxpayer. Thus, *Crummey* trusts would disappear because there would be no advantage in including an artificial right of withdrawal; and the tax law would be the better for it. Neither the

Internal Revenue Code nor the Treasury should invite taxpayers to play charades. The Code ought to reflect an expectation that citizens will turn square corners with their government and it should mark the path of rectitude as precisely as possible.

If Congress can give attention to the language of Section 2503(b) regarding denial of the per donee annual exclusion for gifts of "future interests in property," then perhaps other large issues can also be considered. Is an annual exclusion per donee in the amount of $10,000 ($20,000 if the donor has a cooperative spouse) really defensible at a time when annual federal deficits are enormous? It is true that in terms of purchasing power, the modern equivalent of the original exclusion of $3,000 would be perhaps eight times that figure. That is not to say, however, that such a large amount is the appropriate amount for the annual exclusion. The original [r]ationale was to eliminate the need for Gift Tax returns on Christmas gifts and the like. One may wonder whether the early allowance of $3,000 per donee might not still be adequate for that purpose.

Reexamination of the appropriate amount for the annual exclusion would also suggest reconsideration of the amount appropriate for the unified credit, which replaced the former exemption and was enacted with the Revenue Act of 1976 and became fully operational with a credit of $192,500 a decade later in 1987. The present unified credit, as even insensitive estate planners know, enables the passage of $1,200,000 to the next generation free of estate tax, provided arrangements have been made to utilize fully the separate unified credits available for each spouse of the present generation. When the present level of the unified credit is compounded with the annual exclusion per donee for lifetime transfers it offers wealthy individuals with large families the opportunity to avoid acquaintance with the federal transfer tax on quite substantial sums—millions in fact. It would seem that responsible fiscal policy dictates a more modest level for the unified credit and a scaling back of the per donee exclusion.

But if such stern measures were to be adopted, then additional attention surely needs to be given to the rate structure of the federal transfer tax system. Thanks to an unduly generous unified credit, which has the effect of shielding the first $600,000 (or $1,200,000 for a married property owner) from the transfer tax, the present rate tables move with astounding acceleration from a rate of 0 to 37 percent as the first effective tax bracket. This seems inordinately precipitous. Surely a more modest climb to the maximum rates ought to be reestablished, especially if the estate taxpayer's club is to be enlarged with a smaller unified credit. After all, historically, the rates have progressed from an initial 3% to a maximum of 77%. There is some natural appeal in a gradual elevation of the rate schedule. Moreover, in any reexamination of the rate schedule it should be recognized that the object of the federal transfer taxes is not really to break up the large estates, an early rationalization, but one for which the taxes were never designed. No, the object today is to raise modest amounts of desperately needed revenue. The rate schedules should be revised with that end in mind.

What is being suggested is that with any reexamination of the appropriate amount for the per donee exclusion from the Gift Tax, Congress should also consider the appropriate amount to be sheltered from transfer taxes by the unified credit. Additionally, Congress should adopt a rate schedule that has more than a narrow band of percentage points from the lowest applicable rate to the highest. Surely, someone in the Treasury and in Congress ought to be interested in these issues.

NOTE

Do you agree with Pedrick that *Crummey* represents "a blatant, statutory misinterpretation of Section 2503(b)"? Does the Code always elevate substance over form? For an earlier proposal to eliminate the present interest requirement while denying the annual exclusion for the creation of demand powers and replacing the per-donee amount with a flat per-donor amount, see Kent Mason, *An Analysis of* Crummey *and the Annual Exclusion*, 65 MARQ. L. REV. 573 (1982). For a "more modest" proposal to eliminate the present interest requirement and replace it with a vesting requirement modelled on the provisions of § 2642(c), see F. Ladson Boyle, *Present Interest Gifts in Trust: Donor and Donee Problems*, 29 GONZAGA L. REV. 453 (1993).

Which of the reform proposals excerpted in this Subpart do you find most appealing from the standpoint of tax policy? Which do you think would be most acceptable in today's political environment?

B.   Disclaimers

The excerpts in this Subpart consider the vexing question of how the gift tax should treat disclaimers of property and the proper relationship between federal and state law in answering this question. John H. Martin argues that, contrary to § 2518, treating disclaimers as taxable transfers is simpler, fairer, and more consistent with the goals of the federal wealth transfer tax system. Joan B. Ellsworth takes the opposite tack, arguing that any disclaimer that is valid under applicable state law should also be respected for federal tax purposes.

John H. Martin, *Perspectives on Federal Disclaimer Legislation*, 46 U. CHI. L. REV. 316 (1979)*

* * *

I. THE UNSUCCESSFUL SEARCH FOR UNIFORMITY AND CERTAINTY

A. Policy, Uncertainties, and a Federal Solution

1. Common Law of Disclaimers. The underlying policy given effect in the property-law doctrine of disclaimer is that a person should not be saddled with a burdensome estate or interest against his will. * * *

This freedom to choose and to refuse has long been recognized for transfers by deed or will. But historically the common-law theory governing passage of property by intestate succession overrode the policy undergirding disclaimers. Because of the predominant importance of knowing the new owner of the property from the instant of the prior holder's death, the common-law doctrine of "descent cast" placed title in the heir without regard to the recipient's desires. * * *

Several consequences flow from a state's decision to allow or not to allow a disclaimer in any particular case. An effective disclaimer causes the property to be transferred to another person as if directed to that destination by the original donor. The disclaimant is treated as never having been involved. This "relation-back" approach in turn triggers several consequences beneficial to the disclaimant. Generally, the creditors of the disclaimant cannot reach the property, for the debtor never has any interest in it. If the transfer is by death, an inheritance tax usually cannot be assessed on the receipt by the disclaimant, for such receipt never occurs. Similarly, if the jurisdiction has a gift tax, a relation-back theory would deny the existence of a taxable transfer, for the disclaimant never acquires an interest that could form the subject of a subsequent gift.

Significantly, as these consequences became predictable and certain, they provided reasons for rejecting gifts beyond a desire simply to escape from unwanted burdens or to exercise independence. Creditors could be avoided, or at least be kept from reaching a ready fund; taxes could be deflected or minimized; and the testamentary scheme of the testator could be revised to comply with either wishes not found in a valid will or the family's notion of what was the intended pattern of distribution. In recent years, these new motives seem to have completely overshadowed the original justifications for disclaimers.

2. Pre-1976 Federal Tax Treatment. Until 1976 the treatment of disclaimers for federal tax purposes fairly consistently followed the property-law pattern just sketched. In particular, * * * the pre-1976 federal tax law applied the doctrine of relation back. But the development of federal law regarding disclaimers has been not only parallel to, but also dependent on, local law: favorable application of the federal tax rules was, before 1976, allowed only when the disclaimer was valid under state law. Because the states have prescribed different procedures for effecting a disclaimer, have varied in important respects with respect to the types of interests that may be disclaimed, and have differed across a wide spectrum in prescribing time limits for making the disclaimer, there has existed a very real and unsettling lack of uniformity.

* * *

Dissatisfaction with the variations in tax consequences produced by the differences in underlying state law was the fundamental reason for the revisions in the 1976 Tax Reform Act. * * * Congress intended to set aside the inconsistent tax results caused by ancient state law distinctions such as those prohibiting disclaimer of an interest acquired via intestate succession. It also indicates that Congress sought to eliminate tax benefits arising out of long delayed decisions given effect under local property law solely because indefeasible vesting of the interest has not occurred earlier. Enactment of section 2518 thus represents a quest for the holy grail of uniformity. To some commentators, the crusade has appeared successful. To others, including this writer, the effort fell markedly short of the objective.

* * *

Admittedly, section 2518 is not responsible for all our present difficulties. Indeed, there was nonuniformity in the tax treatment of disclaimers before its enactment. * * * But the new rules were enacted with the promise of resolving the old difficulties, and it is striking not only that they failed to achieve uniformity, but also that they have created new conflicts and complexities for understanding the law of disclaimers. These problems raise questions about the advisability of having enacted section 2518, questions that become even more troubling when we turn to the section's effect on the planning stages of gift and estate transactions.

* * *

III. IN SEARCH OF A MORE EFFECTIVE STATUTE

Given the difficulties section 2518 presents in its current form, it is important to consider how revisions might round off the sharp corners of the statute. Clearly, the current section is preferable to pre-1976 law because it represents progress toward uniformity, and it partially removes some uncertainties concerning the tax consequences of disclaimers, even if it does inject a new level of complexity into the law. Thus, the confusion over the proper application of the new statute, its failure to attain uniformity, and the creation of an atmosphere that encourages complex predeath planning and more extensive post-mortem manipulations all demand a search for modifications Congress might enact to cure these deficiencies.

A. Federal Transfer Mechanism

* * * [M]any of the difficulties with the federal statute stem from the requirement in section 2518(b)(4) that the interest pass "without any direction" by the disclaimant and the lack of any mechanism in the statute for transferring the disclaimed property. On the one hand, if the federal law were understood simply to ignore the local property-law characterization of an attempted disclaimer, the disclaimant might be allowed a marital or charitable deduction, for example, without the requisite transfer ever materializing at the state level. On the other hand, even if the federal statute were understood to allow the disclaimant to make a ministerial direction of the interest, the statute still requires some means of identifying the substitute taker, a requirement that throws the statute back to the vagaries of state law.

One approach to overcoming these difficulties is, of course, for Congress simply to override state law by inserting a transfer rule into section 2518. This transfer mechanism could provide, for example, that if rejection were made within the time and in the manner prescribed, then "the interest shall pass to those who would take if disclaimant had predeceased the creation of the interest." Alternatively, a federal transfer mechanism could be designed to operate only if neither state law nor the instrument creating the interest specifies a substitute disposition. This latter suggestion would both permit diversity according to the desires of the several states and recognize a right in the donor to specify substitute takers, even if it might still encourage drafting in anticipation of disclaimer with the attendant complexity and premium on planning.

The federal transfer mechanism would cause the conflicting state property-law result to conform to the federal standard. It thus avoids the problems created by simply ignoring the state property-law label for federal tax purposes. * * *

* * *

* * * If section 2518 were to contain a transfer provision, the caseload of the federal courts likely would be increased to resolve the disputes over its application. Moreover, the very arguments in favor of a federal system—a government close to the people, the ability to experiment at the local level with new legislation, and the freedom to reflect local preferences and customs—suggest rather strongly that restraint and caution are more appropriate than zeal in developing federal property law, even assuming that development is constitutionally permissible.

B. Other Approaches

Opportunities to improve the operation of the present federal disclaimer statute are available that provide alternatives to creating a federal transfer mechanism. Instead of taking such a radical step, Congress might adopt one of the various proposals for recognizing a disclaimer as valid in those situations in which state law does not shift the property, but the disclaimant transfers the property to the proper next-taker. A number of proposals for disclaimer legislation that antedate section 2518 recommend this kind of a solution. On the one hand, several model and uniform acts, proposed for streamlining the states' property laws on this topic, and a proposal for federal reform by the Section of Taxation of the American Bar Association look to the law of lapse to identify the proper next-taker, which, insofar as federal tax treatment is concerned, would pave the way for a "ministerial direction" solution. On the other hand, the American Law Institute and the Treasury Department have recommended simply that the statute permit the disclaimant to re-transfer the property as he chooses within a reasonable time after the original transfer.

In accordance with the ABA proposal and the tenor of the model and uniform acts, an amended section 2518 could recognize refusals that were not treated as disclaimers at the local level by amending the "without direction" language of section 2518(b)(4) and incorporating a lapse-based specification of who the substitute taker should be. A disclaimer would then be effective if the disclaimant, within the stipulated time period, refused the property and assigned or conveyed the interest to the person(s) who would have taken on lapse. The time when lapse would occur, that is the point at which disclaimant is treated as having predeceased, should be the time the disclaimed interest is deemed created. The transfer by the disclaimant would be essentially a ministerial act, would not be discretionary in the sense of choosing the substitute taker, and thus, in accordance with present law, would not constitute the exercise of control justifying imposition of a transfer tax.

There could, of course, be problems in applying the law of lapse in order to determine the rightful recipient. * * *

* * *

Greater freedom of selection by a disclaimant was proposed in the American Law Institute and in the Treasury Department recommendations. The freedom to select would exist when neither the instrument of transfer nor local law supplies an alternate taker. The ALI recommendation would recognize for federal tax purposes a rejection followed by timely selection of the next recipient even though local law might not characterize the refusal as a disclaimer, indeed even though local law might classify the action as acceptance. The justification for permitting tax-free selection of the substitute taker is to provide "maximum freedom in post-transfer arrangements" and thereby to reduce the premium placed on advance planning of property dispositions. The Treasury proposal would permit the disclaimant to designate as taker only someone to whom the original donor could have made a deductible transfer, i.e., a spouse, a charity, or an orphan.

The draftsmen of the Model Acts and of the ABA Section of Taxation proposals gave specific reasons for not embracing freedom of designation by disclaimant. Such broad authority was simply too much like a power of appointment, the exercise of which necessarily connotes acceptance—with all of its benefits—rather than rejection. The redirection by disclaimant was seen to be at odds with the claim of refusal and rejection.

Such criticisms of a freedom to redirect are undoubtedly on target. The ability to take property in absolute ownership or to transfer it to another who is selected by the recipient is indeed a very broad power. That the decision to accept or re-transfer must be made within a short, nine-month time span does not derogate from the plenary nature of the power. Therefore, if section 2518 were amended to give recognition to a transfer by a disclaimant that shifts the interest to a substitute taker, at the very least the validation should be limited to transfers made to persons identified under some external standard such as the concept of lapse.

A focus on the close relationship between a power of appointment and the disclaimer treatment advocated by the ALI is useful in another sense. Every decision to accept or reject a gift includes the ability to designate oneself as recipient by simply accepting the property. Yet, the power to make oneself the owner of property is the very root of a general power of appointment, and utilizing a general power to shift ownership to another person is fully subject to transfer taxation. Such a connection between a general power, seemingly the obverse of a renunciation, and the disclaimer, which presupposes the right to take for oneself, raises more fundamental questions about section 2518 that may preclude mere tinkering with the statute. Indeed, it is essential to consider the argument that the special treatment for disclaimers should be discarded entirely in favor of emphasizing this ability to accept benefits and hence in favor of subjecting disclaimers to estate, gift, and generation-skipping taxes.

IV. DISCLAIMERS AS TRANSFERS

In essence, section 2518 establishes the rules for giving recognition to the theory of relation back for tax purposes. The failure to obtain uniformity through a single national rule, the substantial problems confronting attempts to create uniformity, and the complexity and importance the section has brought to pretransfer planning suggest that now is the time to consider abandoning relation back—with all its problems—as a rule of federal tax law. Whether to recognize the effect of the relation back seems fundamentally to be a policy decision; certainly there is nothing in the concept of disclaimer that requires the action to be tax-free. To be sure, acceptance by the donee can and should continue to be a necessary element for a valid gift. Rejection should be permitted for testamentary transfers—both intestate and testate—as well as for inter vivos gifts. But it does not follow from recognizing the opportunity for disclaimer that the theory of relation back must be observed. * * * [S]ome jurisdictions do not apply the theory to questions of inheritance taxation and creditors' rights. Therefore, it is appropriate to examine the act of disclaimer and decide whether it is comparable to other actions that are subjected to transfer taxation.

A. Disclaimers and Powers of Appointment

When a person is offered a gift, he must decide whether to take the property (or interest in property) as an owner or to reject it, letting it pass elsewhere. It cannot be denied that the intended recipient can freely make the property his own. This ability to decide is an element of property control that becomes even greater when the recipient has the ability to make a partial disclaimer. If the recipient has the right to pick and choose between portions of a gift or has the ability to sever the gift and, in effect, create new interests, then the action is more than a simple refusal: it is an assertion of dominion over the property. Of course, in either case, the ability to accept or reject is most certainly not full control; until the recipient makes a decision to become an owner of the interest, there is not the full measure of domination. Nevertheless, full, absolute control is not required to precipitate application of a transfer tax.

Given these principles, the treatment of general powers of appointment offers a most persuasive analogy for justifying taxation of disclaimers. The definition of a general power looks to the holder's ability to make himself, his estate, or creditors of himself or his estate the owner of the property. The definition does not focus on whether the donee has a broad power to designate other persons, a narrow power to do so, or any such power at all. That a disclaimant cannot designate substitute takers of the rejected property, therefore, does not distinguish a disclaimer from a general power of appointment. Moreover, possession alone of a general power of appointment is sufficient to precipitate taxation notwithstanding failure to take actual benefits.

* * *

A transfer tax is an excise imposed upon a transfer or shift in ownership rights. Since the disclaimant's act is a necessary step in the ultimate taker's accession to ownership rights, here, as in the case of a general power, it is necessary for tax purposes to look through the relation-back theory that is otherwise applied to the disclaimant's action. In short, since the disclaimant has the discretion to accept property as his own, there undoubtedly exists a voluntary, discretionary act that shifts ownership. Thus, even if, as in the power-of-appointment situation, the tax consequences of the disclaimant's act seem purely a policy decision, consistency demands that the disclaimer be subjected to transfer taxation.

An argument in reply to this line of reasoning is that a power of appointment presupposes a prior acceptance of the power whereas the disclaimer decision comes before that previous acceptance step. Though correct as a matter of theory, in practical terms this distinction uses labels to hide the element of control that exists at that earlier stage. If the realities of the situation are assessed and focus is placed on elements of control, benefit, and enjoyment rather than on labels from the law of property, the rationale for transfer taxation becomes highly compelling.

* * *

C. Other Considerations

1. Tax Policy. Classifying disclaimers as transactions generally subject to transfer taxation would recognize the substantial control and enjoyment implicit in the decision to accept or reject property, and thereby remove an inconsistency in present law. More importantly, such a rule would facilitate attainment of the goals and policies of estate and gift taxation. A primary *raison d'etre* for transfer taxation is to limit the transfer of wealth and, in so doing, to reduce economic inequality.[192] It is the egalitarian impulse, not revenue production, that fuels its momentum and should therefore shape its design.

As disclaimers now operate, however, they offer considerable opportunity for tax minimization and avoidance. The existence of disclaimer possibilities permits delay in allocating shares among family members; this feature in turn allows passage of property to other family members when the named recipient has adequate wealth from other sources. These adjustments in property distribution can be used most often by persons who have sufficient resources to permit the luxury of refusing property. Persons with modest means cannot afford even to entertain the idea. They accept, possess, and use their property, and they suffer the consequences of transfer taxation when the residue passes to the next family member. Disclaimers, then, present opportunities to keep wealth intact. In this respect, they work contrary to the basic purpose of wealth taxation. This policy-defeating feature and the resultant inequity among taxpayers can be corrected by removing the tax-free option offered by disclaimers.

* * *

2. Policy Objections. There are, of course, arguments other than those already noted against this change in the tax approach to disclaimers. * * *

* * *

Double taxation or, more accurately, the prospect of two successive taxes within a short period of time is [a] potential objection. The original donor may be subject to gift or estate taxation. If a disclaimer is treated as a transfer subject to tax law, a second exaction is made shortly after the original one. Yet, not only can this successive taxation occur in nondisclaimer contexts

---

[192]   Another reason, of course, is to raise revenue. *See* Jantscher, *The Aims of Death Taxation, in* DEATH, TAXES AND FAMILY PROPERTY 40, 51 (E. Halbach ed. 1977) for an evaluation of reasons advanced for imposition of estate taxes and the conclusion that the redistributive purpose is its most legitimate objective. * * * *Cf.* Eisenstein, *The Rise and Decline of the Estate Tax*, 11 TAX. L. REV. 223 (1956) * * * (indicating revenue production was the original goal of estate taxation).

when successive transfers take place, there is no discernible policy suggesting that there is anything inherently wrong with two taxes in quick succession. Although the credit for tax on prior transfers[200] mitigates the blow of successive estate taxation caused by two deaths within up to a ten-year period, the policy reflected in that provision responds to the burden of taxes imposed on involuntary transfers. The policy does not and should not apply when the second transfer is voluntary, as in a disclaimer.[201]

* * *

NOTE

Martin advocates subjecting disclaimers to the federal gift tax as a solution to the conflict between state disclaimer statutes and § 2518. Is there another solution that would address the problem of the lack of uniformity without unduly burdening state property law? What other problems would be presented by such an alterative solution?

Joan B. Ellsworth, *On Disclaimers: Let's Renounce I.R.C. Section 2518*, 38 VILL. L. REV. 693 (1993)*

I. INTRODUCTION

* * *

The effectiveness of a disclaimer is dependant on state law. State law determines who will take the transferred property: either the recipient intended by the original transferor or another substituted taker. In addition, state law distinguishes valid disclaimers from all other transfers. A disclaimer is fundamentally different from a voluntary transfer of property because it is a refusal to accept property *ab initio*. The disclaimant is considered to have received no property interest and to have transferred none. Thus, a valid disclaimer results in one gratuitous transfer (from the transferor to the substituted taker) while an invalid disclaimer, or no disclaimer, may occasion two transfers (from the transferor to the would-be disclaimant, and then from the disclaimant to the substituted taker).

This distinction has important federal and state tax ramifications. Where there are two transfers, there are two occasions for the imposition of transfer taxes; but when only one transfer is recognized, the tax burden may be smaller. * * *

* * *

For years the federal tax consequences of a disclaimer depended almost entirely on state law. Because of state variations, there was some inconsistency in the federal treatment of disclaimers, which was viewed as inequitable. In addition, disclaimers sometimes facilitated tax avoidance. To alleviate these problems, Congress enacted Internal Revenue Code (I.R.C.) section 2518, which contains its own definition of a "qualified disclaimer." State law has retained

---

[200]   I.R.C. § 2013.

[201]   An instructive omission is the lack of any such credit when transfers in quick succession are subject to gift tax.

*   Copyright © 1993. Reprinted with permission.

considerable importance, however, even for federal transfer tax purposes. Instead of a pure federal system, the law of disclaimers is now an amalgam of state and federal rules: rules that sometimes conflict with one another, leaving attorneys and their clients in a state of uncertainty and confusion.[13]

This Article * * * suggests * * * that the federal government should no longer be permitted to control the definition of a valid disclaimer. I.R.C. section 2518 ought to be repealed and state laws should be returned to their prior position of pre-eminence in the realm of disclaimers. It is argued that the state law inconsistencies that worried Congress and inspired section 2518 are less significant today and that it is the conflict between federal law and the various state laws that is presently inequitable.

A return to a state-dominated system of disclaimer law has been made possible by the 1986 enactment of the Generation-Skipping Transfer Tax (GSTT). The GSTT is designed to ensure that family wealth is taxed at least once each generation, and it has halted several important tax-avoidance techniques previously used by the very wealthy. * * * [T]he GSTT has reduced the ability of disclaimers to affect tax receipts of the federal government. It has also reduced the need for a federal standard defining valid disclaimers. The GSTT has cleared the way for a meaningful reduction in the level of conflict and confusion presently found in the law of disclaimer.

* * *

VI. SIMPLIFICATION

A. Continuing Conflict

* * * Disclaimants may be subject to a substantial federal tax liability on property that, under state law, is entirely beyond their reach. The federal rules are filled with complexities and uncertainties that are not easily mastered. Similarly, state disclaimer statutes—even those derived from the uniform acts—are not models of clarity, and there is a paucity of case law to aid in their interpretation. The fact that the two systems overlap while operating independently of one another adds to the confusion.

* * *

At one time, the dominance of federal disclaimer law served a valid purpose. In addition to pursuing "uniformity," the stated objective of section 2518, Congress was also seeking to forestall a common tax avoidance technique used by well-to-do families. An adult child would disclaim property passing from his deceased parent so that the property would then pass to the decedent's grandchildren with only one layer of transfer tax imposed. Had the adult child not disclaimed, transfer taxes would have been imposed twice before the grandchildren received the family wealth. This plan can function in situations where the adult child has sufficient property and is willing to forgo an inheritance in order to protect family assets from the taxman. In plain words, disclaimers provided tax loopholes for the rich.

By creating uniform federal disclaimer rules, Congress apparently intended to tighten up on the use of such "planning tools." * * * Congress did not go so far as to disregard state disclaimer law entirely, but it did manage to limit the power of state law disclaimer statutes to frustrate the collection of federal gift and estate taxes. Today, the Generation-Skipping Transfer Tax (GSTT) is quite effective in performing this important function.

---

[13]   For an excellent discussion of the complexity and confusion left in the wake of the new federal statute, see John H. Martin, *Perspectives on Federal Disclaimer Legislation*, 46 U. CHI. L. REV. 316 (1979) * * * .

B. Effect of the GSTT

* * *

* * * The GSTT imposes a tax (calculated at the highest marginal rate of the estate tax) on transfers to any individual who is more than one generation younger than the transferor. Thus, if a transferor gives or devises property to his grandchild, the transfer is subject to two distinct taxes: (1) the gift or estate tax and (2) the GST tax.

This combination of taxes produces approximately the same result as if the transferor had devised the property to his child who later gave it to the transferor's grandchild. Such a two-step transfer is subject to the gift or estate tax twice: once in the transferor's estate, and again when the child transfers the property. Under the new GSTT, the one-step transfer is subject to two transfer taxes as well. * * * The overall effect * * * is to create a system where family wealth is taxed at least once every generation, regardless of the form of transfer.

* * *

Thus, the GSTT has greatly reduced the tax incentives for using disclaimers. Disclaimers can still produce transfer-tax savings, but those savings are quite modest and could have been secured by appropriate planning. For example, where tax benefits such as the GSTT exemption or the unified credit have been overlooked or inadequately utilized by the decedent, family members can sometimes secure the benefit of these statutory provisions by disclaiming. Such use cannot be considered tax avoidance, however, because the disclaimants are merely taking advantage of tax-saving provisions that were deliberately created by Congress for the benefit of taxpayers. The disclaimants are not exploiting loopholes.

Today, section 2518 does little to discourage tax avoidance. Because most pre-1986 trusts have been "grandfathered"—that is, protected from the reach of the GSTT because of their age—section 2518 continues to play a useful role in limiting the tax-avoidance potential of these older trusts. In all other cases, state disclaimer laws and the GSTT combine to adequately protect fairness and the federal fisc. Therefore, for all gifts made after 1986 section 2518 is no longer necessary, and it should be revoked.

C. Simplification for Whom?

Simplification of the tax laws is something everyone approves of—in principle at least. Fairness requires that tax laws be comprehensible. But when simplification produces revenue losses or perceived unfairness in distributive effect, simplification may lose popularity. Furthermore, proponents of simplification may disagree on what is "simple." Federal disclaimer laws were enacted to create greater national uniformity in the tax treatment of citizens of the various states. But uniformity does not necessarily engender simplicity.

Local lawyers who represent an array of clients in diverse matters must question whether section 2518 helps to simplify their practice. Although disclaimers are not a part of their daily routine, these attorneys must master the local disclaimer law (no matter how complex) in order to identify those occasions when its use may be beneficial. When a disclaimer is appropriate, the complexities of federal law must be explored as well, because neither common sense nor any rule of thumb can predict the federal tax results of a valid disclaimer. * * *

Whose simplicity should take priority? * * * [T]he central goal of estate planning [is] appropriate devolution of property * * * , and this is controlled by state law. Federal tax considerations should not be allowed to preempt the field.

* * * Granted, taxpayers can employ estate planning specialists who are fully competent to untangle the relationship between the federal and state rules, but why should such expensive expertise be necessary? * * *

D. Disclaimers as Taxable Transfers

Some commentators have suggested a simplification strategy that is the converse of the proposal made here.[351] They believe that all disclaimers should be treated as taxable transfers. The rationale for this view lies in the analogy between disclaimers and general powers of appointment. Under both concepts, an individual can choose between taking property personally or deferring to another recipient. Initially, Congress had difficulty in determining how to tax general powers, but it was ultimately agreed that the right to acquire property is tantamount to outright ownership. Accordingly, the exercise, release or lapse of a general power is now treated as a taxable transfer.

The same rationale might be applied to disclaimers. A blanket rule defining disclaimers as taxable transfers would put an end to the problem of determining which disclaimers are "qualified." In addition, such a rule would simplify the federal tax laws and would, perhaps, increase revenues. * * *

Imposing a transfer tax on all disclaimers would be unfair and unwise. It would interfere with long-established property law doctrine by creating a corresponding but diametrically opposed tax law doctrine. * * * A better way to reduce conflicts between state and federal disclaimer laws is to eliminate section 2518 altogether and to forgo imposing federal transfer taxes on *any* validly disclaimed property.

E. Fairness for Taxpayers

* * *

Without section 2518, the federal tax consequence of a disclaimer that is valid under state law will be obvious. The transfer will be taxed as if the disclaimed interest had never existed. Property will pass directly from the transferor to the substituted taker, and the transfer will be taxed accordingly. The question of whether the disclaimer is valid will be decided under state law and there will be no federal tax law questions.

It is clear that some federal tax law advantages may be gained by disclaimers. * * * [In some cases] taxpayers may be able to achieve tax savings through the use of disclaimers. * * * If we deny taxpayers the right to perform postmortem planning—that is, the right to take remedial action—we place undue emphasis on sophisticated and expensive representation. * * *

With respect to pre-1986 transactions and "grandfathered" trusts, section 2518 was, and still is, necessary. While not a perfect solution, it does keep some forms of tax avoidance in check. For current and future transfers, however, the GSTT has made section 2518 obsolete. * * * Other than serving as a transition rule to deal with "grandfathered" trusts, section 2518 should be repealed entirely.

The chief advantages of discarding section 2518 are simplicity and fairness. * * *

NOTE

How does Ellsworth justify a more favorable tax treatment for disclaimers than for powers of appointment? For another perspective on the federal tax treatment of disclaimers, see Grayson M.P. McCouch, *Timely Disclaimers and Taxable Transfers*, 47 U. MIAMI L. REV. 1043 (1993) (noting that independent federal requirements of § 2518

---

[351]   *See* * * * Martin, *supra* note 13, at 356-69 (recommending that disclaimers should be considered equivalent to taxable transfers).

serve to prevent taxpayers from "exploiting state property law doctrine as a short-cut to wholesale tax avoidance").

C.   The Scope of the Gift Tax

The excerpts in this Subpart discuss the scope of the gift tax in two contexts. The first two excerpts consider the impact of valuation difficulties on the determination of whether a transfer is a completed gift: Robert N. Macris argues that the open transaction approach is both theoretically and practically undesirable in the gift tax, while Mitchell M. Gans defends such an approach in conjunction with other statutory changes. Subsequent excerpts explore the gift tax's failure to tax various transfers of opportunities from parents to their children: George Cooper criticizes the resulting erosion of the tax base, while Paul L. Caron proposes various statutory reforms to address problems posed by transfers of opportunity.

Robert N. Macris, *Open Valuation and the Completed Transfer: A Problem Area in Federal Gift Taxation*, 34 Tax L. Rev. 273 (1979)*

INTRODUCTION

* * *

There are two prerequisites to the imposition of tax on what is seemingly a transfer of wealth. One concerns itself with timing, and the other with valuation. The gift tax will be activated only when the transfer, in whole or in part, is complete. * * * At the time the transfer is deemed complete, there must be a valuation of the transferred property interest. This process of assigning a value to the transferred property is, of course, basic to the imposition of tax. * * *

Resolution of the question of when a transfer is complete rests on a cessation of "dominion and control" in the transferor. It is only when this termination of control occurs that there is a completed transfer. Either a transfer is complete or it is not. Valuation, on the other hand, is not so clearly defined. The process of valuation encompasses a view to the past and future, as well as to the present. In the vast majority of cases, a reasonable estimate of value can be ascertained. In certain instances, however, value can assume an elusive nature.

* * *

* * * The present state of the law of federal gift taxation demonstrates a muddling of principles with regard to questions concerning valuation and those dealing with completed transfers. * * *

* * *

OPEN TRANSACTION

Open Valuation—Income Taxation

* * *

The classic open transaction involved the income tax in the case of *Burnet v. Logan*.[82] In exchange for stock in an iron company, the vendor-taxpayer was contractually entitled to receive an annual payment contingent upon the quantity of iron ore produced from a certain mine. The issue was whether an estimate of the value of this contractual right should be made, thereby fixing the amount realized as of the date of sale, or whether the sales transaction should be held open, with future receipts applied as a return of capital until the entire basis was recovered, and thereafter as taxable gain. The Supreme Court held that "[t]he liability for income tax ultimately can be fairly determined without resort to mere estimates, assumptions, and speculation. When the profit, if any, is actually realized, the taxpayer will be required to respond."[84]

* * *

The Service has taken the position, with regard to the valuation of contract rights for purposes of imposing the income tax, that a value must be assigned except in "rare and extraordinary cases."[85] * * *

Open Valuation—Estate Versus Gift Taxation

Estate Tax

The problem of speculative valuation and the open transaction also arises, with different stakes, in the estate and gift tax areas. In the context of the estate tax, closed valuation is the rule. The estate tax must be assessed either on the date of death or on the alternate valuation date six months later. Otherwise, the administration of decedents' estates would be subject to inordinate delays while awaiting valuation to become certain. If the administration of an estate were completed despite the existence of a speculative asset (in effect, by assigning a value of zero to that asset), then the tax on that part of the estate would be forever lost. These considerations, therefore, require a valuation of all assets for estate tax purposes, no matter how inexact that valuation may be.

Gift Tax

In the gift tax context, unlike the estate tax, there seems to be no apparent necessity to value a property interest at the time a completed transfer takes place. Imposition of the gift tax can be delayed until the value of the property interest transferred is readily ascertainable. In certain circumstances, however, the ramifications of open valuation may be undesirable. * * *

Potential Avoidance of Transfer Tax

For example, assume that *A* is the owner of a half interest in a gold mine of speculative worth. *A* promises (the promise is enforceable under the applicable state law) to pay *B*, at the end of each year for ten years, *A*'s annual bounty from the mine. Since the promise is binding, there is a completed transfer at the time the promise is made. However, the value of the ten-year interest is uncertain.

Compare the foregoing example to the situation where, instead of the above promise, *A* makes an outright transfer of his half interest in the gold mine to *B*. Again, there is a completed

---

[82]   283 U.S. 404 (1931).

[84]   *Id.* at 412-13.

[85]   Rev. Rul. 58-402, 1958-2 C.B. 15, 16; *see* Reg. § 1.1001-1(a).

transfer; and again, valuation is not certain. In each of the two situations, the gift tax could be levied on *A* annually, depending on the magnitude of the benefit *B* derives from the mine. However, if *A* were to die prior to the end of the ten year term, no further gift tax, of course, could be assessed. The value of the half interest in the mine at the date of *A*'s death would be included in his gross estate in the first hypothetical situation, but nothing would be includable in *A*'s estate in the second situation.

It can be seen, then, that in the second hypothetical, *A* potentially evades both the gift and estate tax. Clearly, in this situation, the government would insist on valuation at the time of the transfer, no matter how imprecise, so that some transfer tax would surely be levied. In the first hypothetical, by contrast, *A*, while effecting a completed transfer, retained a property interest sufficient to require inclusion of the value of the portion of the mine owned by him in his gross estate. Thus, if the transaction is held open and gift tax is levied only upon actual receipts by *B*, there is no danger of a tax-free reduction of *A*'s estate.

Three Modes of Transfer Relevant to Open Valuation

In sum, as far as the transfer tax provisions are concerned, there are three modes of transfer relevant to open valuation. One is effected at death and is subject only to estate tax. The second is an inter vivos transfer on which gift tax is payable, and in which the donor retains no ties to the transferred property sufficient to create potential estate tax liability. The third is an inter vivos transfer which creates a gift tax liability, and which, in addition, gives rise to potential estate tax liability because the donor continues to possess sufficient control over the property so that its value would be drawn into the gross estate.[95] It is only in the third mode that the option of open valuation is available. The crucial question with regard to this third mode is: Should this option be exercisable when valuation is speculative?

Considerations on Utilization of Open Valuation

Desire for Consistency

Logical consistency dictates that if the option of open valuation is available only in one of the three relevant forms of transfer, then open valuation should not be resorted to even where it is permitted. If the transaction must be closed for purposes of the estate tax and if it must be closed for purposes of the gift tax where the transfer is not of a type potentially subject to estate taxation (that is, if valuation, no matter how speculative, must be derived for these two purposes), then it seems that value should be ascertained as well for purposes of the gift tax, even in the situation in which the inter vivos transfer in question can potentially be drawn into the donor's gross estate. Assuming that an identical asset is transferred in all three situations, why should its valuation be necessary in the former two instances, but not in the latter one? Of course, consistency, although desirable, may not be required. Nevertheless, the desire for consistency between the two transfer taxes and, furthermore, within the gift tax itself, should be sufficient to exclude the possibility of open valuation from the realm of gift taxation.

Language of the Statute and the Regulations

Moreover, the scope of the gift tax is to reach all completed inter vivos transfers of property interests. The spirit of the gift tax as it is manifested by the language of the statute and the regulations requires a valuation of these transfers at the time that they become complete. Section 2512(a) mandates that for a gift, "the value thereof at the *date of the gift* shall be considered the amount of the gift." In addition, section 25.2511-2(a) of the regulations states that

---

[95]   The third mode spoken of here is a transfer that will be subject either to gift or estate tax but not both if open valuation is chosen, and potentially subject to both gift and estate tax * * * if closed valuation is chosen.

"[t]he gift tax is not imposed upon the receipt of the property by the donee, [rather the tax] is an excise upon [the] *act of making the transfer*, [and] is measured by the value of the property passing from the donor."

The presence of this language in the statute and in the regulations, without a provision for mitigating circumstances when valuation might be speculative, spawns a theoretical contradiction with the principle of open valuation. A transaction will be held open only because it is determined that a substantial number of the factors on which valuation rests are not quantifiable at the time the transaction is complete. It is only the future that will make apparent what was veiled in the past. In this notion, however, there is a serious dilemma. The future will reveal not only what was obscured in the past, but also a multitude of factors affecting value that were simply not in being at the time of the completed transaction. * * * Accordingly, if open valuation is adopted, then it seems inevitable that the valuation process will include these post-transfer factors. The tension, therefore, is between imprecise valuation at the time of the completed transaction, or precise valuation at some later time when the precision rests on post-transfer elements. In the context of gift taxation, the language of the statute and the regulations necessitates valuation on the date that the transfer is complete. It follows, then, that in the gift tax area, this tension must be resolved in favor of closing valuation when the transfer is complete.

Administrative Convenience

In part, the argument for open valuation rests on administrative convenience; that is, when the factors on which valuation relies are unclear, it is too burdensome for both the government and the courts to assess value and haggle with the taxpayer. On the other hand, open valuation generates its own inconvenience. An otherwise open gift involving a flow of payments to the donee nevertheless requires a reckoning of what has passed to the donee after each successive calendar quarter. The gift tax will be assessed continuously in this fashion until the termination of payments to the donee or until the donor's prior death. In the latter case, the remaining value of the speculative asset must, in any event, be estimated for estate tax purposes. Furthermore, even if the open gift does not entail a continuous flow of payments to the donee, there must be constant vigilance in order for the government to become apprised of any susceptibility to valuation. Hence, the inconvenience of this laborious process must be weighed against the unsuitability of closing the transaction.

Allocation of Risk

In a real sense, open valuation is merely a form of allocation of risk between the government and the taxpayer. Where a transaction is kept open, the government assumes the risk that the transferred asset will depreciate in value because of unforeseeable factors, and the taxpayer assumes the risk that there will be appreciation for the same reason. Objectively, this appears to be an even balance. In addition, though, where a transaction is held open, the government is burdened by a deferral of tax liability. * * *

* * *

Summary: Utility of Open Valuation

In weighing the utility of open valuation, there must be a careful separation of the theoretical and the practical. In a theoretical sense, open valuation is inconsistent with the statute as it now reads because under open treatment the tax is levied on a value derived not on the date of the completion of the transfer, but on some future date of valuation. It is probably because of this theoretical inconsistency that the Service and the courts have confused the concepts of completion and valuation. In an attempt to reconcile the concept of open valuation with the statute, they have often concluded that a gift not susceptible of valuation is incomplete. This conclusion is clearly incorrect. If open valuation is to be adopted without congressional direction, then it must be accepted in the face of this contradiction. The decision to adopt it must then balance the practical, that is, the costs and benefits to the taxpayer and to the government.

TRANSFERS FOR AN INADEQUATE CONSIDERATION

* * *

Measure of Value of the Gift

* * * [A]ny completed transfer of a beneficial interest in property, made for less than "an adequate and full consideration in money or money's worth," will be subject to gift tax, unless made in the ordinary course of business. The tax will be assessed on the difference in value between what is transferred and what is received. This assessment should present no difficulty unless there are questions of valuation. These questions may occur in three contexts: either (1) the transferred property, (2) the consideration, or (3) both the transferred property and the consideration may not be susceptible of valuation at the time of the completed transfer.

"Gift" of Speculative Value for "Consideration" of Certain Value

Consider the following: Suppose that D promises to transfer to A his receipts from a half interest in the production of a speculative gold mine for ten years. Assume that in all probability the ten-year interest will be worth between $30,000 and $70,000, and that A gives D $10,000 in exchange. Assume further that the transfer is not in the ordinary course of business, and that the agreement is binding under state law. Therefore, the transfer is complete. D has relinquished control over his interest in the mine.

As far as valuation is concerned, there are two choices: The transaction can be held open or it can be closed. If the latter is chosen, D will be taxed to the extent that the estimated value of the ten-year interest exceeds $10,000. If the transaction is held open, then the gift tax should be levied on the actual amount of the transfer in excess of $10,000. No tax should be imposed until more than $10,000 from the mine is paid to A. Thereafter, any payments made to A will be taxed to D as gifts in each successive calendar quarter. * * *

"Gift" of Certain Value and "Consideration" of Speculative Value

Assume the same facts, except that A gives D $100,000 in exchange for the promise. Now, there is a completed gift from A to D. If the transaction is closed, then the value of the gift will be the excess of $100,000 over the estimated value of the ten-year mining interest at the time of the transfer. If the transaction is held open, however, the probable value of the gift will lie between $30,000 and $70,000, but there is no way to be certain until the entire ten years elapse. It is only then that the excess in value of the $100,000 over the value of the mining interest will be known.

In the first situation, where the transfer is not susceptible of valuation, but the consideration is fixed, open transaction treatment results in a levy of gift tax on each successive actual transfer in excess of the consideration. But, in the second situation, where the transfer is fixed, and the consideration is not subject to valuation, then, under open valuation it is only when the actual amount of the consideration is determined that the gift tax can be levied. This will present a problem, because, if the donor should die before the termination of the period of payment of the consideration, then there will be escape from transfer tax. Therefore, in this second situation, the transaction must be closed.

Both "Gift" and "Consideration" of Uncertain Value

The third situation is subject to yet another analysis. Suppose that in a transaction not in the ordinary course of business D makes a binding promise to pay to A his receipts from a half interest in a gold mine for ten years, and A, in exchange, makes a binding promise to pay to D his receipts from a half interest in a silver mine for ten years. Assume that the interest in the gold mine is of greater value than the interest in the silver mine, but that the value of both is uncertain. Hence, there is a completed transfer from *D* to *A*.

If the transaction is closed, then the value of the gift will be the excess of the estimated value of the gold mine interest over the estimated value of the silver mine interest at the time of the transfer. An open transaction may present a problem. If the rate of return on each interest varies from year to year, and the return on the interest of greater total value is not of greater value in each and every year, then it will not be possible to assess the gift tax until all contingent payments are made. * * * Thus, if the gift tax is postponed until all payments are made (i.e., if the transaction is held open) and the donor dies prior to this time, then the problem of escape from both the estate and the gift tax is present to the extent that amounts have been actually paid by the donor in excess of those received. Similarly, if, instead of exchanging binding promises, *A* and *D* had actually transferred their respective interests in the mines, *D* would have effected a completed transfer to *A*, no part of which could be drawn into his gross estate. On valuation there is no choice in both situations. If the transfer or a portion thereof can potentially evade both the gift and the estate tax, the transaction must be closed.

* * *

NOTE

Do you agree with Macris that the open transaction approach is necessarily inconsistent with the language of the gift tax statute? Do you agree that disregarding post-transfer events in an open valuation regime would present serious administrative problems?

Mitchell M. Gans, *Gift Tax: Valuation Difficulties and Gift Completion*, 58 NOTRE DAME L. REV. 493 (1983)*

I. INTRODUCTION

Fair market value is the basis upon which transfer taxes are imposed. While ascertaining value is easy for some transfers, it is frequently an imprecise and difficult process. Occasionally, the transferred item is incapable of valuation—either because the transfer is subject to a contingency having a probability of occurrence that cannot be actuarially determined or because some aspect of the transferred item prevents even valuation experts from rendering a reasonable judgment.

Two formats are available for taxing these difficult-to-value transfers. The first alternative is to tax the transfer at the time the transferor severs his control, the point at which transfers are generally subject to taxation. Using this format, the determination of value is necessarily speculative. That is, the process requires taxpayers, the Internal Revenue Service, and the courts to hazard the best guess that the circumstances will permit. The second alternative is to defer the imposition of the transfer tax until the difficult-to-value aspect of the transfer becomes susceptible to more accurate valuation.

---

    *   Volume 58, Issue 3, the *Notre Dame Law Review* (1983), 493-536. Reprinted with permission. © by *Notre Dame Law Review*, University of Notre Dame. The publisher bears the responsibility for any errors which have occurred in reprinting or editing.

In the estate tax context, the former alternative has generally been applied because, unlike the latter, it makes it possible to compute the estate tax within a reasonable time after death, facilitating prompt estate administration. In the gift tax setting, however, a valuation-difficulty rule has evolved, which in some situations defers the computation and payment of the tax where the gift is difficult to value. Since this deferral approach allows the tax computation to be made when valuation is no longer difficult, its application increases valuation accuracy. This article will argue that this increase in accuracy warrants a more expansive application of the valuation-difficulty rule than has thus far been the case.

It has been suggested, however, that the valuation-difficulty rule ought to be categorically rejected in the gift tax context as well because its application would produce results that are incongruous with conventional gift tax theory. Ordinarily, a gift is deemed complete and the tax is immediately imposed upon value at the time the donor severs his control over the gift. The gift tax system therefore normally excludes post-severance events from the tax base. The valuation-difficulty rule, on the other hand, effects a deferral and takes post-severance events into account. This deviation in theory produced by the valuation-difficulty rule can be minimized, it will be suggested, by excluding all post-severance events from the valuation process other than those that merely reveal what was unascertainable at the time of severance.

* * *

II. FORMATION OF THE VALUATION-DIFFICULTY RULE

* * *

The transfer of an interest in property becomes subject to gift tax when the donor relinquishes his control over the property. Where, however, the donor divides his transfer into two time frames—first contractually obligating himself to make the transfer and then discharging his obligation by making the actual transfer of the property—a timing question arises: is the gift complete when the contractual obligation is undertaken or when the property is transferred in discharge of the obligation? The courts have concluded that the gift is complete when the donor's contractual obligation becomes enforceable under state law.

This question resolved, it became necessary to decide whether the gift should be deemed complete where the contractual obligation had a contingent nature. * * *

* * *

* * * [A] gift is not complete at the time that a contingent contractual obligation is undertaken if the contingency is such that the probability of its outcome cannot be actuarially determined. The IRS adopted this principle in Revenue Ruling 69-346.[9] There, a husband and wife, residing in a community property state, entered into an agreement that required the wife to transfer her one-half interest in their community property to a trust to be created under the husband's will. Although the agreement became enforceable when it was executed, the IRS ruled that the wife did not make a taxable gift until the husband's death,[10] when it first became possible to calculate the value of her gift. The IRS formulated the rule as follows:

---

[9]   1969-1 C.B. 227.

[10]   Since a donor's retention of dominion and control over a gift renders the gift incomplete, Treas. Reg. § 25.2511-2 (1958), and since, in the ruling, the wife's dominion and control continued after the agreement was entered into—by spending or saving, she would affect the amount of community property—it is arguable that the conclusion that the gift was incomplete until the husband's death was not dependent upon a finding of valuation difficulty. *See* Macris, *Open Valuation and the Completed Transfer: A Problem Area in Federal Gift Taxation*, 34 TAX L. REV. 273, 294 (1979).

[T]he effective date of the gift for Federal gift tax purposes is the date upon which a promise to make a future transfer becomes enforceable under State law, and not the date upon which an actual transfer of property is made, provided the gift is susceptible of valuation at the time it becomes enforceable.

* * *

III. SCOPE OF THE VALUATION-DIFFICULTY RULE

* * *

* * * [A]ssume that a taxpayer owns a mineral interest located somewhere in the Persian Gulf region. Assume further that the country in which the interest is located is involved in an incandescent war. If the country within which the interest is located does not prevail, the victorious countries may confiscate the interest, depriving the taxpayer of his ownership in the minerals without any compensation. While in this precarious position, the taxpayer makes an outright gift of the mineral interest.

If * * * the valuation-difficulty rule is to be applied in the non-contractual context, the gift is incomplete, since its value is contingent upon the outcome of the war and, therefore, impossible to calculate with any certainty. Putting aside for the moment the wisdom from the policy viewpoint of any rule that would render this gift incomplete, there are difficult practical problems inherent in such a rule in the context of this illustration. If the taxpayer dies after having conveyed his ownership in the mineral interest but prior to the gift having become complete in the tax sense, the transfer of the minerals will have escaped transfer taxation, even though the value of the minerals may eventually prove to be substantial. At the time of the conveyance of his rights in the mineral interest, the taxpayer is not deemed to have made a gift by virtue of the valuation-difficulty rule; at the time of the taxpayer's death, the mineral interest cannot be included in his gross estate, for he will have relinquished all of his control and rights with respect to the property prior to his death. The difficulty here is that although the gift will be deemed complete when its value becomes ascertainable at the conclusion of the war, by our hypothesis that will not occur until the taxpayer has died. Since, under the present transfer tax system, the gift tax does not apply to any transfer when the transferor is dead at the time the gift becomes complete, the gift tax cannot apply here.

Contrast these difficulties, engendered by application of the valuation-difficulty rule in the non-contractual context, with the results that stem from application of the rule to a contractual gift, such as that in Revenue Ruling 69-346. There, the wife contractually obligated herself to make a gift upon the death of her husband of property that would not be determinable until his death. As will be recalled, the IRS ruled that because of valuation problems, the gift was not complete until the husband died. Unlike the hypothesized conveyance of the mineral interest, there was no potential for the complete avoidance of transfer tax created by application of the valuation-difficulty rule * * * . If the wife had died after having entered into the enforceable agreement but prior to the tax gift having become complete (i.e., at her husband's death), she would not have made any transfers pursuant to the agreement, since it required her to make the transfer only if she were to survive her husband. Nevertheless, all of her assets, including those that she transferred pursuant to the agreement, would have been includible in her gross estate. Having survived her husband, she was subject to gift tax; had she failed to survive, the estate tax would have been applicable.

Thus, deferring the taxable gift because of valuation problems will not create the potential for complete avoidance of transfer tax in the context of a promise to make a gift contained in an enforceable contract. Such a contractual gift will become subject to gift tax when valuation can be accomplished, or, if the donor dies prior to the completion of the gift, the property that is the subject of the gift will be included in the donor's gross estate, the donor having control over it at death.

* * *

IV. DEATH-COMPLETION RULE: A PROPOSAL

The valuation-difficulty rule provides a more accurate measurement of the value of a gift and should therefore be applied in as many contexts as possible when the gift is difficult to value. One constraint, however, that prevents expansive application of the rule is that when it is applied to some gifts, tax avoidance can result. This tax avoidance can be eliminated if a provision is adopted requiring all gifts subject to the rule to become complete no later than the death of the donor, thereby preventing any gift subject to the rule from escaping the donor's transfer tax base. Thus, the adoption of such a rule would permit the valuation-difficulty rule to be applied to any difficult-to-value gift without any concern about tax avoidance.

* * *

If, at the time of the donor's death, the gift were still not capable of valuation, a speculative approximation of value would be necessary. This need to speculate, however, is not produced by the valuation-difficulty rule or the rule requiring that the gift be deemed complete by the donor's death, but rather by the notion that events occurring after the transferor's death should not affect the transfer tax base. Indeed, the testamentary transfer of difficult-to-value items requires the same speculative approximation for estate tax purposes. So, unless the notion that post-death events be disregarded for transfer tax purposes is abrogated, speculative approximation will be necessary for those gifts subject to the valuation-difficulty rule that do not become capable of valuation by the time of the donor's death.

* * *

In sum, adoption of this death-completion proposal will make possible an expansive application of the valuation-difficulty rule without permitting tax avoidance. Since application of the valuation-difficulty rule increases valuation accuracy, the rule should be expansively applied, complemented by the death-completion rule to prevent tax avoidance.

V. VALUATION

A. Selecting the Valuation Time Frame

* * *

Neither the Code nor the regulations explicitly indicate the date on which a gift subject to the valuation-difficulty rule is to be valued. Section 2512, the only provision in the Code that addresses gift tax valuation, states that "if the gift is made in property, the value thereof at the date of the gift shall be considered the amount of the gift." But is "the date of the gift" the date enforceable rights are created in the donee under the state law or the date those rights subsequently became capable of valuation? * * *

* * *

* * * If sections 2501 and 2512 are construed as effecting a unified time-frame for both valuation and gift completion purposes, then the amount of a gift subject to the rule will be its value on the date valuation becomes possible. This construction would require all events occurring after the donor had severed control over the gift but prior to valuation becoming possible to enter the valuation calculus. This result, however, violates the inveterate transfer tax precept that all events occurring after the donor has severed control over the given item should not affect the computation of the gift's value.

This violation of transfer tax theory is produced by a clash of three principles: (1) the valuation-difficulty rule; (2) the notion that events occurring after the donor has severed control (post-transfer events) should have no bearing on the valuation process; and (3) the construction of sections 2501 and 2512 as creating a unified time-frame.

To resolve this clash, a comparison of the policies underlying each of these three principles is necessary. As suggested, the valuation-difficulty rule is beneficial, since it permits the accurate measurement of transfers that are inherently difficult to value when initially made. Omitting post-transfer events from the valuation process also serves an important function: donors can compute their gift tax liability at the time that they sever their control over the gift. In contrast, applying the third principle, the unified-time-frame construction, to all gifts subject to the valuation-difficulty rule without any limitation does not fulfill any policy objective * * * . Since a rigid construction is not grounded in any policy objective, at least insofar as gifts subject to the valuation-difficulty rule are concerned, and since the valuation-difficulty rule and the rule excluding post-transfer events from the valuation process do serve important objectives, a flexible approach to the section 2501 and section 2512 time frames is desirable. In other words, while as a general rule it is appropriate to calculate value as of the date the donor severs control over the gift—excluding post-severance events—it is nevertheless appropriate, with respect to difficult-to-value gifts, to calculate value at the time valuation becomes possible, taking into account post-severance events.

B. Revelation v. Non-Revelation Events

Whenever the valuation-difficulty rule is applied, at least one post-transfer event—the ultimate outcome of the contingency inherent in the gift that makes it necessary to apply the valuation-difficulty rule—must affect the valuation. That is not to say, however, that all other post-transfer events must also be included in the valuation process. Indeed, it will be argued that the only post-transfer events that should affect the valuation process are those that reveal the outcome of the contingencies that made it appropriate to invoke the valuation-difficulty rule in the first instance. Such post-transfer events will be termed "revelation events."

The approach suggested here works an accommodation of two conflicting policy objectives. On the one hand, transfer tax theory generally requires that post-transfer events be disregarded. On the other hand, when the valuation-difficulty rule is applied to permit the accurate measurement of a transfer that is difficult to value at the time it is initially made, it is obviously necessary to include in the valuation process the post-transfer outcome of the difficult-to-value contingency. So, the compromise is struck by eliminating all post-transfer events other than the revelation of the outcome of the difficult-to-value contingency from the valuation process.

* * *

C. Neutralization of Deferral

Although the gift having a quantity that can be determined immediately and the gift with an unascertainable quantity superficially appear to be entitled to equivalent treatment, there is a difference between the two, warranting, perhaps, different treatment. The gift whose value is calculable at the outset is immediately subject to tax, while the other does not become subject to tax until its value becomes ascertainable. There is no policy rationale to support the deferral of the tax obligation in one case while requiring an immediate payment of the tax in the other. To remove the deferral, an interest charge * * * should be imposed on the tax obligation. If an interest charge were imposed, the disparity between the two hypothesized gifts would be neutralized.

Of course, the Code does not presently provide for an interest charge. Consequently, gifts subject to the valuation-difficulty rule will enjoy preferential treatment if all non-revelation events are disregarded in calculating value. Unless the Code is amended to provide for an interest charge, this preferential treatment can only be ameliorated by including some post-transfer increases in value, although non-revelation events, in the gift tax base. If the post-transfer increase in value approximates the inflation rate, the deferral will be roughly neutralized (taking into account the relationship between the inflation rate and the appropriate interest rate).

* * *

* * * [I]n the context of * * * many * * * gifts subject to the valuation-difficulty rule * * *, inclusion of the time-value of money in the tax base will neutralize the deferral. On the other hand, for those gifts subject to the rule that do not automatically increase in value as time lapses, an alternative approach must be taken, of which there are basically four.

E. Available Alternatives

First, exclude all non-revelation events from the valuation process and amend the Code to provide for the imposition of an interest charge. From the policy viewpoint, this is the most attractive alternative, since it closely approximates the tax treatment applicable to gifts that are not too difficult to value. * * *

Second, "pick and choose" among the non-revelation events, including in the valuation process only those that approximately neutralize the deferral. * * * A process such as this—where the proper amount of tax to be paid is computed first and then the tax base that will produce this tax is determined—is antithetical to our system of taxation.

Third, exclude all non-revelation events from the tax base. In the absence of an interest charge, this alternative treats gifts subject to the valuation-difficulty rule more favorably by conferring on those who make gifts of this type the benefits of deferral. The disparity between gifts subject to the rule and gifts immediately capable of valuation that is created by this alternative renders it unattractive.

The fourth alternative, which has been adopted by the IRS, would include in the valuation calculus all non-revelation events. Although this alternative does deviate from general transfer tax policy concerning post-transfer events more than the other alternatives, it can be rationalized, perhaps, on the ground that its consequences, which are generally adverse to the taxpayer, are self-inflicted. * * * By selecting a difficult-to-value asset, the donor himself creates valuation doubts, which, since voluntarily created, ought to be resolved against him. The division of risk created by this alternative also makes it attractive. Just as the taxpayer bears the risk that the inclusion of non-revelation events will result in subjecting post-transfer appreciation to tax, the government bears the risk that the inclusion of such events will result in post-transfer depreciation reducing the amount of the gift below its value on the day control is severed. Finally, the inclusion in the tax base of post-transfer increases in value, if approximately equal to the inflation rate, should neutralize the deferral.

Since, however, some assets outperform inflation and other assets do not perform as well as inflation or suffer a decline in value despite inflation, the first alternative, which, unlike the last alternative, provides an accurate measurement of value of the gift on the date control is severed and which imposes an interest charge to neutralize the deferral, is preferable. The first alternative being unavailable without the necessary legislation, however, the last alternative is the least unacceptable one and should be applied to all gifts subject to the valuation-difficulty rule—except, of course, to * * * [certain gifts that can] be stripped of all non-revelation events other than the increase in value attributable to the time-value of money.

* * *

NOTE

What difficulties might arise in applying Gans' distinction between "revelation events" and other post-transfer events? Does Gans make a persuasive case for open valuation in the gift tax area? Compare the "easy-to-value" approach advocated by Joseph M. Dodge:

> The main thrust of my reform proposals seeks accurate valuation of gratuitous transfers by avoiding reliance on estimates of, or speculation about, future events and by analyzing relevant events as they actually occur. Hindsight, in other words, should be used whenever possible. * * * [C]ertain inter vivos transactions that attempt to fix low transfer tax values should be held open until death.

Joseph M. Dodge, *Redoing the Estate and Gift Taxes Along Easy-to-Value Lines*, 43 TAX L. REV. 241, 244 (1988). See the excerpt from Dodge's article in part VII(B), *infra*.

George Cooper, *A Voluntary Tax? New Perspectives on Sophisticated Estate Tax Avoidance*, 77 COLUM. L. REV. 161 (1977)*

* * *

* * * *Intrafamily Fringe Benefits—Diversions of Services and Capital.*

 * * * Any approach whereby a wealthy individual can divert a wealth-generating opportunity to his prospective heirs can fairly be classified as estate freezing, even though the parties engaging in it may not be conscious of the substantial estate planning implications of their actions. There is no doubt * * * that a wide variety of the typical layman's estate planning of this nature is a basic part of the regular activity of many wealthy individuals. Especially if one is an active businessman or investor, opportunities for bringing one's prospective heirs into a profitable activity occur with regularity.

The extensive audit of Richard Nixon's tax returns by the Joint Committee on Internal Revenue Taxation provides a good example of how a child can profit, without gift tax, from parental advice.[61] Patricia Nixon (Tricia) received a substantial sum on reaching her twenty-first birthday in 1967 from a trust fund established on her behalf by Mr. Elmer Bobst, a family friend. She loaned $20,000 of those proceeds to her father in return for his demand note bearing interest at 6% per annum. The father and daughter entered into a claimed oral understanding that this sum would be invested in a Florida land development venture known as Cape Florida Development Co., Inc. in which Mr. Nixon was also making an investment. Tricia was to have no management or control over the investment. The joint investment was made in 1967 for $38,000. In 1972 the property was sold for $150,000 and $65,000 was paid to Tricia as her share of the proceeds.

---

* This article originally appeared at 77 COLUM. L. REV. 161 (1977). Reprinted by permission. This work was also published as a book by Brookings Institution (1978).

[61] JT. COMM. ON INT. REV. TAX, EXAMINATION OF PRESIDENT NIXON'S TAX RETURNS FOR 1969 THROUGH 1972, S. REP. NO. 93-768, 93d Cong., 2d Sess. 147-55 (1974).

This transaction was scrutinized in a tax audit that was as expert and exacting as any ever conducted and, after much discussion and legal analysis, the Joint Committee took pains to say that if the transaction had been properly established with a binding obligation to pay Tricia a fixed share of the profits at the outset, it would be fully recognized for tax purposes. However, the Committee also found that the claimed oral agreement was not sufficiently established by the evidence to be creditable. Mr. Nixon was therefore subject to income tax on the full profit from the deal, and the Committee suggested that the payment of Tricia's profits to her should be treated as a gift from Mr. Nixon. For our purposes the critical point is that there was nothing fundamentally challengeable about the deal. If it had been cleanly carried out it would easily have succeeded in enriching the young woman by $45,000 in a single investment transaction through the exploitation of her father's knowledge and contacts without any gift tax to him.

This transaction is a typical example of what all our interviewees acknowledged was a common and ordinary practice. The extent to which the younger generation in a wealthy family is enriched in this fashion is impossible to estimate, but it is surely an important factor in assuring that the children of wealthy parents themselves become wealthy.

Despite the obvious implications of such diversions for maintaining the level of family wealth from generation to generation, it would be foolhardy to suggest that every such diversion is or should be within the reach of the estate or gift tax. No sensible person would suggest that a tax could be imposed on the giving of parental advice. Frequently, however, these diversions involve more than mere advice, as the parent provides his child with a valuable opportunity which has been created by the parent and whose economic value is a direct reflection of the parent's activities. These additional factors are what turns many family partnerships into effective transfer tax avoidance devices, and they should raise doubts when they appear in other contexts as well.

A striking example of a situation where a parent effectively shifted a portion of the value of his own business activities, as distinguished from merely sharing investment advice, is provided by the case of *Robert P. Crowley*,[64] an income tax case which has impressive estate planning implications. Mr. Crowley controlled a savings and loan association. The operation of this business generated various collateral sources of income—appraisal fees, insurance fees, and abstract and title policy commissions. In 1952, he set up a partnership (later incorporated), Crowley Co., to handle this collateral work. The partnership was wholly owned by Crowley's four children in equal shares, all of which were held in trust by Mrs. Crowley for the benefit of the minor children (ages 19, 16, 14, and 10). The partnership's initial working capital came from $2,000 contributions from each child, funded out of the child's small personal savings account. The oldest son, still in college, had received some training in appraisal work from his father, and he handled such work for the partnership with his father's assistance. The appraisal fees were divided between the association and the partnership. The son also acquired a license as an insurance agent and he handled the insurance needs of the savings and loan association, serving as sub-agent of several general insurance agents. Abstract and title fees were handled similarly. The partnership (later incorporated) generated $57,000 in income from these sources for the children in three years, without any income tax (or presumably, gift tax) to the father.

This case should not be taken to mean that any such diversion will be successful. In the *Crowley* case itself we learn of one instance which goes too far. Mr. Crowley had, prior to setting up his children's partnership, been engaging in a small personal loan business of his own. He tried to divert this business to the children by advancing them money at $2^{1}/_{2}\%$ to be loaned

---

[64]   34 T.C. 333 (1960), *acq.*, 1961-2 C.B. 4. * * *

to his former customers at 6%. The court taxed the income from these loans directly to Mr. Crowley.

The theory of the *Crowley* court was that the various fees for appraisal and insurance services were at least colorably earned by the children while the loan income was strictly payment for use of the parent's capital and not, as the court puts it, "from the performance of services, however meager" by the children. The Internal Revenue Service has acquiesced in this decision without qualification. A prudent tax planner should not be lulled by this acquiescence into total reliance on the Tax Court's "however meager" standard, but the possibilities for tax free diversions suggested by this case need not be ignored either. If a diversion like this, from a business wholly controlled by a parent to minor children, can escape tax, how difficult can it be to divert more subtle opportunities to adult children?[67]

* * * [O]ur interviewees * * * described situations where a parent directed business to a new corporation owned by children, helped it out with inventory, and supported it with his experience in a myriad of ways. In some instances the parent actually served as an officer or employee of the new company and took principal responsibility for running it for a modest salary.

The common factor in all these transactions is the transfer to a child of valuable parental talents and services which are seemingly not recognized as the subject matter of the gift tax. Because this strategy also has income tax avoidance implications, the income tax law has some provisions which could be used to attack more obvious abuses, as where a parent runs a business owned by his children for a grossly inadequate salary. However, these provisions would not cover many of the situations described above, and in any event, what little law there is on the subject suggests that, even where these provisions do apply, their effect does not carry over to the estate and gift tax. That is to say, even if income of a child is reallocated to his parent for income tax purposes to reflect the parent's real contribution to a business, it does not necessarily follow that this income, which still legally belongs to the child, will be treated as having been obtained by gift from the parent.[72] Our interviewees agreed that there were broad opportunities for the rendition of services from parent to child with no real risk of estate or gift tax exposure.

Another form of intrafamily benefit that seems to have escaped the coverage of transfer taxes despite its obvious economic value is loans from parent to child. All of the planners with whom we spoke said that clients frequently loaned funds to enable their children to undertake business or investment opportunities. To the extent that such loans are made at prevailing rates of interest and arm's length regularities are observed, there seems to be no risk of transfer taxation even if the child's credit would not have enabled him to obtain a similar loan from a stranger. * * *

A variation on this loan arrangement, which is also very popular, is for parents to guarantee repayment of loans obtained by children from banks or other third parties. It seems clear that such a gift of credit is not subject to transfer taxation.

Another nontaxable benefit which parents frequently provide for children is the assumption of risk of loss so that children can undertake opportunities which they might otherwise fear. * * * Sometimes the assumption of risk is not rolled into a more complex arrangement but is

---

[67]   * * * There are some obvious non-tax limitations on these diversions of business opportunities imposed by the law of corporate opportunity, the fiduciary obligations of a partner, and the securities laws, but these are hardly comprehensive.

[72]   In Hogle v. Commissioner, 132 F.2d 66 (10th Cir. 1942), income produced by a parent's management of a margin trading account for his children was taxed to the parent, but in a later case the court refused to charge the parent with having made a taxable gift to his children. Commissioner v. Hogle, 165 F.2d 352 (10th Cir. 1947).

simply a direct and unfettered assurance from parent to child. An assurance of this nature was part of the Nixon Cape Florida deal discussed earlier, in that Mr. Nixon guaranteed to Tricia that, at a minimum, he would return her basic $20,000 investment to her. Yet the Joint Committee nowhere suggested that this assumption of risk generated any tax problem.[78]

It is thus possible, with as much facility after 1976 as before, for a parent to devote great effort to locating investment opportunities for his children, to provide the capital to exploit these opportunities, to supply expert personal services which will make the opportunities a success, and to assure that if, after all this, the deal fails, he will pick up the loss—all without any transfer tax liability.

* * *

NOTE

Although many of the specific tax-avoidance loopholes described by Cooper have been closed by Congress or by the courts, others—like the transfer of opportunities—remain. Indeed, in many respects Cooper's voluntary tax thesis is as timely today as when it was first published. For a radically different approach, see Randall J. Gingiss, *The Gift of Opportunity*, 41 DePaul L. Rev. 395 (1992) (characterizing problems of valuing services and opportunity as "insurmountable" and recommending that instead of attempting to reach such transfers the Code should be amended to "exempt closely held businesses from the transfer tax system"); Case Hoogendoorn, *Transfers of Opportunities—An Opportunity to Avoid Transfer Tax?*, 71 Taxes 892 (1993) (arguing that "America's pro-family public policy ought to discourage" attempts to tax transfers of opportunity, and that "[n]o transfer tax system should ever seek to discourage intrafamily economic activity on advantageous terms not otherwise available").

Paul L. Caron, *Taxing Opportunity*, 14 Va. Tax Rev. 347 (1994)*

I. INTRODUCTION
* * *

For over seventy years, Congress has required businesses under common ownership or control to deal at arm's length with each other for federal income tax purposes. In particular, section 482 * * * authorizes the * * * Service * * * to allocate income, deductions, credits, and other allowances among such businesses where necessary "to prevent evasion of taxes or clearly to reflect the income of any such [business]." The goal is to place "a controlled taxpayer on a tax parity with an uncontrolled taxpayer"[4] by preventing "the shifting of income from one commonly controlled entity to another."[5] * * *

---

[78]   If it ever becomes necessary for a parent to make good on a guarantee against loss, a gift will occur at the time that the parent covers the child's loss unless the child obligates himself to repay. * * *

*   Copyright © 1994. Reprinted with permission.

[4]   Treas. Reg. § 1.482-1(a)(1).

[5]   Your Host, Inc. v. Commissioner, 58 T.C. 10, 24 (1972), *aff'd*, 489 F.2d 957 (2d Cir. 1973).

In contrast, Congress has not required parents to deal at arm's length with their children for federal gift tax purposes; there is no gift tax equivalent to section 482 giving the Service a roving charter to filter all dealings between parents and children through an arm's length lens.
* * *

In recent years, however, the Service has begun to * * * [apply] the gift tax in a series of intrafamily transactions that historically were not viewed as appropriate subjects to be taxed. The Service succeeded ten years ago in convincing the Supreme Court in *Dickman v. Commissioner*[12] that a parent who makes an interest-free loan to a child makes a taxable gift of the use of property. In affirming the view that "the gift tax was designed to encompass all transfers of property and property rights having significant value," the Court held that "the gift tax should be applied broadly to effectuate the clear intent of Congress." The decision extended beyond foregone interest from the use of money in interest-free loans to the use of money and property in other circumstances. Although the dissent noted that "[t]aken to its logical extreme, this theory would make the loan of a car for a brief period a potentially taxable event," the majority responded by assuming that the Service would not apply the gift tax in such cases.
* * *

* * * [This Article] argues that *Dickman* inexorably leads to taxing various gifts of opportunity from parents to their children under a judicially-created gift tax version of the arm's length standard of section 482. This Article advocates a series of interstitial statutory reforms that incorporate a variety of income tax analogues more appropriate in the gift tax context than the section 482 arm's length standard.

* * *

III. THE GIFT OF SERVICES

The estate depletion rationale for imposition of the gift tax is tested where parents provide gratuitous services for their children. * * *

* * *

* * * [T]he conventional view is that section 2501(a)'s use of the term "property" excludes services from the reach of the gift tax. Although Parent's estate would be depleted by the compensation he would have received had he performed the services for third parties, the exclusion of gratuitous services from the gift tax base is based on the theory that the tax law should not presume that if Parent did not provide the services to his children, he necessarily would have used the time to provide services to third parties for compensation. Instead, Parent may have pursued other leisure activities that would not have bolstered his estate.

IV. THE GIFT OF THE USE OF PROPERTY

The same theory also supports excluding from the gift tax intrafamily transfers of the use of property: the tax law cannot presume that if a parent does not provide the property to her children, she necessarily would have invested the property and thus augmented her estate. This issue was first raised in the context of interest-free loans and then in connection with the use of money or property in other contexts.

* * *

---

[12]   465 U.S. 330 (1984).

B. The Use of Money or Property In Other Circumstances

* * *

One year after *Dickman*, two commentators lamented the "alarmingly broad" potential application of the Court's holding that "the forbearance of a valuable opportunity" constituted a taxable gift. They suggested that *Dickman* could be extended "to a myriad of other situations that on the surface may not appear to be a transfer of the use of property." In particular, they focused on the possibility that the Service could apply *Dickman* to a variety of estate freeze situations. Their warning proved prescient as the Service began using *Dickman* to subject various estate freeze transactions to the gift tax.

* * *

The most far-reaching extension of *Dickman* has occurred in the context of loan guarantees. Nearly twenty years ago, George Cooper reported the "very popular" practice of parents guaranteeing commercial loans to their children, and stated that it was "clear that such a gift of credit is not subject to transfer taxation."[254] In Private Letter Ruling 91-13-009, however, the Service relied on *Dickman* to take a contrary position.

* * *

* * * In any event, * * * the Service recently withdrew the ruling and "express[ed] no opinion at this time" about the gift tax treatment of the loan guarantee.[268] * * *

* * *

The rulings that have cited *Dickman* over the past ten years demonstrate that the Court's reliance on administrative forbearance was misplaced as the Service has subjected a wide variety of "commonplace transactions" involving "traditional family matters" to the gift tax. The cases that have applied *Dickman* have been unable to effectively constrain the Service in light of the *Dickman* Court's expansive theory of gifts of foregone earnings from the use of property. Instead, Congress has had to clarify specific areas but, by leaving *Dickman* unchecked, has left the Service free to impose the gift tax on transfers of the use of money or property in other circumstances.

V. THE GIFT OF OPPORTUNITY

The administrative and judicial developments of the post-*Dickman* decade * * * reveal both the intellectual poverty of the Court's treatment of the forbearance of a valuable opportunity as a taxable gift and the folly in relying on the Service's discretion as the only check on the extension of this theory beyond the interest-free loan context. The result is a judicially crafted gift tax version of the section 482 income tax standard * * * . The Service's embrace of such a judicially created version of the section 482 arm's length standard applicable to dealings between related corporations presents a number of interpretive difficulties.

A. Problems With Dickman's Section 482 Analogy

The developing gift tax judicial arm's length standard is both narrower and broader than its income tax statutory counterpart.

---

[254]   * * * [George Cooper, *A Voluntary Tax? New Perspectives on Sophisticated Estate Tax Avoidance*, 77 COLUM. L. REV. 161, 186 (1977).]

[268]   Priv. Ltr. Rul. 94-09-018 * * * (Dec. 1, 1993). * * *

1. The Narrower Arm's Length Standard

Although section 482 clearly subjects services to the arm's length gauntlet, the role of gratuitous services is more problematic under the gift tax as a result of *Dickman*. The Supreme Court relied on the estate depletion theory to justify the application of the gift tax to foregone interest on the use of money. According to the Court, although parents have no affirmative obligation to invest money and thereby augment their estates, the gift tax is implicated once they transfer the use of the money to their children. * * * This conclusion calls into question the common understanding of the courts, Service, and commentators * * * that the performance of gratuitous services by parents on behalf of their children is not subject to gift tax. This understanding was based on the theory that even though the parents' estates theoretically would be depleted by the compensation they would have received had they performed the services for third parties, the tax law would not presume that parents necessarily would use the time to provide services to third parties if they did not provide the services to their children. * * *

* * *

2. The Broader Arm's Length Standard

The nascent gift tax arm's length standard also is potentially broader than section 482. In *Hospital Corp. v. Commissioner*,[298] the Tax Court held that section 482 was not applicable to transfers of economic opportunities among controlled corporations. * * *

In contrast, several commentators suggest that *Dickman* may empower the Service to impose the gift tax whenever a parent forgoes an opportunity for the benefit of her children. These commentators add a post-*Dickman* spin to George Cooper's pioneering work almost twenty years ago criticizing the erosion of the transfer tax base caused by the failure to tax such transfers of opportunity.[302] * * *

* * *

Transfers of business opportunities pose the most vexing gift tax challenge in light of the myriad ways parents can transfer wealth to their children in this context. * * * In an important set of companion pre-*Dickman* technical advice memoranda[315] largely ignored by commentators, however, the Service subjected a parent's forbearance of business opportunities to the gift tax.

In these rulings, two Brothers each owned 50% of Corporation engaged in the business of manufacturing and selling steel to domestic and export customers. Brothers set up trusts for the benefit of their children. Brothers, as trustees of the trusts, formed domestic international sales corporations ("DISCs") to conduct the export operations formerly conducted by Corporation. In particular, the DISCs purchased manufactured steel from Corporation and from unrelated suppliers with whom Corporation had previously dealt, and then sold the steel to export customers. The DISCs' export sales activities were carried out by Corporation's personnel using Corporation's facilities pursuant to a supply and service agreement with the DISCs. Corporation charged the DISCs for the services performed by its personnel.

In the first ruling, the Service held that neither section 482 nor the assignment of income doctrine applied to reallocate income from the DISCs to Corporation. In the second ruling, however, the Service noted that "[t]he fact that income was allocated and taxed to the DISCs for income tax purposes should not, as the taxpayer suggests, preclude the application of the gift

---

[298]   81 T.C. 520 (1983), *nonacq.*, 1987-2 C.B. 1.

[302]   * * * Cooper, *New Perspectives*, *supra* note [254], at 181-87.

[315]   Tech. Adv. Mem. 81-36-020 * * * (Apr. 29, 1981); Tech. Adv. Mem. 81-36-005 * * * (June 5, 1980).

tax to the transaction." * * * [T]he Service viewed the transactions as gratuitous allocations of income from Corporation to the DISCs. Brothers thus "gratuitously transferred their interests in [Corporation's] export profits to the beneficiaries of the trusts owning [the DISCs]. Each gift occurs upon completion of a sale through [the DISCs]."

These pre-*Dickman* rulings are significant in several respects. The Service accepted the general proposition that a parent's transfer of a business opportunity to her children is not a transfer of property subject to the gift tax. * * * In any event, the scope of the rulings' exemption for transfers of business opportunities is unclear in light of the Service's position that a parent's involvement in the successful utilization of the opportunity would convert the transfer into one of property subject to the gift tax. The post-*Dickman* experience indicates that the Service would aggressively use post-transfer parental involvement to generate the necessary property interest. In addition, the rulings highlight the Service's willingness to apply the gift tax's arm's length standard in a situation where section 482 does not apply, thus telegraphing the broader potential scope of the gift tax analogue.

B. Rethinking the Scope of the Gift Tax

The post-*Dickman* decade demonstrates the desirability of congressional guidance that incorporates income tax analogues more appropriate to the gift tax treatment of foregone opportunities than the section 482 arm's length standard.

* * *

Several commentators have expressed concern over the failure of the transfer tax system to effectively reach transfers of opportunity. Almost twenty years ago, George Cooper criticized the ability of "a parent to devote great effort to locating investment opportunities for his children, to provide the capital to exploit these opportunities, to supply expert personal services which will make the opportunities a success, and to assure that if, after all this, the deal fails, he will pick up the loss—all without any transfer tax liability."[362] * * *

* * *

Congress should reconsider the blanket exemption of services from the gift tax base through the focus on transfers of "property." Although valuation difficulties and concerns about invading a family's privacy certainly caution against widespread application of the gift tax to parental services on behalf of their children, there is room for statutory reform that targets the most abusive situations. For example, it is one thing for a parent to occasionally provide investment advice to her children, but quite another for a mutual fund manager to resign her position to devote her full time energies to managing her children's stock portfolio. In order to properly apply the gift tax to the latter situation but not to the former, *Dickman*'s use of the foregone earnings principle under the estate depletion theory could be limited to situations where parents provide services to their children for which they have received compensation from third parties. * * *

* * *

The income tax provides further useful analogues for considering the gift tax treatment of the use of property. * * * Although section 7872 resolved perhaps the easiest valuation problem through the use of the applicable federal rate in the interest-free loan context, valuation need not be an insurmountable problem in other situations. For example, the rent-free use of the family car or the family vacation home conceivably could be valued on the basis of the

---

[362]   * * * Cooper, *New Perspectives, supra* note [254], at 187.

existing commercial rental market for such property. However, the practical difficulties of such a valuation approach, combined with the resulting intrusion into family life, make such an approach undesirable. Instead, as Congress has done in various income tax areas, the focus could be shifted to the particular use the donee makes of the property after the transfer.

* * * [I]f the children rent out the family car or the family vacation home to third parties * * * this subsequent use of the property could trigger the gift tax on the initial transfer. Although *Dickman* and section 7872 did not tie a parent's gift tax result to her children's actual use of the money lent to them free of interest, the valuation and privacy concerns support a more limited rule for transfers of the use of other types of property.

These valuation and privacy concerns are obviated where, as in the service context, a parent is in the business of renting the property to third parties. In this situation, imposition of the gift tax is justified under the traditional estate depletion theory, because the parent is foregoing rental income by transferring use of the property to her children. Accordingly, the gift tax could be made applicable whenever a parent provides her children with the rent-free use of such property, regardless of the use to which the children put the property.

The search for guidance is more problematic with respect to the appropriate gift tax treatment of transfers of economic opportunities in general. * * * Transfers of capital opportunities apart from interest-free loans would be beyond the statutory scheme outlined above. Transfers of business opportunities * * * also would not be reached by such gift tax reform. If the Service's broad authority under section 482 is inadequate to reallocate transfers of business opportunities among a corporate family, Congress should make clear that *Dickman* does not give the Service the power in the gift tax context to police similar transfers between parents and children.

* * *

NOTE

Harry L. Gutman and Ronald D. Aucutt have engaged in a spirited debate over the appropriate gift tax treatment of transfers of opportunity. Gutman advocates taxing "foregone economic opportunity," although he intends merely to "present the nature of the issue" without resolving the "myriad of technical problems to be worked out in crafting appropriate statutory solutions." Harry L. Gutman, *A Comment on the ABA Tax Section Task Force Report on Transfer Tax Restructuring*, 41 TAX LAW. 653, 671, 673 (1988); Harry L. Gutman, *A Practitioner's Perspective in Perspective: A Reply to Mr. Aucutt*, 42 TAX LAW. 351, 354 (1989). Aucutt faults Gutman for being preoccupied with "the integrity of the impersonal [transfer tax] 'base,' to the neglect of the people from whom the tax is to be collected"; he criticizes the attempt to tax transfers of opportunity as "simply too intrusive into family relationships." Ronald D. Aucutt, *Further Observations on Transfer Tax Restructuring: A Practitioner's Perspective*, 42 TAX LAW. 343, 348-50 (1989).

PART III:

THE GROSS ESTATE

This Part explores the scope of the gross estate and its role in defining the reach of the estate tax. Subpart A introduces the interrelated themes of inclusion, deduction, and valuation in discussing property owned at death (§ 2033), and Subpart B focuses on joint-and-survivor tenancies (§ 2040). Next, Subpart C considers in detail the "string provisions" (§§ 2036-2038) concerning property transferred by the decedent during life with retained interests or powers. Subpart D deals with survivor benefits under annuities and other contractual arrangements (§ 2039), and Subpart E examines the special treatment of life insurance (§ 2042). Finally, Subpart F addresses powers of appointment (§ 2041).

A.   Property Owned At Death

In identifying the scope of a decedent's gross estate, by far the most important inclusionary provision is § 2033, which reaches "all property to the extent of the interest of the decedent therein at the time of his death." This provision coincides roughly with "probate assets" passing by will or intestacy. Indeed, the remaining inclusionary provisions (§§ 2034-2044) serve primarily as backstops to prevent easy estate tax avoidance through the use of will substitutes or lifetime transfers.

Although the scope of § 2033 is generally well settled, the existence of an includible property interest is often complicated by issues of valuation and potential deductibility. In his article on the estate taxation of the "fruits of crime," William J. Turnier explores these issues in the context of stolen property and contraband. Similar themes run through Bruce Wolk's analysis of the tax treatment of transfers between unmarried couples.

William J. Turnier, *The Pink Panther Meets the Grim Reaper: Estate Taxation of the Fruits of Crime*, 72 N.C. L. REV. 163 (1993)*

* * *

Two recent technical advice memoranda have focused attention on the issue of the appropriate estate tax treatment of property that is the fruit of criminal activity. * * *

Both technical advice memoranda address three basic issues: (1) whether property that is the fruit of criminal activity is includible in the·estate; (2) if includible, what value is properly includible; and (3) whether a deduction should be allowed the estate if such property is either recoverable by the true owner or confiscated by the state. * * *

I. THE RECENT DECISIONS

A. TAM 91-52-005: Stolen Property

Technical Advice Memorandum 91-52-005, dealing with the estate tax treatment of stolen property, presents an extremely interesting set of facts involving the theft of the famed Quedlinburg treasures. The deceased, Joseph T. Meador, while serving as a member of the United States military during World War II, successfully stole a number of works of art from the treasury of the Quedlinburg church in the German province of Saxony-Anhalt. He mailed these objects to himself at his home address in Whitewright, Texas * * * . When his activities were discovered, he was court-martialed and discharged from the military.

* * *

At Meador's death in 1980 he, by will, left * * * the remainder of his property to his sister and brother. * * * No estate tax was filed because the estate [inventory] only listed assets worth approximately $105,000 and a life insurance policy worth $15,000. * * * No mention was made of any of the works of art that were apparently still in the possession of Meador's estate. Some property held by the estate was distributed to his heirs in 1981, and the balance was distributed in early 1983. Shortly thereafter, the decedent's brother and sister obtained the services of an appraiser to examine the works of art. * * * Meador's brother and an agent attempted first to sell some of the art objects in the legitimate art market.

During the course of this effort, Meador's brother and sister were informed by individuals whom they contacted that the property in question had been stolen. * * * Meador's siblings next attempted to sell the manuscripts in the illicit art market. The entire Quedlinburg treasure in possession of Meador's heirs was recently estimated to be worth between $50 million and $100 million in the legitimate art market; a single manuscript, a ninth-century illuminated gospel, was worth $9 million in the legitimate art market. Nevertheless, it and several other lesser items would bring only $3 million in the illicit art market.

Acting in part on the basis of information regarding these attempted sales, a free-lance detective traced the transactions down to their origin in Texas. The Quedlinburg church then commenced legal action to retrieve its property. * * * The Quedlinburg church and a German cultural foundation eventually agreed to pay Meador's heirs a "finder's fee" of $2.75 million for the return of the entire Quedlinburg treasure.

* * *

B. TAM 92-07-004: Illegal Drugs

Less than eight weeks after the publication of TAM 91-52-005, the IRS published TAM 92-07-004, in which it dealt with the estate taxation of illegal drugs. The decedent had long been suspected by local and federal law enforcement authorities of engaging in drug smuggling activities. In January 1987, he arranged for two accomplices to meet him on an unused stretch of interstate highway in Florida. He had intended to fly in at night in an airplane full of marijuana, land on the highway, and turn over the drugs to his accomplices. The accomplices were to have arranged emergency landing lights for the decedent's plane; however, a severe storm resulted in their late arrival at the designated spot. The decedent arrived on time, and the incomplete arrangements for lighting resulted in the decedent's fatal plane crash.

When the police arrived at the crash site, they confiscated several bales of marijuana, weighing a total of 662.5 pounds, which had been smuggled into Florida by the decedent. * * *

* * *

II. INCLUDIBILITY

Section 2033 of the Code provides that "[t]he value of the gross estate shall include the value of all property *to the extent of the interest therein of the decedent* at the time of his death." It is well worth noting that the Code does not speak in terms of ownership or other well-established concepts of various property interests. Congress employed rather general language (i.e., "interest") in describing the reach of § 2033. The regulations indicate that mere beneficial, as opposed to legal, ownership of property is sufficient to result in its inclusion under § 2033. * * *

* * *

In determining whether the possessor of such goods has sufficient rights in that property to justify inclusion in the estate, the IRS, in both TAM 91-52-005 and TAM 92-07-004, resorted to the basic rule that the possessor of property, even one who lacks legal title, has valuable economic interests in that property.

* * *

* * * [I]t is apparent that the possessory interest of a thief represents a valuable property interest that should be included in his estate. * * * For example, a thief who holds a $1 million stolen painting has at least the fair market value of the potential enjoyment of the painting for a limited period of time, a benefit that is admittedly far less than the full fair market value of the property itself. The thief also has the potential to realize the property's full fair market value if he is able to transport the property to a jurisdiction with a favorable statute of limitations, or if the true owner merely lacks due diligence. * * * Thus, the critical issue in the case of stolen property should be that of determining the value of the rights held by the possessor, and not the mere verification of the existence of rights in the property that the possessor can pass to his heirs.

* * * [I]t seems safe to conclude that the same basic principles that apply to stolen property in general also apply to contraband, with the result that even its illegal possession should be held to give rise to a valuable property interest taxable under § 2033.

* * *

III. VALUATION

Under § 2031 of the Code, the gross estate of the decedent consists of "the value at the time of his death of all property" includible in his estate. The statute does not indicate how value is to be determined, but the relevant regulations provide that the value of property is its fair market value, defined as "[t]he price at which the property would change hands between a willing buyer and a willing seller, neither being under any compulsion to buy or to sell and both having reasonable knowledge of relevant facts."

* * *

In addressing the valuation issue with respect to the stolen property involved in TAM 91-52-005, the IRS indicated that it is appropriate to value the stolen works of art in both the legitimate and illicit art markets, and that the appropriate value for estate tax purposes is "the highest price that would have been paid at that time whether in the discreet retail market or in the legitimate art market." * * *

* * *

Although the legitimate art market, circa 1990, assigned a value to the Quedlinburg art treasure ranging between $50 million and $100 million, the decedent's siblings * * * ultimately realized only $2.75 million on the entire Quedlinburg treasure. Leaving aside for the time being the issue of changes in the value of the property from the time of the decedent's death in 1980 to 1990, the first issue to resolve is the relevance of the art objects' legitimate market value of between $50 million and $100 million. This value is irrelevant because it (or its comparable 1980 value) represents the "true owner" fair market value, not the thief's possessory interest value that the decedent had and transferred to his heirs. The thief's possessory interest is reflected by the value range of $2.75 to 3 million that the heirs developed in the illicit market and the reward market. As that value is all the decedent's heirs could hope to receive for the art, it represents the value of the interest conveyed by the decedent to his heirs.

In essence, the use of an illicit market value or the reward value for such property provides a workable mechanism for obtaining a value for the limited property interest which the possessor has in the stolen goods. It is comparable to establishing a discounted fair market value for a situation where the possessor holds property under a clouded title.

* * *

Analysis of the valuation issue with respect to contraband is closely related to the valuation analysis of stolen property. * * * In TAM 92-07-004, the IRS concluded that the 662.5 pounds of marijuana held by the drug-smuggling taxpayer at his death should be valued for inclusion in his estate at the "retail street value" of average grade marijuana in the city area near the crash site.

* * *

Under the facts of TAM 92-07-004, however, the use of retail street value is inappropriate, because that is not the market in which a wholesale distributor would sell his drugs. Although the * * * use of retail values is appropriate for household possessions such as a used automobile, which would be purchased at retail value from a vendor of used cars, it is inappropriate where the items or their composition represent goods an individual would not purchase in the retail market. For example, although a decedent's personal automobile should be valued at retail, if the decedent were also a wholesaler of used automobiles, those cars should be valued in the market in which they would be sold—the wholesale used car market. * * *

* * *

* * * [A] strong argument can be made that the use of "retail street value" is inappropriate for valuing a bulk supply of 662.5 pounds of baled marijuana in the hands of a smuggler. At retail these goods are not sold in bales, but in small packets of an ounce or less. Presumably the baled marijuana was to be sold to suppliers who were to sell it to others in the chain of distribution. * * * Since vast mark-ups occur with contraband as it makes its way from smuggler to eventual retail customers, use of retail street value results in a vast overstatement of the fair market value of these assets in a decedent's estate.

* * *

* * * One possible explanation for the IRS's approach to the issue is its desire to force estates like that involved to disclose fully the nature of the decedent's activities—as a smuggler at wholesale—to avoid retail valuation. This disclosure might result in the forfeiture of all of the decedent's other property holdings under state and federal forfeiture laws. Laudable as such a goal may be, it does not justify inappropriate valuation methods. * * *

* * *

IV. DEDUCTIBILITY AFTER RETURN OR FORFEITURE

Both TAM 91-52-005 and TAM 92-07-004 deal with the issue of whether a deduction should be allowed under either § 2053 or § 2054 when an estate that includes the fruits of crime returns such property to its rightful owner, or surrenders it to authorities who seize it acting pursuant to forfeiture legislation. * * * [I]n TAM 91-52-005 the IRS ruled that because, under Texas law, claims could no longer be filed against the decedent's estate, no deduction could be allowed under § 2053 when the stolen property was returned to the "true owner." In TAM 92-07-004, the IRS disallowed a deduction under either § 2053 or § 2054 on the basis that allowing a deduction for the loss of confiscated marijuana would undermine national public policy against trafficking in controlled substances. * * *

* * *

One of the real difficulties with the public policy doctrine is determining the precise extent of its application. For example, should the doctrine be applied in the case of all forfeitures (e.g., those resulting from illegal gambling, racketeering, moonshining, and dealing in narcotics) or just those involving trafficking in controlled substances? Similarly, does it undermine national policy against theft and dealing in stolen property to allow a deduction to holders of stolen property who are compelled to return the property to its rightful owner?

* * * The lack of clearly articulated standards as to what types of illegal activities are worthy of the added sanction of deduction disallowance results in arbitrary judicial outcomes. * * *

The arbitrary imposition of the public policy disallowance doctrine is compounded by the fact that, once imposed, the impact of the sanction largely depends on a variety of other factors, such as the tax bracket of the taxpayer and the availability of other deductions. For example, take the hypothetical case of an estate that holds $300,000 of legally derived assets and $200,000 of illegal drugs which were seized by the government at the decedent's death. Since this is a non-taxable estate, application of the public policy doctrine to disallow a deduction for the seized assets would result in no added sanction. If, however, the estate, in addition to the $300,000 of legally derived assets, held $1,200,000 of seized drugs, payment of the resulting net $363,000 in estate tax due would totally bankrupt the estate.

Nonetheless, despite any such concerns with arbitrariness, * * * [t]he judiciary * * * can at least be expected to use the public policy doctrine to deny deductions in all cases involving drug trafficking.

* * *

Section 2053(a)(3) of the Code provides that "the value of the taxable estate shall be determined by deducting from the value of the gross estate such amounts . . . for claims against the estate . . . as are allowable by the laws of the jurisdiction . . . under which the estate is being administered." * * *

One major unresolved issue under § 2053(a)(3) is whether the use of the word "allowable," as contrasted with "allowed," indicates that actual payment of the claim is not essential for deduction of a claim under § 2053(a)(3). * * *

* * *

* * * [I]f one is dealing with a return or forfeiture of property where there will be no disallowance based on public policy considerations, a deduction should be allowed if the return or forfeiture was required by local law and was actually accomplished during administration of the estate. For example, a deduction should be allowed for the timely return of stolen property to the "true owner" during administration of the estate. The same result should follow if, for example, the decedent died possessing goods that were subject to claims by customs authorities who, at the decedent's death, were seeking to have the property destroyed for violation of customs rules involving criminal sanctions. If property is confiscated and destroyed during the administration of the estate, a deduction should be allowed under § 2053(a)(3).

Substantial variations in results could occur, however, where claims that do not fall under the public policy disallowance doctrine go unpaid by the estate, or are settled for less than their full value. The IRS * * * would then limit deduction to the amount the estate paid on the claim. The result in TAM 91-52-005 is consistent with this position, since the Meador estate never returned the stolen art works to their rightful owner during the administration of the estate under Texas law. * * * [H]owever, it might be possible to assert that at the decedent's death he held the stolen property that was subject to an "allowable," but not "allowed," claim for its return by the true owner, and hence a deduction should be permitted.

There are several criticisms one could make of this suggestion. First, since knowledge of the stolen property's location by the "true owner" is a prerequisite to his or her attempting by law to recover it, an essential fact necessary for the very existence of the claim as an allowable claim under state law arguably would not be present. Allowance of a deduction in such circumstances would be akin to the estate of a surgeon claiming a deduction for several botched operations that were undetected by patients. Second, even if one accepts the above line of reasoning, the claim could be valued at its true "snapshot" value in light of the facts existing at the date of death. Doing this, we might value the claim as virtually worthless since the "true owner's" ignorance and the heirs' and executor's seeming determination to maintain that condition results in the "allowable" claim having a negligible value. When this negligible value is subtracted from the value of the possessory interest in the stolen property held by the estate, a substantial positive net value will remain. Given heirs or an executor of an honest disposition, a dramatically larger value would be assigned to any such claim. Where the public policy doctrine is not invoked to disallow a claimed deduction, a similar valuation-centric analysis could be made in the case of forfeitable fruits of other illegal activities.

* * *

NOTE

Note the importance of state law in determining the nature and extent of the decedent's "interest" in property. A person in possession of stolen property may have enforceable rights against everyone except the "true owner," and in the case of contraband even the "true owner" may have no enforceable right to possess or transfer the property. Furthermore, as Turnier points out, the estate tax consequences of includibility and deductibility are often closely linked with questions of valuation. A defective title or a claim of doubtful validity may be subject to substantial valuation discounts. Do valuation adjustments offer an analytically sound method of measuring the wealth transferred by a decedent? Which particular circumstances should be taken into account in valuing a decedent's interest in property? To what extent should post-death events be taken into account?

For a discussion of employer-provided death benefits under § 2033, see the article by Bruce Wolk excerpted in Subpart D, *infra*.

Bruce Wolk, *Federal Tax Consequences of Wealth Transfers Between Unmarried Cohabitants*, 27 UCLA L. REV. 1240 (1980)*

INTRODUCTION

In recent years the number of couples living together without formal marriage has increased significantly. Aside from those relationships where the parties provide their own personal expenses and share common household expenditures, cohabitation usually produces a transfer of wealth between the partners. The transfers may simply consist of providing support, or they may extend to the assignment of interests in property; they may occur both during cohabitation and after the relationship terminates. Transfers during the relationship, such as income pooling or provisions for support, will likely be consensual * * * . Even upon termination most transfers undoubtedly occur without judicial intervention. The partners may agree upon a property settlement when they separate, or, if death has ended their relationship, the decedent may have provided for the surviving partner by will. If the cohabitants cannot agree on their property rights upon separation, or if the death of a cohabitant leaves the survivor dissatisfied with the decedent's testamentary disposition, one partner may seek judicial enforcement of perceived property rights.

* * *

I. INCOME TAX CONSEQUENCES

* * *

The adoption of a domestic partnership approach to the taxation of cohabitants is justified by the fact that the present approach to the taxation of spouses is itself based on a partnership model, namely, the community property system. That system rests on the premise that marriage is an economic partnership in which two parties contribute their labor, both within and without the household, and become co-owners of the wealth created by such efforts. Where cohabitants have entered into a similar domestic partnership, it seems appropriate to grant them the same tax treatment as a married couple with an indistinguishable economic relationship.

* * *

III. ESTATE TAX CONSEQUENCES

The death of a cohabitant raises significant federal estate tax issues regarding wealth transfers to the surviving cohabitant. The basic problem is to determine the extent to which the property accumulated during the cohabitants' relationship is to be included in the gross estate of the first to die. * * *

The extent to which property will be included in the decedent's gross estate for estate tax purposes depends on the form of ownership chosen by the cohabitants for their property. If the cohabitants held their property as tenants in common or periodically divided their joint income into separately owned shares, the decedent's gross estate would include the value of the property to the extent of his or her interests. Thus, in general, one-half the value of property held as tenants in common would be included.[245]

Special problems arise if the cohabitants have placed their property in joint tenancy with rights of survivorship. Under Internal Revenue Code section 2040, the full value of joint tenancy property will be included in the gross estate of the first to die, except to the extent that the survivor can prove that he or she contributed property or money toward the acquisition of the property. Moreover, to the extent that the consideration furnished by the surviving joint tenant was attributable to a gift from the decedent it is considered to be a contribution by the decedent and not the survivor.

This approach can present difficult tracing problems. For example, suppose the cohabitants place all of their income in a joint bank account from which, over the years, they withdraw funds not only for personal and household expenses, but also to purchase stocks, bonds, and real estate, all held in joint tenancy. One might take the approach that each cohabitant should be credited with a contribution proportional to his or her share of the deposits to the account. Such an approach, however, fails to take account of withdrawals which may have benefited the survivor and therefore in effect reduced the survivor's contribution. An exact reconstruction of the source of deposits and the use of withdrawn funds over a period of years will generally be impossible. * * *

In an effort to deal with these complex tracing problems, the Tax Reform Act of 1976 created a special rule for certain qualified joint interests between spouses. Under * * * section 2040(b), one-half of the value of a joint tenancy between spouses will be included in the gross estate of the first to die * * * .

Since section 2040(b) is not applicable to joint interests between cohabitants, it represents [an] example of the tax law's use of marital status as a factor in the determination of tax liability. It is unclear why Congress singled out married couples for special treatment, although the legislative history indicates that Congress believed it was "often difficult, as between spouses, to determine the degree to which each spouse is responsible for the acquisition and improvement of their jointly owned property." The staff of the Joint Committee on Taxation also suggested that section 2040(b) will "implicitly recognize the services furnished by a spouse toward the accumulation of the jointly owned property even though a monetary value of the services cannot be accurately determined." Both of these asserted justifications would seem to apply with equal force to cohabitants.

* * * [N]ow that the gift and estate taxes are unified there seems to be little policy justification for retaining the consideration-furnished test of section 2040(a) for any joint tenancy, where the creation of the tenancy constituted a gift. Thus, the special treatment of married couples under section 2040(b) would be best cured by an extension of section 2040(b) to all joint tenancies without regard to the relationship of the joint tenants.

A further problem with respect to joint tenancy property acquired by cohabitants is the question of whether domestic services can constitute consideration furnished for purposes of section 2040(a). Where an income earning cohabitant purchases joint tenancy property with his

---

[245]   If the decedent had title to the property, but the cohabitants' agreement gave each cohabitant present vested rights to one-half of such property, presumably only one-half of the value would be included in the decedent's gross estate. Such property could be analogized to community property. * * *

or her income alone, section 2040(a) treats the income earner as furnishing all of the consideration for the purchase, unless the creation of the tenancy is supported by consideration in money or money's worth furnished by the other cohabitant. If the other cohabitant is not earning income but instead is a homemaker, can it nevertheless be argued that the services rendered constitute adequate consideration? No cases could be found involving cohabitants, but the courts have uniformly held that domestic services performed by a spouse do not constitute consideration in money or money's worth for purposes of section 2040(a).

* * *

* * * Even * * * if there were no legal duty to perform domestic services, allowing such services to constitute adequate consideration might lead to serious erosion of the limitations on the gift and estate tax marital deductions. The relationship of husband and wife is simply not an arm's-length employer-employee relationship. It would be all too easy to characterize payments motivated by love and affection and a natural desire to share as payments for services rendered and thereby reduce estate and gift taxes, despite the fact that the services might well have been rendered out of like impulses without regard to such payments.

The same problem of distinguishing between bargained-for transfers and donative transfers arises with respect to cohabitants. An arm's-length exchange of domestic services by cohabitant A in return for a joint tenancy in the earnings of cohabitant B would presumably constitute adequate consideration furnished by A for gift tax and section 2040(a) purposes. * * *

The problem of adequate consideration is not limited to joint tenancy property. The cohabitants might have agreed that property accumulated during their relationship would be divided at death, whether or not it was jointly held. Following the death of a cohabitant the survivor may therefore have an enforceable claim to property of the decedent. The decedent's estate would want to be able to deduct the claim from the decedent's gross estate for federal estate tax purposes. Section 2053 allows a deduction for "claims against the estate," but in the case of a claim "founded on a promise or agreement" the deduction is allowable only to the extent that it was "contracted bona fide and for an adequate and full consideration in money or money's worth."

Thus, a transfer which during life would be subject to gift taxation does not escape transfer taxation when made at death. * * * Presumably a bona fide arm's-length agreement to perform domestic services in return for a transfer of property at death would give rise to a deductible claim supported by adequate and full consideration in money or money's worth. As in the case of lifetime transfers, however, such agreements between cohabitants may not result from a true arm's-length bargain. Thus it would be necessary to determine what part of the transfer represented compensation and what part represented a bequest, taxing the bequest accordingly. * * *

There is, of course, an analogy between the contractual rights of the surviving cohabitant and certain state-created rights of surviving spouses in common law property jurisdictions. In most such jurisdictions surviving spouses have a right to some fraction of the deceased spouse's property by virtue of their spousal status, even if the will is contrary. This fractional interest, however, is clearly includible in the decedent's gross estate and subject to estate taxation. Ignoring for the moment the effect of the estate tax marital deduction, this type of status-forced sharing at death therefore has the same unfavorable estate tax consequences as contractual sharing between cohabitants in cases where there is inadequate consideration. If the surviving cohabitant's domestic services are held to provide adequate consideration, the cohabitants would actually receive more favorable estate tax treatment than spouses in common law property jurisdictions, at least before the marital deduction is taken into account. Yet, if the surviving spouse had also performed domestic services, there seems to be little reason to distinguish between the two survivors.

In addition to providing a means of eliminating the distinction between married and unmarried couples, the domestic partnership approach would place the transfer taxation of both on a more realistic footing. It would treat the wealth accumulated by married couples and domestic partners as the fruit of an economic partnership that is generated by both partners. This is, of course, the same approach taken by the community property model, which incorporates such partnership notions into state property law itself. Thus the difficult question of "consideration" would disappear, whether wealth transfers occur pursuant to express or implied agreements or by reason of status, because the existence of the economic partnership would justify what amounts to an irrebuttable presumption of consideration.

Congress has in fact adopted the partnership approach, at least in part, by creating the estate tax marital deduction * * * .

The unavailability of the estate tax marital deduction to cohabitants can result in rather large differences in estate tax liability between estates of cohabitants and estates of spouses. * * *

The extension of the estate tax marital deduction to cohabitants would not result in a complete implementation of the domestic partnership approach. * * * However, such an extension would eliminate the gross disparities in tax treatment between domestic partners and married couples * * * . On equitable grounds it is difficult to see why the marital deduction should not be extended to cohabitants, at least where their relationship approaches that of marriage. Although there would be an increased administrative burden resulting from this extension, this burden would be limited in scope since it would involve only a one-time appraisal of the facts of a cohabitation relationship rather than a series of appraisals over time.

* * *

CONCLUSION

* * *

Exactly how to define a domestic partnership is of course a difficult issue, perhaps subject more to political judgment than to logic. Certainly those economic and familial characteristics normally associated with marital relationships should be present for a cohabitation relationship to be considered a domestic partnership. In addition, some minimum period of cohabitation, such as three years, should probably be required in order to reduce the administrative burden of dealing with large numbers of transitory relationships and to discourage the use of the domestic partnership as a tax avoidance device. Finally, same-sex couples meeting these requirements should probably be recognized as domestic partnerships, since the underlying partnership theory is economic and social rather than sexual or procreative.

The extent of the recognition of domestic partnerships for tax purposes also involves difficult policy choices. Ideally, there should be no distinction at all between married couples and domestic partners since the tax policies supporting special treatment for the former apply as well to the latter. However, because marriage can affect tax liability in so many different ways, unfavorably as well as favorably, full recognition of domestic partnerships may create serious auditing problems for the Internal Revenue Service. Therefore it would probably be best to recognize domestic partnerships only for the limited purpose of determining the tax consequences of wealth transfers between cohabitants upon the termination of their cohabitation. The most serious inequities are likely to occur upon termination, since wealth transfers made at that time are likely to be more substantial than earlier transfers. Thus the inter vivos dissolution of a domestic partnership would be treated for tax purposes in the same manner as a divorce, and the death of a domestic partner would be treated in the same manner as the death of a spouse. * * * For transfer tax purposes, transfers upon separation would not result in taxable gifts and transfers at death would qualify for the estate tax marital deduction.

* * *

NOTE

Marriage automatically gives rise to property and support rights and obligations under state law. Can unmarried cohabitants create similar rights and obligations by private contractual arrangement? Which "economic and familial characteristics" normally associated with marriage would prove useful in defining a domestic partnership for federal tax purposes?

Under existing law, interspousal transfers on death or divorce are generally shielded from estate and gift taxes; Wolk recommends that similar transfers between unmarried cohabitants should also be tax-free. Why is the concept of money's worth consideration inadequate to achieve the same result?

B.   Joint-and-Survivor Tenancies

Joint ownership with right of survivorship is widely used as a substitute for a will, especially among married couples. In the case of property held by a decedent and a surviving spouse as joint tenants (or tenants by the entirety), half the value of the property is included in the decedent's gross estate; the same amount is automatically eliminated from the taxable estate by the unlimited marital deduction. (The practical significance of the 50 percent inclusionary rule is thus limited to its impact on the surviving spouse's income tax basis.) By contrast, in the case of a nonspousal joint tenancy, the decedent's gross estate generally includes the full value of the underlying property, except to the extent the property was acquired with consideration furnished by the surviving co-owner.

In the following excerpt, Guy B. Maxfield explores several problems arising under the proportional exclusion rule of § 2040(a). These problems remain largely unresolved for nonspousal joint tenancies, notwithstanding the simplified treatment of spousal joint tenancies under § 2040(b).

Guy B. Maxfield, *Some Reflections on the Taxation of Jointly Held Property*, 35 REC. ASS'N B. CITY N.Y. 156 (1980)*

INTRODUCTION

Beginning with the initial enactment of a Federal estate tax on the value of property transferred at death, Congress chose to single out for specialized treatment property owned jointly with survivorship rights which now appears in Section 2040. This section defines the method for determining the amount of the decedent's interest in such co-owned property which is includible in the decedent's gross estate.

Prior to the enactment of the Tax Reform Act of 1976, the amount includible under Section 2040 depended upon whether the co-owners acquired property (i) by purchase or (ii) by gift, bequest, devise, or inheritance. In the [latter case] an amount equal to the fair market value of the property times the decedent's fractional interest in such property was to be included in the gross estate * * * . In the case of property purchased by the co-owners, however, the value of the decedent's interest in such property was determined by the ratio of the consideration furnished by the decedent for the purchase of the property to the total purchase price of such property * * * . This shift from an inclusion method based on the decedent's interest in property as defined by local law * * * to an inclusion method based upon the decedent's contribution toward jointly owned property acquired by purchase was believed necessary by Congress to prevent the avoidance of the estate tax through inter vivos transfers which were initially not subject to a gift tax and did not divest the decedent of enough control over the property which, from a policy standpoint, would be sufficient to prevent taxation at death. * * *

To implement this decision with respect to jointly owned property acquired by purchase, the statute created a rebuttable presumption that one hundred percent of the consideration for the purchase of the jointly owned property was contributed by the first co-owner to die unless the executor of the deceased co-owner could establish not only the amount of the surviving co-owner's contribution toward the purchase price, but also that such contribution had not been acquired from the decedent by the surviving co-owner for less than adequate and full consideration in money or money's worth. * * *

With the enactment in 1932 of a Federal gift tax on inter vivos transmissions of wealth, the tax law was further complicated with respect to jointly owned property. A transfer of property for less than adequate and full consideration by creation of a joint tenancy with survivorship rights caused the imposition of a gift tax. * * * Although subject to gift tax, such property is also includible in the gross estate of the donor co-owner. Thus, Congress made two critical, but independent tax policy decisions—one for the gift tax and a second, separate decision for the estate tax * * * .

* * * [Section] 2040(b) * * * change[s] the conceptual basis of estate taxation of jointly owned property from a contribution concept to an ownership concept for certain joint interests of spouses * * * .

* * *

AMOUNT INCLUDED UNDER SECTION 2040(a)

As previously stated, Section 2040(a) establishes a presumption that the decedent furnished all of the consideration for the purchase of jointly owned property, thus causing an amount equal to the fair market value of the entire property on the decedent's date of death to be included in the decedent's gross estate. This is so unless the decedent's executor can prove that the surviving co-owner furnished all or a part of the consideration for the purchase of such property. To the extent that the executor is successful in meeting this burden of proof, the value of the jointly owned property to be excluded from the decedent's gross estate depends upon the ratio of the consideration furnished by the surviving co-owner to the total consideration for the purchase of the property as follows:

$$\frac{\text{Surviving Co-owner's Consideration}}{\text{Total Consideration}} \times \frac{\text{Fair Market Value on}}{\text{Decedent's Date of Death}} = \frac{\text{Amount}}{\text{Excluded}}$$

Of course, in those cases where the executor proves that the surviving co-owner furnished all of the consideration toward the purchase of the jointly owned property the value of such property to be included in the decedent's gross estate would be zero.

* * *

A. Property Purchased With Some Debt Financing

The problem with respect to a determination of the respective amounts of consideration furnished where the co-owners finance a part or all of the purchase price is whether the debt should be included as a part of such consideration and, if so, how much should be attributable to each co-owner? For example, assume that husband and wife purchased a residence for $100,000 taking title as joint tenants with a right of survivorship. Each spouse contributed $10,000 in cash as a down payment and the balance of the purchase price was financed with a mortgage for $80,000. If the husband made all of the mortgage payments reducing the principal balance by $20,000 and the property had a fair market value at the husband's death of $100,000, what amount should be includible in the husband's gross estate? If the outstanding mortgage balance of $60,000 at the date of the husband's death is not taken into account, then the wife will be considered to have contributed one-fourth of the total consideration toward the purchase of the property ($10,000 out of $40,000) and $75,000 would be included in the husband's gross estate. On the other hand, if the spouses are considered to have each contributed one-half of the outstanding mortgage then the wife's contribution toward the purchase price would be $40,000 out of a total of $100,000 ($10,000 cash upon purchase and $30,000 of the remaining mortgage balance of $60,000 at death) and the amount includible in the husband's gross estate would be $60,000. The Service has ruled that the [latter] method is the correct approach in those cases where both spouses are jointly and severally liable on the mortgage and, under state law, if either co-owner is required to satisfy the mortgage to an extent greater than one-half, such co-owner is entitled to a contribution from the other co-owner.

* * *

B. Capital Improvements

With respect to expenditures made by the surviving co-owner for capital improvements to jointly owned property, there is no doubt that an amount should be included as a part of the consideration furnished by such surviving co-owner. The question is whether such expended amounts should attract a pro-rata share of the appreciation or depreciation in the value of the jointly owned property from the date of its purchase?[44]

There are at least three possible ways in which the value of the capital improvement could be included as a part of the consideration furnished. The first approach, and the one suggested by the regulations, would be to aggregate the total consideration furnished by the surviving co-owner with respect to the purchase of the property, including that attributable to capital additions, and multiply the ratio of the resulting amount to the total consideration furnished by each co-owner by the fair market value on the decedent's date of death. For example, if each spouse contributed $5,000 toward the purchase of jointly owned property and the husband subsequently made a $10,000 addition to the property when such property was worth $50,000 and on the date of death the property was worth $100,000, the amount includible in the husband's gross estate would be $75,000, i.e., [$100,000 − ($5,000/$20,000 × $100,000)]. This would appear

---

[44]   Perhaps a second question is whether the measure of the consideration furnished, in the form of an addition to jointly owned property, is its cost or the increase in the value of the jointly owned property resulting from such addition. * * *

to increase inequitably the husband's gross estate by inclusion of an amount of appreciation in the value of the property which is in reality attributable to the wife's original contribution to the purchase of the property, and not to the amount expended for the capital improvement. * * * [T]his method may also work to the advantage of the taxpayer depending upon the facts. If, in the above example, the capital improvements had been made by the surviving spouse immediately prior to the decedent's death, $25,000 would have been included in the decedent's gross estate resulting in an inequitable amount of appreciation being excluded.

A second approach would be to exclude from the fair market value of the jointly owned property at the decedent's date of death an amount equal to the amount expended for the capital improvement. This approach, however, ignores any appreciation or depreciation attributable to such capital improvement and seems clearly to be contrary to the intent of the statute.

The final method would be to treat the original property and the capital improvement as "separate jointly owned" property. In applying this method to the above example, the addition of the capital improvement of $10,000 would be equal to one-sixth of the total value of the property after such improvement ($50,000 fair market value plus $10,000 improvement). Assuming that the same ratio in value will continue until the date of the decedent's death, one-sixth of the fair market value of the entire jointly owned property ($\frac{1}{6}$ × $100,000 = $16,666) would be attributable to the capital improvement and included in the husband's gross estate because he furnished all of the consideration for its purchase. That amount of the remainder of the value of the property ($83,334) includible in the husband's gross estate would be determined on the basis of the original contributions of $5,000 each. The decedent would, therefore, include $41,667 attributable to that portion of the property for a total inclusion of $58,333.

Although this method appears to be preferable to the first two methods as it seems more closely to reflect the intent of the statute and is not suscept[i]ble to abuse, it creates several practical problems. * * *

* * *

C. Earnings From Property Attributable to the Decedent

Amounts contributed by a surviving co-owner toward the purchase of jointly owned property will be counted as a part of such co-owner's contribution only to the extent such amounts are not traceable to property acquired from the deceased co-owner for less than an adequate and full consideration in money or money's worth. Thus, if a parent makes a gift to his child of property and thereafter the child creates a joint tenancy with a right of survivorship with the donor-parent in such property or uses such property as his contribution toward the purchase of property the title to which is held jointly with the donor-parent, such property would not be counted as consideration furnished by the child. On the other hand, if the donee-child uses income from property which property was received as a gift to purchase jointly owned property with the donor-parent of the income producing property, such income is not deemed to be property traceable to the donor-parent and is counted as a part of the donee-child's contribution. * * *

A question arises, however, as to whether appreciation in the value of property acquired for less than adequate and full consideration, while held individually by the surviving co-owner, or appreciation in the value of jointly owned property where the surviving co-owner furnished none of the consideration should be considered as a part of such co-owner's contribution toward the purchase of other jointly owned property. * * * For example, assume that a parent gives property with a basis of $15,000 and a fair market value of $25,000 to his child and the property appreciates to $32,500 at which time the child sells the property and purchases other property for $32,500 taking title jointly with a right of survivorship with his parent. The child will be considered to have contributed $7,500 ($32,500 value of single name property less $25,000 value on date of gift) toward the purchase of such property. If, on the parent's date of death, the property has a fair market value of $160,000, the child's contribution would reduce the amount included in the parent's gross estate from $160,000 to $123,077, i.e., [$160,000 − ($7,500/$32,500 × $160,000)].

* * *

D. Consideration in Money or Money's Worth

The regulations under Section 2040(a) state that the contribution to be taken into account is consideration furnished in money or money's worth. * * *

* * *

Money's worth would seem to include the value of property or services as furnished by a co-owner and that is indeed the case. A problem occurs, however, with respect to services furnished by a surviving co-owner in the jointly owned family farm or business. Were these services gratuitously furnished or was there an agreement that the spouse work in the business and receive a share of the profits or compensation which was to be applied against the price of the jointly owned property? * * *

* * * Where the spouses deposited their earnings in a jointly held bank account, the executor must not only establish the amount of deposits by each party into the account but also the amount of withdrawals in an effort to substantiate that the surviving co-owner's earnings were actually applied toward the purchase of the jointly owned property. This presents an almost insurmountable burden of proof, especially where contributions toward the purchase of jointly owned property have occurred over a long period of time; and, as is typically the case, the records which could establish the amount of each co-owner's contributions have been destroyed.

* * *

NOTE

Maxfield observes that, prior to the enactment of § 2040(b), tax advisors generally considered joint-and-survivor tenancies an "undesirable form of ownership, except with respect perhaps to the family residence, household checking account and real property located outside the state of domicile." Why? Do these objections still have force under current law?

Other commentators view the problem of inclusion under § 2040(a) as involving "an identification of what the decedent transferred." *See* Charles L.B. Lowndes & Richard B. Stephens, *Identification of Property Subject to the Federal Estate Tax*, 65 MICH. L. REV. 105, 132 (1966). Does the statute implicitly define the amount includible in the decedent's gross estate by reference to a specific transfer of property? To the extent that the creation of the joint tenancy was treated as a taxable gift, should a corresponding portion of the property be excluded from the gross estate? Compare the proportional exclusion rule of § 2040(a) with the consideration offset rule of § 2043(a).

Recall Bruce Wolk's recommendation, in his article on transfers between unmarried cohabitants, that the 50 percent inclusionary rule of § 2040(b) be extended to all joint tenancies. Is this a good idea?

C.   Lifetime Transfers with Retained Interests or Powers

1. Retained Interests or Powers

From its inception, the estate tax has contained provisions designed to prevent depletion of the gross estate through gratuitous lifetime transfers. The original statute provided for inclusion in the gross estate of transfers made by the decedent "in contemplation of death" or "intended to take effect in possession or enjoyment at or after death." These provisions ultimately evolved into §§ 2035-2038, which generally apply where the decedent transferred property during life (for less than full money's-worth consideration) subject to any of several enumerated interests or powers, i.e., a life income interest (§ 2036(a)(1)), a reversionary interest (§ 2037), or a power to designate beneficiaries or revoke or amend (§§ 2038, 2036(a)(2)); the modern counterpart of the contemplation-of-death provision applies where one of the foregoing "taxable strings" was severed within three years of death (§ 2035).

Charles L.B. Lowndes and Richard B. Stephens provide an overview of §§ 2036-2038, analyzing the scope and operation of each provision. In a separate article, Lowndes explores the tax consequences of various limitations on the exercise of retained powers, and points out several ambiguities and inconsistencies in the treatment of joint powers and contingent powers.

In his article on retained powers, Willard H. Pedrick focuses on the impact of standards and contingencies under §§ 2036 and 2038, and questions the soundness of the judicially-developed "ascertainable standard" doctrine. In a subsequent article, Pedrick calls for a reassessment of the conventional view that a settlor's retained control over trust administration does not amount to "possession or enjoyment" of the underlying trust property.

John L. Peschel addresses a range of problems involving interests or powers retained by a trust settlor. He presents two alternative reform packages—one "tougher," the other "more relaxed"—to highlight the difficulty of accommodating relevant considerations of public policy in identifying the appropriate direction for reform in this area.

Charles L.B. Lowndes & Richard B. Stephens, *Identification of Property Subject to the Federal Estate Tax*, 65 MICH. L. REV. 105 (1966)*

⁂

II. WHAT DID THE DECEDENT TRANSFER?

* * *

B. Transfer with Retained Life Interest

Apparently section 2036 does not impose a tax upon a transfer in which a life estate is retained unless the transferor's life interest persists until his death. However, the amount included in the gross estate under section 2036 is not limited to the value of the decedent's retained interest, but rather extends to the entire interest he transferred during his life in connection with which he retained the life interest. For example, if *A* transfers Blackacre to *B* but retains a life estate, at *A*'s death the full value of Blackacre, as distinguished from the value of his retained estate, will be included in *A*'s gross estate.

An exception is made to the rule that the full value of the property transferred by the decedent during his life is included in his gross estate pursuant to section 2036 if the decedent retained only a contingent life estate after granting to another a life estate which is still outstanding at the decedent's death. In such a case the value of the life estate anterior to the decedent's is excluded from the decedent's gross estate on the theory that this interest in the property was not subject to the decedent's retained interest. Thus, for example, if *A* granted Blackacre to *B* for life, then to *A* for life, then to *D* in fee, and if *A* predeceased *B*, the value of Blackacre less the value at *A*'s death of *B*'s outstanding life estate would be included in *A*'s gross estate. * * *

Section 2036(a)(2) provides for the imposition of a tax where a decedent transferred property and, instead of reserving the possession or enjoyment of the property directly, retained a power (either alone or in conjunction with any person) to designate the possession or enjoyment of the property. For the purpose of determining the amount includible in the gross estate under section 2036(a)(2), the power to designate possession or enjoyment of the transferred property is equated to the direct reservation of possession or enjoyment of the property. That is, section 2036(a)(2) is interpreted as requiring the inclusion in the decedent's estate of the full value of the property to which that power attaches rather than merely the value of the power retained by the decedent. Thus, for example, if *A* transferred property to *T* in trust for *C* for life, remainder to *D* in fee, and if *A* retained power to direct the trustee to accumulate the income from the trust property, the full value of the trust property, not merely the value of the income subject to *A*'s retained power, will be included in *A*'s gross estate.

C. Revocable Transfers

Section 2038 taxes a transfer made by a decedent during his lifetime if the enjoyment of the transferred interest is subject to alteration, amendment, revocation or termination at the decedent's death by virtue of a power exercisable by the decedent either alone or in conjunction with any other person. Although most of the transfers which are taxable under section 2038 are also taxable under section 2036(a)(2), the amount against which the tax is levied under section 2038 is limited to the property interest actually subject to the power, unlike the amount

---

*   Originally published in 65 MICH. L. REV. 105 (1966).

included in the decedent's gross estate under section 2036—the value of the property transferred by the decedent in connection with which he reserved the power. For example, suppose that A transferred property to T in trust for C for life, remainder to D, and retained a power to substitute another beneficiary to receive the trust income during C's life. If A dies survived by C, both section 2036 and section 2038 apply to the transfer. Under section 2036(a)(2), since A retained a power to designate the income from the trust for a period which did not in fact end before his death, the full value of the trust property is includible in his gross estate. However, under section 2038 only the value of the interest subject to A's power, that is, the value of C's life estate, would be included in A's gross estate. Since these alternate sections produce such different results it is quite clear which one the government will seek to apply.

Although it seems settled that under section 2038 the interest subject to the power at the decedent's death is the basis upon which the amount includible in his gross estate is determined, it is not always easy to define precisely the scope of that interest. For example, suppose that A transferred property to T in trust, the terms of the trust being to pay C the income from the trust property during C's life and at C's death to pay over the trust property to D and his heirs. Suppose also that A retained a power to terminate the trust at any time during C's life and to direct the trustee to pay over the trust property to C free and clear of the trust. If A predeceases C, what amount should be included in A's gross estate? It is arguable that only the value of D's remainder should be taxed to A's estate, since A could not in any event deprive C of the enjoyment of the property during his life. However, according to the statute a tax is due when the decedent possessed at his death a power to "change" the "enjoyment" of the transferred property. It would appear that C's enjoyment will be changed if his interest as an income beneficiary is converted into that of an owner in fee simple. Although the point may not have been squarely in issue in *Lober v. United States*,[53] the Supreme Court implied in its decision in that case that the full value of the trust property would be taxed to the decedent's estate in the hypothetical situation.

* * *

D. Transfers Taking Effect at Death

Section 2037 taxes a transfer by a decedent during his lifetime as a transfer taking effect at death if the transferee's possession or enjoyment of the transferred property is dependent upon his surviving the transferor and if the transferor retained a reversionary interest in the property the value of which reversionary interest immediately before the decedent's death exceeded five per cent of the value of the transferred property. Although retention by the decedent of a reversionary interest until his death is a prerequisite for the imposition of a tax under section 2037, the amount included in the decedent's gross estate is not limited to the value of the reversionary interest that lapses at his death, but rather extends to the full value of the property which was transferred by the decedent during his life and which meets the survivorship and reversionary interest requirements. However, only property interests that meet both the survivorship and reversionary interest requirements are included in the decedent's gross estate under section 2037. Thus, if A transferred property to T in trust for C for life, remainder to C's surviving children, with remainder in default of such children to A or A's estate, nothing would be taxed to A's estate under section 2037 as a result of the trust, since the possession or enjoyment of the beneficiaries was not dependent upon their surviving A. C is entitled to enjoy the property as long as he lives, whether or not he survives A. C's children are entitled to possess

---

53   346 U.S. 335 (1953).

the property if they survive *C*, whether or not they survive *A*.[57] Of course, the fact that property is not taxable under section 2037 does not mean that it may not be taxed under some other section of the statute. In the hypothetical case, for example, although nothing will be taxed to *A*'s estate under section 2037, the value of *A*'s reversionary interest in the transferred property will be taxed to his estate under section 2033 as property in which he owned at his death an inheritable interest.

* * *

NOTE

Each of the inclusionary rules discussed by Lowndes and Stephens has its own internal logic; yet, taken together, §§ 2036-2038 present a rather untidy patchwork. A particular power may be subject to overlapping jurisdiction of more than one section; a standard or contingency may have different effects under different sections; and the several sections may produce dramatically different includible amounts. What accounts for these anomalies?

Recall that §§ 2036-2038 evolved from a single statutory provision covering transfers "intended to take effect in possession or enjoyment at or after death." This evolution is chronicled in Louis Eisenstein, *Estate Taxes and the Higher Learning of the Supreme Court*, 3 TAX L. REV. 395 (1948). For a trenchant analysis of the judicial and legislative antecedents of § 2037, see Boris I. Bittker, *The* Church *and* Spiegel *Cases: Section 811(c) Gets a New Lease on Life*, 58 YALE L.J. 825 (1949); Boris I. Bittker, Church *and* Spiegel: *The Legislative Sequel*, 59 YALE L.J. 395 (1950). A detailed examination of §§ 2036 and 2038 appears in Boris I. Bittker, *Transfers Subject to Retained Right to Receive the Income or Designate the Income Beneficiary*, 34 RUTGERS L. REV. 668 (1982).

Charles L.B. Lowndes, *Tax Consequences of Limitations Upon the Exercise of Powers*, 1966 DUKE L.J. 959*

* * *

There are many situations where the existence of a power has important tax consequences under the federal income, estate, and gift taxes. Frequently, existence of a power is the occasion for imposing a tax. Less frequently, it will prevent imposition of a tax. To take a simple situation: Suppose that *A* transfers property to *T* in trust for *C* and reserves power to revoke the trust. Retention of the power to revoke the trust keeps the trust property in *A*'s taxable estate

---

[57]   * * * If only part of the property meets the survivorship and reversionary interest requirements, only that part of the property is includible in the decedent's gross estate. For example, if *H* transferred property to *W* for life, remainder to *H* if he survived *W*, and remainder to *X* if *H* did not survive *W*, and if *H* died survived by *W*, only the value of the transferred property less the value of *W*'s life estate (which is in no way dependent on her surviving *H*) at *H*'s death would be included in *H*'s gross estate. * * *

*   Copyright © 1966. Reprinted with permission.

for purposes of the federal estate tax. It also makes the income from the trust taxable to *A* under the income tax. But it prevents a complete transfer and a taxable gift under the gift tax.

The situations where the existence of a power will attract or repel a tax are fairly well defined. However, the extent to which restrictions upon the exercise of a power will negative the existence of the power for tax purposes is much less certain. For example, in the hypothetical case in the preceding paragraph, suppose that *A*'s power to revoke the trust was conditioned upon his surviving the trustee. Did *A* make a taxable gift when he created the trust? Is the income from the trust taxable to *A* during *T*'s life? If *A* dies survived by *T*, must the trust property be included in his gross estate? The purpose of this article is to explore the tax effects of limitations upon the exercise of powers. * * *

* * *

Impossibility

What little authority there is holds that physical conditions which prevent the exercise of a power do not negative the existence of the power for tax purposes. The leading case is *Commissioner v. Estate of Noel*,[6] where the Supreme Court held that the decedent possessed incidents of ownership in flight insurance on his life which made the insurance taxable to his estate, even though at the time of his death in flight it was physically impossible for him to exercise those incidents. * * *

* * *

Apart from philosophical abstractions, it would appear that the crucial consideration which makes it imperative to treat a power as existing, even though it is physically impossible to exercise the power is the practical consequence of the opposite view. Mr. Justice Black put a judicial finger on the nub of the matter when he said "It would stretch the imagination to think that Congress intended to measure estate tax liability by an individual's fluctuating, day-by-day, hour-by-hour capacity to dispose of property which he owns." Any such rule would not only entail inquiry into the circumstances surrounding the death of each individual decedent; it would tie in tax liability with the adventitious circumstances attending his death, rather than with the extent of his wealth and the property he controlled during his life. A man who is killed in an airplane crash might avoid having his life insurance and revocable trusts taxed to his estate, while another taxpayer expiring more sedately at home in bed would be taxed on these properties.

* * *

Incapacity

* * *

From the viewpoint of sound tax policy, there are, to a greater or lesser degree, the same reasons for holding that legal incapacity does not prevent the existence of a power for tax purposes that there are for arguing that impossibility does not negative the existence of a power. * * * [A] power may be exercised by a guardian, a committee or a court for a person who lacks capacity to exercise the power himself, so it is hard to see any injustice in taxing the power, even though the donee may be personally incapable of exercising it.

* * *

---

6   380 U.S. 678 (1965).

Joint Powers

* * *

* * * The estate tax imposes a tax on powers which were exercisable by the decedent alone, or by the decedent in conjunction with any other person. It does not, however, tax a decedent on property which he has transferred subject to a power to alter or revoke exercisable by one other than the decedent without the decedent's concurrence. * * *

According to the estate tax "any other person" means any other person, including a person possessing a substantial adverse interest in the property subject to a power. Consequently, a trust will be taxable to the grantor's estate if he retained power to alter or revoke the trust, even though the power could be exercised only with the concurrence of a beneficiary of the trust. * * * Ownership of a substantial economic interest in property transferred by a decedent by the person who must concur in the exercise of a power to alter or revoke the transfer, is no real guaranty that the property has passed beyond the transferor's control, where the decedent was free to select the person whose concurrence is necessary to exercise the power. In this connection it is interesting to note that the only part of the estate tax where the fact that a person whose concurrence is required to exercise a power possesses a substantial adverse interest in the property subject to the power assumes any significance is the provision taxing joint powers of appointment. * * * Presumably, the reason why *donated* powers of appointment, which are taxed under section 2041, are treated differently than *reserved* powers taxed under the other provisions of the estate tax, is that the donee of a joint power of appointment does not name the person whose concurrence is required to exercise the power of appointment. Therefore, the fact that the person who must concur in the exercise of the power of appointment has a substantial interest in the property subject to the power which may be prejudiced by the exercise of the power may actually limit the donee's control over the property subject to the power.

* * *

* * * The principal defect in connection with the taxation of powers under the estate tax lies in the failure to tax inter vivos transfers by a decedent where the decedent gave a power to alter or revoke the transfer to someone else. * * * There is no appreciable difference between a transfer in trust which can be revoked by the transferor with the consent of the trustee and a transfer which the trustee can revoke alone. Presumably, the transferor controls his own actions so in both cases the revocation of the transfer depends solely on the will of the trustee. * * *

* * * The estate tax should be amended * * * to impose a tax where power to alter or revoke a transfer is vested in persons other than the transferor. Nor should this tax be limited to situations where the possessor of the power lacks a substantial adverse interest in the transferred property. If this limitation were written into the law, it would be inconsistent with the tax that is imposed where the decedent and a person possessing a substantial adverse interest in transferred property have power to alter or revoke the transfer. Moreover, it is possible for a person to retain control over transferred property even though he gives a person possessing a beneficial interest in the property power to alter or revoke the transfer, if he is careful to give this power to a donee who will comply with his wishes.

* * *

Transfers revocable by the transferor alone or by the transferor in conjunction with a person lacking a substantial adverse interest in the transferred property, are treated as incomplete transfers that are not subject to the gift tax. * * *

* * * According to the Supreme Court's reasoning in *Smith v. Shaughnessy*,[78] however, a transfer is complete for gift tax purposes when the transferred property passes beyond the control of the transferor, regardless of how the transfer is treated under the estate tax. Pursuant to this premise the lower courts have held that a transfer that can be revoked only with the consent of a person possessing a substantial adverse interest in the transferred property is a complete transfer and a taxable gift, regardless of any inconsistency with the estate tax.

Apparently, however, the taxable gift in the case of a transfer that can be altered or revoked only with the consent of an adverse person, is limited to that part of the transferred property whose enjoyment cannot be altered or revoked without the consent of a person having an interest in that portion of the property. * * *

* * *

Contingent Powers

* * *

The exercise of a power may be limited by a contingency which must occur before the power can be exercised. * * *

* * * The regulations * * * provide that a power to alter or revoke the enjoyment of transferred property will not be in existence at the transferor's death and will not be taxed under section 2038, if the exercise of the power is subject to a contingency which has not occurred at the transferor's death. * * *

* * * Although the regulations say that a contingent power is not taxable under section 2038, this concession is qualified by the observation that the power may be taxable under section 2036(a)(2). Inasmuch as most transfers that are taxable under section 2038 are also taxable under section 2036(a)(2), this is an important qualification. For example, suppose that *A* transferred property to *T* in trust to pay the income to *B* for life, remainder to *C* in fee, and provided that if *A* outlived *B*, he should have power to revoke the trust. According to the regulations, if *A* predeceased *B*, the trust property will not be taxed to his estate under section 2038, but it will be taxed under section 2036(a)(2). Furthermore, if immediately before his death *A*'s chance of outliving *B* was better than one in twenty, *C*'s remainder will also be taxable to *A*'s estate under section 2037.

* * *

* * * Although there is not much authority as to the effect of a contingency upon a power to alter or revoke a transfer under the gift tax, it is generally assumed that a contingency limiting the exercise of the power will not prevent a complete transfer and a taxable gift unless the contingency is an event within the transferor's control. * * *

* * *

* * * Some contingencies are obviously within or without the transferor's control, but there is also a gray area where determining whether a contingency is within the transferor's control depends upon how control is defined. * * * Suppose * * * that *A* retains power to revoke the trust if he marries or gets divorced. Is the contingency upon which the exercise of the power hinges an event within or without *A*'s control?

* * * Taxes are imposed upon the existence of a power because of the control which the power gives the owner of the power over the income or property subject to the power. * * * From the viewpoint of the policy underlying the taxation of powers, whether a contingency negatives the existence of a power for tax purposes should depend upon whether the contingency

---

[78]   318 U.S. 176, 181 (1943).

detracts from the control that the owner of the power has over the property subject to the power to an extent that makes it unfair to treat him as owner of the property subject to the power for tax purposes. * * *

* * *

NOTE

Lowndes argues that property transferred subject to a power to alter or revoke should be drawn back into the gross estate, even if the power is held solely by a person other than the decedent. Furthermore, Lowndes sees no reason to carve out an exception for powers held by an "adverse party" or an "independent trustee." Does his argument imply that a third-party power to alter or revoke should prevent a transfer from being complete for gift tax purposes? What would be the likely impact of such a broad inclusionary rule on the drafting of trusts? In discussing contingent powers, Lowndes recognizes the difficulty of determining how far a particular contingency interferes with a power to alter or revoke. What considerations might be relevant in distinguishing "taxable" from "non-taxable" powers?

Willard H. Pedrick, *Grantor Powers and Estate Taxation: The Ties That Bind*, 54 Nw. U. L. Rev. 527 (1959)*

* * *

POWERS OVER CORPUS AND THE ESTATE TAX

By its terms section 2038 returns to the grantor's gross estate all transfers with respect to which he has retained, alone or in conjunction with any other party whether as trustee or otherwise, the power to alter, amend, revoke or terminate. A power in the grantor to revest in himself the beneficial ownership of the transferred property is plainly within the terms of the section. But the language used reaches more than a power to revoke. The language "alter and amend" and the congressional committee explanation thereof indicate that the function of this provision is to reach any power to shift the beneficial interests in the transferred property. Accordingly, it was decided relatively early by the Supreme Court that the grantor need not have a power to retake the property for himself. It is enough if he retains a power to shift the beneficial interests among others. Later decisions made it clear that the power to change beneficiaries could be very circumscribed such as a power to shift the benefits from *A* to *B* and this would still be classed as a taxable power to alter or amend. More recently the Supreme Court in the *Lober* decision[26] has established that not even a change in the identity of the beneficiaries is required—a mere power to withhold or accelerate distribution of corpus is a taxable power to alter or amend if held by the grantor.

* * *

Under the present statute if the grantor can advance corpus to the beneficiary and most certainly if he can choose between beneficiaries for corpus distributions he has retained an estate

---

*   Originally published in 54 Nw. U. L. Rev. 527 (1959).

[26]   Lober v. United States, 346 U.S. 335 (1953). * * *

taxable power. Nor, according to the statute, does it matter that he holds his power as a trustee. Despite the words of the statute, however, there are several lower and intermediate court decisions that in effect immunize certain powers to advance corpus if held by the grantor as trustee. Critical to this judicial exception of certain powers to advance or withhold corpus is the presence of an ascertainable standard. A power in the grantor as trustee to advance corpus "in his discretion" is regarded as governed by no standard and no better it would seem is a power to advance corpus in accordance with the beneficiaries' "best interests." On the other hand a power to advance corpus to meet the beneficiaries' needs, support, maintenance, education, emergencies, to maintain a given standard of living or a fixed income have been classed as powers subject to a fixed standard.

Given a fixed standard such as the use of corpus for support of the trust beneficiary, the doctrine of the cases, expounded by the Second Circuit in *Jennings v. Smith*[34] is that such a canalized power is no power at all because the trustee is a mere ministerial functionary of the equity court. A corollary is that if the contingency under which the power is exercisable has not occurred at the time of the grantor's death, i.e., the beneficiary is not then in want, then the power was not in fact exercisable at the date of the grantor's death and is non-taxable on that ground as well. Despite the considerable number of decisions applying the *Jennings* doctrine to the prejudice of the Treasury in estate tax litigation, however, perhaps it is not as settled as its devotees might hope.

As the case law now stands it is apparently open to a grantor to retain estate tax free a power to advance corpus in his discretion in accordance with an extended list of contingencies: i.e., to maintain a suitable living standard with or without regard to other sources of support, to meet expenses of education, medical care, life insurance protection, emergencies for trust beneficiaries and their families, and perhaps even to equalize wealth as between beneficiaries taking other increments into account. With a little imagination the list can be extended so that in almost every conceivable situation where the grantor would be inclined to advance corpus to a beneficiary or to allocate within a class of beneficiaries he will have discretionary authority under a standard to do so—precisely as if he had retained a power to advance corpus in his discretion. It is difficult to believe that dramatically different estate tax consequences can hang on the formal business of reciting a comprehensive list of contingencies rather than simply entrusting advancements of corpus to the trustee's discretion.

As a practical matter * * * many fiduciary powers subject to a standard do entrust real discretion to the trustee. He is usually more than a mechanical agent. Indeed, it is elementary that the customary powers to invade or to allocate stamp the trust as discretionary in nature. * * *

On the other hand a power in a grantor-trustee to advance corpus to a beneficiary in accordance with the "best interests of the beneficiary" does not cast the trustee adrift on an uncharted sea. Nor for that matter is authority to advance corpus simply in the trustee's discretion an excursion ticket to leave the jurisdiction of the equity court. * * * The matter is simply one of degree but powers to advance corpus on the basis of a continuing judgment by the trustee on the beneficiary's position all fall on the side of discretionary powers under the law of trusts. There may be, depending on the words of the instrument, a greater or lesser ambit of authority but the customary invasion powers for "needs," support and maintenance all involve true powers or discretions vested in the trustee. That is the whole point in the sensible provision of such powers of invasion. * * *

To classify as non-taxable significant powers to alter the beneficial interests in the trust through invasions for support or for the beneficiaries' other general needs on the ground that there are outer limits on the grantor's power of choice and at the same time to hold taxable a

---

[34]   161 F.2d 74 (2d Cir. 1947). * * *

power to invade in accordance with the best interests of the beneficiary or simply in the trustee's discretion is to draw a line not warranted by the provisions of the tax statute or the law of trusts. Section 2038 taxes all power to change beneficial interests—specifically including powers held by the grantor as trustee. This strongly suggests, since all trustee powers are subject to some court supervision, that no importance is to be attached to such control when the grantor holds the power. The relative paucity of trust litigation involving powers of grantor trustees testifies that blood and future expectations for the most part outweigh all the litany of trust doctrine.

* * *

If, as suggested here, neither the law of trusts nor the provisions of section 2038 warrants an exemption from the estate tax of discretionary powers in the grantor to alter beneficial interests what consequences should follow? First, of course, the broad version of *Jennings v. Smith* exempting from estate tax grantor powers to invade in accordance with a standard such as support and maintenance should be abandoned as error. * * *

If the grantor's power to invade is tied to one or two tightly defined contingencies such as a power to use corpus to meet the beneficiary's medical expenses, under the law of trusts he has little or no real discretion and consequently he has no power within the meaning of section 2038. In this narrow application the *Jennings* doctrine is unassailable. Even powers that do involve real discretion such as a power to alter the trust to make provision for any grandchildren born during the grantor's life, though to be classed as a power for estate tax purposes will not generate tax consequences if the contingency has not in fact occurred. * * *

The critical question under section 2038 is whether the grantor did at the time of his death have some power or choice, not necessarily a broad choice, but some discretion to give corpus to this beneficiary or that. If he retains an authority of a continuing nature on contingencies largely to be defined by him to advance corpus in amounts largely to be determined by him then the circumstance that equity might restrain him from wholly unreasonable or irrational acts in the exercise of his authority should not obscure the fact that he has retained a discretionary power exercisable down to the date of his death. A reserved power to advance corpus to meet the beneficiary's needs, or for support or maintenance is treated under the law of trusts as investing a substantial measure of discretion in the holder of the power even though there are standards to govern the exercise of the discretion. Where under the law of trusts such discretion is real and significant, a grantor retaining such discretion should be treated as one who has reserved a power to alter or amend. There would thus be lines to draw but lines more in conformity with the law of trusts and the language of section 2038 taxing all reserved powers including those held in a fiduciary capacity.

* * *

POWERS OVER INCOME AND THE ESTATE TAX

Transfers with a reservation of the income from the property are taxed to the decedent's estate by the terms of section 2036 and since 1931 a right to designate the persons who shall enjoy the income has been equated for estate tax purposes with personal enjoyment of the income by the grantor. It is this section that covers grantor powers to alter beneficial interests in income from transferred property and thus performs with respect to powers over income the function performed by section 2038 with respect to powers to alter and amend. There are similarities in the two sections but differences as well. An obvious difference is the fact that a taxable power of disposition over income under section 2036 renders all corpus producing that income taxable while under section 2038 only the property subject to the power is includible in the gross estate. * * *

There is as well a difference in the form of the language used in the two sections. Section 2036 applies to a right "to designate the persons who shall . . . enjoy . . . the income." It is plain from the structure of the section that the grantor need have no power to take the income for himself and the cases under this section have established, as they have under section 2038, that the ambit of power can be narrow in the extreme and still be a taxable power. Thus discretionary power to shift income from the life tenant to the remainderman or any other power to shift the income from *A* to *B* will be classed as a taxable power to designate who shall enjoy the income. * * *

A power to accelerate a distribution of the corpus of a trust to the beneficiary who would ultimately take in any case may well be a power "to alter or amend" the trust under section 2038 and the Supreme Court in fact so decided in the *Lober* decision. It should not follow, however, that a power to accumulate income for ultimate distribution to the same income beneficiary should be classed as a "right to designate the persons who shall enjoy the income," under section 2036. To "designate the persons" requires a power to choose between different takers. But, it may be said, what of the possibility that the accumulated income might go instead to the estate of the beneficiary, should he predecease the distribution date? * * * The assimilation of an individual with his own estate in other phases of the estate tax, in the marital deduction and with powers of appointment, counsels that accumulations eventually payable to the same person or to his estate might well in all cases be accepted as not amounting to a power to designate the persons to enjoy the income. * * *

One problem that is common to the two sections is the matter of powers related to a standard, such as a power to distribute if needed for support, medical expenses, education and the like. The lower court decisions have treated the problems presented under section 2036 as essentially the same as those arising under section 2038 and have broadly applied the *Jennings* doctrine of the non-taxability to all powers to accumulate or distribute income when governed by a standard. But as seen above in connection with powers over corpus, the *Jennings* doctrine is thought to err in not recognizing that some standard-governed powers in fact lodge a substantial discretion in the holder. If the rejection of the broad *Jennings* doctrine is the sound course, then all retained powers to shift income as between beneficiaries should be estate-taxable where the grantor thereby enjoys a significant continuing authority to decide who is to receive the income, whether he is subject to some broad standard or not. Section 2036 does not by its terms exempt any powers to designate the persons who shall enjoy the income. The only question is what constitutes a right to designate and a practical interpretation is urged. If under the law of trusts the power gives the trustee a significant ambit of authority to decide whether the income shall go to *A* or to *B* the power should be a taxable power when held by the grantor. Thus, a discretionary power in the grantor to accumulate income not expended on support should be viewed as such a power where others will take the accumulated income.

* * *

What the law ought to be in this area apart from the present provisions of section 2036 is another matter. Trusts which authorize the trustee to use income or principal or both for support of the beneficiary are commonly intra-family transfers involving families of substantial means. To use the legal obligation of support as the base on which to rest the taxability of some of these intra-family transfers is quixotic at best. Trusts become taxable or non-taxable largely depending on the competence of the draftsman and his care, or lack of it, in the use of words relating to support. Surely all intra-family transfers, for spouse and minor children, those authorizing support, those authorizing discretionary distributions and those silent on the point, should fare alike. * * *

* * *

* * * [T]he proper issue is not whether there is a standard but whether there is a significant discretion—an actual authority to decide to distribute or to accumulate, to invade corpus or hold it intact, to knowingly shift interests from one beneficiary to another or to decline to do so.

* * *

NOTE

Pedrick criticizes the judicially-developed exemption for retained fiduciary powers that are limited by judicially enforceable external standards. What is the rationale for exempting such powers? If, as Pedrick argues, the line drawn by the courts is "not warranted by the provisions of the tax statute or the law of trusts," what criteria should courts apply? How realistic and reliable is the "law of trusts" in determining whether the decedent retained "real and significant" discretion?

Consider a fiduciary power to make distributions for the "support" of the settlor's dependents. Should the estate tax consequences of such a power depend on whether the decedent or another person is trustee? On whether distributions are to be made from income or corpus? On the terms of applicable state law defining support obligations?

Willard H. Pedrick, *Grantor Powers and the Estate Tax: End of an Era?*, 71 Nw. U. L. Rev. 704 (1977)*

* * *

* * * [T]he Tax Reform Act of 1976 * * * supplies a short and somewhat curious estate tax provision treating the retention of "voting power" over stock as retention of "possession or enjoyment" requiring inclusion in the taxable estate. This new provision should signal the end of the era of permissibility for death tax purposes of nontaxable retention of substantial managerial powers over transferred property.

So sweeping a change in death taxation is not mandated by the literal words of the new provision. The new section, however, should be viewed as requiring reexamination by the Supreme Court of the whole line of cases that have in the past permitted the anomaly of lifetime transfers passing muster for death tax avoidance purposes despite the retention by the transferor of substantial authority over the transferred property. * * *

* * *

A FEW PAGES OF HISTORY

In the modern federal estate tax adopted in 1916, Congress, after arranging for death taxation of such common testamentary substitutes as joint tenancies and life insurance, included in the tax base, as well, lifetime "gifts in contemplation of death" and, in addition, all other "transfers intended to take effect in possession or enjoyment at or after the death of the transferor."

The phrase "transfers intended to take effect in possession or enjoyment at or after the death of the transferor" was inspired * * * . The quality of the inspired tax phrase * * * comes

---

*   Originally published in 54 Nw. U. L. Rev. 704 (1977).

from its very imprecision, its flexibility, its dependence on the interpretative process after the fact to achieve the general objective redefined as time alters the nimble tactics of tax avoidance. Note that the phrase deliberately eschews terms of settled meaning of the law of property such as "interest," "right" or "title" in favor of the broad undefined and nontechnical terms of "possession or enjoyment." Determination of what was a "transfer intended to take effect in possession or enjoyment at or after the death of the transferor" was left to the courts, with all possible flexibility to assure that decedents who had arranged their affairs so as to avoid the appearance of ownership would still pay full tax rates if they had nonetheless postponed till their death full enjoyment or possession of the property by their beneficiaries.

But the Supreme Court proved unequal to the responsibilities placed on it almost from the start. * * * [T]he Court's emasculation of the phrase "transfer intended to take effect in possession or enjoyment at or after death" started very early in the life of the provision * * * .

* * *

The continuing durability of an economically primitive conception of "possession or enjoyment" was demonstrated * * * in the 1972 decision of the Supreme Court in *United States v. Byrum.*[26] In that case, the grantor owned at the outset 71% or more of the stock of three corporations. In 1958, he set up irrevocable trusts for his children or grandchildren, transferring substantial blocks of stock in the three corporations so that he died owning less than 50% of the common stock in two of the corporations and less than 59% in the third. As to each of the trusts, he retained as grantor and not as trustee, power (1) to vote shares of unlisted stock (the stock of his three corporations); (2) to control the investment policy of the trusts (specifically including retention or sale of the three corporations' stock in the trusts); and (3) to remove the trustee and replace it with another corporate trustee. The Commissioner undertook to put the principal of the three trusts into Byrum's taxable estate on the ground that under section 2036 he had retained for his life (1) "the possession or enjoyment of, or the right to the income from, the property transferred," or in the alternative that he had retained (2) "the right, either alone or in conjunction with any person, to designate the persons who shall possess or enjoy the property or the income therefrom."

The "retention of possession or enjoyment" argument was elaborated by the Commissioner in terms of Byrum's power, as the principal stockholder to vote his own stock and that in the trust so as to retain his corporate post as president. But the Commissioner * * * was credited by the Court with conceding that "mere retention of the right to vote shares does not constitute the type of 'enjoyment' in the property itself contemplated by § 2036(a)(1)." So reassured, the Court adhered to the simplistic notion * * * that the type of "enjoyment" covered by the section was "a right to income, use of property itself, or a power of appointment with respect either to income or principal." With this fixation, the Court * * * [concluded] that retention of voting power or other powers of business management was not the retention of "enjoyment" of property. That the grantor Byrum had no reason to be nervous about retaining his post as corporate president was simply classed as a happy and irrelevant accident of fate.

The Government's alternative argument was that grantor Byrum by his reserved voting power had the authority to direct the corporate dividends either to present beneficiaries or withhold them for the remaindermen, and that he therefore had a taxable power to designate the income recipients under section 2036(a)(2). To this, the Court responded that Byrum was not free under the law to do as he chose. In the view of the majority of the Court, a combination of economic forces operating on small businesses and the fiduciary duty owed by a majority shareholder to minority interests meant that Byrum was not in fact or in law free to determine

---

[26]   408 U.S. 125, *reh. denied*, 409 U.S. 898 (1972).

whether the corporate income was or was not to be declared as dividends. A companion proposition that Byrum's power as voter of the corporate stock in election of directors was not the reservation of a "right" under the trust instrument to direct payment of income out of the trust to this or that beneficiary was given some weight. From this complex of reasons, it followed that Byrum had not retained a power to designate the persons to enjoy the income of the trust within the meaning of section 2036(a)(2). A vigorous dissent by Justice White observed that the dividend policy of the three corporations had in fact changed dramatically with the death of the stock voting grantor, Byrum. He argued trenchantly that to permit the Byrum gambit to controlling shareholders of closely held corporations "will open a gaping hole in the estate tax laws."

That *Byrum* did open a considerable breach in the federal estate tax was generally accepted.
* * *

* * *

THE UNSOUNDNESS OF *BYRUM*

But the question persisted whether *Byrum* was an acceptable answer to arrangements to retain the substance of economic control for life and to defer until death passage of economic control of the enterprise to the next generation or its representative.

Byrum in a sense was a two-legged stool—on which a taxpayer necessarily sat with a sense of unease, conscious of a precarious balance. The two legs are the two standards of taxability of section 2036. One, [section] 2036(a)(1), is the "possession or enjoyment of, or the right to the income from, the property." The other, [section] 2036(a)(2), is the "right . . . to designate the persons who shall possess or enjoy the property or the income therefrom."

In a sense, the latter provision, at least in its application to the *Byrum* situation, is relatively straightforward. There could be no doubt that Byrum, by virtue of his retained voting power on the stock in trust together with the stock retained in his own name, did have the naked power to elect directors who would or would not declare corporate dividends in accordance with his wishes. In substance then, he could determine or designate whether the corporate income would go into the trust and then possibly to the current income beneficiaries or to the remaindermen, depending on the corporate trustee's discretion to distribute or accumulate. The arguments of the majority in *Byrum*, that economic constraints and the fiduciary duty of majority shareholders to the minority greatly and really restrict the naked power of the grantor majority shareholder, are simply not very convincing.

On the other hand, the power to designate the persons to receive the income was not reserved to the grantor in the *Byrum* trust, and there was in fact an outside (though replaceable) corporate trustee to decide whether income received by the trust would be paid out or retained. Thus, it is not so clear on the *Byrum* facts that the grantor really did have a right to designate the income recipients. The point that the reservation of power or right did not relate directly to income distribution from the trust thus does have substance.

But perhaps the most troublesome feature of applying the "power to designate" provision to the *Byrum* situation grows out of the fact that a grantor of an irrevocable trust of diversified blue chip securities with no voting control over any of the corporations in which he owns shares would be able to retain complete managerial power over the shares, bonds, real estate and other property in the trust and be unreachable under the language of 2036(a)(2). Such a grantor would have no control over dividend policies through his retained power to vote the stock. The policy concern that owners of closely held corporate stock should not be subject to such invidious discrimination as compared to the owner of a diversified portfolio, is a compelling argument against application of the "power to designate" standard to *Byrum* and similar factual situations.

But that is not the end of the matter. There is the other standard of taxability—the retention of the "possession or enjoyment . . . of the property" under [section] 2036(a)(1). It is true, of course, that * * * *Byrum* relegates this ground of taxability to desuetude.

But surely Congress did intend originally that the "possession or enjoyment" phrase would serve as an independent ground for thwarting tax avoidance transfers where the transferor continues to enjoy the perquisites of ownership. The phrase originally had no limitations other than those to be developed by the interpretative process. It embraced undefined interests, powers and "strings" that might fairly be regarded as amounting to "possession or enjoyment" deserving of taxability to prevent tax avoidance where some of the substance of ownership was retained by the transferor. * * * But the opportunity in 1972 to reconsider the question of the taxability of retained powers of management presented to the Court in *Byrum*'s case was passed by. The Government did not ask the Court to reexamine the question, and the issue simply went by default * * * .

THE TAX REFORM ACT OF 1976—
TAXING RETENTION OF VOTING POWER

In the Tax Reform Act of 1976, however, Congress acted to overrule the decision in *Byrum* because as put by the Report by the House Ways and Means Committee, "[The] Committee believes that the voting rights are so significant with respect to corporate stock that the retention of voting rights by a donor should be treated as the retention of the enjoyment of the stock for estate tax purposes." The House Bill taxed retention of voting rights in the "transferred stock." * * *

To tax only in the case where the transferor retains voting power over transferred corporate stock and to leave untouched a myriad of other techniques by which a transferor can retain managerial power over transferred property would make the tax law quixotic, and grossly discriminatory. What, for example, of the case where the voting power is lodged in preferred stock, limited as to redemption value and income participation and subject in addition to redemption on certain contingencies or after a certain period of time, where the grantor transfers "growth" nonvoting stock with no strings? What of outstanding options to acquire voting stock, which need not be exercised in light of the continuing shadow they cast on management decisions? What of special long term management contracts preserving to the transferor the substance of control without formal power to vote stock? And what of other types of property, unincorporated businesses, partnership interests, real estate and the like?

If a strictly literal interpretation is given to the 1976 addendum to section 2036, nothing more than a technical inconvenience, a limited pothole on the expressway to tax avoidance, results. Congress cannot have intended so ludicrous a result. What Congress did was to add one highly concrete example of retention of managerial power as retention of "possession or enjoyment" in the context of a section that taxes all other modes of retained "possession or enjoyment." Congress surely need not put into the Internal Revenue Code highly individualized descriptions of all the conceivable tax avoidance devices to come from the nimble minds of fertile tax planners. There is too much of that in the Code already. Surely, the Court does not want to drive the Congress in that direction. Now, thanks to the limited response by Congress, the Court has the opportunity to undo at long last the damage it has done to the effectiveness of the phrase "possession or enjoyment" as a tax avoidance provision.

There are at least two approaches that would give the tax avoidance language of "possession or enjoyment" its proper sweep. One interpretation would tax the transferor when authority substantially the equivalent of the kind of power represented by the power to vote stock is retained in whatever form—an application of the "substance" doctrine. The other approach— and that urged here—is that the Court accept the congressional action in the Tax Reform Act of 1976 as persuasive of the need for judicial reconsideration of the *Byrum* doctrine in all its reaches. * * *

* * *

* * * At this stage, the Court should view the 1976 legislation as a legislative plea to reconsider the question of what generally constitutes retention of "possession or enjoyment" so as to achieve an interpretation of the phrase that will harmonize with the specific rule, which was inserted by Congress as an instructive example. Freed of any constraints based on its own prior course of decisions, and reinforced by the clear policy statement from the Congress that retention of managerial power over transferred property can indeed be the retention of possession or enjoyment, the Court should take a large view of the function of this tax avoidance provision.

* * *

ECONOMIC CONTROL AS "ENJOYMENT" OF PROPERTY BY THE WEALTHY

* * * Humans have an impressive ability to consume, and some with means live very opulent lives. But it is a fact of life that the disposition to consume does tend to taper off. It has long been recognized that the fraction of income expended on consumption decreases as the level of income rises.[68] * * * The point is that in thinking of "possession or enjoyment" of property in terms of those who are subject to the federal estate tax, it is indeed primitive and unrealistic to think very long in terms of the beneficial use of income for consumption expenditure.

For persons of means, the advantages that wealth gives in our society are considerable. Wealth or property in our society means power. Whether through ownership of a controlling interest in a corporation or through ownership of a diversified portfolio, wealth gives the holder thereof power and status. To a controlling shareholder, wealth gives authority to command others, to assign their employments, to enjoy their subservience, to enjoy the ability to make decisions and insist on those decisions being carried out. * * *

* * *

In a recent study, Professor Lester C. Thurow has made the same point with force:

> The motive that has been left out of neoclassical economics is that of economic power—within either the family or the community. Whereas consumption possibilities are finite, subject to diminishing marginal utility and severely limited by time budget constraints, economic power is not subject to the same limitations. Appetites for power are larger and may be subject to increasing marginal returns. Great economic power takes no longer to wield than small economic power. If one likes economic power, then one wants to maintain it until death. To de-accumulate assets or to give them away is to give up economic power. The individuals on the *Fortune* list may be sixty-five years of age and may have no possibilities of consuming their own wealth before death, but they have and enjoy economic power. They will leave a fortune at death simply because there is no way to enjoy economic power until death without leaving a fortune at death.
>
> The role of economic power helps us understand why more individuals do not use the tax loophole of transferring their assets before death. The problem is that to do so is to give up economic power. Parents typically fear that

---

[68]   J. KEYNES, THE GENERAL THEORY OF EMPLOYMENT INTEREST AND MONEY 96-97 (1936) * * * .

their children will not give the assets back if they need them (unexpected medical bills, etc.), or they fear that they will not have "respect" or "filial" devotion if the family assets are transferred before death. To give up economic power within the family is to give up one's status and station. Few individuals are willing to give up their economic power even vis-à-vis their own children.[73]

* * *

* * * Surely the conclusion must be that for persons of substantial means, those subject to the federal estate tax, the continued exercise of managerial authority over property is a principal, if not *the* principal means, by which they "enjoy" their ownership of wealth. * * * An irrevocable trust that leaves the grantor with relatively undiminished power of management over the property transferred—power to vote stock, power to sell investments and reinvest, power to sell a business enterprise and reinvest in other channels ought not to be classed as a transfer which divests the transferor of all the "possession or enjoyment" within the meaning of section 2036(a)(1). Nor should any distinction be made between retention of managerial powers over stock in a closely held corporation and retention of managerial powers over any form of investment. * * * Under this view, owners of stock in closely held corporations would be at no disadvantage. All who reserved investment management powers would be taxable. Nor should it matter whether the retained powers of management are retained as grantor or as trustee, a distinction rejected by the House Committee in explaining the retention of voting power provision in the "76" Act. Equity's limitations will not seriously circumscribe the grantor's exercise of managerial authority. Moreover, the extent of the equity court's supervision can be considerably affected by the language of the draftsman reserving managerial authority to the grantor. Letting tax consequences hang on the nature of the boilerplate language used to describe the reserved managerial power would surely be to exalt formalism.

* * *

The Supreme Court of the United States, nudged by Congress in the Tax Reform Act of 1976, should now at last allow the tax avoidance provision of section 2036 to serve its intended object. That means overruling *United States v. Byrum* * * *, root and branch. It means as well, adoption of a stance of flexibility in the interpretation of the section that will enable it to operate to thwart arrangements, however devious, that do in fact secure to the transferor continued exercise of managerial authority over transferred property.

* * *

At long last, we should be nearly at the end of the era during which it has been possible for the owner of capital ostensibly to convey it away for the benefit of his family while retaining important and valued powers and controls over that property, and escaping the death tax in the process. The power to vote stock, to sell it and reinvest, to liquidate investments and undertake new enterprises represents the real stuff of continuing dominion over and enjoyment of capital. By judicial decision reinterpreting the "possession or enjoyment" language of section 2036 now called for by the congressional rejection in the 1976 Tax Reform Act of the *Byrum* decision, we will be brought into an era when the estate tax law will be more honest, have more regard for realities and be more evenhanded in its treatment of owners of property.

* * *

---

[73]   L. THUROW, GENERATING INEQUALITY: MECHANISMS OF DISTRIBUTION IN THE UNITED STATES ECONOMY 141 (1975). * * *

NOTE

Pedrick argues that the 1976 enactment of § 2036(b) can and should be taken as signalling Congressional disapproval of the line of Supreme Court cases culminating in *Byrum*. In his view, a strict, literal interpretation of § 2036(b) represents "nothing more than a technical inconvenience, a limited pothole on the expressway to tax avoidance." An argument can be made, however, that the narrow scope of the "anti-*Byrum*" provision indicates Congressional approval of the Supreme Court's general approach in *Byrum*. See John T. Gaubatz, *The Nontaxation of Nontestamentary Acts: Will* Byrum *Survive the Tax Reform Act of 1976?*, 27 CASE WES. L. REV. 623 (1977). These contrasting views of *Byrum* and its aftermath reflect fundamentally different conceptions of the proper role of § 2036, both under current law and under various reform proposals.

John L. Peschel, *The Impact of Fiduciary Standards on Federal Taxation of Grantor Trusts: Illusion and Inconsistency*, 1979 DUKE L.J. 709*

* * *

III. EVALUATION OF EXISTING LAW

* * * How do the existing income, estate, and gift tax rules fare when tested by various policy considerations? The use of the plural emphasizes that it is not appropriate to reduce the inquiry to a determination whether existing law adequately protects against "tax avoidance." This rubric either constitutes a question-begging label for the basic problem or improperly excludes important considerations affecting the construction of a balanced tax system in this area. To be sure, the dominant question is the extent to which the grantor of an irrevocable inter vivos trust should be permitted the estate and income tax advantages normally associated with such transfers when he has retained some degree of benefit or control. Final resolution, however, must take into account other public policy factors, some of which reflect the goals or legitimate interests of grantors, trustees, and other parties directly involved in the trust.

* * *

On balance, there is a strong argument that the present federal tax rules governing irrevocable inter vivos trusts reflect an inadequate response to these various policy considerations. The problems with the existing system are so diverse that both sides (that is, the tough tax reformer and the person more sympathetic to the interests of the parties directly affected) have ample ground to complain. Since each side can isolate specific problems that indicate that the rules are either too generous or too tough, it is difficult for anyone to stake out a neutral position without making, or at least expressing, an underlying assumption. * * * [T]wo alternative packages for revisions in the present system will be described, one of which makes them tougher and the other, more relaxed. It is believed that many people would agree that the present rules are unsatisfactory but that reasonable people will disagree over which direction reform should take.

A. Tougher Rules

A reader who assigns a high priority to the construction of barriers to tax avoidance among high-income and wealthy individuals will be attracted to this position. Since the irrevocable inter vivos trust is widely used by this group, the present rules would seem to be a ready target for revision. A responsible tough tax reformer will not openly advocate uncertainty or excessive complexity in the rules, but he may feel less sympathy for a target group that has traditionally been able to afford the required professional counseling. He will also be cautious about importation of nontax fiduciary law (where the role of regulation in the public interest is more limited) and will be more willing to assume the worst about the motives of grantors of irrevocable inter vivos trusts. Surely, he will share with his friends on the other side of the fence an appropriate degree of outrage at manifestations of incoherence in the present scheme.

In general, the existing rules with respect to fiduciary standards and identity of the trustee * * * seem to come closer to the tough tax reformer's goals than to his opposite's goals. Nevertheless, some significant leaks in the system could be plugged by explicit legislation.

1. *Estate Tax.* The feature of both sections 2036(a) and 2038 that excludes from the grantor's gross estate the value of trust assets where he had the foresight to pick a third party trustee seems far too generous. Exclusion from the gross estate seems improper when the trustee is given a broad discretionary power to distribute trust income or principal to the grantor. The income tax requirement in section 677(a) that the power at least be shared with a person with a substantial beneficial interest adversely affected by exercise in favor of the grantor seems preferable to the grantor's ability under sections 2036 and 2038 to secure estate tax exemption by appointment of a third party who has no conceivable *pecuniary* reason for resisting grantor advice.

Far more debatable is the question whether the "independent trustee" exception of section 674(c) should be adopted for both estate and income tax purposes when the issue is potential grantor benefit. It would not be unreasonable to retain the income tax distinction that allows an independent trustee exception in the case of broad powers to control beneficial enjoyment among persons other than the grantor, but that narrows the exception in the grantor benefit situations to a requirement of sharing with an adverse party.

With respect to administrative powers, the present law would seem unsatisfactory to the tough tax reformer: Congress, by focusing on a single power in the anti-*Byrum* amendment, has only created an ad hoc exception to the present "common law" interpretation of sections 2036 and 2038; and this common law underestimates the degree of control over beneficial enjoyment attributable to the other powers.[150]

2. *Limited Direct Powers Over Beneficial Enjoyment.* * * * [B]oth the present estate and income tax rules grant a broad exemption when the power of the trustee (even a grantor trustee) over trust income and principal is subject to an ascertainable standard. If the trustee is authorized to distribute trust income or corpus to a beneficiary in such amounts as he deems necessary for such beneficiary's "support and maintenance," the trust is not included in the grantor's gross estate * * * . The ascertainable standard exceptions do have major disadvantages: the unwary draftsman has often stumbled into a trap; the rule has tended to breed litigation, particularly in the estate tax area; and in its pure form (for example, "support and maintenance") the standards may permit too much control over beneficial enjoyment to allow exclusion when similar nonadministrative powers would require inclusion.

---

[150]   *See* Pedrick, [*Grantor Powers and the Estate Tax: End of an Era?*, 71 Nw. U. L. Rev. 704, 718 (1977)]. * * *

3. *Transfer Tax Coordination.* For many years, there has been a consensus that the federal transfer tax rules need to be revised in order to prevent a particular transfer from being subject to both the estate and gift tax. Consequently, any congressional revision of the rules regarding grantor trusts should finally resolve this long standing weakness.

B. More Relaxed Rules

A reader may not only rebel against the inconsistency of the existing rules, but may also feel that they are too restrictive because of a different policy perspective. Thoughtful individuals can hardly be expected to object to rules designed to prevent "unearned" estate and income tax savings from an irrevocable inter vivos trust when the retained grantor benefit or control is substantial. Nevertheless, the present tax system might well appear to reflect "overkill" in that underlying assumptions or requirements overlook the possibility—and perhaps the probability—of bona fide performance by most trustees in meeting their primary fiduciary obligation to the beneficiaries. Even more undesirable is the direct incentive * * * to select a trustee who assures tax protection to the grantor at the cost of undesirable nontax consequences. Furthermore, one can argue in favor of a set of rules that does not operate as a significant disincentive to making lifetime gifts.

1. *Grantor Benefit Trusts.* In general, the advocate of more relaxed tax rules should find it difficult to quarrel with the broad feature of inclusion in the grantor's gross estate under section 2036(a)(1) * * * when the grantor has retained direct and even indirect benefit from the trust income and corpus. Indeed, the advocate may even be forced to agree with the tough tax reformer's objection that the apparent estate tax exemption when a third-party trustee is given a broad discretionary power to make distributions to the grantor is too generous. The inequity of this third-party trustee exemption is highlighted by comparing the estate tax result of two similar trusts. In the first, the third-party trustee has broad discretion in making distributions of income to the grantor and consistently does so for the grantor's support and maintenance. The trust is excluded from the grantor's gross estate. In the second trust, the trustee's discretion is limited: he is required to make distributions to the grantor for his support and maintenance. At least part of the trust will be included in the grantor's gross estate.

* * *

2. *Grantor Control Trusts.* When the grantor does not have direct or indirect access to trust income and principal for personal benefit, an appealing argument can be made that the existing rules should not be tightened excessively and should be refined to reflect less cynical assumptions regarding human behavior.

(a) *Direct distribution powers.* Under sections 2036(a)(2) and 2038, exclusion from the gross estate whenever the grantor does not, alone or in conjunction with another person, have the power to control beneficial enjoyment is inconsistent with the tighter income tax rules that deal with the reality of "friendly trustees." Perhaps the estate tax exclusion should be limited to situations in which some form of independent trustee test is satisfied. * * * With respect to a power subject to an ascertainable standard, a more consistent set of estate and income tax rules should be formulated. The tough tax reformer might insist that the reconciliation be achieved by incorporating into the estate tax provisions the income tax requirement of section 674(d) that neither the grantor nor a spouse living with him can be one of the trustees. On the other hand, a broad exemption for powers subject to an ascertainable standard might be preserved despite uncertainty about its application, on the ground that a grantor who has a careful draftsman should be rewarded for limiting the grantor's string to the property.

A more radical revision of the present rules would involve the wholesale importation of the various exceptions reflected in sections 674(b)-(d) into the estate tax area, including the exceptions permitting possession of limited powers by the grantor. It is not hard to defend these exemptions if one assumes that the typical trustee will approach the exercise of these limited powers over beneficial enjoyment in a bona fide manner with due regard to fiduciary obligations owed beneficiaries with conflicting interests. For some, allowing the grantor to be a trustee would be too generous, even if no independent trustee requirement similar to that in section 674(c) were incorporated into the estate tax laws. However, the advocate of a more relaxed approach to trustee powers over beneficial control can point out that some of the present tax rules make assumptions about typical fiduciary behavior not sustained by any known broad contemporary studies. Preservation of the more restrictive features of the existing rules regarding trustee identity might not be justified in the absence of evidence that trustees are deferring on a wholesale and persistent basis to grantor directions or "suggestions."

One feature of the current income tax rules regarding grantor trusts appears initially to be sound in theory, but closer examination reveals several weaknesses. A grantor can secure protection against income taxation by giving the power over beneficial enjoyment to a person who has an interest in the trust that would be adversely affected by exercise of the power. For example, an irrevocable inter vivos trust, making B trustee, with income payable to A for life in such amounts as the trustee shall determine and then remainder to B causes no problem for the grantor even if the trustee has a power to revoke the trust and revest the property in the grantor. Section 676(a) would not apply because any exercise by B of the power to revoke would adversely affect his own interest in the trust.

B's obvious conflict of interest supplies the justification for the tax exemption; the conflict also creates ancillary problems. First, it is very inappropriate for the federal tax laws to include an exception that creates a strong incentive to select the trustee on a basis contrary to preferred trust policies. * * *

Traditional trust law places a high priority on the trustee's duty of loyalty to the beneficiaries, which is fortified by tough rules regulating self-dealing behavior by trustees. The strength of this policy is illustrated by the prohibition in at least one key state of exercise by a trustee of a power over trust income or principal for his own benefit. Furthermore, assigning fiduciary powers to a person with an adverse interest cures the grantor's federal income tax problem at the cost of creating both estate and income tax consequences for the *holder* of the power. The trustee/beneficiary may be deemed to have a general power of appointment for purposes of including a portion of the trust assets in his gross estate, and the trust income may be taxed to the trustee whether or not distributed to him. The adverse tax effects to the trustee may be inadvertently ignored or underestimated by the less experienced practitioner who sees only the "adverse party" exception as a solution for the grantor's income tax problems. Finally, the application of the adverse party test even for income tax purposes can be a tricky business, and the issue of what constitutes a "substantial" adverse interest has had to be litigated in some marginal situations.

Elimination of the adverse party exception in the income tax area and resistance to its extension into the estate tax area on the grounds of strong contrary nontax policy considerations would probably not be a position favored by those who prefer a relaxed approach to federal taxation of grantor trusts. Nevertheless, such a person might see this apparent step backward in pure tax results as a reflection of a better integration of the nontax factors involved in planning these types of trusts.

(b) *Administrative powers.* Since standard administrative powers held by a trustee (including the grantor) are generally not a major source of estate and income exposure for the grantor, the person advocating a more relaxed tax scheme for irrevocable inter vivos trusts should be satisfied with the current state of the law. Of course, the major exception to this rosy picture is the congressional reversal of the Supreme Court decision in *Byrum* relating to the retained power to vote corporate stock transferred into trust. * * *

* * *

NOTE

Existing tax law relies heavily on applicable state law in determining the nature and extent of a decedent's control over property transferred during life. How realistic are the constraints imposed by a trustee's duties of loyalty and impartiality? Is it unduly "cynical" to inquire whether the trustee has actually exercised independent judgment in administering the trust? Consider how the foregoing proposals advanced by Lowndes and Pedrick would fare under Peschel's criteria for sound tax policy.

---

2. Consideration

A separate set of issues arises in determining the amount includible in the gross estate under §§ 2035-2038, particularly where the lifetime transfer was made for partial consideration. Under § 2043, the includible amount is limited to the difference between the deathtime value of the underlying property and "the value of the consideration received" by the decedent. Charles L.B. Lowndes explores the application of this "consideration offset" in connection with sales of remainder interests.

Charles L.B. Lowndes, *Consideration and the Federal Estate and Gift Taxes: Transfers for Partial Consideration, Relinquishment of Marital Rights, Family Annuities, the Widow's Election, and Reciprocal Trusts*, 35 GEO. WASH. L. REV. 50 (1966)*

* * *

THE ROLE OF CONSIDERATION UNDER THE ESTATE AND GIFT TAXES

* * *

In order to prevent a double tax, the estate and gift taxes provide that inter vivos transfers, otherwise taxable, shall not be taxed to the extent that they are made for adequate and full consideration in money or money's worth. Congress realized that transplanting the concept of consideration from contracts to the estate and gift taxes without any qualifications would encourage tax avoidance. If a man could transfer property for a contractual consideration of nominal value without paying an estate or gift tax, he could get property out of his taxable estate without burdening his estate with the economic equivalent of the transferred property. Consequently, the estate and gift taxes limit the consideration which will prevent a taxable transfer to an adequate and full consideration in money or money's worth, that is, to a consideration which will serve as a substitute for the transferred property in the transferor's taxable estate. * * *

* * *

SOME DIFFICULTIES WITH CURRENT DOCTRINES OF CONSIDERATION UNDER THE ESTATE AND GIFT TAXES

* * *

Partial Consideration

Transfers for an insufficient, or partial consideration, raise two problems. The first involves classifying such a transfer: how is it determined whether a transfer is one for an adequate or for an inadequate consideration? This difficulty is generated by the fact that the statute fails to specify precisely in many situations what is the transfer which is taxed. The second problem concerns valuing the partial consideration for the purpose of determining the amount of the transfer which is taxable.

* * * *United States v. Allen*[14] is an excellent illustration of the problem that may arise in determining whether there is a transfer for an inadequate consideration. The decedent, during her life, transferred property in trust reserving the income from the property to herself for life. Shortly before her death, in contemplation of death, she sold her life estate for slightly more than its actuarial value. The question arose as to what amount, if any, was taxable to her estate because of the trust. Of course, her executor contended that nothing was taxable. The trust property could not be taxed to her estate under section 2036, which taxes transfers with reservation of a life interest, because the decedent's life interest did not persist until her death.[15] The only basis for taxing the property to her estate was the release of the life estate in contemplation of death. According to the executor, however, the transfer in contemplation of death was not taxable because it was a transfer for an adequate consideration. Apart from legal technicalities, it seems obvious that the difference between the value of the property in which the decedent retained a life estate and the consideration she received for the release of the life estate in contemplation of death should have been taxed to her estate. If she had not released the life estate in contemplation of death, the full value of the trust property would have been taxed to her estate. Since the purpose of taxing transfers in contemplation of death is to prevent avoidance of the estate tax, it seems clear that the decedent should not have been able to avoid an estate tax by release of the life estate in *Allen*. Yet, she would have avoided tax on the difference between the value of the trust property and the consideration received for the release of the life estate if the transfer in contemplation of death had been treated as a transfer for adequate consideration. Whether or not the transfer was for an adequate consideration depends on what was transferred. The district court thought that the interest transferred in contemplation of death was the decedent's life estate, and the transfer was, therefore, a tax-free transfer for an adequate consideration. The Tenth Circuit took a more sophisticated approach, holding that the interest transferred by the decedent when she released her life estate was the tax interest attributed to her for purposes of the estate tax, that is, the interest which would have been taxed to her estate had she not made the transfer in contemplation of death. From this point of view, she transferred the full value of the trust property, which would have been included in the gross estate if she had not made the transfer, and the transfer was taxable because made for an inadequate consideration. The amount which was taxed was the full value of the trust property, in which she retained a life estate, less the value of the consideration received for the release of the life estate.

* * *

---

[14]   293 F.2d 916 (10th Cir.), *cert. denied*, 368 U.S. 944 (1961).

[15]   * * * However, in his concurring opinion in *United States v. Allen*, [293 F.2d at 918], Judge Breitenstein said, "As I read the statute, the tax liability arises at the time of the inter vivos transfer under which there was a retention of the right to income for life. The disposition thereafter of that retained right does not eliminate the tax liability."

* * * The second problem in connection with transfers for partial consideration relates to the method of valuing the consideration. Is it valued according to its value at the date of transfer, or the date of the transferor's death, * * * or according to some other method?

The Regulations take the position, which receives support from the language of the statute, and the cases, that partial consideration is valued according to its value at the date of the transfer. This works out satisfactorily under the gift tax, since the property whose transfer is treated as a taxable gift is valued according to the same date. It works badly under the estate tax, however, because it means that the consideration and the transferred property will be valued on different dates. If the taxpayer still owns the consideration at his death and it has increased in value since the date of the transfer, valuing the consideration according to its value at the date of the transfer is unfair to the taxpayer, because it means that his estate will be taxed on the increased value of the consideration at the date of death, although it is only allowed credit against the inter vivos transfer for the lower value of the consideration at the time of the transfer. On the other hand, if the value of the consideration decreases between the time of the transfer and the decedent's death, valuing the consideration according to its value at the date of the transfer is unfair to the Government, because although only the diminished value of the consideration is included in the decedent's gross estate, he is allowed to credit the higher value at the date of the transfer against the amount taxed to his estate because of the transfer.

If there were some guarantee that the decedent would retain the partial consideration received for the inter vivos transfer until his death, it would be fair to value the consideration according to its value at the date of his death * * * . The property transferred and the consideration received for the transfer would then be valued according to the same date, so that the credit allowed against the inter vivos transfer because of the partial consideration would be the same as the amount included in the transferor's gross estate because of receipt of the consideration. The difficulty with this method of valuing the partial consideration arises when the consideration is disposed of by the transferor before his death. Then we encounter the problem (which is avoided when consideration is valued according to the date of the transfer) of determining whether the amount to be subtracted from the taxable transfer is the value of the original consideration or the product of the original consideration and, moreover, what happens when it is impossible to trace the original consideration or its product.

Perhaps the most satisfactory way to handle partial consideration is on a proportional basis; this treats the transfer as a fully exempt transfer up to the value (at the time of the transfer) of the consideration received for the transfer, and as a fully taxable transfer to the extent there was no consideration. For example, if A transferred property worth $100,000 in contemplation of death for $25,000, this would be treated as a tax-free transfer of one-fourth of the property and a taxable transfer of the remaining three-fourths. At the transferor's death, three-fourths of the value of the property at that time (assuming that his estate is valued according to its value at the date of death) would be taxed to his estate. This is the method which is used in connection with jointly held property to determine the extent to which property was acquired by a surviving tenant from a deceased tenant for adequate consideration. Of course, one difficulty in construing the section relating to partial consideration in this way is that, unlike section 2040, dealing with jointly held property, section 2043(a), dealing with inter vivos transfers for partial consideration, does not explicitly prescribe a proportional rule for determining the amount of the transfer which is taxable.

Adoption of a proportional method of handling transfers for partial consideration under the estate tax is fairly simple when the entire property included in the transferor's gross estate is transferred inter vivos. In the preceding hypothetical situation, Blackacre, worth $100,000, was transferred for $25,000 in contemplation of death; the proportionate amounts of the transfer which were taxable and tax-exempt could be computed readily by comparing the value of

Blackacre at the time it was transferred with the amount of the consideration. Where, however, the inter vivos transfer, which triggers the estate tax, involves a different interest than that included in the transferor's gross estate, the problem arises whether the proportionate part of the transfer which is taxable is determined by a comparison between the property interest transferred inter vivos, or the tax interest, which is deemed to have been transferred for purposes of the estate tax. For example, suppose that A in consideration of the receipt of $25,000 transfers property worth $100,000 to T in trust for A for life, remainder to B in fee. Assume further that at the time of this transfer the remainder in the trust property after A's life estate was worth $50,000, and at A's death (the date at which his estate will be valued) the trust property has increased in value to $200,000. What proportion of the trust property is taxable to A's estate? Although it seems clear that, in determining the proportion of the transfer taxable to A's estate, the property transferred and the consideration for the transfer will both be valued according to their values at the date of the inter vivos transfer, it is not clear whether the property interest (the remainder in the trust after A's life estate), or the tax interest which A is deemed to have transferred for purposes of the estate tax (the entire trust property), will be compared to get the proportionate part of the transfer which is taxable. If the value of the remainder which A actually transferred during his life is used to determine the part of the transfer which is taxable under the estate tax, then since the consideration ($25,000) equalled one-half of the value of the property transferred inter vivos ($50,000, the value of the remainder), one-half of the transfer will be taxable. This will mean that at A's death one-half of the value of the trust property at that time, or $100,000, will be included in his gross estate. If, however, A is deemed for purposes of section 2036 to have transferred the entire property in which he retained a life interest for the partial consideration, the proportionate part of the transfer which is taxable must be determined by comparing the full value of the trust property (at the time the trust was created) or $100,000, with the consideration received for the transfer, or $25,000, and three-fourths of the transfer will be taxable, with the result that $150,000 will be included in A's gross estate.

* * *

CONCLUSION

* * *

Consideration has a dual role under the estate and gift taxes. It serves to prevent a double estate tax upon property transferred by a decedent during his life and the consideration received in return for the transfer. At the same time, by injecting the requirement of economic equivalence into the common-law concept of consideration, Congress has attempted to prevent taxpayers from depleting their taxable estates by transfers for nominal consideration. To a certain extent, current conceptions of consideration under the estate and gift taxes fail to achieve either of these objectives. * * *

* * *

With transfers for partial consideration, adequacy of consideration must be measured by a comparison between the value of the consideration and the "tax interest" attributed to the transferor under the estate tax, rather than the property interest actually transferred by a decedent during his life. * * *

* * *

Perhaps the most satisfactory way of handling transfers for partial consideration is on a proportional basis: treat the transfer as a tax-free transfer of a part of the property equal to the value of the consideration (at the time of the inter vivos transfer), and a taxable transfer of the remaining part of the property. It would appear, however, that this proportion should be based upon a comparison of the tax interest attributed to the transferor under the estate tax and the consideration for the transfer, rather than a comparison of the property interest transferred by the decedent during his life and the value of the consideration. * * *

* * *

NOTE

A lifetime transfer made for full money's-worth consideration is expressly exempt from the inclusionary provisions of §§ 2035-2038, but the scope of this exemption is often unclear. In applying § 2035 to the severing of a "taxable string" (e.g., a life estate retained under a previous transfer), the technical issue is whether the adequacy of the consideration should be measured against the value of the severed string or against the value of the property that would otherwise be drawn into the gross estate. In recommending the latter approach, does Lowndes imply that consideration may be adequate to eliminate a taxable gift but may nevertheless be inadequate for estate tax purposes? What is the effect, if any, on Lowndes' analysis of the special gift tax valuation rules of § 2702, discussed in Part V(B), *infra*?

Although Lowndes applauds the Tenth Circuit's decision in *Allen* as "sophisticated," some commentators disagree. *See* Joseph M. Dodge, *Redoing the Estate and Gift Taxes Along Easy-to-Value Lines*, 43 TAX L. REV. 241, 283 (1988) (characterizing decision as "wrong economically"). Are the premises of §§ 2035-2038 concerning inclusion in the gross estate inconsistent with those of § 2043(a) concerning partial consideration?

Consideration also raises problems in connection with certain intrafamily transactions (e.g., a private annuity or a "widow's election"). For detailed discussions of these transactions, see George Cooper, *A Voluntary Tax? New Perspectives on Sophisticated Estate Tax Avoidance*, 77 COLUM. L. REV. 161 (1977); Stanley M. Johanson, *Revocable Trusts, Widow's Election Wills, and Community Property: The Tax Problems*, 47 TEX. L. REV. 1247 (1969); Norman H. Lane, *Intra-Family Sales: Toward a Uniform Tax Treatment*, 41 TAX LAW. 279 (1988).

D.   Contractual Survivor Benefits

Survivor annuities and other contractual death benefits raise special problems which highlight the uneven coverage of the estate and gift taxes. Under § 2039, the value of an "annuity or other payment" payable by reason of surviving the decedent is includible in the gross estate if the underlying "contract or agreement" also provided for lifetime payments to the decedent. Section 2039 is aimed primarily at joint-and-survivor annuities and similar arrangements commonly provided as part of an employment compensation package. The statute, however, is not limited to employment-related arrangements, nor, as the following materials point out, does it reach all death benefits payable by reason of the decedent's employment.

In his article on death benefits, Bruce Wolk discusses the scope of § 2039 and its relationship with other estate and gift tax provisions. He argues that § 2039 should be amended to reach "pure" death benefit arrangements, i.e., those that provide no benefits to the decedent during life. Commenting on the ABA Tax Section Task Force's proposal for inclusion of "[a]ll contractual or statutory survivor benefits economically attributable to the decedent" in the gross estate, Harry L. Gutman points out that the proposal goes well beyond employer-provided death benefits and raises significant issues of timing and valuation.

Bruce Wolk, *The Pure Death Benefit: An Estate and Gift Tax Anomaly*, 66 MINN. L. REV. 229 (1982)*

I. INTRODUCTION

* * *

* * * [A] narrow but significant class of * * * death benefits has * * * managed to escape taxation. The benefits in question are pure death benefits over which the employee has no power to change the designated beneficiary. A death benefit is pure if it provides no payments during the employee's life.[5] Although the Internal Revenue Service has sought to fit the pure death benefit under almost every section of the Internal Revenue Code defining the gross estate for federal estate tax purposes, these attempts have met with only limited success. The exclusion of pure death benefits from the employee's estate opens a significant loophole in the Code's transfer tax provisions. The Service has recently attempted to reach these benefits under the gift tax. These efforts, although ingenious, remain stopgap measures. A comprehensive rethinking of the treatment of employee death benefits is clearly in order.

* * *

II. ESTATE TAX ASPECTS

A. The Limited Scope of Section 2039

The death benefit must be pure—contain no lifetime benefit—if it is to escape estate taxation under section 2039(a). This section includes in the gross estate the value of an annuity or other payment receivable by any beneficiary surviving the decedent under any form of contract or agreement, but only if under such contract or agreement an annuity or other payment was payable to the decedent, or would in the future be payable to the decedent during his or her lifetime.[13] Section 2039 was intended to require inclusion of the value of a survivor's rights in a joint and survivor annuity or similar benefit without resort to the uncertain applicability of the other more general estate tax provisions. By including a retained lifetime interest requirement

---

*   Copyright © 1982. Reprinted with permission.

[5]   A typical benefit provides that upon the death of the employee a specified sum, frequently linked to the employee's salary, is to be paid to a named beneficiary, often the employee's spouse. The payment might be in a lump sum or payable over some period of time.

[13]   The annuity or other payment is included in the gross estate only in proportion to that part of the purchase price contributed by the decedent, but for this purpose, a contribution by the decedent's employer * * * is considered to be a contribution by the decedent "if made by reason of employment." I.R.C. § 2039(b).

in section 2039, however, Congress chose to deal only with the general problem of joint annuities and "not with the whole gamut of arrangements under which an employee, his employer, or both may create benefits for the employee's survivors."

Recognizing that some kind of lifetime payment or benefit was an essential prerequisite to applying section 2039, the Service has sought to find such payments outside the typical context of a joint and survivor annuity. An employer and employee could seemingly avoid the literal application of section 2039 by entering into two separate contracts, one for a pure death benefit, and another for retirement or other lifetime benefits. The Treasury Regulations, however, foreclose this apparent opportunity by providing that the term "contract or agreement" includes "any combination of arrangements, understandings or plans arising by reason of the decedent's employment." The courts have accepted this interpretation.

In *Estate of Fusz v. Commissioner*,[19] the Commissioner took the position that the deceased employee's salary itself constituted an "other payment" sufficient to bring section 2039 into play. Had this view been upheld, all pure death benefits would have been subject to the estate tax under section 2039. The Tax Court, however, rejected this approach and held that the phrase "other payment" is "qualitatively limited to post-employment benefits which, at the very least, are paid or payable during the decedent's lifetime." Since the Commissioner has now acquiesced in *Fusz*, it is clear that a pure employee death benefit, taken by itself, will not be reached by section 2039.

* * *

* * * The inapplicability of section 2039, however, does not resolve the issue of the estate taxation of pure death benefits. In enacting section 2039, Congress did not intend to make it the exclusive statutory provision for taxing employee death benefits; pure death benefits may be subject to estate taxation under one or more of the other estate tax provisions.

B. Section 2033

The Service has sometimes argued that employee death benefits are equivalent to property owned by the employee and therefore are includable in the gross estate under section 2033, but this argument usually fails to impress the courts. Courts base their rejection of the Service's position on a number of theories, depending to some extent on the nature of the particular death benefit before the court. For example, if the employer retains the right to revoke or modify the benefit at any time prior to the employee's death, the courts regard the employee's interest in the benefit as something less than property. Nevertheless, the mere possibility of revocation or forfeiture of an interest does not compel the conclusion that no property interest exists. Moreover, if the employee's death forecloses revocation or forfeiture, what was perhaps a mere expectancy undeniably becomes a property interest of obvious value. Since courts must identify and value interests under section 2033 at the moment of the decedent's death, the possibility that the death benefit plan might be revoked prior to death cannot by itself render section 2033 inapplicable.

Plans under which the death benefit remains discretionary with the employer, even after the death of the employee, present a different problem. The courts and the Service have concluded that because such plans do not create enforceable rights to the death benefit, they represent a mere expectancy and not property under section 2033. Although this result has a certain logical appeal, it ignores the reality of the restraints imposed on employers both by the marketplace for skilled employees and by the need to enhance productivity by maintaining good employee relations. As a practical matter, the employer's ability to withhold the benefit is

---

[19]   46 T.C. 214 (1966), *acq.*, 1967-2 C.B. 2.

largely irrelevant since, for readily apparent business reasons, it would be foolish to do so. Thus, what is technically an expectancy may have substantial value. * * *

* * *

C. The Lifetime Transfer Sections

The federal estate tax reaches more than just the property owned by a decedent. Congress has provided in sections 2035 through 2038 that certain lifetime transfers of property are sufficiently testamentary to justify subjecting the property to estate taxation. * * *

In order to include an interest in property in the gross estate, the lifetime transfer provisions all require that the decedent have "made a transfer" of the "property" interest. * * * In cases in which a decedent purchased a joint and survivor annuity, the courts have had little difficulty in concluding that a "transfer" occurred. The courts disagree on the tax consequence if the employer purchased or provided the benefit. Some courts have refused to find a transfer if the benefit was voluntarily created, discretionary, or forfeitable. A transfer has been found, however, where the decedent qualified for an annuity but elected to receive a reduced annuity to provide his spouse with a survivor's annuity. Finally, if the decedent procured a survivor's benefit from the employer in return for the performance of services during the course of employment, a substantial body of authority provides that the transfer requirement is satisfied.

* * *

1. Section 2035

Before the enactment of the Economic Recovery Tax Act of 1981, property interests transferred by a decedent within three years of death without adequate consideration were included in the decedent's gross estate under section 2035(a). * * *

[In general,] Congress has made section 2035(a) inapplicable to the estates of decedents dying after December 31, 1981. Important exceptions remain, however. * * * Gifts of life insurance, in particular, continue to be covered by sections 2035(a) and 2042. Thus, if one year prior to death a decedent transferred all of the incidents of ownership in a life insurance policy, the entire amount of the proceeds would be included in the decedent's gross estate.

* * *

From the beneficiary's point of view, an employer-provided pure death benefit and an employer-provided life insurance policy are nearly indistinguishable. The only significant difference is that the promise of the employer has replaced the promise of an insurance company. The question therefore arises whether a pure death benefit is a life insurance policy for estate tax purposes.

In the leading case of *Helvering v. Le Gierse*,[111] the Supreme Court held that the essential feature of a life insurance contract is "risk-shifting and risk-distributing." Moreover, the requisite risk-shifting is not limited to contracts issued by an insurance company. * * *

In *All v. McCobb*,[114] however, an unfunded employee death benefit plan was held not to constitute a life insurance policy under section 2039. Given the absence of any premiums or reserves, the court could find no "gamble" with the decedent nor any undertaking to "distribute among a larger group of employees, on the basis of actuarial data from which the appropriate size of a terminal reserve could be computed, the risk of the premature death of a single employee." The court distinguished a mere "promise to pay a sum certain to a named beneficiary upon the death of a retired employee" from a life insurance policy.

---

[111]   312 U.S. 531 (1941).

[114]   321 F.2d 633 (2d Cir. 1963).

Although *All v. McCobb* supports the proposition that a pure death benefit is not a life insurance policy, the court's analysis is subject to criticism. The pure death benefit is not functionally distinguishable from term life insurance. The death benefit, like any other employee benefit, is a substitute for salary, and the employee in effect pays a premium to the employer by accepting the benefit in lieu of cash. The employer makes a gamble just like a life insurance company; an employee who dies prematurely is overcompensated, but an employee who works for many years and then retires is undercompensated. Also, to the extent the employer has more than one employee, the employer can spread the risk to produce, in effect, an annual actuarial cost for providing the benefit. This cost is paid by the services of each employee covered under the death benefit plan.

* * *

2. Section 2038

Section 2038(a)(1) includes in a decedent's gross estate any property interest transferred by the decedent, but which remains, at the date of the decedent's death, subject to the decedent's power, either alone or in conjunction with any other person, to alter, amend, revoke, or terminate the enjoyment of the property interest. It is now well established that the transfer requirement of section 2038(a)(1) is satisfied if an employer provides a death benefit in return for an employee's services. The more troublesome issue has been the degree of power a deceased employee must have retained over the benefit in order to bring it within the reach of section 2038(a)(1).

Although an employee's power to change the beneficiary of the death benefit clearly triggers section 2038(a)(1), an employee may also be able to indirectly affect the beneficiary's interest in the benefit without expressly retaining the right to alter the beneficiary. For example, the employee always retains the power to "terminate" the enjoyment of the death benefit by leaving his or her job. * * *

* * * The act of working is an act of wealth creation. The pure death benefit is a part of the compensation package and represents a deliberate incentive to exercise the power in question, namely to continue employment. Although it is not the only such incentive, the relative level of incentive is not the significant factor. An individual works for compensation, and the decision to work or not to work represents control over the entire compensation package. * * * Thus, the conclusion is incorrect that the power to terminate a death benefit by changing jobs falls outside the scope of section 2038(a)(1).

* * *

3. Section 2037

The Service has successfully relied upon section 2037 to include pure death benefits in the estate of a deceased employee, but its reach can easily be avoided. Under section 2037, property transferred during life by a decedent will be included in the decedent's gross estate if possession or enjoyment of the property, through ownership of the transferred interest, can be obtained only by surviving the decedent and the decedent has retained a reversionary interest in the property that immediately before the decedent's death exceeds five percent of the property's value. * * *

Since the pure death benefit will be paid only if and when the employee dies, the survivorship requirement of section 2037 is automatically satisfied. By drafting the agreement so that the deceased employee does not possess any reversionary interest in the benefit, however, the arrangement can avoid the reversion requirement of section 2037. * * *

* * *

IV. STATUTORY REFORM

The pure death benefit is undoubtedly a proper subject of wealth transfer taxation. The payment to the beneficiary is wealth generated by the decedent's labor, which in principle is no different than the wealth created by the decedent's wages in the form of savings and investments. Although there is no direct cash purchase, the benefit is furnished in exchange for the services of the employee. Whether the employee can select or alter the beneficiaries of the death benefit is not relevant to the issue of whether the employee has made a transfer. The benefit is part of the employee's compensation package, and since it derives solely from the services of the employee, it is appropriate to treat the employee as the transferor.

Having concluded that there is a transfer, one must determine the appropriate time to tax it. If a beneficiary's enjoyment of the property remains subject to the control of the transferor, the property should be taxed upon death as part of the estate since the transfer is inherently testamentary. Even if an employee had no express control over the death benefit, the beneficiaries do not receive anything of substantial value prior to the employee's death that would warrant the imposition of only a gift tax. Although the pure death benefit with an irrevocably named beneficiary is theoretically subject to the gift tax, either at its creation or continuously over its existence, gift tax valuation alone is an inadequate measure of the value of the transfer. Not only is the valuation problem extremely difficult, but the employee's ability to terminate the benefit by ceasing employment represents an inherent control over the benefit that justifies the treatment of any transfer as incomplete until death.

This Article has suggested that the courts could properly interpret section 2038 to include the pure death benefit in a deceased employee's gross estate. Their failure to do so emphasizes the need for statutory reform. The simplest solution would be the amendment of section 2039(a) to remove the retained interest requirement. Although such an amendment would include any contractual pure death benefit in the employee's gross estate, the includability of unenforceable benefits—benefits which remain discretionary with the employer even after the death of the employee—would remain unresolved. * * * In amending section 2039(a), therefore, Congress should specify that the discretionary nature of the death benefit does not preclude its inclusion in the employee's gross estate.

The inclusion of unenforceable benefits in the gross estate, however, raises a potentially serious valuation problem. An enforceable promise by an employer to pay $1,000 per month for three years is certainly worth something more than a similar unenforceable promise. Nonetheless, if the employer has consistently paid the benefits, the value of the possible future payment is clearly greater than zero, since a willing buyer would pay something to a willing seller for the right to receive any payments which are actually made. A reasonable approach toward the valuation of such benefits would be to compute the value of the benefit assuming it were enforceable, then discount that amount by the probability of nonpayment. The contingent nature of an unenforceable employee death benefit is not a justification for excluding it from the reach of the estate tax, since the need to value contingent interests is an unfortunate but frequent feature of the present estate tax system.

As a corollary to subjecting the pure death benefit to estate taxation, Congress should treat the irrevocable designation of a beneficiary and the continued existence of the pure death benefit as an incomplete gift for gift tax purposes. Although the beneficiary has received a current economic benefit of non-zero value, its precise value is indeterminate, and as a practical matter the beneficiary could not sell the right to the benefit. * * *

This statutory scheme, however, results in a transfer tax treatment of pure death benefits diametrically opposite to the treatment of employer-provided life insurance. If the employee assigns the policy, the employer's premium payments are treated as gifts by the employee to the assignee, and the proceeds are not includable in the employee's gross estate. Such profound differences in treatment are difficult to justify, given the essential functional and economic similarities between the two benefits. Congress should therefore subject the assigned group term life insurance policy to estate taxation. This result could be achieved by amending Section 2042 to provide that any incidents of ownership held by an employer in a policy of life insurance on an employee will be attributed to the employee, unless the policy is payable to the employer or is otherwise not intended to be compensation. In addition, a provision should be added to the gift tax statute that would exempt the premium payments from treatment as a transfer for gift tax purposes. * * *

* * *

NOTE

To reach "pure" death benefits, Wolk proposes eliminating § 2039's requirement of a lifetime benefit "payable to the decedent." What function does this requirement serve, and why was it originally included in the statute? *See* Boris I. Bittker, *Estate and Gift Taxation Under the 1954 Code: The Principal Changes*, 29 TUL. L. REV. 453 (1955). Wolk also argues that employer-provided death benefits should be includible in the gross estate even if payment remains discretionary with the employer. For a proposal to include the value of "[a]ll contractual or statutory survivor benefits economically attributable to the decedent" in the gross estate, see American Bar Ass'n, Section of Tax'n, Task Force on Transfer Tax Restructuring, *Report on Transfer Tax Restructuring*, 41 TAX LAW. 395, 411 (1988). This proposal is discussed in the following excerpt.

Harry L. Gutman, *A Comment on the ABA Tax Section Task Force Report on Transfer Tax Restructuring*, 41 TAX LAW. 653 (1988)*

* * *

III. THE TRANSFER TAX BASE

* * *

Under current law, survivor benefits that have, in substance, been purchased by a decedent through an employment relationship may not be included in the decedent's transfer tax base if the benefits are forfeitable at the time death occurs, the decedent never possessed the right to receive benefits during his lifetime, or the decedent did not have the right to designate the beneficiaries. In addition, the value of an action for wrongful death is not, in general, included in a decedent's gross estate because it is not property in which the decedent possessed an interest at his death. Finally, many statutory survivor benefits are not included in the decedent's transfer tax base.

The Report recommends that all "contractual or statutory survivor benefits economically attributable to the decedent" be included in the decedent's transfer tax base at death. The pro-

---

posal is explicitly intended to include not only employer-employee survivor benefits that, for technical reasons, are not presently captured by the statute, but also a number of other benefits—particularly Social Security death benefits—that are currently excluded. * * *

There should be no question that survivor benefits payable as a result of an employer-employee relationship should be included in the transfer tax base of the decedent employee. The value of the survivor benefit represents a payment that is directly attributable to services rendered by the decedent. It is, in substance, deferred compensation, even when it takes the form of insurance proceeds. It is wealth that the decedent effectively chose to receive later rather than sooner and it should not escape taxation.

The treatment of the portion of a wrongful death payment that is determined by reference to the wages the decedent would have earned had life not been wrongfully terminated raises the same issue. Had the decedent not died, an amount equal to the wrongful death payment would have been received by him during his life and, to the extent not consumed, would have been part of his transfer tax base at death. Again, there can be no serious argument that the value of such a payment should be excluded from the transfer tax base of the decedent.

* * *

The Report proposes to include both employment-related and statutory survivor benefits that are "economically attributable" to the decedent. Social security death benefits are mentioned as an example of the latter class. A common sense notion of economic attribution as including amounts earned but not paid during the decedent's life, or payments that act as a substitute for amounts that would have been earned, leads to the conclusion that employment-related and wrongful death proceeds should be included in the decedent's transfer tax base. Another common sense view of economic attribution would include the proceeds of a decedent's investment that are transferred at death if the prior investment has not been treated as a completed transfer. Either rationale can justify inclusion of statutory benefits if they can be thought of as "purchased" by the decedent, or if they serve as a substitute for otherwise taxable nonstatutory investment proceeds. Thus, social security death benefits would be includible if one viewed them as "purchased" by social security tax payments. Similarly, workmen's compensation death benefits would be includible if they are, in substance, analogous to nonstatutory wrongful death proceeds.

In suggesting that the transfer of employment-related survivor benefits remains incomplete until the death of the employee, the Report adopts a hard-to-complete gift rule * * * . If the benefits are forfeitable prior to death, death is the event that eliminates the contingencies. The proper time to complete the transfer, therefore, is at death. Even if the contingencies are satisfied prior to death, however, the decision to treat death as the taxable event is conceptually defensible. * * * [I]f valuation uncertainties preclude taxing benefits as they conditionally accrue, and the conditions relating to growth, rates, and tax base are met, the decision to wait until the benefits are paid before including them in the [decedent's] tax base is neither a tax benefit nor a tax detriment. * * *

* * *

NOTE

Gutman offers two possible "common sense" notions of "economic attribution" to support including statutory death benefits in the gross estate. Are a surviving spouse's Social Security benefits properly viewed as "a substitute for amounts that would have been earned" or as "proceeds of a decedent's investment"? Gutman also suggests a rationale for subjecting death benefits to estate tax rather than gift tax, even if all contingencies are satisfied before death. Would his rationale support similar treatment of life insurance proceeds? What is the basis for the different treatment of death benefits under § 2039 and life insurance proceeds under § 2042?

E.   Life Insurance

The treatment of life insurance for estate and gift tax purposes has remained essentially unchanged since 1954. Under § 2042, proceeds of insurance on a deceased insured's life are includible in the gross estate if the proceeds are receivable by the executor or if the decedent possessed any incident of ownership in the policy at death. Moreover, the three-year inclusionary rule of § 2035, which was made inapplicable to most outright lifetime transfers by the 1981 amendments, remains applicable to transfers of insurance policies on the decedent's life.

The following materials explore the provisions of existing law concerning life insurance and raise several questions about how life insurance should be treated under a unified estate and gift tax system. What rights or interests represent "ownership" of life insurance, when is a "transfer" of life insurance complete, and how should such a transfer be valued? Is life insurance "inherently testamentary"? Does life insurance have distinctive characteristics that justify special tax treatment? Does it invite special forms of transfer tax avoidance?

In 1988 an ABA Task Force, having "failed to develop a consensus" on the tax treatment of life insurance, included a Study Paper, "without recommendation," as an exhibit to its report. *See* American Bar Ass'n, Section of Tax'n, Task Force on Transfer Tax Restructuring, *Report on Transfer Tax Restructuring*, 41 TAX LAW. 395, 416 (1988). Commenting on the Study Paper, Harry L. Gutman recommends the adoption of a premium-payments test to complement the incidents-of-ownership test for estate tax purposes; in addition, he argues that the includible amount should be reduced by any premium payments made by the insured that were subject to gift tax.

In reading the following materials, recall that one of the major tax advantages of life insurance arises from the income tax exclusion of § 101(a). If the tax treatment of life insurance stands in need of reform, should the focus be on the income tax rather than the estate and gift taxes? For an income-tax-oriented proposal, see Robert B. Smith, *Reconsidering the Taxation of Life Insurance Proceeds Through the Lens of Current Estate Planning*, 15 VA. TAX REV. 283 (1995).

Harry L. Gutman, *A Comment on the ABA Tax Section Task Force Report on Transfer Tax Restructuring*, 41 TAX LAW. 653 (1988)*

* * *

III. THE TRANSFER TAX BASE

* * *

* * * The Task Force Study Paper on life insurance * * * correctly notes that:

> It cannot seriously be argued that [current] estate tax rules treat life insurance like [other investments]. [The current life insurance] rules look in part to des- tination of proceeds, in part to the decedent's rights in the policy, and in part to time of transfer. In some respects they are tighter than the rules applicable to other investments and in others more liberal.[64]

The Study Paper suggests a number of alternatives to rationalize the treatment of life insur- ance with survivor benefits and other types of investments.

Proposal A, the core proposal, recommends that, in addition to inclusion under current sec- tion 2042(1), life insurance proceeds on the life of the decedent be includible in the decedent's gross estate if receivable by "his spouse, his ancestors, his descendants, the spouse of any such descendant, or the estate of any such individual." Premium payments and policy transfers would not be completed gifts. The surrender of a policy for cash by an owner described above, how- ever, would constitute a completed gift from the insured to the owner. Special rules are sug- gested for proceeds payable to entities other than estates.

Anticipating criticism that Proposal A would subject to transfer tax the proceeds of insur- ance on the decedent's life purchased by a member of the decedent's family with funds never received from the decedent, while failing to tax the proceeds of insurance purchased by the decedent for the benefit of his mistress, the Study Paper suggests three alternatives that could be adopted in whole or part. First, the current incidents of ownership test could be retained as an additional basis for inclusion. Second, an exclusion could be permitted for insurance "pur- chased by an individual other than the insured with consideration shown to have belonged to such person and never to have been received donatively from the insured." Third, the decedent's transfer tax base could include all insurance on the decedent's life, regardless of the policy owner except for "commercially-grounded insurance."

A wholly different proposal, focused on capturing the increase in the value of insurance resulting from death, would require the inclusion (to the extent not included under section 2041(1) or (2), which would be retained) of "the excess of the insurance proceeds over the value of the policy immediately preceding death."

The Study Paper proposals appear on the surface to present a range of sound pragmatic options. Unfortunately, the Paper fails to articulate explicitly why the adoption of any, or some combination of the proposals would result in a more conceptually sound transfer tax treatment of life insurance. I will explore those questions and offer some conclusions.

One way to approach life insurance is to compare it to survivor benefits. Both represent post-death payments attributable to the decedent, at least in the sense that without a decedent there would be no payment. Life insurance, however, has characteristics that differ from sur-

---

[64]   [American Bar Ass'n, Section of Tax'n, Task Force on Transfer Tax Restructuring, *Report on Transfer Tax Restructuring*, 41 TAX LAW. 395, 438-40 (1988).]

vivor benefits. In the case of survivor benefits, the post-death payments are attributable to something the decedent did—investing either funds or services to produce the post-death payments. Life insurance need not relate to anything the decedent did other than live. Life insurance may be purchased and maintained by individuals other than the insured without any assistance (economic or otherwise) from the insured. This distinguishes it from survivor benefits, and leads to the question of whether identical treatment for life insurance and survivor benefits is appropriate or desirable in all cases.

When the characteristics of the two are similar, the tax treatment should be similar. * * * This logic would lead to the conclusion that to the extent life insurance proceeds are attributable to premiums paid directly or indirectly through property or services provided by the decedent, and the premium payment has not been subject to transfer tax, the proceeds should be included in the decedent's gross estate no matter who the nominal owner of the policy is, and without regard to who receives the proceeds.

The foregoing statement of includibility follows from the decision to treat premium payments as incomplete transfers (the treatment of premium payments recommended in Proposal A). This recommended treatment of premium payments is appropriate if the decedent is the owner of, or possesses the right to benefit economically from, the policy. Depending on how the completed gift rules are resolved, incomplete gift treatment may also be appropriate if the decedent retains the right to control the beneficial enjoyment of the proceeds even if he cannot benefit economically himself. There are, however, situations in which a decedent's premium payment should be treated as a completed gift. For example, when the policy is owned by a third party, the premium payment is an event by which the transferor has irrevocably parted with dominion and control over the transferred funds. In this circumstance the premium payment should constitute a taxable transfer.

If premium payments have been treated as completed gifts by the insured, should the policy proceeds nonetheless be includible in the estate of the insured? The argument for exclusion rests on the notion that life insurance proceeds are simply an investment return. The return is akin to winning a gamble. * * * The fact that the gamble happens to be on the life of the transferor is irrelevant. Thus, if the payment of the premium by the decedent-insured is a completed gift, the transaction should be treated as if the decedent transferred the amount of the premium to the policy owner who then paid the premium. That is the end of the transaction for transfer tax purposes. If this analysis is accepted, insurance proceeds from policies procured, owned, and paid for solely by third parties would, *a fortiori*, be excluded from the decedent's gross estate unless the proceeds were economically available to the estate.

The argument for inclusion when the decedent has paid the premiums takes a number of different forms. First, it is said that life insurance is "inherently testamentary" and, as such, should be taxed at the death of the insured. While the first part of the statement is undoubtedly true, the second does not necessarily follow if the premiums have been subject to tax. The fact that death is the event that causes the payoff does not *compel* one to treat the proceeds differently than any other investment. While one is not *compelled*, however, to treat life insurance differently, one might observe that the failure to include the proceeds, especially when the policy is procured within a short time of death, effectively permits individuals to arrange for a substantial transfer of wealth, tax-free, upon their deaths. It is particularly in this context that some regard life insurance as different than any other investment.

This appearance of tax avoidance is, however, an illusion when viewed in the aggregate. The insurance gamble creates both winners and losers. On the whole, so long as the actuarial tables are correct, the winners and losers balance. It would be incorrect to penalize individual winners (the beneficiaries of those who died early) without some compensating treatment for the losers (those who outlive their actuarial life expectancy).

This is not to say that there is no additional element of value associated with life insurance policies to be captured by the transfer tax. The value of the ability to renew a term policy automatically when the insured is in poor health is an example, particularly if ownership of the policy is transferred after the facts are known. While these special situations should be addressed, they should not affect one's views as to whether life insurance differs in its characteristics from any other investment.

Second, it may be argued that if a purpose of the transfer tax is to "backstop" income by taxing wealth that taxpayers accumulate through income-tax-preferred sources, then life insurance proceeds should be included in the estate of the insured because the proceeds of the insurance are, in most cases, received as tax-free income. The income tax failure, with respect to the protection element of life insurance, is not the tax-free quality of the benefits received, but rather, the nonrecognition of mortality gain and mortality loss. * * *

Third, the exclusion of life insurance proceeds as a simple investment return is defensible only if premium payments constitute completed gifts. It can be argued further that a life insurance purchase should be treated as incomplete because the amount, timing, and existence of the insurance payoff are unknown until the death of the decedent. With such uncertainty, it is possible to leave the transaction "open" until the results can be measured accurately. * * * In the life insurance context there are, as we have seen, situations in which premium payments by the decedent should be treated as completed transfers. Thus, if the insurance proceeds on the decedent's life are included in the decedent's estate and the premiums that purchased the coverage have been treated as completed transfers, the includible amount should be reduced by the premiums attributable to the coverage. * * * Put differently, the premium payments can be viewed as independent savings deposits transferred to the insurance company to hold for payment to the owner of the policy upon the death of the insured, with an additional increment if the insured dies before his life expectancy. The insured's transfer tax base should include either the sum of the amounts transferred to the insurance company, or the amount paid out at death, but not both.

Proposal A avoids double counting by treating premium payments as incomplete transfers. This is an appealing, pragmatic approach to the problem. If it is adopted, however, premium payments attributable to policies that lapse before the decedent's death must be treated as completed transfers at the time the policies lapse. These premium payments are not like forfeited survivor benefits when the decedent never "owned" the forfeited property. Here, the insured actually parted with property *inter vivos* and, if it is abandoned (through lapse of the policy), the tax-free nature of the prior transfers must be corrected.

On balance, I believe there is a rational basis, in view of inherent valuation difficulties and the need to treat insurance policies funded entirely by the insured similarly to survivor benefits, to include insurance proceeds in the gross estate of the decedent-insured with a deduction for the premiums paid that have been treated as completed transfers. Moreover, this rule of inclusion should apply no matter who owns or procured the policy. What is the result if the decedent paid only some of the premiums? The problem may be illustrated by the following example. For purposes of illustration, assume that premium payments by the insured were not completed transfers. Suppose, prior to death, A paid premiums totalling $15,000 on a $100,000 term policy on A's life. B, the owner of the policy, paid $35,000 in premiums. Should the includible amount be the total proceeds less the premiums paid by B ($65,000), the proportion of the proceeds attributable to A's payments ($30,000), or some other amount? There is no sound justification for simply subtracting the premium payments made by B. Moreover, unless one can ascertain the portion of the proceeds purchased by each particular premium payment, proportional inclusion appears to be a sound solution.

The foregoing discussion has developed a conceptual rationale for a premium payments test, a form of which was once in the Code, only to be abandoned by Congress in 1954. I suggest that the premium payments test is analytically sound and that it should be enacted along with * * * "a conclusive presumption that consideration for the policy comes first out of donative transfers from the insured." This presumption will reduce tracing problems associated with a premium payments test.

In recommending the adoption of a premium payments test for inclusion of the proceeds of life insurance owned by third parties, and over which the insured does not possess an incident of ownership, I have rejected the suggestion that all insurance on the life of the decedent be included in the decedent's transfer tax base. Why should insurance proceeds ever be excluded from the insured's transfer tax base?

The issues one would consider in answering this question include one's view as to the nature of the transfer tax, discomfort with selecting the life insurance gamble for special treatment, and assessment of the simplification gains that would be achieved. A blanket rule of inclusion, adjusted to account for premiums paid (or deemed paid) by the decedent, is appealing at a number of levels. It would eliminate any abuse potential; appear relatively simple to administer; remain consistent at a result level with the treatment of survivor benefits; appear to compensate for some failures of the current income tax; and have a plausible, if not widely accepted, theoretical base. Nonetheless, I am reluctant to extend the transfer tax base this far.

First, I do not believe that the transfer tax should attempt to capture all value that exists simply because the decedent exists.[77] Rather, I believe it should attempt capture value that has been *created* by a decedent's services or investments. The premium payment rules developed above properly limit inclusion to proceeds attributable to the decedent's services or investment.

Second, I am unable to distinguish an insurance gamble from any other bet. To be sure, the "insurable interest" requirement restricts the availability of the bet on a decedent's life. This is, however, a question of *who* can play the game, not an issue of substance. Moreover, the fact that most noncommercial life insurance may be held by family members is not relevant to the question whether the proceeds should be included in the decedent's estate. It means only that family insurance transactions should be scrutinized carefully to assure that the insurance is not being used to make tax-free, what would otherwise be a taxable transfer.

Simplification objectives cut in the other direction. If all life insurance were included in the insured's estate, planning opportunities (and the associated transaction costs) would be eliminated and the statute could be simplified. It would, however, be necessary to permit, in addition to the reduction for premiums paid by the decedent that were treated as completed gifts, a reduction for premiums paid by the policy owner. This further adjustment prevents double counting when the owner paid all the premiums. There is no justification for including the owner's investment in the decedent's estate. This adjustment requires a tracing rule that will somewhat complicate the determination of the includible amount. The presumption, however, that consideration for the policy comes first from the donative transfers of the decedent could be applied here as well.

---

[77]   If the tax base is to include value that exists simply because the decedent exists, how should societal status and business contacts and opportunities be treated? Should these elements of value be included within the tax base? Most would, I think, agree that even if timing and valuation issues could be resolved at acceptable levels of administrative costs, these attributes are simply too intangible to be susceptible to a tax on wealth transfers.

Despite the simplification potential of a broad rule of includibility, I do not think it should be enacted. Rather, I recommend a premium payment test as suggested above, together with the retention of current section 2042(1) and some form of the incidents of ownership test.[80]

* * *

NOTE

Gutman notes that his discussion is limited to the "protection element" of life insurance, and indicates that any "investment elements" should, to the extent they can be identified and separated, be treated "the same as any other investment." Under Gutman's proposed premium-payments test, what amount would be includible in the gross estate of an insured who assigned a life insurance policy during life, assuming that all pre-assignment premiums were paid by the insured and all subsequent premiums were paid by the assignee? Recall that Gutman's proposal would require that the includible amount be reduced by any premium payments made by the insured that were subject to gift tax.

Ordinary life insurance may be viewed as a financial asset with three components: (1) term insurance, which covers the risk of the insured's death during the current premium-payment period; (2) a right to continue coverage at a fixed price; and (3) a terminal reserve, which represents an equity investment attributable to premium payments. *See* Douglas A. Kahn & Lawrence W. Waggoner, *Federal Taxation of the Assignment of Life Insurance*, 1977 DUKE L.J. 941, 943-46. Some commentators criticize the notion of proportional inclusion of life insurance proceeds under a premium-payments test, claiming that the effect would be "topsy-turvy" where the policy was assigned by the insured during life: "the greater the number of premiums paid by the insured, the greater the amount of reserve in the policy that should be excluded from his gross estate; yet under the premium payment test, each payment made by the insured prior to the assignment will increase the amount included in his gross estate." *Id.* at 973. Recall that Gutman recommends the adoption of a premium-payments test, coupled with an adjustment for any premium payments made by the insured that were subject to gift tax. Does Gutman's proposal answer the objections raised by Kahn and Waggoner?

The 1981 amendment to § 2035 made the three-year inclusionary rule inapplicable to most outright lifetime transfers. Section 2035, however, preserves the three-year rule for transfers of life insurance on the decedent's life. For discussions of the estate tax treatment of life insurance under existing law, see Harrison S. Lauer, *Estate Taxation of Life Insurance Transfers: The Impact of the Tax Reform Act of 1976 Still Ignored Twelve Years Later*, 41 TAX LAW. 683 (1988); Jeffrey G. Sherman, *Hairsplitting Under I.R.C. Section 2035(d): The Cause and the Cure*, 16 VA. TAX REV. 111 (1996).

---

[80]   The incidents of ownership test should be consistent with the completion rules * * * when the insured is the transferor of the policy; the test should also be consistent with the power of appointment rules when the insured possesses powers over a policy procured and owned by a third party. * * *

F.   Powers of Appointment

In a transfer tax system based on transfers of beneficial interests in property, powers of appointment pose special problems. In a 1939 exchange, Erwin N. Griswold argued that the estate and gift taxes should reach property subject to powers of appointment (including some nongeneral powers), and W. Barton Leach objected that such an approach would merely penalize legitimate property dispositions. The positions staked out by Griswold and Leach continue to define the broad terms of the debate over powers of appointment.

The treatment of powers of appointment has remained essentially unchanged since 1951. A power of appointment (held by a person other than the creator of the power) is normally subject to estate or gift tax only if it is "general"; and the statutory definition of general powers permits the holder to exercise considerable control over the underlying property without incurring estate or gift tax consequences. In formulating their respective reform proposals in the late 1960's, neither the ALI nor the Treasury Department recommended any change in the power-of-appointment provisions.

Those provisions have come up for reexamination in light of the introduction of the generation-skipping transfer (GST) tax in 1976 and its revision in 1986. (The GST tax is discussed in Part VI, *infra*.) The Treasury Department's 1984 proposals would rely primarily on the GST tax rather than the estate and gift taxes in dealing with powers of appointment. Joseph M. Dodge carries this line of reasoning to its logical conclusion and recommends repeal of the power-of-appointment provisions.

Erwin N. Griswold, *Powers of Appointment and the Federal Estate Tax*, 52 HARV. L. REV. 929 (1939)*

* * *

Is it desirable to make the statute applicable to special powers? It is submitted that in general, it is. * * *

The first consideration which suggests the extension of the tax to special powers is the very great facility for evasion and avoidance which is afforded by the statute in its present form. The definition of the term "general power" is not only the subject of recondite refinements, but it is in any event exceedingly narrow. Any power can very easily be made a special power without materially limiting the donee's freedom of choice. * * *

Moreover, even where the power is narrowly confined the special power remains a substantial factor in tax avoidance. By the use of special powers, and an astute application of the common-law Rule against Perpetuities, "a period of upwards of 100 years can be obtained during which . . . there is no new federal estate tax." * * *

Finally, we may well remember that a special power of appointment is what its name indicates, a power to control the enjoyment of property. Despite all the fictions of the past that the donee is just the arm through which the donor acts, the fact is clear that it is the donee who exercises the final control. That his control is not complete is not enough to make it necessary in fairness to lift the tax in all cases. The important fact is that he can alter the legal relationships

---

to property; the ultimate disposition of the property is projected until the time of his death; his act or failure to act is a substantial factor in the process of transmission from the dead to the living; it was he who "affected the course of the succession."

It will of course be objected that special powers of appointment are not mere tax avoidance devices, that they were in full use long before succession and estate taxes were ever heard of, and that they serve a socially useful and desirable purpose in introducing flexibility into family dispositions, and thus, to some extent, counteracting the unfortunately rigid consequences of the dead hand. Such an objection may in part be met by confession and avoidance. The most flexible of all dispositions is a transfer in fee, and it does not for that reason escape taxation when the donee dies. The same is true of a general power. The fact, of course, is that flexibility means projection of control, and termination of control is the chief basis for the imposition of an estate tax. If the testator desires the benefits of extension of control, it may be thought that his property should pay the price as in the case of other dispositions. So far as the estate tax finds its justification as a periodic imposition on the control and transmission of wealth it would seem in many cases to be justified here.

The question is purely one of policy, and there are arguments on both sides. * * * The estate tax is in effect a sort of periodic capital levy, with the periods largely determined by chance. They should not come too close together. This is recognized in the present provision of the law which exempts from the tax property which has previously been subjected to the tax * * * . On the other hand, anything which unduly prolongs the period with respect to any particular property is equally undesirable as long as the tax remains fully applicable to other property. The question, then, is whether the use of special powers makes it possible "unduly" to prolong the period during which there will be no tax. It might be argued that the tax should be imposed whenever property passes from a life tenant to a remainderman—a clear instance of transmission from the dead to the living. To date we have not thought it wise to impose such a tax, although the effect of this is to allow the tax-free transmission of property from one generation to the next. While there is no tax in this situation, it seems reasonable to say that the tax is not postponed "unduly" if it is not applied where there is a life estate followed by a power to appoint to a narrowly defined class, such as would normally take the remainder. It would therefore seem to be desirable to except from the operation of the tax certain special powers in situations where their tax-free use would not postpone the tax for a longer period than in the ordinary life tenant-remainder situation. The need for flexibility may thus be met, without unduly opening the door to tax avoidance, by imposing the tax on special powers generally, but excepting from this imposition any power which could be exercised only among the children of the donor or of the donee, and where the property, in default of appointment, is to be distributed among the class.[134] If such an exception as this is made, it should be provided that only the first exercise of a special power should be excepted, leaving the tax applicable in full to any property subject to delegated special power, and thus eliminating the possibility that through the use of special powers the tax might be avoided for a hundred years or more.

* * *

---

[134]   It might be thought that the exception should be broader or narrower than that indicated. The exception suggested would take care of most of the typical family power situations. The exception might be narrowed to the children of the donee, or, on the other hand, it might be extended to powers to appoint among not more than five, or perhaps ten, named persons. How broad the exception is to be is, of course, purely a question of legislative policy. It would seem, though, that it should not be broader than is necessary to harmonize the primary purpose of preventing tax avoidance with the conflicting desirability of maintaining the possibility of greater flexibility in family dispositions of property.

W. Barton Leach, *Powers of Appointment and the Federal Estate Tax—A Dissent*, 52 HARV. L. REV. 961 (1939)*

* * * I fear that Professor Griswold's attitude, if adopted by those responsible for federal estate tax legislation, would check a current tendency of testamentary draftsmen to use sensible and flexible powers of appointment and cause them to revert to the rigid type of remainders which have so often proved inadequate to meet changing and difficult family situations—all without any appreciable increase in the proceeds of the tax. I submit that a proposed tax which penalizes wise methods of disposition of family funds and tends to force unwise methods has a heavy burden of proof to sustain.

* * *

Professor Griswold asks the question, "Is it desirable to make the statute applicable to special powers?" And he answers, "It is submitted that in general, it is." To whatever extent this answer applies to honest-to-goodness special powers, as distinguished from tax-evasion fakes, this proposal seems to me iniquitous.

Let us take two testators, *A* and *B*. Each has a moderate estate, a wife and three children. Their wills are as follows:

(1) *A* leaves his property in trust for his widow for life, remainder to his children equally. This is a stupid provision from the point of view of the good of the family. Mrs. *A* may survive for years, even decades. The children who are now young will grow up with varying capacities and prospects. There is little to recommend an equal distribution among them predetermined as of *A*'s death.

(2) *B* leaves his property in trust for his widow for life, remainder to such of his children and in such proportions as his widow shall appoint. This is a wise provision. It is quite probable that by the time Mrs. *B* dies the children will have developed in such a way that she will be able to make a reasoned allocation of the property among them on the basis of need; and the special power of appointment allows her to do just this.

At the present time *A*'s and *B*'s estates are treated alike by the Federal Estate Tax. The property is computed as part of the assets of the estate of both *A* and *B*, but not as part of the assets of either of their wives. That is to say, a tax is assessed upon the death of each man but none upon the death of his wife. A tax on special powers would assess another tax on the death of Mrs. *B*, but none on the death of Mrs. *A*. Why? For two reasons: (1) because it is so hard to distinguish a special power from a general power * * * , and (2) because Mrs. *B*, "despite all the fictions of the past," has "affected the course of succession." * * * Let us examine these in order.

I suppose that anyone would concede that ninety-nine per cent of special powers that are created are honest-to-goodness special powers designed for no other purpose than the benefit of a small compact group of close relatives, usually children or grandchildren of the testator. If this, or anything like it, is conceded, I submit that the first reason given above is a trifle extravagant. We are asked to penalize a great majority of sensible, honest dispositions in order that a negligible minority of tax-evaders may not escape. Hardly, it would seem, the course of a wisdom that weighs other things than the desirability of plugging loopholes in the tax structure. But there is no necessity of letting the one per cent slip through. Professor Griswold and I and anyone else familiar with the field recognize the difference between an honest-to-goodness special power and a tax-evasion fake; so the problem is merely one of expression. One pos-

---

sible point of departure for solving this problem of expression is suggested by Professor Griswold * * * . Another might be found in a section drawn for the Restatement of Property by the present writer.[1]

Now to the second reason. There are several "fictions of the past" with relation to powers of appointment but the relationship between the donee of a special power (and I mean an honest-to-goodness special power) and the property subject thereto is not one of them. The donee does not own the property; his creditors cannot reach it; he cannot transfer it to anyone outside the scope of the power; he can derive no personal benefit from the exercise of the power, directly or indirectly. * * * The donee of a special power is in no sense, legal or practical, the owner of the property. He has no interest which he is transferring, legally or practically. To impose a tax where there is a life tenant with a special power is to say that such a person is analogous to an owner rather than to a simple life tenant; and, legally and factually, this is not true.[2]

* * * Professor Griswold suggests that from the proposed tax might be excepted powers to appoint among the children of the donor or the donee and powers where, in default of appointment, the property will go to the objects of the power. If this exception (somewhat amplified—e.g., to include spouse and issue of deceased children) is adopted, it will cover about 99 per cent of special powers; only the tax-evasion fakes will be left outside; and he and I will be in substantial agreement on the issue of special powers. But certainly the way to accomplish such a result would not be to draw a statute taxing all special powers and then excepting 99 per cent of them; the proper method would be to expand the definition of general powers so that it reaches oddities which are the creation only of the tax-lawyer's ingenuity and perform no useful dispositive function within the family.

A tax upon ordinary special powers puts a premium upon unwise family dispositions. Hence, I say, it is iniquitous. It is to the public interest as well as to the interest of those immediately concerned that family funds should be distributed according to need; and a tax which tends to thwart such distribution is prima facie unsound.

---

[1]   "A power is special . . . if (a) it can be exercised only in favor of persons, not including the donee, who constitute a group not unreasonably large, and (b) the donor does not manifest an intent to create or reserve the power primarily for the benefit of the donee." RESTATEMENT, PROPERTY, c. 26, *Powers of Appointment* (separately published, 1938) § 443(2).

[2]   Someone is going to say, "All right, then. Let's impose a tax when an ordinary remainderman succeeds a life tenant." There is a dark hint in Professor Griswold's paper that such a proposal may not be long in coming. * * * It is no matter to be examined in a mere footnote. However, it may be worth while to point out the probable practical consequences, first, of a tax on all special powers and, second, of the possible future suggestion as to life-tenant and remainderman:

(1) If a tax is imposed where there is a life estate with special power of appointment and none where there is a life estate with rigid remainder, the tendency will be to eliminate powers of appointment and cause rigid remainders to be adopted. Net result: No gain in federal revenue, but much loss in wise dispositions of family funds.

(2) If a tax is imposed both where there is a life estate with special power and where there is a life estate with rigid remainder, the tendency will be to eliminate all life estates and remainders. * * * Net result: No great gain in federal revenue, much loss in wisdom and flexibility of dispositions, and transfer of the business of trust companies to life insurance companies dealing in annuities.

Erwin N. Griswold, *In Reply*, 52 HARV. L. REV. 967 (1939)*

* * *

Professor Leach's chief distress is with respect to special powers. He says that the donee "does not own the property." If the estate tax is confined to ownership, the argument has validity. There seems room to contend, however, that one who has the "economic whiphand" over property may be the fit subject for a tax, even if he does not "own" it. But all of this seems quite beside the point. So far as the present discussion is concerned, Professor Leach's dissent is almost entirely a matter of tilting at windmills. For I have not contended that all special powers should be taxed. Nearly all of his argument is expressly directed to special powers of the narrow sort which I have said should not be taxed. The problem of expressing a statute which would draw the line between "an honest-to-goodness special power and a tax-evasion fake" is, I think, more difficult than he makes it out to be. Anyone familiar with tax problems can see the undesirability of a statute which puts it in terms of whether the power is in favor of a group "not unreasonably large." And it seems to come with small grace from one who has counseled the use of the power for tax avoidance to say that "ninety-nine per cent of special powers that are created are honest-to-goodness special powers" and that we should not "penalize a great majority of sensible, honest dispositions in order that a negligible minority of tax-evaders may not escape."

We are agreed that certain special powers should not be taxed, and that others should be. The way to reach that result is to make the statute applicable to all powers, and then to except the category of special powers narrow in scope, though perhaps large in number, where the tax avoidance possibility does not seem to outweigh the family utility of the power device.

NOTE

What sort of tax avoidance did Griswold have in mind when he proposed a broad inclusionary rule for powers of appointment coupled with an exception for "the category of special powers narrow in scope, though perhaps large in number, where the tax avoidance possibility does not seem to outweigh the family utility of the power device"? What is the functional difference between the criteria for taxability offered by Griswold and Leach, respectively? Is it as easy to distinguish an "honest-to-goodness special power" from a "tax-evasion fake" as Leach seemed to think?

The Griswold-Leach exchange occurred under pre-1942 law, when general powers were subject to estate tax only if exercised. For an exhaustive discussion of the background of the power-of-appointment provisions and the problems arising under pre-1951 law, see Louis Eisenstein, *Powers of Appointment and Estate Taxes*, 52 YALE L.J. 296 (part I), 494 (part II) (1943).

AMERICAN LAW INSTITUTE, FEDERAL ESTATE AND GIFT TAXATION (1969)*

* * *

Powers of appointment in a transfer that creates a succession of limited beneficial interests give a flexibility to the arrangement that permits adjustments to meet changed conditions. A rigid and inflexible plan of successive limited interests is likely to be inadequate to meet the conditions of the future under which it will operate. The present transfer tax law is quite liberal in the controls the owner of a limited interest can be given without causing him to be treated as the owner of the appointive assets for transfer tax purposes.

This liberality contributes to the generation-skipping problem * * * . But a tightening of the power-of-appointment rules to cause the powerholder to be treated as the owner of the appointive assets in more situations than at present would simply tend to drive property arrangements into the more rigid mold, if the more rigid mold avoided the burdens of transfer taxation. Therefore, the generation-skipping problem should not be resolved by drawing a different line than now exists in the power-of-appointment area. Rather, a solution should be adopted that applies equally to the rigid and nonrigid arrangements.

The power-of-appointment field has been the subject of extensive review and revisions by Congress on various occasions. It is not believed that a re-examination of the rules as to transfer taxation of powers would be fruitful. * * *

* * *

NOTE

Would Leach agree with the ALI recommendation?

U.S. TREASURY DEPARTMENT, TAX REFORM FOR FAIRNESS, SIMPLICITY, AND ECONOMIC GROWTH, REPORT TO THE PRESIDENT (1984)

* * *

Current Law

A decedent's gross estate includes all property with respect to which the decedent possessed a "general power of appointment" at the time of his or her death. For purposes of this rule, the term "general power of appointment" is defined as a power given the holder by another (rather than a power created by the holder) enabling the holder to appoint the property to the holder or the holder's estate or to creditors of either. The purpose of this rule is to include in a decedent's estate property with respect to which the decedent possessed virtually the same control as if the property were owned outright. Thus, a power will not be classified as a general power of appointment if it can be exercised only in conjunction with the creator of the power or in conjunction with a person having a "substantial interest" in the property that would be adversely affected by the exercise of the power of appointment. Moreover a power will not be classified as a general power of appointment if the ability to exercise the power is limited

---

by an "ascertainable standard" relating to the support, health, education, or maintenance of the holder.

Reasons for Change

The present rules governing general powers of appointment are largely ineffective. They can be circumvented easily by creation of a power that is purportedly limited by an ascertainable standard but that, in reality, gives the holder substantial discretion and control over the trust property.

In addition, present law can often trap the unwary taxpayer. For example, the general power of appointment rule may be invoked where neither the creator of the power nor the donee of the power is aware that a particular power is likely to be construed as a general power of appointment. To a great extent, this uncertainty exists because State law determines whether a limitation placed on the exercise of the power constitutes an "ascertainable standard." Thus, unless a standard is used that is identical with the language of the statute or the regulations, construction of the standard for Federal transfer tax purposes must generally await a construction of the language under State law.

Finally, the general power of appointment rule would in many cases be unnecessary if application of the generation-skipping tax would ensure that a transfer tax is collected at the decedent's generation. * * *

Proposal

The current power of appointment rules would be replaced by a rule treating an individual as the owner of property for transfer tax purposes where the individual possesses a non-lapsing right or power to vest the property or trust corpus in himself or herself. For purposes of this rule a power or right would be treated as nonlapsing if it did not, by its terms, expire prior to the death of the powerholder.

The release of such a power (or the extinguishment of such a power at death) would be treated in the same manner as a transfer by the outright owner of the underlying property. Thus, for example, if the holder of a power releases the power and retains an income interest in the property which would cause a gift of the property to be treated as incomplete, he or she would continue to be treated as the owner of the property for Federal transfer tax purposes.

* * *

NOTE

The "ascertainable standard" exception is subject to criticism on two counts: it undermines the effectiveness of the provisions that impose tax on general powers of appointment; and it is indeterminate in its application to many powers. Does the Treasury Department's proposal offer a satisfactory solution to the problems of ineffectiveness and uncertainty? For recent discussions, see Richard W. Harris, *Ascertainable Standard Restrictions on Trust Powers Under the Estate, Gift, and Income Tax*, 50 TAX LAW. 489 (1997); John G. Steinkamp, *Estate and Gift Taxation of Powers of Appointment Limited By Ascertainable Standards*, 79 MARQ. L. REV. 195 (1995).

The link between powers of appointment and generation-skipping trusts, noted in the Treasury Department's 1984 reform proposals, has prompted one commentator to suggest that the GST tax is better suited than the estate and gift taxes to deal with powers of appointment. *See* Amy Morris Hess, *The Federal Taxation of Nongeneral Pow-*

ers of Appointment, 52 TENN. L. REV. 395 (1985) (pointing out that "shifts in beneficial interest of the permissible objects of the power when the power is exercised or permitted to lapse" constitute taxable events under the GST tax). In light of the GST tax,
have the estate and gift tax provisions concerning powers of appointment become
obsolete?

Joseph M. Dodge, *Redoing the Estate and Gift Taxes Along Easy-to-Value Lines*, 43 TAX L. REV. 241 (1988)*

* * *

VII. POWERS OF APPOINTMENT

Under present § 2041, a decedent must include in her gross estate any property over which
she possessed, at the time of her death, a general power of appointment, either inter vivos or
testamentary, whether exercised or nonexercised. Moreover, the inter vivos exercise, release,
or lapse of a general power of appointment is a deemed transfer for gift tax purposes under
§ 2514, as well as for the "transfer" estate tax provisions. A "general" power held by a person
(the "donee" of the power) is one exercisable in favor of the donee, her estate, or the creditors
of either, but excludes any such power which is held jointly with the creator ("donor") of the
power or an adverse party, or which is limited by a standard relating to the donee's support,
maintenance, health, or education.

The main policy issue with respect to powers of appointment relates to the conceptual distinctions embodied in the current rules. The thesis developed below is that * * * any attempt
to draw a clear decisional line through the domain of powers of appointment is futile because
powers defy meaningful categorization. * * *

It is convenient to start with the assumption that the present law rule requiring inclusion
in the donee's gross estate of property subject to an unexercised general inter vivos power of
appointment is justified on the ground that the donee could have acquired the property during
life, and then proceed with an inquiry into the justification, if any, of the current rule that causes
inclusion in the donee's gross estate of property over which she possesses a general testamentary power of appointment. A general testamentary power is potentially distinguishable
from a general inter vivos power (which is also taxable) in that the donee of a testamentary
power is precluded from obtaining the property for her own benefit during life; on the face of
it, the best she can do is to control its devolution. At the same time, a general testamentary
power is hard to distinguish from a broadly phrased "special" (that is, nongeneral) power of
appointment exercisable in favor of anyone other than the donee's estate or its creditors,
which is presently not taxable. Proposals to extend the estate tax to reach certain special powers inevitably founder on deciding which ones should be taxable.[349] But, once it is decided to
subject special powers to taxation, there is no feasible basis for including some and excluding

---

    [349] *See* Griswold, *Powers of Appointment and the Federal Estate Tax*, 52 HARV. L. REV. 929
(1939); Leach, *Powers of Appointment and the Federal Estate Tax—A Dissent*, 52 HARV. L. REV. 961
(1939). * * * In general, it would seem that a power exercisable in favor of one's lineal descendants,
spouse, and parents is the most valuable type of special power and the best candidate for inclusion in the
category of taxable power.

others, except perhaps to require that the person possessing a taxable power also possess some beneficial interest.[350]

Perhaps the best rationale for the existing rule is that a testamentary power which can be exercised in favor of the donee's estate is available to the donee's creditors; therefore, the general testamentary power could have conferred lifetime economic benefits on the decedent, as is the case with an inter vivos general power. However, it actually does produce such a lifetime benefit only in those cases where it is in fact reached by the decedent's creditors. But, in general, the creditors of a decedent can reach the appointive property only if the testamentary power is exercised by the decedent.

The foregoing raises the issue of whether only exercised general powers should be taxed. If an inter vivos power is exercised in favor of the donee or her creditors, the donee's § 2033 gross estate will have been augmented, and in that case there will be no need for §§ 2041 and 2514. If an inter vivos general power, exercisable alone, is exercised in a non-trustee capacity in favor of a third party, the situation can be viewed as if the power had been exercised in favor of the donee, followed by a transfer to the third party for gift and estate tax purposes, that is, treated as a constructive transfer by the donee of the power. Such a result perhaps can be obtained under present * * * doctrine without reliance on § 2514, although it might be desirable to retain a modified version of § 2514 for the purpose of defining what is a general power for this purpose.[353] On the other hand, it can be argued that the donee of the power is merely the agent of the donor in fixing the ultimate destination of the donor's transfer. As far as case law is concerned, it might be possible to erect a distinction between a true constructive transfer, that is, one in which the property would have eventually been paid or distributed to the donee if the power had not been exercised, and a "pseudo" constructive transfer, that is, one where the property would have gone to another in default of the exercise of the power, which should not be treated as a transfer.[355] Ultimately, the issue here anticipates that with respect to unexercised inter vivos powers, namely, whether property should be attributed to one who never actually owned the property and never would have owned it unless the power had been exercised. In any event, the constructive transfer theory does not justify taxing the exercise of a general testamentary power except (again) to the extent that the creditors of the donee actually obtained the property (because only to that extent has the donee enjoyed the property). With respect to the appointive property which is not obtained by the donee's creditors, the exercise of the testamentary general power has the same effect as the exercise of a testamentary special power. Under state law, the donee's creditors are likely to be able to obtain the appointive property only where the appointive property is security for a debt of the deceased donee or the probate estate is insolvent. A rule limiting inclusion in the gross estate only to the extent the property is reached by the donee's creditors could take the form of an amendment to § 2033. A broader rule that would look to the maximum extent that the creditor could have reached the property possesses a certain logical appeal, but it would be hard to administer and would operate as a trap for the unwary, since knowledgeable estate practitioners would simply avoid drafting general testamentary powers.[359]

---

[350]   * * * Of course, one must then define what constitutes an "interest" for this purpose.

[353]   The definition of general power would exclude any power exercisable in a trusteeship capacity or held jointly with another party * * * .

[355]   Present transfer tax case law probably does not support this distinction. * * *

[359]   The principal reason under present tax law to create such a power is to qualify for the marital deduction under the power-of-appintment exception to the terminable interest rule. * * * This option, however, has been largely rendered superfluous by the QTIP exception to the terminable interest rule. * * *

The foregoing ultimately calls into question the starting point, that is, whether unexercised inter vivos powers should cause the subject property to be included in the donee's gross estate. Unlike a retained power to revoke, where a hard-to-complete rule is necessary to value the amounts actually transferred, no valuation-of-transfer rationale supports the posture of § 2041. * * * In the power-of-appointment situation, the takers in default may well be among the natural objects of the donee's bounty, so that it might make sense not to exercise the power at all. It might be contended, on this basis, that a nonexercised power of appointment constitutes a "constructive" transfer, effective at the donee's death, from the donee to the takers in default. But this argument proves only that the failure to exercise a lifetime power should be subject to the same rules as are applicable to the exercise of a general testamentary power, that is, the property should not be taxed except to the extent it ends up in the hands of the donee's creditors (or the donee personally). In any event, there are alternative possible explanations for failing to exercise the power: The donee might not know about the power or the extent of the property involved; the donee may not feel it is appropriate to exercise it because the property was never hers; the donee may not care enough to exercise it; and the donee may procrastinate or effect a defective exercise. A rule of taxation of such import should not be based on the elusive, and possibly self-serving, state of mind of a dead person. In sum, the taxation of unexercised inter vivos powers can hardly be said to be an essential feature of an estate tax. In the last analysis, the estate tax should not be imposed on a person with respect to property (not transferred by herself) which she might have owned but did not. A fortiori, the gift tax should not be imposed upon the exercise of a general inter vivos power in favor of a third party.

Tentatively, then, a reasonable theoretical case can be made for the repeal of §§ 2041 and 2514. With repeal, the exercise of a general inter vivos power in favor of the donee or her creditors will augment the donee's potential § 2033 gross estate; unexercised powers, and powers exercised in favor of anyone other than the donee personally, would be taxed, under an amendment to § 2033, only to the extent that the appointive property is in fact reached by the donee's creditors or the creditors of her estate.

Practical considerations decisively tip the scales in favor of repealing §§ 2041 and 2514. With their repeal, the distinction between general and special powers of appointment would no longer possess any relevance. The definition of general power under current law is unsatisfactory insofar as it exempts a power to withdraw corpus limited by standards relating to "support," "maintenance," "health," and "education." In practice, the "standards" exception has the effect of making the incidence of § 2041 elective among the cognoscenti, meaning also that it can be a trap for the ignoranti. Nor does it necessarily impose a meaningful limit on the amount that can be withdrawn by the donee. Of course, the standards exception could be repealed, but other means of avoidance would be used, such as naming the spouse, close friend, or close relative of the beneficiary as trustee, and giving such trustee an unlimited discretionary power to invade corpus for the beneficiary, or naming the beneficiary and a nominal adverse party as cotrustees. Indeed, any attempt to "clean up" the definition of general power is likely to be futile, since knowledgeable planners will simply avoid using general powers. * * *

It is conceded that many of the arguments made above—which mostly pertain to the absence of any persuasive rationale for existing or possible distinctions among various types of powers of appointment—might be equally made in favor of taxing the expiration and exercise (etc.) of all powers of appointment. Nevertheless, such is not the case for the bottom line argument, namely, that the estate and gift taxes are taxes on transfers by a decedent or donor, and a person should not be deemed to have owned (and transferred) property just because she could have owned it or appointed it to her estate. If there were no generation-skipping tax, then it might be persuasively argued that the failure to tax powers of appointment would open up a significant loophole. But a failure to tax property by reason of the termination (etc.) of powers of appointment is no worse than a failure to tax property by reason of the termination (etc.) of interests in such property. It is just this type of situation that a generation-skipping tax is designed to reach. Since powers of appointment exist in the context of successive interest trusts, a properly designed generation-skipping tax can do double duty, as it were. Thus, the expiration and exercise (etc.) of powers of appointment, general and special, should trigger a generation-skipping tax, on the same basis as the termination (etc.) of interests. To a major extent, such was the case with the 1976 generation-skipping tax, which was retroactively repealed in 1986 and replaced by a new generation-skipping tax.

However, the 1986 generation-skipping tax apparently moved in exactly the opposite direction by defining "interest" to exclude any power of appointment other than an inter vivos general power. Thus, the termination of a general testamentary power or a special power cannot per se trigger the tax. Of course, if the donee of the excluded power also possessed an "interest," the termination of the power might well coincide with a taxable "interest" termination. Also, the exercise of an excluded power might produce a taxable transfer by terminating an existing interest or triggering a taxable distribution. Finally, a generation-skipping transfer could occur with respect to permissible appointees under an exempt inter vivos special power by reason of their death, or the termination, release, or lapse of the power.

* * *

* * * [T]he fact that the definition of "interest" under the generation-skipping tax includes any general inter vivos power of appointment, without exception by reference to fiduciary standards or co-holders of the power, combined with the ability of the generation-skipping tax to directly or indirectly reach most situations involving special powers of appointment, cements the case for repealing §§ 2041 and 2514. * * *

* * *

NOTE

Dodge argues that "a person should not be deemed to have owned (and transferred) property just because she could have owned it or appointed it to her estate." Why? What justification might there be for retaining the power-of-appointment provisions of existing law?

PART IV:

MARITAL AND CHARITABLE DEDUCTIONS

This Part explores the marital and charitable deductions, which raise issues common to both the gift tax and the estate tax. Under current law, there are no quantitative limitations on the amount of property that can qualify for a marital or charitable deduction, but both deductions are conditioned on compliance with detailed qualitative restrictions concerning the form of the transfer.

A.   Marital Deduction

Transfers between spouses raise special estate and gift tax concerns. Until 1948, when the marital deduction was first introduced, interspousal transfers were fully taxable except to the extent covered by the annual exclusion or made in exchange for money's-worth consideration. The original marital deduction was subject to quantitative and qualitative restrictions reflecting its intended function of equalizing the tax treatment of married couples in community property and noncommunity property states. The scope of the marital deduction was dramatically expanded by the Economic Recovery Tax Act of 1981, which removed the 50 percent ceiling and added the "qualified terminable interest property" (QTIP) provisions. As a result, the marital deduction now shields potentially unlimited amounts of interspousal transfers in qualifying form from estate and gift taxes. The expansion of the marital deduction has also led to renewed scrutiny of its technical provisions and policy underpinnings.

1. Origins of the Unlimited Marital Deduction

Early proposals for abandoning the 50 percent ceiling and relaxing the terminable interest rule emerged from separate studies conducted by the ALI and the Treasury Department; both were published in 1969. The Treasury proposal for an unlimited marital deduction drew a critical response from commentators such as David Westfall, who argue that the problems of the original legislation could be cured by less drastic measures. In response, Jerome Kurtz and Stanley S. Surrey point out that the Treasury proposal would permit property to pass from a decedent to the surviving spouse for life with remainder to the couple's children, at the cost of a single transfer tax. Although the ALI and Treasury proposals were not enacted in 1969, they offer valuable insights into the statutory approach adopted by Congress in 1981.

AMERICAN LAW INSTITUTE, FEDERAL ESTATE AND GIFT TAXATION (1969)*

* * *

The marital deduction has now been with us since 1948. It was originally adopted in an effort to bring about greater equality in the operation of the gift and estate tax laws in community property states and non-community property states. In view of the fact that community property is divided between husband and wife on a 50-50 basis, the marital deduction was limited to about 50% of the donor spouse's estate. More precisely, the gift tax marital deduction is 50% of each gift from one spouse to the other, and the maximum estate tax marital deduction is 50% of the deceased spouse's adjusted gross estate. We will refer to the present rules as "the 50% marital deduction."

The interest of each spouse in community property is ordinarily the equivalent of outright ownership, subject to the managerial control of the community property that may be vested in one of the spouses. In particular, a spouse's interest in community property does not ordinarily terminate on death. Thus, the so-called terminable-interest rule was developed under which transfer to a spouse of certain terminable interests do not qualify for the 50% marital deduction. In other words, generally speaking, the donee spouse must receive an interest somewhat equivalent to outright ownership, for the gift to her to qualify for the marital deduction. The technical requirements to qualify an interest other than outright ownership for the marital deduction are fairly complex, and some of the courts have taken a highly technical approach to these requirements, with the result that many good faith efforts to meet the legal requirements have failed.

In community property states, the marital deduction is not available unless one or the other of the spouses owns some separate property. * * *

1. 100% Marital Deduction

Dissatisfaction with the 50% limit on the marital deduction stems from these concerns: First, it does not achieve complete equality of tax treatment as between community and non-community property states because the marital deduction for lifetime transfers is limited to 50% of the value of each gift to the donee spouse;[18] Second, it still results in the imposition of a transfer tax on the movement of property from spouse to spouse and forces them into an unnatural record-keeping of interspousal transfers if the law is to be complied with; Third, frequently the tax that has to be paid as a result of an interspousal transfer comes at the death of a spouse, a time when significant sources of income may disappear, and hence not a time when a further economic adjustment should be required to pay taxes on the transfer; Fourth, very complex dispositions are necessary to give the surviving spouse on the donor spouse's death the exact 50% that is the maximum marital deduction; and Fifth, in smaller estates, the 50% marital deduction is frequently inadequate to provide the surviving spouse with an adequate tax-free amount.

A 100% marital deduction with no disqualification of community property would eliminate all the concerns mentioned in regard to the 50% marital deduction and bring to full fruition from a tax standpoint the often expressed attitude of husband and wife that the property is "ours" without regard to the technical legal ownership requirements.

---

[18]   Under community property laws half a husband's accumulated earnings, for example, will become his wife's without any taxable transfer, and will thus be removed from his taxable estate even if the wife is the first to die. In a common law state the husband would be left with all the accumulated earnings taxable in his estate, if he survives, unless he had made gifts to his wife before her death.

2. Current Beneficial Enjoyment Test

It is proposed that any transfer (whether the property transferred is community property or separate property) which provides the donee spouse with the current beneficial enjoyment of the property should qualify for the marital deduction to the extent of the full value of the property. In the case of income-producing property, current beneficial enjoyment means the right to receive the income. Thus, a transfer to T in trust with directions to pay the income to the donor's wife for life, with remainder over to designated beneficiaries and with no power in the wife to change the destination of the property on her death would qualify for the marital deduction under the current-beneficial-enjoyment test. This type of trust can be used where the donor spouse wants to protect his children from being left out as a result, for example, of the second marriage of his spouse.

The introduction of the current-beneficial-enjoyment test and the accompanying elimination of the terminable-interest rule might be said to give the common law states some advantage over the community property states, in that in the latter the surviving spouse will end up owning outright, with full control, one half of the community property, whereas in a common law state the same tax benefit can be produced by giving the surviving spouse only a life interest. This is true, but even in a community property state the deceased spouse's half of the community property could also be qualified for the marital deduction by giving the surviving spouse only a life interest therein. Moreover, it would be possible in a community property state, if one spouse can transfer his share of the community property to the other, for a spouse to transfer his share of the community property to the other spouse without any transfer tax cost and then the receiving spouse could deal with the entire property in the same way as in a common law state.

If terminable interests qualify for the marital deduction, then a transfer would be considered to be made by the donee spouse whenever the current beneficial enjoyment ceases. This will be on her death, if she is given a life interest, but may be prior to her death if she is given a current interest until she remarries or for some stated period of time. The property she is treated as transferring on the termination of her current beneficial enjoyment may pass to predetermined beneficiaries. It would not be fair to her to subject her other assets to the payment of the tax assessed on this imputed transfer. Furthermore, the tax on this transfer should be at the top rate for the taxable period involved, so that the tax on other assets transferred by her in such period is not higher than it otherwise would be. So far as deathtime transfers are concerned, this will mean the imputed transfers will always be taxed at the donee spouse's ultimate top rate. So far as lifetime transfers are concerned, however, an imputed transfer in one taxable period, though at the top rate for that period, would affect the beginning rate applicable to transfers in a future period, unless some special rule is adopted to cover this situation. In the usual case, the imputed transfer will not occur prior to death. In the instances where it does, one possibility would be to tax the imputed transfer at what would be the top rate if all the property then owned by the wife were transferred, and to ignore the value of the imputed transfer in determining the rate at which other transfers are taxed.

3. Election as to Time of Imposition of Tax

Under the present marital deduction, there is no election available to pay the tax on a qualified marital deduction gift at the time of the transfer and eliminate from transfer taxation the movement of the beneficial enjoyment out of the donee spouse. Somewhat the same end may be accomplished by giving the donee spouse a benefit that does not qualify for the marital deduction and under which she will not be regarded as the owner for transfer tax purposes. If a change is made to a current-beneficial-enjoyment test, the area of qualified marital deduction gifts will expand tremendously. An election should therefore be given to treat a qualified marital deduction gift as subject to the transfer tax at the time it is made, with provision that no transfer tax would then be imposed on the termination of the donee spouse's current beneficial enjoyment. This would mean that if the entire current benefit were conferred on the donee spouse in the form of a life interest, one half could be taxed at the donor spouse's death and the other half at the donee spouse's death (or any other fractional division), if that appeared desirable in the particular case. Also, the donee spouse could be given the outright ownership of property and an election made to pay a tax thereon (or on some part) at the time of the donor spouse's transfer and, if the property on which the tax had been paid could be traced, no tax would be payable on its transfer by the donee spouse.

* * *

NOTE

Did the original marital deduction accomplish its stated purpose of equalizing the tax treatment of married couples in community property and noncommunity property states? For a discussion of the background and rationale of the 1948 legislation, see Adrian W. DeWind, *The Approaching Crisis in Federal Estate and Gift Taxation*, 38 CAL. L. REV. 79 (1950); Stanley S. Surrey, *Federal Taxation of the Family—The Revenue Act of 1948*, 61 HARV. L. REV. 1097 (1948).

U.S. TREASURY DEPARTMENT, TAX REFORM STUDIES AND PROPOSALS, 91st Cong., 1st Sess. (1969)

* * *

Under present law, a special deduction is permitted both for estate and gift tax purposes for transfers of property from one spouse to another. This deduction is commonly referred to as the "marital deduction." However, there are limitations on the amount of the deduction which may be claimed; in the case of the gift tax the deduction may not exceed one-half of the amount transferred, and [in] the case of the estate tax the deduction is limited to one-half of the adjusted gross estate. Thus, generally, one spouse may transfer up to one-half of his property to the other spouse free of tax.

In order for a transfer from one spouse to another to qualify for the marital deduction under present law, several tests must be met. On a transfer at death, the property must be transferred directly from the decedent to his surviving spouse; the value of the property must be included in the decedent's taxable estate; and she must be given outright ownership (or its equivalent) over the property. These rules have curtailed the use of some natural forms of transfers between spouses. For example, a transfer of property from a husband to his wife with income payable to her for life, and upon her death all remaining property to their children, does not qualify for the marital deduction and is taxed in the husband's estate. In addition, because the deduction is limited to 50 percent of the adjusted gross estate, highly complex drafting arrangements have developed and are used in many estates to insure that no more property than the exact amount needed to utilize the marital deduction passes to the surviving spouse. The result of overqualifying is to leave property in a way in which it is taxable in the surviving spouse's estate without a corresponding deduction in the first decedent's estate. * * *

It does not appear * * * that transfers of property between husband and wife are appropriate occasions for imposing tax. An especially difficult burden may be imposed by the tax when property passes to a widow, particularly if there are minor children. The present system of taxing transfers between spouses does not accord with the common understanding of most husbands and wives that the property they have accumulated is "ours." Furthermore, the distinctions drawn by existing law between transfers which qualify for the marital deduction and those which do not qualify have generated drafting complexities, artificial limitations upon dispositions, and considerable litigation.

In order to reduce the tax burden in the case of small- and medium-sized estates, where the property on the death of the husband must usually provide for the widow and children, to provide flexibility in the planning of transfers between spouses and to reduce complexity, it is proposed that—

> the present 50-percent limitation should be removed entirely and replaced by an unlimited marital deduction to permit almost all transfers of property between spouses to be tax free;
>
> present restrictions upon the types of interests which qualify for the marital deduction should be liberalized;
>
> spouses should be given the power to determine the extent to which they wish the marital deduction to apply and, thus, the extent to which the transferred property will be subject to tax upon subsequent disposition by the transferee spouse.

Under the unified transfer tax there will be an exemption from taxation for the full amount of any property that passes to a spouse, either during the life of the transferor spouse or at his or her death. However, property received by the transferee spouse will, of course, become part of his or her taxable estate, unless consumed.

The proposals for modifying the marital deduction rules will benefit a number of family situations:

(1) The most important case is the one in which it is expected that the surviving spouse will consume part of the capital which she inherits to provide for herself and the children. This would ordinarily be expected where the estate is modest in size or where the widow will face heavy financial demands for educating the children.

In these cases the first spouse to die (typically the husband) leaves his entire estate outright to the spouse. Under present law, only half is deductible, and any part of the estate left at the wife's death is fully taxable when it is left to the children on her death. In effect, the estate is taxed twice, as it passes down to the children. Typically, this does not happen however in very large estates because the husband can be certain that his spouse will not need all of the estate. Thus, he can leave outright to the wife only an amount that will qualify for the marital deduction; and he can give the remainder either directly to the children or in a trust which will not be taxable on the wife's death. Thus, in the estates of wealthy married decedents it is generally possible, under present law, to arrange things so that the family estate is only taxed once as it goes to the children. The unlimited marital deduction will make this result possible even where the husband now has to encounter a double tax because the wife may need the funds.

* * *

(2) The proposal for the unlimited marital deduction, as it applies to the gift tax, will be of advantage where the poorer spouse dies first. Under present law, the minimum tax is paid if the estate is split equally between husband and wife for tax purposes by, for example, tak-

ing a 50-percent marital deduction on the estate of the first to die, paying tax on half, and then paying tax on the other half at the death of the survivor. * * *

This tax saving is lost (except in a community property State) if the poorer spouse dies first. It could be preserved by giving half the property to the poorer spouse during life but under present law the gift tax marital deduction (which is limited to half of the actual gift to the spouse) would involve a tax penalty at the time of gift. The proposal would permit a married couple to so arrange their property holdings that there would be no tax penalty arising from the order of their death. This would also remove an undesirable discrimination between common law and community property States because there is already an unlimited exemption from interspousal "transfers" resulting from creation of community rights.

(3) Another benefit of the proposal arises from the extension of the deduction to all life interests given to the spouse. Under present law, if property is left so that the income of the property goes to the spouse the bequest only qualifies for the marital deduction if the spouse has such control over the property underlying her income interest that it can be considered her property (and taxable at her death). A husband may want to leave the income from his property to his wife but make sure that the property goes on her death to the children. Ordinarily this would imply that the wife has no control over the underlying property and thus the bequest would not qualify under present law for the marital deduction. It is not of significant concern, however, to the Federal Government whether the husband or the wife makes the decision as to who gets the property ultimately. The substance of the proposal therefore is to let an income interest to the surviving spouse qualify for the marital deduction whether or not the spouse controls the underlying property so long as it is agreed that the property will be taxed on the death of the spouse.

In substance, the proposal is designed to provide that property of a married couple will be taxed once as it passes to the next generation, not twice. * * *

* * *

NOTE

If the Treasury's marital deduction proposal is aimed at estates of moderate size where the decedent's property is needed to provide for the surviving spouse and children, why is the deduction not limited in size or conditioned on the existence of surviving dependents? Does the Treasury's proposal place any restrictions on the ultimate disposition of property qualifying for the marital deduction?

The original marital deduction was allowed only if the surviving spouse received "outright ownership (or its equivalent)." Why is it no longer of "significant concern" to the federal government whether the surviving spouse controls the ultimate disposition of the transferred property? Should the marital deduction be designed to facilitate "natural" forms of interspousal transfers? Is it currently so designed?

David Westfall, *Revitalizing the Federal Estate and Gift Taxes*, 83 HARV. L. REV. 986 (1970)*

* * *

II. THE MARITAL DEDUCTION AND GIFT-SPLITTING

The Treasury's proposed revisions of the marital deduction and gift-splitting purportedly:

> reduce the tax burden in the case of small- and medium-sized estates . . . provide flexibility in the planning of transfers between spouses and . . . reduce complexity . . . .

These goals are hardly more controversial than Motherhood and the Flag. The same cannot be said of all of the methods by which the Treasury would pursue them * * * .

A. Removal of Percentage Limitations and Unlimited Gift-Splitting

* * * In support of its unlimited estate tax marital deduction, the Treasury paints a dire picture of the impact of the present fifty percent limitation "where the estate is modest in size or where the widow will face heavy financial demands for educating the children." In such cases, we are told, the husband is typically the first to die and "leaves his estate outright to the spouse." Thus, half is taxed on the husband's death, and a second tax is imposed on whatever remains when the widow dies. Such evocative imagery runs counter to substance in two main respects.

First, the Treasury's unusual view of what constitutes a smaller estate is illustrated clearly in the text of its proposals * * * . Even in an age of affluence, to call an estate of $499,999 "smaller" is surprising. * * *

Second, whatever may have been the practice for wills drawn prior to 1959, it is common practice today to avoid a second tax on the full value of whatever remains when the widow dies. * * * The mechanics are familiar to nearly every lawyer who drafts wills. The wife is given the maximum amount allowable under the marital deduction, either outright or in a trust which meets the statutory requirements, and the balance is placed in a separate trust, usually referred to as the "nonmarital" trust. Contrary to the Treasury's view, the decedent can give the trustee or the widow herself power to use the principal of the nonmarital trust, if it is needed for the support of the widow or her children, without causing the remainder to be taxed in the widow's estate at her death.[63] * * *

If special consideration is due widows who have responsibilities to minor children or who receive smaller estates, an *unlimited* marital deduction is a clumsy tool for the task. It would benefit as well the childless widow who receives a $20 million estate, freeing her from the $6 million tax she now pays. Such largesse hardly finds justification on the basis of need. Rather, tax hardships for widows could be avoided by removing the present fifty percent limitation for the part of the estate below a fixed dollar level. For example, instead of a uniform fifty percent limitation, the ceiling could be one hundred percent of the first $100,000 in the adjusted

---

[63]   Two popular ways to achieve this result include: (1) giving a trustee who has no beneficial interest the power to distribute principal and income among members of a group consisting of the widow and descendants of the deceased; or (2) giving the widow the income from a trust and a power to withdraw principal for her benefit which is so limited as to be outside the scope of section 2041(b)(1)(A) and thus not taxable in her estate when she dies. * * *

gross estate and fifty percent of the excess. If additional relief is required for minor children, this should be achieved through added exemptions for them.

Part of the potential estate tax revenue that is lost as a result of an unlimited marital deduction will merely be postponed until the death of the surviving spouse (or the termination of her interest during her life), but part will be lost altogether. One of the factors commonly considered in determining whether or not to take full advantage of the present fifty percent deduction is the possibility that the surviving spouse may be able to reduce her estate significantly by tax free gifts under the annual exclusion. * * *

* * *

The Treasury also proposes the unlimited deduction to remove the current discrimination in the federal estate and gift tax against spouses in noncommunity property states. The tax on a $1 million estate is larger than the tax on two estates of $500,000 each. Consider a family in which the husband has accumulated property totaling $1 million and the wife, who has no property, dies first. If the husband and wife live in a community property state and the husband's accumulations consist entirely of community property, the property will be divided by operation of law without payment of any gift tax, and each spouse will have an estate of $500,000. In a noncommunity property state the husband will lose all chance to split his estate unless he remarries. Moreover, if the husband seeks to take advantage of estate-splitting before his wife dies, he may only be able to divide his estate before her death at the expense of incurring a substantial gift tax. For this reason the Treasury favors the unlimited gift tax deduction. But * * * there is an alternative method for removing this discrimination.

* * *

* * * [A]s the Treasury proposes, the survivor should be permitted to treat the transfer of any portion of the decedent's estate as a transfer by her, thus permitting an equalization of estates for transfer tax purposes if the richer spouse dies first. To cover cases in which the poorer spouse dies first and to eliminate the particular discrimination discussed above, gift-splitting should be extended to transfers by the surviving spouse during some limited period, such as six months, after the death of the first spouse.

Obviously, the details of any such extension of gift-splitting to transfers after the death of a spouse remain to be worked out. * * * The important consequence of the extension of gift-splitting just described would be to eliminate the present estate-splitting advantage of community property spouses and thus to provide greater geographic uniformity in the application of the estate tax without necessitating an unlimited gift tax marital deduction.

B. The Terminable Interest Rule and Waiver of the Marital Deduction

* * * The most significant practical consequence of the [terminable interest] rule is disqualification of a life estate unless the spouse is given the right to receive "all the income" and a general power to appoint the principal within the terms of the statutory exception to the general rule. Although a terminable interest coupled with the requisite power of appointment will qualify for the marital deduction, the property subject to the power at the death of the surviving spouse will be taxable in her estate.

The Treasury proposes modification of this scheme to allow any income interest bequeathed to the wife to qualify for the marital deduction if the wife agrees to treat the termination of her interest as a taxable transfer by her. This proposal, a response to the frequent litigation stemming from interpretive problems in the present rule and its exception, is a desirable reform which is fully in keeping with the purpose of the rule. * * * Since the modifications remove the problem whether the proper power of appointment has been given or whether the interest is subject to termination on the occurrence of a contingency, the logical expectation is a reduction in controversy.

* * *

NOTE

Westfall criticizes the abandonment of the 50 percent ceiling, but he accepts the modification of the terminable interest rule. Is the proposed modification of the terminable interest rule "fully in keeping" with the purpose of the rule?

Westfall argues that an unlimited marital deduction is a "clumsy tool" to provide relief for a decedent's surviving dependents; he suggests a special exemption for transfers to minor children. The Treasury proposal contained a similar proposal for an "orphan's deduction," which was enacted in 1976 and repealed in 1981. See former § 2057.

Jerome Kurtz & Stanley S. Surrey, *Reform of Death and Gift Taxes: The 1969 Treasury Proposals, the Criticisms, and a Rebuttal*, 70 COLUM. L. REV. 1365 (1970)*

* * *

* * * Under the proposals, the existing 50% ceiling on the marital deduction would be eliminated and a deduction would be allowed for the full amount transferred to a spouse up to the full value of the estate. Lifetime transfers between spouses would also be completely free of tax. Because all transfers between spouses would be free of tax, any gift by either spouse to a third person could be treated as made by either spouse for purposes of calculating the tax. Such gifts could be treated as made equally by each spouse, or unequally, or treated as made entirely by either one or the other.

Another aspect of this proposal would be the expansion of the kinds of transfers which qualify for the marital deduction. Instead of requiring that the transfer be outright to the spouse or that the spouse have a life estate coupled with a general power of appointment as under present law, any transfer of the present ownership, enjoyment, use, or income to a spouse would qualify for the marital deduction so long as the transferor's spouse consents to having the eventual termination of that interest treated as a taxable transfer. Where the transferor's spouse has less than complete power of disposition or control of the property, the tax imposed on termination of the spouse's interest would be collectible only out of the property itself and would not be a personal liability of the spouse.

Furthermore, an election would be given to permit any transfers which qualify for the marital deduction to be taxed at the time of the transfer. If exercised, this election would eliminate taxation upon the termination of the spouse's interest in the property. In this way, the transferor or his personal representative may regulate the amount includible in each estate and thereby achieve whatever saving might be available by dividing the taxation of the transfer between two

---

*   This article originally appeared at 70 COLUM. L. REV. 1365 (1970). Reprinted by permission.

estates, even though all of the property is left in a way which would otherwise qualify for the marital deduction.

* * *

* * * [A]t least one commentator has objected to the proposal on the ground that the suggested broadening of the marital deduction would strongly influence decedents to leave property to their spouses at the expense of their children.

Viewing the marital deduction as a whole, this assertion appears to be wrong. While not enough is known to state with certainty what decedents are now doing, and while predictions of individual response to changed rules always involve conjecture to some extent, the experience of lawyers dealing with estate plans would, it seems, bear out exactly the reverse of what is asserted. That is, the proposals would seem to give less incentive, rather than more, to leave property to spouses. Under existing law, property left to a spouse will qualify for the marital deduction only if the wife has the power to dispose of the corpus of the property in any way she chooses, while under the proposed revisions gifts or bequests to a spouse would qualify for the marital deduction as long as the surviving spouse has the income interest. Therefore, a testator can get the full benefit of the marital deduction without the necessity, which exists under present law, of making the equivalent of an outright transfer to his spouse.

If the argument goes to the matter of the income interest, it presents a somewhat different question. In that connection the argument would be that the availability of the 100% marital deduction would induce testators to give their spouses all of the income from their property, and that this inducement may be undesirable, regardless of the fact that the surviving spouse need not be given control over the remainder. However, in smaller and medium size estates it is common today for testators to give the income from all of their property to their spouses even though only half of the bequest qualifies for the marital deduction. It would appear that the amount of income given to a spouse depends primarily on the testator's appraisal of her needs rather than on the availability of the marital deduction.

Those situations today where a testator would usually not leave an entire income interest to his spouse involve primarily large estates where it is unlikely that the surviving spouse will need more than half the income. In those estates, the availability of the unlimited marital deduction means very little. One must keep in mind that, while the use of a 100% marital deduction could eliminate taxes entirely upon the death of the first spouse to die, the price of such deduction is to place more property in the estate of the surviving spouse. Where the estate is large this would result in the ultimate tax burden being greater, because the advantage of splitting the estate into two parts to be taxed under two separate rate schedules is foregone. The estate tax on two estates of $5,000,000 each is considerably less than the tax on one estate of $10,000,000. Therefore, where the estate is of such a size that payment of tax on the death of the first spouse is unlikely to cause any hardship to the surviving spouse, and where the surviving spouse is unlikely to consume more than half of the estate, there would be significant tax savings by not using the full 100% marital deduction but electing instead to split the estate between the spouses, as is permitted under the proposal.

In balance, then, it would seem that the desire to use the full marital deduction would be greatest in the case of the smaller estates where the saving from splitting the estate is not significant and where there is some likelihood of the surviving spouse consuming over half of the principal. These are the estates where today surviving spouses frequently receive the income from more than half the estate. In large estates, the saving from splitting the estate would seem more important than a deferral of tax on the death of the first spouse to die. Therefore, it appears unlikely that the allowance of a full marital deduction would significantly change existing dispositive patterns so far as the income interests are concerned and would result primarily in tax deferral in those families where more than half the income interest is presently left to the surviving spouse (and also tax reduction compared with existing law if the spouse consumes more than the marital deduction presently allowable).

Another objection made to the marital deduction proposal is that it would lose revenue to married decedents and that if any revenue is to be lost it should be given to married and unmarried decedents alike. The increase in the marital deduction from 50% to 100% would reduce taxes in two cases. First, taxes would be reduced where, under present law, property of the first spouse to die is taxed both in his estate and in the estate of his surviving spouse—those cases where property is left to the surviving spouse in excess of that now qualifying for the marital deduction but where none of the excess property is consumed by the surviving spouse. Second, a reduction in taxes would occur in those cases where the surviving spouse does consume more than the presently allowable marital deduction. Under present law in the first case some property passing to the next generation is taxed twice, and in the second case more property is taxed in the first estate than ultimately passes to the next generation. This aspect of the operation of the estate tax is inconsistent with the goal of taxing wealth once, but not more than once, each generation. Therefore, this situation should be relieved before more general tax relief is granted and this is the result that the proposed marital deduction revisions would bring about.

The estate tax today is levied on the accumulated wealth that a person has left at his death; any savings that he consumed during his life are not subject to the levy. A person who accumulated until middle age, for example, and thereafter consumed his savings is not subject to the estate tax on that consumption. If the consumption is by his widow, it would seem that the same principle should apply and the estate tax should be levied only upon the accumulation remaining after the combined consumption of husband and wife.

* * *

NOTE

The Treasury's marital deduction proposal provoked few objections; as noted by Kurtz and Surrey, it "would benefit many taxpayers and would not directly raise anyone's taxes." Does the marital deduction implicitly increase the relative tax burden on non-spousal transfers? Which taxpayers are likely to derive the greatest tax benefit from the Treasury's proposal?

Which of the following theories provides the strongest support for allowing unlimited tax-free transfers between spouses: Neutral treatment of married couples in community property and noncommunity property states? A "taxable unit" comprising both spouses? A "once-every-generation" transfer tax?

2. The Marital Deduction After ERTA: Issues Under Current Law

The structure and operation of the marital deduction continue to generate debate. The following excerpts raise several issues that arise in connection with the marital deduction under current law.

In the first excerpt, Wendy C. Gerzog launches a feminist critique of the QTIP provisions, arguing that they degrade women by making it possible for husbands to obtain a marital deduction without giving their wives substantial control over the underlying property.

From an estate planning perspective, the QTIP provisions create both opportunities and pitfalls. Mark L. Ascher discusses the "quandary" of an executor who is granted discretion to elect (or forego) QTIP treatment. Despite the much-vaunted "flexibility" of elective QTIP treatment, Ascher suggests that the executor's discretion is frequently constrained by several tax and non-tax considerations which might best be resolved by the transferor. Sheldon F. Kurtz analyzes the impact of the unlimited marital deduction on the use of formula clauses to regulate the size and character of marital bequests. Douglas A. Kahn explores the tax apportionment problems that arise when a surviving spouse claims an elective share of the decedent's property; he argues that the spouse's share, to the extent it qualifies for the marital deduction, should be exonerated from the burden of estate taxes. Finally, in her article on "joint and mutual" wills, Amy Morris Hess addresses the transfer tax problems that arise when spouses agree to leave their property at the survivor's death to designated beneficiaries.

Wendy C. Gerzog, *The Marital Deduction QTIP Provisions: Illogical and Degrading to Women*, 5 UCLA WOMEN'S L.J. 301 (1995)*

* * *

In 1981, Congress enacted both the unlimited marital deduction and the QTIP exception to the terminable interest rule. The unlimited marital deduction reflected a decision to treat a husband and wife as one unit for the purposes of transfer taxation, a decision which paralleled the choice of the married couple as the proper unit for income taxation and solidified the concept that a husband and wife's property is really "theirs." * * *

* * *

* * * Unlike the terminable interest exception for a qualifying income interest coupled with a general power of appointment, the QTIP allows the predeceasing spouse to receive the benefits of a marital deduction without ceding control of the transferred property. Because statistically the majority of predeceasing spouses are men, the QTIP in effect provides a loophole that perpetuates the women-deserve-only-support school of thought by allowing husbands to reap the benefits of the marital deduction without relinquishing control of the ultimate disposition of the underlying property. In so doing, the provisions give an unwarranted tax benefit to married couples based on the fallacy that decisions by the husband are decisions of the marital unit.

* * *

Essentially, the QTIP provisions allow the taxpayer to control the ultimate disposition of the underlying property after the death of, or earlier transfer by, the surviving spouse. They pro-

---

vide that qualified terminable interest property will be treated as if it passed to the surviving spouse * * * although the surviving spouse will receive only a lifetime income interest in the property. * * *

* * *

The current distribution requirement, which merely gives the surviving spouse an income interest, is not a substitute for giving the surviving spouse an ownership interest in the underlying property. Essentially, the current distribution requirement complicates the QTIP without providing a cogent policy basis for allowing the benefit of a marital deduction where the surviving spouse does not own the underlying property.

* * *

The decision to use the marital unit as the proper unit of taxation for transfer tax purposes rests on the concept that married persons share and make joint decisions about "their" property. Thus, the best time to tax that property is when it leaves the marital unit, whether at the surviving spouse's death or at earlier transfer. However, the legislative history behind the QTIP provisions reveals a policy rationale incompatible with at least one of these assumptions: that married persons both decide what they will do with "their" property. Rather, the QTIP statute itself does not require any *joint* decision-making between husband and wife.

The legislative history of the QTIP provisions is replete with expressions of the decedent/donor spouse's fear of transferring the underlying property to his wife. Basically, the decedent/donor is worried that she will not subsequently transfer the property to his children from either that current marriage or from his prior marriages. Yet the QTIP is based on the theory that a couple shares and makes "joint" decisions about "their" property. If that purported rationale for the QTIP were indeed true, there would be no need for such fear. Underlying the husband's fear is the fact that he does not wish to *share* his decision with his spouse but wants unilaterally to control to whom "his" property is transferred when it leaves the marital unit. In other words, without the QTIP statute the decedent would probably utilize the power of appointment exception to the terminable interest rule. However, the decedent is horrified at this option because he sees the recipient spouse as unilaterally controlling the ultimate disposition of *his* property specifically *not* in accord with *his* wishes. He wants his cake (i.e., the tax benefit of deferral), and he wants to eat it, too (i.e., to control who will finally receive the underlying property). The icing covering this cake is Congress's pretense that the QTIP's preferred tax treatment is based on the decision to use the marital unit as the unit of taxation because married persons *share their* property. Evidently, they do not.

* * *

The QTIP provisions degrade women because they were enacted to enable men to control the ultimate disposition of property but nonetheless the provisions qualify QTIP transfers for a marital deduction. The framers of this new exception to the terminable interest rule further degraded women because they assumed that widows would be content with receiving only one of the indicia of property ownership, e.g., current beneficial enjoyment, and would not protest against the enactment of such a provision. * * *

* * *

While the 1981 legislative history is expressed in gender neutral terms, earlier versions of the QTIP evidence a clear gender bias and stereotyping. All examples in both the A.L.I. Proposal and the Treasury Recommendations envision the surviving spouse as a woman, which is, of course, borne out by the statistical evidence. * * *

* * *

* * * Until the enactment of the QTIP provisions in 1981, the marital deduction required that the recipient spouse own, or have the equivalent of ownership of, property transferred to her. In this way, the property would continue to be owned by at least one member of the marital unit and by no one outside that unit.

With the enactment of the QTIP provisions, Congress extended the tax benefit afforded by the marital deduction to transfers of only a life estate to a member of the marital unit and of a vested remainder to third parties outside the marital unit. It did so on the stated rationale that: (1) married couples share decisions about "their" property, and (2) as long as the value of the underlying property would be included in the surviving spouse's estate at her death, the government's right to such transfer tax revenue would not be compromised.

In fact, however, neither of those policies are served by the QTIP provisions. * * * The QTIP provisions clearly do not require that the surviving spouse agree to either the identity of the beneficiary of the underlying property or to the QTIP election itself. Rather, it is the decedent/donor alone who names the beneficiary of the underlying property, and it is the executor who is entitled to make the QTIP election. Likewise, federal revenue is compromised because the very real economic benefit of tax deferral is given to the transferor despite the fact that the property is transferred outside the marital unit at the creation of the vested remainder in a third party. * * *

The only legitimate rationale for allowing married persons to receive the tax benefit of deferral is because a spouse must transfer the underlying property itself to the other spouse. At a minimum, Congress should only allow the marital deduction where the transferor's spouse must agree both to the identity of the recipient and to a QTIP election.

Ideally, Congress should repeal the current QTIP provisions because they degrade women; clearly, the motivation for their enactment was gender-biased, and as applied, even today the QTIP disadvantages mostly widows. The QTIP provisions encourage husbands to transfer less than a full property interest to their wives by providing the donors with a marital deduction based on the value of the underlying property although the husbands actually give their surviving spouses only a life interest in that property.

* * *

NOTE

Repeal of the QTIP provisions, advocated by Gerzog, would leave the marital deduction available for outright transfers and for power-of-appointment trusts. Would such a system tend to improve the lot of married women relative to their husbands? Of women relative to men in general? Do you agree that the "only legitimate rationale" for the marital deduction requires that "a spouse must transfer the underlying property itself to the other spouse"?

According to another commentator, "[u]ltimately, the QTIP in theory and in practice means that wives are not considered worthy of being property owners or of exercising their rights to make wills." Mary Louise Fellows, *Wills and Trusts: "The Kingdom of the Fathers,"* 10 L. & INEQ. J. 137, 159 (1991). *See also* Wendy C. Gerzog, Estate of Clack: *Adding Insult to Injury, or More Problems with the QTIP Tax Provisions*, 6 S. CAL. REV. L. & WOMEN'S STUD. 221 (1996). In a rejoinder, Lawrence Zelenak contends that "Gerzog and Fellows fail to prove their *feminist* case against the QTIP," and suggests that the QTIP provisions should be low on the list of feminist concerns:

> [I]n the overall feminist scheme of things, any arguable injustice caused by QTIPs to affluent (and overwhelmingly white) widows is simply trivial. Critical race feminists argue that many feminists pay too much attention to concerns peculiar to affluent white women; the attack on QTIPs is almost a parody of the kind of feminism to which the critical race theorists object.

Lawrence Zelenak, *Taking Critical Tax Theory Seriously*, 76 N.C. L. REV. ___, ___ (1998). How might feminist critics respond to Zelenak?

Mark L. Ascher, *The Quandary of Executors Who Are Asked to Plan the Estates of the Dead: The Qualified Terminable Interest Property Election*, 63 N.C. L. REV. 1 (1984)*

* * *

ERTA effected vast changes in the qualitative restrictions on the marital deduction by allowing a deduction for "qualified terminable interest property." The primary characteristic of QTIP is that the surviving spouse must be entitled to all of the income at least annually during her lifetime. In addition, no person, including the surviving spouse, can have the power to appoint the QTIP to anyone other than the surviving spouse during the surviving spouse's lifetime.[17] Furthermore, the decedent's executor must elect QTIP status on the decedent's estate tax return. * * *

QTIP gives married persons unprecedented estate planning freedom. Testators can retain control over the ultimate disposition of their property and still obtain the marital deduction. * * *

* * *

The marital deduction is primarily an estate tax deferral device. Although it shields property from estate tax at the death of the first spouse to die, the property is subject to estate tax at the death of the surviving spouse unless spent, given away, or otherwise dissipated prior to her death. * * *

* * *

ERTA allows testators to achieve objectives that previously were unattainable. The testator can control the ultimate disposition of his property by using a QTIP trust to qualify for the marital deduction. When a credit-shelter trust is combined with a transfer that qualifies the remainder of the testator's estate for the marital deduction, generally no estate tax will be due at the testator's death. If both spouses utilize such planning, a couple with combined taxable wealth of $1.2 million generally will pay no estate tax. Therefore, a frequent drafting technique is a two-trust estate plan: a credit-shelter trust designed to exhaust the unified credit of the first spouse to die and to avoid inclusion in the gross estate of the surviving spouse; and a residual QTIP trust designed to qualify for the marital deduction and to control the ultimate disposition of the client's property.

---

*

17   * * * Powers of appointment exercisable only after the surviving spouse's death do not prevent qualification for the marital deduction. * * * Thus, the surviving spouse may be granted a testamentary special power of appointment. * * *

* * *

One reason for the popularity of the full-deferral[61] estate plan is the commonly held belief that deferral of estate tax necessarily produces economic advantages derived from the time value of money. Although the surviving spouse does realize economic benefits from deferral of the estate tax, deferral, if viewed from the perspective of the QTIP remaindermen, does not necessarily work the same magic.[63]

* * *

By wasting the lowest estate tax brackets of the first spouse to die and subjecting QTIP appreciation and income to taxation at the death of the surviving spouse, full deferral can increase dramatically the total tax burden. Thus, full deferral can deplete substantially the family wealth remaining after the death of the surviving spouse.

* * *

For many clients the cost of full deferral is academic. Understandably, many clients wish to defer taxes until they are unavoidable. Moreover, in many situations the surviving spouse is the overwhelmingly predominant beneficiary, and any estate plan that would increase the assets eventually passing to the QTIP remaindermen at the expense of the surviving spouse is inappropriate. * * *

* * *

The surviving spouse, however, may not be the testator's overwhelmingly predominant beneficiary. In an unsuccessful marriage, the testator's desire to provide his surviving spouse with a substantial interest in his estate may be consistent with a primary desire to optimize the QTIP remainder. Thus, drafting for equalization (or some step in that direction) as the primary estate plan may be more appropriate than drafting for full deferral. In other situations—those involving multiple marriages—the surviving spouse must share with others not only the testator's affections, but also the testator's bounty. * * * Similarly, the testator may want his children to receive a substantial benefit immediately upon his death. If the children are required to wait until the death of the surviving spouse, they could predecease the surviving spouse, and, therefore, never benefit from the marital share. * * *

* * *

The estate of the first spouse to die may be highly illiquid, depending on the nature of its assets and the extent of its obligations. Liquidity, in fact, may be one of the estate planner's primary worries if the principal asset is a closely-held business, a farm, or a parcel of unimproved real estate. Full deferral offers relief from one of the major sources of illiquidity, the federal estate tax. * * *

---

[61]   In this Article, "full deferral" means qualification of the entire estate for the marital deduction, subject only to carving out the unified credit equivalent in such a way as not to be subject to estate taxation at the death of the surviving spouse.

[63]   Assume an estate [subject to a] 50% estate tax bracket. If the first spouse to die qualifies property valued at $1.00 for the marital deduction and the property triples in value prior to the death of the surviving spouse (also in the 50% estate tax bracket), the property remaining after the surviving spouse's death is $1.50. If the first spouse to die chooses not to qualify the property valued at $1.00 for the marital deduction, an estate tax of 50 cents is paid. No additional estate tax, however, need be paid at the death of the surviving spouse. The remaining 50 cents, when similarly tripled, likewise amounts to $1.50 after the surviving spouse's death.

Eliminating tax-based liquidity concerns through full deferral, however, may only sweep them under the carpet. * * * [I]f the long-term preservation of a family business or farm is a primary goal of the testator, full deferral should be undertaken only if the deferred liquidity concerns can be resolved prior to the death of the surviving spouse or if the testator is willing to run the risk that they will not be addressed.

* * *

Because full deferral deliberately foregoes the opportunity to utilize the lowest estate tax brackets available to the estate of the first spouse to die, it can deplete the family wealth that remains after the death of the surviving spouse. If the spouses' combined taxable wealth increases after the death of the first spouse to die, full deferral can cause an especially severe depletion because it also deliberately foregoes the opportunity to "freeze" the surviving spouse's estate. But since prepayment of estate tax accelerates a tax that is not due and thereby deprives the surviving spouse of income and access to principal, the vast majority of clients nevertheless opt for full deferral as a primary estate plan. Those who are advised that full deferral can be very costly to their ultimate beneficiaries nevertheless may choose full deferral because they also are advised that their executors will decide whether prepayment of the tax is appropriate by electing or failing to elect QTIP status.

Examination of the questions implicit in the considerations relevant to making the QTIP election, however, reveals that the great majority of those questions properly can be answered only by the testator. Even if the questions involved administrative rather than dispositive issues, the QTIP election would raise difficult issues of fiduciary conduct. * * *

An executor who causes an estate to prepay the estate tax, even in a good-faith effort to optimize the QTIP remainder, probably breaches the fiduciary duty to minimize taxes. The fiduciary also will worry whether he has failed to treat the estate's beneficiaries impartially. On the other hand, a surviving spouse or QTIP remainderman acting as executor may hesitate to exercise the QTIP election for fear that she might breach the fiduciary duty of loyalty by favoring herself. Even if the duty to minimize taxes, the duty to treat beneficiaries impartially, and the duty of loyalty are remitted expressly by the testator, tax-generating partial QTIP elections still will be extraordinarily rare. Therefore, reliance on fiduciary exercise of the QTIP election is likely to fail miserably as an option for achieving post-mortem flexibility. Moreover, reliance on fiduciary exercise of the QTIP election creates income, gift, and estate tax problems that may offset substantially the supposed advantage gained by the theoretical possibility of a partial QTIP election.

An attractive alternative is to direct the executor to make the QTIP election, while providing for disclaimers by the surviving spouse. But because surviving spouses often are unwilling to disclaim property recently left them by their spouses, such a route must be undertaken only when the surviving spouse is the client's overwhelmingly predominant beneficiary or when the client implicitly trusts the surviving spouse with the responsibility of deciding how much marital deduction is appropriate.

The ultimate failure of both fiduciary exercise of the QTIP election and spousal disclaimers to provide post-mortem flexibility derives from the fact that only the testator can determine how much marital deduction is appropriate. The answer necessarily must be a bit of a guess in some cases, and if the testator could make the decision after his death, the answer might be somewhat better. An executor, however, is incapable of answering whether the surviving spouse is the overwhelmingly predominant beneficiary and whether the family business eventually should pass intact to the children. Thus, it is hardly surprising that the executor saddled with such a burden would take the easy way out by electing full deferral and thereby minimize present taxes in favor of the surviving spouse. Similarly, a surviving spouse, only recently separated from the testator, understandably assumes that no disclaimer is necessary to effectuate the testator's wishes.

* * *

NOTE

Ascher points out that the unlimited marital deduction presents the opportunity to reduce the estate tax at the first spouse's death to zero. Why might such a "full deferral" approach ultimately prove more costly than an "equalization" approach? Some commentators advise that "up to an 'equalizer' amount, it always is beneficial to incur more tax in the estate of the first spouse to die than to defer tax until the death of the survivor." Jeffrey N. Pennell & R. Mark Williamson, *The Economics of Prepaying Wealth Transfer Tax*, 136 TR. & EST. 49, 49 (June 1997). Why might the executor nevertheless routinely choose full deferral?

Ascher also challenges the conventional assumption that giving the executor discretion to make a QTIP election enhances flexibility in post-mortem planning. What considerations might influence the executor's exercise of discretion? As Ascher points out, the surviving spouse can cut back the amount of the marital deduction by making a qualified disclaimer; does this provide a reliable solution to the executor's quandary? What is the drafting lesson here?

Sheldon F. Kurtz, *Marital Deduction Estate Planning Under the Economic Recovery Tax Act of 1981: Opportunities Exist, But Watch the Pitfalls*, 34 RUTGERS L. REV. 591 (1982)*

* * *

III. DEFERRAL VERSUS EQUALIZATION

For larger estates having values in excess of the aggregate value of the exemption equivalents of both spouses, transfer taxes cannot be entirely avoided. For these estates the primary transfer tax planning goal is either tax deferral or tax minimization coupled with maximization of the tax sheltering opportunities afforded by the unified credit. Tax deferral is achieved by taking maximum advantage of both the unified credit and marital deduction to the extent necessary to avoid all transfer taxes on the estate of the first spouse to die, so that the payment of any transfer tax is deferred until the death of the surviving spouse. A tax minimization plan, on the other hand, will utilize the progressive transfer tax rate structure by equalizing the value of both spouses' estates. Equalization will be achieved only if a smaller marital deduction is claimed in the estate of the first spouse to die than would be claimed in a tax deferral plan and will result in some transfer tax liability on the estate of the first spouse to die.

* * *

In determining whether the appropriate goal is deferral or minimization, the planner must also consider the highly speculative impact of at least two other factors. First, the planner must consider the consequences of any appreciation in value or consumption of the assets passing to the spouse and the by-pass shelter trust. Second, the planner must consider the consequences resulting from accumulations of income during the surviving spouse's life. Appreciation or consumption of assets left to H in a form qualifying for a marital deduction in W's estate could substantially affect the amount of transfer taxes payable on H's estate. On the other hand, a bequest in the form of a by-pass trust, although taxable to W's estate to the extent it exceeds W's exemption equivalent, will not be subject to transfer taxation upon H's death. Thus, any appreciation on by-pass trust assets will escape transfer taxation at H's death.

* * *

* * * [M]any clients may prefer the deferral plan for at least three reasons. First, the deferral plan maximizes the amount of income available to the surviving spouse, who is often the preferred beneficiary of the deceased spouse. Second, the additional transfer tax costs resulting from deferral are borne by the children and not the spouse. Third, the highly speculative nature of any assumptions regarding appreciation and income accumulation and the possibility of asset consumption make it difficult to accurately forecast what impact changes in asset values will have on the transfer taxes payable on the surviving spouse's estate. * * *

* * *

VI. FORMULA CLAUSES AND DISPOSITIVE FORMATS

* * *

* * * [T]he identity and value of property which a client actually will own at death cannot be determined prior to death. This results from a number of obvious factors including, but not limited to: (i) changes in the identity and value of assets between the date of planning and death; (ii) depletion of assets through personal consumption or gifts; and (iii) the amount of the unified credit in the year of death. Therefore, the use of fixed amount legacies (e.g., I give H $1,400,000) cannot guarantee that the goal of tax deferral or equalization based upon the identity and the estate tax value of property owned at death will be achieved. This purpose can only be assured with certainty by the use of self-adjusting formula provisions.

At least three potential dispositive formats are available to the planner who wishes to utilize a by-pass shelter trust and a qualifying marital deduction bequest to eliminate all estate taxes on the estate of the first spouse to die, deferring all transfer taxes until the death of the surviving spouse. These are:

(1) A true worth pecuniary formula marital deduction qualifying gift coupled with a residuary by-pass shelter trust. The pecuniary marital deduction formula clause may be worded as follows:

> I give to my (husband or wife) if (he or she) shall survive me, a pecuniary legacy in an amount equal to the value of all the property included in my probate estate passing under the provisions of this Will reduced by the sum of (a) all of the funeral expenses, administration expenses and other claims against my estate paid by my Executor from the principal of my probate estate and without regard to whether such items have been allowed as an estate tax deduction in computing the value of my taxable estate for federal estate tax purposes; (b) the value of all property included in my probate estate passing under the preceding provisions of this Will; and (c) the largest amount, if any, which can pass under this Will free of any federal estate tax liability by reason of the unified credit [and] the state death tax credit to the extent consid-

eration of the state death tax credit does not increase any estate, inheritance or other death duty payable to any state * * * , reduced (but not below zero) by the value of any items included in my gross estate as finally determined for federal estate tax purposes passing under the preceding provisions of this Will or outside of this Will which do not qualify for the estate tax marital or charitable deduction and by the amount of funeral expenses, administration expenses and other claims chargeable to the principal of any asset included in my gross estate which are not allowed as deductions in computing the federal estate tax on my estate and by the amount of the adjusted taxable gifts which are taken into account in computing the federal estate tax on my estate. In determining the amount of this bequest, valuation and other determinations as finally determined for federal estate tax purposes shall control. I authorize my Executor to satisfy this legacy in whole or in part with a distribution of cash or assets in kind, provided that any assets distributed in kind shall be valued on their date or dates of distribution.

(2) A true worth pecuniary formula by-pass shelter trust coupled with a residuary marital deduction qualifying gift. The pecuniary by-pass shelter trust may be worded as follows:

If my (husband or wife) survives me, I give to my Trustee, hereinafter named, an amount equal to the largest amount, if any, which can pass under this Will free of any federal estate tax liability by reason of the unified credit [and] the state death tax credit to the extent consideration of the state death tax credit does not increase any estate, inheritance or other death duty payable to any state * * * , reduced (but not below zero) by the value of any items included in my gross estate as finally determined for federal estate tax purposes passing under the preceding provisions of the Will or outside of the Will which do not qualify for either the estate tax marital or charitable deduction and by the amount of funeral expenses, administration expenses and other claims chargeable to the principal of any asset included in my gross estate which are not allowed as deductions in computing the federal estate tax on my estate and by the amount of the adjusted taxable gifts which are taken into account in computing the federal estate tax on my estate. In determining the amount of this bequest, valuations and other determinations as finally determined for federal estate tax purposes shall control. I authorize my Executor to satisfy this legacy in whole or in part with a distribution of cash or assets in kind, provided that any assets distributed in kind shall be valued at their fair market value on the date or dates of distribution.

The same amounts pass to the spouse and the trustee of the by-pass shelter trust under both formulas. In fact, the pecuniary formula marital deduction gift is defined in the same manner as the residue of an estate is effectively defined. * * *

(3) Two residuary gifts, one to a residuary by-pass shelter trust, the other a residuary marital deduction qualifying gift. This can be accomplished by either expressing the by-pass shelter trust as a formula with the balance of the residuary estate passing to the spouse, or vice versa. For example, the will might provide as follows:

All the rest, residue and remainder of my estate, real, personal and mixed, of whatsoever nature and wherever situated of which I shall die seized or possessed and to which I shall be entitled at the time of my death, including any legacies or devises which may lapse or be invalid or for any other reason shall fail to take effect, after the payment of all debts, expenses and taxes, all to be determined in a trust accounting sense, (all of which is hereinafter referred to as my "residuary estate") shall be disposed of as follows:[43]

A. If my (husband or wife) survives me, I give to my Trustee, hereinafter named, that fractional share of my residuary estate determined by multiplying the value thereof by a fraction, the numerator of which shall be equal to the largest amount, if any, which can pass under this Will free of any federal estate tax liability by reason of the unified credit [and] the state death tax credit to the extent consideration of the state death tax credit does not increase any estate, inheritance or other death duty payable to any state * * * , reduced (but not below zero) by the value of any items included in my gross estate as finally determined for federal estate tax purposes passing under the preceding provisions of this Will or outside of this Will which do not qualify for either the estate tax marital or charitable deduction and by the amount of funeral expenses, administration expenses and other claims chargeable to the principal of any asset included in my gross estate which are not allowed as deductions in computing the federal estate tax on my estate and by the amount of the adjusted taxable gifts which are taken into account in computing the federal estate tax on my estate and the denominator of which shall be the value of my residuary estate. In determining the amount of this bequest, valuations and other determinations as finally determined for federal estate tax purposes shall control.

B. I give the balance of my residuary estate to my (husband or wife), or if (he or she) shall not survive me, I give my entire residuary estate (insert alternative dispositive provisions).

* * *

The planner should consider a number of factors, often pulling in different directions, in selecting the format which is best suited for a particular estate. These factors include:

(1) The income tax consequences of distributing assets in satisfaction of bequests under the will.

* * *

(2) Income tax consequences to legatee for income earned by the estate.

* * *

(3) The allocation of appreciation and depreciation earned during estate administration.

Since legatees of pecuniary bequests are entitled only to the dollar amount of the bequest, the benefits of appreciation and the risks of depreciation occurring after decedent's death accrue to the residuary beneficiaries. In light of this fact, in periods of anticipated appreciation in values, it would appear that the marital bequest should be frozen at a pecuniary amount and the by-pass shelter trust carved out of the residue, particularly if the spouse is the primary beneficiary of that trust and will share in the benefits of post-death appreciation in any event. Under

---

[43]   In this clause the residue is expressly defined to take account of taxes. This is called a true residuary clause. The residue could have been defined in a manner which ignored taxes, in which case it would be called a pre-tax residuary clause. * * *

* * * [I]f a pre-tax residuary formula is used, all taxes must be expressly charged against the non-marital share of the residue to avoid a partial loss of the marital deduction. * * *

this format, all appreciation realized during the administration of the decedent's estate would be allocated to the by-pass trust and would escape tax in both spouses' estates. Conversely, if the marital share were carved from the residuary estate in whole or in part, all or a portion of the appreciation realized during the administration of the decedent's estate would be taxed to the spouse's estate. Nonetheless, this analysis, which favors a pecuniary marital deduction gift, may be more illusory than real. The amount of appreciation realized during the administration of a decedent's estate which would escape tax in the surviving spouse's estate if a residuary by-pass shelter trust were used depends upon the lapse between the decedent's death and the time the marital gift is actually funded.

* * *

(4) Ease of administration.

If a format utilizing either a pecuniary by-pass shelter trust or a pecuniary marital gift is adopted, administrative problems arise in connection with the selection and revaluation of assets to be distributed or sold to satisfy the pecuniary bequest. These factors do not necessarily arise if both types of bequests are carved out of the residue unless the executor deems it advisable, for other reasons, to sell estate assets. This is because residuary shares can be satisfied by a distribution of assets in kind, and as long as distributions are proportionate among the shares, distributed assets need not be revalued. Nonetheless, there are at least two problems which arise if both shares are carved out of the residue.

First, state law may be unclear as to whether the executor must fractionalize each asset distributed in satisfaction of residuary shares. If assets must be fractionalized among the residuary shares, the resulting co-tenancies may prove to be an unsatisfactory title holding arrangement. However, this issue is often academic because a well-drawn will generally authorizes the executor to make non-pro rata distributions among the residuary legatees. If the executor is not expressly authorized to make non-pro rata distributions but nevertheless does so at the request of the legatees pursuant to their agreement, the distribution will be treated for tax purposes as if the executor had made a pro rata distribution and the legatees then exchanged the property among themselves. In this fictional transaction, gain or loss might be realized by the distributees.

Second, disproportionate partial distributions could result in a readjustment of the fractional interests of the residuary legatees necessitating further adjustments in the allocation of gains, losses, and income realized subsequent to the partial distribution and revaluation of assets following each partial distribution. * * * These problems suggest that for purposes of ease of administration, carving both shares out of the residue should be avoided.

(5) Identity of assets.

If the estate consists of a significant number of assets which are difficult to value (e.g., real estate or unlisted securities), a format which reduces the number of times assets have to be revalued should be used. If either a pecuniary by-pass trust or pecuniary marital gift is otherwise desirable, use of the pecuniary by-pass trust is preferable where the value of the trust is likely to be smaller than the marital gift. Where the marital gift is likely to be smaller in value than the by-pass shelter trust, however, the pecuniary marital gift should be used. Problems of revaluation, of course, can be avoided if both shares are carved out of the residue and disproportionate distributions are eliminated or kept to a minimum.

* * *

The above discussion of the several factors relating to format selection leads to the conclusion that the preferable format is a pecuniary formula by-pass shelter trust and a residuary bequest to the spouse. * * *

* * *

NOTE

As Kurtz points out, the structure of a marital bequest may be influenced by several considerations other than present-value tax savings. As a practical matter, what difference does it make whether the marital bequest is defined as a pecuniary amount or a residuary share following a pecuniary by-pass trust? Review the formula clauses provided by Kurtz. How do the formulas deal with nonprobate assets included in the gross estate? With taxable gifts made during life? Kurtz refers to administrative complications that may arise in applying a fractional-share formula to non-pro-rata interim distributions during estate administration. For a more detailed treatment of this problem, see Sheldon F. Kurtz, *Allocation of Increases and Decreases to Fractional Share Marital Deduction Bequest*, 8 REAL PROP., PROB. & TR. J. 450 (1973). Why might a corporate executor find a fractional-share formula more convenient to administer than a pecuniary formula?

For recent discussions of planning and drafting considerations involving marital deduction formula clauses, see Lauren Y. Detzel, *The Heart of the Matter—Effective Use of Formula Clauses in Estate Planning*, 30 U. MIAMI INST. EST. PLAN. 16-1, 16-1 (1996); Barry M. Nudelman & Athena A. Panos, *Choosing the Most Appropriate Marital Deduction Formula Clause*, 23 EST. PLAN. 256 (1996). For exhaustive analyses of marital deduction formula clauses, see RICHARD B. COVEY, MARITAL DEDUCTION AND CREDIT SHELTER DISPOSITIONS AND THE USE OF FORMULA PROVISIONS (1984), and Alan N. Polasky, *Marital Deduction Formula Clauses in Estate Planning—Estate and Income Tax Considerations*, 63 MICH. L. REV. 809 (1965). The impact of the 1981 legislation on marital deduction planning is discussed in Joel C. Dobris, *Marital Deduction Estate Planning: Variations on a Classic Theme*, 20 S. DIEGO L. REV. 801 (1983), and in Don W. Llewellyn, *Estate Planning for the Married Couple*, 28 VILL. L. REV. 491 (1983).

Douglas A. Kahn, *The Federal Estate Tax Burden Borne by a Dissenting Widow*, 64 MICH. L. REV. 1499 (1966)*

Renunciation of her deceased husband's will entitles a widow[1] to a specified percentage of the husband's net estate (or a dower interest) in lieu of any benefits she would otherwise have received under the will. The size of the dissenting widow's[3] share differs among the several states, but the normal range is from one third to one half of her husband's net estate. * * * [T]he thrust of the statutory provisions is to protect a widow by giving her an election to take, in lieu of her husband's testamentary gifts, a specified share of his real and personal property remaining after payment of funeral expenses, administrative expenses, and other claims against the estate.

---

*   Originally published in 64 MICH. L. REV. 1499 (1966).

[1]   For convenience, reference in this article is made only to a widow, but the discussion is equally applicable to a widower who is permitted by local law to renounce his deceased spouse's will (or who is entitled to an intestate share of her estate), and thereby becomes entitled to a forced share of her estate.

[3]   As used in this article, the term "dissenting widow" refers to a widow who has renounced her husband's will.

In situations where the decedent's estate is of sufficient size to cause the imposition of federal estate taxes, the question arises whether the dissenting widow's share is computed as a fraction of the decedent's net estate after deducting federal estate taxes, or whether her share is a fraction of the decedent's net estate computed without regard to estate taxes. In other words, is the widow obligated to bear a proportionate part of the federal estate tax liability? This question has become particularly important since the adoption * * * of the marital deduction provisions * * * . It appears manifestly unfair to impose an estate tax burden upon the widow when her share of the estate is excluded from the computation of the tax. * * *

The significance of this problem does not rest solely with determining the size of the widow's share vis-à-vis the other beneficiaries. The resolution of the problem will also affect the size of the estate tax payable to the federal government, since the tax is determined in part by the amount of property passing to the widow that qualifies for the marital deduction. * * *

* * *

I. APPORTIONMENT OF FEDERAL ESTATE TAXES

From its inception in 1916, the federal estate tax law has required that the decedent's executor make the estate tax payments that are due the Government. Because of this provision, the courts in many early cases determined that federal law required that the estate tax be paid out of the residue of the estate without contribution from other probate and non-probate assets. In response to those decisions, the New York legislature enacted a statute in 1930 providing for the apportionment of federal estate taxes, unless the decedent directed otherwise, among the persons entitled to any property included in the gross estate of the decedent for federal estate tax purposes. An increasing number of states have followed New York's example, and have adopted some form of apportionment of federal estate taxes.

* * * In *Riggs v. Del Drago*,[29] the United States Supreme Court * * * upheld the constitutionality of New York's apportionment statute, and resolved beyond dispute that Congress intended that the determination of the ultimate placing of the estate tax burden rest on state law rather than federal law. * * *

* * *

In many of those states that do not have apportionment statutes, the local courts have nevertheless effected an apportionment of federal estate taxes pursuant to the doctrine of "equitable apportionment," which is nothing more than a specific application of the equitable concept of contribution. However, the courts of a number of jurisdictions have rejected this equitable doctrine.

* * *

Assets or interests in assets may be included in a decedent's gross estate for tax purposes, even though they are not subject to probate. Such non-probate assets include life insurance, jointly held property, certain inter vivos transfers, and property over which the decedent possessed a general power of appointment. * * *

* * *

* * * [C]ourts fashioning rules of equitable apportionment properly distinguish between probate and non-probate assets and require contribution only from recipients of the latter, since that result will most frequently represent the unexpressed intent of the decedent. However, the tax apportionment rules enacted by state legislatures have a broader reach and usually require

---

[29]   317 U.S. 95 (1942). * * *

contribution from testamentary beneficiaries as well. Thus, the burden is placed on the testator to indicate a contrary intent if he prefers to exempt certain bequests or devises from estate tax burdens. It is difficult to determine whether that aspect of the apportionment statutes is the product of a legislative determination of the likely intention of a decedent, or whether it is an expression of legislative policy favoring an equitable distribution of the estate tax burden. In any event, the equitable distribution of the tax burden has some visceral appeal, and a testator retains the power to change this result if he wishes to do so by inserting an appropriate tax clause in his will.

There is one area of testamentary disposition that clearly warrants the application of rules of apportionment: the bequest and devise of a fractional share of a decedent's estate to his widow. * * * [T]he widow's share should be exonerated from estate tax burdens to the extent that it qualifies for the marital deduction, since that result would accomplish the intent of the testator in most circumstances. The widow's share is normally exonerated under apportionment statutes, either by express reference or by a provision that any deduction or exemption allowed by reason of the relationship of any person to the decedent shall inure to the benefit of that person. It is more difficult to utilize the doctrine of equitable apportionment for this purpose, but it is this writer's view that it should be so applied. A testator's desire to minimize taxes is no less typical than his desire that non-probate assets participate in the satisfaction of the estate tax obligation. * * *

The unique considerations compelling contribution from the recipients of non-probate assets are perhaps best demonstrated by the fact that it is only as to such assets that the federal government has undertaken to prescribe the manner of apportionment of the estate tax burden * * * . As early as 1919, the federal estate tax law empowered executors to recover contributions for payment of estate taxes from the beneficiaries of insurance on a decedent's life, if the insurance proceeds were included in the decedent's gross estate. * * * In 1942, Congress enacted a similar provision requiring contribution from persons receiving property over which the decedent once possessed a general power of appointment, if such property were included in the decedent's gross estate.[46] In 1948, when Congress adopted the marital deduction provisions for the estate tax, it amended these two apportionment provisions to preclude contribution from insurance proceeds or appointive property which passes or has passed to the surviving spouse and for which a marital deduction was allowed. The two provisions are now set forth in sections 2206 and 2207 of the Internal Revenue Code of 1954 and constitute the only provision for apportionment of estate taxes in federal law. It is difficult to understand why these two types of non-probate assets have been singled out while other non-probate properties included in the decedent's gross estate (such as jointly held property, transfers in contemplation of death, and transfers with retained life interests) have been ignored. The two sections have been criticized as piecemeal legislation, and it has been suggested that they should either be expanded or repealed. An expansion of these provisions to provide for tax apportionment as to all property included in the decedent's gross estate would eliminate both the patchwork of apportionment rules that now apply throughout the fifty states and the difficult conflict-of-laws question whether contribution from recipients of the property of the decedent is determined under the law of the state in which the decedent was domiciled at death or under the law of the state in which the situs of the property is located. * * *

* * *

---

[46] * * * The rule for apportionment is inapplicable if the decedent has made some other provision in his will.

II. APPORTIONMENT AND THE DISSENTING WIDOW'S SHARE

In several instances, courts have treated the existence or absence of apportionment rules as virtually dispositive of a dissenting widow's demand that her share be computed without regard to estate tax liability. However, in a number of cases the courts have held that the computation of the widow's share is determined only by the language of the statute defining her share, and that the applicability of apportionment rules is therefore irrelevant. Since the support given the widow's position by a statutory rule of apportionment is greater than the support provided by the applicability of equitable apportionment rules, the two types of rules should be considered separately.

A. Equitable Apportionment

As noted above, the function of the equitable apportionment rule is to distribute the estate tax burden equitably among the parties owning property or interests in property that was included in the decedent's estate for tax purposes and who therefore benefited from the payment of the tax, since the payment released the federal lien imposed on their property and relieved them of personal liability. To the extent that property passing or having passed to the widow qualifies for the marital deduction, such property does not create any estate tax liability and therefore should be exempted from contributing toward the payment of the tax. In situations where a widow renounces her deceased husband's will, she is entitled to a specified percentage of her husband's net estate (defined in differing terms by the various state statutes), and if the net estate is determined after making an allowance for estate taxes, the widow will, in effect, bear a portion of that tax even though her share is tax deductible. Thus, the question is whether the applicability of the doctrine of equitable apportionment modifies the statutory language describing the dissenting widow's share in situations where such language does not explicitly direct that estate taxes be taken into account.

Initially, consideration must be given to the question whether property which qualifies for the marital deduction (irrespective of whether the property passed to the widow prior to her husband's death, by testamentary disposition, by intestacy, or pursuant to the widow's election) should be required to bear a proportionate part of the estate tax burden. The widow's property that qualifies for the marital deduction is included in her husband's gross estate and therefore is subject to the federal tax lien for payment of estate taxes. In addition, the widow is personally liable for that payment. The widow benefits from the payment of the estate tax to the same extent as the other beneficiaries, and thus it may seem fair that she should bear a proportionate part of the tax. However, the equitable doctrine of contribution requires a sharing of a common burden only by persons whose equities are equal. While the tax liability is imposed on all participants in the gross estate, their equities are unequal, since the widow's share is tax deductible and the others are not. Consequently, where equitable apportionment is applicable, contribution is required according to the participants' share of the decedent's *taxable* estate, and to the extent that the widow's share is deductible, it is not included in the taxable estate, thus exonerating the widow from contributing to the tax burden.

However, exoneration of a widow's deductible share from estate tax liability is not dispositive of the question of the size of her forced share. In instances where a widow renounces her deceased husband's will, she becomes entitled to a portion of his estate computed according to the statutory provisions of the state of her husband's domicile (or perhaps of the state in which the situs of property is located). If her share is computed after allowance for federal estate taxes, the net effect of the computation is to charge her with a portion of the estate tax burden. Nevertheless, the manner of computation turns upon the construction of the specific statutory language defining the dissenting widow's share, rather than upon a determination of whether she should be burdened by the estate tax. Moreover, the rationale of the doctrine of equitable apportionment does not accord with granting equitable treatment to the beneficiaries so much as it does with approximating the unexpressed intent of the decedent; of course, the intent of the decedent is irrelevant in computing a dissenting widow's share.

* * *

In sum, the existence of the equitable apportionment doctrine is not dispositive in favor of a dissenting widow, and, as we shall see, the absence of such a doctrine does not require a decision that is unfavorable to her. Nevertheless, one of the purposes of equitable apportionment, albeit not the primary purpose, is to divide the tax burden among the beneficiaries in some equitable manner, and the net effect of deducting estate taxes before computing the widow's share is inconsistent with that purpose. This inconsistency is not of sufficient magnitude to warrant modifying statutory language defining the widow's share, but where there are other compelling reasons for so doing, the doctrine may buttress the widow's claim.

B. Statutory Apportionment

In those states where the legislature has adopted a statute apportioning estate taxes, the case for computing the widow's share without regard to taxes is far more compelling. By adopting an apportionment statute, the state legislature has demonstrated its desire to have the estate tax burden allocated on an equitable basis, and (in virtually all such statutes) to exonerate the surviving widow's property to the extent that it qualifies for the marital deduction. As noted previously, in most statutes this legislative objective appears to be controlling, even to the extent that it may conflict with the normal intent of the decedent. If the statute defining the dissenting widow's share is susceptible to a construction that would require the computation to be made without regard to estate taxes, that construction should be applied in order to accomplish the legislative policy demonstrated by the apportionment statute. * * *

* * *

III. ADDITIONAL REASONS FOR FAVORING A DISSENTING WIDOW

Apart from the applicability of apportionment rules, there are independent reasons advanced on behalf of the dissenting widow's position, and her share may be freed from an estate tax burden even though no apportionment is available under state law. * * *

A. The Destruction of the Widow's Share

One appealing argument advanced for the widow is that if her forced share is burdened by estate taxes, it may be substantially diminished, or even entirely eliminated, through the inclusion in the decedent's gross estate of non-probate assets. * * * [I]n cases where non-probate assets are included in the decedent's estate, the amount of estate tax liability may exceed the value of the probate estate. The legislative purpose underlying the widow's statutory right of election could be frustrated and in some circumstances entirely nullified if the widow's forced share were rendered vulnerable to diminution from non-probate oriented estate taxes. However, this argument is more persuasive in a jurisdiction which has no apportionment rules than in one which requires contribution from the recipients of the non-probate assets, since in the latter case the widow's share is insulated from the tax liability arising from those assets in which she does not share. * * *

B. The Marital Deduction

The most compelling reasons for disregarding estate taxes in computing the widow's forced share arise from the nature and background of the marital deduction allowance. * * *

* * *

In most circumstances, the property passing to the widow pursuant to her election to take her forced share will qualify for the marital deduction and will therefore reduce the tax burden of the estate. If the widow's share is computed after the deduction of taxes, then she must bear a portion of the estate tax burden even though the property received by her was excluded from the computation of that tax and therefore did not cause any part of its imposition. Of course, if for some reason a portion of the widow's share should fail to qualify for the marital deduction, such portion is not tax exempt and should therefore contribute to the satisfaction of the tax burden, but only to the extent that it is not deductible. The Court of Appeals for the Fourth Circuit once declared that to charge a dissenting widow's share of the estate with the federal tax would be "unfair and unjust" * * * . The Fourth Circuit also placed considerable reliance on the fact that a contrary result would frustrate the congressional purpose underlying the enactment of the marital deduction provision, which was to obtain a geographical equalization of tax treatment by freeing the interest of the surviving spouse in a common-law state from estate taxes so that her treatment would be comparable to the tax treatment afforded citizens of community property states. This consideration has been influential in the decisions of a number of courts.

A significant number of courts, however, have held that the determination of a widow's forced share is controlled by state law, and that the congressional purpose in enacting the marital deduction provisions is irrelevant. These courts point to section 2056(b)(4) of the 1954 Code as indicating that Congress contemplated that a widow's share might be required to bear a portion of the estate tax burden under local law and consequently did not intend to pre-empt the issue. While these decisions are correct in asserting that state rather than federal law controls, they fail to consider the interplay between the congressional act and the policies of the state legislatures. Congress did not adopt the marital deduction provisions for its own selfish reasons or even to further a pervasive national policy favoring widows. In fact, Congress merely reacted to the vigorous complaints of the states regarding the inequality existing before the adoption of the marital deduction provision, and to the readiness of the legislatures in the common-law states to disrupt established property systems in order to obtain desired tax advantages for their citizens. It is difficult to believe that state legislatures would be willing to enact (or seriously consider enacting) an entirely foreign property system (which in most states would substantially enhance the size of a widow's forced share of her husband's estate) solely to obtain tax advantages for its citizens, but after having been granted tax advantages similar to those available in community property states would stubbornly insist upon minimizing the proffered relief. Rather than vigorously asserting the states' independence from the congressional purpose, the courts should consider whether the legislative policy of the state involved encompasses the benefits granted by the marital deduction provision. It is this writer's opinion that the presumption should be made in favor of maximizing the widow's share, unless the legislature has indicated a contrary intent * * * , rather than to presume that the widow's share (and the estate) should not benefit from the marital deduction unless the legislature has affirmatively indicated that it desires that result. * * *

* * *

NOTE

As Kahn points out, there has long been a statutory right of recovery for federal estate taxes attributable to certain nonprobate assets included in the gross estate. *See* § 2206 (life insurance proceeds), § 2207 (property subject to general power of appointment). Since Kahn's article was published, similar provisions have been enacted for additional categories of nonprobate assets. *See* § 2207A (qualified terminable interest property included in gross estate under § 2044), § 2207B (property included in gross estate under § 2036). What arguments can be made in support of, or against, a federal estate tax apportionment statute?

Amy Morris Hess, *The Federal Transfer Tax Consequences of Joint and Mutual Wills*, 24 REAL PROP., PROB. & TR. J. 469 (1990)*

* * *

By far the greatest number of cases dealing with the transfer tax consequences of mutual wills deal with whether property passing under such a will to the surviving testator can qualify for the federal estate tax marital deduction if the testators are spouses. Until the addition of section 2056(b)(7) to the Code in 1981, permitting a naked life estate in property to qualify for the marital deduction, there were essentially three ways that property passing to a surviving spouse could qualify for the marital deduction: it could be transferred outright to the survivor, it could pass in a manner that granted the survivor the interests required by sections 2056(b)(5) and 2056(b)(6), each involving a life estate in a trust or its equivalent together with a general power of appointment over the corpus involved (or a legal life estate with power to consume the principal that had the same characteristics), or it could mirror the disposition described in Revenue Ruling 68-554,[127] which involved a so-called "estate" trust by which the surviving spouse is the sole beneficiary of a trust that is payable to the spouse's estate when the spouse dies. * * *

* * *

Section 2056(b)(7) provides an additional method of passing property to a surviving spouse that will qualify the property for the federal estate tax marital deduction: the "qualified terminable interest in property" (QTIP). * * *

The requirements of section 2056(b)(7) are similar to those of section 2056(b)(5) except that the surviving spouse need not have a power to control the disposition of the qualifying property. Instead, the personal representative of the estate of the first testator to die may elect to have property qualify for the marital deduction in the decedent's estate, provided that the survivor is entitled to all of the income from the property for life and no one other than the survivor may appoint the property to anyone other than the survivor. Property for which such an election is made is subject to taxation when the survivor disposes of it, either by lifetime gift or at death.

The principal impediment to qualification for the marital deduction under sections 2056(a) and 2056(b)(5) of property passing from one spouse to another under a mutual will is that the survivor is contractually bound to transfer the property in accordance with the terms of the

---

[127]   1968-2 C.B. 274.

mutual will. Because of the contractual obligation, the survivor's interest in the property passing under the will is rarely seen as equivalent to outright ownership, and may be construed as no more than a life estate. Section 2056(b)(7) eliminates this impediment. * * * Therefore, the interest passing to a surviving testator under a mutual will should qualify, regardless of the provisions dealing with the remainder, provided that the surviving testator has the requisite income interest and no one has a prohibited power to appoint the property to anyone other than the survivor.

* * *

Prior to the adoption of section 2056(b)(7), difficulties arose in determining whether testators who convey property to a surviving testator absolutely but who also provided for disposition of the property after the survivor's death intended to convey outright ownership to the survivor and, if not, whether the interest conveyed qualified as a life estate coupled with a sufficient power of appointment to qualify for the deduction under section 2056(b)(5). Once a court has determined that a will is mutual, it rarely will find that the will gives the survivor unfettered outright ownership of the subject property, apparently because the court infers that the parties contracted to bind the survivor to preserve the property for the ultimate beneficiaries. * * *

* * *

Several cases have denied the marital deduction in the estate of the first testator to die, even under a mutual will that purported to grant the surviving testator a fee simple but that also contained provisions for those designated to receive the family assets after the death of the survivor. The courts' rationale in each case was that the interest of the surviving testator was limited by the mutual will contract in two respects: The survivor was prohibited from making an inter vivos gift of the transferors' property, and was obligated to preserve the estate for the benefit of the ultimate takers. Consequently, the survivor did not receive an unfettered right to consume the deceased testator's property and, therefore, did not receive a bequest that qualified for the marital deduction [under section 2056(b)(5)]. The courts in each case justified their reading of the mutual will on the ground that it was the only reasonable interpretation of the intent of the testators; that is, the mutual will contract would have been meaningless if the ultimate beneficiaries could not enforce an entitlement to the property against the surviving testator. This interpretation of the intent of the testators of a mutual will is unduly narrow. The same language can be read to indicate that each testator wished the other to have complete discretion to use the property during life, provided only that, if there was anything left to bequeath, it would pass to the named beneficiaries. Thus, the beneficiaries' right against the survivor properly may be construed as limited to preventing transfer of the remaining property to others at the survivor's death, and such a restriction on the survivor would not cause a reduction in or disallowance of the marital deduction.

* * *

Even courts that find that the surviving testator has an unlimited power of consumption under a mutual will must grapple with an unfortunate but universally-held interpretation of the requirements of section 2056(b)(5) concerning the survivor's general power of appointment. Section 2056(b)(5) requires only that the survivor receive an inter vivos or testamentary power, exercisable by the survivor alone and in all events. The Regulations under section 2056 state that an unlimited power to consume property during life is sufficient to qualify the subject property for the marital deduction but that an inter vivos power is not exercisable "in all events" if it cannot be exercised to make a gift of the property.

The critical question, in determining whether any interest qualifies for the marital deduction, clearly should be whether the survivor has an unlimited power to consume during life. If she does, then the property will be includible in the survivor's estate at death under section 2041, and there is no reason to deny the marital deduction at the death of the first testator to die. Unfortunately, courts generally have accepted the Regulation requiring the survivor to have the power to make gifts as a proper construction of the statutory phrase "alone and in all events" in section 2056; indeed, some have explicitly rejected the argument that Congress could not have intended double taxation to occur by denying the marital deduction and requiring inclusion in the survivor's estate.

* * *

Furthermore, whether particular language permits the surviving testator to make gifts may be difficult to determine. * * *

* * *

* * * At issue is the scope of the contract between the testators, a question that must be answered under the applicable state law. Did they contract to leave certain assets to named beneficiaries * * * ? Did they contract merely to leave whatever remained at the death of the survivor? Or did they contract only to leave the testators' assets to the survivor, with the residuary clause meant to function only as the will of the survivor and not as a part of a contract at all? Until a federal court resolves these matters of intent under state law principles of construction, it cannot accurately resolve the federal transfer tax question.

* * *

One of the most frequently litigated questions in this area is the extent to which property held jointly by spouses may qualify for the marital deduction if the spouses have executed a mutual will. Resolution of the question requires a two-part analysis. The federal court must first determine whether the mutual will obligates the surviving testator to dispose of the deceased testator's share of the survivorship property in a particular way. If it does, then the court must determine whether the surviving testator receives a nondeductible terminable interest in the deceased testator's share of the property because of this obligation. The Service initially took the position that a mutual will, speaking as the deceased testator's will, governed the nature of the interest of the surviving testator in jointly held property, and this position prevailed in several decisions. Nevertheless, federal courts generally have held that the jointly held property passes outside the will to the survivor outright. Those courts that have so held uniformly also have held that the jointly owned assets qualify for the marital deduction in the estate of the deceased testator, even if the surviving testator's interest in probate assets subject to the mutual will is concededly nondeductible. Apparently, the Service has conceded this issue and has begun to focus instead on the gift tax ramifications to the surviving testator of the ultimate transfer of the property to the designated remainder beneficiaries.

The courts' analysis of the testators' intent concerning disposition of nonprobate property is rather superficial. The key question is whether the mutual will imposes restrictions upon the survivor's use of the nonprobate property and upon the survivor's ultimate disposition of the property. The resolution of this question turns upon a determination of the intent of the mutual testators. The mutual will may impose restrictions upon the survivor's disposition of the nonprobate property sufficient to disqualify the property for the marital deduction, absent a QTIP election, regardless of whether the nonprobate property passes outside the will for state probate law purposes. If a joint tenancy is severed at the execution of a mutual will, then the testators hold the property thereafter as tenants in common until the first testator's death. The mutual will might be construed to convey an interest in the deceased testator's share of the property to the surviving testator. If that is the case, then the surviving testator's share of the property is not includible in the estate of the deceased testator for transfer tax purposes, and the decedent's share is a probate asset, subject to the terms of the mutual will that govern the transfer of assets generally from the deceased testator to the survivor. Whether the survivor receives a nondeductible terminable interest in the portion that is includible in the deceased testator's estate depends upon a construction of the terms of the will under the analysis that applies to the deceased testator's other property. * * * Mutual wills should not, however, be construed to sever a joint tenancy unless they so state explicitly.

If joint tenancy property is not severed when a mutual will is executed, then the entire property must belong to the surviving testator outright by right of survivorship. If that is the case, and if the mutual will is not construed to impose upon the survivor an obligation to make a future transfer of the property to beneficiaries named in the mutual will, property held jointly by spouses clearly should qualify for the marital deduction, to the extent that it is includible in the deceased testator's estate. To determine whether such a binding obligation exists, a court evaluating the federal transfer tax consequences must determine the terms of the contract between the testators. If the obligation was not previously binding but becomes binding when the first testator dies with a will containing the contracted provisions, then the survivor receives the entire property outright simultaneously with the obligation to transfer it at death to the beneficiaries named in the mutual will. * * * [T]he property would be treated as having passed outright to the survivor under the deed and, therefore, would qualify for the marital deduction. The survivor's obligation to transfer the property to the named beneficiaries at death then would be treated as becoming binding immediately after receipt of the property by right of survivorship. To the extent that such transfer constitutes a completed gift to the ultimate beneficiaries at that time, the survivor would be the transferor. Under this analysis, the property qualifies for the marital deduction in the estate of the first testator to die, but the surviving testator incurs gift tax liability upon the completed gift to the ultimate beneficiaries of a remainder interest in the property at the death of the first testator to die.

On the other hand, if the property is received by the surviving testator subject to an obligation that became binding before the deceased testator died with the mutual will in effect, then the property will not qualify for the marital deduction in the estate of the first testator to die to the extent of the obligation. If the obligation to transfer to others can be valued, and its value is less than the value of the deceased testator's share of the jointly held property, then the difference should qualify for the marital deduction.

If jointly held assets are held to be received by the survivor outright by right of survivorship, and if the mutual will is not construed as imposing a binding obligation on the survivor to make a subsequent transfer, then the property will qualify for the marital deduction in the estate of the first testator to die, as would any probate or nonprobate outright transfer. Such a finding implies that the mutual will directs disposition of the jointly held assets only as the will of the surviving testator and has no effect on the survivor's interest in the assets during life.

Resolution of these issues must occur on a case-by-case basis, through careful examination of the mutual will involved, and cannot be answered by mechanical recitation of the general rules governing title to jointly held property. Unfortunately, there likely will be many instances in which there is no reliable evidence of exactly what the mutual testators intended.

* * *

NOTE

Hess observes that "testators frequently fail to obtain their desired wealth transfer tax results by bequeathing property under a joint and mutual will, and clearly would have been better served had they been advised to use some other implementing document." Does the enactment of the QTIP provisions ameliorate the tax problems arising from a joint and mutual will? If a transfer arguably qualifies for the marital deduction under either § 2056(b)(5) or § 2056(b)(7), why might a taxpayer prefer to rely on the former section? Under § 2056(b)(5), what is the justification for treating probate assets differently from nonprobate assets? Should the surviving spouse's contractual obligation to leave the property to designated beneficiaries at death be analyzed as an encumbrance that merely reduces the amount of the marital deduction? If so, what are the estate tax consequences at the surviving spouse's death?

---

3. Further Reform Proposals

Although the estate and gift tax treatment of interspousal transfers has remained relatively stable since 1981, proposals for further reform continue to flourish. Harry L. Gutman explores the implications of treating married couples as a taxable unit for transfer tax purposes. He proposes a method for aggregating the spouses' separate transfer tax profiles upon marriage and for disaggregating the couple's transfer tax profile upon death or divorce, in order to reduce the estate-splitting advantages available to married couples under current law. Furthermore, Gutman recommends replacing the terminable interest rule with a "current beneficial interest" test along the lines previously proposed by the ALI and the Treasury.

Howard E. Abrams views the terminable interest rule as essentially obsolete. He proposes repealing the terminable interest rule (along with its exceptions) and allowing a marital deduction for the full value of any property in which the surviving spouse receives an interest, as long as the amount of the marital deduction is ultimately recaptured in the surviving spouse's tax base. Recognizing that simple repeal of the terminable interest rule might lead to abusive overvaluation of the deductible interest received by the spouse, Abrams would impose restrictions similar to those developed in the analogous context of charitable lead trusts.

Joseph Isenbergh proposes a radical overhaul of the marital deduction provisions based on the concept of the marital unit as a "notional taxpayer." He recommends repealing the terminable interest rule and allowing an immediate deduction for the value of the interest passing to the spouse. At the same time, he recommends that the existing treatment of QTIP dispositions be retained, so that taxpayers could elect to defer tax on the full value of the underlying property until the termination of the spouse's interest.

In his article on estate and gift tax reform, Joseph M. Dodge views the QTIP provisions as an application of a "hard-to-complete" rule that avoids difficult problems in valuing interspousal transfers of partial interests. He points out that under a "marital unit" theory there is no logical need for the requirement that the transferee spouse receive a life income interest, but notes that lifting that requirement might "be perceived as . . . contravening women's rights."

Finally, some commentators ask whether the marital deduction should be revised to reflect evolving family structures in contemporary society. Joan B. Ellsworth advocates a modified version of the marital deduction in the case of property passing under a "trust for an unmarried survivor" (TUMS).

Harry L. Gutman, *Reforming Federal Wealth Transfer Taxes After ERTA*, 69 Va. L. Rev. 1183 (1983)*

* * *

1. Toward Recognition of the Marital Unit

The transfer tax unit prior to the Tax Reform Act of 1976 was the individual. The marital deduction for property transferred to a spouse in a separate property jurisdiction did not, either historically or analytically, represent a decision to treat the spousal unit where it existed as a taxable unit. Rather, the provision was designed to equate the transfer tax treatment of married residents of separate property jurisdictions with that of married residents of community property jurisdictions. Community property jurisdictions treated property accumulated during marriage as owned one-half by each spouse. The marital deduction, enacted in 1948, granted a deduction to a decedent in a separate property jurisdiction for the value of qualifying property transferred to a surviving spouse, subject to a limit of one-half of the value of the decedent's gross estate. Thus, by using qualifying marital bequests, spouses could generally achieve the community property result of having one-half of the aggregate assets of both spouses included in each one's separate transfer tax base.[127]

In 1976 Congress increased the quantitative limitation on the estate tax marital deduction to the greater of $250,000 or one-half the decedent's adjusted gross estate. The $250,000 deduction was made available to community as well as separate property state decedents. At the same time Congress modified the gift tax marital deduction to allow the full value of the first $100,000 of gifts to a spouse to be deductible. * * *

In ERTA, Congress removed all quantitative limits on the marital deduction, made it available to residents of both community property and separate property states, and expanded the types of interests eligible for deductible status. The substantive effect of these changes is to treat the marital unit as a separate transfer tax unit with respect to interspousal transfers. The abandonment of any quantitative limitation on the amount of a deductible interspousal transfer, particularly when coupled with an individual exemption equivalent of $600,000, brings into sharp focus the question of how the marital unit should be treated with respect to transfers outside that unit. The issue is whether, in light of the implicit recognition of the marital unit as a

---

[127]   The equivalence between married taxpayers in separate and community property jurisdictions was not totally complete. The gift tax marital deduction was limited to one-half the value of the property transferred to a spouse. Thus, inter vivos efforts by spouses residing in separate property states to equalize ownership of property accumulated during marriage could result in a tax liability. In addition, separate property state residents could not achieve the community property result if they did not equalize the ownership of such assets during life and the less wealthy spouse died first.

separate unit for purposes of interspousal transfers, each spouse should continue to be treated as an independent taxpaying unit for transfers outside the unit.

A simple example illustrates the effect of allowing two exemption equivalents. A, a single individual, dies possessing assets of $1,200,000. After application of the $600,000 exemption equivalent, A's estate has a $235,000 tax liability. Assume instead A married B who had no assets. At death A makes a deductible transfer of $600,000 to B, thus equalizing the estates of A and B. As A and B are each entitled to an exemption equivalent of $600,000, there is no tax due at the death of either. The act of marriage has doubled the amount of property owned by one of the spouses that can be passed tax-free by the taxable unit consisting of the two spouses.

The availability of separate graduated rate schedules for each spouse also increases the potential transfer tax advantage gained upon marriage. The marital unit achieves maximum tax savings when the last taxable transfer of each spouse is subject to tax at the same marginal rate. Thus, if C died unmarried possessing assets of $5,000,000, C's estate would incur a transfer tax liability of $2,083,000. If C died married and transferred $2,500,000 in deductible form to surviving spouse D, the transfer tax of each estate would be $833,000, or a total of $1,666,000. The $417,000 difference is attributable to D's additional unified credit of $192,800 plus $224,200 in tax saved by subjecting D's estate to the progressive marginal rate schedule separately.

The tax consequences illustrated by these examples do not arise because ERTA removed the quantitative limitations on the marital deduction. The same basic result occurred if identical marital bequests were made under pre-ERTA law. The pre-ERTA results, however, were thought conceptually acceptable because the pre-ERTA marital deduction was based on the community property model that assumed each spouse was a separate taxpayer owning one-half of the marital property.

The ERTA decision to treat the marital unit as a single unit for purposes of interspousal transfers removes the community property model as the reason for allowing that unit two unified credits and two opportunities to progress through the rate schedule. With the community property justification removed, no reason remains to allow a transferee spouse to take advantage of a separate rate schedule and exemption level with respect to property originally owned by the transferor spouse. This problem could be cured in one of two ways. First, one could maintain the individual as the taxable unit, permit property to be freely transferred within the marital unit, but trace and attribute any transfers outside the unit to the spouse whose earned or inherited assets represented the original source of the transfers. Alternatively, the spousal unit could be treated as a separate unit with transfers from that unit subject to a single rate schedule and exemption level. If neither option is feasible, the current structure would have to be retained.

The first solution is fraught with practical difficulty. The administrative burden of a tracing requirement for spousal property has proved overwhelming. The tracing problem was the principal reason for the 1948 repeal of the 1939 Code provision that attempted to redress the community/separate property imbalance in precisely this way. * * *

If the first option is administratively impractical, one must examine the tentative consequences of treating the marital unit as a separate taxpayer to determine whether such a system is feasible. If a separate rate schedule and exemption level were adopted for marital units, spouses would continue, under the unlimited marital deduction, to transfer property to each other without transfer tax consequences. All transfers by either spouse outside the marital unit would be cumulated and taxed under a marital rate schedule to which a marital exemption equivalent would apply.

A simple example, similar to the one above, can illustrate this system. Assume A, with $1,200,000 in assets, marries B with no assets. Also assume that the marital exemption equivalent is $900,000. If A transfers $300,000 to B at death pursuant to the marital deduction and bequeaths the remaining $900,000 to a trust in which B has an interest insufficient to cause inclusion in B's transfer tax base, no tax liability results because of the $900,000 exemption equivalent. When B dies, none of the $900,000 exemption equivalent is available, and B's estate will have to pay tax on the remaining $300,000 at the marital unit rate. Under the current system, B would incur no transfer tax liability.

Critics will argue that this proposal will create disparities between married taxpayers and single taxpayers. For example, if the spousal exemption level is set at less than twice the single exemption equivalent, this system will overtax the marital unit when each spouse has separately owned property greater than one-half the spousal exemption equivalent.[140] By the same token, where each spouse owns separate property not exceeding $2,500,000, the point at which the maximum marginal tax rate starts, application of the existing rate schedule to aggregated marital transfers subjects their separate property to a rate higher than would apply if the spouses were single. A lower rate schedule for married taxpayers can minimize these disparities, but as long as the rate structure is progressive, it is mathematically impossible to remove all differences.

The income tax experience is relevant in attempting to determine whether the recognition of the marital unit as a taxable unit is worth the concurrent disparities in tax treatment. Income tax literature is replete with discussions of how to tax family income equitably in view of the fact that community property states treat community income as belonging one-half to each spouse and separate property states treat it as attributed to the earner of the income or owner of the asset that produced the income. The income tax solution was the joint return which, in effect, permits married taxpayers to pay twice the tax on one-half of their aggregate taxable income. Thus, the income tax treatment of all married taxpayers with the same aggregate taxable income is equalized no matter how local law apportions the income.

This solution, however, inevitably led to disparities analogous to those that would occur in the transfer tax system. If the rates and tax brackets applicable to married and single taxpayers are identical, married taxpayers filing jointly pay significantly less tax than a single taxpayer with the same amount of income. Applying different rate schedules to single and married taxpayers narrows this gap somewhat. As with the transfer tax, however, it is mathematically impossible for a married couple and a single taxpayer with the same income to incur the same tax liability in a progressive tax system which affords income splitting to married taxpayers.[143]

The income tax accepts disparities between married and single taxpayers to achieve uniform taxation of spousal units. A similarly important goal exists in the transfer tax system: eliminating a tax avoidance opportunity available to married taxpayers with respect to their separately owned property. Congress should be willing to accept similar transfer tax disparities if they are necessary to end unjustified tax advantages. * * *

---

[140] Such a system, however, can result in a windfall to a spousal unit when one spouse possesses property in excess of the single exemption equivalent and the other possesses little or no property.

[143] * * * The income tax literature demonstrates that the goals of progressivity, marriage neutrality, and equal taxation of aggregate spousal wealth no matter how property is held are mutually inconsistent. Therefore, assuming a progressive rate structure, the choice is between marriage neutrality and equal taxation of aggregate spousal wealth. The marital deduction, however, permits spouses, absent rate considerations, to achieve a type of equal taxation through self-help. This fact makes marriage neutrality in the transfer tax context a different concept from income tax marriage neutrality. In the income tax, the concern is to prevent marriage from increasing the tax burden on "nonassignable" income earned by the spouses. In the transfer tax, the concern is to assure that the tax burden on separately owned property does not decrease simply through the act of marriage.

2. A System of Aggregation and Disaggregation

* * * Because a marriage transforms two separate taxable units into a single unit and the termination of marriage reinstitutes the individual as the appropriate unit, use of the marital unit as a taxable unit in the transfer tax requires a system to aggregate and disaggregate the tax profiles of the parties upon either event.

* * *

a. Transfers from the Marital Unit

* * * The following is suggested as the basic structure for aggregating the separate transfer tax profiles of spouses. Upon marriage the prior taxable transfers of the spouses will be aggregated. If aggregate prenuptial taxable transfers are less than the marital exemption equivalent, the aggregate will be the adjusted taxable gift base for subsequent transfers. If aggregate prenuptial transfers exceed the marital exemption equivalent, marriage will not result in tax liability. The spousal unit's adjusted taxable gifts immediately after marriage, however, will be the sum of the marital exemption equivalent and the amount by which each spouse's prenuptial transfers were subject to tax. Any transfer tax paid by either spouse on account of transfers made prior to marriage would be treated as tax paid by the unit for purposes of computing the tax on post-marriage transfers.

The operation of this proposal and the reasons for it are illustrated by the following examples, which again assume that the exemption equivalent applicable to married couples is $900,000 and the exemption equivalent applicable to single individuals is $600,000.

> Case 1: The aggregate prenuptial taxable transfers of the spouses do not exceed the spousal exemption equivalent, e.g., A and B have each transferred $300,000.

Upon marriage this spousal unit would have a separate exemption equivalent of $900,000. The prenuptial taxable transfers of the two spouses would be aggregated, and subsequent transfers would not be traced to the donor spouse. In this case, as A and B have each made $300,000 in taxable transfers prior to marriage, the AB unit has $300,000 of exemption equivalent left. Therefore, the AB unit will be able to make additional taxable transfers of $300,000 before any tax liability results. * * * Once transfers outside the unit exhaust the post-marriage exemption equivalent, they are cumulated without regard to source and subject to tax in accordance with the applicable rate schedule.

> Case 2: Only one spouse made prenuptial taxable transfers, but those transfers exceed the individual exemption equivalent, e.g., A has transferred $700,000, B has made no transfers.

In this case, A's prenuptial transfers resulted in tax liability. Under the proposal, the AB unit will be able to transfer an additional $200,000 before exhausting the marital exemption equivalent. Moreover, as A made a $100,000 prenuptial taxable transfer on which tax was paid, the AB unit will, in effect, be able to transfer tax-free an additional amount equal to the tax previously paid divided by the marginal rate applicable to transfers in excess of the spousal exemption equivalent. For example, if A paid $37,000 in transfer tax on the $100,000 premarital transfer and the marginal rate applicable to the first $100,000 of taxable transfers in excess of the $900,000 spousal exemption equivalent is forty percent, the AB unit could transfer an additional $92,500 after marriage before a tax payment is due.

> *Case 3*: Both spouses have made prenuptial taxable transfers the sum of which exceeds a single individual exemption equivalent, e.g., *A* and *B* have each transferred $500,000.

Because *A* and *B* each had an exemption equivalent of $600,000, the prenuptial transfers in this case did not result in tax liability. Marriage results in aggregate prior transfers of $100,000 in excess of the spousal exemption equivalent. The question is how to account for this excess. Three options are available. First, a $100,000 taxable transfer could be deemed to occur on the date of marriage with the spousal unit deemed to have made $1,000,000 of adjusted taxable gifts for purposes of future transfers. A second option is to impose no tax on the previously transferred excess of $100,000 but aggregate spousal transfers for purposes of future gifts would be $1,000,000. The final alternative is not to tax the $100,000 excess and still consider the spousal unit as having made only $900,000 of adjusted taxable gifts for purposes of future transfer tax liability.

The first option is unappealing. Transfers accorded tax-free status when made should not retroactively lose that character. The second option is more palatable because no tax is imposed retroactively. There is, nonetheless, a form of penalty on post-marriage gifts because the base from which the tax liability for such gifts is computed includes the previously untaxed gifts. The third option adopts the view that status at the time of the gift controls for all purposes. Concededly, this solution would encourage prenuptial gifts up to the amount of each spouse's exemption equivalent. That result, however, is not conceptually objectionable. These rules are designed principally to address the problem of tax-free shifting of ownership of property within the marital unit to take advantage of two credits and rate schedules. Where the source of the prenuptial gift was the separate property of the transferor, there is less harm in permitting two individual exemption equivalents to be utilized. Thus, option three appears the most acceptable solution.

> *Case 4*: One spouse has made prenuptial taxable transfers in excess of the individual exemption equivalent, the other has made prenuptial transfers of less than the individual exemption equivalent; e.g., *A* has transferred $900,000, *B* has transferred $400,000.

The principles developed thus far dictate that marriage have no additional transfer tax consequences. The open question is how to determine the post-marriage adjusted taxable gifts of the *AB* unit. The first alternative is to deny *B*'s unused individual exemption equivalent of $200,000 to the *AB* unit. Post-marriage adjusted taxable gifts would be $1,200,000, the sum of the spousal exemption equivalent ($900,000) plus the amount by which *A*'s prenuptial transfers exceeded *A*'s individual exemption equivalent ($900,000 − $600,000 = $300,000). The other alternative is to make *B*'s unused individual exemption equivalent available to the *AB* unit by reducing the prenuptial adjusted taxable gifts of *A* by the amount of *B*'s unused individual exemption equivalent. Thus, post-marriage adjusted taxable gifts would be $1,000,000, the sum of the spousal exemption equivalent ($900,000) plus the amount by which *A*'s prenuptial transfers exceeded *A*'s individual exemption equivalent and *B*'s unused individual exemption equivalent ($900,000 − [$600,000 + $200,000] = $100,000). In either event, the prenuptial transfer tax paid by *A* would be treated, for purposes of transfers from the *AB* unit, as paid by the *AB* unit.

The first alternative is the better result. If *B* has separately owned property, *B* may avoid losing part of the exemption equivalent by transferring $200,000 of that property prior to marriage. If *B* does not have separately owned property, the allowance of the unused single exemption equivalent to the *AB* unit under the second alternative permits *A* to avoid tax liability by shifting wealth to *B*. This manipulation of the tax system is precisely what a separate spousal rate schedule and exemption level is designed to avoid.

One can therefore develop a manageable system of aggregation for the marital unit. * * * The remaining problem is to disaggregate the taxable gifts of the marital unit upon its termination.

b. Transfers After Marriage Has Terminated

Marriage may terminate due to death or divorce. In the case of termination by death, there is only one remaining member of the unit. The problem is to determine the amount of the exemption equivalent allowed the surviving spouse and the amount, if any, of the adjusted taxable gifts of the spousal unit that will be allocated to the surviving spouse. In the case of divorce, the spousal unit splits into two individual units. One must therefore determine the amount of the exemption equivalent that will be available to each former spouse and how the adjusted taxable gifts of the spousal unit will be allocated between the former spouses.

i. Termination Due to Death

When the death of a spouse terminates the marital unit, two options exist for determining the transfer tax status of the surviving spouse. The first is to allow the tax attributes of marital status to continue after the death of one spouse. The second is to restore to the surviving spouse the unused attributes of individual unit status, at least with respect to property originally owned by that spouse.[145] Avoidance of complexity dictates use of the former approach.

Under the preferred approach, the transfer tax profile of the marital unit, taking into account the deathtime taxable transfers of the decedent spouse, becomes the base for the survivor. Thus, the cumulative taxable transfers of the unit (after application of the rules relating to aggregation upon marriage) become the adjusted taxable gifts of the survivor against which only the spousal exemption equivalent is available.

* * *

ii. Termination Due to Divorce

When divorce terminates the marriage, the spousal unit splits into two individual units. As each may make subsequent taxable transfers, a decision must be made as to the amount of the exemption equivalent each will have with respect to post-divorce transfers and how the adjusted taxable gifts of the spousal unit will be allocated between the former spouses. * * *

The governing principle is that divorce should result in the return to individual status of each spouse. The post-divorce adjusted taxable gifts of each spouse should be the sum of the prenuptial taxable transfers of each plus one-half of the taxable transfers made by the spousal unit. Each spouse should have an exemption equivalent equal to the individual exemption equivalent. One-half of any transfer tax paid by the spousal unit would also be allocated to each. For purposes of computing the tax on post-divorce transfers, all prior adjusted taxable gifts will be treated as if taxed under the rate schedule applicable to individuals.

* * *

4. Transfers of Terminable Interests in Property

Prior to ERTA most transfers of terminable interests in property were not eligible for the transfer tax marital deduction. A "terminable interest" is an interest that will terminate or fail "on

---

[145]   This alternative is based on the assumption that the principal purpose of creating a separate rate schedule applicable to spousal transfers is to eliminate the opportunity to utilize two rate schedules and two exemption levels for property owned by one of the spouses.

the lapse of time, on the occurrence of an event or contingency, or on the failure of an event or contingency to occur." Such a failure must result, however, in that interest passing from the donor to a third party other than the donee spouse for less than full and adequate consideration. The third party must also be able to possess or enjoy any part of the property by reason of such passing.

The pre-ERTA terminable interest rule was designed to serve two functions. Its principal function was to protect the tax base by assuring that a marital deduction would be allowed only for property which, if not included in the tax base of the first spouse, would be subject to transfer tax if disposed of by the donee spouse inter vivos or at death. Its secondary purpose was to assure that donees in separate property jurisdictions received the same ownership interest as donees in community property states. In community property states, a donee spouse by law received outright ownership of one-half of the community property. Because the marital deduction was based on the community property model, it was available in a common-law state only to the extent the donee spouse received outright ownership or its practical equivalent.

ERTA's implicit abandonment of the community property model as the basis for the marital deduction eliminated the secondary justification for the terminable interest rule. The only remaining function of the rule was to ensure that unconsumed spousal property is eventually subjected to transfer tax.[206] A simpler, more carefully tailored rule could have achieved this goal.

Instead of drafting a simpler terminable interest rule, Congress addressed this issue in ERTA by creating a new type of deductible terminable interest—"qualified terminable interest property." Qualified terminable interest property is property from which all of the income is payable at least annually to the donee spouse for life and over which no person has a power of appointment exercisable in favor of any person during the life of the donee spouse other than the donee spouse. Deductible status for qualifying terminable interest property is elective with the donor spouse for inter vivos transfers and with the decedent spouse's executor with respect to testamentary transfers. If deductible status is elected, the value of the property subject to the income interest is included in the transfer tax base of the donee spouse. The inter vivos disposition by the donee spouse of all or part of the qualifying income interest is treated as a taxable transfer of the property to which the interest relates. If the qualifying income interest is retained until death, the value of the property subject to the interest is included in the donee spouse's gross estate. Thus, one spouse may give or leave property for the benefit of the other for life, specify who will receive the property upon the death of the surviving spouse, and defer payment of transfer tax until death of the survivor. The value of the property in which the donee spouse has a qualifying income interest is included in the transfer tax base of that spouse, thereby maintaining the basic principle that any transfer outside the marital unit is subject to transfer tax.

The terminable interest rule is highly complex, and the ERTA solution adds yet another layer of complexity. With ERTA's abandonment of the community property model, Congress could have avoided needless complexity and traps for unwary practitioners by replacing the ter-

---

[206]   The pre-ERTA terminable interest rule not only needed to be reformed to recognize the abandonment of the community property model, but also needed to be changed to conform to the implicit recognition of the spousal unit as the marital unit. Under the pre-ERTA terminable interest rule, Congress imposed a current tax cost on a decedent who desired both to provide for a surviving spouse and to retain control over the ultimate disposition of the property in which the surviving spouse had an interest. Such a disposition would not qualify for the marital deduction and thus would be included in the decedent's transfer tax base. Tax on the transfer would therefore be paid at that time. Once complete deferral of tax on property passing to a surviving spouse became possible under the unlimited marital deduction, there was little reason to impose the tax cost on the retention of control of the ultimate disposition of the property.

minable interest rule with a single rule permitting a deduction for the value of any property in which a donee spouse receives a "current beneficial interest." Both the American Law Institute and the Treasury Department had previously suggested this change. It would have preserved the tax base by providing that the donee spouse would be treated as making a taxable transfer of the underlying property upon the expiration of the donee spouse's interest.

* * *

An alternative to the "current beneficial enjoyment" test as a replacement for the terminable interest rule is to allow a marital deduction for the value, when ascertainable, of any interest given to the donee spouse. The value of any interests in the same property passing to others would be immediately taxable to the donor. This alternative would expand the category of deductible transfers beyond those available under the "current beneficial enjoyment" test. It would also differ in its treatment of an interest that does not pass to the donee spouse by including the value of that interest in the tax base of the donor at the time of the initial transfer. Thus, for example, if A transferred property in trust to pay the income to A's father, F, for life, remainder to A's spouse B, the value of F's life estate would be immediately taxable to A and the value of B's remainder would be deductible. If B died prior to F, the value of the remainder would be included in B's estate. If B died after F, the unconsumed portion of the trust corpus would be included. On the other hand, if A transferred property in trust providing income to spouse B for life, remainder to their children, the value of B's life estate would be deductible and the value of the remainder would be taxable to A at the time of the transfer. At B's death the unconsumed portion of the income distributed from the trust would be included in B's estate.[214]

This alternative to the "current beneficial enjoyment" test basically adopts an "easy-to-complete" rule as the normative principle regarding when a transfer is complete. In other words, it permits fractionalizing property into various temporal elements (which are generally recognized as separate interests in property under traditional property law) and treating each such element as a separate transfer. The tax differences between it and a "hard-to-complete" rule (which provides the conceptual basis for the mechanics of the "current beneficial enjoyment" test) include the timing of the tax payment, the measurement of the value of the various interests, and the treatment of post-transfer changes in value of the underlying property. The "current beneficial enjoyment" rule defers all tax until the disposition of the qualifying ownership interest but includes in the tax base of the donee spouse at that time the entire value of the property from which the current enjoyment was received. The alternative treats the nonqualifying interests as immediately taxable to the donor and therefore excludes from the tax base of both the donor and donee spouse any subsequent fluctuations in value of the property from which the donee receives enjoyment.

Application of the easy-to-complete alternative to even the standard life estate to spouse, remainder to children example discloses a number of problems. First, one must determine the present value of the gift of the remainder interest. This requires both the selection of an appropriate discount rate and a time period over which to apply it. One could, of course, calculate the donee spouse's life expectancy by reference to mortality tables and apply a uniform discount rate to the life expectancy thus determined, but this method still is inadequate. One serious problem is that the accuracy of the discount rate turns on two different variables. The

---

[214]   The rationale for this result would be that the disposition is the substantive equivalent of a purchase of an annuity for the donee spouse and an outright transfer of the present value of the remainder interest to the remainderman.

first is whether the rate, viewed independently of any investment decisions made by the trustee, is correct.[216] A second problem is the extent to which the investment decisions of the trustee may vary the assumptions upon which the rate is based. When this problem occurs, the amount of the gift is mismeasured even assuming an appropriate independent discount rate.[217] Finally, even if the discount rate is correct, the value of the remainder interest is inaccurately measured anytime the donee spouse dies sooner or later than predicted.

One could thus conclude that the easy-to-complete alternative may produce inaccurate and inequitable results even when applied to the most simple cases. The question then is whether the "current beneficial enjoyment" test produces better results at less administrative cost. The term "current beneficial enjoyment" obviously must be defined, and there will doubtlessly be disputes over whether particular dispositions create the requisite current interest in the transferee spouse. Nevertheless, under the "current beneficial enjoyment" test there is no need to fractionalize and value temporal elements of the transfer.[218] Moreover, a trustee's investment decisions cannot affect the measure of the tax base. Current distributions will remain in the tax base of the donee spouse unless consumed. Amounts remaining at the expiration of the donee spouse's beneficial enjoyment will be taxed at their value at that time. Thus, the rule treats all transfers similarly and avoids the measurement vagaries of the alternative.

Some rule to prevent the exclusion from the tax base of interspousal transfers of partial interests in property is still necessary and the complexities of the current rule require revision. The question is whether, in revising current law, one should replace the terminable interest rule with the "current beneficial enjoyment" test or the easy-to-complete alternative. That choice is one of timing, accuracy of measurement, and administrative cost. Balancing these considerations, the "current beneficial enjoyment" test is preferable.

* * *

NOTE

Gutman supports the adoption of a separate rate schedule and exemption level for married couples. How should such a rate schedule and exemption level be structured to minimize discrimination between married couples and individuals? As Gutman notes, invoking the analogy of the joint income tax return, it is "mathematically impossible" to eliminate all differences in a system of progressive rates. Does a high rate of divorce cause special problems under Gutman's proposed system?

Treating a married couple as a separate taxable unit also raises problems of timing and valuation of transfers outside the unit. For example, consider a transfer in trust to pay income to the settlor's spouse for life, with remainder to their children. Should

---

[216]   * * * If market interest rates exceed [the assumed discount rate], the tables undervalue life income interests and overvalue remainder interests.

[217]   Even if the valuation table rate were correct, the trustee could invest in assets with a current yield of less than the table rate, thus reducing the return to the income beneficiary. Assuming appreciation in the property is equal to the difference between the table rate and the actual yield, the executor thereby increases the value of the remainder in that amount.

[218]   This fractionalization will be a formidable task once the disposition departs from the standard life estate/remainder disposition. Similar valuation difficulties led to the 1969 revision of rules governing the allowance of charitable contribution deductions. * * *

the income interest be treated as retained by the marital unit, so that the entire value of the underlying property becomes subject to tax at the termination of the income interest? Or should there be an election to incur an immediate tax? Should it matter whether the trust is created at the settlor's death or while both spouses are still living?

Howard E. Abrams, *A Reevaluation of the Terminable Interest Rule*, 39 TAX L. REV. 1 (1983)*

INTRODUCTION

If a taxpayer dies possessed of *Blackacre* and devises a life interest in it to his surviving spouse, his federal taxable estate includes the full value of *Blackacre* without any diminution for the interspousal transfer. However, if the taxpayer instead devises cash or other property equal in value to the life interest, the taxable estate is reduced by the value of the interspousal transfer. In an estate tax that is based upon the value of a decedent's property without regard to the form that his property takes, this inconsistent treatment of essentially identical devises is troublesome. It is caused by the terminable interest exception to the estate tax marital deduction.

The terminable interest exception has been part of the marital deduction rules since they first were enacted in the Revenue Act of 1948. While the terminable interest rule has changed only slightly in that time, the marital deduction has seen substantial expansion * * * . This expansion of the deduction reflects a major reinterpretation of its role in the estate tax. Originally, the marital deduction was seen as a means of equalizing the application of the estate tax to residents of common-law and community property states; now, it is seen as a fundamental component of the definition of the proper taxpaying entity.

* * *

ORIGINAL UNDERSTANDING OF THE TERMINABLE INTEREST RULE

* * *

The original function of the terminable interest rule was to ensure that community property treatment could only be had by community property like dispositions. For example, a devise by a decedent to his surviving spouse of a life interest does not qualify for the marital deduction if the remainder passes gratuitously from the decedent to another person, "and for policy reasons should not have been expected to qualify, since it in no way resembles the complete interest of the community property spouse." * * *

In fact, however, one type of interest can qualify for the marital deduction without passing outright to the surviving spouse * * * . If a decedent devises property in trust with a life interest in favor of his surviving spouse, the property qualifies for the marital deduction despite the terminable interest rule if three conditions are met: (1) All income from the trust must be payable annually or at more frequent intervals; (2) the surviving spouse must have a power to appoint the trust corpus and this power must be exercisable at least in favor of himself or his estate; and (3) no other person can have a power to appoint the corpus to anyone other than the surviving spouse. By this exception, Congress recognized "one of the customary modes of transfer of property" while imposing restrictions "plainly designed to serve the function of exacting a price for split estate taxation comparable to the price paid in community

---

*   Copyright © 1983. Reprinted with permission.

property states." By dint of an annual enjoyment of income coupled with the specified power of appointment, "the interests of the [surviving] spouse approach complete ownership." * * *

* * *

CHANGING ROLE OF THE MARITAL DEDUCTION AND NEW INTERPRETATION OF TERMINABLE INTEREST RULE

* * *

* * * [T]he Economic Recovery Tax Act of 1981 * * * completed the transformation of the marital deduction. All quantitative limitations on the marital deduction were removed because "a husband and wife should be treated as one economic unit for purposes of the estate and gift taxes." The qualitative limitations imposed by the terminable interest rule were retained, however, with but a single new exception. This exception allows the deduction for property transferred to a trust (known as a Q-TIP trust) in which the spouse has only the right to income, distributable annually or at more frequent intervals. The deduction for such a transfer is allowed only if the estate elects it, and the consequence of the election is that the corpus of the trust is added to the recipient spouse's transfer tax base even if his interest in the trust would not ordinarily justify such an inclusion. The Q-TIP provision is a natural extension of the traditional trust exception to the terminable interest rule given the shift in emphasis from mimicking community property to taxing property only once each generation. * * *

REEVALUATION OF THE TERMINABLE INTEREST RULE

* * *

* * * [T]erminable interests have the characteristic that they are valuable upon creation but may be worthless at the time of the recipient spouse's death. From this, one might conclude that if a terminable interest in fact terminates (that is, becomes worthless by the time of the recipient spouse's death), the spouse's gross estate will include nothing attributable to the terminable interest. Indeed, the terminable interest rule is justified on precisely this ground, for as currently interpreted the role of the terminable interest rule is to deny the marital deduction to an interspousal transfer if the recipient does not have to include the transferred interest in his transfer tax base.

Yet, this conclusion is incorrect. To be sure, the value of the *property* may not be includable in the recipient spouse's estate, but the value of the transferred *interest in property* will be (unless the recipient spouse transfers or consumes it), because the value of the terminable interest will be received by the recipient spouse over time. Consider, for example, the devise by a decedent to his surviving spouse of a life interest in long-term bonds paying a fixed rate of interest each year. The fair market value of the life estate can be computed actuarially by multiplying the annual interest payment times the surviving spouse's expected remaining life and then discounting for the passage of time. For example, if the bonds pay 6% annually on a par value of $100,000 and if the surviving spouse is a male aged 56 at the time of the devise, the fair market value of the life estate is approximately $60,466. The fair market value of the remainder at the time of the devise is $39,534.

Suppose the "overlife" is exactly its expected length, namely, 16 years. At the surviving spouse's death, none of the value of the bonds will be includable to the surviving spouse because the value of the life interest is then zero. However, the spouse will receive some $96,000 of interest on the bonds; this amount, plus amounts earned by reinvesting the interest receipts, *will* be includable unless the recipient spouse transfers or consumes it.

In the absence of a terminable interest rule, there would be a marital deduction of $60,466 and net inclusion of $39,534 to the estate of the deceased spouse. Further, in the absence of transfer or consumption by the recipient spouse, considerably more than $60,466 attributable to the transfer will be includable in the estate of the recipient spouse. As only $39,534 leaves the marital community on the death of the first spouse to die, treating the marital community as a single taxpaying entity requires that a transfer tax on $39,534—neither more nor less—should be payable at that time. As the remaining value of the corpus will leave the marital community at the death of the surviving spouse, only then should a transfer tax be payable on this value. * * *

With the terminable interest rule, however, the incidence of taxation is quite different. Because there is no deduction from the estate of the decedent spouse, a transfer tax must be paid from this estate on the full value of the corpus. On the death of the surviving spouse, the value of the life interest, augmented by compounded interest, will again be taxed. The net effect of the terminable interest rule is thus to tax the value of the terminable interest twice, once in the estate of each spouse.

* * *

The terminable interest rule * * * overtaxes the value of a terminable interest whether the interest entitles the recipient spouse to cash or benefits in kind. The conceptually correct approach is simply to discard the terminable interest rule in its entirety and allow any inter-spousal devise to qualify for the estate tax marital deduction. The deduction should equal the fair market value of whatever interests in property pass from the decedent to his surviving spouse, and a repeal of the terminable interest rule without any other change will effect this result.

* * *

Unfortunately, this conceptually simple approach can be implemented without difficulty only for terms of years, life estates, and other interests terminating at actuarially predictable times. Many interspousal transfers (such as a devise conditioned on a failure to remarry) are conditioned on events whose occurrence cannot be predicted with statistical accuracy. The values of these terminable interests cannot be estimated with reasonable accuracy because the fair market value of a terminable interest necessarily turns on the interest's expected date of termination. * * * Fortunately, there is a solution to this valuation difficulty that seems both equitable and administrable.

* * *

* * * An estate should be given the option of deducting the full value of any property in which the surviving spouse is devised a terminable interest so long as the surviving spouse agrees to include in his transfer tax base an amount equal to the marital deduction claimed by the decedent spouse. If the surviving spouse refuses to agree to this subsequent overinclusion, the estate of the decedent should be allowed a marital deduction for the terminable interest only to the extent that its value can be adequately established.

By allowing this deduction for the full value of the property rather than for only the value of the surviving spouse's terminable interest, the estate is given a deduction in excess of that to which it is entitled. This excess deduction should be allowable only if the surviving spouse is required to include in his transfer tax base an amount equal to the excess plus interest on that excess from the date of the decedent's death until the excess is finally subject to transfer tax. Since the decedent devises only the terminable interest portion of the property to his surviving spouse while a marital deduction equal to the full value of the property is allowed, the excess deduction equals the value of the remainder devised out of the marital community. * * * [T]he value of the excess, plus interest from the date of the decedent's death until the termination of the terminable interest, always equals the full value of the marital deduction claimed by the decedent.[114] Given this relationship, a decedent's estate should be allowed the option of deducting the full value of any property in which he devised a terminable interest to his surviving spouse, so long as the surviving spouse agrees to include in her transfer tax base, upon termination of her interest, the amount previously deducted by the decedent. Hard to value terminable interests can thus be ignored, for all that needs to be valued under this optional approach is the underlying property. Further, the subsequent inclusion to the recipient spouse requires no additional valuation because the amount of that inclusion is simply the amount of the prior deduction.

The * * * Q-TIP provision is similar to this proposal except that (1) the surviving spouse's interest must be a life interest with income payments made at least annually, and (2) subsequent inclusion to the surviving spouse is tied to the value of the property at the time of the termination of the surviving spouse's interest, rather than to the amount of the prior deduction. The requirements that the surviving spouse receive precisely a life estate and that income be paid at least annually * * * seem to reflect no more than an unthinking decision to follow the conditions imposed by the Revenue Act of 1948 on deductible devises in trust, conditions imposed to ensure that the surviving spouse's interest in the trust is comparable to a surviving spouse's interest in community property. Now that Congress has rejected the historical foundations for the terminable interest rule, the limitations imposed by the 1948 Revenue Act on qualifying interspousal transfers of property should be removed rather than perpetuated.

* * * [T]he decision to tie the amount of the subsequent inclusion to the value of the property at the termination of the recipient spouse's interest rather than to its value as of the decedent's death * * * is as little justified. Under the Q-TIP provision, the marital community is taxed on Q-TIP property precisely as if the property were devised in fee to the surviving spouse. While this ensures that the marital deduction cannot be used to exclude property from the estates of both spouses, it imposes an improper burden on the marital community because it fails to reflect the reduced interest devised to the surviving spouse.

One effect of a decedent's decision to divide property between his surviving spouse and a remainderperson is to limit the surviving spouse's ability to profit from subsequent appreciation. * * * [A]ppreciation in property affects the holder of a life estate or other terminable interest only if it causes income to rise, and increased income (unless consumed) adds to the surviving spouse's estate independently. By taxing Q-TIP property as if it were devised to the surviving spouse in fee, the current provision fails to recognize that some part of any future appreciation or depreciation was transferred out of the marital community at the time of the decedent's death.

Consider a devise of an interest in *Blackacre* to a decedent's surviving spouse, a male aged 56 at the time of the devise. If *Blackacre* is worth $100,000 at the time of the devise and rents for 6% of its value per year, the fair market value of the life interest is $60,466. If *Blackacre* appreciates in value to $200,000 immediately after the decedent's death, the surviving spouse

---

[114]   If the actual length of the terminable interest turns out to be t years, the discounted value of the remainder as of the decedent's death is $V(1 + i)^{-t}$, where V is the fair market value of the property and i is the annual interest rate. Therefore, if r is the rate of tax per dollar of includable value, an estate tax imposed at the decedent's death on the present value of the remainder equals $rV(1 + i)^{-t}$.

On the other hand, a tax imposed on the full value of the property equals rV, and if the tax is deferred until the termination of the recipient spouse's terminable interest, then its present value as of the decedent's death is $rV(1 + i)^{-t}$. Thus, an immediate tax on the value of the remainder equals the present value of a deferred tax on the entire property so long as the latter tax is imposed when the remainder becomes possessory * * * .

will benefit from this appreciation in the form of increased annual rental income. The increased rents, however, will be captured by the transfer taxes without resort to the Q-TIP provision (unless the spouse consumes them) because they will be received by the surviving spouse over time. By requiring the surviving spouse to include in his estate the appreciation in the property that accrues during the overlife beyond that amount paid out over time to the surviving spouse, the Q-TIP provision taxes the marital community on that portion of the appreciation inuring to the benefit of the remainderperson only.

* * *

Abolishing the terminable interest rule and modifying the Q-TIP provision will allow a marital community to pay the correct amount of estate tax on all marital property so long as the value of a terminable interest is received by the recipient spouse either in cash or in kind. If, however, a decedent devises to his surviving spouse a terminable interest that accumulates rather than distributes its income, a marital deduction may be used to exempt property from the estate tax of both spouses. * * *

Assume a decedent devises all his property in trust with a life interest to his surviving spouse and remainder over to their children. A direction to the trustee to invest in nonproductive assets would cost the decedent his marital deduction, but a direction to minimize taxes coupled with a broad grant of investment authority to the trustee might accomplish the desired result. Similarly, a devise of underproductive property or closely held stock might maximize the decedent's marital deduction while simultaneously reducing the eventual estate inclusion to the surviving spouse.

* * *

Congress has responded to this abuse in the area of charitable lead trusts by disallowing the charitable deduction unless the charity's interest is an entitlement to a fixed dollar amount per year or a fixed percentage of the corpus per year. Such interests can be accurately valued, and a trustee is unable to limit the charity's actual receipts in favor of the remainderperson by investing in underproductive assets.

Similar limitations could be imposed on interspousal transfers of terminable interests. These restrictions would anticipate most abuses * * * . However, the considerations that inform the structure of an interspousal devise are significantly different from those informing the structure of a charitable devise, and taxpayers might less readily accept limitations on the form of their interspousal transfers than they have accepted the restrictions on charitable lead trusts.

For example, while a taxpayer contemplating a charitable transfer might be influenced by the charity's other funding sources, he is unlikely to provide for an increase in the charity's entitlement if its other sources fail. Similarly, he is unlikely to desire that a charitable transfer be reduced if the charity's outside funding increases. Yet, the same taxpayer might well desire to tie the amount of an interspousal transfer to similar circumstances, particularly if the transfer is made by devise. For example, a taxpayer survived by a spouse possessed of substantial wealth might desire to effect a modest interspousal devise with a provision that the devise should be increased if the spouse's wealth is dissipated. Conversely, a decedent might wish to provide that an interspousal devise be limited if the surviving spouse's needs become reduced. Neither of the above examples can be adequately addressed by resort to charitable lead-like limitations.

If a decedent is willing to devise to his surviving spouse an interest that can only be reduced as circumstances change, the modified Q-TIP proposal will suffice so long as it can be applied to various portions of a single trust. For example, a decedent could devise to his surviving spouse a life interest in all his property, and he could provide that if the spouse's needs are reduced, then the trustee may terminate the spouse's interest in an appropriate percentage of the trust. So long as this termination causes immediate transfer taxation on an amount equal to the same percentage of the marital deduction claimed by the decedent spouse, the marital community is taxed just as if the termination could have been foreseen, valued, and taxed at the time of the devise. Unfortunately, no similar technique exists for taxing interspousal transfers that may increase over time.

The obvious solution is simply to ignore any possible increase in an interspousal devise. While this approach will overtax some marital communities, the overtaxation can be avoided by eschewing interspousal transfers in which the recipient spouse's interest may increase at unpredictable times in the future. While some flexibility is denied to the tax minimizing decedent, it is flexibility unavailable under current law: Interests of this sort do not qualify for the current marital deduction because of the terminable interest rule. Thus, abolition of the terminable interest rule coupled with a modified Q-TIP provision and charitable lead-like restrictions will work no hardship on taxpayers, nor will it significantly restrict the necessary flexibility of estate plans. * * *

* * *

NOTE

As Abrams points out, simply repealing the terminable interest rule and allowing a deduction for the value of interests transferred to a spouse raises valuation problems. Does Abrams' proposal provide an "equitable and administrable" solution without imposing new constraints? Would Gutman agree?

Joseph Isenbergh, *Simplifying Retained Life Interests, Revocable Transfers, and the Marital Deduction*, 51 U. Chi. L. Rev. 1 (1984)*

* * *

* * * As a general proposition, transfers between spouses now pass free of tax. The result is not, however, a total forgiveness of tax, but rather a deferral of tax on transferred amounts that remain within the same generation. Upon the death of the surviving spouse, a transfer tax will ultimately be imposed if the remaining estate is large enough.

* * *

The limitations on the marital deduction ultimately accomplish little more than to channel marital gifts and bequests into specific patterns and to penalize those who commit various footfaults. Combinations of outright transfers and annuities created during life * * * can achieve results comparable to those of terminable interests without incurring a tax penalty. Because there is little reason to discriminate among what are essentially identical transfers, the restrictions on the marital deduction for terminable interests could simply be eliminated.

The general rule of section 2056(a) would then allow a marital deduction for the value of all interests in property passing to a surviving spouse, whether terminable or not. * * *

The bluntest way to simplify things—and possibly the best—would be to repeal all of section 2056(b) (which now both limits the marital deduction for terminable interests and creates "qualified" terminable interests). This change would have only a small effect on the tax cost of transferring wealth within families because it takes away from the IRS little more than does the present allowance of the marital deduction for "qualified" terminable interests.[110] When a "qualified" terminable interest is created under present law, the marital deduction is allowed for the entire value of the property in which the surviving spouse has a life interest (at the cost, to be sure, of the subsequent inclusion of the entire amount in the estate of the surviving spouse). Following the repeal of section 2056(b), however, only the value of the interest in property actually passing to the surviving spouse, i.e., the life interest itself, would be deductible. The additional deferral of tax resulting under section 2056(b)(7) from a marital deduction larger than the actual value of the interest received by the surviving spouse nearly offsets, in most cases, the subsequent inclusion of the entire underlying property in the estate of the surviving spouse.

A subtler simplification of the law would be to repeal the rules barring the marital deduction for terminable interests, while preserving the option of creating "qualified" terminable interests under present section 2056(b)(7). This change would yield a somewhat more flexible tax regime than would an entire repeal of section 2056(b). The resulting rules would allow a deduction for the entire value of property transferred to a spouse subject to a life interest on condition that its value be included in the estate of the surviving spouse. A taxpayer could therefore elect to create relatively more income for the surviving spouse at the cost of a larger transfer tax to be borne later by subsequent heirs.

* * *

A possible concern for the Treasury is that an unlimited marital deduction for terminable interests would leave room for manipulation. For example, life interests could be created in favor of spouses known to be ailing and likely to die soon. Because the ailing spouse will die sooner than would statistically be expected, the remainder interest will be undervalued, thereby allowing a part of the value of the transferor's original interest to pass untaxed. One possible countermeasure, which would cut off most abuse, would be to require inclusion in the estate of a surviving spouse of the full amount claimed as a deduction for any terminable interest transferred by the estate of a spouse having died within the preceding three years.

* * *

Viewed broadly, the unlimited marital deduction has the effect of treating spouses as a single taxpayer with a lifetime equal to the survivor's. In this light, the transfer of a life interest from one spouse to the other can be regarded as the retention of a life interest by this notional taxpayer. Present law, however, treats terminable interests transferred between spouses differently from interests retained by single individuals. Under the general rule, transfers of a terminable interest to a spouse are taxed as though the entire property underlying the interest had been transferred to the remainderman. "Qualified" terminable interests, by contrast, are taxed as though the entire property had been retained by the spouses.

* * *

---

[110]   * * * For a discussion of the terminable interest rule reflecting an analysis parallel to that offered here, see Abrams, *A Reevaluation of the Terminable Interest Rule*, 39 TAX L. REV. 1, 18 (1983).

NOTE

What sort of arrangement does Isenbergh have in mind when he indicates that "combinations of outright transfers and annuities created during life" can be used to circumvent the terminable interest rule under current law? Why might it be desirable to retain some form of QTIP election, even if the terminable interest rule were repealed? Would a three-year inclusionary rule effectively prevent the type of valuation problems identified by Isenbergh?

Joseph M. Dodge, *Redoing the Estate and Gift Taxes Along Easy-to-Value Lines*, 43 TAX L. REV. 241 (1988)*

* * *

* * * [V]aluation is a paramount issue under the marital deduction where the transferee spouse is given a life estate, term of years, annuity, remainder, or other present or future interest in property, and another of such interests is given to a third party, and it is proposed that only the value of the interest transferred to the spouse be deducted. In any such split interest transfer, where one interest in identifiable property is deductible and the other is not, and the deductible interest is overvalued relative to the nondeductible interest, the tax base of both the transferor and the transferee will be erroneously understated. It follows that proposals to simply repeal the terminable-interest rule and its exceptions, which would allow a deduction for the present value of future interests committed to the transferee spouse,[473] would be a godsend to the tax avoidance industry.[474]

* * *

* * * [T]he solution to this type of valuation problem is a hard-to-complete rule. In fact there presently exists a hard-to-complete rule in cases where the transferee spouse's interest comes first, namely the QTIP trust exception to the terminable-interest rule. Under the QTIP rules, a transfer to one's spouse for life, remainder over, results in a deduction for the entire value of the property (not just the value of the interest transferred to the spouse) on condition that the entire unconsumed property appear in the transferee spouse's tax base. Although the underlying theory of the QTIP scheme is sound, some of the QTIP rules could be modified to better accord with their purpose of effectuating a hard-to-complete rule. For example, distributions to third parties during the transferee spouse's lifetime could be permitted on condition that they be treated as gifts by the transferee spouse. In addition, there would be no intrinsic transfer tax rationale for keeping the present law requirement that the surviving spouse have the right to all of the income payable at least annually. * * * Nevertheless, the income requirement probably should be retained in order to carry out the nontax objective of guaranteeing the transferee spouse a minimum of enjoyment of the property. Otherwise, if transferors are given

---

*   Copyright © 1988. Reprinted with permission.

[473]   *See* Abrams, [*A Reevaluation of the Terminable Interest Rule*, 39 TAX L. REV. 1 (1983)]; Isenbergh, [*Simplifying Retained Life Interests, Revocable Transfers, and the Marital Deduction*, 51 U. CHI. L. REV. 1, 29-33 (1984)].

[474]   Thus, persons would transfer large amounts in trust for the spouse for life in cases where the spouse would likely die before his actuarial life expectancy. * * *

the opportunity to defer tax without conferring real and substantial economic benefits on their spouses, the elimination of the income requirement would be perceived as: (1) contravening women's rights, (2) disruptive of family harmony, (3) necessitating that each spouse be represented by an attorney, and (4) undermining public acceptance of the marital deduction for anything other than outright transfers.

* * *

NOTE

Why do the existing QTIP provisions require that the spouse be entitled to all the income from the property, payable at least annually? Why do they prohibit any power of appointment exercisable in favor of any person other than the spouse? Would the "current beneficial enjoyment" proposal be "perceived"—correctly or not—as "contravening women's rights"? Compare Dodge's proposal with Gutman's "hard-to-complete" approach.

Joan B. Ellsworth, *Prescribing TUMS: An Alternative to the Marital Deduction for Unmarried Cohabitants*, 11 Va. Tax Rev. 137 (1991)*

* * *

Given the present state of the law, with its rigid emphasis on the "lawful" marital union, what can be done for the new American family? Are estate planning techniques available to help de facto families that are based on emotional and economic interdependence, but not necessarily on marriage? Are there effective alternatives to the marital deduction?

* * *

* * * Domestic partners may be young or old, they may live with children or without, and their relationships may be heterosexual, homosexual, or nonsexual. The partnership may be newly formed or of long standing. Family assets may be modest in value or of considerable worth, and the property may be distributed equally between the partners or legal title may be vested in one partner alone. The common theme that distinguishes and identifies the nontraditional family is cohabitation with interdependence, but no legal marriage.

* * *

From a transfer tax point of view, the most advantageous property arrangement for an unmarried couple is the 50-50 split. This minimizes the estate tax burden, regardless of which partner dies first, and avoids any gift tax if the partnership is terminated earlier. It may not be possible, however, to achieve a tax-free split of the family assets if one partner initially owns or acquires most of the property. * * *

* * *

Assuming, for the moment, that nontraditional families should not be required to pay more estate taxes than traditional families, can the Internal Revenue Code be revised to achieve such a result? This is a difficult task because we cannot provide new tax benefits to deserving non-traditional families unless we also incorporate barriers to unwarranted tax avoidance. The TUMS* system is designed to achieve both these goals. It provides a useful substitute for the marital deduction while guarding against potential abuses.

In broad outline the TUMS idea is simple: family property that is placed in a TUMS is allowed to escape transfer taxation at the time of transfer. Ordinarily this transfer in trust will occur when one member of a nonmarital domestic partnership dies. At that time, either the personal representative of the decedent or the surviving partner may put the decedent's assets in a TUMS so that no estate tax is then due. The amount of the tax is calculated at the time of bereavement, but it is not paid until a later date. As long as the TUMS continues, net income is paid to the survivor and such income is not subject to estate tax * * * .

* * *

* * * Of course, the resulting deferral is fundamentally different from the regular marital deduction, where all family property consumed after the death of the first partner is allowed to escape transfer taxation forever. Postponement, however, is the major objective here, since that is seen as the most realistic and equitable goal.

When is use of the TUMS appropriate? It is assumed that this quasi-marital deduction should be available when one partner in a functioning nonmarital family dies leaving a surviving partner. Accordingly, it is essential to identify qualifying families. The challenge is to define "unmarried survivor" with precision for purposes of the statute.

Clearly, cohabitation is the salient feature of nonmarital families that require protection. Emotional and economic interdependence are most likely to be found among members of a household, and the benefit of TUMS can reasonably be withheld from individuals who do not reside together. Since it is not intended to give status to casual alliances, a substantial period of cohabitation—perhaps five years—should be prerequisite to formation of a TUMS.

* * *

What about cohabitants who are related by blood: the widowed sisters who spend their waning years together, or the dutiful niece who keeps house for her bachelor uncle? These families should not be precluded from using the TUMS because after years of cohabitation, such couples develop the same interdependencies, and survivor vulnerability as any unrelated couple.

Nevertheless, cohabitation by relatives may create situations where abuse can occur. It is possible that related individuals would reside together primarily for the sake of transfer tax benefits. The extreme case would be the parent/child family. If the parent's assets could be placed in a TUMS for the lifetime of the child, transfer taxes could be postponed for an entire generation. This is clearly objectionable from a policy point of view, since taxing family wealth at least once each generation is a fundamental goal of the transfer tax system.

Any potential for abuse by related individuals can be reduced if the benefit of the TUMS is limited temporally. The TUMS proposal is intended to delay the payment of transfer taxes for a while, but not forever. * * * It is suggested that a fair compromise is to defer all transfer tax payments for five years following the death of a domestic partner. Thereafter, payments may be made on an installment plan in order to further reduce the negative impact on the family.

* * *

---

*   The acronym "TUMS" refers to a "trust for an unmarried survivor."—Eds.

One further restriction must be added, however. It is suggested that the cohabitants should be required to be unmarried—at least, unmarried to anyone except each other—at the time of the decedent's death. * * *

* * *

The gift tax treatment of cohabiting couples is also important, especially where economic pooling of resources occurs during cohabitation. Under current law, expenditures for most items of support are considered to be gifts unless they are for the benefit of persons legally entitled to support by the payor (namely, the payor's spouse and minor children). There is an exception for direct payment of medical and educational tuition costs. * * *

The $10,000 annual exclusion protects pooling arrangements from the gift tax to some extent. But where one partner provides all food, shelter, and clothing (not to mention transportation, vacations, and the like) for the other, less-propertied partner, the annual exclusion may be greatly exceeded. * * *

Some commentators have suggested that the current gift tax exclusion for payment of medical and tuition expenses should be extended to all items of support. This is a sound idea. * * *

* * *

Under the TUMS system, an inter vivos TUMS may be established at any time after the period-of-cohabitation test has been met. No gift tax is payable on contributions made to the TUMS unless a taxable event occurs (i.e., death of the beneficiary or withdrawal of corpus). If cohabitation ceases for a reason other than death, the TUMS can continue, but no new additions may be made. At the death of the donor, the value of the corpus of the trust is included in the donor's estate. If the TUMS continues after the donor's death, with or without the addition of testamentary gifts, estate taxes become due on the same * * * schedule applicable to a purely testamentary TUMS. In each case, the transfer taxes are payable out of trust assets.

* * *

NOTE

Should the concept of the "taxable unit" be expanded to include cohabitants? See Bruce Wolk, *Federal Tax Consequences of Wealth Transfers Between Unmarried Cohabitants*, 27 UCLA L. REV. 1240 (1980), excerpted in Part III(A), *supra*. Does Ellsworth's approach avoid the "fine line-drawing" problem of simply expanding the definition of "surviving spouse" for federal transfer tax purposes? Should transfers within a single generation be generally exempt from transfer tax? Should estate tax deferral (coupled with an interest charge) be generally available to all taxpayers?

B.   Charitable Deduction

Since 1918, the estate tax has contained a charitable deduction for transfers to qualifying organizations. Aside from a 1932 amendment concerning the effect of death taxes payable from a charitable bequest, the only major change in the statute occurred in 1969 with the enactment of limitations on split-interest transfers to charity. In the debate leading up to the 1969 legislation, various income, estate and gift tax abuses involving charitable transfers prompted several commentators to reexamine the purpose and effect of charitable deductions. David Westfall proposes that the estate tax charitable deduction be limited to a percentage of the amount transferred; others urge more drastic changes ranging from complete repeal to the substitution of a flat-rate tax credit. In contrast, Boris I. Bittker defends the deduction, arguing that it provides a sensible adjustment to the estate tax rate structure and contributes to the goal of moderating concentrations of family wealth. George Cooper provides a critical perspective, arguing that even after the 1969 Act the charitable deduction continues to offer unwarranted ȯpportunities for sophisticated estate tax avoidance.

David Westfall, *Revitalizing the Federal Estate and Gift Taxes*, 83 HARV. L. REV. 986 (1970)*

* * *

* * * [I]t is far from clear just what effect a complete repeal of the present estate tax charitable deduction would have on the level of charitable giving. Prospective charitable donors might react in a variety of ways to an increased estate tax.

For example, if the transferor anticipated that his taxable estate would be $1 million if he made no charitable bequests, he could reduce the prospective tax of $289,140 * * * by $31,400 if he bequeathed $100,000 to a charity. Thus, the net cost to the noncharitable beneficiaries of his estate is $68,600. If the deduction were repealed, the net cost would become the full amount of the charitable bequest, $100,000. One possibility is that the donor would not be influenced by the repeal and would still bequeath the full $100,000 to charity, reducing the amount going to noncharitable beneficiaries by the full $31,400 increase in his estate tax. A second possibility is that the repeal would lead the donor to reduce his charitable bequest by the amount of the estate tax increase. Finally, the donor might decide to reduce his charitable gift by more than the amount of the tax increase or to omit it altogether.

To the extent that donors would maintain their level of after-tax charitable giving, the deduction is wholly wasted as a tax incentive for such gifts. To the extent that donors would merely reduce their gifts by the amount of the increased estate tax, the policy question is whether the amount of the increase can be better spent by the recipient charities or by the federal government. Only to the extent that donors would react by reducing their charitable gifts by more than the amount of the tax increase is there a net loss in funds available for public purposes as a result of a denial or restriction of the deduction.

Of course, there is no way to determine with precision how prospective donors would react to the repeal of the deduction, or to alternatives which would reduce its value by limiting deductibility or restricting deductibility to particular types of transfers. But the Treasury has concluded with respect to the income tax charitable deduction that "noneconomic motivations have considerable influence on the level of giving." A similar conclusion appears even more justified with respect to the estate tax deduction—it seems probable that many deathtime charitable transfers are made simply because the decedent is more interested in giving to charity than in giving to any other potential beneficiaries. Thus, the deduction may cost more in lost estate tax revenues than it produces in charitable gifts that would not otherwise be made.

* * *

[I]n order to insure that decedents' estates make some contribution to projects which Congress accords priority, it may be desirable to limit the deduction for all deathtime charitable transfers to a percentage of the amount transferred. * * *

* * *

NOTE

In economic terms, the efficiency of the estate tax charitable deduction can be measured by comparing the amount of induced charitable bequests with the amount of foregone tax revenues. Westfall questions the efficiency of the deduction, but subsequent empirical studies support a more sanguine view. For analysis by two leading economists, see Michael J. Boskin, *Estate Taxation and Charitable Bequests*, 5 J. PUB. ECON. 27 (1976); Martin Feldstein, *Charitable Bequests, Estate Taxation, and Intergenerational Wealth Transfers, in* ESSAYS IN URBAN ECONOMICS AND PUBLIC FINANCE IN HONOR OF WILLIAM S. VICKREY 91 (1976). Even if the deduction turns out to be highly efficient, why might reformers still recommend a percentage limitation? Westfall has characterized the unlimited estate tax charitable deduction as a "luxury," and has raised the question whether the deduction should not be limited to "a percentage of the estate or a percentage of the charitable bequests." Richard B. Covey, Stanley S. Surrey & David Westfall, *Perspectives on Suggested Revisions in Federal Estate and Gift Taxation*, 28 REC. ASS'N B. CITY N.Y. 42, 47-48 (1973).

Boris I. Bittker, *Charitable Bequests and the Federal Estate Tax: Proposed Restrictions on Deductibility*, 31 REC. ASS'N B. CITY N.Y. 159 (1976)*

* * *

The best point of entry into the issue before us is the income tax's percentage limit on the deductibility of charitable gifts, since this is sometimes held up as a model, the absence of such limit from the federal estate tax being viewed as an anomaly that calls for legislative correction. Why does the income tax contain a percentage limit on the deduction of charitable gifts and are these reasons equally applicable to the federal estate tax? * * *

The simplest explanation for the restriction, that it was enacted to prevent a loss of revenue, is not persuasive. The number of persons who give as much as the deductible limit, or who even exceed the biblical tithe, is small; if Congress was ever seriously concerned about a potential drain on the Treasury from an unlimited deduction, that fear should have been allayed long ago by the statistics.

Perhaps the restriction stems, at least in part, from a feeling that taxpayers get satisfactions from their charitable contributions that resemble the pleasures derived from hobbies, vacations, cultural activities, and other personal uses to which they may put their income. In exercising his command over income by making a charitable gift, the taxpayer is sometimes said to get

---

a kind of "psychic income" in the form of personal pleasure and public fame that should not be disregarded in determining his tax liability, even though it cannot be given a precise dollar value. Critics of existing law, indeed, sometimes argue that charitable gifts are simply a form of personal consumption that is no more entitled to a deduction than ordinary expenditures for the cost of hobbies and other personal activities.[22] Other tax theorists are not prepared to go this far, however, because they perceive a "selfless" element in charitable gifts distinguishing them from expenditures for hobbies and other personal activities. But if they also perceive an element of psychic income in charitable gifts, they may wish the tax law to reflect both of these perceptions.

As a device to take simultaneous account of the selfless element and the psychic income in charitable gifts, however, the percentage limit is a crude instrument. Up to the amount of the limit, the selfless element gets full sway, since the deduction is not reduced by any psychic income; on the other hand, amounts above the limit generate no deduction for the donor's generous impulses, implying that they are totally eclipsed by his psychic income. A remedy that would be more suited to the foregoing analysis of the psychological foundations of charitable gifts would be a deduction limited to a specified percentage of each donated dollar.

Another argument that is sometimes offered in support of the income tax's percentage limitation is that in its absence, taxpayers would be able to avoid paying any income tax, no matter how great their income, if they were prepared to donate the entire amount to charity. Since these taxpayers would continue as citizens to enjoy the benefits of the federal government's programs—and not necessarily as ascetics, since they might maintain an expensive standard of living by dipping into capital or using tax-sheltered receipts—this freedom from tax liability, it may be argued, is objectionable.

* * *

These reasons for limiting the deduction for charitable contributions in computing income tax liability—the "psychic income" derived by the donor from such contributions and his continued enjoyment of the benefits of government—are not entirely persuasive. "Psychic income" comes from many sources, but for sound reasons, Congress has never sought to tax it * * *.

Finally, the principal other rationale for the percentage limit (viz., the duty-to-support-the-government argument) presupposes that the benefit of the tax deduction inures to the donor rather than to the donee. But this premise, in turn, rests on still another assumption, viz., that charitable bequests are unaffected by the deduction. If this assumption is invalid, and charitable bequests would be reduced if they were taxed, the unlimited deduction of existing law inures *pro tanto* to the benefit of the charitable donees rather than the donor. Seen in this light, the deduction appears to relieve charitable institutions and their beneficiaries of the cost of supporting the federal government. The wisdom of this policy may be debated, but its impact is certainly altogether different from relieving the *donor* of the burden of supporting governmental services.

* * *

---

[22]   The existence of the charitable deduction, however, undermines the assumption that donating a dollar to charity generates as much satisfaction for the donor as spending the same dollar on himself. To use the terminology of the economist, the deduction has a "price effect," so that it "costs less" to donate a dollar to charity than to spend a dollar on a hobby or vacation. For this reason, if a taxpayer makes a charitable contribution of $1,000, and thereby saves $500 of taxes, it is far from clear that he gets a full $1,000's worth of pleasure or satisfaction; that inference would be justified only if he would have made the contribution even if it had not been deductible. If repeal of the statutory deduction would have led him to spend part or all of the $1,000 on himself, the theory that charitable contributions are indistinguishable from personal consumption would have to be scaled down or abandoned.

Notwithstanding these misgivings about the percentage limitation on the income tax deduction for charitable contributions, I am prepared to accept it arguendo as an embodiment of wise policy. Even on this assumption, I see no case for extending it to the federal estate tax. * * *

Sense can be made of the federal estate tax, in my opinion, only if we disabuse ourselves of the primitive notion that the decedent "pays" the tax. The decedent, I make bold to suggest, leaves this world with nothing, whether the tax is high or low; it is the living persons whom he leaves behind who will enjoy the benefits of his assets and bear the burden of the death tax. The tax, therefore, should take account of *their* circumstances.

To be sure, the legislative decision to impose an estate tax sets limits to the achievement of this objective. To avoid valuing every potential beneficiary's interest in the estate, the federal tax is imposed on the entire estate; the inevitable cost of this simplicity in administration is that the rate of tax cannot be geared to the separate financial situations of the individual legatees. In effect, they are all taxed at an average rate—but it ought to bear a reasonable, even though rough, relationship to their ability to pay.

Many tax theorists favor changes in the death tax area that would refine this relationship, by tailoring the tax more closely to each legatee's personal circumstances. * * * The marital deduction is one such element in the federal estate tax, based on the theory that amounts inherited by a surviving spouse should not be taxed as heavily as transfers to other persons. * * *

The deduction for charitable bequests has a similar function. Far from being an anomaly in the federal estate tax structure, it is, I submit, an appropriate—indeed admirable—device to tailor the tax to the beneficiary's ability to pay. * * * By permitting charitable bequests to be deducted, existing law tacitly, but unmistakably, acknowledges that there is a difference between the beneficiaries of charitable bequests on the one hand, and the members of the decedent's family who receive the bulk of non-charitable bequests on the other. Only by disregarding the obvious can one conclude that the deduction for charitable bequests is a tax loophole, rather than a sensible way of adjusting the rate structure to the realities of life.

When the death tax is viewed as a tax on the recipients of bequests rather than on their deceased benefactor, it becomes evident that the proposed percentage limitation on the charitable contribution deduction would be similar to an income tax on charitable institutions, based on the bequests they receive. The income tax treatment of charitable organizations has been subjected to much criticism in recent years, leading to numerous legislative changes and even more proposals; but to the best of my knowledge, no responsible commentator has ever recommended that contributions should be taxed to the charitable recipient. Yet this is exactly what would happen, albeit somewhat indirectly, if the federal estate tax were amended to restrict the deduction for charitable bequests.

In saying this, I am, of course, assuming that imposition of a percentage limitation would in fact reduce the amount received by charity. If the entire estate is left to charity, this assumption is obviously valid, since only ½ would be deductible, and there is no other source from which the tax on the balance could be paid.[30] If there are other bequests, the effect of a percentage limit is slightly more problematical, but the result is, in my opinion, likely to be similar. Assume, for example, that under existing law a testator plans to leave 20 per cent of his estate to friends or relatives, and the balance, after taxes, to a charity. Assume also that under existing law this plan would result in transmitting 20 per cent to the noncharitable legatees, 5 per cent to the government as taxes, and 75 per cent to the charity. What changes would the tes-

---

[30]   I discard, as wholly unpersuasive for charitable bequests of the magnitude we are discussing here, the possibility that the testator would have scaled down his lifetime consumption in order to enlarge the estate so that the same net amount would go to the charity after payment of the hypothetical tax.

tator be likely to make if the law were changed so that the charitable bequest could be deducted only in part—up to 50 per cent of the estate? Assume that the hypothetical change in the law would increase the federal estate tax from 5 per cent to 20 per cent of the estate—an increase of 15 per cent. Would the testator be likely to cut back the noncharitable bequests by this amount, giving the donees only 5 per cent of the estate rather than the 20 per cent they were to get under the original plan? Or would he be more likely to throw most or all of the entire burden on the charity? The latter seems by far the more likely outcome.

Indeed, he might decide to cut back the charitable bequest by *more* than the amount of the added tax. Under existing law, the unlimited deduction is an inducement to make such bequests: the charity gets more than the testator's other heirs lose. Under the proposed change, however, there is no tax incentive to give more to a charity than can be deducted; the tax result will be the same whether the additional dollars are given to the charity or to the testator's friends and relatives. For this reason, the testator may well be impelled to cut the charity back to the deductible 50 per cent, leaving the balance after taxes to the noncharitable heirs. If this is his reaction, an increase in the tax of 15 percentage points would cause a reduction in the charitable bequest of 25 percentage points. The noncharitable heirs would then get 30 per cent of the estate, rather than the 20 per cent that they would have received under the original estate plan.

If these views about the probable impact of the proposed percentage limit are correct, it is objectionable in two fundamental respects: First, it would impose a burden that cannot be justified on "ability to pay" principles. The federal estate tax * * * is a distinctly upper class tax. * * * The proposed percentage limitation would be felt almost entirely by the largest estates, where it is a virtual certainty that the typical heirs are very high on the income ladder. Taxing charitable bequests (by imposing a limit on the deduction) will, therefore, apply an estate tax rate schedule designed for these wealthy taxpayers to charitable institutions and their ultimate beneficiaries whose economic status is utterly different. No matter how vague the "ability to pay" principle may be, we surely know that there is a world of difference between the average heir to a multi-million dollar family fortune and the run-of-the-mine middle and low income citizen who benefits from bequests to universities, museums, community funds, and other charitable institutions.

Second, if we take into account the role of the federal estate tax as a device to moderate the concentration of family wealth * * * an unlimited exemption for charitable bequests is not only consistent with this role, but actually makes an affirmative contribution to its achievement. By encouraging testators to make charitable bequests, the deduction helps to disperse wealth among a larger group. Indeed, it may outperform the tax itself in this respect, since some testators—as argued above—may reduce their transfers to family members in order to make deductible bequests to charitable institutions. Conversely, if part of the charitable bequest became nondeductible, testators might well prefer, as suggested, to leave more of their property to members of their families, thus increasing, rather than diminishing, the concentration of wealth.

* * *

* * * I have discussed only a small corner of this troubled area, but my principal point— that the burden of death taxes falls not on the decedent, but on the persons and institutions who survive the decedent—has much wider ramifications and, though simple, is often overlooked. Any proposed change in the tax treatment of charities should, in my opinion, be preceded by an analysis of the ultimate burden of the change. It may then become apparent that the added tax will fall on persons least able to bear it—the beneficiaries of charitable institutions. * * *

NOTE

The tax savings generated by a dollar of deduction vary in direct proportion to the taxpayer's marginal tax rate. In a system of progressive tax rates, does the estate tax charitable deduction represent an "upside-down subsidy" for the wealthy? For contrasting views of this question in the income tax context, see Paul R. McDaniel, *Federal Matching Grants for Charitable Contributions: A Substitute for the Income Tax Deduction*, 27 TAX L. REV. 377 (1972); Boris I. Bittker, *Charitable Contributions: Deductions or Matching Grants?*, 28 TAX L. REV. 37 (1972).

Empirical studies indicate that extremely wealthy decedents tend to leave a higher portion of their charitable bequests to educational, cultural, and social welfare organizations than to religious organizations. What would be the likely impact on the distribution of charitable bequests of repealing the charitable deduction, imposing a percentage limitation, or substituting a flat-rate tax credit?

George Cooper, *A Voluntary Tax? New Perspectives on Sophisticated Estate Tax Avoidance*, 77 COLUM. L. REV. 161 (1977)*

* * *

For [wealthy] persons, * * * a major alternative to high transfer tax payments was, as one earthy planner put it, "to do the charitable bit." This can, and frequently does, take the form of bequests to existing charitable organizations. Often it results in the creation of a foundation. Both these routes to charitable giving result in a permanent loss of funds to the family, although that loss can be somewhat mitigated in the case of a foundation by giving the family a continuing role in controlling it. There is, however, a third route to charity which offers just as much in the way of tax saving, and gives a lot more to one's heirs. In fact, it gives the heirs most of the benefits of complete ownership.

The device which produces these marvelous results is known as a "charitable front-end annuity trust" or a "charitable lead annuity trust." In such a trust, property is held to pay a fixed sum annually to charity for a period of time (this is the "front-end" or "lead" period), and at the end of that time full ownership of the property and all income therefrom reverts to noncharitable beneficiaries, such as the heirs of the trust's creator. When property is placed in such a trust, whether by gift or bequest, the creator of the trust receives a charitable deduction for the actuarial value of the front-end annuity interest, determined under Internal Revenue Service tables. For example, if $10,000,000 is put in trust to pay $600,000 per year to charity for twenty-four years, the charitable deduction is $7,530,240. This deduction, roughly equal to three-fourths the estate tax value of the property put in trust, would effectively eliminate three-fourths or more of the estate tax liability on the trust property.

At first blush this tax result seems reasonable enough, since the individual has given up $14,400,000 (24 x $600,000) of income over the twenty-four-year period to obtain a present $7,530,240 deduction, and the difference is the 6% discount factor built into the tables. However, such simple reasoning fails to take account of income tax effects. For persons of such great

---

*   This article originally appeared at 77 COLUM. L. REV. 161 (1977). Reprinted by permission. This work was also published as a book by Brookings Institution (1978).

wealth, a current $600,000 return would produce a net benefit of only $180,000 after taking account of income taxes. That is to say, if the individual had earned $600,000 per year and contributed it to charity, the net sacrifice to him would have been only $180,000 per year in the sense of after-tax income foregone. Thus, the more accurate way of appraising this front-end trust is to say that the individual has given up $4,320,000 spread out over twenty-four years (24 x $180,000), the present value of which is $2,259,072. For this he has gotten an immediate estate tax deduction that, assuming an estate tax rate of 70% * * * , produces an immediate in-pocket benefit from reduced estate taxes of $5,271,168—more than double the amount sacrificed. Viewed in this way, the front-end trust is quite a desirable technique for those who are in the high brackets where this beneficial rate tradeoff occurs. Once the discount factor is cancelled out, the exchange of someone in top estate and income tax brackets essentially becomes one in which for each $100 involved, the Treasury forgives a $70 tax in return for the taxpayer sacrificing $30 to charity.

The benefit from creating a front-end trust is enhanced if one can earn more than the 6% rate built into the tables on property placed in trust. If, for example, the funds are invested in bonds paying 8% interest, $10,000,000 will produce an annual annuity of $800,000 which, from the 6% viewpoint of the tables, is the equivalent of placing $13,333,333 in trust, and the deduction is increased accordingly. If an $800,000 annuity runs for twenty-four years, the charitable deduction computed under the tables is $10,040,320—slightly more than the full amount of the $10,000,000 given to the trust. In other words, it is entirely possible to claim a charitable deduction for the full amount of property placed in trust even though the charity is being given only a temporary interest in the property and the full amount of it is eventually going free and clear to one's heirs.

The front-end trust becomes especially attractive when one realizes that the thing given up, current income for a limited period of time, is a relatively unimportant aspect of property for the very wealthy. Persons in the wealth categories we are now discussing have more current income than they can expend. Beyond a certain point, the real value of greater wealth, is power, control and security. These things are hardly sacrificed at all in a front-end trust. Ultimate total ownership and control after the annuity period provides ultimate security. * * *

* * *

NOTE

The charitable lead trust technique described by Cooper remains popular among estate planners, though the tax savings under current law are somewhat less dramatic than in Cooper's example (due to reductions in the top income and transfer tax rates). Could similar tax savings be obtained with a charitable remainder trust? Do the split-interest rules enacted in 1969 provide an accurate measure of the benefits actually passing to charity? For an exhaustive discussion of charitable remainder trusts in the income tax context, see Leo L. Schmolka, *Income Taxation of Charitable Remainder Trusts and Decedents' Estates: Sixty-Six Years of Astigmatism*, 40 TAX L. REV. 1 (1984).

PART V:

VALUATION

JOHN A. BOGDANSKI, FEDERAL TAX VALUATION (1996)*

Of all the terms used in the federal tax laws, few are as important as "value" and "fair market value."[1] The Tax Court put it nicely in a 1990 decision when it said:

> As must be true of any market-based economy, the concept of fair market value has always been a part of the warp and woof of our income, estate and gift tax laws, and concomitantly the necessity of determining the fair market value of numerous assets for equally numerous purposes has always been a vital and unavoidable function of the tax administrative and judicial process.[2]

This proposition is well-supported by the frequent use of "fair market value" as a measure of taxability in the Internal Revenue Code (the Code) and the Treasury regulations thereunder. A computerized search recently found the term in more than 200 Code sections and more than 2,200 sections of the regulations. And in the case law, "fair market value" is also ubiquitous; for 1994 alone, a similar search turned up more than 270 tax-related court decisions that contained the term.

* * *

NOTE

As Bogdanski notes, every transfer subject to estate, gift, or GST tax must be valued, but the Code has very little to say about general valuation principles. The Regulations define the basic "fair market value" standard in terms of a hypothetical arm's-length transaction between a willing buyer and a willing seller, but the most difficult valuation issues have been left for determination on a case-by-case basis. This Part addresses two recurring problem areas: the impact of control in valuing closely-held business interests, and the treatment of estate freezing techniques involving fragmented ownership.

---

[1]   The process of reducing the worth of goods to an independent standard of value, which in turn eases administration of tax systems, may date as far back as the third millenium B.C. * * *

[2]   Nestlé Holdings, Inc. v. Commissioner, 94 T.C. 803, 815 (1990).

A.   Discounts and Premiums

This Subpart examines the various rationales for allowing valuation discounts to reflect the lack of control inherent in a minority interest in a corporation or partnership. Alan L. Feld discusses the impact of minority shareholder status and argues that courts are often too generous in allowing valuation discounts. Mary Louise Fellows and William H. Painter explore the relationship between minority discounts and control premiums, and propose a statutory solution to the "disappearing wealth syndrome." Their proposal is echoed in the Treasury Department's 1984 recommendations concerning minority discounts. James R. Repetti offers a critical assessment of the "alchemy" of minority discounts under existing law.

Alan L. Feld, *The Implications of Minority Interest and Stock Restrictions in Valuing Closely-Held Shares*, 122 U. PA. L. REV. 934 (1974)*

* * *

I. MINORITY INTEREST

* * *

* * * In the most recent elaboration of its position regarding valuation of stock in closely held corporations, the Internal Revenue Service (Service) listed a series of factors to be taken into account, one of which is the size of the block to be valued.[10] The ruling states that a minority interest, which is not defined, in the stock of an unlisted corporation is more difficult to sell than a similar block of listed stock. It adds that it is equally true that control of a corporation, representing an additional element of value, may justify a higher value for a specific block of stock, so that minority interest presumably is intended to be linked to control.

The principle that there should be a discount for a minority interest is entirely appropriate in a proper case. A minority interest in a corporation controlled by others may be worth significantly less than the liquidation value of the shares. Ownership of shares in a closely held corporation may conveniently be analyzed as composed of three elements of value: the right to a proportionate share of the net wealth of the corporation, or asset value; the right to a proportionate share of distributions from the corporation, or income value; and proportionate participation in the management of the enterprise, or control value. The minority shareholder enjoys the asset value and income value of the shares. But if he is an outsider, he may not enjoy the control value attaching to the shares.

The outsider may have no part in making determinations regarding the day-to-day operating policies of the corporation. * * * A frequently occurring example of the value of participation in operational control is the power of the controlling shareholders to cause the corporation to employ them at reasonable salaries and to refuse to employ the minority shareholders on a similar basis.

---

*   Originally published in 122 U. PA. L. REV. 934 (1974). Copyright © 1974, The University of Pennsylvania.

[10]   Rev. Rul. 59-60, 1959-1 Cum. Bull. 237, 239.

Another element of control concerns the extent to which a shareholder can realize immediately on the asset and income values of his shares. A corporation generally cannot be compelled by a minority shareholder to pay dividends or to distribute assets to a shareholder in redemption of his shares, nor can it be forced to dissolve. The controlling shareholders may restrict or enhance the flow of dividends as the flow benefits them. To the extent they find their control position in the corporation agreeable, they can prevent dissolution of the corporation. If their controlling interest is great enough they may have the power to cause dissolution, should they desire to do so.

Assuming that the majority shareholders will not dissolve the company, the minority shareholder who is an outsider can retire from his undesirable corporate position and realize on his stock in two ways. He can sell the stock to another outsider, in which event the price is likely to reflect a substantial discount by reason of the "captive" position of the investment in the corporation, or he can sell to the insiders. While there may be buyers at a favorable price if the insiders regard it as desirable to eliminate outside participation in the affairs of the corporation, the insider market is normally restricted. On balance it is fair to conclude that the price obtainable by the outsider for the minority shares normally will be substantially less than the pro rata asset and income values.

If, however, the minority shareholder is not an outsider but is part of the group which has effective control over the corporation's activities, the value of his shares is quite different. * * * [T]he value of the shares to the inside minority shareholder is far more likely to approach his proportionate interest in the enterprise than if he were an outsider. Accordingly, little or no minority interest discount is appropriate in such a case.

* * * As the general definition of fair market value, the regulations adopt the widely accepted statement that it is the price at which property would change hands between a willing buyer and a willing seller. When applied to stock in a closely held corporation, however, this general statement can be misleading. Does it suggest that the value put on the shares received by an "insider" donee or legatee should be limited to what a willing outsider would pay for them? If so, the control value of the shares will be ignored and a substantial minority discount applied, although the new shareholder donee or legatee participates actively in control of the corporation. Yet, it is apparent that substantially more wealth has been conferred on the donee than he could obtain simply by reselling the stock interest to an outsider, because an element of the wealth conferred, participation in control, could not be conveyed to an outsider by conveying the shares.

* * *

* * * The courts generally have determined whether the interest transferred is arithmetically a minority interest and then, based on conflicting testimony offered by expert witnesses, have applied some discount from proportionate asset value.

Consider the implications of this legal pattern in the context of a transfer of wealth from one generation to another within a family. Suppose that a parent concerned with the transfer tax seeks to transfer $1,000,000 to his three children. Assume further that both his specific lifetime gift tax exemption * * * and his annual * * * exclusion for each child have otherwise been exhausted. If the parent gave each child one-third of the $1,000,000 he would have aggregate gifts of $1,000,000 on which gift tax would be incurred.

Suppose instead that the donor uses the $1,000,000 to provide the capital for a new corporation in exchange for all of its outstanding stock. If he then transfers one-third of the stock to each child, each gift, under [one] view, should be entitled to a discount for minority interest. If the discount is a conservative twenty percent, each gift would be valued at $266,666, resulting in total taxable gifts of $800,000. * * *

Are the differences in the two gifts great enough to warrant this difference in tax treatment? In one sense, each child will have received something quite different in the two transfers: in the first, $333,333; in the second, a one-third interest in a corporation capitalized with the donor's $1,000,000. This distinction could be significant if there were disagreement as to the management of the corporation, because the interest in the corporation would be worth less than $333,333 to a child who lacked control over the business.

If the family were close, however, each child might enjoy the advantage of consolidated management and might also be able to realize on the funds as needed. In such a case a shareholder who needed money could expect to have his shares either redeemed by the corporation or purchased by the other two shareholders for his proportionate share of the underlying asset value. Alternatively, the shareholders could liquidate the corporation and each would attain directly one-third of $1,000,000.

* * *

Analysis of a minority interest in the corporation might be further refined by examining the relationship of the new owner of the minority interest with the other ownership interests in the corporation. If the others also hold minority interests, no one block of stock has a special control position in the corporation. * * * Each shareholder can, with the aid of others, check the control sought to be exerted by any other shareholder. Minority discount would appear particularly inappropriate here, where the minority "disability" is reciprocal.

But the holder of less than a majority of shares may be a part of a control group which would have control of the corporation even without his participation, i.e., a minority insider. In the event of a dispute between the shareholder and the control group, the group could overrule him. The opportunity to sell his shares may be more limited than in the all-minority interest case. This would appear to be the most appealing case for application of the discount to shares which are held by a member of the controlling group.

Neither the regulations and rulings on the one hand, nor the decided cases on the other, are a substantial help in dealing with these problems. * * *

The potential avoidance of transfer tax, given the confusion in this area, is substantial. It may be illustrated as follows. To return to the father who owns all of the stock of a family holding company, suppose that his gifts are spread over time. He first gives a third of the stock to one son and retains the other two-thirds. The recipient has a minority insider interest of the kind described above. If a minority discount is applied, the shares will be valued at some amount less than one-third of the value of the whole corporation.[30]

Thereafter, in a separate transaction, the father transfers a second one-third interest in the stock of the corporation to another son. Now the shares are held in equal blocks by the three shareholders and should have equal value, one-third of the value of the corporation. The first son's shares have increased in value, to reflect the new dispersion of control in the corporation. By this second gift, then, the father has enriched the second son directly and the first son indirectly. Failure to treat the enhancement in value of the first son's shares as a taxable gift would result in permanent exclusion of the discount from both gift and estate taxes.

If this second gift could be taxed in the amount of both these elements of value, there would be no transfer tax avoidance. * * * The difficulty in taxing this increment of value at the time of the second transfer is that no "property" has been transferred to the first son, while the property transferred to the second son is limited in value to the one-third share given him. The

---

[30]   Presumably, the two-thirds interest in the corporation retained by the father would now be worth a premium over two-thirds of the value of the whole corporation * * * .

cases appear to support this view in rejecting the notion that transferring part of a control block results in a taxable gift greater than the value of the shares to the recipient.

This result cannot be avoided by analyzing the later increase in value in the first son's shares as a transfer incident to the earlier gift. First, both the estate tax and the gift tax apply on a "now or never" basis, imposing tax on the value of the property as best as it can be determined at the time of the transfer. * * * Second, the augmentation in the value of the first son's shares by reason of fragmentation of the control held by the father need not occur incident to a transaction which would otherwise be subject to estate or gift tax. It could as well derive from other kinds of transactions. For example, if the father sold a one-third interest in the corporation to a third party instead of making a gift of the shares to the second son, the control position previously held by the father would disappear, and the value of the shares held by the first son would rise, but with no resultant gift tax.

If no taxable transfer to the first son is deemed to occur when shares are given to the second son, the discount taken on the initial transfer to the first son will be permanently excluded from transfer taxation. This consideration should weigh heavily against applying a discount for minority interests in the case of the "minority insider" where the less than proportionate share of control in the corporation is contingent and uncertain.

The proper response to this situation may be a presumption that a donor or decedent, in making transfers of stock in a closely held corporation which he controls, makes them to transferees who will be a part of the control group of the corporation. In order to establish that a minority discount is appropriate, the proponent of the discount would have to come forward with evidence that the recipient who is claimed to be a minority shareholder actually will suffer the disabilities of an outsider. This burden would generally be difficult to carry where the minority position is reciprocal.

The presumption against minority discount should apply even where participation in control may be limited by the concentration of a majority interest in other hands. Minority discount under these circumstances is likely to result in permanent avoidance of estate and gift tax on the transfer of wealth within the family group. It is not unfair to require the proponent of a minority discount to justify it by more than pointing to percentages and claiming that they "prove" a lack of participation in control.

* * *

NOTE

Feld identifies three elements of value in closely-held business interests: "asset value," "income value," and "control value." How should these elements be measured in ascertaining the value of a particular interest? Under Feld's analysis, what factors are relevant in determining the availability and amount of a minority discount for a particular interest?

Mary Louise Fellows & William H. Painter, *Valuing Close Corporations for Federal Wealth Transfer Taxes: A Statutory Solution to the Disappearing Wealth Syndrome,* **30 Stan. L. Rev. 895 (1978)***

* * *

The 1976 Tax Reform Act made substantive and structural changes in the wealth transfer tax system to ensure further against the evasion of the federal estate tax. * * * In view of * * * the specific concern Congress displayed over tax avoidance devices using lifetime gifts of corporate stock, it is surprising that no consideration was given to the substantial tax savings obtainable through inter vivos gifts of minority interests in closely held corporations. The following hypothetical illustrates the tax avoidance possibility: F owns 51 of the 100 outstanding voting shares of ABC Corporation; his son, S, owns the other 49 shares. If F dies owning the 51 shares, a premium will be added to the value of those shares when the estate tax is assessed to reflect the value of control that accompanies 51 percent ownership of the corporation. The estate is taxed on the control premium irrespective of whether the shares pass to a single beneficiary, who thereby acquires control, or to several beneficiaries, none of whom receives effective controlling ownership.

If F instead had made an inter vivos gift of two shares to S, or to anyone else, the value of the gift for purposes of the gift tax would be discounted to reflect the fact that two shares represent a minority interest in the corporation. * * * [T]he 49 shares remaining will be valued for estate tax purposes to reflect that they, too, represent only a minority interest. Thus, by separating the 51 shares into two different blocks, F avoids subjecting the control premium to a transfer tax. Controlling shareholders of close corporations thus can reduce their estate and gift tax liability through gratuitous transfers of minority blocks of their controlling shares. This tactic may be characterized as the "disappearing wealth syndrome." Wealth disappears in the sense that the donor voluntarily removes from the estate the value of a controlling interest without incurring estate or gift tax liability. This tax-saving device derives from the current method of calculating majority premiums and minority discounts on shares held in close corporations. * * *

I. DETERMINATION OF FAIR MARKET VALUE OF STOCK IN CLOSE CORPORATIONS

* * * [T]he value of the property is generally its fair market value at the time of the transfer. If the stock has no ready market * * * and if no arm's-length transactions have occurred within reasonable proximity to the valuation date, fair market value must be determined by hypothesizing a willing buyer and a willing seller.

* * *

A. The Effect of Control on Fair Market Value

Control of a business essentially is the power to dominate its decisionmaking processes. Those who possess control not only have the power to institute ideas and programs in their self-

---

interest but, more importantly, they can ensure that others cannot use the business and its assets in ways that are contrary to the majority's needs and desires.[32] Thus, controlling shares are valued more highly than minority shares.

1. The relationship of control and ownership.

Although control of a corporation is manifested through a formal decisionmaking mechanism premised on the notion that the owners determine the firm's business and financial policies, control is not inextricably tied to ownership. * * *

* * *

As in publicly held corporations, control in close corporations may not be coextensive with ownership. In the close corporation context, however, the separation of ownership from control does not arise from the dispersion of share ownership; rather, it is a function of the economic power of outsiders and of internal agreements among shareholders. For example, voting trusts frequently have been used to give control of a close corporation to those who hold its senior securities, such as bondholders and debenture holders. In addition to the power of outsiders contractual agreements in many close corporations among the stockholders themselves—such as pooling agreements, voting trusts and irrevocable proxies—permit owners of minority interests to exercise disproportionate influence over the affairs of the company. * * * Thus, increases in the percentage of stock ownership in close corporations do not necessarily result in commensurate increases in the degree and value of control. Rather, the reduction in restrictions on the free exercise of control gives control its value. The value of control for transfer tax purposes, therefore, should increase as the constraints on determining the policies of the firm decrease, regardless of the source of those constraints.

2. Transferability of control.

* * * Control that arises independently of stock ownership * * * clearly is personal to the owner and is nontransferable; the value of such control is not included in the estate for tax purposes.

A different situation exists, however, when control can be transferred by transfer of stock. * * * [A]s long as a controlling shareholder can gratuitously transfer the power of control to another person, the value of that control should be subject to the transfer tax. * * * Ownership of a control block of shares, with the concomitant power to control the assets and management decisions, remains more valuable than ownership of a minority block whether or not the owner of the shares is permitted to retain the control premium upon their sale. Consequently * * * the value of control associated with a controlling block of shares should not escape the wealth transfer tax.

3. Control in the valuation process.

* * * Courts have recognized the importance of control in determining fair market value, and they typically have used the concepts of majority premium and minority discounts in valuing, respectively, controlling and noncontrolling interests in corporations.

---

[32]   "Even absent any contemplated change in management, control increases the value of an investment by protecting it. The power to change the management, even while unexercised, protects the investor with control against an abrupt change by someone else and against a gradual deterioration of the incumbent management. Therefore, in a sense, controlling shares are inherently worth more than noncontrolling shares for reasons relating solely to investment value. * * * " Andrews, *The Stockholder's Right to Equal Opportunity in the Sale of Shares*, 78 HARV. L. REV. 505, 526 (1965).

The very words premium and discount, however, are somewhat misleading when applied to shares of closely held corporations. For example, when used in the conventional sense, "discount" implies the existence of a list price from which the discount is subtracted. Similarly, "premium" suggests a standard price to which the premium is added in determining the sale price. Applying these terms to control and noncontrol blocks of stock seems to imply that, between the discount and premium share prices, an "intrinsic" price exists from which the discount is taken and to which the premium is added. But there is in reality no such price. * * *

* * * [I]n a closely held corporation, different blocks of stock * * * have differing degrees of control * * * . There is no intrinsic price midway between the discount and premium since one merely describes the absence of the other. A minority discount, then, is a corollary of a majority premium and depends on the latter for its validity. A discount for lack of control is only appropriate if the amount discounted already includes a majority premium. * * *

* * * [C]ourts consider four basic methods for determining investment value: capitalization of earnings, dividend-paying capacity, book value, and net asset value. Particular circumstances of each case may require a court to weigh one or more of these valuation methods more heavily than the rest. * * *

The control factor should be considered in the valuation process at two stages—first, when determining how to weigh the various valuation methods, and second, when determining the value of the corporation by the capitalization of earnings method. If a minority interest is being valued, a court should give less weight to dividend-paying capacity, to book value and to net asset value, because the purchaser of a minority interest generally is able to enjoy dividends or the proceeds from liquidation only if such policies are in the best interests of the majority shareholders. The value of minority shares instead can be determined more accurately by giving greater consideration to the company's actual earnings and dividend-paying history.

The capitalization of earnings method is based on two variables: average earnings and the capitalization rate. Proper consideration of control affects these two variables. For example, if the average earnings of a corporation are significantly lower than would be expected for that type of firm, the earnings variable should be adjusted upward when valuing a majority interest. The purchaser can anticipate higher earnings after appointment of more aggressive and competent management. In contrast, purchasers of minority interests generally will be powerless to influence the management and operations of the company. Consequently, the average earnings of a corporation, as actually calculated, should be used even if those earnings are unexpectedly low. Similarly, because control enables an owner to reduce investment risks, the capitalization rate should be higher if a majority interest is being valued than if a minority interest is being valued.

Of course, investment value can be determined either by assuming control and then reducing that figure when valuing a minority interest, or by assuming no control and increasing the determined value when valuing a majority interest. Whichever process is adopted, however, the control assumption must be consistent: A majority premium should not be applied if the value of the company is determined by assuming control and a minority discount should not be applied if the value of the company is determined by assuming no control.

* * *

When valuing stock of a close corporation by comparing the stock prices of comparable, publicly traded corporations, a similar analysis of value and control is necessary. Because quoted prices used in the valuation represent prices of small blocks of stock, no minority discount should be applied. If a majority interest is being valued, however, the price of the stock of a comparable corporation should be adjusted upward to reflect the value of control.

* * *

II. STATUTORY REMEDIES FOR THE DISAPPEARING
WEALTH SYNDROME

* * *

Disappearing wealth occurs in two situations. First, if a controlling shareholder makes one or more inter vivos gifts of minority blocks so that he divests himself of control, the control value of the original block of shares will escape both the gift tax and the estate tax. Second, the value incident to de facto control over a corporation is not subject to the transfer taxes; thus, multiple owners, none of whom have ever possessed voting control of the corporation, can escape taxation for a controlling interest even though they enjoy common interests and exercise working control over the business. * * *

* * *

Consider two individuals, X and Y, each of whom owns a 60 percent interest in their respective family corporations. X dies, leaving her interest to be divided equally between her two children. Y, on the other hand, makes lifetime transfers of 15 percent to each of his two children, leaving the remaining 30 percent to be divided equally between the same two children at Y's death. Because of the unitary approach of the estate tax, X's interest at death will be valued as a majority interest, despite the minority interests inherited by the two children. Y, however, has escaped tax on the transfer of his control value by making the inter vivos gifts to his two children. More equitable tax treatment of X and Y can be achieved by modification of Y's estate tax so as to presume the de facto control held by the recipients of the shares after Y's death, or by full gift taxation of the control transferred from Y's estate through inter vivos gifts.[93]

This Article proposes statutory modifications to provide that any gratuitous transfer of shares from a donor who originally owned a controlling interest in a corporation shall be valued as if they were part of the controlling block. For example, assume M initially owns all 100 shares of XYZ Corporation, and makes the following gifts:

Year	Donee	Number of Voting Shares
1980	Son	20
1982	Husband	20
1984	Daughter	20
1985	Close Friend	20

M dies in 1990 owning 20 shares of XYZ Corporation. At the time of the gifts and at M's death, the corporation had an investment value of $1,000,000, or $10,000 per share, assuming a 100 percent control block, and an investment value of $700,000, or $7,000 per share, assuming a minority block. The proposed statutory amendments would require each gift and the shares owned by M at her death to be valued at $200,000 (20 percent × $1,000,000), rather than $140,000 (20 percent × $700,000). Thus, apart from the ordinary tax advantages of making inter vivos gifts, M is treated no more favorably than a similarly situated taxpayer whose stock is not transferred to family members and business associates until the taxpayer's death.

---

[93]   Full gift taxation is preferable to modifications in the estate tax. Majority owners of close corporations generally do not give stock to persons with interests adverse to the donor's interests. Gifts to parties with similar interests, however, result in preserving the value of control. As a matter of tax policy, a reasonable assumption is that, in practice, inter vivos gifts by majority stockholders in close corporations will be made to parties with interests common to the donor's.

* * *

* * * The disappearing wealth syndrome * * * may take a second form. Even if no single shareholder owns a controlling interest, the interests of a group of stockholders may be sufficiently similar that the group as a unit exercises de facto control of the enterprise. When such de facto control exists, the shares of members of the controlling group are more valuable than if no control existed; this de facto control is not taken into account in valuing the shares. To the extent that members of the controlling group transfer their stock by gift or at death to other persons with similar interests, de facto control is transferred free of any tax because no value in the form of a control premium is assessed against the shares transferred. One solution would be to attribute the ownership of voting shares by related family members and entities when valuing the shares for transfer tax purposes. Under this approach, if A, B and C, who are brothers, each own 30 percent of the outstanding voting shares of XYZ Corporation, after A makes a gift of the remaining 10 percent interest in the corporation to his son, S, the 10 percent interest would be valued as if part of a 100 percent control block because A will be deemed to be constructive owner of all the shares immediately before the gift. Similarly, if A were to die owning a 30 percent interest, it would be valued as if part of a 100 percent control block. * * *

Application of the attribution rules, however, may create harsh results. De facto control is not the equivalent of ownership of actual control. At any time, one of the shareholders may find it contrary to his own interests to agree with the others. Even assuming that initial transferees from a majority shareholder will have common interests and will share jointly in the benefits of control, subsequent transferees are less likely to share those interests. Thus, the control enjoyed by the donor or decedent is tenuous at best, making imposition of a transfer tax inappropriate.

III. FRAGMENTATION OF CONTROL IN GENERAL

* * *

The disappearing wealth problem is not unique to the fragmentation of control of business enterprises, but can arise whenever the owner of an asset transfers to another only some of the rights and powers that attach to ownership of the asset, such as a gift of an undivided interest in a parcel of land.

For purposes of the wealth transfer taxes, all prior gratuitous transfers should be aggregated, and the value of the interest transferred should be based on the value of the asset before it was fragmented. No adjustment in value is needed if the transferor enjoyed only a minority interest before fragmentation. Ownership interests transferred by bona fide sale, rather than gratuitously, should not be aggregated. * * *

* * *

NOTE

As Fellows and Painter point out, several methods are available for valuing shares in a closely-held business. What factors are relevant in determining the relative weight of capitalized earnings, dividend capacity, book value, and net asset value? In theory, should different valuation methods all produce identical outcomes? Under what circumstances would Fellows and Painter attribute ownership of voting shares among "related family members and entities" that exercise "de facto control" of a closely-held business? What additional valuation difficulties arise in the case of a corporation with more than one class of stock?

Why should controlling shares command a premium relative to minority shares? Do controlling shareholders have opportunities to divert corporate earnings and assets for their own benefit at the expense of minority shareholders? If so, can they exploit such opportunities without cost? One commentator, starting from the premise that "the value of a corporation must equal the sum of the values of its parts," argues that "control premiums and minority discounts generally should not be used when valuing closely held stock." Thomas D. Hall, *Valuing Closely Held Stock: Control Premiums and Minority Discounts*, 31 EMORY L.J. 139 (1982). Would Fellows and Painter agree?

U.S. TREASURY DEPARTMENT, TAX REFORM FOR FAIRNESS, SIMPLICITY, AND ECONOMIC GROWTH, REPORT TO THE PRESIDENT (1984)

* * *

Current Law

Property transferred by gift is valued for Federal gift tax purposes at its fair market value, in general the price it would bring in a transaction between a willing buyer and a willing seller, neither being under any compulsion to buy or to sell and both having reasonable knowledge of all relevant facts. Thus, property transferred by gift is not valued by reference to the amount by which it increases the value of the donee's estate, nor is it valued by reference to the amount by which it decreases the value of the donor's estate.

Reasons for Change

In most instances, the value of property transferred by gift will be the same regardless of whether such value is determined by reference to the separate value of the property, the diminution in value of the transferor's estate, or the enhancement in value of the transferee's estate. In other instances, however, these measures of value can vary greatly. This is particularly true in the case of transfers of minority interests in closely held businesses and undivided interests in assets such as real estate. These interests are often valued, for transfer tax purposes, at significant discounts from their pro rata share of the value of the underlying business or asset.

For example, assume that A owns 100 percent of the outstanding stock of X, and that the value of A's stock in X is $1,500,000. If A transfers ten percent of the X stock to B, A may claim that for Federal gift tax purposes the value of the ten percent block of stock is as little as $90,000, reflecting a discount of as much as 40 percent from the proportionate share of the total value of the corporation. If A makes such gifts annually for six years, A may claim that the aggregate gift tax value of the 60 percent interest is only $540,000. Moreover, if A dies holding the remaining 40 percent block, A's estate may claim a minority discount on that stock. If those values are sustained, A has transferred stock worth $1,500,000, but for Federal estate and gift tax purposes has made transfers aggregating only $900,000.

Minority or fractional-share discounts enable taxpayers to structure transfers so as to reduce the aggregate value of property brought within the transfer tax base. This is inconsistent with the underlying purpose of the gift tax, which is to serve as a backstop for the estate tax. Moreover, the overall reduced value of the property as it is reported for transfer tax purposes is inconsistent with economic reality.

Proposal

The value for transfer tax purposes of a fractional interest in any asset owned, in whole or in part, by a donor or decedent would be a pro rata share of the fair market value of that portion of the asset owned by the donor or decedent. Prior gifts of fractional interests in the asset, as well as any fractional interests in the asset held by the transferor's spouse, would be attributed to the donor or decedent for purposes of determining the value of the fractional interest transferred. A fractional interest in an asset would include shares of stock in a corporation, partnership units, or similar interests in a single entity or asset. Rules would be provided to aggregate (or segregate) two different interests in property based upon the criterion of whether the ownership by the transferor of one such interest affects the valuation of the other such interest. * * *

This special valuation rule would apply to transfers of fractional interests, however, only if the donor retains a fractional interest after the gift or has previously made a gift of a fractional interest in the asset. This special valuation rule would also apply for purposes of determining whether a sale by the donor to a related party constitutes a transfer for less than an adequate and full consideration.

The proposal can be illustrated by the following examples.

Example. A owns 60 percent of the outstanding stock of a corporation worth $100x$. A, whose controlling interest is worth $70x$, transfers one-half of his interest to B. The value of the gift for gift tax purposes is $35x$ (i.e., 50 percent of the value of A's 60 percent block of stock). If A retains his remaining 30 percent block until his death, the estate tax value of such block will be 50 percent of the value of a 60 percent block of stock at the date of A's death.

Example. B owns 40 percent of the outstanding stock of a corporation worth $100x$. B's minority interest is worth $30x$, and B transfers one-half of her interest to A. The value of the gift to A would be $15x$, i.e., 50 percent of the value of the 40 percent block possessed by B immediately prior to the gift. However, if B's spouse S owned stock representing 20 percent of the corporation, so that the combined interest of S and B was worth $75x$, the value of the gift to A would be $25x$, (i.e., 33⅓ percent of the value of the 60 percent block held jointly by B and S).

The proposal would contain rules to prevent unfairness or abuse that could result from an individual's acquisition and subsequent transfer of a fractional interest in an asset after having made a gift of a fractional interest in the same asset.

* * *

NOTE

Does the Treasury proposal offer any guidance for measuring the amount of a minority discount in a proper case? Note that the Treasury proposal was not included in the legislation ultimately enacted as the Tax Reform Act of 1986. Moreover, Congress skirted the issue of minority discounts in 1990 when it enacted §§ 2701-2704 concerning estate freezes. Does this suggest that Congress is satisfied with existing law concerning minority discounts?

James R. Repetti, *Minority Discounts: The Alchemy in Estate and Gift Taxation*, 50 TAX L. REV. 415 (1995)*

* * *

III. VALUATION

Because the estate and gift taxes are assessed on the "value" of property transferred, the definition of "value" has significant importance. Value is defined in the regulations as "fair market value," that is, "the price at which the property would change hands between a willing buyer and a willing seller, neither being under any compulsion to buy or to sell and both having reasonable knowledge of relevant facts." The willing buyer and seller are not, however, the donor and donee, but rather are hypothetical people with no relationship to each other. * * *

A. Closely Held Corporations

* * *

The hypothetical willing buyer-willing seller standard is difficult to apply in the context of the closely held corporation because the use of these hypothetical people prevents consideration of the existing relationship between the donor and donee as well as among the donee and other stockholders. Relationships among stockholders of a closely held corporation normally constitute a significant component of value in such a corporation. * * *

In valuing stock in a closely held corporation, the courts generally engage in a multistep process. First, the value of the corporation as a whole is determined. If there is only one class of stock, the value of each share of stock is calculated by dividing the number of shares into that value. An appropriate discount to reflect lack of control and liquidity or an appropriate premium to reflect control then is applied to the block of stock subject to the transfer tax.

Despite the apparently formalistic simplicity of the analytical process, the lines separating the analytical steps are often blurred. * * *

* * *

[Control] offers a number of benefits to a majority stockholder. For example, he can cause the corporation to employ himself or family members. * * * In addition, control of the corporation provides a higher degree of job security for the controlling stockholder or family members than is normally available in the employment market.

Perhaps most importantly, corporate control reduces the intrinsic risk associated with an investment in the corporation. * * * Intrinsic risk is the risk associated with the particular company: generally the risk that it will be mismanaged or looted. * * * Normally, intrinsic risk is minimized by diversification; it also can be reduced by obtaining control. A controlling stockholder can select management that he believes is competent and honest. If they turn out not to be, he can remove them quickly and minimize the damage.

Thus, a stockholder who owns a majority of stock normally will control the board of directors and, therefore, normally will control selection of management, dividend policy and his own employment. This control decreases the risks associated with incompetent or dishonest management, the stockholder's employment security and the timing of cash distributions. Additional benefits of control, however, become available only as the percentage of stock ownership increases. For example, many state statutes require a two-thirds vote of shareholders to liquidate a corporation, sell substantially all the corporation's assets, merge the corporation or amend the certificate of incorporation. The ability to compel liquidation of a corporation or sale of its assets may be valuable if the value of the corporation's assets exceeds the value of its ongoing

---

business. Similarly, the ability to compel or amend a corporation's certificate of incorporation may be valuable if the stockholder wishes to expand the rights or economic benefits of a class of stock.

Because benefits vary with degrees of ownership, it is important that a court identify the degree of control that it assumes in calculating the value of the corporation. * * *

Similarly, when estimating the appropriate amount of discount for a minority interest, it is important to establish specifically what aspects of control that contribute to value are not available to the minority block.[67] For example, if the valuation of the entire company included only the rights to control dividends, employment and management, the court should allow a discount in valuing a minority block to reflect only the fact that the minority stockholder does not have those powers. The discount should not reflect the inability to control liquidation, sale of assets or recapitalization since those factors were not included in calculating the value of the company as a whole.

It is important to note that attempts to value lack of control are complicated further by a trend in many state courts to impose fiduciary duties on stockholders in closely held corporations. Imposition of such duties should slightly reduce the minority discount otherwise allowable. * * * [I]mposition of such duties does not reduce the risk associated with minority ownership to the level that would exist if the stockholder controlled the corporation. Moreover, the cost of litigating an allegedly wrongful act itself would support a minority discount.

* * *

C. Partnership Interests

The method used to value closely held corporations also is used to value partnership interests. Consequently, the courts have allowed minority discounts for interests as limited partners and general partners. The courts, however, do not appear to have been as conscientious in distinguishing subtle aspects of control that partners exert over partnership affairs as some courts have been in the corporate context. * * *

Usually, there are significant differences between the rights and obligations of a minority interest held as a general partner and one held as a limited partner that would justify different minority discounts. The general partner's liability for the obligations of the partnership may justify a larger discount, while the broader rights of the general partner may support a smaller minority discount. The general partner in a limited partnership also generally can participate much more extensively in management than limited partners can. Moreover, a general partner normally has the right to withdraw at any time and receive the value of her partnership interest, less any damages if her withdrawal was in breach of the partnership agreement. * * *

* * *

V. THE LEGISLATIVE AND JUDICIAL RESPONSES

* * *

A. Legislative Response

* * *

Congress has addressed the taxability of transferred opportunities on a rather haphazard basis. * * * Congress has refused through legislation to eliminate minority discounts for the transfer of assets even though the circumstances of the transfer indicated that the owners would work together and, therefore, that control value had not been destroyed. * * *

---

[67]   *See* Fellows & Painter, [*Valuing Close Corporations for Federal Wealth Transfer Taxes: A Statutory Solution to the Disappearing Wealth Syndrome*, 30 STAN. L. REV. 895, 911-12 (1978)] * * * .

* * *

B. The Judicial Response

* * *

The courts have not been responsive to attempts by the Service to address abusive applications of minority discounts. Until recently, the Service took the position, set forth in Revenue Ruling 81-253,[146] that control discounts should not be allowed where a majority stockholder made lifetime gifts of stock to family members. The Service reasoned that had the majority stockholder died holding a majority interest, the stock in her or his estate would have been valued without a minority discount. Because the purpose of the gift tax is to prevent the avoidance of estate taxes through lifetime gifts, the Service argued that lifetime gifts of stock by a majority stockholder similarly should not benefit from a minority discount. The Service also reasoned that when a controlling block of stock is owned by members of a family, "there is a unity of ownership and interest, and the shares owned by family members should be valued as part of that controlling interest." Recognizing that a unity of interest would not exist where family discord existed, the Service also stated that "where there is evidence of family discord or other factors indicating that the family would not act as a unit in controlling the corporation, a minority discount may be allowed."

* * *

[A] string of defeats finally caused the Service to change its litigating posture and revoke Revenue Ruling 81-253, stating "[A] minority discount will not be disallowed solely because a transferred interest, when aggregated with interests held by family members, would be a part of a controlling interest."[164]

* * *

* * * Both the Service and the courts have determined that [the willing buyer-willing seller] standard requires that such actors be hypothetical people rather than the actual transferor and transferee. * * *

* * *

The notion that the identity of the transferee is irrelevant is somewhat circuitous in application. In defining fair market value, the regulations refer to the willing buyer and seller "having reasonable knowledge of relevant facts." A willing buyer certainly would seek to ascertain the market for resale and would discover that the property may have more value to certain purchasers. Thus, for example, while the willing buyer-willing seller test would prohibit the court from valuing a gift or bequest based on the subjective value assigned by the transferee to the property, a willing buyer would consider such subjective value in weighing the amount she would pay for the property since she, in turn, could sell it to the transferee for whom it has more value. The courts, however, have not addressed this circularity, and by ignoring it, are calculating not fair market value, but a somewhat lower value.

* * *

---

[146]   1981-2 C.B. 187, *revoked by* Rev. Rul. 93-12, 1993-1 C.B. 202 * * * .

[164]   Rev. Rul. 93-12, 1993-1 C.B. 202, 203.

VI. ARGUMENTS AVAILABLE TO THE
SERVICE TO CAPTURE LOST VALUE

The Service has employed three other approaches that may accomplish roughly the same objective of trying to capture the transferred opportunity to participate in control. These approaches apply the substance-over-form or step transaction doctrine to combine a series of gifts and bequests that have the long-term effect of transferring control. The Service also has attempted to capture additional value by measuring the "swing vote" attribute of transferred stock. It is likely, however, that these approaches have only limited application and are not very effective in capturing all the value transferred to family members because they easily can be avoided with careful planning.

A. Substance Over Form

One method to capture the control premium where a series of gifts of minority interests is made to a single donee is to apply the substance-over-form doctrine. Disregarding an initial transfer permits a subsequent transfer to be treated as conveying control. * * *

* * *

The paucity of cases applying the substance-over-form doctrine suggests that it is of limited usefulness to the Service in dealing with the transfer of an opportunity to participate in control. * * * A well-advised taxpayer could easily avoid the substance-over-form argument by insuring the existence of circumstances that indicate that a transfer of control in fact had occurred. * * *

* * *

B. Step Transaction Doctrine

The courts also have used the step transaction doctrine to combine gifts made during a short period of time. While the substance-over-form doctrine disregards a transfer, the step transaction doctrine combines a series of transfers into one. Thus, where a majority owner has made a series of transfers to a single donee, the step transaction approach combines those transfers in order to deny a minority discount.

* * *

[T]he step transaction doctrine, like the substance-over-form doctrine, is not an effective tool to combat minority discounts. Planners may avoid the step transaction doctrine by providing sufficient time between transfers and by structuring the gifts in such a way that a joint sale of the gifts is not inevitable.

* * *

C. Swing Vote

A third tool available to the Service to try to capture some of the value of an opportunity is "swing vote" valuation. Even though a block of stock may not represent majority ownership, it still may have disproportionately more value than a smaller block of stock because of the possibility of forming coalitions with other shareholders. * * *

Valuing the relative bargaining posture of a block of stock is difficult, however, because the value depends not only on the size of the block being valued but also on the distribution of the other shares. * * *

* * * [T]he concept of swing value assumes that the owner of the stock being valued will be able to form a coalition with other stockholder groups. * * *

* * *

Family members have an advantage in forming coalitions because group members are more likely to make credible promises when they have a history of dealing with one another and are likely to continue to do so in the future. Repeated contact allows the creation of credible commitments because nonexploiters are able to retaliate in the future against a person who breaks the commitment. Some commentators also have asserted that homogeneity in preferences is another factor likely to result in a stable coalition. Because of shared experiences, family members probably are more likely to have similar preferences.

This learning from game theory has an interesting implication for the current state of law. It shows that in order to determine a realistic swing vote value, the courts must explore two sets of relationships: (1) the relationship of a donee or legatee to the other owners and (2) the relationship of the other owners to one another. The proscription of the willing buyer-willing seller rule that the identity of the transferee cannot be considered means that it will be difficult, if not impossible, to measure swing vote value because the relationship of the transferee to the other owners cannot be considered. Thus, after closer scrutiny, the courts should reject the legitimacy of swing vote value so long as the willing buyer-willing seller rule exists.

If the courts, however, continue to consider swing vote value, there is a distinct possibility that this will result in lower valuations, not higher valuations, as the Service hopes. This will occur if the courts do not focus on the relationship of the transferee to the other owners because of the willing buyer-willing seller rule, but instead focus solely on the relationship of the other owners to each other. The focus on the relationship of the other owners can cause the court to conclude that the other owners will form coalitions. This will further diminish the value of the transferee's stock because, rather than merely being one of several minority owners with no one exerting control, the transferee would be the only minority shareholder with no hope of joining a control coalition.

* * *

VII. A TAX POLICY CRITIQUE OF THE STATUTORY AND JUDICIAL RESPONSES

A. Introduction

The reluctance of the courts and the legislature to tax the transfer of the opportunity to recombine control creates a significant discontinuity between the gift and estate taxes. A taxpayer can avoid the inclusion of the control premium in her estate simply by making lifetime transfers to the same individuals to whom she would have bequeathed the stock.

The discontinuity suggests that either the opportunity to participate in control should be eliminated from the estate tax base where the decedent's bequest divides control among several legatees or, conversely, that the value of the opportunity should be included in the gift tax base where the donor divides control by inter vivos gifts. * * *

* * *

B. Efficiency
* * *

The current discontinuity between the gift and estate tax treatment may create a significant allocational inefficiency if it encourages taxpayers to divide ownership of their companies or other assets in order to reduce transfer taxes in situations where they otherwise would not have done so. This allocational inefficiency would decrease social welfare to the extent the decline in value achieved for gift tax purposes by dividing up an asset reflects a real economic decline in value rather than a transformation of the value.

* * *

* * * [I]t is clearly difficult to measure the allocational effect of the current treatment of minority discounts. While it seems reasonable to assume that, at the margin, the ability to avoid transfer taxes on control premiums would encourage more lifetime gifts of minority interests than otherwise would occur, it is difficult to assess the magnitude of the response. Moreover, it is also difficult to determine whether this impact at the margin has caused a significant decrease in social welfare. * * * It is possible, therefore, that the only adverse impact of the current status is the costs that minority owners will incur in forming a control coalition.

* * *

The analysis of the administrative costs of including an opportunity to participate in control in the gift tax base is comparative. The administrative costs of including the opportunity in both the gift and estate tax base are compared to (1) the administrative cost under the current regime of only including the opportunity in the estate tax base and (2) the administrative cost of not taxing the opportunity at all. The analysis considers the inclusion of the opportunity in the estate and gift tax bases in two forms. The first automatically assigns a portion of the control premium pro rata to minority interests that are transferred by a majority owner where the transferor and family members control the entity or assets both before and after the transfer. This is a form of irrebuttable presumption analogous to the type currently used by chapter 14 in narrow circumstances. The second form is a rebuttable presumption that assigns a portion of the control premium but allows the transferee to show that he will not participate in control. * * * An irrebuttable presumption that includes the control opportunity in both the estate and gift tax bases would result in the lowest administrative costs as compared to the current regime.

* * *

An irrebuttable presumption used to tax the transfer of the opportunity to participate in control would decrease the cost of administering the gift tax because it would relieve the courts, the Service and taxpayers of the obligation to calculate the amount of the minority discount. Instead, they simply would calculate the value of the donor's control block and assign a pro rata portion of that value to the portion transferred by the donor. They could omit the additional step of then calculating the size of the minority discount. The costs of calculating the estate tax should remain unchanged since this is the process that already is used. The estate tax values all the decedent's interests regardless of the manner in which the interests are divided up among legatees or heirs.

The rebuttable presumption would increase the cost of administering both the estate and gift taxes as compared to the current regime. The courts, Service and taxpayers would be required to explore the relationship of the transferee to the other owners and the relationship among the other owners in order to determine whether the presumption that the transferee would participate in control can be rebutted. Since the courts currently do not examine the relationship of the transferee to the other owners, this determination would increase the quantity of analysis required for both the estate and gift tax.

Excluding the control opportunity from both the estate and gift tax base also would have the effect of increasing costs but not by as much as the rebuttable presumption. The costs of calculating the gift tax would remain unchanged since the gift tax base currently excludes the value of control opportunities. The costs of calculating the estate tax for the courts, Service and taxpayers, however, would increase. While under the current scheme, there is no need to calculate the minority discount for each bequest, under this alternative, they would have to calculate the minority discount for each bequest of a minority interest.

C. Equity

Equity usually is analyzed from two perspectives: horizontal equity and vertical equity. Horizontal equity examines whether similar taxpayers are treated similarly. Vertical equity seeks to insure that an "appropriate" distinction is made in the treatment of people who are dissimilar. * * *

* * *

This Article adopts [the] view that the useful inquiry under horizontal equity pertains to the appropriate definition of the tax base and under vertical equity relates to the "appropriate" distinction to make among unequals. In order to determine the appropriate tax base and distinction to make among unequals in designing transfer taxes, it is necessary to determine their purpose or purposes. The formulation of the tax base and appropriate distinction among unequals should be those that best achieve the objectives of the transfer taxes.

Policymakers have not agreed about the fundamental objectives of transfer taxes. * * *

The estate and gift tax may seek to achieve four objectives: (1) to raise revenues, (2) to increase the progressivity of the income tax, (3) to prevent concentrations of wealth in a small segment of society and (4) to prevent families from establishing dynasties. * * *

* * *

* * * [I]ncluding the control opportunity in the gift tax as well as the estate tax base is the best alternative for achieving the objectives of the transfer taxes. Expanding the gift tax base would help prevent the creation of dynasties and concentrations of wealth since it would increase the transferor's gift tax liability. Moreover, expansion of the gift tax base should increase revenues and contribute to progressivity, although the lack of data creates some uncertainty.

D. Recommendations

Although the objectives underlying the transfer taxes are more likely to be achieved if the transfer of an opportunity to participate in control is included in the gift tax base using either a rebuttable or irrebuttable presumption, the latter is a better choice. * * * Given that a donor is not likely to destroy value by dividing up control of an asset among donees who cannot work together, the instances in which the irrebuttable presumption would be overinclusive are probably minimal. Moreover, this overinclusivity also may be offset partially by cases where it is underinclusive, in other words, where an asset is divided among nonfamily members who will cooperate. Therefore, the administrative efficiencies created by an irrebuttable presumption should outweigh any harm caused by its overinclusiveness.

Some may be concerned that enacting an irrebuttable presumption would hinder the efforts of families to retain small businesses. Such a concern would be addressed better by directly providing transfer tax exemptions for the transfer of small businesses to family members, rather than by continuing the present irrational policy towards minority discounts. An exemption would allow families to determine who will control the business based upon sound management principles, not estate and gift tax considerations.

* * *

NOTE

Repetti questions the usefulness of the "willing buyer-willing seller" standard in valuing noncontrolling interests in closely-held businesses. What alternative standard would provide a more realistic measure of value? For a recent proposal arguing that Congress should adopt final-offer arbitration, requiring courts to choose either the taxpayer's or the Service's valuation figure, see Jay A. Soled, *Transfer Tax Valuation Issues, the Game Theory, and Final Offer Arbitration: A Modest Proposal for Reform*, 39 ARIZ. L. REV. 283 (1997).

B.   Estate Freezes

This Subpart addresses the phenomenon of "estate freezes," with particular emphasis on techniques involving family-owned business interests and split-interest trusts. Subpart B(1) explains the operation of preferred equity freezes in the context of family corporations and partnerships. Subpart B(2) explores the background and policy of recent legislative initiatives, and Subpart B(3) offers several perspectives on the status of estate freezing transactions under current law.

1. Preferred Equity Freezes

In a seminal article on "sophisticated tax avoidance," George Cooper explains how under prior law the capital structure of a family corporation could be arranged to shift future appreciation to younger generations at little or no transfer tax cost. William F. Nelson analyzes a similar technique in the family partnership context.

George Cooper, *A Voluntary Tax? New Perspectives on Sophisticated Estate Tax Avoidance*, 77 COLUM. L. REV. 161 (1977)*

* * *

The first major goal of good estate planning is to freeze the size of a client's estate at its current level and divert future growth to the natural objects of the client's bounty. As will be seen, it is far easier to divert future growth than it is to disgorge wealth already accumulated, and good estate planning attempts to get estate freezing action into operation as soon as possible so as to cut off wealth accumulation before it becomes a more serious planning problem. * * *

* * * Where the estate planner has traditionally earned his fee is in accomplishing one or more of three sophisticated goals in gift-giving—preserving continuing control of and benefits from the transferred property in the hands of the client, reducing or avoiding the need to pay immediate gift tax on the transfer, and passing on more of value than meets the taxable eye in the transfer. * * *

---

*   This article originally appeared at 77 COLUM. L. REV. 161 (1977). Reprinted by permission. This work was also published as a book by Brookings Institution (1978).

1. *The Preferred Stock Recapitalization.* Take the case of Dr. Joseph E. Salsbury.[20] Dr. Salsbury was the founder and developer of Salsbury Laboratories * * * . The company was begun on a shoestring in 1927, but by the time of Dr. Salsbury's death in 1967 it * * * was conservatively valued by the Tax Court at more than $13 million. * * *

Dr. Salsbury's estate planning began sometime prior to 1946. By that year, almost two decades after the corporation's founding in 1927, he had transferred 46% of its single class of stock to his wife and two children * * * .

* * * By retaining majority voting control in the corporation, Dr. Salsbury effectively continued in control of the property which he gave to his prospective heirs. He continued to have the power to select all corporate directors and, through them, to choose all the officers who ran the corporation, to fix the salaries of all officers, and to decide when and how much to pay in dividends. This continued control over property through retained voting control of a corporation is not viewed as continuing ownership for the purpose of the estate tax. In addition, since he continued to run the corporation, Dr. Salsbury also achieved the goal of giving his prospective heirs the indirect benefit of a portion of his knowledge and talent free of tax insofar as those personal attributes were used to operate and expand the company.

* * *

* * * [I]n 1946 Dr. Salsbury moved on to a new level of sophistication in his estate planning by undertaking a tax-free stock recapitalization * * * . Pursuant to this recapitalization, all of Salsbury Laboratories' single class of common stock was cancelled, and in place thereof shareholders were issued a combination of new preferred stock and common stock. * * * The preferred stock was divided among shareholders in proportion to their prior holdings of the old common, giving Dr. Salsbury 54% of it. The new common stock was, however, issued almost entirely to Mrs. Salsbury and the children * * * .

The net effect on voting rights of this recapitalization was minimal; Dr. Salsbury's control was preserved * * * . Beyond that, * * * it may fairly be assumed that this recapitalization followed standard patterns. If these patterns were followed, the aggregate value of the preferred stock was approximately equal to the then value of the corporation, and the new common stock had negligible value, embodying only the speculative future potential of the corporation. On this assumption, Dr. Salsbury had no gift tax to pay, but he had successfully shifted to his wife and children the full value of all future corporate growth. In other words, he froze his own estate, and, at the same time, achieved the triple goals of sophisticated estate planning—no loss of control, no current gift tax, and ability to pass on the future benefits of his business acumen free of tax. Moreover, since he retained voting control in the corporation he had the power to decide how much benefit the common shareholders received and when they received it. * * *

The ultimate result of all of this was that when he died in 1967, although Dr. Salsbury had paid little or no gift tax and in fact continued to hold voting control of the $13 million company which he had founded, he actually owned only a limited preferred stock interest which could be included in his estate. This preferred stock was worth, apart from its voting control, only $372,152. The Internal Revenue Service attempted to salvage the situation by arguing that the value of the retained voting control was equal to most of the corporate value, but the Tax Court was unsympathetic and raised the value only modestly to $514,000. The balance of some $12.5 million escaped tax, saving Dr. Salsbury's heirs a potential liability of approximately $7 million. This effectively allowed the business, which was the only substantial asset owned by Dr. Salsbury, to be passed on to the next generation without any meaningful tax burden.

---

[20]   Estate of Joseph E. Salsbury, 34 T.C.M. (CCH) 1441 (1975). * * *

* * *

The problems posed in formulating direct reforms to restrict estate freezing activity become evident when a possible response is considered to the *Salsbury*-type recapitalization * * * . There are four separate transfer tax problems raised by the *Salsbury*-type recapitalization. First, there is the tax-free shift of future growth, which is inherent in any gift. Second, there is the effective way in which this future growth has been separated from present value through the dual-stock structure to maximize tax avoidance. Third, there is the retained enjoyment and control held by the donor parent through his continued ownership of the majority of voting stock. And, fourth, there is the continuing parental contribution to the growth and development of the corporation which is indirectly diverted to the next generation free of tax.

The most obvious locus for reform is the third aspect (retained rights). The Code has long recognized the tax avoidance implications of transfers with retained rights in sections 2036 and 2038, and has dealt with these problems by recapturing the property for purposes of estate taxation, i.e., treating it as if it had never been transferred. Congress could consider attacking the *Salsbury* transaction with amendments to sections 2036 and 2038 which expand the definitions of retained income and control needed to invoke those provisions. As the Supreme Court dryly observed in one of its more enlightened moments, the transfer of corporate property by an individual who retains voting control over the corporation "may properly be said to have left him with more than a memory" of the property. Whether Congress should go so far as to adopt a statutory standard of total amnesia may be questioned. But there is little doubt that the modest anti-*Byrum* provision in the Tax Reform Act does little to prevent a transferor from effectively retaining control over corporate property in which an interest has been transferred. * * *

All these objectives could be accomplished, for example, by an amendment to section 2038 providing that the power to manage or to select the management of a corporation, partnership or other business entity, by exercise of voting rights, contract rights or otherwise, will be considered a power to alter or amend the beneficial enjoyment of all ownership interests in the entity. * * *

Such changes in sections 2036 and 2038 would not, however, really accomplish very much to block the *Salsbury* transaction because the way would remain open to achieve the same ends through the mechanism of a sale rather than a gift. * * * A corporation can be established with the dual-stock structure and the low-value common stock can be sold to the children for adequate and full consideration (which would be nominal given the nominal value of the stock) rather than given to them, thereby completely removing it from the net of sections 2036 and 2038. * * * To combat this, sections 2036 and 2038 might be amended to cover sales to family members, as well as gifts, where a parent retains a defined interest in property. The theory of excluding sales from the scope of sections 2036 and 2038 is presumably that when property is sold the selling parent's estate is not depleted but rather resupplied with equivalent value property. This theory, however, fails to take account of future growth opportunities which are shifted on the sale. Since the shift of this future growth with retained income and control is such an important part of estate tax avoidance, an expansion of sections 2036 and 2038 to cover family sales with retained interests seems essential if we are going to take meaningful action against *Salsbury*-type transactions.

The difficulties in writing this new provision should not be underestimated. There is first the problem of determining how much, if any, credit should be given a purchasing child for his contributions to the future growth and development of the property, especially in a case like *Salsbury* where the child has participated actively for a substantial period. However, under present law we give no credit for this in the case of gifted property recaptured under sections 2036 and 2038, and arguably the problem is so intractable that we have no choice but to follow the same route in sale cases. This would mean that a parent would have to cut all control strings if he wished to avoid risk of having a donee's efforts reflected in the parent's own estate. In other words, it would be difficult for a parent who wished to maintain ongoing dominance of a family business to shift a part of the future growth of that business to a child, even if the child is active in the business and pays for a share in it. That may seem harsh, but it is simply a reflection of the significance of continued dominance. If the parent will not let go of control, the law is justified in treating that control as significant. * * *

* * *

The unfortunate conclusion to be drawn from all of this is that, while it is possible to tax many instances of estate freezing, not all such activity can be covered. Each step toward improving the effectiveness of the transfer tax in this area can have unintended effects impinging upon family relationships. Even if one could be cavalier about these side effects, it is impossible to blink at the fact that political resistance to much expansion of sections 2036 and 2038 in this direction will be severe and the resisters will have cogent arguments to offer.

* * *

NOTE

Cooper presents the *Salsbury* preferred stock recapitalization as an example of "sophisticated tax avoidance" while acknowledging that prior law provided virtually no impediments to such estate freezing techniques. What distinguishes the *Salsbury* transaction from an outright gift of property having a high rate of potential appreciation? Does the rather tolerant attitude adopted by courts in applying prior law suggest that estate freezes were not widely perceived as abusive? If there was no perceived abuse, why did Congress enact former § 2036(c) in 1987 to deal with estate freezes? For another discussion of estate freezing techniques under prior law, see Symposium, *The Estate Freezing Rage: A Practical Look at Planning Opportunities and Potential Problems*, 15 REAL PROP., PROB. & TR. J. 19 (1980). In considering various proposals for statutory reform presented in Subpart B(2), keep in mind Cooper's warning that an expansion of §§ 2036 and 2038 to curb estate freezes would be likely to encounter severe "political resistance."

William F. Nelson, *The Partnership Capital Freeze: Income, Estate, and Gift Tax Considerations*, 1 VA. TAX REV. 11 (1981)*

This article analyzes the partnership as a vehicle for an estate-planning technique referred to metaphorically as "estate freezing." The concept of estate freezing is not a new one: tax planners have recognized for years that transfer tax liability on an assignment of rights to income and appreciation is much easier to limit if the transfer occurs before the income and appreciation accrue, rather than after such accrual takes place.[1] Current inflationary expectations, how-

---

* Copyright © 1981. Reprinted with permission.

[1] *See* Cooper, *A Voluntary Tax? New Perspectives on Sophisticated Estate Tax Avoidance*, 77 COLUM. L. REV. 161, 170 (1977).

ever, are fueling an intensified interest in methods of "freezing" a person's potential transfer tax liability by shifting future income and appreciation on his assets to the natural objects of his bounty. * * *

Estate freezes utilizing corporations or partnerships follow a consistent pattern. In most cases, senior family members exchange rapidly appreciating assets for "frozen" stock or partnership interests. These frozen interests have limited, but preferred rights to future income and appreciation. Junior family members then purchase or receive gifts of "unfrozen" interests in the entity. Holders of these unfrozen interests are entitled to all future appreciation in the value of the corporation or partnership in excess of the limited income preference attributable to the frozen interests. The Internal Revenue Code does not impose transfer tax on this appreciation as it accrues to the common or participating interests, even though such appreciation is accelerated by "leveraging" on the frozen interests.[3]

The primary advantage of an equity freeze is its low cost in tax terms. * * *

Furthermore, * * * the holder of preferred stock or a frozen partnership interest can retain control of the entity without greatly compromising the tax objectives of the freeze. * * *

Of all the vehicles for avoiding transfer tax on shifts of future appreciation, the partnership is the most flexible, the most complex, and the least understood by tax planners and representatives of the fisc. * * *

I. MECHANICS OF A PARTNERSHIP FREEZE

* * *

B. The Partnership Agreement

The partnership agreement that implements a partnership freeze should create frozen and unfrozen interests that are substantially identical in economic terms to the common and preferred stock interests that would be issued if the taxpayer used a corporate vehicle. In drafting such an agreement, the first step is to set up cash-flow distribution and liquidation provisions that achieve the desired economic results. The draftsman then should design income and loss allocation provisions that "track" the predetermined economic arrangement. Thus, in partnership agreements designed to provide liquidation preferences, the income and loss allocation provisions follow, rather than determine, the cash-flow and liquidation provisions.

For example, assume that taxpayer F and his son S decide to use a partnership vehicle for their freeze. They first should draw up the distribution and liquidation provisions of the partnership agreement. The distribution section should provide F with an annual distribution preference computed at the rate of ten percent per annum on F's initial contribution of $50. Under this term, F would receive all nonliquidating cash distributions made during a particular year up to the amount of his annual preference. All nonliquidating distributions in excess of F's preference would go to S. This provision would give F the equivalent of a cumulative dividend preference. The liquidation clause should provide that F will receive all liquidation proceeds up to the amount of his initial contribution, plus any unpaid cash-flow preference that has accumulated. Any remaining proceeds should go to S. This liquidation preference would be analogous to the one attached to preferred stock in a corporate freeze.

* * *

---

[3]   The unfrozen interests are "leveraged" in the sense that the holders of these interests receive not only the income and the appreciation on the assets distributable to them, but also the income and appreciation on the assets attributable to the frozen interests that exceed the fixed return payable to the frozen stakeholders.

The allocation of partnership income and loss in a freeze should follow the economic interests established by the cash-flow and liquidation provisions. The objective of the allocation is to maintain the equality between each partner's capital account[20] and the respective amount that he would receive in an immediate liquidation of the partnership, if it sold its assets for book value. Thus, the agreement in the example should allocate losses to S to the extent of any positive amount in his capital account.[22] Remaining losses then should reduce any positive amount in F's capital account.[23] The agreement should allocate profits to F's capital account up to the amount of his liquidation preference.[24] Profits beyond this amount should go to S. This arrangement would preserve the equality between each partner's capital account and the book value of his liquidation distribution.

* * *

Two variations of the above scheme do not have corporate analogues. First, the frozen partner may receive an enforceable right to a fixed annual distribution, rather than a mere cumulative preference to partnership income and cash flow. This fixed distribution is known as a "guaranteed payment" and, unlike a preference, does not depend on the partnership's cash flow or profitability. Thus, guaranteed-payment rights more closely resemble debt than preferred stock. * * *

The second variation on the above scheme that does not have a corporate analogue is a partnership freeze in which all losses are allocated to the unfrozen interests * * * . This allocation places the frozen partner in a more secure position than preferred stock would, because common stockholders are not liable to preferred stockholders for earnings deficits in excess of common stock equity. Such additional security adds value to the frozen interest, but also converts it into a debt-like arrangement.

II. INCOME TAX ASPECTS OF PARTNERSHIP FREEZES

In structuring a partnership freeze, the tax planner faces three major income tax concerns. First, he must ensure that the freeze vehicle qualifies as a partnership for tax purposes and that the holders of both the frozen and unfrozen interests constitute partners for tax purposes. Second, he must structure the acquisition of the various partnership interests to avoid income tax liability. Third, the tax planner must design the income and loss allocation scheme contained in the partnership agreement so that the scheme is effective for income tax purposes.

* * *

III. TRANSFER TAX ASPECTS OF PARTNERSHIP FREEZES

A. Estate Tax Aspects

The primary objective of an estate freeze is to shift future appreciation out of the frozen stakeholder's estate and into that of an unfrozen stakeholder. In the context of a typical partnership freeze, section 2033 directly includes in the frozen partner's gross estate only the value of the frozen interest at the time of his death. * * *

---

[20]   A partner's capital account is the sum of the fair market value of his capital contributions to the partnership and his allocable share of partnership income, less his allocable share of partnership loss, and less the fair market value of distributions made to him. * * *

[22]   S's capital account is at first economic risk because of F's liquidation preference.

[23]   If F actually receives an allocation of losses, all subsequent profits should be allocated to him until his capital account returns to its original level.

[24]   The amount of F's liquidation preference equals the amount of his initial contribution plus unpaid distribution preferences that have accumulated.

* * *

* * * [The frozen partner's] retention of the indirect economic interest represented by the frozen partnership interest alone should not be sufficient to trigger the operation of either section 2036(a)(1) or section 2038. In such circumstances, the courts should not treat the frozen partner as having "retained" either possession of the partnership assets or income rights with respect to them. * * *

* * *

C. Gift Tax Analysis

* * *

The most difficult gift tax problem in estate freezes is valuation of the frozen and unfrozen interests. The courts and valuation experts have had little experience in valuing the blocks of preferred stock that account for major portions of a frozen corporation's capital, and even less experience in valuing frozen partnership interests. * * *

In valuing preferred stock, experts focus primarily on the stated yield, the income coverage of the stated yield, and the asset coverage of the liquidation preference. In most freezes, the frozen interest accounts for a substantial portion of the vehicle's total equity. The tax planner, therefore, normally will not be able to structure a frozen interest that is worth its "par" or liquidation preference, regardless of how high he makes the yield or preferred return. Valuation experts apply a substantial discount to the interest, because the income and asset coverage of the frozen stakeholder's preferences normally proves inadequate. * * *

To avoid gift tax liability on the differential between the value contributed and the value received by the frozen stakeholder, practitioners have begun to add unusual features to the frozen interests that bolster their value. These features include: voting rights; the right to "put" the frozen interest to the partnership or corporation for an amount equal to the liquidation preference of the frozen interest; the right to convert the frozen interest into an unfrozen interest having a value, at the time of conversion, equal to the liquidation preference of the frozen interest; and the right to liquidate the partnership or corporation and receive assets equal in value to the stated liquidation preference. All of these features should bolster the value of the frozen interest * * * .

The difficulty, however, with all of these added features, except voting rights, is that the frozen stakeholder acquires them solely for the purpose of bolstering value. He generally does not intend to utilize the features later as part of the freeze. In fact, exercise of the features often will thwart the objectives of the freeze. For example, a frozen interest may be worth its liquidation value because of an attached option which permits conversion into an unfrozen interest with a value equal to the liquidation preference of the frozen interest. The objective of the transaction, however, is to shift appreciation out of the frozen stakeholder's estate. He thus will be reluctant to exercise his conversion right, even though failure to exercise it may be against his personal economic interests. The fact that the frozen stakeholder does not intend to utilize the value-increasing features to maximize his own estate raises two questions: first, whether a valuation for gift tax purposes should ignore the added features on the ground that the frozen stakeholder does not intend to exercise them; and, second, whether the presence of features that give the frozen stakeholder the power to participate in freeze income and appreciation will trigger a continuing series of gifts to the unfrozen stakeholders.

As to the first question, the courts probably will not ignore the value-increasing features for valuation purposes merely because the frozen interest holder does not intend to utilize them. The regulations define the value of property, for both estate and gift tax purposes, as "the price at which such property would change hands between a willing buyer and a willing seller, neither being under any compulsion to buy or to sell and both having reasonable knowledge of the relevant facts." Under this definition, the added features clearly must be taken into account in valuing the frozen interest, because, regardless of the frozen stakeholder's intentions with respect to the additional rights, he would take such rights into account in dealing with an unrelated buyer. * * *

Another argument for including the added features in the valuation formula is that such inclusion does not create any opportunities for avoiding transfer tax. If the features increase the gift tax value of the frozen interest, the amount of the frozen stakeholder's taxable gifts upon implementation of the freeze will decrease. The features, however, also will serve to bolster the value of the retained interest for estate tax purposes. Thus, the increased transfer tax at death offsets the decreased tax on the freezing transaction, and the loss to the fisc is simply one of timing.

The second question regarding the effect of adding value-increasing features to frozen interests is whether the frozen interest holder's failure to exercise these rights results in continuing gifts to the unfrozen stakeholders. * * *

* * *

V. CONCLUSION

* * *

It is impossible, at this point in the evolution of the estate-freeze concept, to predict with certainty all of the transfer tax consequences of estate freezes. Analysis of the law as it exists today indicates, however, that the primary transfer tax objective—shifting future appreciation to younger generations without an estate tax cost—is attainable. * * *

Regardless of the effectiveness of these transactions under existing transfer tax law, the Service will scrutinize the freeze concept, and a future legislative change in the rules of the game is not out of the question. * * *

NOTE

Courts have generally refused to apply § 2036(a) to preferred equity freezes involving family-owned corporations or partnerships, on the theory that the transferor's retained interest does not represent enjoyment or control of the underlying corporation or partnership. *See Estate of Boykin v. Commissioner*, 53 T.C.M. (CCH) 345 (1987). Note also that § 2036(b), the "anti-*Byrum*" provision, applies specifically to transfers of stock in a "controlled corporation" but is silent concerning family partnerships.

Nelson discusses several "unusual features" that are used "solely for the purpose of bolstering value" when an estate freeze is initially implemented. Is it true that taking such features into account for gift tax purposes "does not create any opportunities for avoiding transfer tax"? For an excellent discussion of the government's attempts to impose a gift tax on indirect capital shifts resulting from a frozen interest holder's failure to exercise value-bolstering rights, see William F. Nelson & Peter J. Genz, *New Uncertainties in the Equity Freeze: The Impact of* Dickman *On Capital Call Rights And Other Issues*, 63 TAXES 999 (1985).

2. Legislative Initiatives

To deal with estate freezing transactions, Joseph M. Dodge proposes a statutory solution, based on § 2036(a), which would hold such transactions "in suspense" until the final disposition of all the original owner's interests in the underlying entity or property. Dodge's proposal foreshadows the approach adopted in former § 2036(c), which was enacted in 1987, substantially amended in 1988, and ultimately repealed in 1990. The background and rationale of former § 2036(c) are reviewed in a 1990 report by the Joint Comittee on Taxation, which also discusses the "front-end" approach ultimately adopted in §§ 2701-2704.

Joseph M. Dodge, *Redoing the Estate and Gift Taxes Along Easy-to-Value Lines*, 43 TAX L. REV. 241 (1988)*

* * *

* * * [An illusion pertaining to valuation without producing any real economic gain] is the principal aim of many, if not all, buy-sell agreements in which the buyer is a natural object of the seller transferor's bounty, and estate freeze transactions involving a recapitalization of an existing corporate or partnership interest into two forms of equity, one being retained and the other being the subject of an inter vivos transfer.[57]

The above two forms of transactions are similar in that each involves a two step disposition of interests in "underlying" property, namely, an entity or its assets, which is expected to appreciate over time. In the first step, an inter vivos transfer is made of an interest in the underlying property, which interest is undervalued because the true value of the transferred interest will emerge only at a later time; if the future value is speculative or indefinite, so much the better. The retained interest in the same underlying property is "frozen" in value, so that a subsequent transfer of it (typically at the transferor's death) will be undervalued relative to the now-flowering value of the interest previously transferred to the donees. By transferring the underlying property in two steps, in which the interest transferred at each step is undervalued, all appreciation in the underlying property accruing subsequent to the first-step transfer and prior to the second-step transfer is shifted to the transferee without any imposition of transfer tax on the appreciation. Since these devices do not create economic value as much as conceal it, one should not have any qualms about designing rules to defeat them.

---

[57] Here the wealthy person owning a business or controlling interest therein reshuffles her ownership interest, retaining high fixed yield securities (typically preferred stock) with a constant value that soaks up most of the value of the original ownership interest, and engineering the transfer of equity securities to the natural objects of her bounty. The idea is to fix the value of the donor's estate and to shift future appreciation to her donees. Since the appreciation is speculative, and would need to be reduced to present value in any event, and since the value of the original property has mostly been absorbed into the interest retained by the transferor, the gift element attributable to the transferred equity interest is typically claimed to be very low. *See generally* * * * Cooper, *A Voluntary Tax? New Perspectives on Sophisticated Estate Tax Avoidance*, 77 COLUM. L. REV. 161, 195-204 (1977); * * * Nelson, *The Partnership Capital Freeze: Income, Estate, and Gift Tax Considerations*, 1 VA. TAX REV. 11 (1981) * * * .

1. Buy-Sell Agreements

The aim of a buy-sell agreement entered into during the property owner's life is frequently to "fix" the future estate tax value of the property at a value below the anticipated date of death fair market value of the property by requiring the current owner and her estate to sell the property to the designated purchaser for a predetermined or formula price. The contractual restrictions inherent in this type of buy-sell agreement have the effect of depressing or freezing the property's value in the owner's hands; by the same token, the putative purchaser is granted an economic right of considerable value, namely, the ability to buy the property in the future at what is anticipated to be a bargain price. When the donee purchases the property from the decedent's estate at the depressed price after the decedent's death, the property ceases to be subject to the restrictions and therefore is instantly restored to its true fair market value.

Adherence to the "greater of the two" valuation principle [i.e., "the greater of what the transferor had or what the transferee received"] would require that buy-sell agreements and similar contractual restrictions on the decedent and her estate in favor of a donee be completely disregarded, at least if the contractual restrictions disappear at or by reason of the decedent's death either because they lapse or because the obligation to purchase following the decedent's death is mandatory on both parties. As discussed below, there is considerable justification for imposing the greater of the two rule in those buy-sell situations where the "purchaser" is really a gratuitous transferee.

Under gift tax theory, a present agreement to limit future value in favor of a natural object of the transferor's bounty, by enabling the latter to buy from the estate at a discount from true fair market value, constitutes a present gift. Although applicable in principle to the imposition of a restriction under a buy-sell agreement, such a rule would be virtually impossible to enforce in practice, as the amount of the present gift would be the present value of the future excess of fair market value over the price fixed by the agreement, and this excess, if any, in most cases, would not presently be ascertainable.

Under the "open gift" doctrine, the Service might attempt to hold this type of gift in suspense until the value of it can be determined. * * * But the same end result of taxing the aggregate transfer partly under the estate tax (the value as fixed by the buy-sell agreement) and partly as a delayed gift (i.e., the bargain purchase element) can be attained more simply under the estate tax alone by including the value of the property in the person's estate at its full fair market value without regard to the restriction. * * *

The same result obtains if one analogizes the imposition of a buy-sell agreement in favor of a gratuitous transferee to a transfer of property with retained income interest under § 2036(a)(1) of the estate tax. The owner of the property retains the income from it up to her death. The gratuitous donee purchaser has the equivalent of a remainder interest by having a right (and perhaps an obligation) to obtain the property at the owner's death for less than the property's fair market value. Moreover, the owner has surrendered the right to give or bequeath the property to anyone other than the purchaser. It is true that the purchaser pays the purchase price to the owner's estate, but the purchase price simply represents partial consideration under § 2043(a) which would operate as an offset against the amount includable under § 2036. * * *

* * * [I]t might be argued that there is no gratuitous transfer of the bargain purchase element because the bargain purchase arose out of a commercial dealing. However, if the buyer is a natural object of the deceased's bounty, and the purchase price is to be figured on a basis other than the fair market value at the time of the transfer, it seems obvious that a gratuitous transfer is involved, even if there might also be a "business" purpose. It may be necessary to impose a statutory definition of a "natural object of the decedent's bounty" to include, for example, the decedent's spouse and descendants plus any person who is an heir or next of kin of the

decedent, either at the decedent's death or at the time the agreement became binding.[67] It is conceivable (if highly improbable) that even the price term in a sale to a relative under a buy-sell agreement might be primarily motivated by commercial considerations, and the decedent's estate should be allowed to prove that this was the case. * * *

2. Estate Freezes

Turning to the estate freeze recapitalization, the planning goal here again is to fix the value of a retained preferred income interest that will be included in the donor's estate and to shift future growth to the equity interest given away. Moreover, by retaining control of the underlying entity, the donor can adopt policies that will directly contribute to the future appreciation of the interest given away. The problem for the Service is that the true amount of the gift of the equity interest is difficult to ascertain at the time the gift is made, because a value must be assigned to future appreciation * * * . Thus, although the Service will attempt to assign significant value to the equity interest given away, conventional valuation principles render this a difficult task, at best.

The typical estate freeze transaction bears a strong economic resemblance to a § 2036(a)(1) transfer, with income to the donor for life, remainder over at the donor's death, except that present § 2036(a)(1) does not apply because the income from the retained preferred interest is not "from" the transferred property (the equity interest). True, the transferred equity interest might be viewed as an interest in the entity's underlying assets, and the retained preferred interest can be viewed as representing a right to income from the same assets, but there is no authority for piercing the entity veil in the transfer tax area.

* * *

Nevertheless, the rationale underlying § 2036 * * * is also apropos to the estate freeze situation. In brief, that rationale is this: When a transfer occurs with a retained interest, the net amount actually transferred can be accurately determined only by holding the transaction open until the retained interest expires, which typically occurs at the transferor's death. The usual estate freeze transaction does not involve an interest that terminates at death. Yet, the value of the transferred interest might more accurately be valued at the transferor's death than at the time of gift; the interest's potential for appreciation and income can be better evaluated with the benefit of hindsight. * * *

If existing law is inadequate to cope with the estate freeze recapitalization, a statutory change is in order, which might best take the form of an amendment to (or adaptation of) § 2036. Essentially, such a provision would be triggered by any disposition of an interest in property which was created as the result of a prior or contemporaneous restructuring of existing property (or an interest therein) into two or more interests that differ with respect to income, liquidation, or control rights. Once triggered, the provision would treat a transferred interest as not being completed for transfer tax purposes until all interests ever owned by the transferor in the underlying property have been disposed of by the transferor (which typically will occur no later than the transferor's death).[76] When the transfer of the whole is deemed com-

---

[67]   Thus, a sibling is unlikely to be the natural object of the bounty of a deceased who was survived by children or grandchildren, but, if the decedent had no descendants, a sibling might well fit the bill * * * .

[76]   If the (equity) interest is sold rather than made the subject of a gift, any consideration received should be treated as partial consideration for the aggregate of interests in the underlying property deemed transferred at (or before) the transferor's death, and not full and adequate consideration for the particular interest transferred. Without such a rule, the proposed statutory solution would be easy to avoid, given the relative small value of the transferred (equity) interest at the time of "sale."

plete, the retained and gifted interests would be aggregated together as one for federal transfer tax purposes and valued as of the time of the last transfer, and thus the valuation issues raised by the bifurcation into two types of equity interest would simply disappear. * * *

* * * [T]here is no fundamental unfairness in holding a transfer in suspense until all interests of the transferor in the underlying property have been disposed of. The ideal solution might be to look to the future to determine what the future gift of uncertain present value really is, and then to discount such gift back to the present and impose the gift tax. But of course it is not possible to do this with any degree of accuracy. Nevertheless, valuation accuracy can be achieved (or greatly improved) by holding the transfer in suspense until such time as it can be valued. The amount of the gift can then be discounted back to the time the gift was made, but, in order to compensate the government for the delay in collecting the tax when it was "really" due, the discounted amount would be compounded forward to the present. Since the discounting and compounding forward would exactly cancel each other out, that leaves simply the amount of the transfer as of the time it is ultimately capable of valuation.

Finally, it might be thought that the perceived problem and the proposed solution assume appreciation of the initially-transferred equity interests, and, if appreciation does not occur, the government will come out behind. However, transferors are unlikely to attempt an estate freeze recapitalization unless they anticipate that such future appreciation will occur. If it does not, the likely cause will be an excessively high fixed rate of return on the retained preferred interest which will reappear in the transferor's potential § 2033 estate. If the underlying property truly goes bad, the government will be deprived of transfer tax revenue, but it is appropriate that transfer taxes do not apply to the extent that a transaction actually results in economic waste. A rule that renders estate freeze recapitalizations pointless for transfer tax purposes will reduce tax motivated behavior that creates economic potential.

* * *

NOTE

What features do buy-sell agreements and estate freezes have in common that set them apart from other sequential transfers of interests in property? Should transfer restrictions in a buy-sell agreement be viewed as analogous to restrictions on control arising from minority shareholder status? For a recent discussion of transfer restrictions, see Roger R. Fross, *Estate Tax Valuation Based on Book Value Buy-Sell Agreements*, 49 TAX LAW. 319 (1996).

Dodge recommends a statutory approach modelled on § 2036(a) to deal with buy-sell agreements and estate freezes. In fact, Congress enacted former § 2036(c) shortly before Dodge's article was published. Can Dodge's recommended approach be accommodated within the existing estate and gift tax structure? Recall Cooper's earlier warning about the difficulties of drafting an effective, workable, and politically acceptable statute.

JOINT COMMITTEE ON TAXATION, FEDERAL TRANSFER TAX CONSEQUENCES OF ESTATE FREEZES (JCS-13-90), 101st Cong., 2d Sess. (1990)

* * *

III. TRANSFER TAX CONSEQUENCES OF ESTATE FREEZES PRIOR TO 1987

A. General Description of Estate Freeze

An "estate freeze" is a technique that has the effect of limiting the value of property held by an older generation at its current value and passing any appreciation in the property to a younger generation. Generally, the older generation retains income from, or control over, the property.

To effect a freeze, the older generation transfers an interest in the property that is likely to appreciate while retaining an interest in the property that is less likely to appreciate. Because the value of the transferred interest increases while the value of the retained interest remains relatively constant, the older generation has "frozen" the value of the property in its estate.

In one common form, the preferred stock freeze, a person owning preferred stock and common stock in a corporation transfers the common stock to another person. Since common stock generally appreciates in value more than preferred stock, the transferor has "frozen" the value of his holdings in the corporation. Future appreciation is not subject to transfer tax.

An estate freeze can be achieved with almost any kind of property, including interests in active businesses, listed stocks, real estate and art. The older generation may retain a variety of rights in a freeze transaction. Retained rights may include, for example, the right to vote stock, to receive income from property, or to control or use property. The retained right also may be the right to a fixed or variable amount, sometimes known as a "capital call" right. A capital call right may include (1) a right to "put" the frozen interest for an amount equal to the liquidation preference of the frozen interest; (2) a right to liquidate an entity and receive assets; or (3) a right to convert the nonappreciating retained interest into an appreciating interest.

The retained rights in an estate freeze may be structured to lapse or terminate, particularly at death. Retained rights often involve discretion regarding the amount, timing, or fact of payment.

* * *

IV. TRANSFER TAX CONCERNS RAISED BY ESTATE FREEZES

Estate freezes raise three basic transfer tax concerns. First, because frozen interests are inherently difficult to value, they can be used as a means of undervaluing gifts. Second, such interests entail the creation of rights that, if not exercised in an arm's-length manner, may subsequently be used to transfer wealth free of transfer tax. Third, "frozen" interests may be used to retain substantial ownership of the entire property while nominally transferring an interest in the property to another person.

A. Undervaluation of Initial Transfer

Estate freezes provide an opportunity for undervaluation of the initial gift. * * *

Undervaluation may occur because the transferor claims a value for the transferred property lower than the amount a willing buyer would pay for the interest.[58] Freezes involve the cre-

---

[58]   Indeed, the very application of the willing-buyer, willing-seller standard to certain property rights held by related parties may be problematic. In most families, family relationships rather than contractual rights determine how and when property will pass.

ation of interests that are inherently difficult to value for several reasons. First, proper valuation of common and preferred classes must reflect the risks and potential returns for each class over time. This is because a significant part of the value of a residual interest in [a] corporation with classes having different preferences may consist of its value as an option (i.e., its right to future appreciation in excess of the amount needed to satisfy the claims of the preferred stock, without being subject to the same risk of loss borne by the preferred). This option value may be substantial * * * and can be understated if the common stock is valued by subtracting the discounted present value of the anticipated dividends on the preferred stock from the total value of the corporation. * * *

Second, even if one assumes that the value of the common stock can be determined by subtracting the discounted value of the cash flow provided for by the preferred stock from the value of the corporation, the discounted value itself can be difficult to ascertain. Even if the features of the closely held preferred interest are identical to those found in public markets, differences between the two types of securities make comparison difficult. * * * [T]he need of publicly traded companies to have continued access to the capital markets creates an incentive to pay dividends on preferred stock that may be absent for the closely held company. Further, publicly traded preferred stock is inherently more liquid than is comparable stock of a closely-held company. * * *

Moreover, the features of a preferred stock issued in a freeze often vary substantially from features contained in publicly traded stocks. Stock issued in a freeze may lack features common to publicly traded comparables (such as a cumulative right to dividends) or contain features missing from such comparables (such as discretionary capital call rights).

These valuation difficulties create the possibility that inconsistent valuation assumptions will be used to value a preferred interest. Taxpayers may use favorable assumptions in valuing the retained preferred stock at the time of the freeze and unfavorable assumptions in valuing such stock at death.

Undervaluation also may result from the failure to value properly restrictions or options to buy property. Fixed price and book formula options may be valued without taking into account likely appreciation in the property. Options granted in exchange for services may be valued on a mistaken assumption that the parties are dealing at arm's length. Bilateral options exercisable at death may be valued without regard to the different life expectancies of the parties.

Further, undervaluation may result from the use of Treasury tables valuing annuities, life estates, terms for years, remainders and reversions. Those tables are based on assumptions regarding rates of return and life expectancy that are seldom accurate in a particular case, and therefore, may be the subject of adverse selection. Because the taxpayer decides what property to give and when to give it, use of tables, in the aggregate, more often results in undervaluation than in overvaluation.

B. Subsequent Transfers

Creation of frozen interests in property also permits the transfer of wealth free of transfer tax through the subsequent exercise or nonexercise of rights with respect to the enterprise. Even if the transferred property is properly valued at the time of the initial transfer under the willing buyer, willing seller standard, wealth may be transferred thereafter if the rights are not exercised in an arm's-length manner. This may occur if, after the transfer, either transferor or transferee acts or fails to act or causes the enterprise to act or fail to act. It is unclear under present law whether such exercise or nonexercise results in a gift. Even if it does, it is virtually impossible for the IRS to monitor all post-transfer action or inaction with respect to such rights.

Closely held businesses provide many opportunities for subsequent transfers of wealth. Such transfers may occur through legal rights created at the time of the freeze transaction. For example, wealth may pass from a preferred shareholder to a common shareholder if the corporation fails to pay dividends to the preferred shareholder. Even if the preferred stock is cumulative, such failure results in a transfer equal to the value of the use of the money until the dividend is paid. Or, by exercising conversion, liquidation, put or voting rights in other than an arm's-length fashion (or by not exercising such rights before they lapse), the transferor may transfer part or all of the value of such rights.

* * * Similarly, the failure of a life tenant to exercise his rights to use the property can have the effect of transferring wealth to the remainderman. * * *

C. Disguised Testamentary Transfers

Third, the retention of a frozen interest may be used in order to retain enjoyment of the entire property. Enjoyment may be retained through a voting right, a preferred interest in a partnership or corporation, an income interest in a trust, a life estate in property, or a right to use property. In such cases, the transfer is, in reality, incomplete at the time of the initial transfer and, if the frozen interest is retained until death, the transfer is testamentary in nature.

Failure to treat a testamentary transfer as such gives the donor the advantage of favorable rules applicable only to gifts—such as the annual exclusion and tax-exclusive gift tax base. In addition, early utilization of the unified credit increases its present value. These benefits are appropriate only when the transferor has parted with substantial ownership of the transferred property.

V. PRESENT LAW: CODE SECTION 2036(c)

In the Omnibus Budget Reconciliation Act of 1987 (1987 Act), the Congress addressed the estate freeze transaction by including the value of the appreciating interest in the decedent's gross estate and crediting any gift tax previously paid (Code sec. 2036(c)). Such inclusion effectively treats the transfer as incomplete for transfer tax purposes during the period of the freeze. Thus, section 2036(c) addresses the possibilities of initial undervaluation, subsequent transfer of wealth, and retention of substantial ownership by postponing a final determination of transfer tax until the frozen interest passes.

* * *

VI. GENERAL CRITICISMS OF SECTION 2036(c)

A. The Merits of an Incomplete Gift Approach

One criticism of section 2036(c) regards the merits of using an incomplete gift rule for estate freezes. Critics of such an approach argue that regardless of the possibilities for initial undervaluation and subsequent transfer, the gift tax assessed when the transfer is made should finalize the transfer tax consequences of the transaction. They also argue that frozen interests should be regarded as separate property rather than the retention of substantial ownership of the enterprise. Further, they argue that section 2036(c) does not adequately implement an incomplete gift rule because it only credits the gift tax on the initial transfer rather than eliminating such tax entirely. Thus, the donor has in effect prepaid his estate tax without interest.

Proponents of an incomplete gift approach argue that estate tax inclusion is the surest means of providing a proper valuation and avoiding problems attendant to subsequent transfers. They note that such a rule achieves roughly the same effect as treating the transaction as a gift initially—taxation of appreciation is offset by the benefit derived from deferral of tax. They stress that an incomplete gift rule is the only means of addressing the problem of inherently testamentary transfers. Some suggest modifying section 2036(c) to eliminate the initial gift tax while others justify the initial tax on administrative grounds.

B. The Breadth of Section 2036(c)

Critics of section 2036(c) note that the section extends far beyond the preferred stock freeze to a wide variety of family transactions. They argue that such breadth creates uncertainty and hampers planning by family members. They note that section 2036(c) can trap unwary taxpayers undertaking common business transactions such as the lending of money or the provision of services. They believe that further modification of the statute would create undue complexity.

Others counter that freezes may be performed through a wide variety of devices—partnerships, trusts, options and interests in property—and argue that a broad scope is necessary to reach these devices. They note that in the family context many common business transactions operate to transfer wealth. They assert that present-law safe harbors protect most common business transactions with limited transfer tax avoidance potential and that additional safe harbors could be enacted if necessary.

C. Effect on Small Business

Critics of section 2036(c) observe that the provision makes it more difficult to transfer a closely held business between generations. They note that a family is sometimes forced to sell the business in order to pay estate tax. They argue that the creation of special rules for family transfers is unfair and that entrepreneurs play an important role in our society.

Supporters of section 2036(c) note that the provision does not discriminate against small businesses, but in fact treats all transfers of assets alike. They also argue that the donative character of many intrafamily transactions justifies the application of a special standard to them. They argue that all types of wealth should be [subject] to the same transfer tax.

Supporters of section 2036(c) also note that small business owners already receive estate tax relief through the unified credit, special valuation rules for real property, sales treatment of redemptions to pay death taxes, and rules allowing deferred payment of estate taxes. They argue that additional relief for family businesses is better granted to small business generally through modification of these provisions rather than limiting relief to persons engaging in estate freeze transactions.

VII. DESCRIPTION OF DISCUSSION DRAFT RELEASED MARCH 22, 1990

* * *

The discussion draft would repeal section 2036(c), under which the transfer is incomplete until the freeze ceases. Rejecting the characterization of freeze transactions as testamentary, the discussion draft generally substitutes for section 2036(c) a set of rules intended to modify the gift tax valuation rules in such a way as to more accurately value the initial transfer. Such rules operate by adopting valuation assumptions that take into account the likelihood that related parties will not exercise rights in an arm's-length manner.

* * *

NOTE

Congress initially responded to the problem of estate freezes by adding § 2036(c) to the Code in 1987. That provision, as amended in 1988, was triggered when the owner of an "enterprise" made a lifetime transfer of property representing a "disproportionately large share" of "potential appreciation" while retaining "an interest in the income of, or rights in, the enterprise." Section 2036(c) had no effect on the timing or valuation of the initial transfer; however, when the owner ultimately disposed of the retained interest during life or at death, the previously transferred interest was revalued and drawn back into the transfer tax base. For a critical analysis of § 2036(c), see Karen C. Burke, *Valuation Freezes After the 1988 Act: The Impact of Section 2036(c) on Closely Held Businesses*, 31 WM. & MARY L. REV. 67 (1989). The new provision provoked vehement opposition from business owners and estate planners, and was repealed in 1990 simultaneously with the enactment of Chapter 14.

---

3. Estate Freezes Under Current Law

James R. Repetti examines the special valuation rules of §§ 2701 and 2704, and compares the detailed statutory treatment of equity freezes with the absence of specific rules for minority discounts. Another view is offered by Louis S. Harrison, who concludes that these provisions effectively eliminate valuation abuses associated with business estate freezing techniques. Finally, Grayson M.P. McCouch discusses the impact of § 2702 on split-interest trusts.

James R. Repetti, *Minority Discounts: The Alchemy in Estate and Gift Taxation*, 50 TAX L. REV. 415 (1995)*

* * *

* * * Congress has adopted rules to prevent shareholders or partners from transferring the opportunity to participate in future appreciation of corporations or partnerships in transactions commonly referred to as "estate freezes." In the typical estate freeze, an older generation transfers ownership rights to a younger generation that are likely to appreciate in value while retaining interests that are unlikely to appreciate.[114] Because the value of the retained interest is not likely to appreciate, the older generation has "frozen" the value of property that will be includable in its estate. Any future appreciation in the transferred interest will escape taxation.

For example, in a classic estate freeze, an older generation transfers common stock to the younger generation and retains preferred stock with a fixed dividend right. Even if the company becomes more profitable, the preferred stock will not appreciate because of its fixed dividend right. The future appreciation in common stock will not be subject to the estate or gift tax.

Congress first sought to address this problem in 1987 by adopting 2036(c). Because 2036(c) was deemed too vague, Congress repealed it in 1990 and replaced it with 2701. In general, 2701 deals with abuses in calculating the value of the transferred interests, the common stock in the above example.[120] It assumes that the value of the common stock equals the value of all stock interests, common and preferred, minus the value of the preferred stock. The pre-

---

[114]   STAFF OF JOINT COMM. ON TAX'N, 101ST CONG., 2D SESS., FEDERAL TRANSFER TAX CONSEQUENCES OF ESTATE FREEZES at 9 (Comm. Print 1990).

[120]   *See* Louis S. Harrison, *The Real Implications of the New Transfer Tax Valuation Rules—Success Or Failure?*, 47 TAX LAW. 885, 892-94, 903-07 (1994) * * * .

ferred stock generally is treated as having a zero value if the corporation is a "controlled entity" unless the preferred stock has a cumulative right to receive dividends. A "controlled entity" is defined as a corporation or partnership in which at least 50% of the total voting power or fair market value of the equity interests are owned immediately before the transfer "by the transferor, applicable family members, and any lineal descendants of the parents of the transferor or the transferor's spouse."

Note that 2701 assumes that, where the transferees have voting control and are family members, they will maximize the transferred value. The requirement that dividends be cumulative in the context of a family-controlled entity, in effect, creates an irrebuttable presumption that the family members will work together to increase the value of the transferred interest after the taxable transfer by causing the company not to pay dividends. Congress apparently has not been willing to assume, however, that family members will work together with respect to other management matters. Section 2701 does not affect the availability of minority discounts. The regulations under 2701 continue to allow a minority discount in calculating the value of the transferred interests that would have been allowed prior to the adoption of 2701.

* * *

Estate planners also have used the concept of disappearing value by employing formal legal rights that lapse upon the death of the holder. Frequently, a taxpayer would hold stock in a family owned corporation or an interest in a family owned partnership that would include the right to liquidate. If the corporation or partnership had valuable assets, that right may cause the stock or partnership interest to be more valuable than it would have been without a liquidation right. In order to minimize the value of the partnership interest or stock in the taxpayer's estate, the liquidation right would lapse upon the taxpayer's death.

The lapse of the liquidation right could result in a substantial diminution in the value of assets held by the estate and, therefore, a significant decrease in estate tax. Note, however, that the lapse would have no adverse economic impact on the legatees or other family members because the family's control of the partnership or corporation would allow the family to liquidate the business at will. For example, in *Estate of Harrison v. Commissioner*,[124] the taxpayer and the Service stipulated that a limited partnership interest in a partnership that held valuable real estate, oil and gas interests and marketable securities would have a value of more than $59 million if accompanied by a liquidation right but only $33 million without a liquidation right. The court held that because the taxpayer's liquidation right lapsed upon death, the limited partnership interest should be valued at the lower amount even though the taxpayer's family continued to control the partnership.[126]

The legislative response to *Estate of Harrison* was 2704(a), adopted as part of a major revision of the estate and gift taxes in 1990. Section 2704(a) provides that, in certain situations, the lapse of a voting or liquidation right with respect to an interest in an entity is a transfer for estate and gift tax purposes. The amount of the transfer is the reduction in value attributable to the lapse.

Section 2704(a) applies where the holder of the lapsed voting or liquidation right and the holder's family control the entity immediately before and after the lapse. The holder and holder's family must be able to liquidate an interest that the holder held and could have liquidated prior to the lapse. In determining whether the interest could be liquidated after the lapse, restrictions on liquidation that may be removed by the holder or holder's family are disregarded.

---

[124]   52 T.C.M. (CCH) 1306 (1987).

[126]   The court rejected the Service's argument that the lapse of the liquidation right had transferred "something of value" to the taxpayer's two sons who were the only other partners because the Service had stipulated the value of the son's partnership interests had remained the same after the lapse. *Id.* at 1309
* * * .

In effect, 2704 assumes that there has been no diminution in value when a liquidation right lapses, because the family, viewed as a whole, still has the power to liquidate the entity.

* * *

Section 2704(a) also applies to a lapse of any "voting right." Voting right is defined as "a right to vote with respect to any matter of the entity," for example, the right of a general partner to participate in partnership management. The holder of a lapsed voting right in a family controlled entity is treated as having made a taxable transfer. Again, the value of the transfer is the difference between the value of all interests in the entity held by the taxpayer before the lapse and the value of such interests after the lapse. Where the lapse of voting rights results in the holder losing control of the entity, the amount transferred should include the value of the control premium.

One remarkable aspect of 2704(a) is that it, in effect, creates an irrebuttable presumption that family members will cooperate. It assumes that the transferor's voting or liquidation right has not disappeared but rather has been transferred to family members. Thus, in the narrow context of voting and liquidation rights, Congress has done what it refused to do in the broader context of minority discounts for assets held by family members. Indeed, Congress was very careful to point out that it did not intend to change the treatment of minority discounts or other discounts under present law.

* * *

NOTE

. Is the treatment of voting and liquidation rights under § 2704(a) consistent with Repetti's recommendation, reproduced *supra* in Subpart A, concerning minority discounts? Why did Congress avoid addressing the valuation of minority discounts in § 2704? Compare Repetti's view of §§ 2701 and 2704 with the somewhat more enthusiastic appraisal in the following excerpt.

Louis S. Harrison, *The Real Implications of the New Transfer Tax Valuation Rules—Success or Failure?*, 47 TAX LAW. 885 (1994)*

* * *

III. VALUING RETAINED RIGHTS IN THE CORPORATE OR PARTNERSHIP SETTING UNDER CHAPTER 14

* * *

B. Application of the Valuation Mandate

* * *

The following example illustrates [the operation of § 2701]. *P*, an individual, holds all 1,000 shares of corporation *X*'s stock, which is voting common. The fair market value of *P*'s family-held interest in *X* is $1,500,000 * * * . *P* decides to engage in an estate freeze under section 2701 and causes *X* to issue, in a tax-free transaction, 1,000 shares of 8%, $1,000 par value

---

cumulative preferred stock, which bears an annual cumulative dividend of $80 per share. The preferred stock also allows the holder to put all of the stock to X at any time for $1,500,000. P transfers all of the common stock to P's children and retains only the preferred stock. Under section 2701, the gift tax value of the common is determined by subtracting from the value of the family-held interests, $1,500,000, the value of P's retained preferred stock * * * . The preferred stock consists of two applicable retained interests, the dividend right and the put right; accordingly, the stock is valued pursuant to the special valuation rules set forth in section 2701 * * * . The put right is valued at zero because it is an extraordinary payment right. In contrast, because the dividend right under the preferred stock is cumulative, the preferred stock is ascribed a value for these purposes. The value of the dividend right, and therefore the retained preferred stock, could approximate $800,000. The gift tax value of the transferred common is thus $1,500,000 less $800,000, or $700,000 * * * . Because all of the common has been transferred, no minority discount is applicable * * * , and the value of the common is not further reduced.

C. Elimination of Corporate and Partnership Valuation Abuses

Section 2701 eliminates the two common valuation abuses of pre-Chapter 14 business estate freezes. First, section 2701 assumes that discretionary rights will go unexercised. To the extent that these rights are attached to preferred stock, they are given no value for gift tax purposes.

Second, section 2701 prevents the estate freeze accomplished by ascribing a value to an asset held by a donor, allowing that donor to retain that value, and thereafter allowing all increases in value in the asset to pass to one or more donees. Prior to section 2701, one method used to achieve this type of freeze in the corporate setting was for a donor to create two classes of stock: a preferred class retained by the donor, which had discretionary nonlapsing put, liquidation preference, or other rights that could be valued in such a way as to equal the current fair market value of the corporation; and a common class of stock transferred to the donees.

Section 2701 mandates that if the rights under the preferred class of stock can be exercised (or not exercised) at the donor's discretion, then the value of the transferred common stock carries with it the full value of the corporation. In essence, for gift tax purposes the donor will be treated as having retained no equity interest in the company. Accordingly, there is no retained interest that can be frozen.[133]

A freeze could also be obtainable prior to section 2701 when a donor retains only the right to receive a stream of annual payments from the transferred property. Theoretically, a freeze occurs if the donor receives aggregate payments equal to the fair market value of the donor's retained interest (at the time the freeze was undertaken). But if the donor receives, in total, aggregate payments in excess of that amount, then the donor has in actuality received a portion of the increase in the value of the partnership or corporation (i.e., a portion of the net profits). In that instance, not all growth in the value of the entity will pass to the nonfrozen interest and, at best, the donor will have only partially frozen the donor's retained interest.

---

[133]   Not only will a freeze be unachievable in this situation, but it could result in * * * double taxation because the full value of the corporation has been transferred for gift tax purposes during life, but the transferor is confronted with an estate tax on the value of the retained preferred stock at her death. * * *

* * *

To account for this type of inequity, Congress in section 2701(e)(6) provided that regulations are to make appropriate adjustments for the subsequent transfers, or inclusions in the gross estate, of any applicable retained interest valued under section 2701(a). * * *

Prior to section 2701, [a] freeze could have been achieved when the donor retained non-cumulative preferred dividends. Through donor-exercised control of the corporation, the corporation could be certain to issue aggregate dividends less than or equal to the initial calculated value of the donor's retained preferred dividend right.

Section 2701 eliminates this type of freeze. First, noncumulative preferred stock is valued at zero. Accordingly, the retention of noncumulative preferred stock cannot form the basis of a freeze because that retained interest is valued at zero for gift tax purposes.

Second, in order to be ascribed a value for gift tax purposes, the preferred stock must result in a qualified payment right, or such a right must be electively presumed to exist. But even though the preferred stock in this instance will be given a value for gift tax purposes, a full freeze will still not be obtainable. This is because the holder of the preferred stock will receive aggregate payments in excess of the initial value of the retained interest.

The starting point for this analysis is with the methodology used in valuing the qualified payment right. That right is no more than an infinitesimal string of constant payments. Although the Code and regulations provide no express guidance on how to value these payments, the regulations implicitly contemplate that the payments will be valued like an annuity, at an assumed discount rate. * * *

Generally, the lower the discount rate, the greater the value of the retained interest, and therefore the lower the value of the gift of the transferred interest. Hence, a discount rate related to existing market rates, such as the prime rate, is more beneficial from a transfer tax perspective than, say, one based on a junk bond rate.

The Code and regulations provide no guidance as to what discount rate to use in valuing the retained qualified payment right. The section 7520 rate, used in other gift and estate tax contexts, is not necessarily the most realistic discount rate. Nor is a discount rate tied to a market rate; dividend rights in a closely held business context are more uncertain than those in a publicly traded corporation. * * *

* * *

To the extent the corporation's rate of earnings exceeds the discount rate used in valuing the retained preferred stock, that excess rate will inure to the benefit of the holders of the transferred common stock. Hence, as to that excess, there is a minimal freeze created but that is not abusive because the reverse could also occur. If the corporation's earnings are at a rate less than the discount rate used in valuing the retained preferred stock, then there will actually be a reverse freeze, or a transfer tax loss. That is, the retained interest will increase at a rate in excess of the rate of increase of the transferred interest.

* * *

V. CONCLUSION

* * *

Through the enactment of a complicated system of rules and procedures, Chapter 14 has effectively addressed [estate freezing] abuses. For valuation purposes, gifts made in the business context * * * are now the functional equivalent of outright, lifetime gifts of full interests in property. Although there are limited exceptions to that conclusion, those windows of opportunity are narrow and not abusive. The valuation rules set forth in Chapter 14 are fair and accomplish their mission to further consolidate the unification of the estate and gift tax system.

NOTE

The legislative history of Chapter 14 indicates that Congress intended to curb abusive estate freezing techniques without hindering nonabusive "standard intrafamily transactions." Does § 2701 achieve its announced goal of ensuring "more accurate gift tax valuation of the initial transfer" through "well defined and administrable" rules? Does § 2701 avoid the problems of complexity, overbreadth and vagueness that plagued former § 2036(c)? The following excerpt explores the impact of Chapter 14 on estate freezing techniques involving split-interest trusts.

Grayson M.P. McCouch, *Rethinking Section 2702*, 2 FLA. TAX REV. 99 (1994)*

* * *

II. VALUATION UNDER GENERAL PRINCIPLES

Section 2702 is aimed primarily at a few tax-driven techniques involving transfers with retained interests. A classic example is the so-called grantor retained income trust (a "GRIT"), by which the donor makes a gift of property subject to a retained income interest for a limited term. * * *

* * *

* * * When beneficial enjoyment of property is split into a term interest and a remainder, the property's value is apportioned among the interests. Since the combined interests represent complete ownership of the property, the value of each interest generally is derived by subtracting the value of the other interests from the value of the entire property. Thus, the values of the respective interests are interdependent, and any uncertainty or inaccuracy in the valuation of one interest indirectly affects the valuation of the other.

If the limitations and conditions affecting possession or enjoyment of the underlying property can be estimated reasonably, the gift tax value of a term interest or remainder is determined by discounting the future payments to present value under Treasury tables based on prescribed discount rates and mortality assumptions. * * *

A simple GRIT illustrates the impact of the tables on the gift tax value of split interests. Assume that A, age 70, transfers property worth $100,000 in trust to pay income to herself for a term of 15 years with remainder at the end of the term to her nephew B or B's estate.[18] If the applicable discount rate is 10%, the value under the tables of A's retained interest is $76,061 (the present value of 15 annual payments of $10,000 each), and A has made a gift of $23,939, the value of the trust property less the value of A's retained income interest. A can reduce further the amount of the gift by retaining the right to receive the trust property at the end of the 15-year term in the event she is not then living.[20] * * *

---

*   Copyright © 1994. Reprinted with permission.

[18]   The special valuation rules of § 2702 do not apply because B is not a "member of [A]'s family" within the meaning of that section. * * *

[20]   A might retain this additional interest because the trust corpus will be included in her gross estate for estate tax purposes in the event she dies before her retained income interest expires. Retention of the conditional interest in trust corpus therefore reduces the gift tax without significantly increasing the potential estate tax. * * *

* * *

* * * [T]he values of the interests in trust income and corpus are only as accurate as the assumptions built into the tables. Three of those assumptions raise special concerns in the context of A's GRIT. First, the tables assume that the trust corpus remains constant in value and that the trust's entire investment return takes the form of current income. Any assumption concerning the allocation of investment return to income or corpus is unreliable because that allocation normally depends on subsequent actions of the trustee in administering the trust. For example, assume that the trustee of A's GRIT properly invests the trust corpus of $100,000 in stock that generates $9,000 of capital appreciation and $1,000 of dividends annually.[25] Although A actually receives annual income of only $1,000, the tables value her retained income interest as a stream of $10,000 annual payments and produce a corresponding undervaluation of the remainder transferred to B.

A second, analytically distinct problem concerns the assumed discount rate (rate of return). In determining the present value of a split interest, the tables apply a uniform discount rate indexed to the prevailing rate of return on federal obligations. Since the expected return on an investment reflects the type and degree of risk of the investment,[28] the discount rate assumed by the tables is almost certainly unrealistic in any particular case. For example, if the discount rate is unrealistically low, the tables distort the relative present values of split interests. In the case of A's GRIT, this distortion might benefit the government, since an understated discount rate produces an artificially low value for A's retained income interest and thus overvalues the remainder transferred to B. The distortion would benefit A, however, if she retained a right to fixed payments rather than an income interest.

Finally, the tables assume that each individual has a life expectancy consistent with the national mortality experience. This assumption is unrealistic because it takes only age into account, and disregards other factors that indicate a longer or shorter life expectancy for a particular individual. As a result, the tables may produce distorted values for split interests conditioned on survival or nonsurvival. For example, in the case of A's GRIT, if A enjoys unusually robust health and expects to live longer than the average 70-year-old, the tables may produce an unrealistically high value for her retained interest in corpus (conditioned on her death within 15 years) and a correspondingly low value for the remainder transferred to B.

In sum, the tables reflect assumptions about income and corpus allocations, rates of return, and mortality risks that diverge from actual outcomes in particular cases. This does not raise serious concerns as long as valuation risks are allocated fairly between taxpayers and the government. The opportunity for abuse arises when valuation risks are skewed systematically in favor of taxpayers. * * * [T]axpayers (who usually have superior information concerning the factors affecting value in particular cases) tend to structure transactions to exploit the tables and reduce the gift tax value of transferred interests.

* * *

---

[25]   In theory, the trustee may be constrained in its investment and allocation decisions by a duty of impartiality. * * *

[28]   The expected return on an investment represents the arithmetic mean of probable outcomes and reflects the risk of loss (default risk). The variance or dispersion of probable outcomes (volatility risk), to the extent that it cannot be eliminated by diversification, commands a market risk premium. The market risk premium is reflected in a lower present value, and a correspondingly higher discount rate, for the investment. * * *

Assume that, in the case of *A*'s GRIT, *A* retains the right to receive the trust property at the end of the 15-year term if neither *B* nor any of *B*'s issue is then living. In *Robinette v. Helvering*,[54] the Supreme Court refused to allow any reduction in the amount of a gift for a similarly conditioned retained interest because the donor failed to offer "any recognized method by which it would be possible to determine the value" of the interest. * * *

* * *

Although the impact of *Robinette* on the apportionment of value in the initial transfer is well settled, the subsequent treatment of a retained interest having no ascertainable value remains unclear. Specifically, a problem of double taxation arises if the value of the retained interest, having already been subjected to gift tax in the initial transfer, enters the transfer tax base again during life or at death. * * *

* * *

As a practical matter, the problem of double taxation * * * seldom arose before the enactment of section 2702. Transfers in trust normally can be structured to avoid subjecting the same beneficial interest both to a gift tax in the initial transfer and to an estate tax at death. Where [the so-called "string" provisions of §§ 2035-2038] draw a previously-taxed gift into the gross estate, section 2001(b) generally mitigates the risk of double taxation. An acute problem of double taxation normally arises only where a donor subsequently transfers a retained interest that was valued at zero in the initial transfer. This troublesome situation is likely to become increasingly common as a result of section 2702.

III. VALUATION UNDER SECTION 2702

In response to valuation abuses involving split-interest transfers, Congress, in 1990, enacted section 2702, which provides special rules for apportioning the value of trust property between retained and transferred interests. A few defined types of retained interests continue to be valued under the tables. The special rules value most other retained interests at zero, thereby indirectly increasing the gift tax value of interests transferred in the initial transfer. Section 2702 thus may be viewed as an expanded application of the principle of *Robinette*. * * *

A. Initial Transfer

The scope of section 2702 is defined by reference to three interrelated elements: a trust, a transfer, and a retained interest. For purposes of section 2702, a trust includes any arrangement that splits beneficial ownership of property into successive interests, i.e. a term interest and remainder. The statute applies when a living donor transfers a beneficial interest in trust property to or for the benefit of a member of the donor's family. The special rules apply for gift tax purposes in valuing interests retained by the donor (or an "applicable family member") in the underlying property. * * *

Section 2702 serves a limited function of apportioning value for gift tax purposes between interests that are retained and transferred in the initial transfer. Based on the notion that the aggregate value of all beneficial interests in the trust equals the value of the trust property, the regulations derive the value of transferred interests by subtracting the value of retained interests from the value of the trust property. Thus, in focusing on the valuation of retained interests, the special rules indirectly control the valuation of transferred interests for gift tax purposes. By limiting the value of retained interests, the special rules set a floor on the amount of the gift in the initial transfer. The special rules have no effect, however, on general principles governing the timing or extent of gift completion.

---

[54]   318 U.S. 184 (1943).

Under section 2702, a "qualified" retained interest is valued under the tables, and any other retained interest is generally valued at zero. A term interest is qualified only if it confers a right to receive payments in fixed amounts (an annuity interest) or payments equal to a fixed percentage of the annually-determined value of the trust property (a unitrust interest); in either case, the amounts must be payable at least annually, for a term equal to the holder's life, a specified term of years, or the shorter (but not the longer) of those periods. A remainder is qualified only if it confers an unconditional right to receive property in which all other interests are qualified interests. The requirements are intended to ensure that the holder of a qualified interest will actually receive distributions that can be valued realistically under the tables. Conversely, denying value to nonqualified interests reduces opportunities for manipulating the tables.

* * *

Section 2702 substantially reduces the gift tax advantages of retaining nonqualified interests in transfers subject to the special rules. Split-interest transfers remain viable as transfer tax avoidance techniques, however, where the special rules do not apply.[93] Even under section 2702, the mandatory use of the tables to value qualified interests offers substantial planning opportunities to the extent that the tables reflect unrealistic assumptions concerning actual rates of return and life expectancies. Assume that A, age 70, transfers property worth $100,000 in trust to pay a qualified annuity of $10,000 to herself for 15 years or until her prior death, with remainder to her child C or C's estate. If the applicable discount rate is 10%, A's retained annuity is valued at $60,307 and the amount of A's gift to C is $39,693.

* * * [T]he tables reflect an assumption that the trust property will produce a 10% annual return that will match precisely the $10,000 annuity payments to A, leaving property worth $100,000 for C at the end of the term. If the property actually produces a 12% annual return and A survives the 15-year term, C will receive property worth $174,559 rather than $100,000 at the end of the trust term. * * * The tables thus produce a substantial undervaluation of A's gift, and this undervaluation increases in proportion to the length of the term. The effect is even more accentuated if the annuity payments increase in amount over the term.

If the rate of return on trust investments is lower than the assumed rate, a donor can manipulate the special rules by retaining a qualified reversion. * * *

A similar distortion may arise if A has an unusually short life expectancy, even if the underlying property actually produces precisely the assumed rate of return. * * *

B. Subsequent Treatment of Retained Interests

After the initial transfer, the value of a retained interest is no longer determined under the special rules; in a subsequent transfer, the interest is valued under general principles. * * * In the case of a retained nonqualified interest, * * * the two valuation methods raise a problem of potential double taxation. * * *

As in *Robinette*, the problem stems from applying inconsistent valuation methods to the same interest at different times. One possible approach would be to eliminate the inconsistency by applying the special rules in the subsequent transfer. If a retained interest was valued at zero in the initial transfer, this would produce the same effect as simply excluding the interest from the transfer tax base in the subsequent transfer. Although this approach may achieve a pragmatic result in particular cases, it exacerbates the inconsistency between the special rules and general principles concerning the timing and valuation of transfers, and offers no viable general solution to the problem of double taxation.

---

[93]   For example, the special rules do not apply if the donee is not a member of the donor's family, * * * , or to certain transfers of property to be used as a personal residence. * * *

The section 2702 regulations provide a special adjustment to mitigate the problem of double taxation. The adjustment takes the form of a reduction in the donor's cumulative taxable gifts upon a subsequent transfer of a nonqualified interest that was valued under the special rules in the initial transfer (a "section 2702 interest"). In general, the adjustment is available only with respect to a section 2702 interest that was held by the donor at the time of the initial transfer. Moreover, the adjustment becomes available only when the donor makes a subsequent transfer of the section 2702 interest during life or at death; if the donor simply retains the interest until it expires, the adjustment is lost. The regulations limit the amount of the adjustment to ensure that the amount ultimately included in the transfer tax base on account of the section 2702 interest is at least equal to the value of that interest (determined under general principles) at the time of the initial transfer. * * *

* * *

In sum, the section 2702 adjustment attempts to compensate for the unfavorable valuation assumptions introduced by the special rules in the initial transfer. In determining the amount ultimately included in the transfer tax base with respect to the section 2702 interest, the adjustment raises several problems. The amount of the adjustment does not reflect distributions actually received by the donor, even though such distributions may replace all or part of the section 2702 interest in the transfer tax base. Moreover, the adjustment does not purport to compensate the donor for the lost return on any increase in gift tax caused by the special rules between the time of the initial transfer and the subsequent transfer.[154] At a more general level, the section 2702 adjustment introduces considerable complexity and uncertainty while failing to provide an adequate remedy for the distortions caused by the special rules in the initial transfer. Thus, section 2702 falls far short of its goals of simplicity, accuracy and fairness.[155]

* * *

V. CONCLUSION

* * *

Section 2702 responds to [valuation abuses involving split-interest trusts] by sharply limiting the availability of the tables and imposing an unfavorable zero-value assumption on many retained interests. This approach, however, is flawed in concept and implementation. On one hand, the zero-value assumption builds in fresh valuation distortions which often remain uncorrected, notwithstanding the elaborate compensating adjustments provided in the regulations. On the other hand, the continued use of the tables in valuing qualified retained interests, personal residence trusts and gifts to nonfamily members leaves considerable room for sophisticated transfer tax avoidance. Thus, section 2702 has redirected many of the old abuses into new channels.

At a more fundamental level, section 2702 injects complexity and inconsistency into a gift and estate tax system already badly in need of reform. By focusing narrowly on valuation in the initial transfer, section 2702 exacerbates preexisting disparities between the gift and estate

---

[154]   Indeed, the timing effect is magnified where the increase in taxable gifts caused by the special rules pushes other taxable gifts made by the donor between the initial transfer and the subsequent transfer into higher brackets. Even if the amount of taxable gifts is subsequently adjusted, § 2702 may indirectly increase gift taxes payable with respect to interim gifts that are completely unrelated to the initial transfer.

[155]   The legislative history indicates that chapter 14 is intended "to assure more accurate gift tax valuation of the initial transfer" and to deter abuse through "a well defined and administrable set of rules," without hindering nonabusive "standard intrafamily transactions." * * *

taxes. The use of split-interest trusts to avoid transfer taxes could be curbed far more effectively by moving toward an integrated gift and estate tax system. Specifically, a uniform tax-inclusive base and consistent rules governing completion and valuation would eliminate most of the differences in transfer tax cost between split-interest transfers and outright transfers made during life or at death. Although these reforms would represent only a first step toward full integration, they would render section 2702 obsolete while making the gift and estate tax system simpler, fairer, and more neutral.

NOTE

McCouch notes that § 2702 has substantially reduced the transfer tax advantages that were available through GRITs and similar arrangements under prior law. However, he criticizes § 2702 for exacerbating "preexisting disparities between the gift and estate taxes" and for redirecting "old abuses into new channels." Would full integration of the estate and gift taxes resolve the problem of split-interest trusts? How would the other estate freezing techniques discussed earlier in this Subpart fare in a fully integrated transfer tax system? Proposals to integrate the estate and gift taxes are discussed *infra* in Part VII. A thoughtful and thorough analysis of split-interest transfers under § 2702 appears in Mitchell M. Gans, *GRIT's, GRAT's and GRUT's: Planning and Policy*, 11 VA. TAX REV. 761 (1992). For a discussion of GRITs and similar techniques under prior law, and a proposal foreshadowing the approach adopted in § 2702, see F. Ladson Boyle, *Evaluating Split-Interest Valuation*, 24 GA. L. REV. 1 (1989).

PART VI:

GENERATION-SKIPPING TRANSFERS

Long before the initial enactment of a generation-skipping transfer (GST) tax in 1976, it was widely recognized that trusts could be used to insulate property from estate and gift taxation for several generations. The early debate over generation-skipping transfers is reflected in the Treasury Department's 1969 proposals, which are explained and defended by two of their principal architects, Jerome Kurtz and Stanley S. Surrey, in response to critics like David Westfall who share the proponents' view of the need for reform but view the Treasury proposals as combining "a high degree of complexity with partial ineffectiveness." A more fundamental attack is launched by Gilbert Paul Verbit, who challenges the premises of the 1976 statute as well as its technical approach.

To some extent, the versions of the generation-skipping tax proposed by the Treasury in 1969 and enacted by Congress in 1976 have been eclipsed by the current GST tax, which was enacted in 1986. However, the early debate concerning the purpose and structure of a generation-skipping transfer tax remains relevant in assessing the strengths and weaknesses of current law and in evaluating alternative approaches to generation-skipping transfers.

The current GST tax reaches transfers made directly to persons at least two generations below the transferor's generation, as well as terminations and distributions that shift beneficial enjoyment of trust property to such persons. As a practical matter, a taxpayer may be able to "opt out" of the GST tax by deliberately incurring a gift or estate tax. Jonathan G. Blattmachr and Jeffrey N. Pennell discuss several techniques for achieving this result, and point out some hidden advantages of the "Delaware Tax Trap."

Proposals for further reform continue to flourish. John T. Gaubatz recommends transforming the GST tax into "the engine driving the transfer tax." His system would impose a flat-rate "generation-shifting transfer tax" on transfers to younger-generation beneficiaries, unless the transferor elected to incur an integrated version of the regular estate and gift taxes. In contrast, Leonard Levin and Michael Mulroney suggest that the GST tax might serve as the foundation for a federal rule against perpetuities, supplanting the traditional role of state property law in this area. Finally, Howard E. Abrams views the GST tax as unnecessarily broad in scope and complex in operation. He argues that the main focus of the GST tax should be on direct skips, and that the problems of interests and powers in trust property should be addressed within the framework of the existing estate and gift taxes.

Jerome Kurtz & Stanley S. Surrey, *Reform of Death and Gift Taxes: The 1969 Treasury Proposals, the Criticisms, and a Rebuttal,* 70 COLUM. L. REV. 1365 (1970)*

* * *

* * * There is an aspect of equity in estate taxation * * * that involves a notion of periodicity. If a given amount of wealth is, in one situation, subjected to the estate tax on three occasions over a one-hundred year period, and another accumulation of wealth of equal amount is taxed only once every hundred years, it seems obvious that the two accumulations are treated inequitably as compared to each other. While complete equity in the frequency of imposition cannot be achieved in the estate tax since its imposition depends on death, which is unpredictable, it is nevertheless clear that notions of fairness require some approximation of time equivalence. Some illustrations may help.

If an individual with an estate of $10,000,000 (ignoring deductions, etc.) leaves it to his two children equally, the estate tax will be about $6,000,000 and his children will each get $2,000,000. Assuming that the children then live on the income from their inheritances without affecting principal, each of their estates will pay an estate tax of about $750,000 when the property passes to their children, so that the latter will, in total, inherit $2,500,000 of their grandfather's wealth. If, on the other hand, the grandfather is well advised and leaves his money in trust paying the income to his children with the remainder to his grandchildren, he will pay an estate tax of $6,000,000, the same as in the first case, but the estate tax on the death of the children will be entirely avoided. The grandchildren will therefore take $4,000,000. The amount passing to the grandchildren will thus be over 50% greater in the second case than in the first, although the effect of the two transactions over the two generations is otherwise essentially the same. This effect can be considerably magnified by using transfers which keep property in trust for more than one generation and thereby avoid the tax on more than one intervening death.

Skipping one or more generations for estate tax purposes does not necessarily involve skipping generations as far as enjoyment of the assets is concerned. An intermediate trust beneficiary while alive may enjoy the income, control investments, obtain principal needed for his support, * * * and be able to give principal to others by will—all without incurring estate or gift taxes * * * .

Not only is there clear discrimination between estates of equal initial size in this situation, but there is also a crippling effect on progressivity. This effect occurs because the generation-skipping transfers described are generally available only to large estates. Smaller estates generally cannot take advantage of this type of transfer because of the need of the intervening generations for the principal. Since the tax-saving possibility in generation-skipping transfers is available primarily to larger estates and is increasingly available the larger the estate becomes, it results in reducing the progression of real effective rates or in eliminating entirely progressivity over large segments of the estate tax.

Estate tax returns filed during the 1957-1959 period show that in estates of over $1,000,000, 25% of assets were transferred in generation-skipping form (19% in trust and 6% outright), but that only 9% of the assets in estates of less than $300,000 were transferred in that form. In the over $1,000,000 group, about 80% of all assets involved in trust arrangements were transferred on a generation-skipping basis. Of the decedents who had estates of over $2,000,000

---

*   This article originally appeared at 70 COLUM. L. REV. 1365 (1970). Reprinted by permission.

and who used trusts, only 25% used trusts that were not in generation-skipping form; 77% of the decedents with estates of less than $500,000 did not use such trusts.

* * *

* * * Under the proposals a substitute tax would be imposed on transfers that skip one or more generations. This tax is designed to ensure that there would be the same total tax on such a transfer as there would be if the transfer had been made to the intervening generation and then by the intervening generation to the ultimate donee. The tax would apply whether the transfer were in trust or outright. The substitute tax would not be a penalty imposed on the generation-skipping transfer, but rather—as the name implies—a tax to take the place of the actual tax that would otherwise be skipped. There are several methods available for computing the substitute tax due under various circumstances. If a member of the intervening generation is alive at the time of the transfer to a donee in the subsequent generation, the member may elect to treat the transfer as if he had received the property himself and had retransferred it to the transferee. * * *

Under this proposal, a generation is considered skipped whenever the donee is more than one degree in family relationship below the transferor, and the substitute tax would apply whenever one or more generations were skipped. * * *

If the transfer, rather than being outright, were made in trust, the intervening generation—the parents of the donee—could, but would not be required to, make the election at the time of the transfer; the election could be made at any time prior to the death of the survivor of the transferee's parents. In the interim, transfers out of the trust to the remote generation would be considered generation-skipping transfers. Once a parent of the transferee makes the election, he would be considered to be the settlor of the trust for purposes of applying the substitute tax. The amount of the gift for purposes of calculating the tax due from the electing parent would be based on the value of the trust corpus at the time of the election.

The election would produce the same tax result that would obtain if the transfers were actually made to the member of the intervening generation and then retransferred by him. However, it is essential that this system be elective because the election does impose a tax liability on a member of an intervening generation who never, in fact, receives the property outright. To handle the situation where no election is made, the Treasury proposal contains a provision designed to achieve essentially the same result, but the provision is, of course, less exact.

Where no election is made, the substitute tax is imposed on the donor at the time of the gift at a rate equal to 60% of the donor's marginal rate. * * * [B]y calculating the substitute tax at 60% of the marginal rate an attempt is made to approximate what the effective rate of tax would be if the skipped generation had made the transfer. * * *

* * * Where the transfer is in trust and no election has been made to pay the substitute tax, the tax will become payable by the trustee when distributions are made to the remote generation * * * .

* * *

Several witnesses argued that the generation-skipping proposal would discourage transfers in trust, presumably because most generation-skipping transfers are in trust. This effect is claimed to be undesirable because, it is asserted, most of these long-term trusts are created primarily for non-tax reasons. Again, whether one can say that the generation-skipping proposal would discourage long-term trusts or simply remove the tax consideration in creating them depends on one's point of departure. It is clear, however, that the generation-skipping proposal is designed to make the transfer tax impact on long-term trusts neutral by removing the present tax advantages now accorded such trust[s]. If there are non-tax reasons for using a long-term trust—and there certainly will be cases where this is so—the trust can still be used. The creation of long-term trusts is not prohibited nor is it penalized; the transfer tax advantage is simply removed. Whatever non-tax advantages there are will still remain. But it is difficult to see—and the critics conspicuously do not furnish elaboration on this point—why the existence of valid non-tax reasons for the creation of a long-term trust becomes an argument in favor of the very substantial tax advantages now accorded those trusts.

Another argument made against the generation-skipping proposal is that the aggregate revenue loss under the present rules is small. However, the generation-skipping proposal is not designed primarily to raise revenue. It is aimed primarily at achieving equity. While the aggregate revenue loss may be small, the tax advantage to a particular family using these arrangements can be very great indeed and the advantage increases as the family wealth increases. The issue is thus not one of absolute revenue but rather is one of relative unfairness. * * * The generation-skipping proposal is in many respects a proposal to prevent the erosion of the progressivity in the estate tax. No one has yet made the argument that the present system permitting generation-skipping transfers is fair.

Other arguments against the generation-skipping proposal are largely question-begging. Thus, it is said that generation-skipping trusts involving two generations are rare and there is no reason, therefore, to upset everyone for a few cases. This argument, of course, can be turned upside-down since only the few affected would be upset. * * * Others point to cases in which a decedent's children may be dead so that the natural beneficiaries of his estate are his grandchildren, or to cases in which the decedent simply does not like his children, and ask why a generation-skipping tax should be imposed in these cases. But these situations and others like them lie at the fringe of this problem. By far most generation-skipping transfers occur where both children and grandchildren are alive, where both are liked by the decedent, and where the children share in the enjoyment of the property during their lives. The basic tax rules must be constructed to deal with these normal situations, and the pattern of those rules should not be decided by the fringe cases. Nor should the fringe cases be treated in a different fashion, once the basic decision is made to impose a tax on the time pattern of every generation. Some assert with force that Congress has not yet said that its policy is to tax once every generation. The fact remains, of course, that the proposition now being urged upon the Congress is that taxing once each generation is the equitable way to apply a transfer tax.

* * *

The aspect of complexity is actually relevant only in relation to the proposal to meet the tax escape created by generation-skipping transfers. The solutions adopted in the proposal are complex.[80] But the complexity arises from the challenge presented by the generation-skipping arrangements themselves. Those arrangements are complex matters, for the draftsman must often project himself almost a hundred years into the future and try to perceive and handle all contingencies. It is asking far too much that such a complex situation be dealt with in comparatively simple fashion by the tax law. Of course, among various effective tax solutions the choice would go to the least complex. But, so far, that choice does not seem open, for no other avenue of solution appears to offer the prospect of closing the escape afforded by these arrangements.

When a sophisticated aspect of estate planning is involved and that aspect is one far removed from the ordinary transfers of assets from one generation to the next, the tax policy governing that aspect must also be sophisticated. Tax policy must permit the arrangements to

---

[80]   See Westfall, [*Revitalizing the Federal Estate and Gift Taxes*, 83 HARV. L. REV. 986, 1006-13 (1970)], commenting on the complexity of the proposal and also on why simpler solutions do not solve the problem. * * * Professor Westfall proposes another system designed to deter single generation-skipping.

be used for whatever non-tax purposes they may serve, but it must not permit them to be avenues of tax escape. Less complex tax solutions may be welcome, but those who desire to use these complicated arrangements cannot argue that because there will be *complexity* there must be *tax immunity*.

* * *

NOTE

Kurtz and Surrey illustrate the generation-skipping problem with a comparison between successive outright bequests and successive life estates. Tax consequences aside, are the two dispositions sufficiently similar to justify similar tax treatment? If so, why not simply amend § 2033 to reach property in which the decedent held a life estate? *See* Stanley S. Surrey, *An Introduction to Revision of the Federal Estate and Gift Taxes*, 38 CAL. L. REV. 1, 20-21 (1950). More generally, if there are gaps in the existing estate and gift tax system, is it necessary to superimpose a separate tax to fill those gaps?

David Westfall, *Revitalizing the Federal Estate and Gift Taxes*, 83 HARV. L. REV. 986 (1970)*

* * *

"Normally, a family's accumulated wealth is passed from parent to child and is subject to a transfer tax at each generation."[111] However, transferors can avoid this once-a-generation tax by making gifts to grandchildren or more remote descendants, thus skipping intermediate generations. Sophisticated forms of generation-skipping involve trusts or other arrangements which allow successive beneficiaries, including the settlor's children, to enjoy the income and often portions of the principal without being treated as owners for transfer tax purposes.

The extent to which a trust beneficiary may be given substantially unfettered control and enjoyment of trust property without attracting estate or gift taxes is not as widely recognized as it should be. * * * Trusts are being set up not for the traditional purposes of protecting financially inept widows or orphans or profligate descendants, but rather to ward off the federal tax collector.

Of course, the period which such trusts may last is usually limited by the local version of the Rule Against Perpetuities, but with a judicious selection of measuring lives, the rule ordinarily will permit a trust term of eighty to one hundred years. In some states a longer transfer tax holiday is possible. * * *

The impetus for reform derives added support because generation-skipping transfers are only effective in avoiding taxes for generations which do not exhaust the accumulated wealth of the prior generation. An estate planner normally will not resort to complicated trusts * * * unless substantial amounts of the accumulated wealth would otherwise merely be passed on

---

[111]   [U.S. TREAS. DEP'T, 91st Cong., 1st Sess., TAX REFORM STUDIES AND PROPOSALS, pt. 3, at 388 (Comm. Print 1969)].

from children to grandchildren without benefiting the children. If the children consume all of the accumulated wealth, the generation-skipping trust offers no tax advantage because the children's estates will not in any case be subject to a tax on account of the wealth transferred by their parents. Thus, the benefits of generation-skipping accrue only to those families whose standard of living will be least affected by an increased estate tax.

But the evils of generation-skipping arrangements are not limited to tax avoidance. The indirect social costs may be as large as the taxes the arrangements avoid. The favored tax treatment channels valuable resources into irrevocable trusts which may continue for eighty to one hundred years. The draftsman who creates such a trust has a major responsibility. He must foresee and provide for a wide variety of possible developments in the family's affairs and in economic conditions which may alter detrimentally the situation of the beneficiaries or the locked-in trust property. If the draftsman does his work carelessly, he may affect many lives adversely. Moreover, in addition to the normal administrative costs of complicated trust arrangements, ambiguities of expression in trust agreements may take a staggering toll in litigation, costly both to the individuals concerned and society as well. Uncertainties as to the ownership and management of potentially productive assets may remain unresolved for years, inhibiting the use and enjoyment of the trust property.

The Treasury's proposed substitute tax on generation-skipping transfers, a response to the definite need for reform, unfortunately combines a high degree of complexity with partial ineffectiveness. * * *

* * *

* * * In skilled hands, * * * the tax on generation-skipping transfers would not preclude the effective use of long-term trusts to minimize estate taxes. It should be evident * * * that the tax need never be more than that which would have been paid if the property had been given to the skipped generation, and indeed may be substantially less. * * *

The tax advantages and complexities * * * should not rule out use of the substitute tax altogether. Indeed, it appears to be the best method that has been devised to deal with multiple generation-skipping—transfers to great-grandchildren or more remote descendants. * * * [T]he various alternatives which have been proposed from time to time * * * suffer from one or more major objections. Taxing the termination of life estates * * * does not deal with transfers under which the skipped generation receives no interest in the property. Although it is easy to tax life estates if the interests of the beneficiaries are fixed, there is no simple solution for discretionary trusts which does not either invite avoidance or involve burdensome complexity. Narrowing the definition of nontaxable powers of appointment * * * does not deal with generation-skipping unless the skipped generation receives some power over the property, and it creates an artificial incentive for the employment of non-family fiduciaries who in fact may be quite responsive to the wishes of family members. Finally, more radical departures, such as the accessions tax, would discard over a half century's experience with the present estate tax in favor of an unfamiliar alternative with complexities of its own.

Although the Treasury's proposed substitute tax is currently the best, and probably only effective, means for dealing with the tax avoidance of multiple generation-skipping, it seems undesirable to extend the complexities to single generation-skipping. The revenue increase might well be outweighed by the confusion in estate planning and administration. Instead, we should encourage transferors to avoid generation-skipping transfers altogether. This could be achieved by creating a preferential rate for transfers to children of the transferor which do not involve generation-skipping, either because the child receives outright ownership or a general power of appointment, either of which will cause him to be taxed as owner.

* * *

The Treasury proposal will still be needed with respect to generation-skipping transfers to nondescendants of the transferor and multiple generation-skipping transfers, but the complexities of the proposal are much more bearable when applied only to these transfers, which offer a greater opportunity for tax avoidance and accrue nontax costs as well.

NOTE

How serious are the "indirect social costs" that Westfall identifies in connection with generation-skipping trusts? Does the current GST tax effectively neutralize the tax incentives for creating long-term, multi-generation trusts? Would Westfall's proposal to reduce tax rates on tax-vested transfers to children produce its own set of "indirect social costs"?

Gilbert Paul Verbit, *Annals of Tax Reform: The Generation-Skipping Transfer*, 25 UCLA L. REV. 700 (1978)*

INTRODUCTION

* * *

The major purpose of this Article is to examine whether the generation-skipping transfer is a tax avoidance problem, and, if so, to what extent and in what sense. * * *

* * *

II. THE 1976 TAX REFORM ACT

* * * [T]he 1976 Tax Reform Act rejected the * * * idea that outright gifts or bequests which skipped a generation be taxed. The 1976 Act imposes a tax only where there is a trust (or its equivalent) "which provides for a splitting of the benefits between two or more generations which are younger than the generation of the grantor of the trust." The 1976 Act adopts the English approach of taxing various generation-skipping transfers at the termination of the beneficial interest, thus rejecting the idea of taxation at the time of the transfer into trust. The rate of taxation is normally the marginal rate of the holder of the beneficial interest. * * *

* * *

III. TOWARD A CONCEPT OF TAX EQUITY

A. When is a Beneficiary an Owner?

The House Ways and Means Committee justified the imposition of the tax on generation-skipping transfers as aimed primarily at achieving equity. Although the Committee did not define "equity" it chose to illustrate the concept by noting that the extent of the beneficial enjoyment over trust assets and income that one might enjoy without having the trust corpus included in one's estate was virtually indistinguishable from outright ownership of the trust corpus, a situation which would have resulted in inclusion of the trust assets in the estate. The prin-

---

ciple of equity * * * is simply that "if an individual whose situation and attributes are x ought to pay the same tax t, then . . . every other individual having the identical x ought to pay the same tax t." In the present case, the Ways and Means Committee indicated that its "bill provides generally that property passing from one generation to successive generations in trust form is to be treated, for estate tax purposes, substantially the same as property which is transferred outright from one generation to a successive generation."

The phrases "in trust" and "outright" may, however, mask greater differences than at first appear. Whether there is inequity present depends upon one's view of how similar or dissimilar the two situations are. Some differences in the position of the beneficiary who receives his bequest outright (BO) and the beneficiary who receives only the trust income for life (BI) are readily apparent. BO can devise the corpus; BI cannot. BO can invest the corpus however he likes; BI cannot. BO is entitled to both the income and capital gain earned by the assets; BI receives only ordinary income since under the usual trust provisions capital gains are added to the corpus. BO can squander capital on yachts and homes on the Riviera; BI cannot. Thus, the case for including the full value of the trust corpus in the estates of BO and BI is not as obvious as the Committee would have us believe. If, however, BI is given access to and power over the disposition of the trust corpus this narrows the gap between BI and BO and adds validity to the proposition that they ought to receive the same estate tax treatment. This is the real problem bothering tax reformers: the extent of dominion which a beneficiary could exercise over the corpus of a trust without being considered the "owner" of the trust for estate tax purposes. As the Ways and Means Committee report pointed out, the corpus will not be included in the estate of a beneficiary

> even when the beneficiary under the trust has: (1) the right to receive the income from the trust; (2) the power to invade the principal of the trust, if this power is subject to an ascertainable standard relating to health, education, support, or maintenance; (3) a power (in each beneficiary) to draw down annually from his share of the principal the greater of 5 per cent of its value or $5000; (4) a power, exercisable during life or by will, to appoint any or all of his share of the principal to anyone other than himself, his creditors, his estate or the creditors of his estate; or (5) the right to manage the trust property by serving as trustee.

Few would deny that a beneficiary with such an array of powers has an interest approaching "outright" ownership. The difficulty is, however, that the statute has not responded to this view of the problem. In short, if property rights (1)-(5) are the premise, the statute is a non sequitur. The tax exemptions for the power to invade corpus pursuant to an "ascertainable standard" and the power to invade corpus on a "5 and 5" basis result from exceptions to the definition of general powers of appointment contained in § 2041 of the Internal Revenue Code. * * * The power to invade corpus according to "an ascertainable standard" is explicitly removed from the definition of a general power of appointment by section 2041(b)(1)(A) and the "problem" created by this subsection could easily have been eliminated by repealing it. So too, the "5 and 5" exception could have been eliminated by simply repealing the second sentence of section 2041(b)(2). No new chapter 13 was needed. * * * Thus, despite the recitation of the powers over corpus which a beneficiary could enjoy prior to the enactment of new chapter 13, it is clear that its elaborate provisions were necessary solely to reach the interests of income beneficiaries. We must therefore return to the question of whether equity requires that income beneficiaries be treated as "owners" of the corpus.

* * * If equity is judged in terms of tax avoidance possibilities or total tax revenue "lost," it is not at all clear that excluding the value of the trust corpus from an income beneficiary's

estate will result in greater avoidance and a greater revenue loss than would an outright owner's ability to take advantage of the many other tax avoidance devices [e.g., lifetime consumption or gifts] foreclosed from the income beneficiary. * * * Is it "equitable" to treat a person with an infinite variety of estate planning devices available in the same manner as a person who has none at all? This characterization may be overstated since income beneficiaries can be granted the power to invade corpus. * * * The "lost" estate planning advantages of the income beneficiary may not be lost at all if the income beneficiary has non-trust assets to use for inter-vivos gifts and the marital deduction. The difficulty is that we do not know whether these observations are valid—there is no available data to test them—and therefore we cannot know whether the tax planning benefits of the trust device are fully offset by the loss of other tax avoidance opportunities. If this is the case, there would be no need for a new chapter 13.

B. Taxation Every Generation

Another concept of equity used to support the generation-skipping transfer tax is based on the premise that estate taxes are designed to tax wealth every generation and that generation-skipping transfers are "inequitable" because they undermine this principle. This inequity is in turn heightened by the fact that only wealthier taxpayers can afford to cut off their children from trust assets. Thus, "families with moderate levels of accumulated wealth may pay as much or more in cumulative transfer taxes as wealthier families who utilize generation-skipping devices." Even a casual reading of the preceding exposition may leave the reader puzzled, for if it is a cardinal principle of the estate tax that property be taxed at every generation, how can that principle be reconciled with the fact that Congress has rejected proposals to tax outright gifts from grandparent to grandchild? Instead of a principle, the taxation every generation concept is an empirically derived observation. Since the estate tax is levied at death, and given the fact that death marks the end of a generation, the estate tax is levied once a generation. The correct statement of the general premise, therefore, is that the estate tax is levied on transfers made at death. The fact that death also marks the end of a generation is coincidental.[125] Thus, there is no such principle as taxation at every generation and taxpayers have always been free to arrange their affairs so as to avoid this result.

* * * [I]f the *status quo ante* was inequitable because families with moderate levels of accumulated wealth could not afford to split benefits between generations, the new Act has made it worse. Ironically, it has the result of increasing inequity in the estate tax law by closing the avoidance possibility to those who must provide in testamentary dispositions for their children first, then their grandchildren, while leaving it open to the very wealthy who are able to make direct bequests to their grandchildren because their children are already well provided for. Tax planners have not waited long to advise their clients that "layering"—creating trusts for different generation levels—will now be an important feature of estate planning.

C. Measuring the Tax

Another concept of "equity" used in death tax analysis derives from the incidence of the tax. It is generally accepted that estate taxes fall primarily on the heirs. But these taxes take lit-

---

[125]   *See* Kurtz & Surrey, [*Reform of Death and Gift Taxes: The 1969 Treasury Proposals, the Criticisms, and a Rebuttal*, 70 COLUM. L. REV. 1365, 1369 (1970) (characterizing "periodicity" as an "aspect of equity in estate taxation")]. * * * While it may be clear to the authors that equity requires some approximation of time equivalence, it is not clear to the present writer. * * * As Vickrey pointed out, by making transfers of wealth taxable at death the system adopted an irregular time interval for the incidence of the tax. *See* [Vickrey, *An Integrated Successions Tax*, 22 TAXES 368 (1944)]. Passing off this obvious fact as a bar to "complete equity" and then arguing that "notions of fairness" require adjustments to offset the statutory scheme seems a rather tall order.

tle account of the situation of those who pay. Thus, poor heirs receiving large bequests pay higher rates of taxation than rich heirs obtaining small bequests. "Is a tax borne by one group . . . but measured by the amount bequeathed by another, just by our standards? The answer must be negative."[130] The new tax on generation-skipping transfers does nothing to ameliorate this, for in addition to the tax based on the testator's wealth, it imposes a tax based on the wealth of the "deemed transferor," a party who will not only not bear the incidence of the tax but whose wealth—the tax base—may have absolutely no connection with the property being taxed.

D. Clarity and Complexity

Complexity in the tax law is also a source of inequity. * * * Complication in the tax laws puts a premium on expert tax advice, the availability of which can be directly correlated with the wealth of the party seeking advice. The more complicated the tax provision, the more likely it will work to the short-run economic advantage of the tax bar and the ultimate economic advantage of its wealthy clients. Few would maintain that the tax on generation-skipping transfers furthers tax equity by avoiding complexity. * * *

Not unrelated to the goal of equity is that of neutrality. In the words of the Ways and Means Committee, "the tax laws should be neutral and . . . there should be no tax advantage available in setting up trusts."[135] This is not a new idea with regard to generation-skipping transfers. In 1946 Eisenstein, for example, suggested that by adopting the English system "we would make a significant stride toward the ideal that the choice of a trust or outright gift should not be determined by tax considerations."[136] Although this statement has often been repeated, it must strike the reader as a totally inadequate guide to action. Estate and gift tax considerations will become irrelevant only when the estate and gift tax system is repealed. The best one can hope for by piecemeal change is to reduce the tax advantages of one form of disposition over another. Presumably this is what Eisenstein and others meant. The 1976 Act has not significantly reduced the tax advantages in setting up trusts. Trusts continue to offer potential tax savings as well as other non-tax benefits. * * *

IV. THE ESTATE TAX RETURN STUDIES

The only available empirical data on the use of generation-skipping devices is found in a study of 1957 and 1959 estate tax returns directed by Professor Carl S. Shoup of Columbia University. * * *

What was Congress, or for that matter the outside observer, to make of this data? If one favored the view that there was a "generation-skipping problem," one could point to the estimated revenue loss of $267 million due to the use of generation-skipping techniques. Moreover, it could be argued that the wider use of generation-skipping trusts by millionaires than by those leaving smaller estates was regressive and discriminatory. On the other hand, opponents of legislative action rested on the principle *de minimis non curat lex*. In particular they could cite the fact that even for millionaires outright bequests to family members exceeded bequests in generation-skipping form by ten to one. While hundreds of millions of dollars are certainly nothing to sneer at, Shoup was able to characterize the estimated revenue loss as "relatively small." In fact on the basis of his study, Shoup was led to "wonder why the wealthier citizens of the country do not take greater advantage of the tax savings to be derived from long-term trusts."[160]

---

[130]   Harriss, [*Sources of Injustice in Death Taxation*, 7 NAT'L TAX J. 289, 295 (1954)].

[135]   [H.R. REP. NO. 1380, 94th Cong., 2d Sess. 47 (1976).]

[136]   Eisenstein, [*Modernizing Estate and Gift Taxes*, 24 TAXES 870, 872-73 (1946)].

[160]   [CARL S. SHOUP, FEDERAL ESTATE AND GIFT TAXES 169 (1966)].

One can safely conclude only that the data enable both sides to make respectable arguments concerning the existence of a generation-skipping "problem" and that it would take an extensive analysis of possible criteria against which the data could be measured before a conclusion might be reached. * * *

CONCLUSION

A reasonable conclusion that might arise in the mind of the reader is that new chapter 13 should be repealed at the earliest opportunity, for it represents the end product of the legislative process at its worst. The focal point for analysis to support this conclusion must be the Report of the House Ways and Means Committee. In its purported "Reasons for Change" the Committee presents the reader with a jumble of code words—"equal treatment," "transfer taxes every generation," "inequities," and "tax neutrality"—whose meaning, let alone relationship to the statute, is less than clear. * * * It is difficult to take seriously legislation enacted without reference to any data indicating the existence of a "problem."

* * *

Our examination of the generation-skipping transfer problem suggests clearly what ought to be done. Reasonable men could surely conclude that the pre-1976 power of beneficiaries to reach corpus was so great a quantum of ownership that the corpus ought to have been included in the beneficiary's gross estate. As indicated earlier, the simple way to achieve the necessary change in the tax law is to amend § 2041 by eliminating subsections (b)(1)(A) and the second sentence of (b)(2). That having been done, Congress could direct its attention to the "problem" of the income beneficiary. * * *

* * *

NOTE

In the absence of a GST tax, what steps, if any, would Verbit recommend to deal with "the 'problem' of the income beneficiary"? Would he accept a GST tax that implemented a once-a-generation tax more systematically? Verbit criticizes the 1976 statute for failing to reach direct transfers to grandchildren. Does the treatment of such transfers as "direct skips" under the current GST tax answer this criticism? Note that the current GST tax imposes no greater burden on a transfer to a great-grandchild than on a transfer to a grandchild.

Jonathan G. Blattmachr & Jeffrey N. Pennell, *Using "Delaware Tax Trap" to Avoid Generation-Skipping Taxes*, 68 J. TAX'N 242 (1988)*

* * *

Because the stated maximum estate and gift tax rate is never greater than the flat GST rate, often it will be desirable to cause either the estate or gift tax to apply rather than the GST. * * *

Unfortunately, opting for estate or gift tax inclusion rather than generation-skipping transfer taxation is not always desirable. * * *

* * *

* * * [E]state plans must be drafted to provide sufficient flexibility to determine which system of tax will be most favorable, by providing an opportunity to subject trust property to the estate or gift tax rather than the GST, as appears best at the time of the appropriate taxing event.

EXPOSING GS PROPERTY TO ESTATE OR GIFT TAX

The most common methods by which property that otherwise would be subject to the GST regime may instead be exposed to estate or gift tax are (1) by discretionary distributions from the trust to the beneficiary, (2) by the trustee exercising discretion to grant a general power of appointment to the beneficiary, (3) by a trust provision directing that distributions be made to the beneficiary pursuant to a formula distribution provision, or (4) by granting the beneficiary a formula general power of appointment, the exercise or lapse of which is treated as a taxable transfer under Section 2041 or 2514. Unfortunately, several problems affect each of these common approaches.

For example, formula provisions are difficult to draft. The factors affecting the amount described under the formula potentially include the applicable rates, surtaxes, credits and exemptions, the ability to avoid all taxation through proper planning at the time of the applicable taxable event and so forth. * * * With respect to discretionary provisions, many trustees express a reluctance to exercise discretion to make distributions to a beneficiary, or to grant a general power of appointment, for fear that either decision may change the ultimate beneficiary of the trust property, thereby subjecting the trustee to litigation by a disappointed potential recipient. * * *

The determination whether property should be exposed to estate or gift tax rather than the GST is complicated, and a fiduciary could face liability for making the "wrong" decision. Further, the transferor may not want to arm the trustee with these powers, because granting a general power of appointment to a beneficiary or invading the trust and paying the property outright to the beneficiary may cause the property to be deflected away from those the transferor wanted to benefit.

* * *

THE "DELAWARE TAX TRAP" ALTERNATIVE

An alternative, requiring no exercise of fiduciary discretion, is to rely on the so-called "Delaware Tax Trap" of Sections 2041(a)(3) and 2514(d). These arcane and little known sections provide that property subject to a nongeneral power of appointment will be includable in the estate of the powerholding beneficiary (or will be subject to gift tax upon exercise) to the

---

extent the power is exercised to create another power of appointment that "can be validly exercised so as to postpone the vesting of any estate or interest in [the] property, or suspend the absolute ownership or power of alienation of [the] property, for a period ascertainable without regard to the date of creation of the first power." In more simple terms, exercise of a nongeneral power of appointment to create a new power of appointment that has the effect of postponing the period of the Rule Against Perpetuities converts the nongeneral power of appointment into a taxable power.

* * *

The underlying reason for the original adoption and application of Sections 2041(a)(3) and 2514(d), and the key to the ways to exploit them, is the Rule Against Perpetuities. The Rule as applied to trusts generally requires trust corpus to vest in some beneficiary within a period measured by the life of some person alive when the trust was created, plus 21 more years. Granting any testamentary power of appointment or a presently exercisable nongeneral power of appointment will not, in most states, constitute the requisite vesting for perpetuities purposes, nor extend the original perpetuities period.

In most jurisdictions, however, the grant of a presently exercisable general (PEG) power of appointment is regarded as if it were a vesting of the property subject to the power because the holder of such a power may immediately appoint the subject trust property to the holder personally, meaning that alienation of the property is no longer suspended. In addition, the powerholder may presently exercise the power to appoint the property in further trust, with a new perpetuities period beginning with that exercise. And, most important, under a unique feature of Delaware law, the grant of a presently exercisable *nongeneral* power of appointment has the same effect as creating a PEG power in most other states. * * *

WHICH NEWLY CREATED POWERS TRIGGER THE TRAP?

Although Sections 2041(a)(3) and 2514(d) were originally enacted to prevent estate tax avoidance through successive exercises of, and creation in others of new, *nongeneral* powers of appointment, these provisions also appear to apply to the creation, by exercise of a nongeneral power, of a presently exercisable *general* power of appointment (the PEG power) if creation of the new PEG power begins a "new" perpetuities period without regard to the creation of the original nongeneral power. This is the case under most states' Rule Against Perpetuities.

* * *

* * * If this interpretation is correct, then the Delaware Tax Trap is applicable in *any* state in which a PEG power extends the period of the Rule Against Perpetuities, and creates the opportunity to trigger the trap to work the intended shift of tax liability from the GST to the estate or gift tax.

HOW THE TRAP OPERATES

To illustrate, assume that Parent (*P*) created a trust for the benefit of Child (*C*), giving *C* a nongeneral power to appoint the remainder at death among *C*'s descendants in such shares as *C* selects, either outright or in further trust and allowing creation of new powers of appointment. Without exercise of this nongeneral power, eventually the trust must vest in order to avoid violation of the Rule. But assume that, consistent with the terms of the nongeneral power granted to *C* and with local law, *C*'s will exercises the nongeneral power to extend the trust and, among other things, grants a PEG power of appointment to *C*'s youngest living descendant. By this simple exercise, *C* begins a "new" period for purposes of the Rule, applicable with respect to the extended trust. If properly done, the trust could be further extended by successive similar exercises of newly created powers of appointment, in each case creating new PEG powers of appointment—all "kicked off" by *C*'s exercise of the original nongeneral power. Under Section 2041(a)(3), *C*'s exercise of the nongeneral power of appointment in this case causes the trust property subject to the new PEG power to be includable in *C*'s estate as if *C* had a general power of appointment, even though the trust property would not otherwise have been includable in *C*'s estate (that is, if the power had been exercised in some other manner or not at all).

In effect, then, arming *C* with this nongeneral power of appointment in a generation-skipping trust, intended to continue in further trust until required to terminate under the local Rule Against Perpetuities, allows *C* to decide whether to allow the GST to apply or, by proper exercise, to cause the trust property to be includable in *C*'s estate to the extent *C* creates a PEG power of appointment in another beneficiary.

* * *

CONCLUSION

In some cases it will be preferable to expose property to estate or gift tax rather than GST. In other circumstances the converse will be true. While a given result may be obvious in some cases (such as if death of the beneficiary is imminent), in most cases the appropriate result will not be clear until long after the plan has been crafted. * * * Granting the beneficiary (or allowing the trustee to grant) a nongeneral power of appointment that may be exercised to grant others a PEG power, the exercise of which causes a new period to begin for purposes of the Rule Against Perpetuities, provides the greatest flexibility for GST purposes. * * *

The Delaware Tax Trap does not, however, represent the exclusive method to invoke the "best" tax result. If the beneficiary is incapable of exercising the nongeneral power due to incompetency, a trustee invasion power may be the next best method to add trust property to the beneficiary's estate. Thus, many drafters will want to consider whether such a power also ought to be included in well-drafted generation-skipping plans, for fall-back planning purposes. Together, the nongeneral power and the trustee's discretion ought to provide sufficient flexibility to best confront the question of which tax to incur, with a minimum of exposure to the fiduciary.

NOTE

Blattmachr and Pennell identify hidden advantages in the "arcane and little known" provisions of §§ 2041(a)(3) and 2514(d). Why might it sometimes be desirable to incur a GST tax rather than an estate or gift tax? For a fuller discussion of planning considerations, see Jonathan G. Blattmachr & Jeffrey N. Pennell, *Adventures in Generation-Skipping, or How We Learned to Love the "Delaware Tax Trap,"* 24 REAL PROP., PROB. & TR. J. 75 (1989). Another commentator has urged the repeal of §§ 2041(a)(3) and 2514(d), arguing that they have been rendered superfluous by the enactment of the GST tax. See Ira Mark Bloom, *Transfer Tax Avoidance: The Impact of Perpetuities Restrictions Before and After Generation-Skipping Taxation*, 45 ALB. L. REV. 261, 307 (1981). What are the arguments in favor of and against preserving these provisions?

John T. Gaubatz, *A Generation-Shifting Transfer Tax*, 12 VA. TAX REV. 1 (1992)*

This Article * * * proposes a rewriting of the Federal gift, estate, and transfer taxes, currently contained in Chapters 11 through 14 of the Internal Revenue Code of 1986, into two complementary taxes—a flat-rate "generation-shifting transfer tax" (GST tax), and an elective, progressive-rate, "integrated transfer tax" (IT tax).

* * *

I. WHY, WHAT, AND WHEREFORE

* * *

B. Recasting the Transfer Tax

* * *

The basic design of the proposal has its genesis in the current generation-skipping transfer tax. This tax, if shorn of the $1 million exemption, is an extremely effective vehicle of taxation. It is so effective, in fact, that one of the primary estate planning devices is to make transactions taxable at the intervening generation, so as to avoid the generation-skipping transfer tax. It further has the advantage that it does not usually apply until the possessory interests of the intervening generations have ceased. Thus, it requires only a single return when the intervening generation's interests terminate. The tax result does not depend on the timing of the creation of the interests, but on their possession, and thus the tax is relatively form-independent; a bequest under a will of a transferor is handled much the same as the termination of a reserved life estate in the transferor.

C. Other Considerations

If the goal of the transfer tax is to tax property when it shifts between generations, the generation-skipping transfer tax provides an attractive model. All that would be required to turn it into the necessary tax is to change it from a generation-skipping transfer tax into a generation-shifting transfer tax. That could easily be done by defining the taxable transfer (direct skip, taxable termination, or taxable distribution) as occurring when property passes one, rather than two, generations below the generation of the transferor. It would be that simple. Indeed, the only major disadvantage of the generation-skipping transfer tax as a model is that it structurally is fairly incompatible with a progressive rate schedule, as was discovered in attempting to implement the 1976 version of the tax. Further, although a flat rate is attractive from a simplicity point of view, a flat rate set high enough to have the impact of reducing dynastic concentrations of wealth would be politically intolerable if applied to the upper middle class, whose primary preoccupation is the accumulation of resources for education, retirement, and medical needs. This weakness of the generation-skipping transfer tax is currently overcome by exempting from the tax transfers that are estate or gift taxable at the intervening generation. This allows the transfer to be taxed using the progressive rate schedule applicable to those taxes, while avoiding the problem, inherent in the 1976 version of the generation-skipping transfer tax, of having to calculate a tax based on the rate structure of a "deemed transferor."

Using the application of the existing estate and gift tax systems insures that there will be a knowing taxpayer who has the burden of calculating the progressive tax if the maximum GST tax is to be avoided. For the same reasons, this "out" suggests a way to avoid the weakness of

---

the GST tax if it were used at the first generation—provide an alternate tax, with a progressive rate schedule, which could be applied as an alternative, and put the burden on the taxpayer to elect into the alternative tax. In short, this proposal replaces the existing gift and estate taxes with a single progressive tax, which will be called an Integrated Transfer (IT) tax, applicable at the election of the transferor or other appropriate party or his or her executor.

As will appear, the proposed structure avoids much of the existing complexity of the "string" provisions (currently located in sections 2035 through 2042 of the Code), the marital and charitable deductions, and the annual exclusion.

D. Inclusionary Provisions, Deductions, Credits, and Exclusions

1. Inclusionary Provisions

The proposed tax does not require provisions similar to the current "string provisions" to insure taxation of appreciation to the time of the transferor's death or other termination of the grantor's interest in the property. If any of the beneficiaries, including the transferor, who are entitled to receive current distributions are in the transferor's generation, no tax will apply to the creation of the trust or other multiple-interest transfer. Because the GST tax does not apply to transfers into trust unless all of the beneficiaries are shift persons one or more generation younger than the transferor, trust interests will not be taxed until there is a termination of all of the interests held by beneficiaries, including the transferor, who are either in the transferor's generation or in a previous generation. This would only happen on termination, or on distribution of trust assets to a younger generation beneficiary. Thus, there is an automatic delay in the application of the tax, which is exactly what the "string provisions" were designed to accomplish. The separate treatment of life insurance, pensions and other contract rights under the current Code is simplified by treating them as trust equivalents, so that taxation of interests created by them is delayed until the termination of prior interests unless all interests are owned by the same generation.

Transfers of business interests and value manipulation through multiple classes of stock and partnership interests continue to be a problem that is difficult to solve. The proposal adopts the principle inherent in *Robinette v. Helvering*.[89] As does the current Chapter 14, the proposal requires that transactions be in a recognized form if any portion of the transferor's interest in the business is to avoid taxation when he makes a current transfer of an interest in the business to a shift person.

2. Deductions

Because transfers within a generation are not taxed, and the transferor's spouse is defined to be in the same generation as the transferor, no transfer to a spouse is taxed. This makes complex marital deduction provisions unnecessary. On the other hand, the tax abuse sought to be avoided by means of the current complexity of those provisions is avoided by not treating the creation of trusts as a taxable event in the usual case. Thus, for example, a trust for the surviving spouse until death or remarriage would not constitute a taxable event, but the trust, including any appreciation, would be taxed when the surviving spouse died or remarried. Yet this occurs without needing any of sections 2056, 2041, or 2044 of the Code.

Similarly, because charities are defined to be in the same generation as the transferor, outright transfers to charity would not constitute direct shifts, and, therefore, would not be taxable. Charitable lead trusts would not be treated as current transfers because the charity is assigned to the transferor's generation, and the trust is therefore not a shift person. As a result, the trust would become taxable only on the termination of the charity's interest. This means that the

---

[89]   318 U.S. 184, 186-7 (1943).

types of valuation abuse sought to be avoided under current sections 2055, 2522, and 2642(e) of the Code with respect to such transfers should not arise.

In the case of a charitable remainder trust, no tax problems would arise if no income beneficiary were in a generation younger than the transferor; if there are no younger generation beneficiaries, there would be no taxable transfer. If all income beneficiaries were younger than the transferor the creation of the trust would be taxable as a direct skip, because the charity's future right would not be an "interest" for the purposes of determining whether all of the trust's beneficiaries were shift persons. However, the proposal would treat the entire value as passing to the shift persons unless the trust were in the form of an annuity trust, unitrust, or pooled income fund, using the approach of Chapter 14 with respect to grantor-retained interests. This should effectively prevent valuation games. At the time of termination of such a trust, the charitable interest would pass tax-free; the property would not then pass to a shift person, because the charity is defined to be in the transferor's generation.

* * *

3. Credits

The currently complex credit situation is simplified. The tax on prior transfers (TPT) credit, with its percentage phase-out, is avoided, because the proposed tax more appropriately handles the problem. If the prior decedent is of the current decedent's generation or below, the prior death did not create a taxable event. If the prior decedent was in a higher generation, the transfer should be taxable because of the generation-shift, even if such shifts happen close upon each other. Indeed, the tax is designed to produce a double tax on transfers that skip generations.

* * *

4. Exclusions

Abuse of the per-donee annual exclusion should be reduced under the proposed tax, because the proposal limits the exclusion to direct skips not in trust, apart from trusts for minors. Thus, exclusions for life insurance trusts, with their attendant withdrawal powers, would not be allowed. * * *

* * *

III. A BRIEF ANALYSIS OF THE ADVANTAGES
AND DISADVANTAGES OF THE PROPOSED GST/IT TAX

The proposed GST/IT tax system would have five major advantages over the current formulation of transfer taxation. First, it better assures that all property will be taxed once each generation. Second, it better avoids taxation within a single generation, and thus better assures that property will be taxed no more than once each generation. Third, it avoids the problems of double reporting and double coverage endemic in the current system. Fourth, it makes some of the more complex provisions of the current Code unnecessary. Finally, it does all this without requiring estate planners to learn concepts not already familiar to them, and without a significant impact on the revenue generated by the transfer tax.

A. Advantages
* * *

1. Taxation Once Each Generation

The proposed combined taxes are more effective than the existing transfer tax at insuring taxation once each generation in a variety of ways. First, the annual exclusion is limited to transfers not in trust. This restricts the amount that can pass to a lower generation beneficiary tax-free through leveraging. A similar impact is achieved with respect to life insurance through defining the insured as having an interest in the policy which terminates at his or her death. This means that the insured's death triggers the GST tax on the policy proceeds if the policy beneficiary is in a younger generation. No longer will it be possible to leverage excludable gifts of premium payments into untaxed receipt of the policy proceeds.

Second, because the proposed GST tax applies to each shift between generations, whether the shift is direct or in trust, the tax effectively deals with multiple-generation gifts without reference to an additional tax system. The tax merely defines each generation shift to be another taxable event. Third, by adopting a "hard to complete" approach, the tax more surely catches any appreciation between the time of the "transfer" and the time transferors, or others in the transferor's generation, actually lose control over, or the benefit of, the property.

2. Avoiding Multiple Taxation Within a Single Generation

The primary way in which the proposed tax avoids multiple taxation within a single generation is by defining the taxable event as the termination of the interests of a higher generation. This makes taxation of transactions within a single generation impossible—something not currently true with respect to gifts and bequests to parents, siblings, cousins, and others in the transferor's generation. The effect is heightened by redefining downward the generation of the transferor whenever the property is taxed, in much the same way in which the current generation-skipping transfer tax upgrades generations. The reassignment of the transferor to a younger generation means that subsequent transactions with respect to the property within that younger generation will not trigger application of the tax—thus preventing double-taxation within the generation.

3. Avoiding Double Reporting and Coverage

The proposed GST tax clearly distinguishes between transactions that are currently taxable, and those that will be taxable in the future. It does this by excluding from the definition of direct shifts transactions that have current generation beneficiaries who hold present interests. Thus, such transactions can only produce taxable terminations or distributions in the future. In this way, the proposed tax avoids the current problem of double reporting.

The proposal also avoids most, if not all, of the problems of overlapping provisions currently found in the Code's "string provisions" of the estate tax. The proposed tax contains only three definitions of taxable transfer—taxable terminations, taxable distributions, and direct skips. To the extent that the three are not inherently exclusive of each other, the proposal makes them so. Further, the IT tax is expressly exclusive of the GST tax, and itself contains only one inclusionary section, thereby preventing overlap.

4. Timing of Gifts

As a general matter, a tax should not create a positive pressure for a particular type of estate planning, i.e., the tax results should, as much as possible, be independent of the method used. Thus, a gift to a child should produce approximately equivalent tax results as a bequest of similar property to the same child, or the child receiving a distribution from a trust established by the transferor. The proposed tax uses the same system to tax all transfers, and tends to treat the creation of successive interests as incomplete—thus delaying until the time of possession the taxation of the transfer to the remaindermen. For example, if an individual transfers property to a trust, retaining the income from the trust for life, and giving the remainder interest to his children, the transfer is incomplete under the proposed GST tax. The transaction cannot be a taxable termination or distribution, because no trust interest has terminated, and there has not been a distribution from a trust. There has not been a direct skip, because the grantor, who is a current generation beneficiary, has an interest in the trust. Thus, the trust will not be taxed until the grantor's life estate ceases, whether because of his death or his disposing of it earlier.

A taxable termination will then occur, and the tax will apply. The same would occur if the grantor did nothing, and executed a will leaving his property to his children. In this way, the proposed tax allows inter vivos techniques to be used as an effective substitute for testamentary gifts without a different tax result.

* * *

NOTE

Under Gaubatz's system, transfers would be taxable only if made to beneficiaries at least one generation below the transferor's generation. What is the justification for exempting transfers to beneficiaries in the transferor's generation or a higher generation? Would Gaubatz's proposal ensure that tax was imposed at each generation?

Gaubatz would permit the transferor to elect to incur an "integrated transfer tax" in lieu of a generation-shifting transfer tax. Aside from obtaining the advantages of the unified credit and low rate brackets, why might the transferor make such an election?

Leonard Levin & Michael Mulroney, *The Rule Against Perpetuities and the Generation-Skipping Tax: Do We Need Both?*, 35 VILL. L. REV. 333 (1990)*

I. INTRODUCTION

* * *

* * * [W]here federal taxation touches the passage of assets to and through succeeding human generations, the federal tax law has served as a mechanism for limiting the ability of the wealthy to continue to control their assets over periods of time which Congress has deemed unreasonable. Guided by the imperative to raise federal revenue and by the desire to limit inordinate amalgamation of wealth through inheritance, Congress utilized the tax system.

This use of the tax system is part of one of two parallel movements which has developed in recent times: the ongoing dismantling or prevention of restraints on property alienation as a matter of state real property law, and the federal estate tax-oriented disincentives to the untaxed accumulation and perpetuation of tangible and intangible wealth. The development of these movements is apparently based on a similar societal concern: the impermissible concentration of wealth occasioned by legal rules that order the transmission of wealth as a result of death. A comparison of the two movements, wholly dissimilar in origin and application but arising from the same policy, suggests that select elements of each could be combined in one system.

One of the primary methods of preventing restraints on the alienation of property is embodied in the Rule Against Perpetuities. The Rule applies its sanction in an all-or-nothing fashion; either the interest is left totally unaffected or it is entirely invalidated. One of the primary disincentives to the untaxed accumulation of wealth is the generation-skipping tax. This tax, at least to a limited extent, applies its sanction incrementally. A comparison of the two measures raises an interesting question: What if an incremental approach were applied in the perpetuities area? Also, since the generation-skipping tax in part encourages the end it is conceptually designed to discourage, namely, the appreciation in value of property held by the same family through succeeding generations, should it be revised? And if yes, could such a revised statute also further the purpose served by The Rule?

* * *

III. THE GENERATION-SKIPPING TAX: A FEDERAL PERPETUITIES RULE

* * *

Congress was concerned with the ability and proclivity of the wealthy to avoid the generation-by-generation impact that the estate tax had on persons who were unable to tie up substantial assets in the form of a generation-skipping trust. When Congress enacted the generation-skipping tax it looked to the effect of The Rule which limited the duration of trusts.

* * * [B]oth the generation-skipping tax and The Rule have the same purpose: they seek to coerce property owners to arrange their affairs so that transfers of property will occur after their deaths. While the aim is the same, the penalty for failure to comply differs. With the generation-skipping tax, the absence of an actual transfer event gives rise to a deemed transfer event and the wealth passing downstream is diminished by the amount of the tax. Under The Rule, the penalty is to void the arrangement and thereby recast it in a form in which alienation is not impermissibly fettered. As a result, under the current generation-skipping provisions, if a testator purports to create successive life estates for various generations, the tax would be triggered on the death of each successive generation having a life estate even though the interest of the life tenant was not inheritable and therefore not subject to an estate transfer tax.

Moreover, the tax is levied on "direct skips." This means that even if a prior generation receives no life interest, a generation-skipping tax is triggered by a direct gift to a person who is more than one generation below the donor whose parents are alive at the time of the gift. The tax is levied as each generation becomes entitled to distribution, and it is at the highest available estate tax rate, currently fifty-five percent.

Congress' overt embrace of the public policy against allowing economic perpetuities in the transfer tax area was not all-encompassing. The 1986 Act revision of the generation-skipping tax provided an exemption of up to $1 million for each individual transferor who makes a generation-skipping transfer. To implement the exemption, specific property is identified as exempt and thereafter all subsequent appreciation in value of that exempt property is immune from the generation-skipping tax.

For example, assume the grantor transfers $1 million in trust for his or her grandchildren and allocates the full amount of her exemption to the trust. Thereafter, no part of the trust will ever be subject to the generation-skipping tax, even if it eventually appreciates in value ten-fold.

The exclusion is obviously at complete odds with the general policy of the generation-skipping tax, and it can be expected to encourage long-lasting inflexible trusts, with The Rule as their only temporal limitation. And because, at least as Congress viewed it, only the wealthy can be expected to tie up assets of the magnitude required to take full advantage of the exclusion, the provision points firmly in the direction of encouraging undue accumulation of wealth in the hands of a few.

IV. SO WHAT?

* * *

* * * [P]roperty held under alienation strictures improperly detracts from the mobility of wealth to meet the needs of current owners where those needs could not have been forecast by the original owner. In addition, taxing the devolution of control of wealth from one generation to another without regard to the legal formalities of transfer causes each generation to contribute to the satisfaction of the national federal tax burden with greater uniformity and equality.

There is an implicit quantitative assumption involved in applying this policy. The larger the amount of wealth that can be accumulated or restricted within the present frameworks of the tax system and The Rule, the greater is the presumed level of societal concern. When the amount involved is relatively small, arguably no substantial public interest is impaired, even if the amount is tied up over an inordinate period of time. * * *

* * * On its face, The Rule is an all-or-nothing sanction: The Rule either is or is not violated. A case may fall within the prohibition of The Rule even though the amount involved is so small that its public policy impact is minimal. * * *

In a sense, the generation-skipping tax is also an all-or-nothing sanction. After overreaching the limits of the available exemptions, a single rate is applied. No gradations are available.

Both The Rule and the tax can "cut," but when they do it is with a very dull blade. Undoubtedly that is the result of the failure to clearly articulate, in other than a historical or highly reactive manner, the policy that underpins both.

Is there a better way to address the perceived goals of the policy? Since The Rule and the generation-skipping tax have the same policy target, why sustain both? What if a single system could be devised that is sensitive to the degree of the public interest involved while it continues to further the desired policy?

A taxing scheme seems to be particularly suitable for such a system. The tax rate might vary based not only upon the amount involved but also upon the potential length of time that the trust or other device for tying up the property is likely to remain in effect. This procedure might call for a merger of the present estate, gift and generation-skipping taxes, and the total abandonment of The Rule.

Instead of a generation-skipping tax at one stiff rate, graduated rates could apply based on the number of generations which stand between the beneficiary and the original testator or donor. Moreover, any exemption might be temporarily limited in time to a single generation so that, regardless of amount, the tax would be triggered for future generations. The tax rate might be set ultimately to reach a confiscatory level so that it would operate similarly to the flat prohibition of The Rule. But to account for the direct proportional relationship between the amount involved and the degree of societal concern, the tax would only reach that point in graduated stages. It would thus be incrementally more expensive to tie property up through several generations and the disincentive would increase with the potential amount involved.

In the case of direct skips or gifts directly to a junior generation (whose ancestors remain alive), an additional surcharge of twenty-five percent of the normal tax might be levied for each generation skipped, beginning at the immediate succeeding generation of the testator's or donor's children (or the equivalent generational level). Again, this tax structure might maintain a limited exemption for a single generation. If the gift were of successive interests to several generations, such as a trust which provides income in turn for children, grandchildren and beyond, the present generation-skipping tax might be retained so that as each generation succeeds to the trust interest a new tax would accrue, calculated at the same graduat[ed] rate as though the gift had been given directly to such beneficiaries from the settlor or testator.

* * *

The regime just outlined would render The Rule unnecessary as a means of social control over property owners' efforts to tie up wealth for excessively long periods after their deaths. * * *

* * *

The suggested reform would shift primary responsibility for control to the federal government's tax sector. In view of the increase in geographic mobility, as evidenced by the fact that people tend readily to change their domiciles from one state to another, the degree of uniformity that such a shift would produce is entirely desirable.

A uniform rule of the sort proposed here would cost the states nothing, and their domiciliaries would gain the benefit of being able to plan their affairs by reference to only one set of complex rules instead of two. The federal government would lose no revenue; indeed a revenue gain might well occur. True, the Internal Revenue Service would have the responsibility of administration, but that burden would be an incremental rather than an exponential increase over that which it currently bears under the present generation-skipping tax.

The resulting tax statute would be complex. But from the standpoint of the property-owning taxpayers affected, or more precisely their professional advisors, at present both The Rule and the generation-skipping tax are separately complex, particularly when The Rule itself is not uniform in its manifestations among the states, and the effective planner for mobile clients must now attempt to foresee which states' rules might apply in the future.

* * * [I]t is not a quantum leap to use the federal tax structure to further the public policy of regulating the alienation of property presently in the hands of future decedents. Such a system, it is submitted, would curb unacceptable modes of excess wealth accumulation without unduly restricting socially acceptable processes of wealth distribution under established rules of inheritance.

NOTE

Levin and Mulroney perceive a common social policy of limiting wealth concentration as animating both the GST tax and the Rule Against Perpetuities. They propose combining the federal estate, gift and GST taxes into a single transfer tax which would be imposed at graduated rates according to the amount involved and the number of skipped generations. Consider the challenges faced by the drafter of such a tax statute. Might a combined transfer tax be attractive as a matter of tax policy, regardless of the fate of the Rule? Why might the states choose to retain some version of the Rule for property law purposes? Some states have adopted the Uniform Statutory Rule Against Perpetuities, which has had repercussions on the effective date provisions of the GST tax. See Ira Mark Bloom & Jesse Dukeminier, *Perpetuities Reformers Beware: The USRAP Tax Trap*, 25 REAL PROP., PROB. & TR. J. 203 (1990) (discussing problems before promulgation of final regulations); Jesse Dukeminier, *The Uniform Statutory Rule Against Perpetuities and the GST Tax: New Perils for Practitioners and New Opportunities*, 30 REAL PROP., PROB. & TR. J. 185 (1995).

Howard E. Abrams, *Rethinking Generation-Skipping Transfers*, 40 Sw. L.J. 1145 (1987)*

* * *

This Article will demonstrate that cascading life estates and similar arrangements present no generation-skipping abuse. In fact, the need for any kind of generation-skipping tax is much smaller than has been thought: if a generation-skipping problem exists, it occurs only in transfers akin to the direct skip. Yet, these direct skip transfers are precisely the transfers that do not fit into the proposed alternatives to chapter 13. Once the generation-skipping problem is reoriented to focus on the direct skip, drafting a simple generation-skipping tax becomes possible.

* * *

II. RECONSIDERING THE GENERATION-SKIPPING PROBLEM

A. Cascading Life Estates

Consider first the paradigmatic generation-skipping problem: a devise to the child for life, then to the grandchild in fee. Conventional wisdom considers such a multigenerational transfer to be an avoidance device because two generations of beneficiaries after the transferor enjoy the devised property although only a single federal transfer tax is imposed. Under this analysis the child is the tax-favored beneficiary because the federal government imposes no federal transfer tax when the child dies.

This analysis, however, is flawed: a federal transfer tax is imposed on the child. Assume, for example, that the devise consists of $100,000 in long-term bonds paying a fixed ten percent interest each year. Assume further that the child is sixty years old at the time of the devise so that the discounted value of his life estate, determined actuarially, is about $75,000. The value of the grandchild's remainder, therefore, equals about $25,000.

Upon the child's death none of the corpus of the devise, that is, no part of the bonds, is includible in the child's estate. The interest payments the child received from those bonds, however, are includible in the child's taxable estate under the general estate tax inclusion rule of section 2033. Thus, if the child survives for precisely his actuarially predicted 14.5 years, his estate will include some $145,000 of interest received during his life. If the child invests that amount during his life, a total of about $300,000 will be included in his taxable estate. Thus, the child pays a transfer tax.

To be sure, had the child received the bonds in fee, his gross estate would have been greater than this includible amount by $100,000. On the other hand, the child did not enjoy all the benefits of fee ownership. Had interest rates declined so that the value of the bond rose, only the remainder-beneficiary, the grandchild, would have profited from the increase. The child surely enjoyed much of the value of ownership of the bonds, and his gross estate will reflect about three-quarters of fee simple ownership. The child, however, did not enjoy all the rights of fee simple ownership, and so the child's estate appropriately does not include the full value of the corpus.

The child's estate arguably will not be increased by the value of the life estate if the property consists of a homestead or other property that does not produce income. Even in such a case, however, equivalent value will be included in the child's estate because by living cost-free in the devised homestead, the child will have saved the housing costs that, but for the devise, would have diminished his estate. These savings effectively will increase the child's transfer tax base unless the child consumes them during life.

---

*   Copyright © 1987. Reprinted with permission.

What if the child does consume these savings? Has the child's action improperly eroded the transfer tax base? The value of the life estate was in the child's transfer tax base, but the child removed it in the only tax-free way possible, by consuming it. A taxpayer can always lessen his transfer tax liability by increasing his consumption; the very nature of a transfer tax permits no other result.

* * *

Is this potential for consumption meaningful? Suppose that each child in the case of the outright devise had been willing to commit irrevocably to consuming no more than the income interest from the devised property. In that case, each child could have used some of the devise to purchase a single life annuity. The child could have immediately given the remainder of the devise to the grandchildren, perhaps in the form of a trust accumulating all income until the death of both children. If these steps had been followed, then the amount subject to transfer tax as to each child would have been reduced from the value of the corpus of the property to the value of the grandchild's remainder. By forgoing the potential for additional consumption, thereby forcing the remainder interest to skip their generation, the children could thus have reduced their transfer taxation substantially. If the remainder interest truly skips a generation, the generation-skipping fight should not be about inclusion of the corpus in the intermediate generation's estate but only about taxation of the generationally remote beneficiary's remainder interest.

Further refining the comparison to capture all the elements of the life estate reveals that only the value of the remainder skips a generation. If the grandparent devises property outright to his children, then the children have the discretion to purchase an annuity. If the children receive only a life estate, they have no such discretion. The arrangement that best captures all the characteristics of a life estate, yet that involves only fee simple interests, is the devise of an annuity by a grandparent to his children, with the remainder of the grandparent's estate placed in trust, the corpus and all accumulated income from the trust to be divided among the grandchildren upon the death of the last child.

With this bifurcated devise each child will enjoy and include in his gross estate only so much of the devise as remains unconsumed at death, as well as any other property owned by the child and not consumed during life. Furthermore, the remainder devised to the grandchild is equivalent to a direct skip of the actuarially determined value of the remainder at the time of the grandparent's death. Surely the portion devised to each child in the form of a lifetime annuity would be free of all generation-skipping tax. Since a devise of a life estate to the children followed by the remainder to the grandchildren is the economic equivalent of this bifurcated devise, no generation-skipping tax should be imposed on the actuarially determined portion of the trust devised to each child. Thus, the only generation-skipping issue presented by a devise including an intervening life estate is whether the actuarially determined value of the remainder interest should be subject to an extra tax. Stated differently, should the implicit direct skip be taxed twice?

B. Powers of Appointment

Before considering the propriety of subjecting a direct skip to a generation-skipping tax, consider the other generation-skipping arrangement captured by the 1976 law, the generation-skipping trust with powers over the trust given to members of an intervening generation. Do such arrangements pose a transfer tax problem? Consider a devise of property that remains in trust for the life of the child, then goes to the surviving grandchildren in fee. The child receives a power to accumulate interest or distribute it among the grandchildren during life and also receives a testamentary power to appoint the trust corpus among grandchildren. In this case, the intervening generation, the child, has no interest in the devised property but has powers over it.

Should such a devise be subject to a generation-skipping tax? Consider first a tax that does not tax direct skips. The instant devise consists of a direct skip augmented by an intervening power; if the intervening power does not trigger the generation-skipping tax, the devise will be subject to only a single estate tax. Imposing a generation-skipping tax on this devise amounts to saying that the child's power over the trust corpus is sufficiently akin to ownership to justify a second tax, a tax that would be payable had the child received the corpus in fee.

Determining when powers over property should be taxed as ownership of property is a question that arises in connection with all transfer taxes, not just with a generation-skipping tax. Current law equates a power over property with ownership for purposes of imposing estate and gift taxes only if the power rises to the level of a general power of appointment as defined by section 2041(b)(1) of the federal estate tax law. Should such a definition be imported into a generation-skipping tax?

The answer is "no" for the surprising reason that such a definition would be redundant; if taxable powers are uniformly defined for the federal estate, gift, and generation-skipping taxes, and assuming that the generation-skipping tax does not apply to simple direct skips, then the generation-skipping tax is wholly superfluous. Any power over property created in an intervening generation will either be taxed as outright ownership under the estate and gift taxes or else the power will fail to rise to the level of a taxable power, and the intervening generation will therefore avoid all estate, gift, and generation-skipping taxes.

The gift of property in trust for the benefit of a grandchild with the child having the power during life to distribute or accumulate interest is an example. Under current law the power that the child has over the trust property does not rise to the level of a general power of appointment, and the child will not be treated as owner of the trust for federal estate or gift tax purposes. If the generation-skipping tax used the same definition of a taxable power, then this power given to the child would also escape taxation under the generation-skipping tax. On the other hand, if the definition of a taxable power were changed for estate and gift tax purposes to include the child's power, then the value of the trust corpus would be includible in the child's taxable estate, unless the corpus were subject to the gift tax during the child's life. With this redefinition of taxable powers, no generation-skipping tax is needed because the estate and gift taxes would capture the child's power over the property. Indeed, this example as well as the prior one should serve to prove that, if direct skips are not subject to a generation-skipping tax, then the power of appointment provisions of the federal estate and gift tax laws, governing the transfer taxation of powers over property, are the only generation-skipping provisions needed; no additional taxing structure should be added.[52]

* * *

Why did the Tax Reform Act of 1976 bring with it a "Tax on Certain Generation-Skipping Transfers" rather than a tightening of the definition of a general power of appointment? Professor Casner's study for the ALI in 1969 rejected a rewriting of the powers of appointment provisions. The study asserted that liberal provisions allowing powers of appointment to escape taxation gave needed flexibility to multigenerational arrangements. Yet if one accepts this argument in favor of nontaxable flexibility, and remembers that only the case of a generation-skipping tax that excludes simple direct skips from its reach is under consideration, the generation-skipping tax is nothing but an amendment to the power of appointment provisions

---

[52]   See Verbit, [*Annals of Tax Reform: The Generation-Skipping Transfer*, 25 UCLA L. REV. 700, 724-25 (1978)] * * * .

that redefines the taxability of powers held by an intervening generation. Does such an amendment make sense?

An amendment to the power of appointment provisions such as this does not make sense because the relationship of donor and donee generations has no effect under current provisions of the estate and gift taxes. Some powers over property ought to be taxed as ownership, and reasonable persons can disagree over where the line distinguishing taxable powers from nontaxable powers should be. Once that line is drawn, however, no reason exists for drawing a second line for intergenerational transfers. * * * So long as a system of transfer taxation exists as to direct transfers, generationally blind transfers with intervening powers present an issue that should be the concern only of the estate and gift tax powers of appointment provisions.

Accordingly, if Congress decides that direct skips should not be subject to a generation-skipping tax, the generation-skipping problem boils down to rethinking the definition of a taxable power of appointment. On the other hand, Congress might determine that direct skips should be subject to a special generation-skipping tax. If Congress so decides, how substantial a problem is created by a direct skip coupled with a power given to a member of an intervening generation? The answer, surprisingly, is that the problem disappears entirely.

Reconsider the devise of property for the benefit of a grandchild with substantial powers over the trust corpus given to the child. If direct skips are subject to a generation-skipping tax, the trust corpus will be subject to the generation-skipping tax independent of the child's powers. Thus, powers given to intervening generations need have no impact on the design of a generation-skipping tax that imposes a tax on simple direct skips.

III. DIRECT SKIPS AND GENERATION-SKIPPING TAXATION

The analysis presented above makes clear that the generation-skipping problem is not one of plugging loopholes in the estate and gift taxes; neither transfers with an intervening life estate nor transfers with intervening powers present a generation-skipping problem beyond that posed by the simplest generation-skipping transfer, the direct skip. Accordingly, imposing a generation-skipping tax on direct skips cannot be justified, as a necessary corollary of a generation-skipping tax generally aimed at more complex transfers, despite assertions by the Treasury, the ALI, and the drafters of the Tax Reform Act of 1986 to the contrary. Direct skips are the core of the generation-skipping issue, and if they are to be taxed, the justification for doing so must be faced squarely.

It is often asserted that direct skips are available only to the very wealthy because most taxpayers cannot afford to disinherit a generation. Since direct skips substitute for two or more transfers that do not skip generations, some argue that double taxation of direct skips is necessary to make the transfer tax system neutral among taxpayers. This plea for tax neutrality presupposes that direct skips are sufficiently similar to a series of outright nonskipping transfers to warrant multiple imposition of the transfer taxes. Yet, a direct skip certainly is not identical to a series of nonskipping transfers * * * .

A frequent justification for imposing a tax on direct skips is that double taxation of direct skips ensures periodicity of transfer taxation regardless of the form of a taxpayer's gift or devise; yet, the estate and gift taxes are not periodic or generational taxes. * * *

* * *

IV. SIMPLIFYING THE GENERATION-SKIPPING TAX

* * *

A. Tax-Free Direct Skips: Rethinking Powers of Appointment

If direct skips are not subjected to a generation-skipping tax, then generation-skipping transfers with powers given to members of intervening generations, with or without intervening interests, present a possible abuse of the transfer tax system. The proper resolution, however, is not to enact a generation-skipping tax, but rather to broaden the definition of a taxable power of appointment for estate and gift tax purposes. As that definition currently stands, a power over property is equivalent to outright ownership only if the power can be exercised in a way that effectively permits direct or indirect beneficial enjoyment of the property by the power holder. Such a power is called a general power of appointment.

* * *

Broadening the definition of taxable powers may force transfers into narrow and less flexible forms, but in reality no modification of the taxing system forces any taxpayer to adopt any form of transfer. To be sure, the creation of discretionary powers will likely decrease if the powers are taxed as the equivalent of ownership, but that decrease will simply reflect the inevitable consequence of eliminating a tax loophole. Despite the protests of estate planners to the contrary, equating powers to affect the beneficial enjoyment of property with outright ownership reduces tax avoidance but not wealth transfer flexibility.

* * *

B. Taxing Direct Skips: One Possible Answer

A decision to tax simple direct skips obviates the need to tax powers over property, but introduces two new issues: (1) when should the tax on generation-skipping transfers be imposed, and (2) at what rate should simple direct skips be taxed? The second of these issues has no easy answer.

No timing issue exists for the simplest of direct skips, namely transfers such as those from grandparent to grandchild in fee with no intervening delay. For such transfers the only opportunity for a generation-skipping tax to apply is at the time of transfer. A more complex conveyance including implicit direct skips, though, can offer at least two plausible opportunities for imposition of a generation-skipping tax. For example, consider the devise of property in trust by the grandparent for the benefit of the child for life and then to the grandchild in fee. The grandchild's interest in the trust can be estimated at the time of the devise, and a tax could be imposed immediately on that estimated value. On the other hand, taxation could be deferred until the grandchild actually takes possession of the remainder. The latter method of taxation minimizes horizontal inequities between taxpayers arising from actuarial fluctuations; that is, it minimizes the danger of taxing different members of the same generation differently. For that reason this method is the preferable choice.

If the generation-skipping tax has a flat rate, then taxation at time of transfer will, *ex ante*, equal taxation at time of receipt. For example, if the trust corpus is $100,000 and the child is sixty at the time of the devise, then the child's life expectancy is about 14.5 years, making the grandchild's actuarially determined interest in the trust about $25,000. At any constant rate of taxation the present value of a tax on $25,000 today equals the present value of a tax on $100,000 in 14.5 years. Thus, whether taxation occurs at the time of transfer or at time of receipt should make no difference to the federal fisc.

For more complex arrangements actuarial estimation of the value of a direct skip becomes impossible. For example, consider a devise in trust with income payable to either the child or the grandchild, as the trustee decides, and with the remainder going to whomever of the grantor's descendants the trustee appoints by will. Neither the value of the grandchild's income interest nor the likelihood of the remainder going to a generationally remote descendant of the grantor can be estimated with any degree of reliability. Accordingly, taxation should be deferred until the trust income or corpus is distributed to the grandchild or some other beneficiary. So long as all amounts are taxed as they are distributed and at a constant tax rate, no tax is avoided by this mechanism.

* * *

V. THE CURRENT PROPOSALS: WHAT WENT WRONG

A generation-skipping tax excluding direct skips from its reaches is redundant: outside the direct skip arena, whatever generation-skipping problems that exist should be corrected through the powers of appointment provisions of the estate and gift tax law. In addition, subjecting direct skips to the generation-skipping tax merely requires that transfers to remote beneficiaries be taxed as such beneficiaries receive distributions of cash or other property. If either form of a generation-skipping tax can be implemented so easily, why are the proposals so complex?

The answer can be traced to why we have proposals for a generation-skipping tax in the first place. Both the Treasury and the ALI argue in favor of a generation-skipping tax as a backstop to the estate and gift taxes. They see the paradigmatic generation-skipping transfer as a series of cascading life estates * * * . The Treasury and ALI seek to recharacterize and tax such transfers as if the property passes from generation to generation in fee simple absolute.

In the case of cascading life estates this recharacterization is not difficult; each life tenant becomes the deemed transferor vis-à-vis the next beneficiary. Such recharacterization, however, subjects the entire property to the generation-skipping tax even though only a portion of the property, the actuarially determined value of the remainder-beneficiary's interest, skips a generation. In other words, when the recharacterization is easy, it is also inappropriate.

The crux of the generation-skipping issue is the direct skip, and such transfers do not easily fit into this recharacterization mold. * * *

* * *

The treatment of multigenerational skips causes further unnecessary complexity. The proposals try to recharacterize transfers to very remote beneficiaries as a series of simple generation-skipping transfers, transfers that are then further recharacterized as a series of non-skipping gifts or devises. At each level the proposals struggle to determine whether the fictional transactions are more like testamentary transfers subject to the estate tax, or more like lifetime transfers subject to the gift tax. In fact, though, direct skips, whether of one or several generations, are unlike testamentary or lifetime transfers of an intermediate generation deemed transferor. Once that concept is accepted, multigenerational direct skips can be taxed in the simple geometric way.[126]

The problem is not that the drafters at the ALI or the Treasury have recharacterized poorly, but instead that they chose to recharacterize at all. All generation-skipping transfers can be analyzed as a combination of intervening terminable interests, intervening powers, and direct skips. Intervening terminable interests are adequately addressed by the existing transfer taxes. Intervening powers present no difficulties of their own: if the generation-skipping tax exempts direct skips, then the powers of appointment provision should address intervening powers; if the generation-skipping tax applies to direct skips, then intervening powers become irrelevant. Taxation of generation-skipping transfers is the taxation of direct skips, and direct skips cannot be fitted into the recharacterization mold dominating the current proposals.

---

[126]   For example, if the generation-skipping tax on direct skips is 50%, and ignoring the possible application of a generation-skipping zero bracket, a double skip should be taxed at a rate of 75%, a triple skip at a rate of 87.5%, etc. * * *

The debate on the propriety of a generation-skipping tax should focus on taxation of direct skips. If imposition of a wealth tax at least every generation is appropriate, then a new tax on direct skips is needed. If not, then a reexamination of the estate and gift tax powers of appointment provisions is needed. In no event, though, should we continue to treat the generation-skipping issue as a loophole in the current transfer tax system to be filled with complexity and confusion.

NOTE

Abrams argues that the GST tax should focus exclusively on direct skips, since terminable interests and powers of appointment pose no separate generation-skipping problems. Does this mean that the statutory provisions concerning taxable terminations and taxable distributions are redundant? Why might the drafters of the GST tax statute have chosen not to revise the existing estate and gift tax treatment of interests and powers? Did they simply misunderstand the scope of the generation-skipping problem?

PART VII:

INTEGRATING THE ESTATE AND GIFT TAXES

Since the inception of the modern gift tax in 1932, commentators have expressed dissatisfaction with the lack of coordination between the estate tax and the gift tax. The following materials explore the sources of friction between the two taxes as well as the major proposals for structural reform of the existing transfer tax system.

A.   Responses to the Dual Tax System

Before the Tax Reform Act of 1976, the estate and gift taxes were separate in both form and operation. Each tax provided its own independent base, rate schedule, and exemption. Moreover, the two taxes often overlapped in their application to a single transfer because there was no consistent rule for determining when a transfer became complete for estate and gift tax purposes. This "dual" tax system evoked numerous proposals for "integrating" the estate and gift taxes, as well as for "correlating" them with the income tax.

An influential early proposal for integration and correlation was prepared by a five-person Advisory Committee to the Treasury Department and by the Office of the Tax Legislative Counsel. This study, completed in 1947 and published the following year, recommended modifications to the existing estate, gift, and income taxes with the goal of creating a "unified and coherent system of taxation."

The ALI estate and gift tax project, completed in 1968 and published the following year, presented studies and recommendations under two alternative models. One model assumed that the existing dual tax system would be retained, while the other assumed the introduction of a "unified" estate and gift tax system. The ALI put forward both models without stating a preference for either one.

Some commentators perceived the advantages of a uniform completion rule but resisted the notion of unifying the transfer taxes. For example, Charles L.B. Lowndes proposed a "hard-to-complete" rule which would prevent completion of a transfer for gift tax purposes as long as the same transfer would be drawn back into the transferor's gross estate at death. Lowndes' proposal was consistent with a dual tax system; indeed, he strenuously objected to a unified system on the grounds that it would "remove[] the tax differential in favor of inter vivos gifts" and would "mean scrapping a half century of effort dedicated to refining the estate tax to its present point of perfection."

On the other hand, the Treasury Department's Tax Reform Studies and Proposals, completed in 1968 and published the following year, drew heavily on the ALI's proposal for a unified transfer tax system. The Treasury Department's proposals proved controversial. In response to opponents of a unified system, Jerome Kurtz and Stanley S. Surrey, two of the principal architects of the proposals, explained and defended their position.

U.S. Treasury Department, Federal Estate and Gift Taxes: A Proposal for Integration and for Correlation With the Income Tax (1947)

* * *

If an integrated transfer tax is to operate successfully, the concept of an *inter vivos* transfer must be defined as precisely as possible. Generally speaking, it should be immaterial, for purposes of an integrated transfer tax, whether a disposition during life is deemed complete and taxable at one point of time or another. In either case the total tax burden will be approximately the same because of the cumulative basis for determining the applicable rate of tax. The date of completion of a transfer is nevertheless a crucial factor for two reasons. First, since one merit of the transfer tax is the elimination of the present overlapping of estate and gift taxes, such date determines the single taxable event which gives rise to liability for payment of the transfer tax. Secondly, under the proposed systems for correlation of income tax consequences, such date marks the shift of liability for tax on income thereafter accruing from the transferor to the transferee. * * *

* * * The various types of *inter vivos* dispositions of property, other than outright transfers, may be conveniently segregated for purposes of analysis into [the following] categories:

(1) Dispositions subject to a power to change the beneficial enjoyment of the property;

(2) Dispositions whereby the transferor retains a reversionary interest in the property;

(3) Dispositions whereby the transferor retains the right to a possible distribution of the income of the property * * * .

A particular disposition may easily fall within one or more of the above categories, but for purposes of explanation, it is assumed that a disposition represents merely one of them.

1. Dispositions Subject to a Power to Change Beneficial Enjoyment

It is proposed under this heading that a transfer shall be deemed incomplete and therefore not subject to transfer tax if the transferor, any other person, or both retain a power of revocation, alteration, amendment, or termination enabling a change in the beneficial disposition of the property or the income therefrom. The transfer is rendered complete when all such authority finally comes to an end. If the power ceases during life, the transfer tax is incurred in the calendar year in which such cessation occurs. But if the power is outstanding at the transferor's death, the transferred property is treated as part of his taxable estate at death. A power held solely by another person, however, does not render a transfer incomplete if such person is authorized to vest the property in himself as well as others. In a similar connection, a power to change the beneficial disposition of the property does not postpone the completion of the transfer if such power is exercisable solely by will by a person other than the transferor.

Finally, a transfer is deemed complete even though the transferor or others have power (a) to distribute or apply income to or for a current income beneficiary or to accumulate it for him; (b) to apply principal to or for the benefit of the income beneficiary of such portion; or (c) to effect a combination of these results.

The precise scope of the foregoing recommendation may be more easily appraised by comparing it with the existing gift- and estate-tax rules. At present a transfer is incomplete for gift-tax purposes if the transferor, either alone or in conjunction with a person lacking a substantial adverse interest, is empowered to revoke the transfer, to designate new beneficiaries, or to alter the relative interests of the named beneficiaries. * * * On the other hand, if such a power over beneficial enjoyment is held by the transferor in conjunction with a person having a substantial interest adverse to another disposition, or is held solely by a person other than the transferor, the transfer constitutes a completed gift. * * * Insofar as the estate tax is concerned, a transfer is taxable at death if the transferor alone or in conjunction with any person is authorized to change the enjoyment of the property through the exercise of a power to alter, amend, revoke or terminate. If the power is held solely by a person other than the transferor, the property subject to the power is not includible in the transferor's gross estate, unless a power to revest the property in him is exercisable in accordance with some standard enforceable in a court of equity, and not as the donee may freely determine. * * *

If the gift tax rules are placed alongside those proposed under the integrated transfer tax, it is evident that the line in certain instances has been moved over so that transfers which would now be deemed completed gifts would be considered incomplete under the proposed transfer tax. This shift is caused primarily by two factors. First, the proposed revision drops the substantial adverse interest concept which is now a significant element in the determination of gift tax liability, inasmuch as this concept is not responsive to the actual controls retained by a transferor through familial and financial ties. Since the substantial adverse interest concept was eliminated from the estate tax law in 1924, the proposed transfer tax and the estate tax are thus identical in their treatment of a power held by the transferor alone or in conjunction with any other person.

Secondly, the proposed revision eliminates the distinction between a power held by the transferor in conjunction with another person and a power held solely by the other person. The present distinction assumes that a transferor exerts more influence upon another person as co-holder of a power rather than as transferor. * * * [H]owever, any such distinction is unjustifiable and is self-defeating if avoidance is to be justly dealt with. * * * Accordingly, where the power to change the beneficial disposition of the property resides solely in a person other than the transferor, the integrated transfer tax seeks to establish a clear-cut rule that such a power postpones the completion of the transfer until death unless the power is relinquished at an earlier date.

* * *

While continued dominion and control may be manifested through others, a point is reached where it is fair to conclude that they have generally come to an end. Hence it is provided that if a person other than the transferor is free to vest the property in himself, the transfer is complete. Such a transfer is not appreciably different from one which directly vests outright ownership in the other person. It is further provided that if a power in another person to change the beneficial enjoyment of the property may be exercised only by will, the transfer is equally complete. Admittedly, a donee of a testamentary power may be amenable to persuasion to such an extent that he will revest the property in the transferor or his estate. But such a power, when held by another, is not, as a rule, a ready means of assuring a continuing dominion in the transferor. * * *

The recommendation also provides that certain powers, which allow for a limited type of shifting in beneficial enjoyment, shall not render the transfer incomplete. Thus, the transferor will be required to pay a transfer tax at the time of transfer, and will thereafter be relieved from tax on the income from the transferred property, where he or another person has the power to distribute income to or for the benefit of a current income beneficiary or to accumulate it for future distribution to him. * * * [I]t is true that if distribution of income is withheld and the current income beneficiary of a trust dies prior to the expiration of the trust, the accumulations may ultimately pass to an alternate taker. Such a power of accumulation, however, is very limited in scope since its operation as a method of adjusting beneficial enjoyment depends upon the untimely death of the current income beneficiary. It is also provided that a transfer shall be deemed complete despite a power in the transferor or another person to pay over any portion of the principal to the current income beneficiary of such portion. Such a power of invasion undoubtedly permits continuation of dominion over the transferred property. It is believed, however, that transferors should not be entirely precluded from attempting to meet the needs of changing circumstances, such as a sudden emergency which requires immediate invasion of principal to assist the current income beneficiary. This consideration, it is felt, warrants the creation of a distinction between a limited power to invade and other powers to shift beneficial enjoyment.

* * *

2. Dispositions Reserving a Reversionary Interest in the Transferor

Under this heading the following provisions are recommended:

(a) A transfer shall be deemed incomplete if the property or the income therefrom must revert to the transferor or his estate after the expiration of any period of time;

(b) A transfer shall be deemed incomplete if the property or the income therefrom may so revert to the transferor or his estate and no beneficiary can obtain possession or enjoyment of the property during the transferor's lifetime.

These suggestions for change require a brief explanation of existing law.

If a transferor at the present time, in making an *inter vivos* disposition of property, provides that the property is to return to him or his estate after a specified period of time, a gift tax is imposed upon the value of the interests granted to others. If the property does not revert to him prior to his death, an estate tax is imposed upon the value of the reversion at the date of death. If there is a similar reversionary interest only in the income, the actuarial value of such lesser interest is taxable at death. The draft accompanying this report would withhold the imposition of any transfer tax until death unless the reversionary interest were released before death. There are two reasons which suggest the appropriateness of the recommendations. First, a transfer tax should strive as much as possible, for the sake of simplicity in application and convenience of administration, to apply at one particular time to a disposition as a whole. One might say that such single application is of the very essence of an integrated transfer tax. If tax is imposed at several stages, difficulties are bound to arise, especially with regard to the valuation of interests preceding the reversion. Secondly, the recommendation follows very naturally from the income tax treatment proposed with respect to the same type of transfer. Since it was felt that income tax should be imposed upon the transferor, a suggestion that such a transfer be treated as a completed gift was rejected. * * *

A problem of much greater importance under the existing estate and gift taxes is presented by a reversionary interest in the grantor or his estate which is contingent in character. Such an interest arises where the property may or may not return to the grantor, depending upon whether or not he survives the income beneficiaries. The gift tax consequences where such a reversionary interest is present are generally clear. A gift tax is payable upon the value of the entire property less the value of the reversionary interest (*Smith v. Shaughnessy*, 318 U.S. 176 (1943)), or upon the value of the entire property if the reversionary interest cannot be valued according to recognized actuarial methods of computation (*Robinette v. Helvering*, 318 U.S. 184 (1943)). If the property is thereafter included in the gross estate at the transferor's death, a credit is allowed for the gift tax paid.

* * * [I]f a transferor provides that the property is to return to him if he is living at the death of the income beneficiaries, the value of the property, less the value of any outstanding life estates in others, is includible in the gross estate. The typical situation is one in which the transferor provides for a life estate in his wife, a remainder to their children if he predeceases his wife, and a reversion to him if he survives her. Inasmuch as the ultimate receipt of the remainder is dependent upon the beneficiaries' survival of the transferor, it is taxable * * * as a transfer intended to take effect in possession or enjoyment at or after the transferor's death. *Helvering v. Hallock*, 309 U.S. 106 (1940). On the other hand, where the passing of a remainder interest is not dependent upon the transferor's death, such interest is not subjected * * * to an estate tax despite the transferor's reservation of a reversion. Such a case may be illustrated by a transfer in trust providing for a life estate in the transferor's wife, a remainder to their surviving issue, and a reversion to the transferor or his estate in the absence of such issue.

The foregoing principles have provided the basis for the recommendation made with respect to contingent reversionary interests. Under the proposed provision, where the transferor reserves such an interest, the basic question is whether any beneficiary can obtain possession or enjoyment of the property during the transferor's lifetime. If the answer is in the affirmative, the entire property is subjected to transfer tax at the time of transfer. If the answer is in the negative, the transfer tax is postponed until death. In neither case is allowance made for the value of the reversion or of any outstanding life estates. In this manner there is but one taxable event and difficult problems of valuing "slippery and elusive" interests are avoided. * * *

Contingent powers to dispose of property are not far removed from contingent reversionary interests. A transferor may provide, for example, that if the initial life beneficiary predeceases him, the transferor is authorized to appoint the property as he sees fit. At present a transfer subject to a contingent power of appointment is a taxable gift measured by the value of the property less allowance for the possibility, actuarially computed, that the transferor may be able to appoint the property. * * * The estate-tax treatment of such transfers, however, is considerably unsettled under the decisions. * * *

Because of the similarity between contingent reversionary interests of the *Hallock* variety and contingent powers, the proposed revision provides that no transfer tax is payable by reason of either until the transferor's death. * * * It should be noted, however, that not all contingent powers would be subject to these rules. The rules are intended to cover only taxable powers to change the beneficial enjoyment of the property. Thus, a power to accumulate income or to accelerate payment of corpus for the benefit of the current income beneficiary would not be taxable, whether contingent or not.

3. Dispositions Reserving to the Transferor a Right from the Income of the Transferred Property

The revision proposes that, in general, a transfer shall be deemed incomplete as long as the income is or may be distributed to, or held or accumulated for future distribution to, the transferor. This recommendation is derived from the present provisions * * * taxing the income of such a transfer in trust to the transferor. Two important differences should, however, be noted. First, the concept of the substantial adverse interest has been eliminated, for the reasons heretofore noted. Secondly, the revision proposes to treat a transfer as completed even though the income from the property is or may be applied for the support of the transferor's dependents, or to the payment of premiums upon policies of insurance on the life of the transferor. * * *

* * *

NOTE

In the income tax context, the primary issue is likely to be whether a particular item of income for the current year is taxed to the donor or the donee. By contrast, in the transfer tax context, the choice of a completion rule is likely to affect not only the timing but also the valuation of the transfer. Can a single concept of "completed transfer" adequately serve the various purposes of the transfer taxes and the income tax?

The Treasury's 1947 study played an important role in a lively debate on the merits of integration. For further discussion of early reform proposals, see George T. Altman, *Integration of the Estate and Gift Taxes*, 7 LAW & CONTEMP. PROBS. 331 (1940); Adrian W. DeWind, *The Approaching Crisis in Federal Estate and Gift Taxation*, 38 CAL. L. REV. 79 (1950); Erwin N. Griswold, *A Plan for the Coordination of the Income, Estate, and Gift Tax Provisions With Respect to Trusts and Other Transfers*, 56 HARV. L. REV. 337 (1942); Joseph S. Platt, *Integration and Correlation—The Treasury Proposal*, 3 TAX L. REV. 59 (1947); Robert W. Wales, *Consistency in Taxes— The Rationale of Integration and Correlation*, 3 TAX L. REV. 173 (1947); William C. Warren, *Correlation of Gift and Estate Taxes*, 55 HARV. L. REV. 1 (1941).

AMERICAN LAW INSTITUTE, FEDERAL ESTATE AND GIFT TAXATION (1969)*

* * *

Under present law, a lifetime arrangement with respect to property may or may not be a completed gift for gift tax purposes. Moreover, even though the arrangement involves a completed gift for gift tax purposes, it may not remove the value of the property from the donor's gross estate for estate tax purposes. This treatment of such completed lifetime gifts—in other words, the area of double transfer taxation—has been thought to be necessary to prevent lifetime transfers that have some of the characteristics of a deathtime transfer from escaping the higher estate tax rate schedule. The gift tax paid on these transfers that are also subject to estate taxation will give rise to a credit against the estate tax assessed on the same transfer * * * .

It is proposed * * * to eliminate this double taxation area by treating every arrangement as involving either a lifetime transfer or a deathtime transfer, but never both. Such elimination will simplify the transfer tax structure.

Under a unified tax, the ultimate tax liability is designed to be approximately the same whether a transfer occurs during life or at death. Hence, the line between lifetime and death-time transfers can be drawn wherever is most convenient. * * *

1. Retained or Granted Powers

Often a transferor retains (or confers on a trustee or another) power to determine later the ultimate disposition of property transferred by him. In such cases, it is proposed that under a unified tax the existence of a power in a lifetime arrangement should not prevent a transfer from being completed for transfer tax purposes unless (1) the power can be exercised in favor of the transferor, and (2) the power is exercisable by him alone or in conjunction with one who does not have a substantial interest that would be adversely affected by the exercise of the power.

The acceptance of this policy in the power cases under the unified tax would result in a completed gift in many cases that would be subject to estate taxes today. It would allow a transferor to retain many strings on a transfer and nevertheless get the value of the future growth out from under transfer taxation, as long as the strings do not permit the transferor to pull the property back to himself. This easy-to-complete-gift policy that is possible under a unified tax is regarded by some as one of the most attractive features of such a tax. * * *

* * *

Though a lifetime arrangement may be a completed gift under the power tests, it may be an incomplete one for one or another of the reasons noted below. * * *

2. Retained Current Beneficial Enjoyment

It is proposed that a lifetime arrangement under which the transferor retains the current beneficial enjoyment of the transferred property be regarded as an incomplete gift even though the interests of others in the transferred property on the termination of the current beneficial enjoyment are irrevocably fixed. This is a change from present law, under which an irrevocable transfer of property with income retained by the transferor involves a completed gift of the remainder interest for gift tax purposes. The transferred property is also included in the transferor's gross estate for estate tax purposes (I.R.C. Sec. 2036), with a credit for some or all of the gift tax paid * * * . In eliminating the double tax area, this transfer has been placed on the uncompleted gift side of the line with the result that it would be taxed as a transfer only at the time the current beneficial enjoyment ends. This would make these arrangements possible without the transferor diminishing his holdings by the payment of a transfer tax at the time the arrangement is established. * * *

3. Retained Reversionary Interest That is Certain to Become Possessory

It is proposed that if the transferor retains a reversionary interest that is certain to become possessory he be treated as making a completed gift of only the interests that precede his reversionary interest. Any interests subsequent to his reversionary interest would be treated as transferred only upon the termination or transfer of the reversionary interest. The retained reversionary interest that is certain to become possessory is close to the retained-current-beneficial-enjoyment case insofar as interests that follow the retained interest are concerned and the two should be treated similarly. * * *

* * *

NOTE

For a detailed discussion of the ALI project, see John H. Alexander, *Federal Estate and Gift Taxation: The Major Issues Presented in the American Law Institute Project*, 22 TAX L. REV. 635 (1967); A. James Casner, *American Law Institute Federal Estate and Gift Tax Project*, 22 TAX L. REV. 515 (1967); Donald McDonald, *Unsatisfied at Any Price—A Summary of the Proposals Presently Under Consideration in the American Law Institute: Federal Estate and Gift Tax Project*, 21 TAX LAW. 329 (1968).

Charles L.B. Lowndes, *Common Sense Correlation of the Estate and Gift Taxes*, 17 U. FLA. L. REV. 507 (1965)*

* * * One easy step * * * which would eliminate most of the complexities connected with the gift tax and materially simplify estate planning, is an amendment to the gift tax providing that transfers should not be taxed under the gift tax as long as they are subject to the estate tax.

A simple example will point up the purpose of the amendment. Suppose that *H* transfers property to *T* in trust to pay the income from the property to *S* until *S* reaches age 35, and then to distribute the trust property to *S*. If *S* dies before attaining age 35, the trust property is to be distributed to his surviving issue, or, if he dies without issue, to *W* in fee. What are the gift tax consequences of the trust if *H* retains power to revoke the trust with the consent of *W*? This depends in the first instance upon whether *H* has made a complete transfer and a taxable gift, which depends in turn upon whether *H* can revoke the trust only with the concurrence of a person possessing a substantial adverse interest in the trust property. If *W* possesses a substantial adverse interest in the trust property, *H* has made a taxable gift; but not otherwise. Whether or not *W* possesses a substantial adverse interest in the trust property depends upon whether she has a substantial chance of succeeding to the trust property. This is, of course, a question of fact that turns upon the circumstances surrounding the transfer. If *W* is *S*'s mother and at the time the trust was created *S* was a young married man 30 years of age with two healthy children, *W*'s chance of succeeding to the property is probably so remote that she does not possess a substantial adverse interest in the trust and *H* did not make a taxable gift. If, however, at the time the trust was created *S* was unmarried and childless and in extremely bad health, it is quite possible that *W* would have a substantial adverse interest in the trust and *H* has made a taxable gift.

But even assuming that *W* has a substantial adverse interest in the trust does not solve all of the gift tax problems connected with the creation of the trust. There is still the question of the amount of the gift which *H* has made. According to *Camp v. Commissioner*[4] a transfer that the transferor can revoke with the consent of a person possessing a substantial adverse interest in the transferred property is a complete transfer and a taxable gift only to the extent of the interest that cannot be revoked without the consent of the owner of the adverse interest. According to that decision, therefore, *H* has made a complete gift only to the extent of *W*'s contingent remainder, which raises the difficult question of valuing the remainder.

Let us add one more factor and assume that the power, which *H* retained to revoke the trust, was limited to a power to revoke the trust in its entirety. In this situation there is dicta in the *Camp* case to the effect that there is a taxable gift of the entire trust property upon the theory

---

[4]   195 F.2d 999 (1st Cir. 1952).

that it is impossible to revoke the trust without prejudice to the interest of the person required to concur in the revocation. Consequently, there is the further problem whether *H*'s power was a power to revoke the trust in whole or in part, or was limited to a power to revoke the trust in its entirety.

The point of the proposed amendment to the gift tax exempting transfers under the gift tax as long as they remain subject to the estate tax is that it would eliminate these problems. A transfer is taxable under the estate tax as long as it may be altered or revoked by the transferor either alone or in conjunction with any other person including a person possessing a substantial adverse interest. If, therefore, transfers taxable under the estate tax were exempted from the gift tax, revocable transfers would not be taxed under the gift tax and these problems would not arise.

* * *

POSSIBLE OBJECTIONS TO THE PROPOSED AMENDMENT

If the purpose of the gift tax is to prevent avoidance of the estate tax by taxing inter vivos transfers that might be used to get property out of the taxable estate, it seems obvious that there is no reason to subject a transfer to the gift tax as long as it remains subject to the estate tax. * * *

* * *

A MORE DETAILED LOOK AT THE PROPOSED AMENDMENT

The actual mechanics of the proposed amendment to the gift tax would be very simple. It would specify that the transfers taxable under sections 2036, 2038, 2039, 2040, 2041, and 2042 of the estate tax would be exempt from the gift tax as long as they remained subject to the estate tax. Section 2036 taxes transfers with a reservation of life interest. Section 2038 taxes revocable transfers; section 2039 certain survivor benefits; section 2040 jointly held property; section 2041 powers of appointment; and section 2042 life insurance.

* * *

The projected amendment * * * fails to exempt a transfer taking effect at death, which is taxable under section 2037 of the estate tax, from the gift tax. The reason [is] that in many cases it is impossible to tell whether a transfer will be taxed as a transfer taking effect at death when the transfer is made. Two elements are required for a transfer taking effect at death: the possession or enjoyment of the transferee must be dependent upon surviving the transferor. In addition, the transferor must have retained a reversionary interest in the transferred property, which immediately before his death was worth more than five per cent of the value of the transferred property. Due to the fact that the valuation and comparison of the reversionary interest and the transferred property must be made at the transferor's death in order to determine whether the five per cent requirement has been complied with, it is impossible in many cases to tell whether a transfer will be taxed as a transfer taking effect at death until the transferor's death. This seems to make it desirable to tax the transfer initially under the gift tax and then refund the gift tax if the transfer is later taxed under the estate tax, and include the refund in the transferor's taxable estate. * * *

There is an alternative solution for the problem of exempting transfers taking effect at death from the gift tax, which seems preferable, although it involves amending the definition of a transfer taking effect at death. The requirement of a reversionary interest in connection with a transfer taking effect at death is easier to justify on historical grounds than it is as a matter of logic and policy. The 1949 Technical Changes Act dispensed with the reversionary interest for a transfer taking effect at death, and defined such a transfer as a transfer where the transferee's possession or enjoyment was dependent upon surviving the transferor. This makes a good deal of sense if the reason for taxing the transfer is the fact that possession or enjoyment of the transferred property is held in suspense until the transferor's death. If this is the real justification for the tax, it is difficult to see that anything beyond a difficult problem of valuation is added by requiring a reversionary interest worth more than five per cent of the value of the transferred property in addition to survivorship for a transfer taking effect at death. If the tax is based upon ownership of the reversionary interest it would appear that the tax should be limited to the value of the reversionary interest. Regardless of the wisdom of redefining a transfer taking effect at death solely in terms of survivorship, if this were done, then it would be possible to tell whether a transfer was or was not a transfer taking effect at death at the time the transfer was made. Consequently, transfers taking effect at death could be exempted from the gift tax as long as they remained subject to the estate tax.

* * *

Under the proposed amendment the exemption from the gift tax would be limited to the period that the transfer remained subject to the estate tax. This is necessary to prevent a transfer from escaping both taxes. For example, if A transferred property to T in trust for C for life, remainder to D, and retained the power to revoke the trust, the transfer would not be taxable under the gift tax. If, however, A were later to release his power to revoke the trust he would make a taxable gift at that time.[20] Otherwise, A could avoid both the estate and gift taxes by creating a revocable trust and later divesting himself of the power to revoke the trust in a fashion that would not incur the estate tax. In this connection it is also pertinent to note that there might be a taxable gift when income from a transfer exempted from the gift tax because it was taxable under the estate tax was paid over to the donee entitled to the income. For example, when the trustee in the hypothetical example earlier in this paragraph paid over the income from the trust to C before A released his power to revoke the trust, there would be a taxable gift of the income from A to C. After A released his power to revoke the trust and the income passed beyond his control, any further income payments would not, of course, constitute taxable gifts.

The principal advantage of amending the gift tax to exempt transfers from the gift tax as long as they remain subject to the estate tax is that this would eliminate a number of the problems that arise in administering the tax and determining when there has been a taxable transfer. This becomes apparent from a brief examination of the effect of the proposed amendment on the various inter vivos transfers taxed under the estate tax that would be exempted from the gift tax.

Transfers with a reservation of a life interest or retention of a power to designate the income from, or possession and enjoyment of, the transferred property, which are taxed under section 2036, would no longer be taxable under the gift tax as long as they remained subject to the estate tax. This would mean that when a man gave away property in which he retained a life estate, it would not be necessary to value the remainder he parted with in order to determine the amount of the gift. In the case of a transfer in which the transferor retained the power, either alone or in conjunction with any other person, to designate the income from, or the possession or enjoyment of, the transferred property during his life, there is at the present time the possibility of a taxable gift not only of the remainder after the grantor's death, but of the intervening estate, if he can exercise his power only in conjunction with an adverse interest. For example,

---

[20] This is, of course, what happens at the present time, since the creation of a trust that the grantor can revoke without the concurrence of a substantial adverse interest is an incomplete transfer that is not taxed under the gift tax, until it is completed by termination of the power of revocation. * * * Under the proposed amendment, however, even the creation of a trust that the grantor could only terminate with the concurrence of a substantial adverse interest would be an incomplete transfer that would not be taxable under the gift tax. The inter vivos release of the power of revocation would, however, be a taxable gift.

suppose that *A* transfers property to *T* in trust to pay the income to *B* for life, then to *C* for life, and upon the death of the survivor of *B* and *C* to distribute the trust property to *D* in fee, and retains power to alter the income beneficiaries of the trust with *C*'s consent. *A* has made a gift of the remainder. The extent to which he has made a taxable gift of the income interests depends upon the substantial adverse interest factors that determined whether there was a taxable gift in the revocable trust situation discussed at the outset of this article. By correlating the gift tax with the estate tax on transfers taxable under section 2036, all of these problems can be eliminated since there will be no gift tax as long as the transfer remains subject to the estate tax.

The gift tax problems connected with revocable transfers were noted at the beginning of this discussion, when it was pointed out that these problems could be eliminated if the gift tax were amended to exempt transfers taxable under the estate tax. To provide a completely satisfactory solution for the taxation of revocable transfers, however, a further amendment should be made to the estate tax definition of a revocable transfer. At the present time a revocable transfer is defined by section 2038 of the estate tax as a transfer where, at his death, the transferor possesses power to alter, amend, revoke, or terminate the possession or enjoyment of the transferred property, either alone or in conjunction with some other person. This definition should be amended to define a revocable transfer as one revocable by any person. There is no substantial difference between a trust that the grantor can revoke with the consent of another person and a trust revocable by the other person alone. In both cases the grantor has control over his own actions and revocation of the trust is dependent upon the will of the other person alone. There is only a verbal difference, for example, between a trust that the grantor can revoke with the consent of the trustee and a trust revocable by the trustee alone. Many commentators have pointed out the absurdity of taxing a trust that can be revoked by the grantor only with the consent of a beneficiary of the trust, and exempting a trust revocable by a trustee, or a person lacking any adverse interest in the trust, alone. The income tax defines a revocable trust in terms of a trust revocable by the grantor or a nonadverse party or both. A similar definition should be written into the estate tax, except, of course, since the estate tax imposes a tax upon a trust revocable by the grantor with the consent of an adverse party, the estate tax should be extended to trusts revocable by any person, including those possessing a substantial adverse interest in the trust property.

Redefining revocable transfers under the estate tax to include transfers revocable by anyone will not only improve the estate tax, it will have a valuable side effect in connection with the proposed amendment to exempt transfers taxable under the estate tax from the gift tax. At the present time one of the most confused areas of the gift tax is the taxability of a transfer revocable by one other than the transferor. For example, suppose that *A* transfers property to *T* in trust to pay the income to *B* for life, remainder to *C* and empowers *T* to invade the trust property in his discretion for the benefit of *A*. Has *A* made a taxable gift? * * * If there is no taxable gift here, it would seem that the cases holding that this is a complete transfer immune from the estate tax will have to be reexamined. Although the estate and gift taxes are not mutually exclusive and the same transfer may be taxed under both taxes, they certainly should be mutually inclusive; it should not be possible to avoid both taxes, but a transfer that is not taxed under one tax should be taxed under the other. It is almost inconceivable that if a transfer revocable by one other than the transferor is not going to be taxed under the gift tax, it will long continue to be immune from the estate tax. By amending the definition of a revocable transfer to include transfers revocable by one other than the transferor and adopting the proposal to exempt transfers from the gift tax as long as they remain subject to the estate tax we can clear up all of these problems. Transfers revocable by anyone will be subject to the estate tax. They will not be taxed under the gift tax as long as they remain subject to the estate tax. At the present time section 2036(a)(2) taxes a retained power to designate the possession or enjoyment of transferred property as long as the power is vested in the transferor alone, or in the transferor in conjunction with some other person. Presumably, it would be desirable to conform section 2036(a)(2) with section 2038 by eliminating the requirement that the power must be "retained," and extending the tax under section 2036(a)(2) to a power vested in any person.

* * *

NOTE

Does Lowndes' proposal completely eliminate the possibility of double taxation? Is it possible to do so without opening opportunities for avoidance through transfers with retained interests or powers?

U.S. Treasury Department, Tax Reform Studies and Proposals, 91st Cong., 1st Sess. (1969)

COMPLEXITY UNDER PRESENT LAW

The lower rates applicable to lifetime transfers create an incentive to make what essentially amount to testamentary transfers in forms which are intended to appear as lifetime transfers. The separation of the gift tax has thus necessitated the creation of elaborate rules for determining which tax should apply to situations in which a donor transfers property during his lifetime but retains until death some interest in it or some opportunity to recover it. As a consequence, under the present dual transfer tax system complexity and controversy often prevail. Slight differences in the form of lifetime transfers often lead to substantial differences in the amount of tax which must be paid.

In general, under present rules, a lifetime transfer under which the transferor retains sufficient beneficial enjoyment of, or control over, the property transferred is treated for transfer tax purposes as an incompleted transfer. For example, assume A transfers securities in trust for B, but A retains the right to receive the dividends for the rest of his life, or A transfers in trust for the benefit of B, but A retains the right to retake the property for himself or retransfer it to some third person. If such a transfer remains incomplete (i.e., the transferor still retains beneficial enjoyment or control) at the death of the transferor, the property is included in his gross estate subject to estate tax. However, any gift tax which was paid at the time of the purported lifetime transfer is allowed as a credit against the estate tax liability, and is itself excluded from the gross estate for estate tax purposes. The general policy underlying these rules of present law is known as the "hard-to-complete-gift" rule.

UNIFIED TRANSFER TAX

To eliminate the distinction in tax treatment between lifetime and deathtime transfers, it is recommended that the estate and gift taxes be combined into a single [unified] transfer tax. Under this system a single exemption and a single rate schedule would be made applicable to the total wealth subject to transfer taxation. The same rate schedule would apply to both lifetime and deathtime transfers. Thus, the transfer tax liability upon death would be directly related to the total amount of wealth transferred during lifetime. The exemption and the rate bracket applicable to transfers at death would be based, respectively, upon the extent to which the overall exemption was absorbed by lifetime gifts and on the rate bracket attained upon lifetime transfers. * * *

In addition to eliminating the dual rate base, the unified transfer tax would further equate lifetime and deathtime transfers by providing rules for computing the tax on lifetime transfers so that, in effect, the tax is paid out of the property transferred, as is the case with transfers at death. Thus, the proposal provides for computation of the tax on lifetime transfers by valuing the gift ("grossing-up" the gift) so as to include the amount of the tax within the amount of the gift upon which the tax is computed. A simplified table would be available to compute the grossed-up transfer, so that taxpayers would not be burdened by complex calculations.

* * *

Taxable and Nontaxable Transfers—In General

Under the unified transfer tax the complexity of present law will be largely eliminated and it will be possible to shift to an "easy-to-make-a-complete-gift" rule as compared with the "hard-to-complete-gift" rule under present law described above. This is so because under the unified transfer tax the overall tax cost of transfers will be approximately the same regardless of whether they are made during lifetime or at death. Since the excessive advantages under present law for lifetime gifts would be eliminated, the tax avoidance possibilities in attempting to have an incomplete transfer qualify as a completed lifetime gift would also be eliminated. Thus, transfers which under present law are not sufficient to remove the subject property from the transferor's estate, may be treated as completed transfers under the unified transfer tax.

Under the unified transfer tax, transfers, whether during lifetime or at death, which are subject to a tax at the time of the initial transfer are referred to as "included transfers." Those dispositions which are not taxable events at the time of the initial transfer are referred to as "excluded transfers." The treatment of the significant types of included and excluded transfers is summarized below. The tax is imposed upon the aggregate amount of lifetime transfers in each year; at death the tax is levied against the aggregate amount of transfers at death plus any transfers made during the calendar year of death. In all cases the rate of tax would be determined by cumulating the current transfers with transfers made in prior years.

* * *

Transfers with Current Beneficial Enjoyment Retained

Under present law, an irrevocable transfer under which the transferor retains the right to current beneficial enjoyment for some limited period of time, such as his life, is treated as a transfer of a future interest which may be subjected to a gift tax. If the transferor still has the right to the current beneficial enjoyment when he dies, the full value of the property in which his retained interest existed is includable in his gross estate for estate tax purposes, with a credit allowed against the estate tax for the gift tax previously paid.

The unified transfer tax would simplify existing law by providing that a tax would be imposed only once, when the current beneficial enjoyment terminates. Thus, a transfer under which the transferor retains the current beneficial enjoyment is treated as an excluded transfer. The situation is viewed as if there had been no transfer at all; the transfer, in effect, does not take place until the current beneficial enjoyment terminates by death, lapse of time, transfer, or the occurrence of some contingency. If, however, the transferor wishes to pay the tax at the time of the initial transfer on the basis of the then value of the property he may elect to do so and the property would not again be subject to tax upon the termination of current beneficial enjoyment.

Example.—If *A* transfers certain property in trust to pay the income to *A* for his life, then the principal to *B*, the transfer would be an excluded transfer since *A* has retained beneficial enjoyment. When *A* dies there is an included transfer from *A* to *B*, the property being valued as of *A*'s death. However, *A* may elect to have the initial transfer in trust treated as an included transfer. If such an election were made there would not be an included transfer upon *A*'s death. * * *

Transfers with Reversionary Interest Retained

Under present law, some transfers under which the transferor retains a reversionary interest are not treated as completed transfers. At the time such a transfer is made a gift tax is imposed upon the value of the entire property reduced by the value of the transferor's reversionary interest. If, at the time of death, the value of the reversionary interest exceeds 5 percent of the value of the property and beneficial enjoyment of the property is conditioned upon survival of the decedent, the entire value of the property at death is included in the decedent's gross estate with a credit allowed for the gift tax previously paid.

Under the unified transfer tax the treatment of transfers with retained reversionary interests is greatly simplified. If the reversionary interest is a contingent interest (i.e., the property will revert back to the transferor only if some contingency is satisfied) then the full value of the property will be taxed as an included transfer at the time of transfer. If the reversionary interest is not contingent but the property is certain to revert at some future date, then only the interests which precede the retained reversionary interest will be treated as included transfers. The reversionary interest and any interest which may follow it will be excluded transfers at the time of the initial conveyance.

Example 1.—*A* makes a transfer in trust, the income to be paid to *B* for *B*'s life, then if *A* survives *B*, to *A* for *A*'s life, then the principal to go to *C*. If *A* dies before *B*, the beneficial enjoyment (i.e., the income) from the property will not revert to *A*. Thus, *A*'s reversionary interest is a contingent interest, and the entire amount of the property transferred by *A* is an included transfer.

Example 2.—*A* transfers property in trust, the income to be paid to *B* for 10 years, then the principal to revert back to *A* and his heirs. Since the property is certain to revert back to *A* (or to his heirs if he should die) after 10 years (i.e., there is no contingency), only the 10-year interest in *B* is taxed as an included transfer at the time of the initial transfer.

Transfers with Power of Appointment Retained

Under the unified transfer tax a transfer with power of appointment retained will be a completed gift (i.e., an included transfer) except to the extent that the transferor will be certain to be treated as the owner of the transferred property (under the rules described above) when the power is exercised, released, allowed to lapse, or terminated. Many lifetime transfers that are not completed ones under present law would be completed ones under this proposal. For example, under present law a transfer under which the transferor retains the power to designate who may enjoy the benefits of the transfer, even though he cannot benefit himself by any exercise of the power, is not a completed gift for Federal gift tax purposes. This change can be made under a unified tax system because treating such lifetime transfers as completed ones does not permit any significant tax avoidance.

* * *

NOTE

Are there situations in which an overlap between the estate and gift taxes might reasonably be tolerable, or even desirable, in an integrated system? Consider how the ALI and Treasury proposals would deal with such an overlap (e.g., a reversionary interest subject to a condition which may or does in fact occur). Also, consider how the respective proposals would deal with discretionary trusts and with retained powers that are disregarded under current law (e.g., powers exercisable solely by a third party or subject to an ascertainable standard).

Opponents of the Treasury's proposals argued that preferential gift tax rates were necessary to encourage lifetime gifts. In response, Jerome Kurtz and Stanley S. Surrey challenge the premise that such tax incentives are necessary or desirable. For subsequent discussion of the differential estate and gift tax rates, see the articles by Harry L. Gutman and Paul B. Stephan III in Subpart B, *infra*.

Jerome Kurtz & Stanley S. Surrey, *Reform of Death and Gift Taxes: The 1969 Treasury Proposals, the Criticisms, and a Rebuttal*, 70 COLUM. L. REV. 1365 (1970)*

* * *

I. THE ESTATE AND GIFT TAXES

* * *

B. The Existing System

* * *

3. *Lifetime Gifts.* * * * [T]he existing estate and gift tax system * * * favors lifetime gifts over testamentary dispositions. * * * [T]he existing system provides this favoritism in an irrational and inequitable manner.

The existing favoritism is a result of three separate factors. First, the existing gift tax is calculated from a separate rate schedule distinct from the rate schedule applicable to the estate tax. Second, the gift tax rates are lower than the estate tax rates. And third, the tax base is different. * * *

Since the taxation of gifts is based on a rate schedule completely separate from the estate tax rate schedule, total wealth transfers by an individual may be divided between lifetime transfers and testamentary transfers with each type of transfer taxed independently on a schedule beginning at the lowest rates. The aggregate transfers made by an individual can thus be split between two rate schedules and therefore taxed at rates unrelated to the individual's total transfers of wealth. The total tax will depend on how much of the total amount transferred is subject to the gift tax and how much is subject to the estate tax. * * *

The second, and perhaps most obvious factor favoring lifetime gifts over death transfers is that the gift tax rates are 25% lower than the estate tax rates in each bracket. * * *

The third factor favoring lifetime gifts is that the tax bases for the estate and gift taxes are different. This factor is somewhat more subtle in its operation and therefore is frequently overlooked, but for the very wealthy it provides the most significant saving for lifetime gifts. The base to which the estate tax is applied is the aggregate property owned by the decedent before diminution by that tax, whereas the base for the gift tax is the net amount transferred to the donee. * * *

* * * Where the tax bracket of the transferor is very high, the fact that the gift tax itself is not included in the base makes an enormous difference. Because the tax rates themselves increase as the size of the transfers increase, the failure to include the tax in the base, i.e., the failure to "gross up," is of increasing advantage as the amount of a transferor's assets increases. * * *

---

*   This article originally appeared at 70 COLUM. L. REV. 1365 (1970). Reprinted by permission.

* * *

III. OBJECTIONS TO THE PROPOSALS

* * *

B. Effect on Lifetime Gifts

One of the most frequently voiced criticisms of the Treasury proposals is that the unification of the estate and gift taxes into a single transfer tax system would discourage lifetime gifts. The major premise of this argument, in some cases specifically stated and in some cases simply assumed, is that there is something worthwhile about lifetime gifts, that tax incentives are needed to offset the natural reluctance to make such gifts, and that the tax incentives provided under the existing system are desirable.

* * *

* * * Even if one admits that lifetime gifts ought to be encouraged—and this question will be discussed later—there are certainly more equitable ways of providing this encouragement than the way the existing system does it. No one has yet come forward to justify a system that encourages gifts by very wealthy donors by granting them tax reductions many times greater than those granted to the less wealthy. If the making of gifts is a socially desirable act to be encouraged as a matter of federal tax policy—a premise open to substantial question—then it seems that it should be encouraged to the same extent for all. The arguments of the critics, however, seem to be that the existing system encourages gifts, and the proposed changes do not; therefore, the proposed changes are bad. A more constructive approach, assuming the premise that encouragement is desirable, would be to argue that the existing system does encourage them but in an inequitable way, while the proposed revisions eliminate all encouragement; therefore, we should try to design a system which encourages gifts in an equitable way and to a fair extent.

The only way to provide for an equitable encouragement of gifts is to adopt a unified transfer tax system with gross-up for lifetime transfers and then allow some percentage discount in the rate applicable to gifts as compared to death transfers. The amount of the discount would depend on how much encouragement to lifetime gifts was thought desirable.

The argument usually advanced to support tax incentives for lifetime gifts is that it is to the advantage of the government to have property moved into younger hands, for the young will tend to be more venturesome with such capital and thus improve the economic climate by increasing the mobility and risk-taking capacity of that capital. More persuasive, however, is the counterargument that the Government is not appropriately concerned with the rate of transfer of wealth from parents to children and should leave such matters to family decision, or at least that it is not so concerned as to provide tax incentives to affect whatever may be a family's natural inclinations in such matters. In any event, whether the consequence above asserted for lifetime gifts is true or not in a particular case at least depends to a large extent on the subject matter of the gift and on its form. Most lifetime gifts are of marketable securities placed in trust, and they are made at a time when the donor is quite elderly. A gift to a trust extending for a long period of time seems little different in terms of economic mobility and risk-taking than continued ownership by the donor. The beneficial donee in this case does not have control of the property and its management is likely to be at least as conservative as it was in the hands of the donor. If one is in favor of encouraging lifetime gifts, it would surely be worth analyzing just what kinds of gifts are to be encouraged. Perhaps outright gifts are more to be encouraged than gifts in trust.

To say that the existing system is preferable to the proposed revisions because it encourages lifetime gifts and the proposal does not is thus to ignore both the basic problems at which the revisions are aimed and the questions which must be explored in a consideration of whether the tax system should be deliberately structured so that it operates in a nonneutral way to encourage lifetime gifts. In this regard, it is difficult to conceive of the Congress adopting a policy of encouraging lifetime gifts through a direct subsidy approach. Suppose, for example, someone were to propose that the federal government pay grants directly to those wealthy parents who make gifts to their children while the parents are alive, with the largest federal grants going to the wealthiest parents. Presumably the suggestion would never seriously be considered as a legislative proposal. Yet that is precisely the effect of the existing estate and gift tax system when the tax savings accorded to lifetime gifts under that system are translated into direct subsidies.

* * *

NOTE

Kurtz and Surrey criticize the incentives under the transfer tax system for lifetime gifts rather than bequests. Should their analysis also consider the role of gifts and bequests under the income tax as well? See the articles by Harry L. Gutman and Paul B. Stephan III excerpted in Subpart B, *infra*.

B. Reforming the "Unified" Tax System

Even after the "unification" of the estate and gift taxes in 1976, tax policy debate continues to focus on persistent disparities between the two taxes. In particular, the disparity between the "tax-inclusive" estate tax base and the "tax-exclusive" gift tax base continues to provide preferential treatment for lifetime gifts. Moreover, in the absence of a consistent timing rule for determining when a transfer becomes complete, a single transfer may be subject to both gift and estate tax. A recurring theme in the following materials involves the interrelationship between the definition of the tax base and the formulation of a uniform completion rule.

One approach to integration, recommended by the Treasury Department in its 1969 proposals and reiterated in a 1984 report, calls for a "gross-up" of the gift tax rates to compensate for the "tax-exclusive" gift tax base, coupled with some form of a uniform completion rule to replace §§ 2036 through 2038. An alternative approach is advanced by Joseph Isenbergh, who proposes that the gross-up be accomplished at death under an expanded version of § 2035 which would apply to gift taxes paid on all lifetime gifts. Theodore S. Sims compares the two approaches, and defends the Treasury's approach on grounds of simplicity and neutrality.

Under a fully integrated tax system, a transfer should normally be subject either to gift tax or to estate tax, but not to both. Thus, any proposal to integrate the estate and gift taxes raises a fundamental question of timing: What difference does it make whether an integrated transfer tax is imposed during life or at death? Alvin C. Warren, Jr., demonstrates that, if certain assumptions are met, the timing of the tax does not affect its present value.

In his comment on the ABA Tax Section Task Force's 1988 Report on Transfer Tax Restructuring, Harry L. Gutman builds on Warren's insight and points out that the choice between a uniform "easy to complete" or "hard to complete" rule, if not distorted by a systematic preference for lifetime gifts, should turn primarily on considerations of convenience and administrability. Gutman is especially critical of the ABA Task Force for accepting the continuing preference for gifts. In his comment on transfer tax reform, however, Paul B. Stephan III points out that a preference for lifetime gifts can be accommodated (if deemed desirable) in a unified system, as a means of offsetting the entrenched preference for deathtime transfers under the income tax. Finally, Joseph M. Dodge endorses a hard-to-complete rule, primarily on the ground that this will promote more accurate valuation of transferred and retained interests than the existing rules.

Note that all of the above proposals were advanced before the enactment of the special valuation rules of §§ 2701 and 2702 (discussed in Part V(B), *supra*). Consider the impact of those rules on prospects for further integration.

U.S. TREASURY DEPARTMENT, TAX REFORM FOR FAIRNESS, SIMPLICITY, AND ECONOMIC GROWTH, REPORT TO THE PRESIDENT (1984)

* * *

Current Law

In General. Under current law, the estate tax and the gift tax (referred to collectively as transfer taxes) are imposed using the same graduated rate structure. Under this unified rate structure, the marginal transfer tax rate applicable to any taxable transfer is determined by taking into account all prior transfers, whether made during lifetime or at death. * * *

* * *

Although imposed at the same nominal rate as the estate tax, the gift tax is not imposed on the same tax base as the estate tax. The estate tax is imposed on the entire amount of the taxable estate, with no deduction or exclusion from the base for the portion of the estate that goes to pay the tax. Because the estate tax base includes the amount used to pay the tax, the estate tax is said to be imposed on a "tax-inclusive" basis. In contrast, the gift tax is imposed on a "tax-exclusive" basis (i.e., only the amount of property that actually passes to the donee is subject to tax). * * *

* * *

Completion of Gift. Present law contains a complex set of rules governing when a transfer is complete for purposes of applying the gift tax. In general, these rules provide that a gift will not be complete unless the donor has so parted with dominion and control over the property that he or she no longer possesses any power to change its disposition, whether for the donor or another.

Transfers within three years of death. Any gift tax paid with respect to a gift made within three years of a decedent's death will be included in the decedent's gross estate for Federal estate tax purposes. In the case of a transfer by the decedent of the incidents of ownership of a life insurance policy on the life of the decedent within three years of death, the amount includible in the decedent's estate will be the proceeds of the policy rather than its value at the time of the gift. In effect, these rules cause any taxable gifts made within three years of the donor's death to be subject to tax on a tax-inclusive basis, as if the property had been retained by the donor until his death (although post-gift appreciation is not brought back into the donor's gross estate).

The Retained Interest Rules. Because of the preferential tax treatment afforded to transfers by gift, the role of the gift tax as a backstop to the estate tax can be fully realized only if rules exist that prevent the structuring of a testamentary transfer in a form that qualifies such transfer for gift tax treatment. When applicable, the retained interest rules require the full date-of-death value of the transferred property (offset by any consideration received by the decedent on the initial transfer) to be included in the donor's estate. Such value will thus be subject to tax on a tax-inclusive basis, although a credit is given for any gift tax paid at the time of the original conveyance of the property. The most important of these rules are described briefly in the following paragraphs.

Transfers with retained beneficial enjoyment. There must be included in a decedent's gross estate the date-of-death value of any property transferred during his lifetime by gift if the decedent retained for his lifetime possession or enjoyment of the property or the right to the income from the property. This estate tax rule applies even though the decedent reported the underlying transfer as a taxable gift and paid a gift tax on all or a portion of the value of the property.

Transfers with retained control. A decedent's gross estate includes the fair market value of property previously transferred by gift where the decedent has retained for his lifetime "the right . . . to designate the persons who shall possess or enjoy the property or the income therefrom," or "a power . . . to alter, amend, revoke or terminate" the transfer. As a practical matter, these two inclusion rules often provide overlapping coverage.

The premise of these two provisions is that the power to determine the ultimate recipient of the property, or to control the time or manner of enjoyment of the property by the recipient, is a sufficient ownership interest in the property to cause it to be treated as if owned by the transferor. Thus, these provisions can apply even though the retained power did not give the decedent the power to revoke the transfer or otherwise to revest title in himself.

Reversionary interests. Also included in the decedent's gross estate is the value of any interest in property with respect to which the decedent has previously made a transfer and has retained a proscribed reversionary interest. This rule applies only if the value of the decedent's reversionary interest immediately before the death of the decedent exceeds five percent of the value of the property.

Reasons for Change

Notwithstanding the policies supporting full unification of the estate and gift taxes significant tax incentives remain for individuals to make lifetime gifts. Arguably, some of these tax advantages are justifiable because of practical considerations. * * * The application of the same progressive rate schedule to all transfers, without adjustment for post-transfer appreciation in the value of the property, may * * * be justified because of simplicity and because a lifetime transfer deprives the donor of the use of the property and the use of any money used to pay gift tax on the transfer.

On the other hand, some of the advantages of lifetime gifts cannot be justified either on grounds of tax policy or administrative convenience. Specifically, neither tax policy concerns nor administrative convenience support application of the gift tax on a tax-exclusive basis while the estate tax is computed on a tax-inclusive basis. Such a rule hampers the overall fairness of the transfer tax system because the individuals it benefits are those who can afford to give away a significant portion of their property during life. Those individuals who are unable or unwilling to make lifetime gifts, and who therefore retain their property until death, are subject to tax at a higher effective rate.

In addition, the preferential treatment accorded lifetime gifts encourages individuals to make lifetime transfers solely to reduce their overall transfer tax burden. The transfer tax system should not treat an individual wishing to retain his or her property until death either more or less favorably than it treats an individual wishing to make lifetime gifts.

Finally, the preference given lifetime gifts has resulted in a complex and often arbitrary set of rules that attempt, with uneven results, to prevent taxpayers from taking unintended advantage of the preference. In some cases, these rules do not fully remove the preference given to lifetime gifts; in others, the rules are punitive and cause transfer tax consequences that are more severe than if the individual had not made a lifetime gift.

Proposal

Unification of Gift and Estate Taxes

The gift tax would be computed on a tax-inclusive basis. Under this system, the gift tax payable on a transfer of a fixed net amount to a donee would be determined by calculating the gross amount that, when subject to the transfer tax rate schedule, would be sufficient to pay the gift tax on the transfer and leave the net amount for the donee. Stated differently, the amount of the gift would be "grossed up" by the amount of the gift tax payable with respect to the transfer. The tax imposed on a decedent's estate would be computed by adding the amount of the decedent's taxable estate to the sum of the decedent's adjusted taxable gifts and the gift tax paid by the decedent.

In order to prevent taxpayers from having to make somewhat complicated gross-up calculations, the gross-up factor would be built into the rate table contained in the statute. Under this method, the stated rate applicable to gifts would be higher than the stated rate applicable to estates, but the effective rate imposed on a net transfer would be the same regardless of whether subject to the gift tax or the estate tax. * * *

* * *

Simplification of Rules Pertaining to Completed Gifts and Testamentary Strings

Application of the gift tax on a tax-inclusive basis would eliminate the major disparity between the transfer tax treatment of lifetime gifts and transfers at death. Therefore, it would be possible to eliminate the rule requiring inclusion in the gross estate of gift taxes paid on transfers made within three years of death. The complex retained interest rules would be replaced with a simpler set of rules determining when a transfer of less than an entire interest constitutes a completed gift for Federal transfer tax purposes. These new rules would ensure that a transfer is subject to gift or estate tax but not to both taxes. * * *

Retained beneficial enjoyment. The proposal would simplify present law by providing that a transfer tax would be imposed only once when the beneficial enjoyment retained by the donor terminates. Thus, if a donor makes a gift of a remainder interest in property, but retains the intervening income interest, no gift would occur until the termination of the donor's income interest. At that time, the property would be subject to gift or estate tax at its full fair market value. Because the transferor would be treated as the owner of the property during the interim, any distributions made to beneficiaries other than the transferor would be treated as transfers when made.

The transferor would continue to be treated as owner of the property for all transfer tax purposes. Such treatment would foreclose any opportunity for tax avoidance through the transferor's repurchase of the remainder interest free of gift tax.

* * *

Revocable transfers. The rules of present law would continue with respect to any transfer where the transferor retains the right to regain possession or enjoyment of the property. Such a transfer would be treated as incomplete for gift and estate tax purposes, and would be treated as complete only when the transferor's retained right or power to revoke terminates. Distributions from the property to beneficiaries other than the donor would be treated as gifts when made * * * .

Retained powers. In determining whether a gift is complete for transfer tax purposes, the proposal would treat a retained power to control the beneficial enjoyment of the transferred property as irrelevant where the power could not be used to distribute income or principal to the donor. Thus, the fact that the transferor as trustee or custodian can exercise control over the identity of the distributee of the property or over the amount or timing of a distribution would be irrelevant in determining whether a gift is complete (although such factors may be relevant in determining whether the transfer qualifies for the annual gift tax exclusion). Under this rule, a transfer would be complete for gift tax purposes where the grantor creates an irrevocable trust but retains the absolute right to determine who (other than himself) will receive the trust income or principal.

Reversionary interests. Current rules regarding retained reversionary interests would be replaced by a rule that disregards reversionary interests retained by the grantor in valuing transferred property for Federal gift tax purposes. The existence of the reversionary interest would be relevant only for purposes of determining the timing of the transfer for estate and gift tax purposes.

If the donor makes a gift of property for a term of years or for the life of one or more beneficiaries, and if the donor retains a reversionary interest that is more likely than not to return the property to the donor or his or her estate, the transfer would be treated as incomplete. Interim distributions of income or principal (or the value of the use of the property) would be treated as gifts by the donor on an annual basis. On the other hand, if it is more likely than not that the reversionary interest will not return the property to the donor or his or her estate, the transfer will be treated as complete and the full fair market value of the property will be subject to gift tax, without reduction for the actuarial value of the reversionary interest. If the donor dies with the reversion outstanding, the value of the reversionary interest will be excluded from the donor's estate, whether or not the reversion terminates at that time. If the property reverts to the donor prior to his or her death, the donor would have the right to retransfer the property at any time free from additional gift tax liability. If not retransferred during the donor's lifetime, the property would be excluded from the donor's estate. In order to prevent disputes arising from the reversion and subsequent retransfer of fungible assets, however, the proposal would require the donor to place the reverted property in a segregated account in order to benefit from the exclusion.

The determination of whether a reversionary interest is more likely than not to return property to the donor during his lifetime generally would depend on the life expectancy of the donor and the anticipated duration of the intervening interest. For example, a reversion following a term of years less than the donor's life expectancy or following the life of a beneficiary older than the donor would be more likely than not to return the property to the donor. Similar actuarial determinations would be made for multiple intervening income beneficiaries. * * *

* * *

Analysis

Application of the gift tax on a tax-inclusive basis would remove the primary tax incentive for lifetime gifts and therefore would make tax considerations a relatively neutral factor in the decision whether to dispose of property during one's lifetime or to retain it until death. However, the proposal would provide greater fairness in the application of the transfer tax system because all persons paying the transfer tax would do so on the same tax-inclusive basis. Finally, by removing the major incentive for disguising testamentary transfers as lifetime gifts, the proposal would permit the simplification of the rules governing when a transfer is complete for estate and gift tax purposes.

The proposed rules for determining when a transfer is complete would ensure that each transfer is subject to estate or gift tax, but not to both taxes. By delaying the imposition of transfer tax liability until the donor's interest terminates, the proposed rules would reduce the number of instances in which it is necessary to consult an actuarial table to value the transfer of a partial interest in property and would provide greater accuracy in the valuation of the transferred interest.

* * *

NOTE

Compare the approach outlined above with the Treasury's 1969 proposals. Has the Treasury's position evolved in light of the 1976 "unification" of the estate and gift taxes?

Joseph Isenbergh, *Simplifying Retained Life Interests, Revocable Transfers, and the Marital Deduction,* 51 U. CHI. L. REV. 1 (1984)*

Sections 2036, 2037, and 2038 of the Internal Revenue Code contain several long-standing rules of estate taxation designed to preserve the taxable estate from erosion. Section 2036(a)(1) pulls back into the taxable estate the value of property transferred before death subject to a retained life interest, thus exposing to taxation interests in property that would otherwise expire with the decedent. The apparent theory of this rule is that one who has enjoyed property for life and has controlled its subsequent disposition ought to be treated at death as its owner. Section 2037 returns to the estate transfers taking effect at death in which the decedent had a reversionary interest. Sections 2036(a)(2) and 2038 reach transfers subject to revocation, amendment, or other control by the transferor.

* * *

* * * Though justified under earlier forms of the transfer tax laws, [these rules] are now little more than sources of unnecessary complexity and could therefore be repealed without creating substantial new possibilities of tax avoidance. In addition, to offset the greater attractiveness of certain lifetime gifts that might result, the transfer tax base should be enlarged to include in the estate all gift taxes paid during life. * * *

I. RETAINED LIFE ESTATES

* * *

If gift tax rates and estate tax rates were flat and identical, there would be no tax advantage (assuming proper valuations and no differences between the estate tax and gift tax bases) to the transfer of remainders with retained life interests, even without any special rule governing this pattern.[21] * * *

* * *

The source of the tax advantage offered by the transfer of a remainder is twofold. First, there is a "bracket effect." The present gift of a remainder (a future interest) makes use of the lower graduated brackets. When the remainder is valued by being discounted back to the present, there is a foreshortening of its future nominal value (of $5 million) to a present value of $2.5 million. These two values are equivalent in present terms, but the taxes on the future and the present amounts are not. The future tax on the high bracket portion of the future transfer (i.e., the amount above $2.5 million) is itself not discounted back to present value to determine the present tax. Rather, a present tax is determined based on lower bracket amounts. * * *

Second, there is a "tax base" effect. Under present law, the gift tax and the estate tax are each imposed on a different tax base. The amount of a taxable gift does not include the gift tax itself, which is paid by the donor as a percentage of the net amount received by the donee. By contrast, the estate tax base does include the estate tax: the tax comes out of the amount of the taxable estate itself. The exclusion of the gift tax from the gift tax base means that gifts are taxed at a lower effective rate, despite the "unified" rate schedule for gifts and transfers at death adopted in 1976. Although this discrepancy was partly remedied by section 2035(c), added to the Code in 1976, gifts made more than three years before death continue to be taxed at a lower effective rate because of the tax base effect.

* * *

Repeal of section 2036(a)(1) [would put] the remainder with retained life interest on the same footing as more cumbersome alternatives * * * . Moreover, the repeal of section 2036(a)(1), even in the absence of other statutory change, would not make the use of retained life interests an automatic choice for taxpayers. The earlier payment of tax would continue to be a potentially costly step, and the reluctance of many to surrender full ownership of their wealth during life would probably not give way to pure tax considerations, especially if these were less than compelling.

If, in addition to the repeal of section 2036(a)(1), the statute were amended to blunt the tax base effect, the tax treatment of retained life interests would be brought more nearly into parity with that of transfers at death. A simple change toward this end, which meshes easily with the repeal of section 2036(a)(1), would be the inclusion of all gift taxes paid during life in the taxable estate. Section 2035(c) already requires such inclusion (or "gross-up") for gift taxes paid on transfers within three years of death. A small change in the language of section 2035(c) would extend this rule to all transfers made during life.

The bracket effect would not be reduced under this regime. While this effect can be considerable in some cases, it is in all events limited, and can never loom large in the transfer of dynastic fortunes. * * *

---

[21]   There might even be a disadvantage in transferring a remainder if the discount rate applied in valuing the remainder were too low compared with the rate appropriate to measure the time value of the tax payment itself. * * *

Repeal of section 2036(a)(1) and the inclusion of gift taxes paid in the estate, without more, would still leave the problem of "deathbed" transfers. Someone in declining health might transfer remainder interests shortly before death. If these were valued on the assumption of a normal life expectancy (known to the grantor to be unlikely), substantial transfer tax savings could result under the tax regime proposed here. One possible countermeasure would be to value transfers made in the last three years of life as though life expectancy at the time of transfer were zero.[61] Remaining possibilities for manipulation would be slight.

Broader problems of valuation and enforcement could also result from the tax regime proposed here. For example, it might be tempting to transfer future interests during life at highly understated values. The present rule of section 2036(a)(1) "polices" such maneuvers by requiring that the property transferred subject to a retained life interest be included in the taxable estate at its value at the time of death. Without such a rule, the IRS could end up with only one chance—i.e., the lifetime transfer itself—to tax the transfer between generations at an appropriate level.

This potential abuse is simply an aspect of the ubiquitous and largely irreducible problem of valuation of lifetime transfers, an area where taxpayers often have the upper hand.[62] * * *

II. REVOCABLE AND OTHER TRANSFERS

Once gift taxes paid during life are added to the taxable estate, the present statutory treatment of reversions and revocable interests also becomes largely unnecessary. * * *

[Sections 2036(a)(2), 2037 and 2038] of the Code have long and complex histories and their existence largely reflects the absence of any gift tax in the early period of transfer taxes. * * *

If lifetime gifts are taxed at essentially the same rates as transfers at death, taxpayers gain from the deferral of tax on revocable transfers. There is no reason why all transfers of beneficial interests in property including revocable gifts should not be taxed since a revocable gift certainly confers the benefit of the time value of the gift until revocation on its recipient. Exactly how much of a benefit depends on the intention of the grantor. This uncertainty, however, goes to the value of the gift, not to the existence of a gift in the first place. Since the maker of a revocable gift has the key to its value in his own hands, it is entirely reasonable to resolve any uncertainties of valuation against the grantor and to tax revocable and amendable gifts during life at the same value they would have if made unconditionally.

* * *

CONCLUSION

Retained life interests [and] revocable transfers * * * do not permit the avoidance of tax to an extent that justifies either the complexities induced by the rules limiting these devices or the constraints imposed by these rules on otherwise legitimate methods of estate planning. So long as all transfers of value during life and at death are subject to tax at uniform rates, the advantage of reducing the nominal amount of a transfer taking effect in the future by making it now is essentially offset by the necessity of paying a tax today in dollars of more immediate value.

---

[61]   This countermeasure would cause remainders subject to retained life interests transferred during the 3-year period to be included in the unified tax base * * * without discount. The transfer tax consequences would therefore be the same as if the entire amount had remained in the estate at death.

[62]   Taxpayers have the upper hand in such matters of valuation because they can (and do) make transfers of property the value of which may depend on subsequent events within their control or even on their own efforts. * * *

Present law, however, still does not achieve effective uniformity of rates, because the gift tax itself paid on most lifetime transfers escapes taxation. If the transfer tax base were enlarged to include all gift taxes paid during life—a principle already partly in place under section 2035(c)—much of sections 2036, 2037 [and] 2038 * * * could be sent to a well-deserved rest.

NOTE

Isenbergh argues that §§ 2036-2038 would become largely superfluous if all gift taxes paid during life were included in the gross estate. Some commentators, however, believe that such "radical surgery" would "remove some vital organs." W. Leslie Peat & Stephanie J. Willbanks, *A Page of Logic Is Worth a Volume of History: The Treatment of Retained Interests Under the Federal Estate and Gift Tax Statutes*, 8 VA. TAX REV. 639, 672 (1989). What role, if any, remains for §§ 2036-2038 in a unified estate and gift tax system?

Theodore S. Sims, *Timing Under a Unified Wealth Transfer Tax*, 51 U. CHI. L. REV. 34 (1984)*

* * *

I. THE DIFFERENCE BETWEEN GIFT AND ESTATE TAXATION

More lenient taxation of lifetime gifts, even under uniform gift and estate tax rates, arises from a disparity in the tax bases to which those rates are applied. * * *

* * * For convenience, the estate tax base may be described as "tax-inclusive," whereas the gift tax base is "tax-exclusive"; or, as it is sometimes put colloquially, the gift tax does not impose a "tax on the tax." The result is that, for equivalent after-tax transfers, the gift tax base is systematically smaller than the estate tax base. Thus, where nominally identical tax rates apply to apparently equivalent transfers, a lifetime wealth transfer is taxed at a lower effective rate than is a comparable transfer at death.

* * *

II. SOME CONSEQUENCES OF
MORE LENIENT TAXATION OF GIFTS

* * *

The benefits of congressional tolerance of a comparatively lenient gift tax will ineluctably accrue to those willing to make outright gifts. Nevertheless, Congress has remained anxious to confine more lenient taxation to transfers that "truly" are lifetime gifts, and to forestall its extension to what are substitutes for, or in effect are, transfers at death. The resulting tension is manifest in a complex statutory scheme that deters various efforts to capitalize on advantageous taxation of gifts. Indeed, from its very inception, the estate tax has struggled with the treatment of outright gifts apparently motivated by the imminence of death (and of transfer taxation in any event)—so-called "deathbed gifts"—and with the treatment of lifetime gifts "with strings attached."

* * *

For present purposes the important point is that the machinery with which we police the use of "strings attached" lifetime transfers is a principal source, possibly the principal source, of complication in our transfer tax system. Since lifetime wealth transfers can so readily be deployed to achieve what are essentially testamentary objectives, such complications are an inevitable feature of a system that tolerates comparatively lenient taxation of lifetime gifts. Ridding the system of these problems has been a major focus of most studies of transfer tax revision.

* * * [T]o the extent that we continue to tax gifts more leniently than we do estates, that fact alone will (and should) influence the extent to which, as a matter of policy, lifetime gifts are made "difficult" or "easy" to complete for transfer tax purposes, and will affect the degree of complication in the system. Conversely, achieving true neutrality in the taxation of lifetime transfers and transfers at death might allow the choice of rules to be made solely on grounds of administrability, and therefore holds out the possibility of substantial estate tax simplification. * * *

III. METHODS OF ELIMINATING THE DIFFERENCE BETWEEN GIFT AND ESTATE TAXATION

* * *

* * * The [1969] *Treasury Proposals* * * * proposed altering the computation of tax on a lifetime gift, at the time the gift was made, so that it would equal the tax associated with an identical private wealth transfer when made through a decedent's estate. Although not actually set out in the *Treasury Proposals*, the kind of adjustment the Treasury had in mind can readily be specified. For any given nominal tax rate, t, the adjustment consists of dividing by $(1 - t)$ the gift tax value of a gift.[99] The quotient is the "taxable" gift. * * * This approach, which Congress declined to incorporate into the 1976 Act, generally is referred to as "grossing-up" the gift.

* * *

With respect to those lifetime transfers to which it applies, section 2035(c)—like the "gross-up" approach advocated by the Treasury—can operate to equalize the taxation of gifts and estates. * * *

In its existing form, however, section 2035(c) is more limited than the "gross-up" advocated in the *Treasury Proposals*; it applies only to transfers within three years before death. Even where it does apply, moreover, it differs from the *Treasury Proposals* in the matter of timing. The Treasury would have levied a tax-inclusive tax at the time of a gift; the existing system continues to levy a tax-exclusive gift tax, relying on section 2035(c), where it applies, to tax the gift tax at the transferor's death. Putting aside the three-year limitation of existing law, however, it appears that both section 2035(c) and grossed-up taxation of gifts restore the same number of dollars to the transfer tax base. As a consequence, either approach might form the basis for unifying the gift and estate tax bases.

IV. COMPARING THE METHODS OF UNIFYING THE GIFT AND ESTATE TAXES

Given two different ways of achieving a unified gift and estate tax base, is there a principled basis for choosing between the two, assuming Congress should be disposed to legislate in this area? * * * The object of this part of the article is to demonstrate that the approach advo-

---

[99]   Given a taxable estate E and a tax rate t, the estate tax is tE and the estate after tax is $E - tE$, or $E(1 - t)$. For an equivalent after-tax gift of $E(1 - t)$, when taxed at rate t, also to attract tax of tE, it first must be divided by $(1 - t)$. * * *

cated by the Treasury in 1969 is superior to section 2035(c) in achieving neutrality in the taxation of comparable wealth transfers. * * *

[This conclusion] is advanced in the face of a discernible reluctance to tax gifts in the same way that we tax estates, as the approach advocated in the 1969 *Treasury Proposals* would require. In part, this reluctance reflects a general apprehension about discouraging lifetime wealth transfers unduly. This apprehension is fortified by the perception that, when an individual transfers wealth by lifetime gift instead of waiting until death, the resulting acceleration of the transfer tax payment increases the real tax cost of making the transfer. Requiring also that gift taxes be computed in the same way as estate taxes, the argument proceeds, would render the increase in tax cost excessive.

In some sense, this apprehension can be viewed as reflecting a desire to tax lifetime gifts preferentially.[115] If, however, the objective is simply to avoid discrimination against lifetime giving, such concerns are misplaced. In financial terms, a tax paid now undeniably has a higher real cost than a tax of identical amount not payable until sometime in the future. But by the same token, a gift made now is of greater value to the recipient than a transfer of the same amount not made until some later date. A sound comparison of the two must take account of the fact that, in terms of financial value, the earlier gift is effectively larger. Thus, the higher real cost of the tax liability associated with an earlier gift, even when taxed on exactly the same basis as a later gift, simply reflects the transmission of more real value to the recipient.

* * *

Conversely, the process of discounting implies that, expressed in nominal values, a gift made now will be smaller in amount than a financially equivalent transfer at death. Correspondingly, the tax imposed on a present gift should have a lower nominal value than the tax imposed on a financially equivalent transfer at death. * * *

In other words, the mere fact that gift tax payments are made earlier than estate tax payments is not a sound basis for taxing gifts more leniently than estates. Comparisons involving values expressed consistently—either by reducing all transfers and tax payments, whenever made, to present value, or by extending them all to their value as of some future date—are more reliable as a guide to whether consistent taxation has been achieved. Similarly, a comparison of the operation of grossed-up taxation and taxation under section 2035(c) should focus consistently on present or future values.[120]

A. Transfers with Retained Life Estates

* * *

[Assume that a transferor (*T*) has wealth of $100 available for transfer, and that a 40% tax is levied on each dollar transferred. If *T* makes an outright bequest of $100, having consumed all the income earned during life, *T*'s beneficiaries will receive $60 after tax at *T*'s death. Alternatively, suppose that *T* creates an irrevocable inter vivos trust of $60, retaining a life income interest, and pays a gift tax on the actuarial value of the remainder; an estate tax will be imposed at *T*'s death. It is assumed that *T*'s life expectancy and the appropriate discount rate used in valuing the transferred remainder are such that each dollar payable on the anticipated date of *T*'s death is worth 50 cents today. The amount of the gift tax may be taxed either at the time of

---

[115]   Such a desire, however, is not invariably regarded as being incompatible with a unified transfer tax. * * *

[120]   The analysis in the text implicitly assumes that it is appropriate to use identical rates to discount the value of future accessions to wealth and future tax liabilities. * * *

the gift (under a tax-inclusive gift tax) or at death (under section 2035(c)). The difference in timing affects the financial value of the combined transfer taxes.]

If we tax lifetime transfers and transfers at death identically, the government should (to use our simplifying assumption about rates) take 40% of the tax-inclusive value of whatever T transfers whenever and however he transfers it. It should take nothing of what T chooses to retain. Thus, when T elected to live off the income from $100 and to leave $100 at his death, * * * in effect he chose to retain half the value—the "income" half—attributable to having $100 in hand at the time he made that decision. The remaining $100 of principal, ultimately due to be transferred, was also ultimately due to be taxed. What is more, since T elected to consume the "income half," the burden of the tax was destined to fall on the "remainder" half of the value attributable to having $100 now. That "remainder" half has a present value of $50, and a value at the time it is expected to pass to T's estate of $100, leaving $60 (after tax at 40%) for T's beneficiaries.

When, instead, T chose to create the remainder by lifetime transfer and to pay the transfer tax himself, he paved the way for shifting the incidence of the tax. Instead of the tax being paid by T's estate, thereby depleting the wealth that passed to T's beneficiaries after estate tax, its discounted equivalent was paid as gift tax by T. That payment, in contrast with the creation of the remainder, actually depleted T's wealth, thereby reducing the value of the income T could expect to receive during the balance of his life.

By substituting a gift tax payment for an equivalent estate tax payment, of course, T only *potentially* shifted the burden of the transfer tax to himself. He still retained the option of taking subsequent steps to offset his payment of the gift tax. Assuming that the lifetime creation of the remainder had attracted gift tax of $20 under the gross-up approach * * * , T could have compensated for his payment of the tax by thereafter consuming the $20 of principal that remained in his possession. But when T elected instead to restrict future consumption to his remaining income, he completed an incremental transfer of wealth. He actually sacrificed, in favor of his beneficiaries, the right to receive the income from the $20 paid as tax for the duration of his expected remaining life. * * *

* * *

* * * The implication of these examples is that, under the gross-up approach to taxation of lifetime gifts, the incremental wealth transfer created by T's foregoing the income on the gift tax payment is itself taxed (on a tax-inclusive basis) at the 40% transfer tax rate * * * . By contrast, taxing the gift as under current law and postponing until death the inclusion of the gift tax in the transfer tax base—thereby deferring a portion of the tax on the lifetime gift—exempts the incremental transfer from tax.

* * * Regardless of the value of the assets in which a remainder is created by lifetime transfer, where creation of the remainder operates to transfer more than the anticipated after-tax value of the transferor's estate, the gross-up approach taxes the incremental transfer. Section 2035(c), in contrast, yields taxes with a combined value that usually equals, and never exceeds, the estate tax that would have been paid in the absence of the lifetime transfer. In short, when applied to lifetime transfers with retained life interests, the approach advocated by the Treasury in 1969 would tax lifetime gifts consistently with existing taxation of transfers at death. Section 2035(c) does not.

* * *

NOTE

For further discussion, see Joseph Isenbergh, *Further Notes on Transfer Tax Rates*, 51 U. CHI. L. REV. 91 (1984). Isenbergh suggests that "the discount rate used to value the present cost of a tax paid in the future (in effect, the time value of tax deferral) should probably be greater than the discount rate applied to the amounts of the actual transfers themselves." *Id.* at 93. Why might the present value of future estate tax costs (or savings) be discounted more heavily? If the amount of gift tax paid were compounded to arrive at a future value to be included in the gross estate under § 2035(c), should the interest rate be the same as the rate of return on the underlying property? If not, should it be higher or lower?

Alvin C. Warren, Jr., *The Timing of Taxes*, 39 NAT'L TAX J. 499 (1986)*

It has recently been suggested in a variety of contexts that under certain conditions deferral or acceleration of a tax will not affect its present value. If the required conditions are satisfied, the effect of such a tax will not depend on when the tax is levied. * * *

* * *

II. ESTATE AND GIFT TAXATION

Consider an individual who has $100, which is invested at a rate of return such that, if no income is consumed, the principal will double by the individual's expected date of death. She plans, however, to consume all the income from the investment for the rest of her life and leave the $100, minus transfer taxes, to her children. Current law would tax a testamentary transfer more heavily than a lifetime gift that is equivalent in present value, because the estate tax is included in the tax base, while the gift tax is not.

In 1969 and again in 1984, the Treasury proposed that this difference between gift and estate taxation be eliminated, with the gift tax also levied on a gross basis. Assuming an estate tax rate of 40 percent, our transferor could leave her children $60 after taxes of $40 on a testamentary transfer of $100. If the gift tax were also levied on a gross basis at 40 percent, she could give her children $30 now as an equivalent lifetime gift. That gift would require an immediate gift tax payment of $20, computed as follows: The net gift of $30 would be converted (or "grossed-up") to a gross gift of $50, which is $30 divided by 1 − t where t is the gross tax rate: $30/(1 − .4) = $50.[10] Forty percent of a gross gift of $50 yields a gross gift tax of $20 and a net gift of $30.

After making the gift of $30 and paying a gift tax of $20, the transferor would retain $50, leaving the parties with assets equal in present value to those they would have after a pretax testamentary transfer of $100: The transferor's retained $50 is the present value of the income that would be produced on principal of $100 for the remainder of her life, because assets will dou-

---

[10]   Levying a tax *t* on a pretax gift G yields a tax of *t*G and a net gift N of G − *t*G or G(1 − *t*). If N equals G(1 − *t*), then G equals N/(1 − *t*). Because the tax is the product of the gift and the tax rate, the same result could be obtained by grossing up the rate, rather than the gift.

ble in value by the transferor's death under our assumed rate of return. Similarly, the $30 received by her children after gift taxes is, in terms of present value, equivalent to an after-tax testamentary transfer of $60. And the $20 gift tax collected by the Treasury is [the] equivalent in present value of $40 collected from the estate.[11]

Again in terms of simple algebra, a transferor with assets of A can leave her children $(1 - t)A(1 + r)^y$ in value at her date of death with either an immediate lifetime gift or a testamentary transfer, where t is the uniform gross transfer tax rate, y the years remaining until the transferor's death, and r the annual after-income-tax rate of return to all parties. If the gift is made immediately, the children receive $(1 - t)A$ after gift taxes, which will compound to $(1 - t)A(1 + r)^y$ by the transferor's death. If the gift is made at death, the transferor can put aside A today, which will compound to an estate of $A(1 + r)^y$, leaving $(1 - t)A(1 + r)^y$ for the children after payment of estate taxes. As long as the tax rate is the same under the estate and gift taxes, and is applied on a consistent (here gross) basis, the transfer taxes will not affect the choice between making a gift earlier or later if the transferor and her children have the same investment opportunities and face the same income tax rates. Differences in income tax rates will, of course, affect the family's after-tax return, but the source of such differences would not be the transfer taxes.

If, as proposed by the Treasury, the gift tax were levied on a gross basis, that tax would thus become a method for fully prepaying the estate tax under our assumptions, which do not yet include graduated rates. Adoption of the Treasury proposal would continue the process of "unifying" the two taxes begun by the adoption of a single rate schedule and a unified exemption in 1976.[12]

* * *

CONCLUSIONS

As suggested by their common algebraic formulation, the relationships described above can be generalized into a single principle: *The present value to a taxpayer of a consistently defined tax will be the same whether the tax is deferred or accelerated, as long as the tax rate remains constant and the base of a deferred tax increases over time by the rate of return generally applicable to investment of proceeds available after payment of an accelerated tax.* The foregoing * * * examples indicate that identification of equivalences of taxes in present value can be useful in several ways.

First, present value equivalence can help identify tax treatments that achieve neutrality regarding taxpayer choices. If the assumptions identified above, such as a constant tax rate, are fully satisfied, * * * transfer taxes levied on a consistent gross basis would not distort the choice between lifetime and testamentary gifts * * * .

Second, where the conditions for equivalent present value are not satisfied precisely, approximate equivalences may suggest that particular tax provisions are not as distortionary as they first appear, due to the roughly compensating effects of apparently different treatment. * * *

Third, present value equivalences can suggest alternative taxing structures that might be used to accomplish the same or similar ends, such as * * * the gift tax as a means of prepaying the estate tax * * * .

---

[11]   Equivalence to the government assumes that the Treasury would discount at the after-income-tax rate of return. * * *

[12]   *See* Sims, *Timing Under a Unified Wealth Transfer Tax*, 51 U. CHI. L. REV. 34 (1984); Isenbergh, *Simplifying Retained Life Interests, Revocable Transfers, and the Marital Deduction*, 51 U. CHI. L. REV. 1 (1984).

Finally, and perhaps most importantly, specifying the exact conditions necessary for equivalence in present value can elucidate the limitations of conclusions based on equivalences that are not approximated under current law and prevailing institutional arrangements. Tax rates, for example, both differ across taxpayers and change over time. Formulation of tax policy often involves judgment about just how far the specified conditions deviate from a very complex economic reality. For example, * * * graduated rates would eliminate the present value equivalence of estate and gift taxes levied on a gross basis, because even under the same graduated rate schedule, the estate tax would apply to larger, compounded, transfers than would an earlier gift tax. The remaining difference in result might, however, be acceptable in the interest of simplicity, since full achievement of equivalent treatment under the transfer taxes could require revaluation of all lifetime gifts at the time of the transferor's death.[28] * * *

NOTE

Consider the assumptions underlying the conclusion that deferral or acceleration does not affect the present value of a transfer tax. Are these assumptions met under existing law? Would they be met under any of the proposed versions of an integrated estate and gift tax system?

Harry L. Gutman, *A Comment on the ABA Tax Section Task Force Report on Transfer Tax Restructuring*, 41 TAX LAW. 653 (1988)*

* * *

III. THE TRANSFER TAX BASE

* * *

A. The Gift and Estate Tax Base

* * *

Under current law, the tax base for *inter vivos* transfers is the value of the property transferred. If the transfer results in gift tax liability, the gift tax paid is not included in the gift tax base. In contrast, when a transfer occurs at death, the tax is paid from the wealth disposed of at that time. Thus, the estate tax base includes the tax due on account of the transfer.

If one accepts the principle that the tax system should not favor one form of giving over another, lifetime and deathtime transfers should be treated identically. Accordingly, the tax base for lifetime transfers should include the tax generated by the transfer.[18]

---

[28]   * * * Date-of-death valuation of lifetime gifts would also require that credit be given for any previous gift tax payments, also compounded to a date-of-death value.

*   © 1988 American Bar Association. Reprinted with permission.

[18]   The same conclusion may be reached by a different analysis. If one agrees that a tax should be imposed on the net wealth depletion resulting from a transfer, and an inter vivos transfer results in a tax liability, payment of the tax further depletes the transferor's wealth. Thus, taxes paid with respect to lifetime transfers must be included as part of the value of the transfer.

The failure to "gross-up" the gift by including the gift tax generated by the gift results in a preference for lifetime giving. This preference can be quantified and expressed as a rate reduction. When expressed on a tax-inclusive basis, if the maximum estate tax rate is 50%, the equivalent gift tax rate is 33⅓%.[19] A preferential rate applicable to lifetime transfers encourages such transfers and, therefore, violates the tax policy goal of allocative neutrality. Moreover, a preferential rate for lifetime giving requires one to focus more carefully on the question of when, in a unified transfer tax structure, a transfer should be treated as complete.

The Report acknowledges the foregoing but nonetheless concludes that a uniform transfer tax base is inappropriate for three reasons. First, it asserts that many believe a preference for lifetime gifts creates social and economic benefits because it "causes business and investment capital to be moved into the hands of younger, more vigorous owners." The Report cites no authority for the proposition that lower gift tax rates encourage any significant amount of capital to be shifted to "younger, more vigorous owners," and I am not aware of any empirical studies that support this claim.

Lower gift tax rates may encourage lifetime as compared to deathtime transfers, but it is doubtful that many of those transfers result in "vigorous" risk taking. Property transferred to younger generations is often transferred in trust. Trustees operating under fiduciary constraints cannot be "vigorous" risk takers. Furthermore, outright gifts, I believe, are often used principally to support consumption expenses of donees rather than their speculative investments. It is true that a lower gift tax might encourage the earlier transfer of ownership interests in closely-held businesses. It is not clear, however, that either society or the economy benefits because of an earlier, rather than later, transfer. Moreover, if there is a societal benefit to be derived from the earlier transfer of interests in closely-held businesses, or transfers that result in more vigorous risk taking, and the federal government seeks to offer incentives for such transfers, the encouragement should come through a more calibrated policy than adopting a rate reduction applicable to all lifetime gifts.

The second reason proffered for retaining current law is that "[if] the gift tax is regarded as an advance payment of estate tax," the lower gift tax "may be analogized to a discount for early payment." As demonstrated by Professors Warren and Sims,[22] this assertion is simply wrong. The present value of a transfer tax payment does not vary relative to when it is paid if neither the tax rate nor the tax base vary between payment dates and the property grows at the same rate without regard to when the tax is paid.

The Report's final argument in favor of a tax-exclusive gift tax base is that, given other features of the current income and transfer tax structure, the preference for lifetime gifts compensates roughly for the fact that a donor's basis for property transferred by gift carries over to the donee (with an adjustment for gift tax attributable to the appreciation in the transferred property), while property obtained from a decedent receives an estate tax valuation date basis for income tax purposes and may be eligible for estate tax relief provisions that are not available for lifetime transfers. This "two wrongs make a right" argument is no more persuasive in this context than in any other.[24] It is disappointing that the Task Force was unable to agree on the obvious proposition that if the problem is disparate income tax basis rules for lifetime and

---

[19]   A net gift of $100 taxed at 50% results in a gift tax of $33.33. Expressed as a percentage of the property transferred, the gift tax rate is 33⅓%.

[22]   Warren, [*The Timing of Taxes*, 39 NAT'L TAX J. 499, 499-500 (1986)]; Sims, *Timing Under a Unified Wealth Transfer Tax*, 51 U. CHI. L. REV. 34, 57 (1984).

[24]   For a more eloquent articulation of the Task Force's argument against rate unification, see Stephan, *A Comment on Transfer Tax Reform*, 72 VA. L. REV. 1471, 1480-90 (1986).

deathtime property transfers, the solution is a consistent income tax rule rather than a compensating, base-eroding transfer tax preference.[25]

* * *

IV. STRUCTURAL UNIFICATION

* * *

As the Report notes, structural unification is not a new issue. The technical problem is to determine when a transfer should be treated as complete (a synonym for "taxable"). The Report recommends a relatively "easy-to-complete" gift rule pursuant to which a transfer is complete unless the transferor "can recover the transferred property, through exercise of a power retained by him or conferred by him upon another" or "will receive the income from the transferred property, or can do so through the exercise of a power retained by him or conferred by him upon another." In general terms, only the direct or indirect reservation of a power to revoke the transfer or receive the income from the transferred property will render a transfer incomplete. Thus, a transfer with an express reversionary interest is complete, as is a transfer in which the transferor retains the power to control the beneficial enjoyment of the transferred property.

I want to emphasize that I believe the proposal to be an improvement over current law, but *only if* the estate and gift tax bases are the same. Unless the estate and gift tax bases are uniform, the proposal results in a lower tax rate than is presently the case for *inter-vivos* retained future interest transfers and transfers in which the transferor has retained the power to control beneficial enjoyment of the transferred property. In such a world, a transfer should remain incomplete until the donor has given up all opportunity to benefit economically from the transferred property and has no power to affect its beneficial enjoyment. If the estate and gift tax bases were uniform, I would favor early completion for retained powers transfers in which it is clear that the transferor does not possess the power to alter the amount available to the beneficiaries, but later completion for retained interest transfers and those transfers in which the decedent has, directly or indirectly, reserved a power that enables him to affect the amount available to the beneficiaries.

As a general proposition, a transfer should be treated as complete when a transferor has irrevocably parted with his entire interest in the subject matter of the transfer. This rule is easy to apply in the garden variety situation in which a transferor disposes of all or some defined share of his total interest in the property, e.g., a one-half undivided interest in an income or remainder interest in a trust. It is also easy to apply to revocable transfers. Its application, however, is less clear in the following situations:

(a) transfers in which the transferor has retained an economic benefit, commonly in the form of a life estate, an estate for years, or a reversionary interest;

(b) transfers over which the transferor has retained the power subsequently to direct the economic benefits of the transferred property; and

(c) transfers in which the transferor has nominally parted with the property but has retained the substantive ability to affect the subsequent value of the transferred interest.

---

[25]   Given the A.B.A. Section of Taxation's prior performance with respect to this issue, it is not surprising that this Task Force could not reach a consensus. *See* Hoffman, *Role of the Bar in the Tax Legislative Process*, 37 TAX L. REV. 411, 438-92 (1982).

A. Retained Economic Benefit

* * *

1. Retained Life Estate

Assume *A* transfers property in trust, retaining the right to the income for life, remainder to *B*. *A* has transferred a discrete, identifiable interest in property—the "corpus" of the trust. *A*'s present transfer of the corpus, however, will not be possessed by *B* until *A*'s death. Should *A*'s present transfer of a discrete interest in property that will be possessed by *B* only in the future be treated as a completed transfer when made?

The tax stakes here involve the proper measurement of the value of the remainder interest and the treatment of post-transfer changes in value of the trust corpus. If the transfer of the remainder interest is deemed complete at the time the trust is funded, *A* will have made a gift at that time of the present value of the remainder interest. Application of the principle that a transferor is to be taxed only once with respect to any particular transfer means that the corpus of the trust is thereafter removed from *A*'s transfer tax base. There are no further transfer tax consequences at *A*'s death; the fact that the value of the corpus may fluctuate is irrelevant.

The alternative view of this transaction would not permit the separation of the transfer into its component temporal parts. As a consequence, the transfer will be incomplete (nontaxable) until *A*'s death; only at that time has *A* parted with his entire interest in the transferred property. Thus, the entire value of the transferred property will be included in *A*'s transfer tax base at death; no transfer tax event would have occurred prior to that time.

The first view of the transaction is described as an "easy-to-complete" gift rule. It is simple to apply in the situation hypothesized. The amount of the gift is the actuarial value of the remainder interest. This ease of application, however, masks a number of difficult issues involving the accurate calculation of the present value of the remainder interest. Furthermore, the rule can be manipulated to produce inaccurate results. An easy-to-complete rule is a tax planner's dream because the opportunities to "beat" the valuation tables abound.

The second view of the transaction is described as a "hard-to-complete" gift rule. It does not permit fractionalizing transferred property into its temporal elements, even if traditional property law would recognize each temporal element as a separate interest in property. The hard-to-complete rule does not avoid the need to define the quantum of retained benefit that will result in its application. Under the hard-to-complete rule, however, only the types of benefits that invoke the rule need be defined. There is no need to value those benefits. Moreover, a trustee cannot, through investment decisions, produce a mismeasurement of the taxable transfer. Current distributions of trust income will remain in the tax base of the transferor unless consumed. Amounts remaining in trust at the time of the expiration of the transferor's retained interest will be taxed at their current value at that time. Thus, in this type of transfer, the hard-to-complete gift rule treats all transfers similarly and avoids the measurement vagaries of the easy-to-complete rule. It is a better rule and was properly recommended by the Report.

2. Reversionary Interests

Assume *A* transfers property in trust to pay the income to *B* for life, reversion to *A* or *A*'s estate. Two questions arise. First, when will the transfer to *B* be taxed? Second, what remains in *A*'s transfer tax base after the transfer? The Report recommends that this transfer be treated as wholly complete. Thus, the transfer is taxable in full when made and nothing remains in *A*'s transfer tax base. As the Report recognizes, however, if the property reverts to the transferor it will be included in his transfer tax base twice unless a compensating adjustment is made.

The Report's proposal is conceptually incorrect in treating the value of the reversionary interest as a completed *inter vivos* transfer. There are two conceptually correct alternatives. The transfer of the income interest could be treated as complete when property is transferred to the trust. The present value of the income interest would be determined and that amount would be A's taxable transfer. Subsequent distributions of income from the trust would not affect A's transfer tax profile. Alternatively, the initial transfer would be treated as incomplete and then each distribution from the trust would be treated as a taxable transfer by A. The former rule contains all the previously identified defects of the easy-to-complete gift rule. The latter, while accurately measuring the transfer made by A, introduces administrative complications not present in the application of the hard-to-complete gift rule to transfers with retained economic interests. The decision whether to adopt the hard-to-complete rule will depend, at least in part, on whether the additional administrative costs exceed the benefits of accurate measurement of the transfer.

The choice between the selection of an easy or hard-to-complete gift rule for the intervening interest will also affect, as a conceptual matter, the residual amount in A's transfer tax base. The easy-to-complete gift rule explicitly separates the property transferred into components. Since under that rule, the gift at transfer is the value of the income interest transferred, from the date of the transfer until A actually comes into possession of the underlying property again, A's transfer tax base logically includes only the value, at any point in time, of the reversionary interest. Thus, if A dies before B, A's transfer tax base will include the present value of the reversionary interest. Under a hard-to-complete rule, A's transfer tax base includes, at death, the entire corpus of the trust. The underlying basis for the hard-to-complete rule—that property cannot be separated into temporal segments for transfer tax purposes—makes A's death the event that completes the transfer of the remaining value of B's income interest and the reversion.

* * * Unless the costs of administering the hard-to-complete rule are excessive, it is difficult to see why the transfer tax system should permit the potential for erosion of the tax base that the easy-to-complete rule would permit.

* * *

As in the case of transfers in which economic benefits are retained from the outset, measurement errors can be corrected retroactively by adjusting the transfer tax base to conform with what actually happened. An accurate retroactive adjustment system is, of course, the application of the hard-to-complete gift principles to determine the correct amount of the transfer. If the hard-to-complete rule is to be used to adjust retroactively for errors in the easy-to-complete rule, one might ask why it was not adopted as the governing rule in the first place.

A further difficulty with the use of the easy-to-complete rule in the context of contingent reversionary interests arises if the contingency cannot be valued. Here, the presumptive answer is to treat the entire value of the property as the initial taxable transfer. But this solution is correct only if the transferor does not regain possession of the property. When the transferor regains possession of the property, the transferor's wealth base had been depleted only by the amounts that have been distributed to the intervening beneficiary. The balance, to the extent it had previously been taxed as a completed transfer, should not re-enter the transferor's tax base. Once again, a mechanism must be created to avoid this double counting.

No matter what rule is selected with respect to the general treatment of transfers involving contingent reserved future interests, situations will arise in which, on the basis of actuarial data or specific facts and circumstances, a determination can be made that the probability of repossession is remote. In these situations, the general rule could be modified to treat the initial transfer as wholly complete. There would, however, have to be a mechanism to unwind the transaction if the transferor subsequently regained possession of the property.[93]

The choice between the Report's proposal and a hard-to-complete gift rule is not obvious if the gift and estate tax bases are the same. On balance, I prefer a hard-to-complete gift rule with an exception for the limited number of transfers in which the value of the transferor's retained future interest is *de minimis*. * * *

B. Retention of the Power to Control Beneficial Enjoyment

Assume *A* irrevocably relinquishes the right to benefit personally from transferred property, but retains the right, either alone or in conjunction with others, to designate the ultimate transferee, the time the transferee may enjoy the benefit of the transferred interest, or both. When should such a transfer be treated as complete?

This question poses another fundamental issue in the design of a transfer tax. Once a transferor has relinquished all direct or indirect right to the economic benefits of the property, the transferor's wealth, as commonly understood, has been depleted by the total amount of the transferred property. If the tax is to be imposed at the time a transferor's wealth is depleted, the fact that the ultimate beneficiaries of the transferred property are unknown should be irrelevant and the transfer deemed complete. Under such a rule, the critical issue would be the definition of that point at which no economic benefits are retained.

On the other hand, it could be argued that so long as the transferor retains the right to determine the beneficiaries of the transferred interest, or the time or manner of their enjoyment of the property, he has not really parted with sufficient control over the property to conclude that, for transfer tax purposes, his estate has been depleted. In other words, "depletion" does not occur until *all* rights over the transferred property are relinquished.

Neither of the foregoing is obviously "correct." As a historical matter, transfers in which the ultimate ownership of property was not settled until the death of the transferor were taxed under the estate tax. That treatment arose, however, in a context in which there was no gift tax, and continued in a context in which the gift tax rate was lower than the estate tax rate. The same conclusion is not compelled under a unified transfer tax structure when equivalent tax rates and bases apply to *inter vivos* and deathtime transfers. If the estate tax base remains tax inclusive and the gift tax base tax exclusive, however, the resulting rate preference for lifetime transfers will cause taxpayers to prefer early completion.

If the gift and estate tax bases are the same, as I have strongly urged, the choice between the two would turn principally on administrative concerns. Early completion requires a single return at the time of the transfer; later completion requires that a return be filed by the transferor each time a distribution is made from the transferred property. This factor would tend to favor earlier completion, which I agree should be the rule when the transferor has retained only the power to control beneficial enjoyment.

C. Retention of the Ability to Affect the Value of the Transferred Interest

Recall the example in which *A* transferred nonvoting common stock to her children, but continued to own all the voting stock of a closely-held corporation. With respect to this example, I concluded that the post-transfer appreciation should remain in *A*'s transfer tax base. The

---

[93]   This discussion assumes that a transfer will be wholly complete when the possibility that the transferor's retained interest will become possessory is remote. It ignores the issues involved in defining the circumstances leading to a determination of "remoteness" adequate to invoke the rule. * * *

problem now is to determine when transfer of the nonvoting common stock and the related appreciation should be treated as complete.

There are three choices. First, in any situation in which the transferor retains control over the growth of the transferred property, the transfer remains wholly incomplete until the transferor relinquishes that control. Second, the initial transfer of the property can be treated as complete and the aggregate post-transfer growth treated as an additional transfer when control is relinquished. Third, the initial transfer of the property can be treated as complete and each annual increase in value until control is relinquished would constitute an additional transfer.

I have noted above that it makes no economic difference when a transfer is taxed so long as the tax base, tax rate, and growth rate are the same. If these conditions are satisfied, the selection of the completion rule would turn on administrative considerations, which in this case would favor the first option. That option would also be preferable if the conditions for neutrality are not satisfied and a lower tax results from early completion.

* * *

NOTE

Gutman argues strongly against adopting an "easy-to-complete" approach as long as the gift tax continues to be imposed at a lower effective rate than the estate tax. Like Sims, he perceives a uniform transfer tax base as an important step toward a more neutral and simpler transfer tax system. For a subsequent exchange between Gutman and Ronald Aucutt, a member of the ABA Task Force, see Ronald D. Aucutt, *Further Observations on Transfer Tax Restructuring: A Practitioner's Perspective*, 42 TAX LAW. 343 (1989); Harry L. Gutman, *A Practitioner's Perspective in Perspective: A Reply to Mr. Aucutt*, 42 TAX LAW. 351 (1989). In the following article, Paul B. Stephan III defends preferential gift tax rates as a means of compensating for the disparate treatment of lifetime and deathtime transfers under the federal income tax.

Paul B. Stephan III, *A Comment on Transfer Tax Reform*, 72 VA. L. REV. 1471 (1986)*

* * *

* * * [T]he case for a unified rate structure is weaker than the Treasury and its supporters have realized. One of the principal justifications for a separate tax on the transfer of wealth is that it plugs gaps in the income tax base. While this insight is important, too few analysts have taken the next step of thinking about how the transfer taxes can complement the income tax. Preserving a rate differential between gifts and deathtime transfers is one way of offsetting the income tax's discrimination between gifts and bequests.

* * * The centerpiece of the Treasury's simplification project for the estate and gift taxes is base integration, i.e., elimination of the reinclusion rules that currently treat some transfers as both gifts and bequests. But base integration can be achieved without rate unification. Slight expansion of the estate tax base, coupled with a rule excluding from gift taxation all transfers eligible for estate taxation, will produce a simple and administrable transfer tax while preserving a rate differential. * * *

* * *

II. THE CASE AGAINST RATE UNIFICATION

The assertion that gifts and testamentary transfers are functionally the same and therefore should have equivalent tax consequences ignores one of the strongest arguments in favor of transfer taxation. The transfer taxes supplement the income tax by reaching asset appreciation that largely escapes income taxation. Other, more direct ways of subjecting this appreciation to income taxation—such as treating transfers as realization events or using carryover basis for bequests—have proved impossible to implement. But the income tax, although friendly to both gifts and bequests, clearly favors the latter. If the transfer taxes are meant to complement the income tax by offsetting the income tax favors that gifts and bequests enjoy, they should correspondingly discriminate in favor of gifts.

A. The Link Between Income and Transfer Taxation

* * *

* * * [T]he income tax preferences for gifts and bequests differ significantly. The donor of appreciated property pays no income tax on the gain that accrued during his ownership, but the donee takes over the donor's basis ("carryover" or "transferred" basis) and thus will include the donor's gain in income when the property is sold or exchanged. The tax advantages of carryover basis, as compared to a rule treating a gift as a realization event, are only deferral of taxation until the donee sells or exchanges the property and calculation of the tax by reference to the donee's potentially lower marginal rate.

* * *

By contrast, when appreciated property is inherited or is otherwise eligible for inclusion in the decedent's taxable estate, the beneficiary acquires a new stepped-up basis equal to the current value of the property. As a result, the beneficiary can dispose of the property without including the decedent's gain in income. If wealthy persons plan their dispositions so as to realize losses during life and retain their appreciated assets until death, the stepped-up basis rule amounts to a complete forgiveness of income tax on most asset appreciation held by persons wealthy enough to leave their capital untouched. * * *

If the estate tax is simply another way of collecting the income tax that should be paid on unrealized appreciation, then the gift tax should account for the different income tax consequences of gifts. Although some tax should fall on gifts, because the deferral and deflection favors are not insignificant, the burden should be less than that on testamentary transfers, which enjoy the more valuable income tax preference of complete exclusion. * * *

Consider how the current transfer tax preference for gifts relates to marginal income and transfer tax rates. * * * [T]he preference increases with the amount of the transferor's taxable wealth. * * * This relation, although seemingly perverse in terms of progressivity, makes sense if one assumes that transferors with greater wealth tend to be matched with transferees who have higher income tax rates. * * * The income tax's discrimination against gifts weighs more heavily on donees with higher marginal income tax rates, as the cost of the lost basis step-up is tied to the level of income taxation. Therefore, increasing the preference with the amount of the transferor's taxable wealth makes up for the discrimination against gifts that grows with income. * * *

B. Objections to the Income Tax Argument

Although the link between the income and transfer taxes seems powerful, there are several objections to using the income tax's discrimination against gifts to justify the gift tax's lower rates. First, it is by no means clear that the transfer taxes serve only to correct for the income tax's nonrealization rules. Cash gifts and bequests as well as transfers of unappreciated property come under the transfer taxes, although property held in this form enjoys no particular income tax preference. Moreover, the rate structure of the transfer taxes is not connected to rates under the income tax, as a purely complementary tax presumably would be. And to the extent the transfer taxes have purposes other than filling in for the income tax, they need not take account of distinctions, like that between gifts and testamentary transfers, that matter in the income tax.

Although these objections have superficial appeal, they ignore the practical effect of the transfer taxes and the distribution of unrealized gain among the population. * * * Although incomplete, available evidence suggests that much of the unrealized appreciation that escapes income taxation because of the gift and bequest nonrealization rules belongs to the relatively small class of persons who possess sufficient wealth to come under the transfer taxes. The converse of this observation—that most persons with enough wealth to worry about transfer taxation possess substantial unrealized appreciation—is also well documented. The bottom transfer tax rate, which is higher than the top income tax rate, can be characterized as a combination of the highest possible income tax plus an interest charge for the deferral privilege resulting from nontaxation of unrealized gain. While there is no doubt that the transfer taxes are both under- and over-inclusive if compared to an income tax rule treating gifts and bequests as realization events, the fit is not preposterous * * * .

Another response to the income tax-transfer tax link is that two wrongs do not make a right—that the use of stepped-up basis for assets includible in the transferor's taxable estate is indefensible and should be repudiated, not woven further into the fabric of federal taxation through offsets in the transfer tax. Elimination of the income tax preference for holders of appreciated assets has been on the agenda of reformers for decades, and Congress took the first step when it instituted carryover basis for testamentary transfers in 1976. * * *

But as it turned out, Congress lacked the commitment to sustain even as incomplete a reform as carryover basis, which it retroactively repealed in 1980. Stepped-up basis for testamentary transfers now seems a permanent part of the landscape * * * . At present only second-best solutions seem possible, and among these the transfer taxes appears to be the best.

* * *

* * * [I]f the income tax is going to attach some consequences to the distinction between gifts and testamentary transfers, a normative argument of sorts can be found to help in the sorting. It seems reasonable to believe that the rich—that is to say, people who have sufficient disposable wealth to be concerned about the transfer taxes—are relatively risk-averse when it comes to their excess capital. This assumption may seem counter-intuitive at first, because one might expect the average person to take the greatest chances with money that he does not need. But risk-taking is for most mortals the necessary counterpart of higher rates of return, and it is the rich who presumably are least concerned with the growth of their disposable wealth. We may expect the rich to take fewer risks simply because they are least dissatisfied with the rate of return on low-risk investments.

If this intuition about the wealthy is correct, it should follow that the dispersion of their wealth through gratuitous transfers will place capital in the hands of people more willing to take chances. In the case of closely held businesses, for example, we associate an intergenerational turnover of management with innovation and provide some income tax incentives to speed up the changing of the guard. Seen in this light, the transfer tax preference for inter vivos gifts may have welfare benefits, as it can nudge wealth out of the hands of aging owners and into the possession of younger, more productive entrepreneurs. * * *

A different objection to a gift tax preference is the problem of adverse selection. The income tax favor to testamentary transfers has value only to the extent an asset has appreciated in value or, stating the obverse, the income tax penalty on gifts disappears for assets whose value corresponds to basis. * * * In reality, the wealthy can give away unappreciated property, for which there will be no income tax penalty but a transfer tax preference, and live off appreciated assets during life.

Consider an individual owning asset A, worth $1,000,000 with a basis of $1,000,000, and asset B, also worth $1,000,000 but with a zero basis. Assume that the individual regards $1,000,000 as the amount of surplus wealth he can dispose of either during his life or at death. Under current law he can make an immediate transfer of asset A, enjoying the lower gift tax rate without sacrificing any income tax benefits for the transferees. He will borrow against asset B, consuming the principal amount of the loan and using the investment income from the asset to pay interest on the loan. If, at death, this individual has borrowed against the full value of asset B he will have no taxable estate, because the debt offsets the value of B, and he will still avoid income taxation because B can be sold (with a stepped-up basis) to pay off the loan.

To the extent that the amount of unappreciated property owned by the rich is greater than their disposable wealth, the adverse selection objection is compelling. But the assumption that many individuals meet this condition seems too strong. It is not easy to accumulate wealth while the value of one's property fails to grow, especially during periods of inflation. The power to make gifts from unappreciated assets while consuming appreciated property during life undoubtedly allows some taxpayers to reduce the effect of the income tax penalty for gifts, but this capability means only that the transfer tax preference should be less than the income tax penalty on gifts. * * *

* * *

III. BASE INTEGRATION WITHOUT RATE UNIFICATION

Even if a transfer tax preference for gifts is otherwise desirable, the question remains whether the costs associated with the preference outweigh its benefits. Once a favored category of transfers exists, taxpayers will try to wrestle transactions into it. The reinclusion rules illustrate how costly it can be to screen out transfers that masquerade as gifts but should not qualify for the preference. If such rules are the necessary price of a rate differential between gifts and bequests, the mischief they create may justify ignoring the other arguments for favoring lifetime transfers.

But the present reinclusion rules are not the only means of protecting the integrity of the gift tax base. A one-tax-per-transfer, hard-to-complete system can cabin the gift preference while achieving the benefits of base integration. * * * The rate differential is not the source of mischief in the transfer taxes and can coexist with a less complex and fairer system.

* * *

Consider a system that treated as taxable gifts only transfers that have no testamentary aspects. It would include in the transferor's estate all property transferred during life if any interest or power were determined by reference to his life; all other transfers would fall under the gift tax. As in current law, the retained-power trust would be picked up only by the estate tax, because the power exists until the transferor dies. Distributions from the trust would constitute taxable gifts, as under current law. * * * Retained-income transfers as well as transfers with retained reversions would be taxed only at the transferor's death, not twice as under the present system. Transfers that the current system treats only as gifts even though the transferor imposes ex ante restrictions that last until his death—e.g., a trust where the income accumulates during the settlor's life with distribution to his surviving issue at the time of his death—instead would be taxed at the higher estate rates.

This hard-to-complete system not only would eliminate the current mare's nest of reinclusion rules, but would limit the gift tax rate preference to transfers that are consistent with the normative reason for distinguishing gifts and bequests. Transfers subject to conditions that limit the donee's power to take risks with the property generally would be subject to the higher estate tax rates unless the conditions lapsed during the donor's life. * * *

* * *

NOTE

Stephan notes that the transfer taxes "supplement the income tax by reaching asset appreciation that largely escapes income taxation." Although it would be more direct to tax this appreciation through the income tax, Stephan claims that such reforms have proven to be "impossible to implement." Would the hard-to-complete system he prescribes be any easier to implement? Are there good reasons to pursue this indirect transfer tax reform rather direct income tax reform?

Joseph M. Dodge, *Redoing the Estate and Gift Taxes Along Easy-to-Value Lines*, 43 TAX L. REV. 241 (1988)*

* * *

* * * The main thrust of my reform proposals seeks accurate valuation of gratuitous transfers by avoiding reliance on estimates of, or speculation about, future events and by analyzing relevant events as they actually occur. Hindsight, in other words, should be used whenever possible. For example, the ultimate transfer tax effect of inter vivos transfers with retained interests should be suspended until the retained interest expires or the transferor dies, whichever occurs first. Similarly, certain inter vivos transactions that attempt to fix low transfer tax values should be held open until death.

* * * An intractable line-drawing problem is best resolved not by attempting to refine it, but by defining it away with rules that make line-drawing irrelevant * * * .

* * *

III. TRANSFERS WITH RETAINED INTERESTS
* * *

B. Ironing Out Sections 2036(a)(1) and 2037
* * *

2. The Retention Requirement

Several problems arise, particularly under § 2036(a)(1), with respect to the statutory requirement that an interest be "retained" by the transferor.

---

a. Discretionary Trust for Benefit of Settlor

Assume that A creates an irrevocable trust, income to A or accumulated in the trustee's discretion for A's life, remainder to B. In this form, the trust is not includable in A's gross estate under § 2036(a)(1). * * * The trust is excludable because the transferor has not *retained* the income from the transferred property. For the same reason, an irrevocable trust in which the trustee has the discretion to pay corpus to the settlor is not includable under § 2037.

The above raises the issue of whether the current construction placed upon the retention concept is justified. The argument pro is that the concept of "retention" should serve legitimately to restrict inclusion in the gross estate to those transfers in which income or corpus from the transferred property returns, or might return, to the transferor by reason of the mandatory terms of the transfer or by the exercise of a power of control held by the transferor. Inclusion is not warranted where the property or the income therefrom can return to the transferor only through an independent act of the transferee or other party (other than the transferor). * * * The concept of a testamentary transfer that should be included in the transferor's gross estate entails the notion of a "string" on the transfer held by the transferor personally; if the transferor is powerless to pull the string, the transfer can be said to be not truly of a testamentary nature.

On the other hand, in a discretionary trust for the benefit of the settlor, possession or enjoyment of the property or the income therefrom does not become fixed until the settlor's death. Nor has the settlor irrevocably given up everything. * * * In a discretionary trust, the settlor is a beneficiary designated in the instrument of transfer by the settlor herself, and there is likely to be no other income or corpus beneficiary during the settlor's lifetime. The trustee is likely to know the settlor personally and either to have benefitted economically through commissions and other business connections or to be related to, or even under the influence of, the settlor. * * * The point is that the concept of "retention" plausibly could be conceived of as encompassing the situation where the transferor, in or incident to the instrument or act of transfer, designates herself as a permissible recipient of income or corpus.

Turning to practicalities, it will be observed that, in a discretionary trust for the settlor, the trust is not included under § 2036 or § 2037 even if a substantial amount of income or corpus is in fact distributed or paid to the settlor. It might be supposed that the settlor in such a case has the cake while her estate eats it too, but the opposite turns out to be the case. The inter vivos transfer will have been fully subject to gift tax, with no reduction in the amount of the gift, since no interest has been retained. The income and corpus actually received will augment the transferor's § 2033 gross estate. Thus, at least part of the transfer will be subject to transfer tax twice. Moreover, the exclusion for twice taxed transfers does not apply because the estate inclusion occurs under § 2033, rather than § 2036 or § 2037.

On the other hand, if the property were not subject to gift tax but was included under § 2036 or § 2037, the income or corpus received up to death would have augmented the settlor's potential § 2033 gross estate. Taxing the property only at death under § 2036 or § 2037 does not duplicate taxation under § 2033 of amounts received prior to death; the value of the property included under § 2036 or § 2037 is determined with reference to the future income from the property, and amounts received before death are something else. * * *

Tentatively, then, there is a good pro taxpayer case for subjecting discretionary trusts for the benefit of the settlor to a hard-to-complete rule.

Given again a discretionary trust for the benefit of the settlor, under present law, the gift and estate tax results are flip-flopped if, under state law, the settlor's creditors can reach the income or corpus. This rule produces confusion in that the results depend on the application of state law which, on this point, is often uncertain, varies according to time and place, and hinges on attenuated subtleties. This confusing doctrinal area would be eliminated totally as a problem area if the broader concept of retention (as discussed above) were adopted, since the same result of estate inclusion would occur regardless of state law.

Modifying the retention requirement along the lines suggested above, along with simplifying the law with respect to retained powers, would serve to overcome the extreme formalism in estate and gift tax law that often defies, or at least ignores, reality. Thus, in a discretionary trust for the benefit of the settlor, the settlor may be able to reach the income or corpus at will by means of her familial or economic influence over the trustee. However, the courts refuse to inquire into such matters, even in cases involving irregularities in the administration of trusts, by hiding behind the rules pertaining to trustees' fiduciary duties under the law of trusts. * * * [I]f the trustee in fact accedes to the settlor's influence and pays income and corpus to the settlor, the argument that the settlor did not retain any interest because of the discretion granted the trustee under the trust instrument is simply wrong, because the trustee's exercise of discretion in favor of the settlor would be virtually unassailable in a court of equity. If the idea of "retention" were modified to include any possibility that income or corpus would be paid to the settlor under the instrument of transfer, the gap between formalism and realism would close and, at the same time, the courts would not need to enter the quicksand of trying to determine whether the settlor actually controlled or influenced the trustee.

* * *

c. Settlor as Beneficiary Under Fiduciary Standards

Another difficult issue with respect to the retention requirement pertains to trusts in which the trustee is to pay income or corpus to the settlor according to standards such as support, welfare, comfort, and the like. The doctrine in this area is—and must inevitably be—confusing. In one case, the settlor was held to have retained the right to income where the standard was happiness, the theory apparently being that such a standard was so broad as to give the settlor the equivalent of the right to demand all of the income. However, a narrower standard, such as support, would equally appear to confer an enforceable right on the beneficiary to compel distributions. * * * Other kinds of standards, such as health, education, and financial emergency, are distinguishable in that they imply irregularity and fluctuating amounts. Indeed, such standards verge on being contingencies, and should perhaps be treated accordingly. * * *

The waters are muddied by cases which hold that the result is reversed if the phrase "in the trustee's discretion" (or some variant thereof) precedes the standards. * * * The purported justification for the current rule is that there is a meaningful difference between a case in which the settlor beneficiary can enlist the aid of a court of equity to compel the trustee to make distributions and a case in which the best that can be obtained is a direction that the trustee not abuse its discretion or act in bad faith. Actually, however, where discretion is given for administering a standard, the test is the narrower one of whether the trustee has acted beyond the bounds of reasonable judgment, unless the discretion conferred is absolute or unfettered. * * *

In short, under present law the resolution of cases involving a power limited by a standard to pay income or corpus to the settlor hinges on the kind of attenuated subtleties that are confusing, lacking in predictability, and breeding of litigation. Moreover, as noted earlier, resolving cases according to the law of trusts implies retreat into a nether world often divorced from the reality of the operation of a particular trust. If, on the other hand, the concept of "retention" encompassed a pure discretionary trust for the benefit of the settlor, as suggested above, there would also follow a simple and predictable rule for these "standards" cases: The trust would be taxed at its estate tax value rather than its gift tax value, provided that the amount includable might be limited with reference to the maximum extent to which the trustee could exercise its powers in favor of the settlor consistently with the most liberal construction of the trustee's power.

* * *

C. Statutory Reform for Future Interest Transfers

The reforms suggested above would improve doctrine at the margin but they would be insufficient to foreclose some significant tax avoidance abuses involving transfers with retained interests * * * . [C]urrent law typically mismeasures the amounts actually transferred to others, sometimes to the point of taxing the same thing twice. The type of major statutory reform proposed below, namely, enactment of a hard-to-complete rule for all split-interest transfers involving a retained interest * * * , will cure both the major abuses and the doctrinal problems.

* * *

The policy argument in favor of the hard-to-complete rule is that it will defeat present estate planning techniques in which taxpayers seek, often successfully, to save taxes by outsmarting the assumptions built into the actuarial tables. The tables are based on the assumption that the results average out in the long run as between the government and taxpayers as a group. It is true that everyone dies eventually, but not everyone makes inter vivos transfers with retained income interests. It can be surmised that sophisticated tax advisors lead clients into such transactions with an awareness of the opportunities for tax avoidance that can be obtained by beating the actuarial tables, especially when it comes to life expectancies. A hard-to-complete rule will block this route to tax avoidance.

Illegitimate tax avoidance aside, a hard-to-complete rule assures accurate valuation of the interests that eventually pass to the grantor's donees. Accurate valuation will work to the advantage of taxpayers (as well as of the government) in cases where that is appropriate. Moreover, considerations of equity among transferors require that accurate measurement be made of the gratuitous transfers actually made by each.

Moving beyond the standard right-to-income situation, the concern for accurate measurement especially mandates adoption of a hard-to-complete rule for discretionary, "standards," and contingent trusts for the grantor's benefit. Thus, § 2036 should be reformulated (and a corresponding gift tax rule added) to include in the value of the gross estate all transfers where, under the terms of the instrument of transfer, income may, now or in the future, be payable to the transferor. * * *

* * *

Suppose A creates a trust of $1 million, income to B for life, reversion to A * * * . If the actual income yield is greater than that built into the actuarial tables * * * , or if B outlives her life expectancy as built into the tables, then A will succeed in removing more from her § 2033 gross estate by way of the gift of the income interest, in present value terms, than * * * she is charged with for gift tax purposes.

The same analysis holds true if A's reversion is contingent on surviving B, with a contingent remainder over to C if A predeceases B. Moreover, for gift tax purposes A can still subtract the value of the reversion from the total gift that is taxable, even though such reversion will disappear at A's death if A predeceases B.

* * *

* * * [T]he undervaluation of the gift of the income interest may or may not be balanced out by an overvaluation of the reversion or remainder included in the gross estate. Even if the reversion or remainder is overvalued for estate tax purposes, that raises a wholly separate issue from that of the undervaluation of the gift of the income interest, since the two are valued at different points in time. If interests can be valued accurately, the opportunity to do so should not be foregone. By adopting a hard-to-complete rule, misvaluation of both the income and remainder (or reversion) interests is avoided.

Any misvaluation of the income interest that ran from the date of the gift to the date of the transferor's death is corrected under the hard-to-complete rule by treating the gift of the income interest (and other interests as well) as being incomplete but treating each actual distribution from the trust as being a present gift from A to B. If the income interest expires prior to A's death, the property will return to A's § 2033 gross estate, and A will not have been charged with any gifts that never occurred. If the income interest continues past A's death, the problem is whether to treat the transfer as being complete at A's death or to wait until some later event such as the expiration of B's income interest or the taking in possession of A's reversion. If A's reversion expires at her death, the answer is simple: The transfer is completed at A's death, because there are no excludable (or deductible) interests following A's death. Both interests are transferred at A's death. Under the hard-to-complete rule—in contrast to the operation of present §§ 2033 and 2037—B's outstanding income interest is not subject to gift tax as such (although distributions prior to A's death are gifts to B), and hence B's interest is not excludable as of A's death since the transfer is complete only on A's death. If, on the other hand, A's reversion does not expire at her death, the issue must be faced of whether the transfer should be held open until the reversion is either extinguished or comes into possession. But it easily resolves itself. If the reversion subsequently expires, ignoring it would have been justified at A's death. If the reversion comes into possession (to A's estate), ignoring it would again have been appropriate because the property is simply retransferred to A's heirs or legatees (or paid to the creditors of A or her estate); if the property was already taxed at A's death in full, taxing it again later is pointless. Either way, taxing the entire property at the decedent's death is justified. To hold otherwise here would be inconsistent with the long-standing policy of not holding transfers open in cases where the transferor has not retained any interest (or power) just because all interests have not yet vested.

Once it is decided to hold the transfer open in the manner described above, it would not matter what the value of the settlor's reversion was at the date of death. Therefore, the present 5% rule of § 2037 would of necessity be repealed. The issue of the remoteness of the reversion might possess relevance when the transfer is made, since, if the reversion was sufficiently remote, it might be appropriate not to hold the transfer open but to treat it as being complete in full when made. * * *

* * *

The hard-to-complete rule for retained reversion transfers would not make any reference to actuarial tables. Results would track with actual transfers, not, as often happens under present law, * * * on might-have-beens and impossible possibilities. Present § 2037 could be completely repealed, since it would be absorbed into an expanded successor to § 2036 that holds a transfer open on account of any possibility that the transferor, under the instrument of transfer, might receive either income or principal from the transferred property.

* * *

D. Conclusion

The lesson to be drawn from the foregoing is that retained income interests and reversions should trigger a hard-to-complete rule, not so much because the retained interest approximates ownership of the transferred property, but because a hard-to-complete rule assures accurate valuation of the transfers as and to the extent that they actually occur. * * *

* * *

IV. TRANSFERS WITH RETAINED POWERS

* * *

A. Problems Under Present Law

* * *

[E]xisting law posits a dubious distinction between "administrative" powers and "dispositive" powers, the former being per se immune from the reach of §§ 2036-2038. An administrative power is a power relating to investments or the determination of what receipts and disbursements are allocable to income and corpus, as opposed to a power explicitly pertaining to distributions of income and corpus. On the face of things, administrative powers can be used to shift enjoyment of a trust between the income and remainder beneficiaries. Examples include investing in depleting assets or growth stock, allocating corporate distributions between income and corpus, maintaining (or not maintaining) a depletion or depreciation reserve, and allocating expenses to income or corpus.

The basis of the rule exempting administrative powers is that "trustee powers given for the administration or management of the trust must be equitably exercised * * * for the benefit of the trust as a whole." But a platitude is no substitute for analysis. It is not at all certain that administrative powers explicitly drafted to override conventional principles of the law of trusts would be significantly limited in their exercise by a court of equity. Moreover, only a tiny minority of cases will ever be brought in a court of equity against a settlor-trustee, especially where the beneficiaries are closely related to each other and to the settlor-trustee.

The administrative powers exception in turn spawned the *Byrum* problem, wherein a settlor could transfer stock of a closely held corporation to a trust and control the flow of income to the trust by exercising control over the corporation.[300] Congress responded by enacting § 2036(b), but that provision is inadequate, since it is limited to situations where the settlor retained the right to vote the transferred stock. It fails to reach the situation where the settlor can control the flow of dividends by voting nontransferred stock.

Finally, the law under §§ 2036(a)(2) and 2038 is especially murky in the situation where the settlor trustee holding a power to accumulate income or invade corpus is subject to a broad distributive standard such as "happiness" or "welfare," with courts reaching different results on what appear to be similar facts. Unlike analogous situations, the outcomes do not appear to depend on whether the standards are rendered only indirectly enforceable in a court of equity by insertion of "in the trustee's unfettered discretion," or words of like import. On the merits, many of these decisions seem dubious in that the settlor trustee's dispositive powers were not subject to meaningful restriction. Not only is that true when analyzing the law of trusts, it undoubtedly would be seen to be more so if the courts bothered to inquire into how these trusts actually operated in practice. However, the courts consider only legally enforceable rights to be relevant; actual power is not.

Ultimately, the "dispositive standards" doctrine has the effect of rendering §§ 2036(a)(2) and 2038 "elective" to settlors; prudent draftsmanship virtually assures avoidance of these sections while leaving the settlor trustee with substantial dispositive control.

B. Reforming Present Law

There are three possible ways of dealing with transfers with retained powers. One is to continue, but modify, the present approach which aims to fix a certain quantum of control above which there is deemed to exist a state of "substantial ownership" sufficient to justify a hard-to-

---

[300]   United States v. Byrum, 408 U.S. 125 (1972).

complete rule. Although certain of the existing doctrinal difficulties could be patched up along these lines, the substantial-ownership approach is inherently unworkable. Unlike interests, which can be defined, weighed, and measured, powers resist formal categorization and quantification. The significance of a power is affected by a multitude of factors, such as its nature (to sprinkle, accumulate, invade, add beneficiaries, appoint remainders), its scope (how many interests and persons might be affected), whether it exists singly or with other powers, whether it is held solely or jointly (and, if the latter, the identity of the other holders), whether it is contingent or can be exercised at any time, whether and to what extent it is subject to control by a court of equity, and whether the power is held directly or indirectly. A facts-and-circumstances test capable of considering all of the foregoing is not appropriate for a wealth transfer tax; it promotes uncertainty and breeds litigation. The alternative of trying to reduce the factors into a set of rules would be extremely difficult and undoubtedly arbitrary. * * *

A second approach would be to apply a hard-to-complete rule to all transfers in which the transferor retains any dispositive or administrative power, including all transfers in which the transferor is or might be trustee. It is no objection to say that such a rule would prevent a settlor from being trustee. Of course she could be trustee; the only difference would relate to when the transfer would be taxed. Under a transfer tax system that is truly neutral between gift and estate transfers, it will not matter if the transfer is taxed when made or when the power is extinguished, except for the fortuitous fact of any discrepancy between the property's future economic yield as compared to estimates thereof used to value the property at the time of transfer.

It will also be objected that a retained power to alter beneficial interests is not as "valuable" as a retained interest. The answer is that, to a person of great wealth who is materially well off, a retained power is likely to be as valuable as a retained interest. If the power were not important, it would not have been retained. * * *

The third alternative is to treat transfers with retained powers (other than to revoke) as always being complete when made. * * * It will be objected that such a rule will allow a wealthy transferor to have her cake and to eat it too, that is, as having given away property when really she has kept substantial enjoyment of it. Of course, whether a given transfer involves the retention of substantial enjoyment might be somewhat difficult to answer; as mentioned above, a case by case substantial ownership approach is unsatisfactory. But there is an answer that cuts deeper. As indicated earlier, the real reason for imposing a hard-to-complete rule on all transfers with retained interests is not that any retained interest approximates ownership. * * * Rather, transfers involving retained * * * interests, and revocable transfers, must be subjected to a hard-to-complete rule in order to accurately determine the exact amount of the transfer from the transferor to the transferees. However, valuation is not an issue with respect to transfers with retained powers to affect beneficial enjoyment. In these cases it is absolutely clear that the property and the income therefrom is committed to persons other than the transferor * * * . Thus—and to repeat a point made above in discussing the hard-to-complete rule—under a neutral transfer tax system, there is no opportunity for tax avoidance here except as might result from the vagaries of the market subsequent to the transfer.

There are some administrative advantages attendant to an easy-to complete rule. First, a hard-to-complete rule would inevitably generate attempts to avoid it by way of "indirect" powers exercised through corporations and other entities and individuals. * * * Second—and perhaps a more general formulation of the first point—an easy-to-complete rule would effectively obviate any need for "rule" distinctions in this area. Third, if a hard-to-complete rule were enacted here, all distributions to persons other than the transferor would be completed transfers, and it might be somewhat difficult for the compliance system to keep track of these transfers, especially if the gift tax exemptions are no longer available. Fourth, there would be no need to examine the issue of whether a given power was "retained" under the transfer. Fifth, it would no longer be necessary to decide whether certain powers, not mentioned in the instrument of transfer, were within the scope of a hard-to-complete rule.

* * * [I]t seems that the easy-to-complete approach * * * for transfers with retained powers affecting beneficial enjoyment has merit, although the case for a hard-to-complete rule is virtually as compelling. Either would be preferable to the current unhappy situation. * * *

* * *

NOTE

Dodge considers "substantial ownership" as a criterion for measuring the degree of control represented by retained powers. He rejects this approach as "inherently unworkable," however, noting that "[u]nlike interests, which can be defined, weighed, and measured, powers resist formal categorization and quantification." Are the problems concerning completion and valuation more intractable in the case of retained powers than in the case of retained interests? Can these problems be resolved "by defining [them] away with rules that make line-drawing irrelevant"? For a recent proposal to adopt a uniform "hard-to-complete" rule for estate and gift tax purposes, see James M. Spica, *Federal Transfer Tax Treatment of Actuarial Appreciation*, 42 DRAKE L. REV. 123 (1993).

PART VIII:

ALTERNATIVE TAX SYSTEMS

Part VIII explores the feasibility and desirability of alternative tax systems that have been proposed to replace or supplement the existing wealth transfer taxes. They are considered in the following order: (1) an accessions tax; (2) an income tax; (3) a consumption tax; (4) a wealth tax; and (5) a bequeathing power succession tax.

A.   An Accessions Tax

An accessions tax, first proposed by Harry Rudick,* would be imposed on the recipient's cumulative lifetime gifts and inheritances. William D. Andrews, the Associate Reporter for the Accessions Tax Proposal to the American Law Institute's Federal Estate and Gift Tax Project,** describes the rationale and operation of an accessions tax and focuses on problems arising from transfers in trust. Edward C. Halbach, Jr., presents an accessions tax as an alternative to the existing wealth transfer taxes.

William D. Andrews, *The Accessions Tax Proposal*, 22 TAX L. REV. 589 (1967)***

* * *

An accessions tax is an excise tax on the transfer of property by gift or on death, but imposed on the recipient rather than the donor or the decedent's estate. Like a transfer tax, the accessions tax would have a graduated rate schedule; but the rate is graduated according to the aggregate taxable accessions of the recipient from all sources, without regard to other property owned or disposed of by the donor or decedent. Thus an accessions tax may bear more heavily than a transfer tax in the case of a single person inheriting from several sources, while it will bear less heavily when a single estate is divided among several recipients without accessions from other sources.

This difference in rate graduation is the most important distinguishing characteristic of an accessions tax. It is this difference that led Rudick to assert the accessions tax would be more

---

*   Harry J. Rudick, *A Proposal for an Accessions Tax*, 1 TAX L. REV. 25 (1945); Harry J. Rudick, *What Alternative to the Estate and Gift Taxes?*, 38 CAL. L. REV. 150 (1950). Rudick's proposal was criticized in Richard D. Kirschberg, *The Accessions Tax: Administrative Bramblebush or Instrument of Social Policy?*, 14 UCLA L. REV. 135 (1966). *See also* CARL S. SHOUP, FEDERAL ESTATE AND GIFT TAXES (1966).

**   *See* AMERICAN LAW INSTITUTE, FEDERAL ESTATE AND GIFT TAXATION 446-589 (1969).

***   Copyright © 1967. Reprinted with permission.

consistent with the purpose of federal transfer taxes to promote dispersion of wealth. Others have suggested that rate graduation in accordance with the circumstances of the recipient is fairer, or at least more rational, than graduation according to the wealth of transferors, simply because the recipient probably bears the burden of the tax in any event.

* * *

SUMMARY DESCRIPTION

Accessions

Accessions are defined generally as including all property received by way of gift or inheritance. More specifically, accessions include the receipt of life insurance proceeds if the insured retained incidents of ownership; the receipt of employee benefits by an employee's survivors after his death; the amount of property acquired by the survivor in a joint tenancy in excess of the portion contributed by him or on which he was taxed when the joint tenancy was created. With several minor exceptions, and one major exception, the events that represent included transfers by the transferor under the unified transfer tax represent accessions to the transferee under the accessions tax proposal.

The major exception is a transfer in trust. In the accessions tax proposal no accession is ordinarily deemed to occur on account of the creation of a trust or the transfer of property to a trustee. On the other hand, a distribution from a trust, whether of income or corpus, is treated as an accession to the distributee from the settlor. This rule applies even after the settlor's death, and it applies to testamentary as well as inter vivos trusts. There are various exceptions and qualifications, described below, but the accessions tax proposal is built around the concept that ordinarily the distribution of trust property, rather than contribution to the trust, is the taxable event.

Exclusions and Deductions

There is a complete exclusion of interspousal accessions. There is an exclusion of money or property received (and expended) for current consumption, and on top of that an annual per donor exclusion for outright inter vivos gifts of up to $1,500 (which will cover $3,000 from a married donor if nothing is received from his spouse). The annual exclusion is inapplicable to transfers at death and to trust distributions. There is a lifetime exemption of $24,000 (described as a zero per cent bracket in the rate schedule) applicable to taxable accessions from all sources.

No exclusion is necessary for charitable contributions; charitable organizations are simply exempt from the tax. On the other hand, there is need to provide an exclusion for charitable distributions if it is thought desirable to exempt them from the tax.

A deduction is also provided of 40 per cent of the amount of any accession from a parent, parent-in-law, sibling, child, or parent of a deceased parent ("immediate relations"). The effect of this deduction, like that of the 50 per cent marital deduction under the present gift tax, is to make the effective rate of tax on accessions from these people lower than that on accessions from other sources ("remote accessions"). The reasons for this rate differential are described below in the discussion of the rate structure.

Computation of Tax

The tax is computed and paid annually. Each year's tax is based on the year's taxable accessions, but the rate, which is graduated, depends on a taxpayer's cumulative total of taxable accessions during his whole lifetime. The mechanics of computation are exactly the same as under the present gift tax: read the tax in the table for the taxpayer's taxable accessions for the taxable year and all prior years; then read the tax in the table for the taxpayer's taxable accessions in prior years only; the tax for the current year is the excess of the former over the latter.

* * *

The Special Estate Tax on Property Left in Trust

Part of the accessions tax proposal is that there be, in some cases a separate tax on property left in trust. This tax is imposed only in the case of decedents who leave moderately large estates ($500,000, excluding property left to or for a spouse or charity); and only if a significant amount ($100,000) is left in trust. The tax is imposed only on property left in trust (including property still held in any inter vivos trusts created by the decedent during his lifetime), but at a rate determined by reference to the decedent's whole probate estate. * * * The special estate tax paid on any trust is made the basis for a credit against accessions taxes on subsequent distributions from the trust. The effect of the credit is to make the special estate tax operate principally as a device for prepayment of accessions taxes on trust distributions, not as an instrument for imposing any substantial additional tax burden. The purpose is simply to curb the otherwise unlimited opportunity for tax deferral that would exist under the general rule that trust property is taxed on the way out of the trust, not on the way in.

TRUST BENEFICIARIES

The treatment of trust beneficiaries—the fact that generally a tax is imposed only on the distribution of trust property, not on the creation of the trust or the vesting of a beneficiary's interest—is perhaps the central structural feature of the accessions tax proposal. This rule and the reasons for it will now be examined in greater detail.

Exceptions and Qualifications

There are several exceptions and qualifications to the rule that trust beneficiaries are taxed only on distributions of the trust property:

1. Any person interested in a trust is permitted to elect, as of the end of any taxable year, to be treated as having received a distribution of the property in the trust. The consequences of such an election are (i) that the amount of the property in the trust is deemed to be an accession to the person making the election; (ii) that the person making the election will not be taxed on subsequent distributions from the trust, and any other person subsequently receiving a distribution from the trust may treat it as an accession from the person who made the election; and (iii) that any property in the trust on the death of the person making the election will be part of his taxable estate for purposes of the special estate tax on property left in trust. * * *

2. If a person sells an interest in a trust, the sales proceeds are to be treated like a distribution from the trust on account of such interest. The purchaser will not be subject to accessions tax on subsequent distributions to him; and if he causes distributions to be made to someone else the distributions will be accessions from the purchaser, not from the creator of the trust.

3. If a trust beneficiary is permitted to enjoy his interest by occupation or direct use of trust assets rather than by the distribution of income, then the value of such use shall be treated as a distribution from the trust for accessions tax purposes.

4. If a trust beneficiary at any time has a general power of appointment over the trust property, then he shall be treated as having received a distribution of the property subject to the power, and subsequent distributees of the property and the income therefrom, may treat it as if the powerholder were the creator of the trust. A general power of appointment is defined in much the same way as under the unified transfer tax, except that it does not include a power that can only be exercised on death.

5. * * * [A] trust income beneficiary may elect to establish a fixed rate of tax or to pay up his accessions tax in advance on the actuarial value of his interest.

* * *

The Tax Deferral Problem

The general rule for taxing trust beneficiaries gives rise to the problem of tax deferral. Thus if property is left by A on his death to a trustee to pay income to B for his life and then to distribute the corpus to B's issue, no accessions tax is payable by any beneficiary with respect to the trust corpus until B's death. A tax would have been payable on A's death if the property had been left outright to B; and under a transfer tax, the tax would have been payable on A's death whether the property were left outright to B or in trust. Under the accessions tax proposal therefore, the trust disposition can be said to defer the tax on the trust corpus for the period of B's lifetime.

This result has been considered to be unacceptable in the case of large estates. That is the reason for imposing the special estate tax on substantial trust dispositions. Insofar as the special estate tax operates as a prepayment of accessions taxes all that is deferred is the final reckoning by which trust property is accounted for as an accession to a particular beneficiary.

Tax deferral is not considered to be a serious problem in small or middle-sized estates, however, because the corollary of deferral is inclusion in the tax base of all income (including capital appreciation) during the period of deferral. In the case given above, for example, income distributions to B during his life will be subject to tax as accessions to B from A. If the trust assets are invested to produce capital appreciation rather than (or in addition to) current income, the government will share in that too by virtue of valuing the corpus on B's death, not A's, for purposes of taxing the transfer to B's issue. Neither the income nor the capital appreciation would be taxed under a transfer tax imposed at the time of A's death.

* * *

The Possibility of Taxing Trust Interests as Accessions on Vesting

Consideration has been given to the possibility of treating certain trust interests as accessions when they arise, or vest, or vest in possession. It could be provided, for example, as under some of the state inheritance tax laws, that any vested present interest should be valued and taxed as an accession when it vests in possession. Or it could be provided that any indefeasibly vested interest, present or future, is to be valued and taxed as an accession upon vesting. The rule could even be extended to embrace certain sorts of contingent interests if the contingency does not prevent the making of a reasonable valuation.

In the case of any interest taxed as an accession, subsequent distributions would not be regarded as accessions; distributions on account of untaxed interests would continue to be taxed as accessions under the general rule.

The arguments in favor of this alternative are simple and straightforward:

(i) An interest in a trust is property; and some interests, at least, should be treated like other property. A person is richer—better off—after being made a trust beneficiary than before; an accessions tax—which is after all a tax on enrichment by gift, bequest, or devise—should not ignore that fact. Like other property, many interests in trusts can be valued and even sold if necessary.

(ii) This alternate treatment would operate, pro tanto, to reduce the problem of tax deferral. Indeed, in the simple case where A leaves property in trust granting a life estate to B and remainder to C and his heirs, this treatment could be made to eliminate the problem of tax deferral altogether by taxing both B and C, each on the value of his interest, immediately on A's death.

The objections to this method of taxing trust interests are less obvious:

(i) The idea of taxing trust beneficiaries on the value of their interests at the time the trust is created cannot, after all, be carried very far. There is no feasible way, for example, to tax the beneficiaries of a discretionary trust on the value of their interests at the time the trust is created. Even under nondiscretionary trusts there are many beneficial interests that it would be impractical to tax at the creation of the trust. * * * On the whole it seems no more objectionable to discriminate between trust interests and other kinds of property than it would be to distinguish trust interests that are vested (and not subject to partial divestiture) from those that are subject to various sorts of conditions.

Furthermore, if taxpayers wanted tax deferral the effect of taxing certain interests prior to distribution might be simply to drive settlors and testators into creating discretionary trusts solely to avoid immediate imposition of a tax.

(ii) There would be a substantial problem of raising funds to pay the tax if a life estate or remainder interest were treated as an accession upon vesting. It would be unfair to provide for the payment of accessions taxes out of the trust assets because different beneficiaries may have very different tax rates. If, for example, the life beneficiary is in a high tax bracket while the remainderman is in a low accessions tax bracket, payment of both taxes out of the trust corpus would be unfair to the remainderman; there is no reason why his ultimate take from the trust should be reduced by payment of a tax at the life tenant's accessions tax rate. * * *

* * *

In one sense the whole matter of waiting until distribution can be viewed as meeting this problem of liquidity by allowing a trust beneficiary to make payment in kind. A trust beneficiary who pays no tax on the vesting of his interest, but who must thereafter pay tax on each distribution to him on account of his interest, has in effect assigned a portion of his interest (the portion being determined from time to time by his applicable tax rate bracket) to the government. Thus the effect of deferral is similar to that of a system which would require the trust beneficiary to account for the value of his interest as an accession, but then permit him to pay the resulting tax by way of a partial assignment of his interest in the trust. Indeed this is precisely the rationale underlying the provision which allows a trust income beneficiary to establish a fixed rate of tax with respect to income distributions.

(iii) Any proposal to tax trust beneficiaries upon the vesting of their interests would introduce substantial problems of valuation. The impossibility of valuing some trust interests, indeed, is what would prevent any thoroughgoing system of taxing trust beneficiaries on the creation of the trust. There is no feasible way to value the interests of beneficiaries in a discretionary trust. But even in the case of beneficiaries with vested life income or remainder interests accepted valuation techniques are unsatisfactory. * * *

Existing valuation techniques are also deficient, of course, in that they fail to take account of differences in investment policy affecting the relative values of income and remainder interests.

Deferral of tax until distribution has the effect of solving valuation problems through a wait and see technique. A life beneficiary in poor health will only be taxed on what she actually receives; and the remainderman whose interest is enhanced by the life tenant's ill health will have to pay the tax on the full value of the trust property at the date when his interest falls in.

(iv) Insofar as ultimate tax burdens are concerned, tax deferral is not a serious problem. The deferral of tax is accompanied rather generally by a compensating increase in the amount that becomes subject to tax. Indeed with graduated rates the increase in amount of tax tends to overcompensate for the effects of deferral.

(v) If tax deferral is a problem it is a problem of interrupting the flow of tax revenues, or of postponing the liquidation of estates, not a problem of undertaxation of trust beneficiaries. As such the problem can be much better taken care of through the device of the special estate tax, which is imposed directly on trust assets, than by taxing beneficiaries prospectively on the value of their interests.

Indeed, the special estate tax can be thought of, in a sense, as an alternate method of taxing the creation of trust interests, designed to eliminate the problems that arise from trying to tax the trust beneficiaries directly. The special estate tax meets the foregoing objections because (i) it is based on the whole value of property in the trust, not just the value of certain interests; (ii) it can be paid out of trust assets, with subsequent readjustments to prevent a tax at one beneficiary's rates from impairing another beneficiary's interest; and (iii) it need not depend on valuation of beneficiaries' interests—and even if it is based on the valuation of individual interests it is only a tentative tax, in effect, which will be finally readjusted in such a way as to correct for errors in valuation.

* * *

Elective Treatment of Property Left in Trust

The proposal permits any interested person to elect to be taxed as if property left in trust had been left outright, or distributed, to him.

There will be three principal reasons for making this election. The first would be that if a beneficiary expects ultimately to receive most of the property in a trust, he may elect to be taxed under this section in order to avoid inclusion in his accessions tax base of income and capital appreciation prior to distribution of trust property to him. The second reason would be to take advantage of the lower rate of tax applicable to transfers from parent to child. * * * The third reason for electing to be taxed would be to reduce or avoid the special estate tax imposed on property left in trust.

The purpose of permitting this election is to make the tax as neutral as possible with respect to the choice between a trust and an outright disposition of property. The dual rate structure and the special estate tax are both intended to compensate for certain advantages that a trust might otherwise have over an outright disposition. This election will prevent either of those provisions from overcompensating, by making it clear that a trust will never result in the sacrifice of tax advantages that would have resulted from an outright disposition to the current trust beneficiary.

An election to be taxed on undistributed trust property can be made only with respect to the whole value of specified trust assets or on the basis of the actuarial value of an income interest. * * * The reason this sort of election has not been extended, in this proposal, to remaindermen and holders of other interests except current income interests, is that it creates substantial problems of valuation and of adverse selection. * * *

Sale of an Interest in a Trust

The purpose of the general rule governing trust beneficiaries is to postpone the tax until their interest is reduced to immediate enjoyment. Ordinarily, the reduction to immediate enjoyment occurs upon the distribution of funds or property by the trustee to the beneficiary. If the beneficiary sells his interest, however, that constitutes a reduction to enjoyment, and there is no reason to postpone the tax beyond that point. Therefore the sale proceeds are treated as an accession and taxed to the same extent that a distribution of the sold interest would have been taxed.

Use of Trust Assets by a Trust Beneficiary

The deferral of tax on a trust beneficiary until distribution depends upon two propositions: (i) that a trust beneficiary's enjoyment of his interest only occurs as distributions are made to him, and (ii) that the government will be compensated for deferral by the fact that all investment returns during the period of deferral will enter into the accessions tax base. Both these propositions would be violated if a trust beneficiary were permitted to use the trust property in kind—as when a trust beneficiary is permitted to occupy a residence held in trust for him—

unless the use is treated as the equivalent of a distribution. Any direct use of trust assets by a beneficiary is therefore treated as a distribution for accessions tax purposes. * * *

* * *

THE SPECIAL ESTATE TAX ON PROPERTY LEFT IN TRUST

The general treatment of trust beneficiaries in the accessions tax proposal is predicated on the proposition that the advantages of tax deferral in small and moderate estates are offset by the increase in tax that ultimately results from including investment gains in the tax base. The increase in tax will prevent any great tax-motivated increase in the use of trusts; and it will compensate the government for such deferral as does occur.

Unlimited tax deferral would be unacceptable in the case of very large estates, however, for a number of reasons:

(1) In very wealthy families the distribution of trust property might be put off more or less indefinitely. In such families dominion may be more significant, marginally at least, than consumption, and many aspects of dominion can be effectively exercised without ever taking property out of trust. * * *

(2) One of the purposes of taxing transfers on death may be to promote the reasonably prompt and orderly liquidation of very large estates. This effect could be avoided under the accessions tax, standing alone, by leaving property in trust.

(3) From a fiscal standpoint the delay in revenue collections with respect to property left in trust may be undesirable even if ultimate collections are larger. * * *

(4) Even if the deferred tax on trust distributions is larger, the opportunity to avoid any immediate tax on property transferred in trust would be likely to have a disproportionate psychological impact on some testators. In order to make the tax factor as nearly neutral as possible with respect to the choice between a trust and an outright gift or bequest it may seem desirable to provide for some immediate tax on a transfer in trust. This will tend to equalize immediate as well as ultimate tax burdens on the two sorts of transfers.

Accordingly, the proposal includes a special estate tax on property left in trust. The special estate tax is payable only if a decedent leaves at least $100,000 in trust. Thus a man and wife can leave up to $200,000 in trust without paying any special estate tax. Moreover, the special estate tax operates, as will be seen, largely as a prepayment device rather than as a true additional tax.

The Taxable Estate

The property on which the special estate tax is imposed—the taxable estate—is defined by the following rules:

(a) Except as hereinafter provided, any property left in trust under the decedent's will is included in the taxable estate.

(b) Except as hereinafter provided, any property transferred by the decedent to a trustee during his lifetime, together with all income and proceeds therefrom, if still held in trust as of the date two years after the decedent's death, is included in the taxable estate.

* * *

* * * It is contemplated that the special estate tax will be paid out of assets included in the taxable estate. If the tax is paid wholly or partly out of assets not otherwise included in the taxable estate, then the amount so paid shall be included in the taxable estate.

The general purpose in defining the taxable estate is to include all property which would be taxed as an accession to someone from the decedent if it had been left outright on the decedent's death.

* * *

The general purpose in computing the special estate tax is to arrive at an amount which represents a reasonable, conservative approximation of the amount of accessions taxes that are being deferred. * * *

* * *

* * * [T]he rules protect against the imposition of a special estate tax that is too high in relation to the accessions tax rates of any beneficiary with a qualified present interest; and against the imposition of a special estate tax at too high a rate in view of the number of the decedent's issue. With these qualifications a crude approximation, simply arrived at, seems adequate.

Credit Against Subsequent Accessions Taxes for Special Estate Tax Paid

In the case of distributions (or other taxable accessions) from a trust that has been subject to the special estate tax, a credit shall be allowed against the accessions taxes payable by the distributees in accordance with the following rules:

(1) A credit ratio is computed for any trust upon payment of any special estate tax, which will be applicable, except as hereinafter provided, to all distributions from the trust. The credit ratio is the amount of special estate tax paid, divided by the amount of property left in the trust immediately after payment of the tax. For this purpose property in the trust is taken at the same value as was used in computing the special estate tax.

Thus, for example, if a special estate tax of $200,000 were paid out of a $1,000,000 trust, the credit ratio would be 25 per cent (200,000 ÷ 800,000).

(2) The credit ordinarily allowable with respect to any trust distribution (or other taxable accession) is the amount of the distribution multiplied by the trust credit ratio. Thus, if a trust with a credit ratio of 25 per cent makes a distribution of $10,000, a credit of $2,500 is allowable against the distributee's accessions tax. The amount of the allowable credit is itself treated as an accession. Therefore, in the case given, the distributee would report a taxable accession of $12,500 and claim a credit against accessions taxes of $2,500.

(3) If the credit allowable with respect to a trust distribution exceeds the distributee's accessions taxes due on account of the distribution, it may, nevertheless, be applied as a credit against accessions taxes due on account of other accessions in the same or subsequent taxable years. No refund (or offset) is allowed, however, of accessions taxes paid (or due) for prior taxable years.

(4) The total amount of credit allowable on distributions from any trust is limited to a dollar amount equal to the special estate tax paid plus six per cent simple interest. Rules are provided to govern the computation of this limitation.

The purpose of the credit is to make the special estate tax operate principally as a device for prepayment of accessions taxes, rather than a source of additional tax burden. The credit ratio scheme is a simple device for allocating the credit proportionately among the accessions taxpayers who receive distributions from the trust. It also serves to give recognition to the fact that a dollar of tax paid earlier casts more of a burden than a dollar paid later, since the credit ratio applied to all distributions from a trust throughout its duration will ordinarily produce more dollars of credit than the dollars of tax paid. The credit ratio device also serves to protect the government against investment losses; if trust assets are lost so that distributions and resulting accessions taxes are eliminated, at least the government will keep whatever amount was paid in special estate tax.

When the credit allowable on a distribution exceeds the accessions tax payable by the recipient, no refund is allowed. To this extent the special estate tax is not a pure prepayment device, but serves also to set a kind of floor, or lower limit, on the rate of tax applicable to property passing through the trust.

THE ACCESSIONS TAX RATE STRUCTURE

The accessions tax is imposed at rates that are graduated in relation to a taxpayer's lifetime cumulative aggregate of taxable accessions. The mechanics of computation are exactly analogous to those employed to compute the gift tax under present law.

The rates are further varied according to the relationship between the taxpayer and the transferor of a particular accession, accessions from immediate relations being taxed at lower rates than accessions from others. Immediate relations are defined as the taxpayer's parents, parents-in-law, children, and siblings, and parents of a deceased parent of the taxpayer if the parent was deceased at the time the transfer was made. (The taxpayer's spouse is not defined as an immediate relation because accessions from the taxpayer's spouse are wholly exempt from any accessions tax.)

* * *

If a taxpayer has had both remote accessions and accessions from immediate relations, the tax is computed by aggregating accessions from all sources; deducting 40 per cent of the amount of the accessions from immediate relations; and then applying the rate schedule for remote accessions to this reduced amount. This mechanism has the effect of basing graduation of the aggregate of taxable accessions from all sources while offering different rates for accessions from different sources. * * *

* * *

Reasons for the Dual Rate Structure

The dual rate structure is designed to try to establish or restore some degree of tax neutrality between the giving of property to children and to grandchildren. For this purpose the dual rate structure offers a lower rate schedule for application to transfers from parent to child, to compensate for the natural tax advantages that attach to a transfer from grandparent to grandchild under an accessions tax.

The natural tax advantages that attach to a transfer from grandparent to grandchild are several. * * * The accessions tax is intentionally designed so that the taxes will be lower if property is distributed among a larger number of people. By leaving property to his grandchildren a man can bring their lifetime exemptions into the computation of taxes due on his death, and cause part of his property to be taxed at rates determined by the grandchildren's lifetime cumulation of accessions which is likely to be less than his children's. The tax inducement to give to grandchildren is even more immediate when gifts in trust are considered. * * * Under the rules in this proposal, for moderate estates, a trust has the further effect of deferring any tax until distributions are made from the trust.

There are several reasons why some compensation is needed to offset the natural advantages of giving to grandchildren under an accessions tax. First there are reasons relating to incentives and social policy—there do not seem to be any adequate reasons of policy for creating the very strong incentives a single rate accessions tax would offer to pass over children in favor of grandchildren. * * * Second there are reasons of equity. There do not seem to be any satisfactory reasons of equity why tax burdens should be substantially higher * * * because a family's wealth moves from one generation to the next instead of being put in trust or left from grandfather to grandson. * * * Third there are reasons of finance. While exact estimates are impossible it appears that rates under a single rate accessions tax would have to be set quite high to offset the erosion of the tax base that would result from an increase in giving to grandchildren under such a tax. A dual rate structure therefore makes it possible to propose lower rates from parental accessions than would be possible under a single rate schedule.

The dual rate structure does not eliminate the natural advantages of giving to grandchildren under an accessions tax. * * * But the dual rate structure does represent a relatively simple way to give a compensating tax advantage in the case of gifts to children. It thus operates to make the tax more nearly neutral, in this vital area, than it otherwise would be.

* * *

A very important aspect of the accessions tax proposal is the elimination of some of the most intractable problems that have arisen and persisted under the existing gift and estate taxes, and with which any proposal for a tax on transferors must be concerned. A brief mention of some of those problems is in order.

(1) The problem of telling a lifetime transfer from a transfer taking effect at death disappears under an accessions tax. As with a unified transfer tax, there is no rate differential predicated on the distinction between a lifetime transfer and a transfer at death. But even the problem of timing—when is a transfer in trust sufficiently complete to be taxed—disappears under an accessions tax because only trust distributions are taxed in any event.

(2) The problems of defining a qualifying interest for marital deduction purposes are virtually eliminated. Under the accessions tax proposal any accession from a spouse is exempt, and there is no need to judge limited or divided interests because no tax arises, from which to grant an exemption, until distribution of trust property. * * *

(3) Problems of qualification and valuation in relation to the charitable deduction are largely eliminated, or at least reduced in importance, under an accessions tax.

(4) Problems concerning the treatment of transfers in trust under which the transferor retains a reversionary interest, especially a contingent reversionary interest, are eliminated under an accessions tax.

(5) The matter of defining when a transfer by one spouse may be attributed and taxed to the other—the whole matter of gift splitting—is virtually eliminated under the accessions tax, because the rate of tax is not dependent on the amount of property transferred by an individual transferor.

* * *

This central structural change—the taxation of trust distributions instead of contributions—while only prompted by the shift to an accessions basis of taxation, has the effect of eliminating some of the thorniest, most persistent technical problems that have plagued the gift and estate tax, in various forms, from the beginning. * * *

* * *

NOTE

As Andrews points out, an accessions tax would significantly change the treatment of transfers in trust. Under current law, a gift or estate tax is imposed on the donor or decedent's estate at the time a transfer in trust becomes complete. In contrast, an accessions tax with respect to trust transfers would normally be imposed on the recipient only upon the receipt of distributions. Lorence L. Bravenec and Dennis R. Lassila see this as a "significant problem" with Andrews' accessions tax proposal. Lorence L.

Bravenec & Dennis R. Lassila, *An Accessions Emphasis for Federal Estate and Gift Taxes*, 24 TAX NOTES 1069, 1070 (1984). Does the "special estate tax" proposed by Andrews adequately address this problem? In a later article, Andrews contends that it would be "relatively simple" to impose a withholding tax on the creation of a trust which could then be credited against the accessions tax on subsequent trust distributions. William D. Andrews, *What's Fair About Death Taxes?*, 26 NAT'L TAX J. 465, 469 (1973).

Edward C. Halbach, Jr., *An Accessions Tax*, 23 REAL PROP., PROB. & TR. J. 211 (1988)*

* * *

GENERAL NATURE OF THE TAX

In essence, an accessions tax is collected from the *recipients* of gratuitously transferred property. The amounts of the levies are based on the recipients' circumstances and transfer tax histories rather than on those of donors and estates. The tax differs from an inheritance tax (also imposed on transferees) in two primary respects. First, it is based on the taxpayer's cumulative accessions from all sources over an entire lifetime, with its exemption and any rate graduation applied accordingly. Second, the tax, as contemplated here, would normally tax funds or assets as they reach the recipients (for example, free of trust), not when those beneficiaries' interests are created in some future-interest or uncertain form. Thus, generally at least, a recipient would report actual receipts from gifts, estates and other donative sources in any year in which allowable annual and marital exclusions are exceeded or inapplicable. * * *

* * *

POTENTIAL ADVANTAGES AND PROBLEMS OF THE TAX

* * *

A traditional * * * argument for an accessions tax is premised on basic fairness: that it facilitates equitable allocation of burdens among those who in a realistic sense bear the tax. * * *

Under a system that is oriented toward *transferors* (that is, donors and estates), like the present system, the tax on any given amount of receipts is greater for a recipient who takes from one transferor than for a person who receives that same amount of property from several transferors. This discrepancy in treatment is present as well under *transferee*-oriented systems that take the form of an inheritance tax. Furthermore, under *transferor*-oriented systems, a person who inherits a particular amount as one of several successors to a larger estate is taxed more heavily than a recipient of the same amount would be taxed as the sole beneficiary of a smaller estate.

By way of contrast, under an accessions tax, persons whose total accessions are similar in amount would be taxed similarly. This similarity of treatment would result regardless of differences either in the number of sources from whom transfers are received or in the number of other recipients with whom estates are shared.

* * *

Deductibility and Completeness Issues Disappear

Some stubborn problems that are familiar under the present system would virtually disappear under an appropriate accessions tax format that focuses almost entirely on actual receipt.

One category of such problems is illustrated by difficulties that have been the source of a long, unproductive struggle in the qualification and valuation of both marital deduction and charitable deduction transfers. Similarly, issues about the qualification of specific gift transfers for annual exclusions virtually disappear. * * *

There is also a second category of problems that essentially disappear under an accessions tax. These problems involve the drawing of lines between transfers during life and those that are effective at death, and other issues about when a transfer is to be treated as completed. * * *

The essence of the solution to these various types of problems, and therefore the key to the simplicity of an accessions tax, is found in the fact that when a transfer occurs the system has no need for immediate identification of recipients and interests to be taxed. This follows from the fact that the tax is not on the transfer but on the receipt. It is therefore not imposed until the recipient comes into possession or receives a distribution. Nor does the right to any exemption or exclusion from tax have to be determined until that time. Consequently, qualification requirements, valuation problems and associated issues simply do not arise. Essentially, then, the wait-and-see approach inherent in an actual-receipt form of the tax just naturally would leave these matters behind rather than in the way.

Problems of Deferral

Potentially troublesome problems of tax deferral result from that same decision not to impose the accessions tax until there is actual distribution from a trust and receipt by a trust beneficiary. The main problem, however, *tends* to be handled simply and naturally by self-adjustment. Compensation to the government takes the form of an automatic expansion of the eventual tax base. The enlarged base will include income and appreciation arising during the deferral period—values that would not have been included in the initial amount of the accession had there been no deferral.

* * *

Interspousal "Accession Splitting" (cf. Traditional Estate Splitting)

The traditional gift and estate planning problem of estate or wealth splitting, as it exists in the present transfer tax system, would disappear with the adoption of an accessions tax. An inverse problem arises, however, involving what might be called "accession splitting" between transferee spouses.

* * *

* * * [A] transferor might be induced to divide gifts or bequests between transferee spouses. * * * Unless this opportunity is neutralized, an accessions tax would reward accession splitting through planning that, for example, divides between X and X's spouse a substantial inheritance that would otherwise have been left to X alone. Conversely, if the law allows such an opportunity, it would effectively penalize a transferor's failure, unwillingness or inability (such as if X does not marry until after the transferor dies) to take advantage of this interspousal accession splitting.

A solution to this problem that is both neutral and equitable may require aggregating such split accessions in the spouse who was related to the transferor, or possibly the opposite—that is, allowing an accession to be treated as split * * * whether or not the disposition was in fact made that way. It does not, however, seem desirable to let the accessions tax treatment be finally determined by the way the transferor makes the transfer * * * .

* * *

A New Problem: Conscious "Accession Scattering"

In most typical estate plans, it would be natural to have some "scattering" of accessions among recipients other than spouses (usually, among a transferor's children). Under ordinary circumstances at least, the results of this behavior would be unobjectionable from a policy standpoint. * * *

On the other hand, it is doubtful that there is a persuasive social policy justification (or a real and substantial economic power-sharing justification) for the tax system to reward and thereby encourage estate plans that property owners would not otherwise desire, involving bequests of large amounts of wealth to more remote descendants at the expense of children. Furthermore, as a practical matter, * * * even the deliberate, planned dispersion of estates among numerous recipients in several generations is substantially counteracted in the long term by cumulation of accessions in the transferees. * * *

How does this cumulation occur? In simplest terms, as descendants "multiply" when transfers are made to lower generations, there will also be a multiplication of the number of ancestors from whom accessions can be expected to be received and cumulated over the lifetimes of those recipients. * * *

* * *

* * * [T]here is a shortcoming * * * inherent in any system that tolerates generation skipping * * * . That is, with scattering by giving to grandchildren, collections would, in effect, occur once every other generation. This problem is not peculiar to an accessions tax but, as in any other system (unless it is to be ignored), calls for "correction" by a special levy on generation-skipping dispositions.

* * *

SPECIFICS OF THE TAX

* * *

Taxation and Definition of Accessions

* * *

The contemplated accessions tax would be imposed annually * * * on all taxable accessions by a U.S. citizen or resident, and possibly on others who receive transfers from citizens and residents. "Taxable" accessions are those in excess of the recipient's exemption. "Accessions" are non-excluded receipts by way of gift, testate or intestate succession, and other covered transfers. * * *

* * *

Receipts *by* charities would not be subject to the tax; and receipts by individuals *from* charities pursuant to their charitable purposes are also not accessions. In addition, there would be an unlimited exclusion for interspousal transfers. These types of exclusions would be altogether uncomplicated in the accessions context.

The tax would also offer an annual exclusion, which could quite practically be more restrictive than under the present donor-oriented tax. It should be limited to medical and tuition payments and $5,000 worth of gifts annually from each of an unlimited number of donors, with a continuation of gift splitting by donor spouses. The exclusion would *generally* not be available for receipts by reason of the transferor's death or for trust distributions * * * . For simplicity, neutrality and equity reasons, however, outright bequests should be treated as gifts made in the year of the testator's death, with the usual exclusion amount limit and gift splitting privilege. Because of the trust rule and the absence of an accession until the time of actual receipt, the annual exclusion rule would generally have no need for a present-interest concept. * * *

* * *

* * * [A]ccessions would generally be defined to include the forms of wealth transfer reached by the present system, with adaptations that seem useful and workable under an accessions tax system. * * * The most obvious and fundamental adaptation would be with respect to trust interests, for which distribution/receipt (not transfer) would be the taxable event.

The critical principle for identifying gratuitous (or "wealth") transfers for most purposes would still be the absence of adequate "consideration in money or money's worth." The principle would, of course, be adapted to look for value given by the recipient rather than value received by the transferor. * * *

Assets subject to a nonlapsing general power of appointment or withdrawal would be accessions to the powerholder at the time the power becomes presently exercisable, such a power being equivalent to complete ownership and receipt of the underlying assets. * * *

* * *

Neutrality in Accessions by Married Persons

* * *

A transferor who would normally leave an inheritance entirely to a particular beneficiary may be tempted by the basic, unqualified accessions tax concept to leave that inheritance partly to that beneficiary and partly to that beneficiary's spouse. * * *

* * *

Initially, it seemed appealing to allow spouses the option of splitting * * * any accessions received by either of them. Further consideration surfaced an array of complexities and equity-neutrality problems, as did consideration of a plan that would allow spouses to make a prompt, actual division of property following an accession in order thereby to permit a split of the accession for tax purposes. Ultimately, however, these concerns (centering around the equity objective of similar treatment for persons similarly situated), including concerns arising from fortuities of timing, seemed to favor the approach of aggregating any split accessions in the "related" spouse. * * *

* * *

"Scattering and Skipping": Policy and Treatment

* * *

* * * [G]eneration skipping and likely forms of accession scattering are but different manifestations of the same phenomenon * * * .

* * *

* * * [T]he solution chosen should produce, as nearly as feasible, the same result in a skip situation as the result that would occur if the property had been left to and taxed to a recipient in each successive generation, one at a time, down to the generation in question. The same result, however, cannot be achieved with this precision without (1) determining, in a substitute levy, the appropriate accessions tax rate(s) and any remaining exemption(s) for the "skipped"

generation(s), as well as (2) determining the available exemption and applicable rate(s) for the remote recipient in question. * * *

* * *

An appropriate model would require a two-step computation of the tax on generation-skipping accessions. This procedure can simply be illustrated by a transfer that skips a single generation. First, as a substitute for the tax in the skipped generation, a special generation-skipping levy would be calculated * * * . Then the levy on the recipient's accession, reduced by the amount of the substitute levy, is computed as if the remaining amount were a regular accession by the recipient, who applies the regular exemption/rate schedule to determine the amount of exemption consumed or the amount of tax due. If this second step shows a tax, it is added to the substitute levy * * * to produce the full tax to be imposed on the generation-skipping accession.

* * *

Deferral: Problems and Solutions

Deferred imposition of the tax at the time of actual receipt is the key to what makes so many traditional problems disappear under an accessions tax of the type contemplated here. * * *
* * * [T]here are two quite different types of concerns associated with deferral. * * *

* * *

First, there are what might be called taxpayer concerns. These are concerns over the prospect that, under an accessions tax, (1) most trusts would be penalized and (2) the after-tax utility of trust benefits would be distorted over a beneficiary's lifetime. That is, a trust's beneficiaries would unjustifiably suffer (1) from tax-base expansion (that is, heavier overall taxation) and (2) from distorted timing of the tax toll (that is, early payments favored at the expense of later payments), both of which result from deferral under a progressive exemption/rate structure. * * *

* * *

The second concern might be called a socioeconomic policy concern. Long-term deferral, if not counteracted, would permit the perpetuation of concentrations of wealth, and even growth of those concentrations through untaxed accumulations. This would be an obvious matter of concern if the concentration were to represent socially significant economic power, but it should also be a concern if deferral offers a special privilege and an inequitable (that is, an unjustified) advantage for those who use trusts, especially those who are induced by this potential lack of neutrality to use trusts when they otherwise would not. * * *

* * *

The Taxpayer's Problem: Overcompensation

* * *

Fortunately, both * * * types of taxpayer disadvantages may be cured by a properly designed election. * * *
Under a flat-rate accessions tax, the election would allocate all or any part of the beneficiary's unused exemption to a trust, or to an independent share of a trust. Under a graduated tax, the election could also assign rate brackets to a trust or share. * * *
A beneficiary would be first allowed to make this election on any return filed after the beneficiary's interest becomes a present one, that is, one under which the beneficiary is entitled or eligible to receive distributions currently. * * *

If *A* elects to allocate her exemption in an amount equal to the corpus value of the trust or independent share, this would exempt all distributions she receives (whether of income or principal) from the trust or share * * * . In addition, distributions to *A*'s (or her spouse's) issue or their spouses, whether during *A*'s lifetime or at or after her death, would be immunized from the substitute generation-skipping levy for her generation, just as if the accessions had come from *A* to the descendant who (or whose spouse) received the distribution. Thus, under the election, the substitute levy for *A*'s generation is avoided, just as if distribution had first been made to *A*, covered by her exemption, with *A* then giving or leaving that property to her descendants. More generally, * * * the allocation would cause the trust to be treated as if the corpus had initially been left to *A* who transferred it in trust for herself and for others.

For fear of undesirable manipulation, and to avoid inequity and intrusiveness, the law should not allow cooperative, non-propertied friends and relatives, "compensated" only by limited benefits, to be used as unwarranted sources of elective exemptions that would allow generation-skipping transfers to escape substitute levies as property passes down to genuine, lower-generation objects of the original settlor's bounty. Therefore, accessions by lower-generation beneficiaries would be exempt from the substitute levy only as long as: (1) the distributees are the descendants or spouses of the descendants of the electing beneficiary or his or her spouse; or (2) the electing beneficiary had the prerogatives of an owner (such as a largely unrestricted power to withdraw or appoint inter vivos or, in the case of remainder distributions, the rough equivalent of a testamentary general power). Generally, then, absent such virtual ownership, despite an elective allocation by *A*, distributions to persons who are not *A*'s (or her spouse's) descendants or the spouses of such descendants are not treated as accessions from *A*. They are treated as what they are—accessions from the original transferor. * * *

If *A*'s election allocates an exemption amount that is less than the entire value of the trust corpus at the time, the complete shelter described above could apply to any trust or share that is separated out and independently administered by the trustee in the amount of that allocation. If the trust corpus exceeds *A*'s exemption allocation and an appropriate part of the trust cannot be administered as a separate trust or share, a fractional "exemption ratio" would be determined * * * .

Then an "exempt amount" would be determined each year applying that exemption ratio * * * to *all* trust distributions made that year to all distributees, not just to distributees who are covered (that is, protected) by *A*'s election. To the extent of *A*'s "exempt amount," the full amount of distributions to *A*, her spouse, her descendants or any others eligible to be covered by her election would be protected. * * *

* * *

The Public Policy Problem:
Perpetuation of Economic Power and Privileges

* * *

The broader public policy concerns that arise from deferring taxation of significant trust wealth until the time of distribution call for a special response. * * *

Without special provision, * * * the use of trusts and the accompanying deferral would permit long-term preservation and expansion of family economic power and control. This is generally deemed objectionable when economically and socially significant wealth is involved and when the payment of taxes—hence the government's "compensation" for deferral—would be exacted only upon distribution. In addition, there should be some concern for the impairment of horizontal equity and the loss of neutrality that follow from extending special privileges only to those who have used—or have been induced to use—the trust device * * * .

These concerns are aggravated by the possibility of indefinite or extended postponement of the tax in some states or by the possibility of heavy accumulations being involved. * * *

* * *

* * * [A]lthough conceptually out of harmony with the accessions tax, the solution discussed here, an estimated tax, does not abandon the accessions tax method of determining ultimate tax liabilities and collections. All that is involved is a prepayment in order to deplete an economic base that would otherwise be artificially preserved by the use of trusts, and even the time value of the prepayments can and should (like benefits of deferral) be accounted for through the system chosen.

* * *

The solution in this report calls for prepayment of an estimated tax on trust accessions. It would apply to all but "owned" trusts—that is, those in which a beneficiary is treated as owning (and is therefore taxed as having received an accession of) all or an identifiable portion of the corpus of a trust. The value of all non-"owned" trusts created by a given decedent (whether inter vivos or by will) and still in existence at the imposition date are to be aggregated. * * *

* * *

After determining the amount of the estimated tax for the aggregated trusts of the transferor in question, that amount would be paid from and apportioned among the included trusts and their independent shares in proportion to their respective imposition-date values reduced by the exclusion amounts * * * applicable to each. * * *

As accessions occur through trust distributions and the true accessions tax is imposed, credits based on estimated-tax prepayments would be allowed against the distributees' accessions taxes. A credit ratio would be established for each trust or independent share, and that ratio would continue to determine credits allowable to distributees until the trust terminates. * * *

* * *

An additional estimated tax on major trust holdings would be imposed at each "change of generation" during the existence of long-term trusts. * * *

* * *

NOTE

Halbach earlier urged the adoption of an accessions tax in Edward C. Halbach, Jr., *Accessions Tax Favored*, 4 TAX NOTES 29 (1976). *See also* Eugene Steuerle, *Equity and the Taxation of Wealth Transfers*, 11 TAX NOTES 459 (1980) (arguing that accessions tax is theoretically superior to estate tax as complement to general income tax). John T. Gaubatz points out that an accessions tax would require a greater number of tax returns and might raise liquidity problems for recipients of tangible property. John T. Gaubatz, *A Generation-Shifting Transfer Tax*, 12 VA. TAX REV. 1, 55-56 (1992). Do these administrative concerns detract materially from the advantages of an accessions tax?

B.   An Income Tax

Several commentators suggest reform of the income tax rules relating to gifts, bequests, and inheritances as an alternative to the current wealth transfer taxes. John K. McNulty proposes repealing § 102, which excludes gifts, bequests, and inheritances from the recipient's gross income. Lawrence Zelenak and Joseph M. Dodge support replacing the "stepped-up" basis rule of § 1014 with an approach that taxes gains at death rather than an expansion of § 1015's carryover basis rule to include transfers at death. Charles O. Galvin prefers either approach compared to the current system.

John K. McNulty, *A Transfer Tax Alternative: Inclusion Under the Income Tax*, 4 TAX NOTES 24 (1976)*

To reform the estate and gift tax system, I suggest that those levies be repealed and that gifts or bequests be taxed to the recipients under the income tax laws. The change, I believe, would result in greater simplicity and fairness than would reform of the existing estate and gift taxes.

WHY HAVE WE EXCLUDED GIFTS AND BEQUESTS FROM INCOME?

Why should the recipients of gifts and inheritances be taxed on those receipts as income? One answer lies in the fact that gifts and inheritances really do constitute income to the recipients, both in an economic and in a legal and Constitutional sense of the word "income." * * *

* * *

For a great many years, gifts and inheritances have been excluded from the federal income tax's definition of gross income by a statutory exclusion, presently found in Section 102 of the Internal Revenue Code. The exclusion may historically have stemmed from a fear that the term "income" as used in the Sixteenth Amendment did not comprehend gifts and inheritances, but rather was limited, in the language of early United States Supreme Court opinions, to "gain, derived from capital, from labor, or from both combined." * * * The exclusion for gifts and inheritances has continued beyond the time when these constitutional doubts have receded.

Gifts and inheritances may also have been excluded from income to "keep the Tax Commissioner out from under the Christmas tree." That is to say, considerations of administrative expediency and psychological factors and matters involving ability to pay may have suggested that the receipt of a gift or bequest should not be a taxable event. * * *

ADVANTAGES OF TAXING GIFTS AND BEQUESTS AS INCOME

To tax gifts and bequests as income would expand the base of the income tax and comprehend in that tax, with its graduated rates, annual computation, and other structural characteristics, items of accretion to net worth that belong in the base of the income tax because, just as much as income earned from personal efforts or investments, such items really do provide financial gain to the recipients and increase their ability to pay tax.

To tax the receipt of gifts and bequests as income changes the *identity* of the taxpayer in comparison with our present system. Under present federal transfer tax law, the donor of the

---

*   Reprinted with permission. Copyright © 1976. Tax Analysts.

lifetime gift or the decedent who transfers property at death is the taxpayer. The tax owing is computed by measuring the amount of the gift, in conjunction with other gifts made by the taxpayer during life or at death, and imposing a tax upon this base, subject to certain exemptions and exclusions. In other words, the amount of tax owing is measured by the capacity of the donor to confer a gratuitous benefit upon the donee.

* * *

The proposal to tax gifts and inheritances to the recipient rather than to the transferor means that the amount of tax paid will be geared to the taxpaying ability of the recipient, rather than that of the transferor, and would be determined by the income tax rates and other rules, rather than the rules of the federal estate and gift taxes. In some respects, this proposal resembles the proposal for an "accessions tax," which, however, would determine the amount of tax owing by the recipient according to the amount of donative transfers received by that person during his or her life, without regard to the other income or wealth of the recipient.

The proposal to tax gifts and inheritances as income would adjust the tax owed to the ability to pay of the recipient, taking into account that recipient's income from all sources. This proposal has the advantage of fairness, at least to those who view the federal income tax as the fairest tax in the federal taxing system and as one that somehow gets at ability to pay better than any other tax, whether at the state or local or federal level (except perhaps a theoretical wealth or expenditure tax, or a hypothetically comprehensive and all-inclusive income tax, none of which is administratively feasible or likely to be enacted in the foreseeable future).

Another advantage is that the rate of tax on gifts would be the same as the rate on bequests, which would be a change from the disparity in rates of the present transfer taxes, a disparity that gives rise to much tax planning, controversy and administration and compliance costs.

Still another advantage may lie in the redistributive effects of the proposal. Although it would be premature to advance a definite conclusion about distributional effects, a likely surmise would be that taxing gifts and bequests as income would lead to less concentration of wealth and wider distributions of property given during life or at death, and to lower income taxpayers, compared to the effects of present transfer taxes.

SOLUTIONS TO SOME MAJOR DISADVANTAGES

One supposed disadvantage of taxing gifts and inheritances as income is that a taxpayer might, once in his or her lifetime, receive a large gift or bequest all of which would be taxable in one year and subjected to the graduated rates of the income tax law. If this were to happen, the result might be to put a very heavy tax burden on such a recipient compared to someone else who receives the same amount in gifts or inheritances over a number of years, and thus is in much the same overall position as the first taxpayer. * * *

* * *

Another possible disadvantage of taxing gifts and inheritances as income might be thought to be the necessity for reporting birthday gifts and holiday transfers and many other small exchanges that would heavily burden taxpayers to report or which would largely go unreported and thus untaxed. The answer to such an argument is to include in the income tax law an annual exclusion or a lifetime exclusion of a certain amount. As a result, the tax authorities would not have to "sit beneath the Christmas tree" or make liars out of taxpayers who inadvertently or otherwise failed to report the small transfers that take place, particularly within a family context, and which are not presently taxable under the federal gift and estate taxes.

The effect of adding a special gift and bequest exclusion or exemption in the income tax law would be to inject a small additional complexity in that law. However, the benefits derived

in the form of repealing the lengthy estate and gift tax laws and imposing a fairer tax on donative transfers and improving the integrity of the income tax itself by extending it to an item of
income that for many years has been exempted, more than outweigh the slight disadvantages
in amending Section 102 and possibly the income averaging provisions.

It is likely that some additional statutory enactments would be necessary to cope with the
complicated transactions that taxpayers have learned to construct as ways of minimizing or
avoiding the present federal transfer taxes. Serious thought would have to be given to the problem of trusts, revocable transfers, gifts disguised as loans, transfers with retained powers of
alteration or amendment, annuities, life insurance, powers of appointment, future interests and
the many other problems dealt with by * * * the estate and gift tax law * * * .

It would be overly optimistic to imagine that transfer taxes could be repealed and nothing
substituted for them when gifts and bequests are made taxable as income. However, the nature
of the new structure—the taxation of gifts and bequests as income rather than as transfers taxable to the transferor—would mean that the legislation necessary to prevent escape or undue
deferral or shifting of tax would be less expensive, as would the administrative promulgation
of regulations and the enforcement of compliance under present law.

* * *

NOTE

McNulty is certainly correct that the recipient of a gift or bequest enjoys an
increase in wealth. How might the shift from a wealth transfer tax (which is nominally
imposed on the transferor) to an income tax (on the recipient) affect the tax cost of
making gifts and bequests relative to consumption?

Marjorie E. Kornhauser also has called for the repeal of § 102, arguing that "it is
inconsistent with both the current economic understanding of income and the goals
of the income tax." Marjorie E. Kornhauser, *The Constitutional Meaning of Income
and the Income Taxation of Gifts*, 25 CONN. L. REV. 1, 52 n.188 (1992). *See also*
Joseph M. Dodge, *Beyond Estate and Gift Tax Reform: Including Gifts and Bequests
in Income*, 91 HARV. L. REV. 1177 (1978); Charles O. Galvin, *Taxing Gains at Death:
A Further Comment*, 46 VAND. L. REV. 1525 (1993). If gifts and bequests are treated
as taxable income to the recipient, what are the appropriate income tax consequences
to the transferor?

Lawrence Zelenak, *Taxing Gains at Death*, 46 VAND. L. REV. 361 (1993)*

I. INTRODUCTION

If a taxpayer sells property for more than the property cost him, the gain realized on the
sale is subject to income tax. If a taxpayer makes a gift of appreciated property, the donee takes
the property with the donor's basis, so the appreciation will be taxed when the donee sells the
property. But if a taxpayer dies owning appreciated property, the appreciation is not taxed at

---

death, and the basis of the property becomes its fair market value at death. The result is that the appreciation is never subject to income tax. * * * The President's Budget estimates the annual revenue loss from the failure to tax gains at death at more than $25 billion. Current law is objectionable also for its lock-in effect: elderly taxpayers are discouraged from disposing of appreciated assets, because if they hold the assets until death, the appreciation will escape income taxation permanently.

This tax forgiveness did not originate as a conscious policy decision. Rather it occurred almost accidentally from the combination of two ideas that were accepted instinctively during the early years of the income tax: that the mere transfer of property at death did not constitute a realization of gain or loss on the property, and that fair market value basis for heirs was appropriate to prevent taxation of capital, because "'capital' was thought to refer to some tangible thing, whatever its value, rather than to a monetary account keeping track of what has been taxed."

Defenders of the current system have justified it on the grounds that the step up in basis is "paid for" by the estate tax on the appreciation. It is true that appreciation that escapes income tax may not escape estate tax, and the estate tax rate may even be higher than the income tax rate. Nevertheless, there are two problems with this argument. First, the step up in basis applies even to property that is not subject to estate tax (because of the unified credit or the marital bequest deduction). Second, and more important, the income and estate taxes are distinct, both conceptually and practically. Conceptually, there is no reason why appreciation transferred at death should not be subject to both taxes—to the income tax because it is gain, and to the estate tax because it is a gratuitous transfer. Practically, gratuitously transferred income is generally subject to both taxes. If a taxpayer sells appreciated property during life, the gain is subject to income tax, and if at death he transfers the proceeds of the sale (reduced by the income tax paid) to his beneficiaries, the estate tax will apply as well. The treatment of appreciation at death thus produces inequity between taxpayers who realize income during life, and those who transfer unrealized appreciation at death. The inequity is both horizontal (discriminating between different taxpayers of similar income and wealth) and vertical (favoring wealthy taxpayers because a greater portion of their income tends to be in the form of unrealized appreciation transferred at death).

If Congress desires to eliminate the permanent forgiveness of capital gains tax at death, it could do so either by providing that the basis of property transferred at death carries over to heirs and beneficiaries, or by taxing gains at death. During the process that led to the enactment of the Tax Reform Act of 1986, virtually every base-broadening reform with significant support among tax policy experts was discussed by Congress and the administration. The one glaring exception was the forgiveness of gains tax at death. This omission would be astounding, but for some history.

As part of the Tax Reform Act of 1976, Congress enacted Section 1023 of the Internal Revenue Code, which generally provided a carryover basis (rather than a Section 1014 fair market value at death basis) for inherited property. Congress added the carryover basis provision to the Act very late in the legislative process, with little opportunity for either input from interest groups or careful technical drafting. Affected taxpayers and their representatives harshly criticized it, on both technical and policy grounds, and in 1980 it was repealed retroactively. Regardless of one's views on the merits of carryover basis, its short unhappy life was one of the greatest legislative fiascoes in the history of the income tax. This was recent history in 1986, and it is understandable that Congress lacked the fortitude to revisit the issue so soon.

In the past few years, interest in this area slowly has reawakened. As memory of Section 1023 recedes, as pressure to raise revenue without raising rates increases, and as the remaining opportunities for significant base-broadening reform diminish, it becomes more likely that Congress eventually will revisit the area. And when Congress does, it seems much more likely (for reasons discussed below) that it will tax gains at death, rather than revive carryover basis. * * *

* * *

II. THE BASIC POLICY OPTIONS

A. *Choosing Between Carryover Basis and Taxing Gains at Death*

Either carryover basis at death or a death gains tax would prevent the permanent avoidance of gains tax that occurs under current law. At the theoretical level, the argument for carryover basis is that postponing tax until an actual sale of the property avoids the need to appraise the property and imposes tax at a time when the taxpayer is likely to have cash available to pay the tax. The arguments for gains tax at death are that it appropriately limits the maximum deferral possibility to a single lifetime; it enforces the principle that income should be taxed to the person who earned it; it imposes tax at an ideal time in terms of ability to pay (because the decedent has no use for the amount due as taxes, and whatever the heirs or beneficiaries receive is a windfall); and, unlike carryover basis, it solves the problem of lock-in. Congress will not choose, however, between the two approaches based on such theoretical considerations. Rather, the key issues will be the complexity of administering the two approaches and the relative amounts of revenue they would raise.

The most serious administrative difficulty—proof of basis—would loom equally large under either system. In other respects, however, a death gains tax would be somewhat simpler to apply than carryover basis. Carryover basis would create a new problem for executors, because their fiduciary duties would require them to make not only an equitable distribution of value among beneficiaries, but also an equitable distribution of basis. A death gains tax does not present this problem, because all assets (other than assets going to a surviving spouse, if the system permits deferral of gains on such assets) receive a fair market value basis following the imposition of the tax at death. In addition, carryover basis requires the maintenance of basis records across unlimited numbers of generations; a death gains tax does not.

* * *

More important than the modest simplicity advantage of tax at death over carryover basis is the much greater revenue effect of tax at death. The Congressional Budget Office (CBO), for example, estimated that taxing capital gains at death would raise $17.0 billion over four years (1994 to 1997), while carryover basis would raise only $5.2 billion. * * *

* * *

B. *Taxing Gains at Death: Revenue Implications and Policy Choices*

* * *

* * * At least one commentator has suggested replacing the transfer taxes with a capital gains tax imposed on gifts and bequests of appreciated property.[54] * * * [I]t is unclear whether the revenue lost by repealing the transfer taxes could be replaced entirely by taxing capital gains at death. Assuming, however, that the change could be made revenue neutral, would it be a good idea? The change might appeal to an "academic desire for tidiness," because it rationalizes the

---

[54]   Professor Galvin suggests repealing the transfer taxes and replacing them with either a capital gains tax imposed at the time of gifts and bequests, an accessions tax, or some combination of the two. [Charles O. Galvin, *To Bury the Estate Tax, Not to Praise It*, 52 TAX NOTES 1413 (1991).]

[57]   For discussion of this issue, see George Cooper, *A Voluntary Tax? New Perspectives on Sophisticated Estate Tax Avoidance*, 77 COLUM. L. REV. 161 (1977).

income tax by eliminating perhaps its most glaring loophole. In addition, it repeals a transfer tax system always objectionable for the many omissions from its base.[57]

Notice, however, that the potential tax base for a capital gains tax on gratuitous transfers is substantially smaller than the potential tax base for a transfer tax system—smaller by the amount of the cost bases of the assets gratuitously transferred. Moreover, at current rates the capital gains tax (twenty-eight percent top rate) will raise less revenue from a given dollar amount of tax base than will the transfer taxes (rates ranging from thirty-seven to fifty percent). Thus, for the capital gains tax to raise as much revenue as the transfer taxes, with a smaller potential base and lower rates, it must include in its actual base a much higher percentage of its potential base than do the transfer taxes. Although some of this might be done through loophole closing, the vast majority would have to be done by using much lower exemption amounts than the $600,000 transfer tax exemption created by the unified credit. Thus, assuming revenue neutrality, replacement of the transfer taxes with a capital gains tax on transfers would result in a major shift of tax burden away from the wealthy and the upper middle class, and onto the middle class.[60] I would oppose the regressivity inherent in such a change, and it seems likely Congress would agree.[61]

In addition to its regressivity, the change would result in increased complexity. The need for valuation of gratuitous transfers would remain, and the need to determine the basis of all gratuitous transfers would arise. More significantly, these burdens would be imposed on many middle class transferors currently not subject to the transfer taxes.

As an alternative, of course, Congress could retain the transfer tax system, but use the revenue raised from the new capital gains tax to reduce the transfer tax burden, either by raising the exemption amount or by reducing rates. If Congress keyed the exemption to the new capital gains tax to the transfer tax exemption, it would impose no new tax burden (either in terms of tax liability or the compliance burden) on the middle class. Moreover, the exemption would improve horizontal equity among the affluent taxpayers above the exemption levels, because all of them now would be subject to tax on their capital gains.

* * *

VI. CONCLUSION

Considering the amount of attention that has been given to base-broadening tax reform options since the mid-1980s, the virtual absence of consideration of reforming the treatment of gains at death has been appalling. The brief and unhappy life of carryover basis may explain the status of Section 1014 reform as the dog that did not bark. But well over a decade has passed since the repeal of carryover basis, and it is time for Congress to revisit the area. When it does so, it will find that taxing gains at death is a more attractive option than carryover basis. It also will find that, although there are difficult choices to be made among simplicity, fairness, and revenue concerns, it is possible to design a death gains tax that is workable, fair, and raises substantial revenue. Consideration of such a tax should be high on Congress's tax agenda.

---

[60]   Despite the relatively small amount of revenue they raise, the transfer taxes supply a large part of the progressivity of the federal tax system. Michael J. Graetz, *To Praise the Estate Tax, Not to Bury It*, 93 YALE L.J. 259, 269-73 (1983). This contribution largely would be lost if the transfer taxes were replaced by a capital gains tax.

[61]   Robert B. Smith, *Burying the Estate Tax Without Resurrecting Its Problems*, 55 TAX NOTES 1799, 1803-04 (1992), argues that the base broadening that would be necessary to replace the transfer taxes with capital gains taxes would not be feasible politically because of its impact on the middle class.

NOTE

James B. Lewis has called Zelenak's proposal "sound tax policy." James B. Lewis, *A Socratic Approach to the Deathtime Gains Tax*, 59 TAX NOTES 580, 580 (1993). Others worry about the difficulty of determining basis under Zelenak's proposal. *See* Donald Samuelson, *Carryover Basis: The Greatest Fiasco in Federal Taxation History?*, 59 TAX NOTES 703 (1993).

Joseph M. Dodge, *Further Thoughts on Realizing Gains and Losses at Death*, 47 VAND. L. REV. 1827 (1994)*

I. INTRODUCTION

Professor Lawrence Zelenak has put forth a detailed proposal for repealing present Section 1014 of the Internal Revenue Code, which gives a decedent's successor a basis equal to the estate tax value of property at death. * * * Repeal of Section 1014 alone, however, does not solve the problem, because it must then be decided whether the decedent's basis should carry over to her successors, as presently occurs under Section 1015 with respect to inter vivos gifts, or whether a gratuitous transfer should be treated as a realization event, with the amount realized deemed to be the fair market value of the property at death. Professor Zelenak favors the deemed-realization approach. I concur in this view, wholly apart from the fact that the carryover basis approach was tried and repealed.

* * *

II. THEORETICAL CONSIDERATIONS

At the theoretical level, the first issue is what is wrong with Section 1014 and the second issue is whether it should be replaced by a carryover basis rule or a deemed-realization rule.

A. Arguments Against Repeal of Section 1014

There exist only three possible arguments against repeal of Section 1014. One is that Section 1014 is necessary to preserve the integrity of the exclusion for bequests and inheritances. The second is that imposing both an income tax and a transfer tax upon a gratuitous transfer is excessive death taxation. The third is that "realization" is a necessary predicate for the existence of income, and that death is not a realization event.

1. Preserving the Integrity of the Exclusion for Bequests and Inheritances

* * *

On the theoretical level, the "integrity of the exclusion" rationale for Section 1014 is only as strong as the underlying rationale for the Section 102 exclusion itself. A compelling case can be made for the repeal of Section 102 and the inclusion of gratuitous receipts in income.[11] Because repeal of Section 102 is not immediately likely, it will suffice here to look at the possible rationales for Section 102.

---

[11]   *See generally* Joseph M. Dodge, *Beyond Estate and Gift Tax Reform: Including Gifts and Bequests in Income*, 91 HARV. L. REV. 1177 (1978); Marjorie E. Kornhauser, *The Constitutional Meaning of Income and the Income Taxation of Gifts*, 25 CONN. L. REV. 1 (1992). * * *

There are two possible historical rationales that can be dispensed with in short order. The first is that gratuitous transfers received are a taxpayer's original endowment and, therefore, are "capital" rather than "income." This means of distinguishing principal from income derives from the law of trust accounting * * * . However, there is no reason why income taxation should follow trust accounting principles. The modern concept of income refers to accessions to wealth, a category into which the receipt of gratuitous transfers clearly falls.

A second possible historical rationale is that the Section 102 exclusion was enacted in contemplation of the later enactment of an estate tax. * * * Today, the estate and gift taxes have such large deductions, exclusions, and credits that they impinge on less than ten percent of the population, whereas the income tax is nearly universal. Thus, it is unrealistic to view the Section 102 exclusion as being "made up for" by the estate and gift taxes.[21] Moreover, the two taxes are wholly separate in concept, since the estate and gift taxes are "second" taxes on amounts previously subject to the income tax. * * *

* * *

* * * [T]he only rational basis of Section 102 is to avoid double taxation of the same item to two taxpayers. This rationale clearly does not support the "integrity of the exclusion" argument for Section 1014, because the latter goes beyond avoiding double taxation to eliminating gain from the system entirely. In fact, the Section 102 approach to the double taxation issue, which is to tax the donor rather than the donee, supports the deemed-realization solution.

2. Would Deemed Realization Produce Excessive Taxation?

Under a deemed-realization system, it is conceivable that a zero basis asset would be subject to the highest income tax rate (39.6 percent), the highest gift or estate tax rate (fifty-five percent), and the highest generation-skipping tax rate (fifty-five percent). This looks like horrendous confiscatory taxation—and then some. However, because the income tax owed would be deductible from the estate or gift tax base, and the estate or gift tax would be subtracted from the generation-skipping tax base, the rates would not be cumulative. Thus, the maximum aggregate tax rate would be 87.75 percent, whereas without the deemed-realization tax the aggregate tax rate would still be 79.75 percent. Thus, in the worst case scenario—which makes the implausible assumption of a zero basis asset—the deemed-realization tax would impose an incremental tax bite of only about twelve percent.

Under present law, taxpayers who realize gains before death can end up paying all three taxes. Thus, Section 1014 enables some taxpayers to avoid a tax to which other taxpayers are subject. * * *

* * *

3. Death is Not a Realization Event

It is argued that there can be no income without realization, and that death is not a realization event, nor should it be treated as a realization event, because it is involuntary. However, all three components of this argument beg the question.

* * *

That death normally is considered to be involuntary is irrelevant. There is no general tax principle that involuntariness yields an exemption or other tax benefit beyond those that Congress chooses to confer. Tax benefits contingent on involuntariness take the form of allowances for additional unforeseen expenditures or deferral of tax on account of premature realizations.

---

[21]   Repeal of Section 102 might raise upwards of $100 billion per year. * * *

An exemption for all unrealized gains bears no relation to any incremental costs incurred by the decedent or her successors; such costs, in fact, are treated separately under the tax system. Similarly, the accelerated realization theory only justifies deferral, not exemption. But, unlike the situation with involuntary conversions of property, taxing gains at death should not be viewed as any kind of undue acceleration of tax, because for the decedent there is no tomorrow; it is either then or never. Of course, the tax system could waive taxation of gains at death in favor of a carryover basis rule, but that raises the next issue, namely, whether the gains should be taxed to the decedent or the decedent's successor.

B. Why a Deemed-Realization Rule?

Once the repeal of Section 1014 is decided upon, it is then necessary to decide whether the carryover basis rule of Section 1015 should be extended to death-time transfers or whether both gift and death should trigger a deemed-realization rule. Tax policies support the latter alternative. Those policies include: (1) the internal logic of an income tax; (2) economics; (3) ethics (fairness); and (4) distributive justice.

The internal logic of an income tax posits that the same dollars should be neither taxed to, nor deducted by, a given taxpayer more than once. Neither approach would violate this norm. A deemed-realization rule would not produce double taxation of the transferor any more than in the common situation where a taxpayer sells gain property and spends the proceeds on personal consumption. The question is whether the gain or loss should be attributed to the transferor or to the transferee. Aside from Section 1015, carryover basis rules apply when entities and owners engage in tax-free exchanges and transfers. In these cases, the owners and entities are alter egos. Here, a carryover basis rule prevents gain from disappearing as it moves from one pocket to the other. Essentially the same rationale justifies Section 1015's carryover basis rule for inter vivos gifts. These rationales do not apply to the death situation, because the decedent's successor no longer can collaborate with the decedent to reduce taxes on the former. Moreover, the better way to curb tax avoidance, especially with respect to gifts, is to treat the gift as a realization event.

As to whether the pretransfer gain or loss should be attributed to the transferor to whom it accrued or the transferee, the general thrust of the income tax in general (as opposed to a consumption tax) is to tax transferors, because they controlled the gain or loss and the gain or loss is measured with reference to the investment of the transferors. The argument that the transferee is the one who enjoys the gain proves too much: it is an argument for taxing the donee on the full amount or value of the receipt. Moreover, a carryover basis rule would allow the shifting of losses to donees. But it is nonsense to treat the donee as incurring any loss on the transaction as a whole, because the donee is always better off as the result of the receipt.

By "economics," I mean neoclassical economics and the concept of economic efficiency, which is usually expressed by the term "neutrality." According to optimal taxation theory, death is the ideal time to impose a disproportionately heavy tax, since the tax would affect economic choices only minimally. Yet, the most neutral income tax with respect to investments would be one that abolished the realization principle entirely and with it the preference for capital gains. Thus, as a general proposition, unrealized appreciation and depreciation, at least of liquid assets and perhaps of all assets, should be incorporated into the tax base annually. The deemed-realization rule lies far closer to that norm than a carryover basis rule, which would allow indefinite deferral of gain. A deemed-realization rule also would be much more potent in combating the lock-in effect. Finally, adoption of a deemed-realization rule would have the salutary effect of increasing revenue that can be balanced by lower rates in general and/or the elimination of preferences for capital gains.

By "ethics," I am referring to tax fairness among individual taxpayers, commonly expressed by the (inadequate) expression "horizontal equity." The basic idea is that individual taxpayers should contribute to a government that performs redistributive and public good functions according to their respective abilities to pay. In general, "ability to pay" refers to economic resources under the taxpayer's control, whether in cash or in kind. In the present context, unrealized appreciation generally constitutes ability to pay; whether nonliquid assets should fall in this category is an issue to be considered below. Aside from the possibility of a concession to nonliquidity, the ability to pay dictates that the transferor be subject to tax on net unrealized appreciation, preferably as it accrues. A deemed-realization rule would conform to ability to pay more readily than a carryover basis rule, although even the deemed-realization rule falls short of the ideal.

By "distributive justice," I refer to the effect of tax rules on the distribution of income or wealth among various classes in society. * * * [D]istributive justice is rarely given independent weight in tax policy discussions, except in the context of rates, tax rules with respect to transactions associated with certain economic classes, or situations where it is hard to tell whether tax base rules accurately reflect ability to pay. In any event, a deemed-realization rule for inter vivos gifts clearly will have a more progressive effect than a carryover basis rule, because it is safe to assume that donors are generally wealthier than donees.

In the case of death-time transfers, the actual tax cannot be borne by the transferor, who is now dead, but can be borne only by transferees. There is no guarantee that the transferees are otherwise well-off. Thus, the distributive justice preference for a deemed-realization rule over a carryover basis rule here is somewhat indirect: one can assume that wealthy transferors tend to have well-off successors (after accessions), and that taxes on transferors generally reduce inherited wealth, which is somehow less worthy or useful than earned wealth and more in the nature of a windfall.

It might be said that the same point applies with equal respect to the ability-to-pay norm. However, in that case the tax is viewed as being imposed properly on the party who controlled the unrealized appreciation. In the context of distributive justice, what counts is the economic effect of the tax on various income groups. But this point (again) is an argument for including the full amount of gratuitous transfers in the income tax base of transferees, an argument that is out of bounds in the context of the present discussion.

A carryover basis rule is wholly inadequate under ability-to-pay and progressivity norms (not to mention horizontal equity) because it results in differential taxation among various transferees receiving identical amounts according to the fortuitous circumstance of differing bases attached to the various properties. This disparate basis problem is avoidable in theory by figuring out the aggregate basis of all properties transferred and then allocating the aggregate basis pro rata among the various transferees. This solution involves design and computational difficulties, however, and it simply cannot be applied to inter vivos transfers. More fundamentally, any basis assigned to any successor misstates the successor's investment in the property. Finally, the allocation of basis only operates among a given decedent's transferees; it does not eliminate basis disparities among all recipients of death-time transfers.

* * *

NOTE

Why do you think Congress decided not to include unrealized gains in income at death, both in 1976 and in 1986? One commentator noted, in connection with the Zelenak and Dodge proposals, "the wide gap between those teaching taxes and those who think they would be the chief victims of taxing gains [at death]." *See* Charles Davenport, *ABA Tax Section Meeting: When Death Isn't Absolution*, 59 TAX NOTES 854, 855 (1993).

Charles O. Galvin, *To Bury the Estate Tax, Not To Praise It*, 52 TAX NOTES 1413 (1991)*†

* * *

In this final decade of the twentieth century, I believe that the wealth transfer system has run its course and should be decently interred. If it serves the cause of progressivity or wealth redistribution—and I doubt that it really does—this objective can be attained with greater efficiency and fairness in the income tax system. I am not unaware of the literature of distinguished commentators urging retention and expansion of the transfer tax system;[5] I believe, however, that major reform effort in this area is shelved for some time to come. Political realities are such that significant executive or legislative action is remote. * * *

Assuming, therefore, that the system is not likely to change from its present form, I urge consideration of its elimination on the following premises.

1. The target population to which the wealth transfer system applies is only a minuscule percentage of the total population, and there is little probability of broadening that base.

2. Even within the small target population, a minimum of planning can offer opportunities for substantial transfers of wealth without tax.

3. Among those within the target population subject to the tax, the results under the current system can be extremely unfair between and among estate owners similarly situated; horizontal and vertical equity are lacking.

4. The revenue lost from the elimination of wealth transfer taxes could be offset by the adoption of either one, or both, of the following changes in the income tax system:

(a) the recognition of gain (or loss) at the time of gift or at death; or

(b) the recognition of income to the recipients of gifts, devises, bequests, or inheritances.

* * *

---

†   * * * With due respect, Professor Galvin expresses his indebtedness for the title of this paper to Professor Michael J. Graetz * * * for his article entitled *To Praise the Estate Tax, Not to Bury It*, 93 YALE L.J. 259 (1983). * * *

5   *See, e.g.*, * * * Graetz, *To Praise the Estate Tax, Not to Bury It*, 93 YALE L.J. 259 (1983); * * * Gutman, *Reforming Federal Wealth Transfer Taxes After ERTA*, 69 VA. L. REV. 1183 (1983); * * * Robinson, *The Federal Wealth Transfer Taxes—A Requiem?*, 1 AM. J. TAX POLICY 25 (1982). * * *

NOTE

Robert B. Smith agrees with Galvin that the wealth transfer tax system should be eliminated because "it needs extensive reform to be effective and the needed reform is unlikely to be undertaken," but disagrees with Galvin's proposal to subject gifts and bequests to the income tax. Robert B. Smith, *Burying the Estate Tax Without Resurrecting Its Problems*, 55 TAX NOTES 1799, 1799 (1992). For Galvin's response, see Charles O. Galvin, *Burying the Estate Tax: Keeping Ghouls Out of the Cemetery: A Reply to Professor Smith*, 56 TAX NOTES 951 (1992). *See also* Charles O. Galvin, *More Reasons To Bury the Estate Tax*, 59 TAX NOTES 435 (1993).

C.   A Consumption Tax

Edward J. McCaffery presents a "liberal" justification for replacing the current income and wealth transfer taxes with a "consumption-without-estate tax." Anne L. Alstott, Eric Rakowski, and Douglas Holtz-Eakin offer separate responses to McCaffery's proposal.

Edward J. McCaffery, *The Uneasy Case for Wealth Transfer Taxation*, 104 YALE L.J. 283 (1994)*

* * *

My argument follows three basic steps: (1) The current gift and estate tax does not work, is in deep tension with liberal egalitarian ideals, and lacks strong popular or political support. (2) While the failure of the status quo may suggest a stronger wealth transfer tax as an alternative, such an answer suffers from two distinct problems: (a) a stronger tax is neither practical nor popular, and (b) given the many imperfections of the real world and the likely consequences of a strengthened transfer tax, such as reduced work, reduced savings, and increased inequality in consumption, a stronger wealth transfer tax may not be preferable even on ideal liberal grounds. (3) Motivated by the first two points to think through matters more deeply, we can arrive at alternative tax systems that both comport better with liberal first principles and fit well with the implicit spirit of our actual practices and beliefs, without any form of estate tax at all.

* * *

II. THE LIBERAL EGALITARIAN CASE FOR (AND AGAINST) WEALTH TRANSFER TAXATION

Over the years, proponents of estate taxation have advanced many reasons for the estate tax, including revenue raising, "backing up" the income tax system, and breaking up large concentrations of wealth. I discuss these rationales, all of which are of questionable justificatory strength when held up against the reality of the existing legal regime, in passing. In contrast, support for the estate tax has drawn its greatest strength from philosophical foundations and

---

*   Reprinted by permission of The Yale Law Journal Company and Fred B. Rothman & Company from *The Yale Law Journal*, vol. 104, pages 283-365.

intuitions, recently advanced by such liberal egalitarian political theorists as John Rawls, Ronald Dworkin, and Bruce Ackerman. I proceed directly to these philosophical arguments to set out the liberal case for wealth transfer taxation.

* * *

* * * [T]he liberal egalitarian case for some form of wealth transfer tax is intimately linked with the "fair equality of opportunity" ideal. This principle * * * holds that people of equal abilities and aptitudes "should have the same prospects of success regardless of their initial place in the social system, that is, irrespective of the income class into which they are born."[35] * * *

* * *

* * * I level five distinct though related criticisms of the general liberal egalitarian support for the estate tax. * * *

First, the current income-plus-estate tax system undercuts its own best theoretical support. Liberal egalitarianism is concerned with, among other goals, mitigating unequal starting points. The actual gift and estate tax regime, however, encourages frequent, large, *inter vivos* gifts, systematically excluded from the income tax base, and it thus can dramatically undermine the pursuit of equal opportunity and level playing fields. * * * Further, the current, and indeed any, wealth transfer tax encourages consumption, or the personal use of wealth. * * * In encouraging *inter vivos* gifts and large-scale consumption by the rich, the current estate tax is illiberal.

Second, no feasible wealth transfer taxation system, under both practical and political constraints, can support the liberal egalitarian ideal. * * *

* * * The third argument is that even [an improved estate] tax is inappropriate in a nonideal world. * * * As noted above, the current, ineffective system of wealth transfer taxation may exacerbate intra-generational inequality by encouraging large *inter vivos* transmissions and increased consumption by the rich. A confiscatory wealth transfer tax, on the other hand, would result in even greater inequality in consumption, as well as diminished savings. These effects might predominantly harm the lower classes both by interfering with prior liberties, as large-scale consumption by the rich may well do, and by lowering general standards of living, as diminished capital would almost certainly do. * * *

Fourth, it is possible to make out a strong argument against wealth transfer taxation sounding in *ideal* theory. The traditional liberal egalitarian tax scheme * * * presumes that individuals are entitled to their "earnings," but views the private possession of "unearned" wealth as uniquely and particularly inimical to, or at least in severe tension with, liberal egalitarian values. * * * [M]y fourth argument is that, even if wealth is indeed "fairly earned," society may nonetheless have objective, political reasons for opposing estate taxation. Simply put, * * * liberal society likes earnings and savings, both of which contribute to a certain metaphoric "common pool," and only or at least especially suspects use, particularly the large-scale, rapid dissipation of capital by the wealthy. * * *

On this view, wealth transfers from the wealthy may even be, ironically, the preferred liberal result. Because liberal society likes earnings and savings on objective political grounds, but does not like excessive private use, it must allow the rich to pass on their wealth * * * .

* * * I now arrive at my fifth argument: The best feasible liberal tax system features no wealth transfer tax at all. The plan that I believe best responds to liberal egalitarian ideals, as mentioned above, is a progressive consumption-without-estate tax. * * * Whereas any estate tax encourages use and punishes thrift, a progressive consumption tax appropriates "private" wealth at precisely the moment when an individual is about to use it excessively for personal

---

[35]   [JOHN RAWLS, A THEORY OF JUSTICE 73 (1971)].

purposes. * * *

* * *

The five arguments can now be summarized and related as follows. (1) The current estate tax is porous, ineffective, and counterproductive on purely liberal grounds. (2) No stronger version is popular or practical, in part because (3) the liberal theory supporting an estate tax does not fit in a nonideal world where individual earnings lack presumptive, decisive moral weight, and in part because (4) our objective, political values, even under ideal conditions, lead liberal society to approve of work and savings and only or at least especially to disapprove of the wanton private use of resources, and any wealth tax is perverse on these scores. (5) Therefore, our practices have been moving, at least inchoately, toward a progressive consumption-without-estate tax. If we more consciously and consistently implemented what our practices suggest, we would have a better liberal egalitarian system than any featuring a wealth transfer tax. By meeting our objective values and changing the very meaning and hence the dangers of the private possession of wealth, we achieve in the end a happy convergence between liberal egalitarian theory and our actual practices.

III. THE ESTATE TAX: LAW, EFFECTS, AND CONSEQUENCES

* * *

The general subject of capital formation and its relationship to estate taxation is controversial. While commentators have long noted the possibility that a wealth transfer tax might adversely affect the capital stock, advocates of wealth transfer taxation have responded with two sometimes intermingled lines of attack. One is the categorical claim that the aggregate capital stock does not matter, or alternatively that the stock is ample at any particular moment in time. A second line of attack features skepticism about the empirical effects of the tax on actual private decisions.

* * *

* * * Whatever one thinks of the complicated social question of the optimal savings rates and capital stock, more savings would help reduce the cost of capital and increase productivity, ultimately resulting in higher wages. Since wages are the key element of the tax base, * * * capital enhancements should increase the general tax base. More important, capital stock may improve intra-generational opportunities. * * * Capital itself may help all of society, perhaps especially the working classes, even though it is apt to be concentrated in the hands of the wealthy. * * *

* * *

One might object that a negative effect on capital will obtain under any effort to tax wealth or to redistribute resources generally, so that the capital stock theme is simply an argument against "progressivity" or even against distributive justice itself. Any redistributive attempt will diminish the incentives of the most wealthy—without question a critically important class when it comes to capital accumulation—to work or save. All such redistributions will also involve moving wealth in the direction of those with lesser propensities to save. Therefore, the argument runs, a concern over capital proves too much and is doomed to be "conservative" or illiberal.

* * * [T]his argument * * * reflects a failure to think through the normative distinction between the possession and use of wealth. If we progressively tax the use of wealth, we will not necessarily chill its private accumulation. Nor will we necessarily move capital into the hands of those with greater propensities to consume. As we shall see later, a progressive consumption tax is a way of protecting a "frugal capitalist class" while penalizing only the "self-

indulgent aristocracy." Indeed, taxing the use of wealth changes the very meaning and dangers of private possession. * * *

IV. THE (LIBERAL) FAILURES OF THE ESTATE TAX

* * *

A. Behavioral Incentives

* * *

* * * The estate tax may be exerting adverse incentive effects on the consumption-savings and work-leisure decisions of the very wealthy, an extremely important class for purposes of both capital accumulation and prior liberal principles. * * *

* * *

For the very wealthy, the economic effects of any estate tax regime favor consumption over savings, and leisure (which can be considered the consumption of nonwork) over work. Many tax policy commentators, especially those who argue for more progressive estate taxation, presume that the very wealthy accumulate wealth for its own sake; that is, that they are wholly inelastic to any tax rate. An equally compelling story, however, is that the very wealthy are negatively elastic * * * .

Furthermore, the antiwork and antisavings incentives may extend down to the donee level. By encouraging *inter vivos* gifts, the wealthy young receive their wealth, or become certain of its ultimate receipt, early in life. This wealth may undercut their incentives to work and save. * * *

On the other hand, a complete and efficacious shutting down of wealth transfers may increase work and savings incentives at the lower generations, with possibly beneficial effects on capital. Such a complete confiscation, however, would surely impact incentives at the donor level. * * *

B. Distributive Effects

* * * [S]ome commentators have argued that the estate tax is concerned with "breaking up large concentrations of wealth." * * *

* * * A nagging practical question, however, is whether we can truly bar the transmission of wealth. If we cannot, a gift and estate tax regime may not make sense. We have seen that the present regime *encourages* frequent, early, and aggressive gift giving as a way to beat the estate tax. This fact of induced tax avoidance undercuts the equal-opportunity goal, and possibly even the concerns about wealth concentration. * * *

* * * If we tighten the gift and estate tax by closing the loopholes, we run the risk of harming capital accumulation, which itself will have adverse distributive effects. If we take steps to protect the capital stock, the combined policy may increase inequality of consumption. We have not necessarily achieved a better, fairer society if the ownership of assets is more equal, but the use of wealth is less so. * * *

Whatever one might think of these theoretical and design-based arguments, there is solid evidence that the gift and estate tax regime is not effectively fostering a better overall distribution of wealth. In the United States, wealth concentration generally has been constant throughout this century, despite the presence of a nominally steep gift and estate tax regime.[148]

---

[148] *See* [Henry J. Aaron & Alicia H. Munnell, *Reassessing the Role for Wealth Transfer Taxes*, 45 NAT'L TAX J. 119, 122-27 (1992)] * * * ; *see also* [Michael J. Graetz, *To Praise the Estate Tax, Not to Bury It*, 93 YALE L.J. 259, 271 (1983)] * * * .

* * * [I]t is not implausible that the current system actually causes some of the real problems of maldistribution, at least by constraining the evolution of better, more liberal tax systems.

* * *

V. LOOKING FOR ALTERNATIVES: TOWARD A POLITICAL THEORY OF TAX

* * *

B. A Consumption-Plus-Estate Tax

* * *

* * * [A] common recommendation for a comprehensive tax system is a broad-based consumption tax supplemented by a wealth transfer tax. * * *

A difficulty with the consumption-plus-estate tax system is that the estate tax turns out to be in tension with many, and possibly all, of the underlying norms of consumption tax theory. * * * [T]hree classes of justifications emerge, each of which sits uneasily with an estate tax.

First, supporters of consumption taxation argue that the consumption tax is more "efficient" than the income tax. This efficiency claim * * * consists of two separate strands. The major efficiency claim is that the consumption tax is efficient because it does not distort the savings-consumption decision. More technically, this claim reduces to the argument that there is less total deadweight loss under the consumption tax than under the income tax or any alternative tax regime. * * *

The minor efficiency claim is that there is market failure leading to an overly low savings rate. * * * This second type of efficiency claim does not bear especially on estate taxation, since almost all such claims refer to life-cycle or precautionary savings and typically involve the lower or middle classes. Nevertheless, the point does underscore the inherent difficulties and costs of looking to any but the wealthy to increase private savings.

A second and distinct argument is that the consumption tax will increase the aggregate level of savings. This argument is not technically an efficiency claim because it does not look to some function of individual preferences. Rather, this second claim is more in the nature of a macroeconomic, merit-good argument: More savings will benefit society regardless of individual preferences at any moment in time. * * *

A concern with the aggregate capital stock would look to the total, or uncompensated, elasticity of savings. Such total elasticities of bequest savings, however, may also be high. * * * Bequest savings may once again be the best vehicle to look toward, and the worst to tax, in any effort to increase aggregate capital. * * *

A third set of arguments involves fairness claims * * * . Perhaps the strongest moral argument for the consumption tax is * * * that a consumption tax charges a levy on what a taxpayer removes from the public "pool" for her own, private, preclusive use * * * . This * * * position is consistent with a general aversion to excessive private consumption * * * .

* * * [I]f a concern about monitoring consumption indeed underlies the moral appeal of the broad-based consumption tax, tacking on an estate tax undercuts and counteracts that concern. If we have some moral or political reason for disliking private, preclusive consumption, perhaps particularly the excessive, conspicuous consumption of the very wealthy, it seems odd to be encouraging such consumption with an estate tax. The estate tax may increase inequality of consumption, presumably the precise social space of most concern to consumption tax advocates, while decreasing the productive contributions of work and savings.

* * *

Use presents a different, indeed *opposite*, paradigm from work or earnings alone. It is use that takes away from others—from third parties or from the "common store"—and diverts resources to private preferences. Use represents an imposition by the individual on the collective. Those who do not want to interfere with earnings under just systems may indeed care about use and be willing to interfere with it. * * *

Of course, there are questions and problems. If parties capable of high earnings insist on spending all of their earnings, society faces a choice between the good of work effort and the bad of excessive private, preclusive use * * * . But if an individual is willing to work and save and consume her high earnings prudently over many years, or even pass them on to her heirs, then society can avoid passing judgment on her earnings *per se*. We can, in short, minimize and alter the class of people as to whom we must make a trade-off between productivity (a social good) and inequality (a social bad); we can burden only the decadent consumers or spendthrifts among the most productive. Those productive parties not spending their wealth irresponsibly are serving the public good and need not be overly taxed.

* * *

There are fairness arguments for the consumption tax other than the various "common store" arguments. Perhaps the most common is the horizontal equity point that compares the saver to the consumer and asks why the former should be "double taxed." * * *

* * *

* * * [W]hile a consumption tax is attractive on liberal grounds * * * , adding any transfer tax is highly questionable under the three broad sets of claims supporting the consumption tax model. The first two economic arguments clearly seem to counsel against tacking on an estate tax. Various fairness claims also counsel against the tax. A wealth transfer tax induces or rewards behavior that the consumption tax is intended to discourage: consumption, leisure, and *inter vivos* giving. It is thus hard to get to the consumption-plus-estate tax position from a consideration of consumption tax norms alone.

Perhaps for this reason, liberal advocates of a consumption-plus-transfer tax model generally proceed from a different direction. They accept the consumption tax, for one or another of the above reasons, *despite* what they perceive as its major vice: its tolerance of large stores of private, unevenly distributed wealth. The estate tax is intended to be an antidote to the consumption tax, since it supposedly reaches the lifetime accumulations of wealth that the consumption tax explicitly condones. Under this view, the estate tax is a means of "leveling the playing field" to preserve meaningful and prior notions of equality, quite apart from concerns about efficiency or wealth maximization. * * *

There are, however, problems with this particular compromise. The consumption-plus-estate tax model becomes deeply schizophrenic, even oxymoronic; we are "saving" the consumption tax model from its critics by undermining exactly those reasons why we should have supported it in the first place. * * *

C. A Progressive Consumption-Without-Estate Tax

* * * We have seen that the status quo, with its flawed income-plus-estate tax, is not working in theory or in practice. We have seen that there is much that is popular and normatively attractive in consumption tax theory, but that what is most appealing in this alternative tax scheme is in tension with any wealth transfer tax. We have seen that our practices have in fact resisted any meaningful estate tax. Finally, we have seen that an objective, political, liberal perspective approves of work and savings, while only or at least especially questioning excessive private use. All of these ideas lead to my fifth and final liberal argument against an estate tax: the desirability of a progressive consumption-without-estate tax.

The plan derives in part from economic thinking, which has shown us that any real-world scheme of wealth transfer taxation is apt to encourage *inter vivos* gifts, or to discourage work effort and capital accumulation among the wealthy, or to do both. The answer also draws in part from an exploration of the intuitions lying behind advocacy of the consumption tax model. I presume that a basic intuition * * * has been that the use of wealth, and not its mere possession, is what really concerns liberal society. This position is the core of what I am taking to be the consumption tax's principal fairness claim. * * *

* * *

* * * [P]rivate savings have some distinct virtues. Private savings result from possession without use, which in turn implies productive work effort. * * * [P]rivate wealth can undergird social, macroeconomic progress. Private wealth can also counterbalance government power, and private investment decisions are typically more efficient than public ones. * * *

* * * Repealing the estate tax may in fact be one of the most efficient and even just ways to increase capital * * * . The very presence of the estate tax induces certain unjust behavior, such as large *inter vivos* gifts and large-scale consumption by the rich. More to the point * * * is precisely the possibility that we can use the tax system to *ensure*, or at least to regulate, the "frugality of the capitalist class." The state can do what individuals otherwise might not, of their own accord: guarantee that only the frugal get to keep their large amounts of private wealth. * * * [T]he curtailment of self-indulgence without a general burden on frugality or accumulation is, of course, *exactly* what the progressive consumption-without-estate tax aims to do. * * *

Recall the * * * conjecture that the estate tax effects a transfer from those with a greater propensity to save to those with a greater propensity to consume, thereby lowering the capital stock. An initial instinct may be that this loss is an unavoidable feature of all redistribution; all ethically appropriate redistributions take from the rich and give to the poor. But this thinking is not true once we distinguish between use and possession. Taxing the use of wealth is a way of allowing the most efficient savers to hold on to their capital, while at the same time serving many, if not all, liberal egalitarian ends. Private savings may be the most efficient way to increase the capital stock, * * * and an increased capital stock will have progressive effects, intra- as well as inter-generationally. Moving toward a progressive consumption-without-estate tax may be the "best" way—the most fair and efficient—to increase private savings while still monitoring private use. * * *

To be sure, two rather large sets of problems remain. First, there appear to be equitable and political issues involving the concentration of power accompanying private wealth and investment decisions, and some benefits flow from possession alone. Second, as the liberal egalitarian case reminds us, the use of wealth by those deemed to have "earned" it may not be as offensive as any use of such wealth made by subsequent generations, although skepticism over the relevance or meaning of "earnings" weakens this point, perhaps fatally. These objections are common and well founded; the key response is that we do not need an estate tax to deal with either issue.

As to the first point, a combination of progressive rates and investment regulation under a nominal "consumption" tax can check the liberal dangers of possession alone. A progressive consumption tax changes the very meaning and hence the risks and dangers of private "possession." * * * [O]ne might consume or exercise power directly through investment; this is possession *qua* use. * * * But we can readily enough deal with that problem by compelling the private saver to save in certain forms—a blind trust is a limiting example, but any qualified form of savings accounts will do—in order to get the benefits of the nontaxation of savings. Such vehicles can preserve the efficiency of decentralized decisions while checking abuse, much as the loose form of government oversight of the current pension and charitable activity sectors now does. * * *

As to the second problem, of inheritance and inequality, we can deal with the issue of use by later generations through modifications in the consumption tax's rate structure. * * * While society no doubt has some concerns over the possession of unearned wealth by later generations, and such concerns may be greater than those over possession alone at the earlier generation, the concern vis-à-vis the later generation may once again be even greater when it comes to use. * * * Yet under current law, society places no burden on the act of consumption by an heir; we exert no control whatsoever over how or when heirs spend their wealth. Under a progressive consumption-without-estate tax, this hands-off attitude would change, and we can change it even more fundamentally with a separate rate schedule on spending out of inherited wealth.

Details as to the precise rate schedule will of course need to be worked out, and they may require difficult and ultimately somewhat arbitrary decisions. * * *

* * *

The above discussion has led to a specific comprehensive tax reform proposal: a progressive consumption-without-estate tax, possibly supplemented by a separate and higher rate structure on spending out of gifts or bequests, and a regulatory regime loosely monitoring nominally private investment decisions. * * *

* * *

* * * [T]here is no conclusive *a priori* reason to tax all sources or uses of wealth under the same rate schedule. As suggested above, we could modify the progressive consumption-without-estate tax plan by having separate rate schedules on earned income and inherited wealth. The earned income schedule might feature lower rates to be solicitous to labor-leisure trade-offs, and to isolate out the burden of higher rates for consumption out of capital, or noncurrent period earnings. The schedule on inherited wealth would feature steeper rates to discourage consumption out of this source and to serve liberal egalitarian goals of equality of opportunity. Of course, we would need practical details such as tracing rules. I envision a simple scheme: Consumption is deemed to come out of current period earnings, savings attributable to prior period earnings, and inheritance, in that order. But I mean to leave precise details to another day. A basic idea is that a separate and higher rate schedule on spending out of inherited capital will actually move the proposal toward the logic of an accessions tax, i.e., one that taxes donees, not donors. In this sense, we can think of the proposal as a type of consumption-model accessions tax. Unlike an accessions tax, however, the tax is not levied on the act or at the time of transfer; instead, the tax is postponed, deliberately, until the time of ultimate consumption, consistent with an ethical focus on use.

* * *

VI. THE CASE AGAINST DOING NOTHING

* * *

* * * We do know some things. We know, for example, that wealth inequality remains rather severe, regardless of the presence of a nominally steep gift and estate tax. We know that the estate tax raises little revenue, in absolute or relative terms, with or without adjusting for administrative costs and possible income tax losses. We know that individuals are making large *inter vivos* gifts, and that they are taking many other steps to avoid the sting of the tax. We know that the tax features high marginal rates, against which general economic theory cautions. We know that large public and private resource costs are involved in implementation and enforcement of the estate tax. We know that there is general concern about the level of American capital accumulation, and that the capital stock has important intra-generational effects. And we know that wealth transfer taxation is not popular, even though it applies only to a tiny segment of society.

These known facts ought to cast some doubt on the received wisdom and heighten the call for alternative approaches. The case for a change of approach is all the more compelling when we can reason our way toward alternative means for furthering liberal goals and achieving some of the aims that matter to wealth taxation advocates, such as greater equality of opportunity and the improved welfare of the lower classes. Questioning the estate tax does not require that we fall into naive libertarianism or the comforting arms of trickle-down theory. We can design a tax system that constrains the private use of wealth without creating all of the perverse incentives and resource costs of the status quo. This is the point of the progressive consumption-without-estate tax. Is not this—or something—worth a try?

* * *

NOTE

In testimony before the Senate Finance Committee, McCaffery characterized himself as "an unrequited liberal, in both the classical and contemporary senses of the word, whose views on social and distributive justice might best be described as progressive." Edward J. McCaffery, *Rethinking the Estate Tax*, 67 TAX NOTES 1678, 1678 (1995). In what sense is McCaffery's proposal "liberal"?

Anne L. Alstott, *The Uneasy Liberal Case Against Income and Wealth Transfer Taxation: A Response to Professor McCaffery*, 51 TAX L. REV. 363 (1996)*

I. INTRODUCTION

* * * Professor Edward McCaffery argues that the United States should repeal its federal income and estate taxes and replace them with a progressive tax on consumption. * * * Professor McCaffery's novel claim is that his proposal is grounded in liberal egalitarian political theory * * *.[5] In this Article, I argue that Professor McCaffery's argument, although provocative and interesting, is not persuasive. * * * Professor McCaffery's particular recommendations * * * rest on normative claims that are in tension with basic liberal principles and on empirical predictions that rely on a strained reading of the available economic evidence.

* * * Professor McCaffery * * * argues that neither an estate tax nor an income tax is a prerequisite for distributive justice in a liberal egalitarian regime.[8] Instead, he contends, a progressive consumption tax would best promote liberal objectives.

The defining characteristic of a consumption tax is that it removes from the tax base income that is saved or invested (for example, in financial investments like stocks or bonds or in real investments like plant and equipment). A consumption tax, by definition, taxes only income spent on current, personal consumption (for example, on cars, food and travel). By

---

*   Copyright © 1996. Reprinted with permission.

[5]   * * * Like Professor McCaffery, I use the terms "liberal egalitarian" and "liberal" interchangeably; thus, the liberal principles considered here exclude, among other things, libertarian theories.

[8]   *See* [Edward J. McCaffery, *The Uneasy Case for Wealth Transfer Taxation*, 104 YALE L.J. 283, 289-97 (1994)].

deferring tax on saved income until the money is spent, a proportional consumption tax essentially exempts the earnings on the investment from taxation. A progressive consumption tax of the kind Professor McCaffery advocates would offer significant tax benefits to savers while penalizing those with high levels of consumption spending. In contrast, an income tax encompasses both consumed and saved income, and an estate tax taxes all inherited wealth, whether saved or consumed.

* * * Some prominent proponents of consumption taxation have recommended an additional tax on wealth, for instance, an estate tax, in order to preclude an undue advantage for the rich, who own a disproportionate share of capital and income from capital. * * *

* * * I argue that Professor McCaffery's argument is untenable at three key points. First, Professor McCaffery contends that traditional liberal theory has ignored an important distinction between the possession and the use of wealth, and that it is primarily the use, or consumption, of wealth that is objectionable on grounds of equality of opportunity or political liberty. * * * A closer examination shows that Professor McCaffery's argument discounts the significant political, economic and social power that possession of wealth confers. His claim ultimately turns on an ethically unconvincing characterization of private savings and investment as liberal values. * * *

Professor McCaffery's second argument concerns the economic effects of the estate and income taxes. He argues that liberal society appropriately values work and savings, which a consumption tax would encourage but which income and estate taxation discourage. In addition, he claims, the economic gains created by repeal of the income and estate taxes would tend to increase, rather than reduce, economic equality. Professor McCaffery's economic case rests on an overly optimistic account of the relevant empirical evidence and relies on comparisons of an idealized consumption tax with the flawed, real-world income and estate taxes.

Finally, Professor McCaffery defends his interpretation of liberal egalitarian principles by reference to current social practices. He argues that liberal political theory has inappropriately ignored public opposition to the estate tax and contends that, in this case, public opinion is an appropriate guide to liberal egalitarian ideals. Social interpretation is, however, a tricky business, and Professor McCaffery's overly simple reading of public opinion and political rhetoric comes dangerously close to equating illiberal sentiments with liberal principles.

* * *

* * * Although Professor McCaffery apparently does not intend a general attack on redistribution, his moral and economic arguments bear an uncomfortable resemblance to familiar claims made by opponents of redistribution. Left unanswered, Professor McCaffery's arguments could offer unwarranted (though unintended) theoretical support for an illiberal political agenda. * * *

* * *

II. UNEASY NORMATIVE CLAIMS: THE LIBERAL VALUE OF SAVINGS

Inheritance and the private accumulation of wealth create a classic dilemma for liberal theory. Liberal theory typically values liberty, equality of opportunity, and fairness in distribution, but these goals are not always mutually consistent. Permitting inheritance and the accumulation of wealth serves the goal of liberty by allowing people to reap the rewards of their efforts and to dispose of their wealth as they choose. Inheritance can, however, erect barriers to fair equality of opportunity and political liberty by giving some people an unearned head start in life. * * * Thus, there is an inevitable tension between the goal of maximizing individual liberty—including the liberty to accumulate wealth and to pass it on to one's heirs—and the goal of preserving *equal* starting points for everyone.

* * *

Professor McCaffery adopts * * * liberal goals but argues that traditional liberal policies strike the wrong balance among them. He argues that the income and estate taxes discourage work and savings, which a liberal society appropriately values. An initial problem with Professor McCaffery's statements about work and savings is that they seem simply to recreate the classic liberal dilemma. Replacing the income and estate taxes with a progressive consumption tax would allow workers and their heirs to keep more of their earnings (at least if they save rather than consume them) and might encourage more work and savings * * * . But liberal principles suggest strongly that one instead might "value work and savings" in a more meaningful sense by attempting to ensure fair equality of opportunity and political liberty for all workers, and by limiting the economic advantages that attend particular kinds of work that the market values highly. Thus, the challenge for Professor McCaffery is to explain why promoting work and savings is important enough to override competing liberal concerns.

* * *

As an initial matter, it is useful to clarify that, although Professor McCaffery often speaks of "work and savings" in a single breath, in fact, he is most concerned with savings. * * *

A. The Untenable Distinction Between Possession and Use

One key component of Professor McCaffery's argument is that traditional liberal theory has overlooked a crucial distinction between the possession and use of wealth. * * *

The first problem with this argument is that the distinction between possession and use of wealth simply will not bear the normative and analytic weight Professor McCaffery places on it. The boundaries between "possession" and "use" are not well-defined, and, contrary to Professor McCaffery's claim, the "mere possession" of wealth is quite rightly a subject of liberal concern. The unavoidable difficulty is that private wealth remains a source of current social, economic and political power that goes beyond the potential use of wealth for consumption. In addition to the social and political influence that wealth creates, the possession of wealth confers significant economic security; one need not consume wealth to bask in its benefits. The result is that Professor McCaffery's proposal would leave significant leeway for the exercise of economic privilege by the rich.

* * *

Professor McCaffery anticipates the criticism that private possession of wealth can confer political and economic power even when it is not actually spent. In response, he suggests one intriguing substantive change in property law, but he describes it in a single paragraph and overlooks both its institutional complexity and its inconsistency with the rest of his normative argument. He argues that the power conferred by possession of wealth could be curbed by requiring private savers to save through blind trusts or other limited savings vehicles. * * *

Far from resolving the issue, this proposal simply highlights the difficulty of channeling privately-held wealth into truly public projects. The proposal * * * raises a host of serious institutional and normative questions that Professor McCaffery does not consider. For example, creating a huge and influential new class of powerful financial intermediaries raises significant issues about the exercise of financial power by the managers of these trusts, who might assume for themselves the power that wealth confers. * * *

* * *

* * * [T]he blind trust proposal is also incompatible with Professor McCaffery's own objectives. * * * The blind trust device, by definition, would deprive investors of the power to direct and manage their investments and to play a personal role in adding to their accumulated

wealth. Surely that deprivation would tend to discourage work and savings by breaking the linkage between work and reward. The blind trust device would constrain investors to be only passive holders of wealth and (presumably) would allow them to take an active role only in enterprises in which they hold no significant stake. The magnitude of the empirical effect is uncertain, of course, but no more so than other economic effects about which Professor McCaffery is concerned. * * *

Thus, the blind trust proposal raises more problems than it solves. If owners of wealth view control over reinvestment as an important incident of wealth, the blind trust is a "tax" on wealth of exactly the kind that Professor McCaffery finds troubling. * * *

B. The Murky Depths of the "Common Pool"

The second problem with Professor McCaffery's argument is that it mistakenly treats private savings as a liberal value. Professor McCaffery lionizes the "frugal capitalist," who contributes to the "common pool" of savings, and he disparages the "decadent consumer" who depletes that pool. * * *

The common pool is a favorite metaphor among consumption tax advocates, who typically argue that savings benefit society as a whole.[47] The problem with Professor McCaffery's appropriation of this argument, however, is that the common pool idea is grounded in utilitarian, rather than liberal norms. Liberal egalitarian theory provides no rationale for preferring savings over consumption but instead seeks to allow the greatest possible leeway for individuals to pursue their own visions of the good—whether those life plans involve savings *or* consumption. Thus, although contributions to overall social well-being may carry greater weight in a utilitarian scheme, which might value highly any contribution to overall economic output, the common pool metaphor is not a convincing *liberal* justification for a moral judgment in favor of savings over consumption, particularly when such a judgment would ignore the inequalities of opportunity and political power that wealth creates and preserves.

The common pool metaphor also significantly overstates the unique public benefits of savings. Professor McCaffery invokes the concept of "public good" several times in describing the benefits of the common pool, but private investment is certainly not a public good in the conventional, economic sense of a commodity that can be used by some without diminishing its availability for others. Even accepting a looser use of the term "public good," it is not at all clear why private consumption is an "imposition" on the "collective" when private investment is not. * * *

* * *

Even if one agrees that private savings and investment may have long-term social benefits, Professor McCaffery does not explain how private savings create a unique benefit for the collective. * * *

* * *

Thus, the basic problem is that Professor McCaffery's argument overstates the liberal value of savings. Liberal theory provides no moral rationale for privileging private savings over consumption, and there is no particular reason to believe that savings is a unique social good. Although liberal theory acknowledges the advantages of the market in allocating resources to provide goods that people want, it requires that the market operate within the confines of just background institutions that mitigate disparities in wealth.

---

[47]   *See* Thomas Hobbes, Leviathan 238-39 (Richard Tuck ed., Cambridge Univ. Press 1991) (1651); Nicholas Kaldor, An Expenditure Tax 99-100 (1955); [John Rawls, A Theory of Justice 278 (1971)].

* * *

D. Accommodating Inevitable Imperfections
in Liberal Institutions

[Another] element of Professor McCaffery's argument concerns the imperfection of liberal institutions. Professor McCaffery begins by noting, quite correctly, that fair equality of opportunity and just social institutions are not achieved (and may not even be achievable) in the real world. * * * [T]he traditional liberal response has been that, despite these imperfections, society should use the limited available measures (for example, tax and transfer policy) to mitigate disparities in equality of opportunity.

Professor McCaffery, in contrast, invokes the imperfection of real-world institutions to argue for abandoning altogether efforts to mitigate inequalities in inherited wealth. He points out that the estate tax does not address lifetime inequalities in wealth attributable to market outcomes and may even exacerbate lifetime inequalities in consumption, because estate taxation may encourage the wealthy to spend during their lifetimes. He concludes that a consumption tax is appropriate, because "[i]t now becomes possible that inequality in use is more offensive, even to prior liberal values such as the fair equality of opportunity, than is inequality in possession."

This is a peculiar conclusion, for three reasons. First, the argument once again relies on the possession-use distinction * * *. Second, although it is troubling in liberal terms that the current estate and income taxes do relatively little to curb the lifetime influence of wealthy individuals, it is not at all clear that a recognition of persistent inequalities should lead to dismantling redistributive institutions rather than to strengthening them. * * * Third, even if one agreed with Professor McCaffery that large-scale, lifetime consumption is particularly objectionable, the appropriate remedy would seem to be the imposition of a progressive consumption tax on wealthy consumers in addition to—not instead of—the income and estate taxes. The income tax already taxes both consumed and saved income, but it would be possible to levy an additional consumption tax (perhaps at progressive rates with a very high exemption level) to discourage the worst displays of conspicuous consumption.

Professor McCaffery also recognizes that one response to the limitations of the current income and estate taxes would be to strengthen them, but he rejects that possibility for reasons of economic incentives and political feasibility. * * * The political argument is that there is no public appetite for higher estate taxes. As a descriptive matter, this may or may not be true, but, at a minimum, this is a rather one-sided claim: Professor McCaffery dismisses the possibility of improvements in the current income and estate taxes but overlooks the political factors that could distort or constrain a consumption tax as well. * * * [I]t is likely that the same antitax forces that have weakened the estate and income taxes also would be brought to bear in minimizing the impact of a progressive consumption tax on the most powerful consumers. * * *

Professor McCaffery also suggests another solution, arguing that the progressive consumption tax might incorporate a higher rate of tax on consumption funded from inherited wealth. * * * Although Professor McCaffery sets aside issues of implementation, in fact, these practical problems highlight some significant and inevitable tensions between the proposal and Professor McCaffery's main argument. The key issue is when consumption is deemed to come from inherited wealth. * * * Professor McCaffery also argues that, if inherited wealth is particularly objectionable in a liberal regime, consumption out of inheritance could be taxed at particularly high rates. Although Professor McCaffery might coherently argue for such a tax as a compromise between his objectives and the objective of taxing inheritance, the argument at a minimum should acknowledge the significant tensions between the proposal and the primary argument * * * that *any* tax on inheritance inappropriately penalizes savings relative to consumption.

III. UNEASY ECONOMIC CLAIMS: THE COSTS OF REDISTRIBUTION

Another key component of Professor McCaffery's argument concerns the economic effects of the income and estate taxes. Liberal theorists have long struggled with a second classic dilemma: Taxes on income and wealth may facilitate redistribution but, by discouraging work and savings, could ultimately work to the detriment of even the least advantaged. Well aware of this tradeoff, liberal egalitarians have traditionally sought to balance the ethical claims for redistribution against its economic costs.[75] * * *

Professor McCaffery's surprising claim is that his proposal can circumvent this classic dilemma of redistribution. Replacing the income and estate taxes with a progressive consumption tax, Professor McCaffery argues, would both increase economic output and promote economic equality. In effect, Professor McCaffery's argument is that the conventional liberal economic wisdom is wrong and that taxes simultaneously can promote work and savings, enhance equality of opportunity and mitigate unfair disparities in wealth. A closer examination reveals, however, that Professor McCaffery's analysis overstates the likely economic costs of income and estate taxation and fails to consider some economic costs of consumption taxation. Thus, it is questionable whether his proposal would produce even the aggregate economic gains he claims. Even more troubling in liberal terms, he fails to establish that his proposal would produce a distribution of economic gains that would benefit the least advantaged.

* * *

A. The Uncertain Effects of Taxation on Work and Savings

The foundation of Professor McCaffery's case is the proposition that taxation has significant effects on work and savings. Professor McCaffery argues strongly that there is a consensus that high income tax rates are "inefficient and ultimately wasteful" because they lead high earners to reduce work effort significantly. In fact, the effects of income taxes on labor supply are highly uncertain. Economic theory teaches that an income tax both discourages work (through a "substitution effect" that makes work less attractive than leisure) and encourages work (through an "income effect" that leads people to work harder to make up the lost income). Empirical estimates of the effect of income taxes on work effort vary widely, and there is no consensus that the income tax has dramatically reduced aggregate labor supply.

Professor McCaffery claims that the estate tax also discourages work, but again both the theoretical prediction and the empirical evidence are uncertain. The estate tax might reduce work, if bequests are an important motivation for work, but once again the competing income effect might lead workers to work even harder in order to leave the same after-tax bequest. In addition, taxing inheritance might increase work effort among heirs. Professor McCaffery provides little empirical evidence to support his claim, and the actual effect of the estate tax on work effort remains uncertain.

* * *

Professor McCaffery also argues that the income and estate taxes reduce savings, but this proposition too is controversial. * * * There is even less evidence on the effects of the estate tax on savings. In theory, the estate tax, like the income tax, may discourage saving by reducing the return on savings, but again there is a competing income effect that might lead savers to save more in response to taxes. Although it seems likely that people save for a variety of reasons—to provide for old age, to insure against economic calamity and to provide for one's

---

[75]   For an analysis of these issues in the context of the estate tax, see [Michael J. Graetz, *To Praise the Estate Tax, Not to Bury It*, 93 YALE L.J. 259, 264 (1983)] * * * .

heirs—at the moment, there is no economic consensus on the relative importance of the bequest motivation for savings or on the actual magnitude of the estate tax's impact on savings.

What is clear, however, is that other fiscal policies and monetary policies directly influence savings, and that their effects may dwarf those of the income and estate taxes. * * *

Professor McCaffery notes that the estate tax also may reduce aggregate savings by transferring wealth from rich donors, with a higher propensity to save, to the government or to recipients of transfer payments, with a lower propensity to save. Any redistribution from richer to poorer presumably has this effect. * * *

The broader point is—once again—that there is nothing intrinsically good about savings or bad about consumption, without specifying in more detail how savings serve liberal norms like liberty, equality of opportunity or security for the least advantaged. Although savings may promote long-term investment and economic growth, the question of the "right" rate of savings is notoriously difficult when taken seriously. * * *

Finally, at several points, Professor McCaffery argues that the estate tax is objectionable because it encourages the rich to engage in inter vivos giving and lifetime consumption, which Professor McCaffery characterizes as "illiberal" effects. * * * First, [this] argument simply describes some additional goals that may be in tension with one another but offers no reason for choosing one over another. On liberal grounds, it is not immediately clear why unlimited inheritance should be permitted in order to avoid encouraging lifetime gifts or conspicuous consumption. Second, once again it is important to remember that potential incentives do not necessarily translate into behavioral changes of any significant magnitude * * * . Professor McCaffery argues that gifts and consumption patterns are "undoubtedly sensitive" to tax rules but offers little in the way of empirical evidence. One might expect the rich to respond to tax incentives, but many people would be reluctant to save taxes by giving away or consuming the social and economic power that their wealth confers * * * . Finally, the asserted tradeoff also assumes the impossibility or undesirability of reform * * * .

B. Distribution * * *

The second component of Professor McCaffery's economic argument concerns the impact of the estate tax on the distribution of income and wealth. * * *

* * * Even if the estate tax does reduce the capital stock, the government might adopt other policies to increase savings and counteract that result. Thus, repealing the estate tax is not the only, or even the obvious, route to increasing the capital stock. Other plausible policies include, for example, savings subsidies that could encourage increased life-cycle savings to offset reductions in bequest savings. * * * Thus, a conscious governmental policy might choose to tax inherited wealth, as a liberally-disfavored source of savings, and to make up the economic differential elsewhere by encouraging savings distributed in a more egalitarian way. These alternative policies raise a host of empirical questions, but, at the very least, they deserve closer attention in a liberal program for encouraging savings.

* * *

* * * Even if repealing the estate tax would increase the capital stock and raise U.S. workers' wages, Professor McCaffery does not consider how the aggregate increase in labor's aggregate share of national income would be allocated among different classes of workers. * * * Which workers would benefit from an increase in the capital stock? For example, suppose that repeal of the estate tax would increase the incomes of the richest 10% of the population while reducing the incomes of the richest 1%. That sort of change is equality-enhancing in a narrow quantitative sense but is not normatively compelling in liberal terms, because it may do little to enhance equality of opportunity or to improve the circumstances of the least

advantaged. These are questions, not answers, but they are fundamental issues that Professor McCaffery's proposal should take into account.

* * *

D. A Leap of Faith

Thus, Professor McCaffery's economic case against the estate tax is built on a shaky empirical foundation. Taking into account these substantial empirical uncertainties, Professor McCaffery's real claim is that potential reductions in savings brought about by the income and estate taxes are sufficient to warrant repeal of all forms of taxation on capital and income from capital. The available evidence suggests that Professor McCaffery's conclusion rests as much on intuition as on empirical fact.

* * *

* * * Replacing the income and estate taxes with a progressive consumption tax has the clear potential to increase inequalities of income and wealth, to perpetuate for generations even greater inequalities of opportunity, and to exempt wealthy investors from their obligation to help finance the cost of government. Professor McCaffery is eager to take action: He argues "The Case Against Doing Nothing" by urging, "Is not this—or something—worth a try?" On this evidence, I think the answer is "no." Repealing the income and estate taxes could indeed "do something" quite serious by eliminating important redistributive institutions. * * * The existence of empirical uncertainty should not prod us into action for action's sake: Trading uncertain benefits for likely harm is not a wise course.

IV. UNEASY SOCIAL INTERPRETATION: THE DANGERS OF POPULISM

Professor McCaffery structures his argument against the estate tax as a response to an initial "puzzle": Despite its secure place in liberal theory, the estate tax has not garnered popular support in the United States or elsewhere, and existing wealth transfer tax regimes are limited in scope. Professor McCaffery argues that the solution to the puzzle is that liberal political theorists have misconstrued their own principles: "The people are not illiberal; their liberal leaders have failed them." Professor McCaffery justifies his concern with public opinion by characterizing his theory as "political and interpretive." A "political" theory of tax is one that "takes seriously the idea that legal and economic rights and institutions are human-made; that tax rules are, so to speak, up for grabs," and an "interpretive" theory "looks for norms in society's actual practices and beliefs."

Although Professor McCaffery is surely right that any sensible and appealing version of liberalism must pay close attention to society's values, in this case, Professor McCaffery's social interpretation is not careful enough. While practices may indeed reflect deep normative judgments, social interpretation is a delicate task, and the interpreter of social practices also must be an alert critic. An overly simple reading of current practices may elevate unthinking prejudices or narrow self-interest to the level of principles of justice. * * * Professor McCaffery's approach to social interpretation * * * accepts too readily casual public opinion as an authoritative source of liberal values.

The first problem lies in determining what "the public" believes. Public opinion polls provide one source of information, and Professor McCaffery cites the results of several polls that indicate public opposition to estate taxes. Public opinion polls are a questionable source of data, however. It is well known that poll results depend critically on the precise question that is asked. * * * The reported unpopularity of the estate tax may be similarly malleable: The public may reflexively reject a "tax" of any kind, but the answers might well differ if the question asked about compelling the richest 1% of society to contribute a fraction of their wealth to the cost of important government services.

Further, even if the poll results are accurate, uneducated public opinion may not be a reliable source of ethical guidance. Professor McCaffery considers but rejects the idea that the public is "too ill informed for our implicit practices to mean much of anything at all." * * * The deeper problem is that there is no particular reason to think that public opinion necessarily reflects liberal values. * * *

Setting aside public opinion polls as a questionable source of information about society's deepest beliefs, one might look instead, as Professor McCaffery does, to the content of the tax laws. Professor McCaffery argues that "our actual tax systems are at best only weakly progressive, and at worst not progressive at all" and concludes that "[p]ractical liberal politics have gotten our objective social values wrong." Once again, however, social interpretation is considerably more complex than Professor McCaffery acknowledges. In fact, the law sends severely mixed messages. While the current income and estate taxes are not as comprehensive as they might be, they have remained in the law for many years and have exhibited greater and lesser degrees of progressivity. * * *

Another problem in social interpretation is to accord the proper weight to even clear statements of public values. For example, it is easy enough to find political speeches that extol work and savings as American values, but, once again, accepting these statements at face value and characterizing them as necessarily "liberal" is surely naive. Public statements about the value of work and savings often support illiberal policies or obscure a complex political agenda. * * *

* * *

Professor McCaffery * * * argues that " * * * [n]either envy nor any 'soak the rich' populism can explain the [estate] tax's unpopularity and its practical evisceration, here and in other democratic societies." What Professor McCaffery ignores, however, is that populism need not take the form of soak-the-rich "class warfare." Another kind of populism that is even more dangerous to liberal egalitarian ends may now be politically ascendant: A distinctly American, anti-tax, "soak-the-poor" populism * * * . At its very worst, the lionization of work and savings is the self-serving rhetoric of the uneasy middle class * * * .

VI. CONCLUSION

* * * I have argued * * * that Professor McCaffery's current policy proposals reflect an unduly sanguine interpretation of the existing evidence and a willingness to take significant risks with potentially illiberal outcomes. * * *

* * *

* * * Although the contours of liberal institutions are not carved in stone, and it is worth exploring the merits of alternative arrangements, any convincing liberal alternative must comport with liberal egalitarian commitments to equal liberty, equal opportunity and an appropriate regard for the least advantaged. Professor McCaffery's proposal does not meet those criteria. It would limit redistributive possibilities from the revenue side, and his arguments relating to work, savings, public opinion and the capital stock emphasize the costs of redistribution while downplaying the liberal egalitarian case for mitigating disparities in opportunities and economic power. * * * [Professor McCaffery's] proposals ultimately are unpersuasive as a liberal approach to taxation.

NOTE

McCaffery insists that his argument is not "narrowly consequentialist," nor "specifically economic," but rather "a normative and a moral argument." Is he correct in asserting that he and Alstott share the same "broad ends" and that their disagreement is essentially one over "means"? *See* Edward J. McCaffery, *Being the Best We Can Be (A Reply to My Critics)*, 51 Tax L. Rev. 614, 615-16, 619 (1996). Other commentators also question the empirical foundation of McCaffery's argument. *See* Michael J. Graetz, The Decline (and Fall?) of the Income Tax 268 (1997) (noting McCaffery's failure to offer "one shred of evidence" to support his argument that repeal of estate and gift taxes would "increase the wages of the least advantaged members of our society").

Eric Rakowski, *Transferring Wealth Liberally*, 51 Tax L. Rev. 419 (1996)*

I. INTRODUCTION

Liberalism is a woolly doctrine, a canopy sheltering a colorful array of theories about the legitimate scope of state power and the just distribution of social resources and opportunities. Notwithstanding their lush variety, Edward McCaffery claims that liberal theories display a surprising double unity.[1] Virtually all of them, he says, favor a redistributive tax on gifts and bequests, especially on transfers of wealth from older to younger generations. Yet, they all err in advocating a tax on gratuitous transfers. Liberal theorists stand united in unwittingly betraying the ends to which they are committed, by embracing a tool to reduce wealth disparities that does more harm to core liberal values than the good it accomplishes. In lieu of contemporaneous taxes on gifts and bequests, Professor McCaffery contends that liberals should call for taxes only on the expenditure of wealth or income for noninvestment purposes. They should, however, probably support a heavier tax on these expenditures if the money spent can be traced to a gift or bequest rather than to some other source.

* * * I argue that [Professor McCaffery's] methods for deriving and justifying a set of liberal principles against which to measure proposed taxes are ill chosen or applied too casually. I further contend that some of the crucial premises on which he relies in defending the abolition of wealth transfer taxes—most especially, the claim that work and saving are objectively good and that extravagant consumption is objectively bad—have no place in leading liberal theories and should not command allegiance.

* * * Professor McCaffery's progressive consumption tax with higher rates on the personal use of unearned wealth is one defensible way of resolving the clash of values that ought to shape taxes and state spending. But most liberals will not think it the right way. It will not please those who value current equality of resources or well-being more highly than Professor McCaffery does, and who would be more reluctant to leave present people worse off so that their children and grandchildren, who would presumably be better off anyway, might reap a larger benefit. It also will likely repel liberal egalitarians who doubt the accuracy of Professor McCaffery's lightly defended empirical assumptions about the responsiveness of rich people's

---

*   Copyright © 1996. Reprinted with permission.

[1]   *See* Edward J. McCaffery, *The Uneasy Case for Wealth Transfer Taxation*, 104 Yale L.J. 283 (1994) * * * .

work and spending habits to changes in wealth transfer taxes. To convince liberals to abandon estate and gift taxes, Professor McCaffery needs a more compelling moral argument and better behavioral evidence than he supplies.

II. PROFESSOR MCCAFFERY'S CONCEPTION OF LIBERALISM

Professor McCaffery offers two distinct justifications for the claim that liberalism's views about individual liberties and social justice favor a consumption tax without a tax on wealth transfers * * * . The first relies on what he calls a "political-interpretive" theory of taxation, which attempts to tease out lessons for tax policy from the predominantly liberal principles that allegedly suffuse our laws, political institutions, and public opinion. Professor McCaffery's second justification appeals to the views of paradigmatic liberal philosophers. * * *

A. The Political-Interpretive Approach

* * *

Even if Professor McCaffery were right in claiming that most Americans today deplore taxes on all gifts and bequests, * * * that fact alone cannot ground an argument that wealth transfer taxes are unjust or immoral. The political-interpretive approach Professor McCaffery urges collides with Hume's familiar point that it is impossible to deduce what ought to be from what is.[6] * * *

In determining which legal changes are possible, one cannot ignore popular sentiment with respect to the law, along with its history and current expression. Likewise, in determining which legal changes are warranted, public opinion regarding some issues is crucial to fixing what the law ought to be, given our commitment to democratic legitimacy. * * *

But the question Professor McCaffery is trying to answer, as I understand his project, is divorced from these considerations of political expediency and legitimacy. The question is not which policy it would be wise for a member of Congress to back if she were vying for votes, or what she is beholden to do in her representative capacity. The question is what justice or morality demands in the way of wealth transfer taxes, taking certain facts about human motivation and ability as given. This is the question that a citizen or an independent-minded public official attempting to make up her mind about these issues must answer. Knowledge that other people hold one or another view might stimulate her thinking, but it certainly offers no confident answer as to where her thinking should tend.

* * *

Of course, from the perspectives of both legislators and citizens, it might not matter that people subscribe to different moral premises if they endorse the same conclusions. And an academic addressing his argument only to liberals might ignore their discordant theories if the theories all funnelled into a single set of legal rules. But if agreement on outcomes is imperfect, as it certainly is with regard to wealth transfer taxation, then a political approach to setting policy rests on slippery soil. Either it means nothing more than counting heads and letting the majority prevail, or it amounts to taking sides without, by hypothesis, any normative reason for choosing a particular position, because the invocation of a substantive ethical principle would betray what Professor McCaffery has described as the political cast of his approach. Neither alternative has much to commend it if one's goal is constructing the soundest normative position rather than a stable political compromise.

* * *

---

6   DAVID HUME, A TREATISE OF HUMAN NATURE 469-70 (L.A. Selby-Bigge ed., 2d ed. 1978).

C. The Elements of Professor McCaffery's Liberalism

Four propositions stand out in Professor McCaffery's account of liberalism. All of them help contour his proposal. * * * These four propositions * * * seem the most prominent supports underlying the vision of liberalism from which Professor McCaffery extracts his tax recommendations.

1. Equality of Material Wealth

Liberal egalitarians typically believe that justice requires those who are lucky through no merit of their own to share the material benefits of their uncourted good fortune with those who are blamelessly worse off. They disagree on the extent to which good and bad luck that is not the result of voluntary gambles imposes a duty on those who fare better to help those whom fortune cheats, as well as on the extent to which whatever principle of redistribution they endorse should yield to competing values. Likewise, their views diverge over whether inequality is itself an evil, or whether inequality is only to be deplored when it signals that those who are worse off could have their situations improved by giving them some of the resources possessed by those who are better off. Furthermore, liberal egalitarians have not coalesced around a common measure of the respects in which people ideally ought to be made equal or more equal than they now are; the issue remains contested.

Nevertheless, a stout battalion of liberal philosophers favors the redistribution of wealth to make people's prospects more nearly equal. To be sure, not all do. * * * But Professor McCaffery is right to insist that an overwhelming number of liberal *egalitarians* agree that justice demands greater equalization than nature supplies of people's chances to acquire and achieve. Because gifts and bequests are a salient cause of existing inequalities of wealth, particularly when they pass from parents to children, philosophers who advocate reducing disparities in luck to make opportunities more equal are inclined to limit gratuitous transfers by taxes or other devices.

* * * Because liberal egalitarians focus on what individuals have or have not chosen, on what they are responsible for through their efforts and risk taking as opposed to what has come to them unbidden, they generally support an accessions tax on donative transfers rather than a tax on the total value of an estate, a tax on a donor's lifetime giving or an increase in income tax rates across the board.

2. Political Liberty

The second liberal proposition on which Professor McCaffery calls is that the state should discourage or forbid actions that threaten fair democratic political participation, the exercise of individual liberties, or a competitive market economy. This proposition has a broad following. It approves government efforts to limit the political or market power of wealthy individuals. * * *

* * * The argument for estate and gift taxes cannot lean heavily on this second liberal proposition without demonstrating that wealth transfer taxes are better at curing these ills than alternative measures are. Professor McCaffery does not attempt this comparison. He therefore seems right in acknowledging this liberal worry but not relying on it in any important way in making the case for his tax plan.

3. Conspicuous Consumption

The third proposition on which Professor McCaffery grounds his case for a consumption-without-estate tax is both much more controversial and, for him, far more important. He maintains that a liberal state may curb "large-scale or conspicuous consumption" for "objective" political and ethical reasons * * * .

* * *

For someone who adheres to a political-interpretive approach, a ban on "large-scale spending" on personal projects, or especially heavy taxation of that spending, seems an awkward proposition to endorse. There is little evidence that this view is popular, and it seems no accident that it has never been cemented in American law. As for Professor McCaffery's second test for liberal lineage—the ideas of typical liberal thinkers—he fails to name a single liberal philosopher who defends the claim that self-indulgent personal spending properly may be restrained, or ought to be restrained, by a liberal state.

* * *

* * * As traditionally conceived, liberalism protects people's freedom to make mistakes with their property and their lives once they have satisfied any obligations of justice and fair cooperation they owe to others. Professor McCaffery has not explained why this traditional conception is mistaken. Nor has he explained why, if it is, the correct view implies that consumption past a certain point should be prohibited or taxed at a high rate, regardless of how someone spends his money. His reasoning seems to support, instead, a tax targeted at the consumption of luxuries.

* * *

4. The Objective Goodness of Work and Saving

Professor McCaffery's other highly controversial premise resembles its predecessor and is open to similar objections.

> [E]ven if wealth is indeed "fairly earned," society may nonetheless have objective, political reasons for opposing estate taxation. Simply put, and finessing metaphysical questions over desert and entitlement, liberal society likes earnings and savings, both of which contribute to a certain metaphoric "common pool" . . . . Earnings and saving each represent goods to the liberal majority, whereas use represents an individual imposition on the collective and is therefore not a liberal good. Put conversely, claims of inequality are most compelling vis-à-vis the use of resources; the justice of earnings is logically and ethically distinct from the justice of use.

* * *

If the idea * * * is that people should be encouraged to work and save because these activities produce capital that in time will augment other people's consumption and that they should be nudged to do so even given a just distribution of resources, then the argument is apparently that the state should seek to improve the welfare of the poor *more* than justice requires. Yet, it is difficult to imagine what *liberal* reason there might be for tampering with what is assumed to be a just allocation of the benefits and burdens of social life. Professor McCaffery asserts the possibility of such a reason, but he does not state it plainly or offer an argument for it. To the extent that his recommended tax scheme depends on it to show its superiority over rival approaches, it is unlikely to win the assent of many liberal egalitarians.

5. Summary

Of the four propositions that Professor McCaffery alleges are central to the liberal egalitarian position, only the first two—the claim that a liberal state should redistribute income to promote equality of material resources and of opportunity and the claim that it should safeguard political and economic liberties—have garnered widespread support from liberal philosophers. Some liberal writers argue that these two propositions yield a powerful case for stiff wealth transfer taxes when conjoined to observed facts about human motivation and behavior. That claim may or may not be true; a great deal depends * * * on the theory of distributive justice to which one subscribes and the empirical hypotheses one believes are correct. * * * [I]f Professor McCaffery needs to rely on claims about the appropriateness and perhaps the desirability of a liberal state's legislating to advance the allegedly objective ethical value of work and saving and to combat the objective ethical disvalue of flagrant consumption, he will find that few liberals are willing to follow him. * * * They will hold their ground because the values to which Professor McCaffery appeals, in their judgment, would compromise rather than supplement a liberal egalitarian theory of justice.

III. WHY, WHEN AND HOW MUCH SHOULD A LIBERAL STATE TAX TRANSFERS OF MATERIAL WEALTH?

* * *

* * * [G]overnments make some citizens pay to help others, with the aim of redistributing wealth and the opportunities it affords. This is the principal justification liberals give for taxes on gratuitous transfers.

* * *

A. Professor McCaffery's Proposed Progressive Consumption Tax With a Possible Deferred Progressive Accessions Tax

Professor McCaffery claims that "[m]any, and maybe all, of the normative problems with the private possession of wealth turn out to relate to possession *qua* actual or potential use." * * * Professor McCaffery arrives at "a specific comprehensive tax reform proposal: a progressive consumption-without-estate tax, possibly supplemented by a separate and higher rate structure on spending out of gifts or bequests, and a regulatory regime loosely monitoring nominally private investment decisions."

Professor McCaffery does not say by what standards, and using what administrative machinery, the state should regulate the investment of property obtained by gift or bequest. He describes as "a limiting example" a requirement that property secured in this way be placed into a blind trust to gain the benefit of deferred taxation, but says that "any qualified form of savings accounts will do." It is hard to believe, however, that Professor McCaffery would, on further reflection, insist that people place their inheritances into designated savings vehicles to postpone taxation. For example, it would be contrary to the ends he lauds to require heirs to a family business to sell the enterprise and put the proceeds in a bank to defer taxes. The disincentive to giving and investing (by both donors and recipients) created by government controls, along with the inefficiencies and compliance costs they would create, would have to be weighed against whatever benefits Professor McCaffery perceives investment regulation to have. Yet, aside from the suggested savings accounts, which might be mandated for gratuitous transfers of cash and securities—though not without loss and certainly not in the case of most other gifts—Professor McCaffery offers no clue as to how he would strike the balance between liberty to invest and community control.

Nor does he say how high tax rates ought to be as a matter of justice. * * * Given his arguments, the top marginal rate almost certainly would have to exceed 40% on the consumption of earned income until well after the transition to a consumption tax.

A second, higher rate on the consumption of assets received as gifts or bequests, Professor McCaffery notes, would be equivalent to "a type of consumption-model accessions tax." It differs from a conventional accessions tax in that the tax would be levied, not at the time wealth was transferred, but only once it was used. Professor McCaffery envisions "a simple scheme: Consumption is deemed to come out of current period earnings, savings attributable to prior period earnings, and inheritance, in that order," although he wishes "to leave precise details to another day." He declines to say whether something like the scheme he describes is desirable—whether higher rates ought to be imposed on the consumption of wealth received gratuitously.

Professor McCaffery's description of his proposal leaves numerous questions unanswered. He does not disclose how much weight he assigns to the pursuit of equality of consumption, or even why he values equality of consumption. It is even more unclear why he values equality *only* of consumption. Professor McCaffery seems to believe that the feelings of security, power and self-respect that people typically experience when they own considerable wealth, regardless of whether they spend it, should be ignored or given scant weight in determining whether people are treated as equals. But he never addresses the question of why this substantial source of people's well-being and of their perceptions of inequality at best should play a trifling part in specifying justice's demands. It is a salient omission.

In addition, Professor McCaffery does not explain why a liberal egalitarian community might endorse a higher rate of tax on the consumption of unearned wealth than on the consumption of earned wealth. He proposes a dual-schedule consumption tax without saying plainly why consumption made possible by unearned wealth should be taxed more heavily than consumption with a different pedigree, even though the two constitute equivalent withdrawals from the stock of social resources. * * *

Professor McCaffery speaks only of one schedule of taxes on the consumption of wealth obtained by gift [or] bequest. It is unclear whether he does so because he favors a uniform set of rates without exceptions, or whether he has just not engaged in the fine-tuning that would be necessary in fleshing out a comprehensive reform proposal. Many would favor making special provision for generation-skipping transfers,[60] distinguishing relatives from other recipients, or taxing lightly (or not at all) transfers to needy parents, disabled children, and other groups whose expenditures are not frivolous or politically destabilizing.[62]

Professor McCaffery does not discuss the various administrative problems his proposal would encounter, but state regulation of private investment decisions by recipients of inherited wealth—a surprisingly illiberal and probably unworkable suggestion, if it had any teeth—is not the sole difficulty. Recordkeeping and monitoring could pose larger problems. * * *

* * *

B. Methodological Issues

Assessing the normative appeal of Professor McCaffery's proposal is daunting * * * . [T]he proposal itself is exceedingly indefinite. Not only is it unclear exactly what he is recommending in the way of taxation—What would the basic rate structure look like? Would there be one set of rates or two? What limitations would be imposed on investments?—but [he does] not indicate how revenue obtained for the purpose of redistribution should be spent. It is impossible to evaluate the justice of any tax scheme without knowing how the proceeds will be used.

* * *

---

[60]   * * * [See] William Andrews, *The Accessions Tax Proposal*, 22 TAX L. REV. 589, 613-27 (1967); Edward C. Halbach, Jr., *An Accessions Tax*, 23 REAL PROP., PROBATE & TRUST J. 211, 214-15, 227-29, 240-70 (1988). * * *

[62]   * * * *See* Mark Ascher, *Curtailing Inherited Wealth*, 89 MICH. L. REV. 69, 127-32 (1990).

In the remainder of this Section, I discuss several matters of distributive justice that bear crucially on the design of wealth transfer taxes and examine, to the extent that it is possible to tease out his views, Professor McCaffery's stand with respect to them. * * * I assume throughout that liberal egalitarians are at least suspicious of gifts and bequests, because, to a significant degree, they typically represent accessions to someone's resources that the recipient did not earn through her efforts or decisions. Liberals might conclude that the benefits of permitting gratuitous transfers of wealth outweigh the damage to their egalitarian goals, but I assume that they find these unearned accessions prima facie objectionable. The question, then, is why gifts and bequests should be permitted and, if they are allowed, why they should not be taxed heavily, to spread material good fortune more widely than donors desire. * * *

C. Work, Savings and the Plight of the Poor

* * *

2. Professor McCaffery's Main Worry

The tendency of wealth transfer taxes to depress the productivity of potential donors and to induce them to save less and spend more on noncapital assets provokes Professor McCaffery's chief objection to levying estate and gift taxes when wealth is transferred. These effects, he says, furnish a decisive reason to oppose wealth transfer taxes, but it is clear that capital formation's "important effects on intra- as well as intergenerational well-being" are for him the leading reason to scupper estate and gift taxes. Although "a complete and efficacious shutting down of wealth transfers may increase work and savings incentives at the lower generations, with possibly beneficial effects on capital," Professor McCaffery appears convinced that the dampening effect on potential donors' incentives to work and save wisely would be substantially more powerful than the spur to potential recipients' industry and savings. On balance, less would be devoted to capital investment, which would mean that trickle-down benefits to poorer workers would dry up and future generations would be less richly endowed than if wealth could be transferred without impediment. * * *

3. * * * Challenges to Professor McCaffery's Claims

Professor McCaffery's assertion that liberal egalitarians should oppose wealth transfer taxes because of their effects on work effort, saving, and the welfare of indigent laborers is open to [two main empirical] challenges. * * *

a. Impact on Work Effort and Saving

The first empirical challenge concerns the degree to which people who were capable of earning and saving would leave a smaller surplus of production over consumption if donative transfers were taxed than if they bore no tax but their subsequent consumption was taxed at prevailing consumption tax rates (or, as Professor McCaffery appears to favor, at above-normal rates). * * *

* * * Professor McCaffery offers no concrete evidence of how wealthy individuals and people able to earn high incomes would respond to higher wealth transfer taxes. * * * Given that his argument depends crucially on the assumption that both earnings and, more importantly, savings evince a strong negative elasticity with respect to estate and gift tax rates, the paucity of support he offers for this assumption is surprising. Professor McCaffery notes that wealthy individuals spend considerable sums on legal advice to reduce their estate taxes. But the fact that they are rational enough to spend a certain sum of money to obtain even larger tax savings tells us next to nothing about whether talented or rich people would react to higher estate taxes by working harder and saving more, so that they could sustain the after-tax value of the legacies they leave, or whether they would instead labor less or spend more on themselves, pass-

ing on less to their children. Many writers who favor strengthening our wealth transfer tax regime suppose, contrary to Professor McCaffery, that even if gift and estate taxes were increased substantially, high earners would continue to work much as they now do and wealthy people would still invest almost as much as they currently do, so that intergenerational savings would not decline dramatically. Professor McCaffery offers little reason to think their contrary views mistaken. * * *

* * *

In arguing that his proposal will not curtail work and saving as much as alternative taxes on wealth transfers, Professor McCaffery poses the key question for himself as follows, "why is not the chilling effect on capital accumulation or work effort equally strong under the progressive consumption-without-estate tax (especially with a higher rate schedule on spending out of inheritance) as it is under the more commonly recommended consumption-plus-estate tax, or even under the income-plus-estate tax system?" Sadly, this question misses the central issue. Professor McCaffery is free to compare the special consumption tax on unearned wealth he favors to an estate tax. What is far more important is that he compare it to what most liberal egalitarians consider its principal competitor: a progressive accessions tax levied when wealth is transferred. Professor McCaffery avoids this comparison without offering any explanation. Its omission is significant.

* * * When one expands the range of options from a simple estate tax to more attractive alternatives to Professor McCaffery's consumption tax, his argument falters.

First, he says, "the rate structure [of his consumption tax proposal] would encourage dispersion among bequests, as donors saw the lower rates that were available to a wider range of donees." This is true, and it gives his plan an edge over an estate tax. It offers no advantage, however, over an accessions tax, an inheritance tax (which, unlike an accessions tax, is not based on cumulative receipts), or the income taxation of gifts and bequests at donees' rates,[88] all of which base tax liability on donees' receipts rather than the overall amount of wealth transferred by a single donor.

* * *

In the end, Professor McCaffery's case for preferring a tax on donees deferred until consumption to an accessions tax imposed when wealth is transferred or to the income taxation of wealth transfers is very thin. He defends a plan that has no clear advantage over these alternative taxes, judging from the reasons he offers. At the same time, it possesses what some liberal egalitarians regard as the serious drawback of leaving untouched the value that many recipients derive from the mere possession, prior to use, of donated wealth. Whether deferring taxes until gifts or bequests are used for personal consumption would increase work and invested savings significantly is ultimately an empirical issue, but Professor McCaffery's observational evidence and speculative reasoning instill little confidence in his forecast.

b. Trickle-Down Benefits to the Poor

Notwithstanding these deficiencies, assume for a moment that Professor McCaffery is right. Work effort and private saving would increase, thanks to the substitution of a targeted progressive consumption tax for a wealth transfer tax. The second serious empirical challenge to Professor McCaffery's proposal stems from uncertainty about the effects of this presumed increase in work and saving. Professor McCaffery avers that greater toil and investment by able workers and wealthy individuals will augment the wages of the poorest workers or, less

---

[88]   * * * *See, e.g.,* John K. McNulty, *A Transfer Tax Alternative: Inclusion Under the Income Tax,* 4 TAX NOTES 24 (June 28, 1976) * * * .

directly, enhance government benefits flowing to them now and in the distant future more than an accessions tax or an estate tax would. * * *

Why believe him? Professor McCaffery provides no detailed data in support of his claim. He appears to rely instead on the widely accepted idea that increased private capital investment will augment the return to labor, boosting wages over time, and that one effect of heightened growth rates will be hugely elevated real wages decades hence. Transferring wealth to the poor now, in what I take to be Professor McCaffery's view, injures workers in the long run, because it throttles socially beneficial work and investment by those best able to produce and save, and it puts money in the hands of people more inclined to spend than invest. * * *

* * * It also might happen that any increase in investment caused by Professor McCaffery's plan, relative to other options, would hurt the very poorest while yielding larger benefits to members of higher economic groups. It is impossible to say for sure. The upshot of this second empirical challenge is merely that Professor McCaffery has not constructed a tight case for the conclusion that his consumption-without-estate tax would be best for those groups whose welfare he deems most important.

* * *

IV. CONCLUSION

What is most unsettling about Professor McCaffery's call for a progressive consumption-without-estate tax is its indefinite and ungrounded character. Professor McCaffery never makes clear which principles of distributive justice he endorses and why he does so, nor does he offer much proof, based on experience and controlled observation, that some type of consumption tax with a deferred accessions tax will implement a particular collection of liberal egalitarian ideals most effectively. This is not the way to argue for fundamental law reform. * * * No collection of moral values, and no concrete reform measure, will command universal assent, but that is surely no reason to refrain from articulating a set of principles and proposals and seeing how people respond. As a society, we need to reach a decision, even if we ultimately choose to keep what we have. In approaching that choice, we gain more from understanding what divides us than from papering over our differences, hoping the cracks won't show.

NOTE

Rakowski observes that "[l]iberal egalitarians typically believe that justice requires those who are lucky through no merit of their own to share the material benefits of their uncourted good fortune with those who are blamelessly worse off." Does the justification for taxing gratuitous transfers rest on the ground that such transfers are due to "uncourted good fortune" rather than "merit"? Some commentators argue that liberal egalitarians may find "the normative foundation of distributive justice in the simple idea that a community should promote the well-being of its badly-off members." *See* Liam B. Murphy, *Commentary: Liberty, Equality, Well-Being: Rakowski on Wealth Transfer Taxation*, 51 TAX L. REV. 473, 474 (1996). How might liberal egalitarians strike the balance between the claims of present and future generations?

Douglas Holtz-Eakin, *The Uneasy Empirical Case for Abolishing the Estate Tax*, 51 TAX L. REV. 495 (1996)*

I. INTRODUCTION

* * * Recently, Professor Edward McCaffery has [launched] a broad assault on the foundations of the U.S. system of estate and gift taxation.[2] His basic themes are that the estate tax markedly distorts individual incentives, fails to meet its distributional objectives and raises little revenue in the process. In short, the estate tax represents the worst sort of tax policy.

In this brief review, I reconsider the economic underpinnings of Professor McCaffery's critique. It is common to organize economic discussions by whether they are focused on efficiency (the alteration of economic incentives and decisions introduced by taxes) or devoted to equity (the change—direct and indirect—in economic well-being stemming from a tax). I follow this scheme and convey four key points.

First, from an efficiency perspective, the bulk of Professor McCaffery's critique has *nothing* to do with the estate tax. Instead, it centers on the economic distortions introduced by taxes on the return to saving and investment. These efficiency issues are important, but they are not unique to the estate tax and there does not yet exist a professional consensus regarding their resolution.

Second, with regard to equity issues, very little can be said with confidence regarding the distributional consequences of the estate and gift tax. This is a hard, perhaps hopelessly hard, question of tax incidence.

Third, in examining both the efficiency and equity implications of the estate tax, it is not appropriate to consider the estate tax in isolation. The "optimal" estate tax depends critically upon the freedom with which one may adjust each of the available instruments of government policy—taxes, government debt and outlays—toward the variety of policy objectives.

The final point is to stress that the evidence necessary is not available to resolve many of the key issues. Reason is not sufficient; the crucial economic responses to estate tax incentives need to be isolated and measured. The resulting evidence then may provide insight into the appropriate design of tax policy relating to intergenerational transfers. The existing evidence is too meager, however, to adjudicate the opposing positions.

II. ESTATE TAXES AND THE THEORY OF TAX POLICY

* * *

C. Implications for the Optimal Estate Tax

Should estates be taxed? Or should the estate tax be abolished? * * * In his critique of the estate tax, Professor McCaffery argues that "a strong wealth transfer tax system runs counter to deep-seated human motivations." But his preferred alternative—a consumption tax—runs counter to the equally deep-seated motivation to consume more, better and a greater variety of goods and services. And a lifetime earnings tax runs counter to the deep-rooted work habits of humans everywhere. In short, the government has to tax something. Is there anything special about estates?

* * * [T]he answer revolves around four points. First, are gifts and bequests different from other forms of consumption (especially old-age consumption)? From the perspective of economic efficiency, "different" centers on the responsiveness of consumption and bequests to the tax itself. Suppose that taxing (or subsidizing) consumption results in a substantial change in

---

[2]   *See* Edward J. McCaffery, *The Uneasy Case for Wealth Transfer Taxation*, 104 YALE L.J. 283 (1994).

the amounts that individuals consume. In this instance, the distortion of incentives produces a substantial impact on behavior itself: Individuals are induced to do something that they would not choose to do in the absence of the tax. Alternatively, behavior could be relatively fixed; the tax might produce little change in behavior. In the face of a need to raise revenue, it would be preferable to choose taxes that have as little impact on decisions as possible.

Viewed from this perspective, the key issue is whether bequests are more or less responsive to taxes than consumption is. If they are less responsive, it is tempting to tax estates even more heavily than other consumption as an *efficient* means by which to raise revenue.

The second consideration is the relationship between current and future consumption. * * * [T]he key difference between an income tax and a consumption tax is the effect on the prices of current consumption versus future consumption (and bequests). Professor McCaffery proposes to eliminate the estate tax; but even more telling, he proposes to eliminate the income tax as well. * * * [T]he majority of [his] argument revolves around the generic arguments associated with the choice between a consumption tax and an income tax. "Generic" does not imply unimportant. This debate lies at the heart of fundamental tax reform and is central to the design of future tax policy. But these arguments are not unique to the estate tax, and they can not be adjudicated with respect to the estate tax in isolation from the larger currents of reform.

The third question revolves around the "unit" of taxation. The discussion thus far has looked at the lifetime of each generation as the appropriate time period and unit of taxation. * * *

* * * [I]t may be that the focus on generation-by-generation tax effects is simply too short. First, it may be the case that generations interact in ways that preclude analyzing either the old or the young in isolation. * * * Without a firmer understanding of the nature of the intergenerational "exchange," it is not possible to decide firmly on the appropriate tax treatment of these transactions. * * *

Using each generation as the appropriate "unit of analysis" could be misleading from another perspective as well. One might argue that the entire dynastic family is the appropriate unit of taxation. Under this view, one would likely exclude from tax consideration any transactions that occurred within the tax unit (for example, tax transfers between spouses are currently tax-exempt). The use of an estate tax in this kind of setting is quite literally simply a tax on the accumulations of the dynastic family.

The fourth key point in designing the optimal tax policy is distributional objectives. Clearly, defenders of the estate tax lean heavily on the notion that the redistribution of wealth via the estate tax is valuable enough to offset any inefficiency introduced by attempts to alter bequest behavior.[23] In general, one expects that efficiency objectives and equity goals conflict. Interestingly, Professor McCaffery argues that the usual efficiency versus equity tradeoffs do not apply. Rather, he asserts that the current estate tax both fails to improve the distribution of income and wealth and is inefficient.

In this regard, it is important to delineate among alternative distributional objectives. One objective may be to achieve a more equal distribution of lifetime personal consumption, perhaps through a progressive consumption tax. This would be consistent with eliminating both the income tax on capital and the estate tax, both of which serve to tax the return to wealth accumulation * * * . Intergenerational transfers would be taxed only when consumed by their recipient. Alternatively, one could define gifts and bequests to be a portion of "consumption." If so, tax policy would continue to eliminate the capital income tax, but would tax the bequest or gift

---

[23]   *See, e.g.,* Michael J. Boskin, *An Economist's Perspective on Estate Taxation, in* DEATH, TAXES AND FAMILY PROPERTY 65 (Edward C. Halbach, Jr. ed., 1977).

upon its transfer. Professor McCaffery focuses exclusively upon altruism as the foundation of bequest behavior, but more selfish motives are possible; if so, taxing bequests as a form of consumption purchase would be entirely appropriate.

Another distributional objective would focus on income. If so, an estate tax could serve a variety of purposes. First, when paired with an earnings tax, it might serve as the workhorse tax on the returns to capital accumulation (although this role is inconsistent with the current large exemptions). That is, it might be a convenient, ex post means by which to tax the return to investment.

Second, it might serve as a "backstop" to capture taxes on accumulations that are missed by imperfections in the income tax system. In any event, if the goal is to redistribute income, it is unlikely that a consumption tax will be sufficient; the rich simply do not consume a large enough fraction of their income.

In the end, it is not possible to decide the appropriate estate tax without simultaneously considering the structure of the income tax, the behavioral foundations of intergenerational transfers and some sense of the empirical magnitudes. * * *

III. HOW PERNICIOUS IS THE ESTATE TAX?

In basic terms, Professor McCaffery argues that the estate tax leads to reduced work, reduced savings and increased inequality in consumption; I consider each of these potential impacts in turn. The economic damage created by the estate tax stems from the distortion of bequest behavior. Hence, before coming to a judgment regarding the estate tax, it is useful to review briefly the state of knowledge regarding the underlying motivation for bequests and transfers.

A. Behavioral Foundations of Intergenerational Transfers

Intergenerational transfers constitute an important part of aggregate wealth accumulation, but exactly how large is a matter of some dispute. In the life cycle model of saving, capital accumulation stems solely from the decision of individuals to consume below their income during their working years in order to finance consumption during their retirement. In this view, intergenerational transfers are not central to the saving motives of individuals and the accumulation of the wealth in the economy. Laurence Kotlikoff and Lawrence Summers, however, estimate that life cycle motives account for a minority of aggregate wealth accumulation; at the extreme, as much as 80% is due to the desire to leave intergenerational transfers such as bequests.[29] This conclusion is open to question; Franco Modigliani argues instead that the life cycle model accounts for as much as 80% of accumulation.[30] Taking the mid-point suggests that intergenerational transfers account for roughly one-half of wealth accumulation, thus highlighting their importance to the overall path of productivity and real wage growth in the economy.

Transfers, however, are at the heart of the distribution of resources as well. On average, such transfers increase economic inequality. If all transfers were eliminated, inequality in lifetime income would reflect only inequality in labor incomes, which is much lower than inequality in total income.

Thus, while the revenues associated with the estate tax are minor, the economic stakes are quite large, making it important to understand their behavioral foundations.

---

[29]   See Laurence J. Kotlikoff & Lawrence H. Summers, *The Role of Intergenerational Transfers in Aggregate Capital Accumulation*, 89 J. POL. ECON. 706 (1981).

[30]   See Franco Modigliani, *The Role of Intergenerational Transfers and Life Cycle Saving in the Accumulation of Wealth*, 2 J. ECON. PERSPECTIVES 15 (1988). * * *

1. Motives for Transfers

A very simple explanation for bequests is that they are largely "accidental." That is, individuals save for life cycle or precautionary reasons, but die before consuming their entire wealth accumulation. In such circumstances, bequests may constitute a large fraction of wealth accumulation despite the fact that there are no links across generations. Notice that, in this setting, an estate tax has *no* behavioral impacts. It represents a nondistortionary source of revenue that permits the government to lower the use of other, distorting taxes.

Accidental *gifts* are hard to imagine, however; hence, it is necessary to develop approaches that link generations in a more direct way. Initial work on transfer motives focused on the altruism model * * * , in which individuals care about the welfare of family members. Transfers take place to equalize utility among family members. At the limit, if preferences are identical and there is no income lost as a result of transfers, transfers will flow from high- to low-income members, and post-transfer income will be equalized. It is this view of gift and bequest behavior that lies at the heart of Professor McCaffery's view of the estate tax. The estate tax serves to make more difficult the intended intra-family redistribution, leading to the substitution of inter vivos gifts and intricate estate tax avoidance strategies. Notice that, in this setting, an estate tax interferes with the desire to produce *intrafamily* equality in resources. The degree to which overall inequality is increased or decreased, however, depends upon the degree to which inequality is greater within families or between families.

* * *

A second type of explanation focuses on exchange-based motives for transfers. In this view, transfers serve as "payment" for services such as visits, telephone calls and the like or for the purchase of insurance against consumption shortfalls. Finally, transfers also may serve to overcome market imperfections, such as in the provision of credit.

Since these approaches essentially equate transfers with market transactions, tax policy toward gifts and bequests would be driven by the same considerations as those that typically enter in the policy calculus, that is, the degree to which the tax leads to an inefficiently small amount of the purchased activity (for example, visits) and the extent to which it meets distributional objectives.

But which of these potential motivations for inter vivos gifts and bequests is right? Or, more realistically, how much does each type of motivation contribute to overall transfer behavior? To shed light on the issue, I turn now to an assessment of the alternative explanations for transfers.

2. Testing Models of Transfers

* * *

* * * From the perspective of the dynastic family, the estate tax acts as a tax on capital accumulation; as noted above, Professor McCaffery's critique is, in many ways, a critique of capital taxation per se. Conditioned upon an overall level of wealth accumulation by the dynastic family, however, in an altruistic framework, bequests will rise to offset taxes on estates, ceteris paribus, thereby leaving the post-tax estate at the desired level. Hence, the overall effects of the estate tax are quite complex, even in the altruistic approach.

* * *

What can one learn from the research thus far? Clearly, it does not point conclusively to a single explanation for transfer behavior; indeed, it is unrealistic to assume that a single explanation will ever emerge. There appear to be several plausible motives for transfers of wealth across generations, and no single "smoking gun" explanation dominates the others. It seems quite unlikely, however, that the extensive intergenerational links are consistent only with the simple models of altruism that lie at the heart of Professor McCaffery's critique. Accordingly, it is essential to reevaluate the behavioral effects of the estate tax under a wide variety of alternative scenarios. It may be the case that such an evaluation will not overturn the basic critique of the estate tax. But the possibility remains that a richer understanding of the behavioral foundations might lead to a more vigorous defense of the estate tax.

B. Labor Supply

The estate tax reduces the ability to transform a dollar of labor earnings (or other income) into a dollar of resources for the recipient of the bequest. In this way, the tax is no different in kind from the current income tax or a consumption tax * * * . The rates of taxation are quite substantial, however * * * . Hence, one might suspect that the estate tax is capable of producing substantial distortions in labor supply.

Two aspects of the empirical setting argue against a substantial labor supply effect. First, the bulk of labor supply occurs at relatively young ages. * * * For young workers, the appropriate calculation requires offsetting the earnings *now* with the present value of tax liability in the *future*. The impact of such discounting can be quite striking. For example, a $55 tax liability at age 70 would be perceived as a $17 tax to a 40-year old worker. In short, at the time the vast majority of labor supply decisions are made, few workers will envision eventually being liable for estate taxes. And for those few that do face future estate taxes, current disincentives do not appear overwhelming.

Moreover, for the vast majority of workers, there appears to be little disincentive effects from tax policy. Broadly speaking, an enormous literature devoted to understanding the link between wage taxation and labor supply has found little effect for prime-age, primary workers. Thus, for main workers, there appears to be little disincentive effects of note.

Among other workers, however, there appears to be substantially more responsiveness. Second earners, participants in income support programs and others appear quite responsive to tax rates in deciding whether or not to participate. Several recent studies have suggested that the tax increases embodied in the 1993 Budget Act had substantial effects upon high income men and women, exactly the population most likely to be affected by the estate tax. These latter studies argue for caution in dismissing the labor supply effects of an estate tax. But, as stressed earlier, they also argue against a casual acceptance of a progressive consumption tax as a superior alternative.

C. Saving

A theme of Professor McCaffery's critique is the detrimental effects of the estate tax on the accumulation of wealth, and the loss of the "beneficial effects of capital." For clarity, however, it is important to separate two issues: the interference of the estate tax with private decision-making and the aggregate level of capital accumulation.

With regard to the latter, the appropriate estate tax depends critically upon the full range of policy instruments available to the government. In principle, the government could "choose" the aggregate level of capital accumulation through a policy of systematic budget surpluses. Alternatively, it could enact a series of balanced budgets that incorporated "capital grants" as a systematic element of expenditure programs. Each alternative would remove the burden of achieving the socially "right" level of capital accumulation from the estate tax, which could be targeted to other (for example, distributional) objectives. This is another manifestation of the recurring theme that it is not appropriate to decide the correct estate tax in isolation from other policy decisions.

The second issue is the degree to which the estate tax interferes with private decisions regarding the accumulation, allocation and disposition of saving. Given the discussion thus far, it comes as little surprise that few clear answers emerge. Despite its transparent importance and the efforts of the research community, the behavioral foundations of saving decisions remain murky.

* * * [T]he efficiency consequences of Professor McCaffery's proposed alternative (a progressive consumption tax) may differ little from the current system. Put differently, the role of the estate tax in distorting capital accumulation decisions may be relatively minor.

D. Inequality

To most observers, the estate tax *is* about redistribution. But the redistributive aspects are quite unclear. As Professor McCaffery points out, the structure of the estate and gift tax invites two behavioral responses to mitigate the redistributive features. First, parents may substitute inter vivos transfers for bequests, either in the form of gifts or in kind transfers such as college expenses. Second, they may undertake a variety of legal maneuvers (for example, an estate tax freeze) to hasten the transfer process and minimize the tax liability. In each case, the behavior serves to avoid the redistributive possibilities of the tax.

There is a deeper question of redistribution that is unexplored. Consider the example of a simple excise tax on the sale of a specific good. While the legal liability to remit the tax lies with the seller, she will attempt to shift the tax through some combination of higher prices to consumers or lower payments to workers and suppliers. The ultimate incidence of the tax, the ultimate change in the distribution of income, depends upon the myriad adjustments of prices, purchases, sales and the like in the economy.

The estate tax is no different. Viewed in this context, the effect of the estate tax on the distribution of income and wealth is quite complex, and does not end with a simple accounting of gifts received during a child's lifetime, tax payments to the government and estate proceeds distributed. Instead, one must fully incorporate the effect of the gifts, taxes and bequests on labor supply, consumption and saving among both the young and old over time. For example, the receipt of a bequest appears to lower the labor supply of recipients, leading to changes in the profile of lifetime earnings, consumption and net saving among the young. On a large scale, this, in turn, will affect the return to saving and work and alter the distribution of income.

From a research perspective, the unfortunate news is that these effects take place on a generational scale, making it difficult to discern the effects in a straightforward fashion. Instead, one must piece together the impacts, a task not yet complete enough to permit any real confidence in one's understanding of the distributional consequences of the estate tax.

IV. CONCLUSION

Should the estate tax be abolished? This review suggests a nice, firm "maybe." The equivocation stems from the nature of the argument. First, much of Professor McCaffery's critique derives from the economic distortions introduced by taxes on capital income. The magnitude of these distortions is open to debate, and the estate tax plays a relatively minor role in contributing to these distortions. Second, the distributional consequences are essentially unknown, as this is a very difficult question of tax incidence. Of course, the fact that the consequences of the tax are unknown is hardly a ringing endorsement of the status quo. But neither does it argue that one has clear grounds for eliminating the estate tax. Next, eliminating the estate tax cannot be considered in isolation, as the role of the estate tax depends upon other tax, spending and debt policies of the government. In particular, since there are many policies that may contribute to (or detract from) national saving, it is incomplete to argue for the elimination of the estate tax solely on the grounds that it reduces saving.

Is the estate tax perfect? Clearly not. Tremendous ingenuity and effort is devoted to avoiding estate tax liability. From the larger perspective of tax policy, however, the case has not been made that these distortions are quantitatively important to the labor supply, capital accumulation and other decisions at the heart of economic performance. Policy makers are far from having the evidence necessary to resolve many of the key issues.

NOTE

McCaffery finds himself in "substantial agreement" with Holtz-Eakin. *See* Edward J. McCaffery, *Being the Best We Can Be (A Reply to My Critics)*, 51 TAX L. REV. 614, 616 (1996). For further commentary on the issue of whether gratuitous transfers should be taxed within the consumption tax base, under a separate tax on wealth or wealth transfers, or not at all, see DAVID F. BRADFORD & U.S. TREASURY TAX POLICY STAFF, BLUEPRINTS FOR BASIC TAX REFORM (2d ed. 1984) (proposing that gifts and bequests be taxed separately rather than included in transferor's consumption tax base); Joseph M. Dodge, *Taxing Gratuitous Transfers Under a Consumption Tax*, 51 TAX L. REV. 529 (1996) (arguing that gifts and bequests should be taxed in the transferor's consumption tax base); Lawrence Zelenak, *Commentary, The Reasons for a Consumption Tax and the Tax Treatment of Gifts*, 51 TAX L. REV. 601, 613 (1996) (concluding that "[w]here you end up depends on where you start"); Carolyn C. Jones, *Treatment of Gratuitous Transfers: Unraveling the Case for a Consumption Tax*, 29 ST. LOUIS U. L.J. 1155 (1985).

D.   A Wealth Tax

A wealth tax has received extensive scholarly attention from several quarters. George Cooper introduces the notion of a wealth tax and discusses various advantages and drawbacks. Daniel Q. Posin examines the operation of a wealth tax. Lester C. Thurow and Barry L. Isaacs offer contrasting views concerning the economic and administrative aspects of such a tax. Gilbert Paul Verbit adds an international perspective to the debate.

George Cooper, *Taking Wealth Taxation Seriously*, 34 REC. ASS'N B. CITY N.Y. 24 (1979)*

A wealth tax is a tax on the net value of a person's assets rather than on the annual income flow from those assets. It is a tax on total net worth, imposed periodically. * * *

* * *

* * * [O]n those rare occasions when American writers have looked at the wealth tax dispassionately, they have, to put it politely, given it the brushoff. It is periodically raised as an interesting theoretical construct, usually in the writings of economists, but not given extended consideration.

This attitude seems strange since wealth taxes are staple parts of the general taxing systems of many developed Western democracies which we normally think of as following sensible, or at least rational, economic policies—including, among others, West Germany and the Netherlands, as well as all the Scandinavian countries. * * *

The fact that all these countries do something does not necessarily mean it is right for us, but it did convince me that there might be more to the wealth tax than superficial examination had suggested. * * * I have * * * developed a measure of respect for the wealth tax as a plausible part of any modern taxing system. * * * My goal is not to convince you of its worth—I am not entirely convinced myself as you will see—but to get you to take it seriously.

TWO TYPES OF WEALTH TAXES

We must start with an open mind on the subject. That is difficult for some people to do when the subject is taxing wealth. As I said, most people don't think of themselves as wealth-holders, but those who do can easily become apoplectic at the idea of taxing it. * * *

* * *

I don't mean to suggest that these people don't have a point worth considering. They do. * * * [Nevertheless, the] successful European experience with wealth taxes teaches us, at the very least, that such taxes are not fundamentally incompatible with capitalism. It is certainly true that a wealth tax is likely to be a progressive tax, but it will not necessarily make the overall tax burden more progressive than now (that depends on what else is done when a wealth tax is adopted), and it certainly need not lead to confiscation.

We might clear up this point at the outset with a little definition. There are two, fundamentally different, kinds of wealth taxes. One is designed to be paid out of capital, presumably with the goal of eroding existing capital ownership; this we may call a "capital-directed" wealth tax. The other is designed to be paid out of income, presumably with the goal of improving the system of income taxation; let's call that an "income-directed" wealth tax.

The two kinds of wealth taxes are similar in most respects, but there is a big difference in that most critical part of any tax—the rate. Income-directed wealth taxes are, by definition, necessarily fixed at low rates. They cannot exceed a reasonable rate of return on capital after allowing for regular income tax liabilities. Capital-directed wealth taxes, of course, have no inherent rate limit.

All of the European wealth taxes are clearly on the income-directed side of the line. The rates range from a flat .7% in Germany to a progressive rate scale in Sweden going up to 2.5%. The median rate in Europe is around 1%. Moreover, these low rates are accompanied in all but Germany by a ceiling provision which guarantees that the combined income tax-wealth tax burden does not exceed a designated percentage of income.

* * * That does not mean that a capital-directed tax is inherently out of the question. But capital-directed taxation is the nuclear weaponry of tax policy, and any government that plans to use it had better pick the time and place carefully and be prepared for full-scale war.

To put it simply, the two types of wealth taxes are, despite their apparent similarities, qualitatively different animals, yielding very different benefits and generating very different problems. We must keep the distinction carefully in mind.

THE CASE FOR THE WEALTH TAX

Having drawn this important distinction, let me now turn to the central question: Why should we consider a wealth tax of either sort?

In considering the case for a wealth tax, I am going to speak this evening only in terms of its role in our present Federal taxing system, which is dominated by a broad-based personal income tax. * * *

The classic argument for the wealth tax in this context was made by Nicholas Kaldor in 1956 tax reform proposals submitted to the Indian government.

> The main argument in equity for the tax is that income taken by itself is an inadequate yardstick of taxable capacity as between property owners. The basic reason for this is that the ownership of property in the form of disposable assets endows the property owner with a taxable capacity as such, quite apart from the income which that property yields. This is best shown if you compare a beggar who has neither income nor property with the position of a man who keeps the whole of his wealth of say Rs 10,000,000 in the form of jewelry and gold. Judging their capacities by the test of income alone, the taxable capacity of both is nil. Quite apart from such an extreme case, it should be evident that as between people who possess property and income in different proportions, income alone is not an adequate test of ability to pay; nor can that capacity be assessed by a tax based on property alone. . . . [O]nly a combination of income and property taxes can give an approximation to taxation in accordance with ability to pay.[13]

* * *

* * * Kaldor's argument has * * * important relevance here. Hoarding may not be a popular American pastime, but preventing, concealing, eliminating, avoiding and otherwise sheltering taxable income certainly is. There are some investors who simply draw interest on savings accounts, but many more who angle for capital appreciation so that they may pay only a capital gains tax at most and better yet pay no income tax at all while passing accumulated fortunes on to their children. Alternatively, they use their assets to invest in tax shelter deals which generate negative taxable income. Or, they invest in ways that will produce valuable returns not covered by the income tax, for example in a hobby business which produces psychic returns, or in a business whose major object is to provide a job for the investor's son or daughter. An aggravating aspect of this situation is that the opportunities to avoid income tax in this way are likely to be directly related to wealth. That is, the richer you are the more likely you are to be able to forgo current money income in favor of deferred gain or psychic returns. * * *

It is sometimes suggested that the estate tax is the answer to this avoidance, assuring that the hoarder pays at least some tax on his accumulated appreciation. But that doesn't work either, thanks to estate freezing techniques, the process whereby appreciating assets are diverted to children before most of the appreciation occurs.[16]

* * *

A wealth tax would not prevent this, but it would at least assure that a minimum tax at a reasonable rate was paid annually by the children of wealthholders engaging in such transactions.

So far we have been talking about income tax equity. Everyone is in favor of that, and it makes a strong case for an income-directed wealth tax, but it does not provide much support for a capital-directed tax. Now we turn to an argument which is a little more sticky, the justification, based more on social policy than equity, for a capital-directed wealth tax. The tax is advanced with much fervor by its proponents as a mechanism for attacking concentrated wealth.

---

[13]   N. KALDOR, INDIAN TAX REFORM; REPORTS OF A SURVEY (1956).

[16]   Cooper, *A Voluntary Tax? New Perspectives on Sophisticated Estate Tax Avoidance*, 77 COLUM. L. REV. 161, 170-186 (1977), discusses these techniques at length.

It is difficult to blink the fact that wealth in the United States is distributed in an extraor-dinar[il]y uneven way, much more unevenly than the distribution of income. According to the most sophisticated estimates, the top 5% of the adult population in the United States has 44% of the wealth, the top 1% has 27%, and the top .5% has 21%. Even worse is the concentration of investment assets, since homes account for most of the wealth of the bulk of the population. The top half percent of the adult population owns an astounding 49% of all privately-owned corporate stock.

* * *

It is frequently argued that this concentrated economic power needs to be attacked; that substantial wealthholders shape our landscape, define in large measure the allocation of our resources, and control our politics. There is unquestionably a substantial measure of truth in these accusations. Although I am not paranoid enough to believe the most baroque versions of the argument, at the very least it calls for a frank recognition of this power of wealth and gives substantial support to the equitable "additional taxpaying capacity" arguments for a low rate wealth tax made earlier.

* * *

A wealth tax, which is, in a sense, simply a recurring annual version of the estate tax, is much more difficult to avoid. * * * The effectiveness of the wealth tax, as compared to the estate tax, is perhaps best expressed by a photographic metaphor. Taxing wealth with the estate tax is like trying to photograph a recluse with an old single-plate view camera, while giving him some advance clues as to when you are going to take the shot. Barring unforeseen circum-stances, he will probably be able to hide behind a tree at the critical moment. But the wealth tax is like a movie camera following him around all his life. It is difficult to keep hiding from it forever.

This, then, is the argument for a capital-directed tax. It can do a more effective job of accomplishing the same goals as the estate and gift tax. The rates would, of course, be set much lower than existing estate tax rates to reflect annual imposition, but the objective would be to have as much capital-eroding effect as the estate tax is supposed to have.

* * *

THE PRACTICAL PROBLEMS OF THE TAX

* * *

At hearings on his country's wealth-tax proposal, Prof. G. S. A. Wheatcroft, the leading British tax scholar, acknowledged that a wealth tax was theoretically superior to an income tax on investment income, but he raised the problem which bothers everyone:

> As far as I am concerned, I would just put the whole thing in one word, "val-uation," and leave it at that.[24]

In other words, how can we value everything annually? Let me suggest an outrageous response to Prof. Wheatcroft, and then try to justify it. I think valuation would be less of a problem under an annual wealth tax than it already is under our existing estate and gift taxes. I think the "val-uation issue" is an argument for the wealth tax because this tax does more to solve existing val-uation problems than it does to create new ones.

---

[24]   [II Select Committee on a Wealth Tax, Report and Proceedings of the Committee 555 (1975)].

The valuation procedure under a wealth tax would of course commence with a self-assessment return as under our existing income and transfer taxes. The concern about valuation problems under the wealth tax stems from the assumption that this tax will then require us each year, and for every taxpayer, to go through the same process we now go through in assessing the estate tax for the much smaller group of decedents. If true, this would create an impossible administrative burden and would be ample grounds for rejecting the wealth tax.

However, what seems to be ignored in making this assumption is that the agony of estate tax evaluation is a product of two things—the high rates involved and the fact that it is a once-in-a-generation controversy—both of which change dramatically with the wealth tax. When every dollar of valuation means 70 cents of tax, you are going to get a lot of resources thrown into the fray, especially when there is no second chance. But only a lunatic would devote the same effort year in and year out to valuations for a wealth tax of a few percent. Possibly, a taxpayer might fight hard in one year to establish a precedent for how his assets ought to be valued and what factors ought to be emphasized, but that precedent, once established, would likely be followed in ensuing years. The Service has more important things to do than refight the same battle every year. Indeed, the initial controversy would possibly cover several years at once, since the likelihood of recurrent issues under a wealth tax makes multiple-year audits a sensible policy. * * *

Moreover, the fact that a wealth tax deals with repeated small-impact valuations in lieu of a single high-impact valuation, has an even more profound significance than merely reducing the level of controversy from year to year. It means that, in place of subjective attempts at perfection in valuation, we can comfortably shift to more objective, formula-based techniques that can be applied almost automatically. * * * [W]e could expect that very few persons would bother to contest a reasonable formula. Unless the formula was drastically wrong, the stakes would not be high enough to challenge it, and there would always be the comfort that what is a little off in one direction in one year might be a little off in the other direction the next year. We could also reinforce the tendency to use the formula by barring subjective values unless shown to vary from the formula by more than a fixed percent, say 20%.

If this casual attitude toward valuation shocks you, you might reflect a moment on how accurate are the valuations we get today with our subjective adversarial process. Competing experts commonly come up with valuations for such things as untraded securities that are so different you might well ask if they looked at the same company. * * * For taxpayers who can afford to match the government, the result is usually pretty good, too good for my taste. But for taxpayers with less at stake, the result may well turn out unfairly to them. A compromise could well be built into a formula, * * * which would be fairer to all.

Moreover, * * * even if the estate tax valuations reached in the current way were perfect, which they surely are not, they would be inherently arbitrary because they represent the value in a single fortuitously selected year. The company might have been worth double or half in the next or preceding year because of general changes in the market or specific events relating to the company. The decedent probably held the stock for years and the beneficiaries will also likely hold it for a while. What conceivable sense is there in making massive tax burdens turn on the value in one particular year selected by the fickle hand of death? It is difficult to imagine any wealth tax valuation process that could help but be more fair than this.

To put these valuation issues in better perspective, let's look for a moment at specific classes of assets.

The largest single category in terms of aggregate value is real estate. As of 1972, almost a third of privately-held wealth was in the form of real estate * * * . Realty poses difficult valuation problems, as we all know, but in a sense it is the easiest of all from the viewpoint of practical administrative burdens. Every single piece of real estate in the country is already being valued and, in most cases, is already being taxed at rates higher than those likely to be imposed by a national wealth tax. There is no new administrative burden, only an administrative *opportunity* to improve and modernize the existing systems which are often admirable but more often wretched. The time is especially ripe for doing this because modern computer techniques for real estate valuation have been developed * * * which are fast and simple to use and capable of giving results as or more accurate and reliable than traditional techniques.

* * *

The next most important category of property is corporate stock, which constitutes 20% of all privately held assets and almost half (47%) of the holdings of the richest 1% of the population. Much of this is traded stock, as to which valuation is simple. For the untraded securities, I suggest that standard formulae be used, subject to the right of either side to demand subjective valuation. * * *

Most of the remaining major classes of assets are relatively easy to value and do not raise any particular administrative problems: bonds (4% of all holdings), cash (8%), and debt instruments (2%). The most troublesome remaining category is non-business, non-investment, personal property, including household furnishings, jewelry and art.

There is, admittedly, no entirely satisfactory manner of dealing with this property. In terms of pure theory, all assets ought to be in the tax base, just as all income including fringe benefits and the imputed rental value of a washing machine ought theoretically to be in the income tax base. But we are talking practically, and that means there must be some manner of avoiding the need to account for and value every last dishtowel. A basic general tax exemption—the wealth tax's zero bracket amount, if you will—would be a significant contributor to mitigating this problem because it would drastically cut down the number of families subject to the tax. * * *

Still, it does not seem worthwhile to worry about the dishtowels of even the super rich, and we would undoubtedly have additional exemptions for much non-business personal property in dollar floors and exempt categories.

The formulation of the precise exemptions is troublesome. A broad exemption eases administration and reduces equity, a narrow exemption does the opposite. But we should not exaggerate the significance of the equitable problems raised by a broad exemption. The opportunities for tax avoidance through investment in art or jewelry, even if it is totally exempt, would be essentially self-limiting because of the non-income producing nature of these assets and because the simple pressures of supply and demand would naturally tend to make such investments less and less attractive. Nor are the economic implications of diverting funds to art all that serious, since the purchase of art does not consume resources but merely shifts cash from one person to another. For these reasons, and on the assumption that a new tax should start as simply as possible, I think it makes sense to err on the side of administrative ease in this marginal area and grant a broad exemption for most non-business, non-investment property, or at least for all such items below a very high floor. * * *

* * *

* * * Trusts were originally developed as tax avoidance devices and they survive in large part as tax avoidance devices. As a consequence they create endless problems for most broad-based taxes, notably the income tax and the estate tax, and the wealth tax will be no different. There are a variety of ways to deal with the trust question. To some extent this may require trusts to adapt if they want to minimize tax consequences * * *, but these adaptations need not bar any of the legitimate goals of trusts.

Here are some specific suggestions, which are not intended as a definitive answer but to indicate some possibilities. The straight-forward solution, to treat trusts as separate taxable entities, is too generous if there is any substantial zero bracket amount or progressivity in the wealth tax rates. However, if a workable multiple trust consolidation rule could be formulated it might be feasible to treat consolidated groups of trusts as taxable entities. One approach to consolidation is suggested by regulations recently adopted under the income tax, where the same problem of artificial multiple trusts arises. The British Board of Inland Revenue suggested a different plan which seems promising—consolidate all trusts created by a single settlor. This gives one extra zero bracket per settlor, but only one, and the trust zero bracket should be set rather lower than that for individuals.

An alternative to consolidation for trusts, also proposed by the Inland Revenue, is to levy a tax on each trust, but to deem the trust assets to be owned by specific persons and calculate the tax according to the wealth status of the deemed person. For simple trusts, the deemed person would be the income beneficiary. For an accumulating discretionary trust with beneficiaries, there are a number of options for deeming. The Inland Revenue proposed to use the settlor's wealth as the reference point; the Law Society favored using the wealth of the wealthiest potential beneficiary. In each case, of course, the outside person would be only a deem in the trustee's eye; the trust itself would always pay the tax. To the extent this deeming caused harsh results, the British proposal left it open for the trustee to change the deemed person by making actual distributions of income. Still another alternative is to tax trusts at an arbitrary rate when they accumulate and then to recompute the tax when distributions occur. * * *

* * *

So far we have been talking about the practical problems of tax design and administration—largely the problems of the government. However, there is a very important practical problem for taxpayers that cannot be ignored. Where does a taxpayer whose assets are not generating current income get the money to pay his tax—the liquidity problem. But here again, as in the case of valuation, I think the wealth tax is not the creator of liquidity problems but the solution to them.

Liquidity is not a problem unique to the wealth tax. In addition to being a hot issue in local property taxation, it received much attention with respect to the estate tax in the 1976 Tax Reform Act. Liquidity problems are particularly severe under the estate tax because of its very high rates. The severity would be much less under a wealth tax because of its inherently lower rates. Moreover, a capital-directed wealth tax should be accompanied by an elimination or substantial reduction of the estate tax. The wealth tax would thus become a built-in mechanism for paying a portion of present low estate tax obligations in a series of small installments spread out over many years rather than in one large installment. * * *

On the other hand, if repeal or reduction of the estate tax does not accompany adoption of the wealth tax, then the wealth tax should be limited to the income-directed class. Its rate would have to be very low, around 1% if the European tradition prevails, and it should be accompanied by reduction in top bracket income tax rates. In these circumstances, while there would surely be sympathetic cases, it is difficult to believe that the low-rate wealth tax would cause intolerable liquidity burdens on very many taxpayers. Of course, persons with large holdings in Krugerrands, gold bullion, or other nonexempt unproductive property would be under some pressure to sell off a portion or shift to more productive investments. If so, I assume this would be a beneficial and desired result of the tax.

The only liquidity problem area of real concern under an income-directed tax is the situation of farmers and owners of closely-held business who can't easily sell small portions of their assets and, justifiably, do not want to liquidate their entire operation. Indeed such cases are so sympathetic that we may tend to exaggerate how much of a problem they are. As a practical matter, any business has to be generating some income—you can't stay in business if you are losing money indefinitely. If this income year in and year out is only enough to cover the value of the owner's services, the capital value of the business is not likely to be very great and the wealth tax should be minimal or nonexistent. Only a business producing a fair return over and above the value of the owner's services is going to have high capital value and be subject to a significant wealth tax. Moreover, even for such a business, there might well be aspects of the valuation formula which would tend to hold down capital value for wealth tax purposes. * * *

* * *

In sum, I believe this analysis indicates that the wealth tax is practical. It is inherently no more difficult to administer nor harsher than an estate tax except for the issue of more frequent assessment. On closer examination it seems to me that frequent assessment may well make the tax easier to administer rather than more difficult, and less harsh on taxpayers. In any event, the practicality issue is not all one-sided. There are tradeoffs and the balance is at least not clear. Moreover, it is not really fair to look at the wealth tax alone and ask if it imposes unreasonable burdens. The tax should be viewed as an alternative to other reform measures since it is a substitute for more complex provisions attacking income and estate tax loopholes. * * *

* * *

* * * [T]he wealth tax is unlikely to have any dramatic effect on our overall national economic life. The wealth tax will affect equity and it may seriously affect some people's capital, but it is not going to have major macroeconomic repercussions unless its rates are set higher than any of us find imaginable. Nonetheless, some modest effects may be foreseen, and I will briefly comment on those.

One economic argument for the wealth tax is that it is more economically efficient than an income tax. * * * The wealth tax * * * directly rewards and encourages seeking high returns. The wealth tax rate effectively goes down as the rate of return increases because the wealth tax on a given amount of capital is fixed without regard to return. This simple and neutral manner of encouraging risk-taking seems much preferable to the complex pattern of incentives evolved under our income tax law, and it is presumably a desirable aspect of wealth taxation.

However, the wealth tax is also accused of a rather sinister effect, the erosion of the national stock of capital. At the present time, when national concern about "capital formation" runs high, this is tantamount to accusing the wealth tax of being contrary to apple pie. However, despite its superficial logic, there is not really much to this accusation.

Much of any wealth tax will be income-directed and paid out of income, including that newly gained by persons who shift to more productive investments in response to the tax. To the extent it is capital-directed, the burden of the tax will be offset, in part, by the reductions in high bracket income and estate and gift tax rates. The only serious erosion of capital that is plausible will occur in the case of heirs who may for the first time find themselves paying a substantial tax. * * *

A LIMITED PROPOSAL FOR AN INSTALLMENT PAYMENT ESTATE TAX

All in all, it seems to me that a well designed wealth tax, set at a basic low, income-directed, rate with a supplemental, capital-directed, rate on gratuitously received wealth, could be a valuable addition to the United States tax structure * * *.

* * *

In the case of the broad-based, income-directed tax, there are related, but alternative, tax innovations which may be superior in accomplishing the claimed objectives. While there are a variety of equitable concerns which justify an income-directed tax, the major one is the tax freedom accorded to unrealized capital gains. An annual form of capital gains tax, which reaches capital gains as they accrue rather than waiting for realization, would be a much better targeted method than the wealth tax for taxing holders who substitute capital appreciation for ordinary income. This annual capital gains tax also would eliminate lock-in problems. Of course, the major reason we do not have an accrual capital gains tax is because of the perceived impracticability of annual valuation. Once that problem is solved, as it would have to be in preparing for a wealth tax, we might well conclude that the accrual capital gains tax would make better use of annual valuation data than a broad-based wealth tax.

When we turn to the capital-directed tax on gratuitously received wealth, the justification for the tax is not so tenuous. Indeed, the case for a limited wealth tax on gifts and inheritance, and covering only the wealth classes now subject to the estate tax, is sufficiently strong that I would urge its early adoption. The adoption of a wealth tax on this limited class of people and property raises no constitutional problem and breaks no new conceptual or political ground. We are already committed to imposing a stiff capital-directed tax on gifts and inheritances; the wealth tax would merely go the extra step of assessing this tax in a recurring periodic form rather than as a single payment tax.

* * *

What would this limited wealth tax look like? The basic idea would be to follow gratuitously received property in the hands of recipients and impose a recurring tax on it at relatively low annual rates in lieu of part or all of the estate and gift tax. However, it would not do simply to impose this new tax on the dollar value of transferred property at the time of death or gift. If we did only this, we would have failed to make any change which addressed the estate-freezing problems which have been identified as a major gap in present estate and gift tax coverage. The only way to do something about estate freezing—the technique whereby property with low current value but high appreciation potential is given from parent to child—is to allow the wealth tax base to grow with increases in value of gifts and inheritances.

This obviously calls for a tracing system, and my instinctive reaction when I realized this fact was to recoil in fear of having to create a monster. However, on further reflection, I do not think the tracing problems are unmanageable. The critical need in order to do something about estate freezing is to follow the actual gift or inheritance only so long as the actual property remains in the hands of the recipient. During that time there is no difficulty in tracing. Once the particular property is sold to a stranger, the heir has, by definition, terminated his opportunity to gain from latent value in the property and from parental manipulations of it. The heir is then, so to speak, on his own in trying to make a go of it; he is no longer riding on parental coat-tails.

When property is sold we can stop tracing and simply take the dollar value received as a substitute in the tax base. Of course, it would not be desirable merely to freeze the wealth tax base at this dollar value either. For one thing, if we did so the recipient would be under great pressure to sell the property as soon as possible to cut off future appreciation in his tax base. Moreover, given the seeming inevitability of inflation, and the natural opportunities to earn appreciation and other returns on property, the freezing of the tax base at any time would mean that the full real value of the inheritance was gradually being lost to the base. It would be reasonable therefore to say that once the particular inherited property was sold the taxpayer would substitute in his wealth tax base an amount equal to the amount realized on sale adjusted upward by an annually prescribed rate of increase. At a minimum, this would be the rate of inflation, but it could and probably should be somewhat more to allow for a full fair return. The rate of interest on U.S. government securities might be a good reference point. If the taxpayer is able to earn more than this rate, all to his credit; the wealth tax would not treat that as part of the inherited tax base, nor would lesser earnings reduce the base.

That, then, is the basic system. The wealth tax base each year includes the current value of all property ever actually received by gift or inheritance, plus an amount equal to the aggregate dollar value of gifts or inheritances sold in prior years as adjusted for a prescribed rate of increase. In addition, since this tax is in theory a capital-directed tax, it might also be appropriate to subtract from the tax base each year the amount of wealth tax paid in prior years.

This system should work for the majority of cases. It would permit a simple calculation of · taxable wealth each year and impose a fair extra burden on those who fall heir to fortune. Annual valuation would be needed only for inherited assets, and even for those only so long as held by the heir. The only possible unfairness is in the case of a recipient who becomes too poor to meet the tax. As a fallback protection, it may be reasonable to permit any taxpayer whose actual aggregate wealth—inherited and personally saved—falls below the amount * * * nominally computed as the adjusted value of his inheritance, to adjust his tax base down to actual value and use that as a base for future adjustments. This downward adjustment need be made only at the election of the taxpayer, and it would be the only instance in which valuation of non-inherited property would have to be made.

* * *

This limited wealth tax will not solve all the problems raised by the existing inadequate and loophole-ridden taxation of wealth, but at least it will make a start, which is all anyone can ask. It is not free from problems, of course, and one of the greatest is its name. Anything labelled a "wealth tax" is likely to raise the hackles of too many for it ever to get fair consideration on the merits. Therefore let us call the proposal an "installment payment estate tax," which is a correct description and yet less provocative. I hope you will give it some thought.

NOTE

Why does Cooper believe that a wealth tax "does more to solve existing valuation problems that it does to create new ones"? Do you agree? Why does Cooper believe that a wealth tax "is unlikely to have any dramatic effect on our overall national economic life"? Do you agree? David J. Shakow has tentatively advanced "the possibility that we replace our current individual income tax with a wealth tax." In an ongoing research project, he hopes to demonstrate several significant propositions in connection with the proposed wealth tax:

> It is practical to value the assets subject to the tax.

> The economic consequences of such a tax will be more favorable than those of the current income tax.

> The burden of the tax will correlate more closely to economic income than the current income tax.

> The tax will not raise undue problems of liquidity in respect of taxpayers.

David J. Shakow, *Taking Wealth Taxes More Seriously*, U. PA. INST. FOR LAW & ECON. WORKING PAPER NO. 235 (June 1997).

Daniel Q. Posin, *Toward a Theory of Federal Taxation: A Comment*, 50 J. AIR L. & COM. 907 (1985)*

* * *

HOW A WEALTH TAX WORKS

The wealth tax is levied as a percentage of the taxpayer's net worth. For reasons that I will discuss below, the wealth tax should provide a credit for income taxes paid. The literature on this subject describes two forms of the wealth tax. I believe, however, for reasons set forth below, that the two forms are really one and the same. * * *

The two forms of the wealth tax have various names. I will call them for convenience the weak form and the strong form. The weak form of the tax is limited to a relatively small percentage of the taxpayer's net worth. It is designed to exact a tax of less than a normal rate of return from the taxpayer's capital. Rates for this weak form of wealth tax generally hover around 1% or less of the taxpayer's capital subject to the tax.

The strong form of the tax is designed, according to the traditional view, to take more in tax from the taxpayer's capital than is produced by a normal rate of return less income taxes paid. The rate for the strong form is therefore significantly higher than the rate for the weak form. The strong form is said to be a tax directly on capital, according to the traditional view.

* * *

Some numerical examples may serve to illustrate:

Example (1). Let us say T has capital subject to the tax of $100,000. If this $100,000 is invested in high-grade corporate bonds paying 10% interest, T's annual income from this capital will be $10,000. Let us assume further that T is in the 50% marginal income tax bracket. Therefore on T's $10,000 interest income, he must pay income tax of $5,000. Let us say also that T is subject to a "weak" form of the wealth tax, which is imposed at the rate of 1% on his investment. By virtue of this tax, T must pay an additional $1,000 in tax. Thus T's income after the income and the wealth tax is $4,000. The tax has been paid out of the income from the bonds. On this set of facts, a wealth tax has operated like an additional income tax on investment income.

Example (2). The facts are the same as in Example 1, except that T is now subject to a "strong" form of the wealth tax. In this case let us assume that the wealth tax is at a rate of 7% of capital. Once again, T has interest income from his corporate bonds of $10,000. Being in the 50% bracket, he pays income taxes of $5,000. However, on account of the strong form of the wealth tax, he now also owes $7,000 of wealth tax (7% of $100,000). His total tax is $12,000, which he cannot pay solely out of income. Thus he must dip into capital to come up with the extra $2,000. He now has only $98,000 invested. This is the confiscatory aspect of the strong form of the wealth tax, according to the literature.

This analysis, however, is flawed. The day a 7% wealth tax is imposed the value of T's corporate bonds will drop. By how much will they drop? Assume for simplicity that all potential buyers of these bonds are also in the 50% marginal income tax bracket. The bonds continue to pay their fixed amount of $10,000 per year. The income tax on that amount continues to be $5,000. However, no one would pay $100,000 for those bonds if the net after tax return was a negative $2,000. Therefore the bonds must drop in value by enough to lower the wealth tax to $5,000. The bonds will then drop from $100,000 to a value of $71,428. (7% of $71,428 equals $5,000). This is a one-time drop. Thereafter, the bonds will continue to trade at around

---

*   Copyright © 1985. Reprinted with permission.

that price and move up and down according to market factors, such as changes in interest rates. In reality, the price will not drop all the way down to $71,428, because some of the potential purchasers of these bonds are not in the 50% marginal bracket. Thus, a taxpayer in the 30% marginal bracket might find these bonds attractively priced at or near $100,000. This would be so because his income tax would be $3,000 and his wealth tax would be $7,000, if the bonds had a value of $100,000. The bond would not have to drop very much in value for them to have a net positive return to this taxpayer.

What this discussion demonstrates is that there is no such thing as the "strong form" of the wealth tax. There is no such thing as the wealth tax actually being a tax on wealth. The wealth tax, no matter what its rate, will always be payable out of income from the taxpayer's capital subject to the tax, because the property will drop in value to reflect the imposition of the tax.

Of course, in the case of a wealth tax with a relatively steep rate, such as the 7% in the example above, taxpayers in the 50% marginal bracket have undergone a relatively stiff "tax" on their capital in the sense that their capital has undergone a one-time drop in value on the occasion of the first imposition of the tax. That is a different matter entirely, however, from saying that a wealth tax of relatively high rate is paid out of capital. * * *

Consider, for example, X, an individual, whose wealth is entirely tied up in $10 million worth of undeveloped forest lands. These lands generally appreciate 10% every year. X has no salary and owns no income producing assets. X occasionally sells off some land to meet his modest living expenses. On these facts X has little income (only what may be realized on his occasional land sales). Therefore X pays an inconsequential amount of income tax (assume for simplicity that he pays no income tax). Assume X is subject to a 7% wealth tax. On these facts X has unrealized appreciation on the value of his land of $1 million (10% of $10 million) and pays a wealth tax of $700,000 (7% of $10 million). Thus where X pays little or no income tax, the wealth tax even at a relatively high rate does not cause the value of his assets to fall (at least not to him or others not paying much in income taxes). Indeed, the wealth tax has led to a relatively reasonable result, that a taxpayer of great wealth who would not have otherwise paid any taxes at all, in fact paid some taxes. * * *

This discussion leads to the conclusion that a reasonable way to impose a wealth tax of some significant rate is to allow a credit or a partial credit against the wealth tax for income taxes paid with respect to the capital involved. If that were done, then in our Example 2 above, T, having paid $5,000 in income taxes on his investment income, would only pay $2,000 more in wealth taxes to reach his 7%. That would still leave him with a $3,000 after tax return. However, the taxpayer X, above, who owned the forest land, would derive no benefit from the credit for income taxes paid, since he pays no income taxes. As we have discussed, it is appropriate that the wealth tax reach him more heavily.

This discussion has assumed a wealth tax of 7%, which is very much higher than what I would propose * * * . Yet even with this relatively high rate, the tax, when combined with a credit for income taxes, works effectively and in a non-confiscatory manner, not overtaxing those who are already paying substantial taxes on income from their capital and yet reaching those who are not otherwise taxed.

* * *

NOTE

What is the difference between the "weak" and "strong" forms of a wealth tax identified by Posin? Why does Posin believe that "there is in fact no strong form of the wealth tax"?

Lester C. Thurow, *Net Worth Taxes*, 25 NAT'L TAX J. 417 (1972)*

* * *

* * * In most situations, an optimal tax structure will require income taxes, consumption taxes, and taxes on *net worth.* * * *

II. PERSPECTIVES ON TAXATION

A. The Social Welfare Function Approach

If the social welfare function approach is used, the appropriate tax base or bases depend upon an analysis of the different types of social benefits that flow from economic activity and society's distributional objectives concerning these benefits. Potential benefits fall into two broad categories. Individuals receive economic benefits from (1) consuming economic goods and services and from (2) their power to control economic resources. Consumption is a measure of how much an individual takes out of the economic system. Wealth is a measure of an individual's potential power to control the use of economic resources. Given social concerns about both the level and distribution of these two sources of personal benefits, taxes (positive and negative) must be levied on both consumption and wealth.

Wealth, however, is composed of two major components—human capital and physical capital. In an economy where each factor of production is paid its marginal product and where human and physical assets earn exactly the same rate of return for each individual (as they would in a perfect market), income can be used to measure each person's wealth. Each man's wealth is calculated by capitalizing *his* current and future income at the common rate of return on investment. If society regards human and physical capital as indistinguishable and wishes to achieve some desired distribution of wealth, income is an appropriate base. Any desired distribution of wealth can be obtained with some tax on income since the tax will itself be capitalized in determining the value of wealth. If society has different goals about how it would like to see human and physical wealth distributed (most societies seem more worried about equality in human wealth than they are about equality in physical wealth) society needs separate taxes on human wealth (of earnings) and physical wealth (of realized and unrealized returns on physical wealth). In this case, society would need an earnings tax, a tax on physical wealth, and a tax on consumption.

As a result, society should tax whatever economic elements appear in society's social welfare function. If society is concerned about consumption, physical wealth, and human wealth, society must have at least three separate taxes.

B. The Individual Utility Function Approach

In the individual utility function approach, taxes are levied based on individual utility functions rather than social welfare functions. Based on our vision of economic man, the appropriate tax base is the simple summation of consumption expenditures, human wealth, and physical

---

wealth. Such a base springs from an analysis of our actions. Economic man adjusts his consumption and savings decisions so that the marginal benefits from $1 of savings is equal to the marginal benefits from $1 of consumption. Since savings is merely a change in net worth, the marginal benefits from wealth and consumption are brought into equilibrium. Being a rational investor, he also equalizes the marginal benefits from investments in human capital and physical capital. As a result, the marginal benefits from consumption, physical capital, and human capital are equal for each person. As they are all equally beneficial, he should be taxed at some common rate on each. Since each unit of consumption and wealth provides benefits, all units should be taxed. As a result, the proper tax base is consumption plus wealth. The appropriate tax base is not consumption plus increments to wealth—i.e., an income tax.

C. The Efficiency Approach

An efficient tax system is one that avoids excess burdens and does not permit individuals to shift taxes that were destined for them onto other individuals. To the extent that taxes result in a lower GNP rather than higher tax revenue for governments, they are inefficient. To the extent that taxes can be shifted to other individuals, they are inefficient since they do not lead to the desired post-tax distribution of economic resources. Such excess burdens are substantial in our current tax system. * * * Studies also indicate that the current tax structure permits substantial amounts of tax shifting. * * *

Although excess burdens and shifting cannot be completely eliminated, they can be substantially reduced. Reductions are brought about by reducing the opportunities for individuals to avoid taxes by altering their patterns of economic activities. * * *

As a result, efficiency considerations demand a tax structure that covers all of the major forms of economic activity. In theory, taxes on consumption, earnings, physical wealth, and leisure would all be necessary. All of them would have to be carefully balanced to avoid excess burdens and shifting.

As a result, I would argue that each of these three perspectives on taxation would lead to a comprehensive set of taxes rather than reliance on any one tax. * * * [N]et worth taxes are part of such a comprehensive package * * * .

III. EXISTING WEALTH TAXES

Although they are usually regarded as historical anomalies, the United States has vestiges of a system of wealth taxes. Historically, the property tax was designed as an instrument to tax wealth. Since all wealth was held in the form of land or buildings in the middle ages, the property tax was a comprehensive tax on wealth. With the development of modern economies, however, property now constitutes only 40 per cent of net worth. As a result, a tax that was once able to control the distribution of wealth has become inadequate. Since the importance of property varies from portfolio to portfolio, the property tax cannot be used to create society's desired distribution of wealth. In addition, its use creates horizontal inequities among individuals with the same total wealth.

Such horizontal inequities are often used as arguments against the introduction of a progressive property tax. As the opponents point out, progress in the rate structures makes the horizontal inequities greater in the upper ranges of net worth. What they neglect to mention is that it also reduces the inequities in the lower ranges of net worth. Whether the changes in the vertical distribution of wealth produced by a progressive rate structure are worth the increased inequality in the upper ranges of wealth and the reduced inequalities in the lower ranges of wealth is a matter for debate, but it is certainly not axiomatic that progression makes the equity problem worse. Depending upon * * * social welfare preferences it may make equity conditions much better.

What can be said, however, is that there is no way to use a tax on 40 per cent of net worth to control the distribution of wealth and that such a tax leads to biases in the selection of investment assets. One solution to these distortions is to abolish all remaining wealth taxes; the other solution is to introduce a comprehensive system of wealth taxes.

If one examines property taxes closely, it is clear that the major problems do not spring from the technical difficulties of assessing the value of property accurately. The problems spring from political difficulties. Assessments are not made frequently or friends are given favorable assessments. Such difficulties are real and may be insurmountable, but let us not describe them as economic or technical difficulties.

Estate and gift taxes are also wealth taxes. They are not a device for controlling the distribution of wealth in any particular year or in any one generation, but they are a tax for controlling the intergenerational distribution of wealth. While annual wealth taxes have always been frowned upon in American political rhetoric, death taxes hold an honorable place in our pantheon of sacred symbols. According to our revolutionary forefounders, man should be allowed to keep what he earns, but should not be allowed to inherit privileges that he did not earn. Our 4th of July rhetoric would in fact lead us to a 100 per cent inheritance tax. Everyone starts off in the economic race of life from an equal position.

* * * As a practical matter, the estate and gift tax as it is presently constituted has little impact on individual incomes and almost no impact on the distribution of wealth.

The potential usefulness of the estate and gift tax depends upon the desired degree of equality in society's optimum distribution of wealth. The more infrequent the interval of taxation, the less equality the instrument is capable of achieving. With long intervals between tax collections individuals have time to build up their wealth and to use their economic power. A once-in-a-lifetime wealth tax is capable of yielding less equality than a once-every-5-years wealth tax. The latter, in turn, can yield less equality than an annual wealth tax.

If society's desired distribution of wealth is not too equal, it can be achieved with wealth taxes at infrequent intervals. A severe tax could be levied once in each individual's lifetime (at death) or a lower tax could be levied at 1- or 5-year intervals. The choice depends upon other factors such as the different impacts on saving, ease of collection, and the maximum amount of economic power an individual should be allowed to accumulate and exercise in his lifetime. Frequent wealth taxes can prevent any individual from accumulating too much economic power, while estate and gift taxes can only affect averages. Once in a lifetime taxes leave open the possibility that a few individuals will have enormous wealth, but it will be wealth that they accumulated, and not wealth that they inherited.

* * *

* * * [E]ven a very severe estate and gift tax would not place much of a potential constraint upon the maximum amount of wealth an individual could possess. Combined with savings out of earned income, individuals would still accumulate large fortunes.

Severe estate and gift taxes, however, would probably have a noticeable effect on the distribution of income. First, they would severely limit the number of individuals with wealth in the hundreds of millions. No one knows how many of these fortunes rest upon substantial initial inheritances, but many of them presumably fall into this category. Given the actual distribution of net worths and the almost complete absence of estate and gift taxes, it is also clear that many individuals must consume substantial proportions of their inheritance and its earnings, or they must receive low rates of returns on their investments. If this were not the case, the distribution of wealth would be even more unequal than it is.

Currently, the 7.5 per cent of the population with net worths in excess of $50,000 have 59.1 per cent of total net worth, and the top 2.5 per cent of the population with net worths in excess of $100,000 have 44 per cent of total net worth. The elderly are heavily represented among this latter group. Those over 65 years of age account for 37 per cent of the wealth of the group with net worths in excess of $100,000. Inheritance taxes that prevented this wealth from being passed on to other wealthy individuals might substantially reduce the concentration of wealth.

Let us assume for the moment that existing patterns of inheritance are such that all of the wealth of the upper 2.5 per cent of the population is either transferred to other individuals already in the upper 2.5 cent of the population, or is given in such large lumps that the receiver moves into the upper 2.5 per cent (i.e., individual inheritances are at least $100,000 and on average are just as large as current average net worths among the top 2.5 per cent). Moving to a system where no individual would inherit more than $50,000 from all sources would substantially alter the concentration of wealth under these circumstances. * * * [A] severe inheritance tax might have a substantial impact on the distribution of wealth.

At the same time, it is clear that a once-in-a-lifetime wealth tax is not a sensitive instrument for achieving society's desired distribution of wealth. It is too infrequent to place much of a constraint on an individual's wealth, although it might be an effective instrument for affecting the general shape of the wealth distribution. The choice between an effective estate and gift tax and a more frequent wealth tax comes down to a choice between whether society just wants to affect the general shape of the wealth distribution, or whether it wants to prevent individuals from having massive net worths and the economic power that goes with large fortunes. In the former case, an inheritance tax is a good instrument; in the latter case, a more frequent wealth tax must be used.

IV. TECHNICAL ARGUMENTS AGAINST TAXES ON NET WORTH

The variety of technical arguments as to why a net worth tax cannot be levied is only exceeded by the emptiness of most of these arguments. They are really just camouflage for the substantive argument that wealth should not be taxed.

* * * [M]ost wealth is held in easily accessible forms and ownership can easily be determined if the tax is applied at the national level. In any case, all of these items are now supposedly taxed in our system of property taxes and estate and gift taxes. In addition, given a larger zero rate bracket, * * * the tax would apply to very few individuals * * * .

Often wealth taxes are attacked on the grounds that they will force illiquid wealthy individuals to sell some of their assets. This charge is to some extent true, but to the extent that it is true it is irrelevant. If a wealth tax were in existence, individuals would know of its existence and could plan to have the necessary degree of liquidity in their portfolios. To the extent that the problem arose from an infrequent wealth tax (say an inheritance tax where the giver did not plan his portfolio properly), the problem can be eliminated by allowing generous spreading provisions. There is no doubt that some individuals would be forced to sell assets. This is precisely what a wealth tax is all about. Wealth taxes are designed to control the distribution of wealth. They are not designed to allow every individual to keep that degree of wealth that he would like.

Double taxation arguments are often mentioned, but they are completely fallacious. Any time you have both an income tax and a consumption tax, the same dollar is taxed more than once. The purpose of taxation is not taxing dollars equally, but generating society's desired after-tax distributions of wealth, consumption, and income. Individuals, not dollars are to be treated equitably but even they are not to be treated equally. To the extent that dollars need to be taxed more than once to bring this about, they should be taxed more than once.

As a result, it is not possible to dismiss net worth taxes with technical arguments. We can decide that we do not want to tax wealth, but we cannot force that result by claiming that net worth taxes are inherently unworkable.

V. SOME NECESSARY COORDINATION

Depending upon society's interest in economic growth and the nature of the net worth tax adopted, net worth taxes would require carefully balanced consumption taxes to avoid distortions in economic activities and to avoid excess burdens. If society wanted to discourage shifts toward consumption and at the same time collect a progressive net worth tax, it would need to institute a progressive consumption tax to act as a countervailing incentive. To completely eliminate shifts into consumption activities, the consumption tax should be just as progressive as the net worth tax. With such a countervailing tax, an individual would pay exactly the same sum in taxes regardless of whether he decided to consume his net worth or whether he decided to maintain his current investments.

Without such countervailing consumption taxes it is possible to argue that net worth taxes would lead to a slower rate of savings, investment, and growth. With such countervailing taxes, it is not possible to make this argument. If it is desired, consumption taxes can be made more onerous than net worth taxes. With such taxes it would be possible to increase the rate of savings, investment, and economic growth while at the same time collecting net worth taxes.

VI. CONCLUSIONS

The interconnection between "technical matters" and "political matters" is nowhere more clear than it is in the area of wealth taxes. Because professional tax economists and tax lawyers have been willing to testify that wealth taxes were beyond the [pale] of "technical feasibility," the public has not considered whether it does or does not want a system of net worth taxes. * * * [I]t would probably be possible to command majority political support for the proposition that "Americans should not be allowed to inherit great wealth." * * *

While net worth taxes would raise additional revenue, they primarily focus attention on the equity issue—an issue that technical testimony has helped to avoid for the entire post-war period. At what point should society stop its wealth from becoming concentrated in the hands of a minority? We are quick to pose the question for other societies (particularly underdeveloped countries that we are aiding) but slow to pose it for ourselves.

* * *

NOTE

Thurow recommends a net worth tax as part of a package of complementary taxes. Why does he favor a net worth tax over a tax on wealth transfers or accessions? For a proposal to introduce an inheritance tax in addition to Thurow's recommended tax package, see C. Ronald Chester, *Inheritance and Wealth Taxation in a Just Society*, 30 RUTGERS L. REV. 62 (1976).

Barry L. Isaacs, *Do We Want a Wealth Tax in America?*, 32 U. MIAMI L. REV. 23 (1977)*

* * *

V. GENERAL PRINCIPLES: THE CONTROVERSY

A. Arguments for a Wealth Tax

Certain individuals believe that extraordinarily large concentrations of wealth in the hands of a relative handful of individuals is out of keeping with modern societal notions of proper wealth distribution. Others consider the perpetual existence of huge private fortunes, with their concomitant plutocratic control of economic power, as a threat to the very continuation of democratic government. Generally speaking, the principal justification adduced for any wealth tax—whether its primary objective is to break up or check the growth of large concentrations of wealth, or to serve as an alternative to higher progression of a currently progressive income tax structure[62]—is that wealth yields benefits above and beyond the income derived from it. It thus confers upon its possessor additional taxable capacity which equity requires to be taken into account. The classic case used to illustrate the proposition is the contrast between the opulent rajah, whose wealth consists entirely of $10,000,000 worth of gold and jewels, and the beggar who possesses neither income nor property. Comparing the two on the basis of income alone, neither has any taxable capacity. But when we take into account the rajah's ability to convert a portion of his assets for current consumption, clearly he is better off than the beggar.[64] Even looking at individuals whose income-wealth comparison is far less severe, the fundamental situation remains the same. Thus, two persons with families of equal size, each with $10,000 annual income, are not equal in taxable capacity where one has over $1,000,000 in the bank while the other only $10,000. The former clearly has greater economic security as well as a greater ability to meet unfavorable contingencies. He can spend beyond his current income even to some point of extravagance, knowing that he has considerable sums on which he can rely. A certain feeling of esteem is also gained from the mere possession of such wealth. Thus the basic inadequacy of progressive income taxation as the near exclusive source of revenue is that it protects rather than redistributes wealth. * * *

Another argument in favor of a wealth tax is that it would contribute to a more productive use of capital insofar as the tax would be levied irrespective of yield. This should promote the movement of capital out of non-income producing assets such as cash, precious metals, jewels, and uncultivated land, as well as low income producing ones such as certain bonds and securities. * * *

---

*   Copyright © 1977. Reprinted with permission.

[62]   Practical considerations may impose limits on the degree of progression obtainable with income, spendings, and succession taxes alone. If still steeper progression is desired, a tax on net wealth may provide a possible method of topping off the tax structure. Such a net wealth tax would not be considered an important element in the revenue system, but rather a means of achieving a redistribution of wealth at the top of the scale more rapidly than is possible with the other taxes alone. . . . Such a net worth tax would be an acceptable substitute for the continuation of the graduation in the upper ranges of income, spendings, or succession taxes.

VICKREY, AGENDA FOR PROGRESSIVE TAXATION 362-63 (1947).

[64]   N. KALDOR, INDIAN TAX REFORM 20 (1956).

A final argument advanced for net worth taxation is that it promotes a greater efficiency of income tax administration. This is done by providing information on capital values which can be used to cross-check the accuracy of income tax returns, thus discouraging concealment of the income from invested wealth because of the greater likelihood of detection.

B. Arguments Against a Wealth Tax

While it is suggested by some that the general arguments against a wealth tax are reducible to concerns about practical difficulties in administering the tax and the possible adverse economic consequences, particularly on saving,[70] the arguments are in fact more numerous. * * * Materialistic wealth has always been an extremely incomplete index of taxable capacity, since it does not consider the human resources of individuals who depend on earnings from personal services. A wealth tax concerns itself only with the status quo and not how the situation arose in the first place, suggesting that if all wealth were taxed as it was transferred into new ownership, the claim that wealth represented additional taxable capacity would no longer stand. * * *

There is no definition of what constitutes an unacceptable wealth distribution. Wherever there is a relatively high exemption limiting the application of a wealth tax, it is indicative only of the point at which wealth accumulation may be considered unacceptable. But to tax wealth only when it reaches a certain level proves that it is not aimed at ownership of wealth per se, but only at excessive inequalities of wealth. This would tend to weaken the equity argument of additional taxable capacity unless it too was intended to apply only to excessive concentrations of wealth.

* * * The argument that great concentrations of wealth bring power to those who possess them might suggest that the power be controlled, not necessarily that the wealth itself should be confiscated or broken up.

It has been said that those who decry inequalities in wealth distribution often advance such criticism only to hide their basic envy and political discontent. Discrimination of this sort against a wealthy minority of a population without any criteria for limiting the extent of such discrimination is incompatible with the governing principles of democracy and the rule of law. A majority of persons should not be able to decide the appropriate limit on another citizen's wealth. * * *

Those who seek to justify the wealth tax on equitable grounds fail to consider the significance of the fact that income from different kinds of property of the same value can still differ greatly. Taxes levied on the basis of property values discriminate against those whose income yield on investments is negligible. The lead time for enterprises to become productive can be lengthy, causing an individual who holds shares in such an investment to pay a tax based on the market value of his shares, notwithstanding that no dividends may be payable for years. He is thus forced to consume his capital to meet his tax liability.

VI. ADMINISTRATIVE PROBLEMS ATTENDANT TO A WEALTH TAX

A. Introduction

A wealth tax bears great similarity to that form of general property taxation which has existed at one time or another in every nation, including our own, since ancient times. A property tax differs from a wealth tax insofar as property taxes are generally imposed on the gross value of the property, primarily real property, while a wealth tax takes into account the outstanding liabilities of the taxpayer so as to arrive at a net figure. Thus, the wealth tax is levied on the particular person involved, but the property tax is levied on the property itself.

* * *

---

[70]   * * * Thurow, *Net Worth Taxes*, 25 Nat'l Tax J. 417, 421-23 (1972).

Most experts * * * criticize property taxation, particularly with regard to its assessment. The principal difficulty inherent in property tax administration lies in the absence of a market transaction: without a sale, assessments must be based on fallible human judgment. Property taxation is undoubtedly made easier whenever the number of appraisal tasks are kept to a minimum. Even then, despite notable improvements in property tax administration in some areas, discrimination and inequity remain. Insofar as the wealth tax would be administered on the federal level without the luxury of a narrow property tax base, assessment difficulties are almost certain to become more acute.

B. Threshold Level and Assessment Costs

The administratively desirable threshold liability level for incidence of a wealth tax depends to a great extent on the purpose of such a tax. Where * * * the purpose is both to reduce undue concentrations of wealth and to provide tax relief to lower and middle income groups, a high threshold * * * is justified. A high threshold has the added benefit of reducing the number of individuals liable to the tax. * * *

Consistent with American practice regarding other tax assessments, self-assessment undoubtedly would be followed. This is probably necessary to prevent the collection of such a tax from becoming an impossibly massive undertaking. Additionally, since a high exemption threshold is envisaged, wealth tax liability could be handled on the basis of a single return for both income and wealth taxes. The assessment itself would require a detailed and rather complicated form, however, the filling out of which would constitute a hidden cost of the tax.

In addition to the administrative costs to the government and to the taxpayer, any change in tax incidence which will increase the burden on some while reducing it on others, bears close scrutiny because it may bring enough resentment from the former to cause them to act contrary to the design of such change. It may be argued that a tax policy deliberately directed at the elimination of large private fortunes will induce a significant number of hitherto law abiding taxpayers to evade such levies or to act even more unpredictably. The underlying premise is that while the threat of detection is a factor inducing tax compliance, attitudes toward the tax system—particularly concerning the equity or fairness of the system—may be even more important. A significant number of wealthy individuals may even decide to emigrate with their wealth to countries more hospitable to the acquisition and accumulation of large fortunes.

It has been suggested that the use of wealth tax values for the purpose of other taxes offers important savings in administrative and compliance costs through useful cross-checks. This alone would never justify the imposition of such a tax, however, particularly because a wealth tax would add complexity to our already complex tax laws. Significant revisions would be necessary to accommodate taxing the wealth held in trusts and closely held corporations. * * * It may be difficult to determine who owns the capital upon which the tax will be assessed. * * *

C. Discovery of Assets

In theory at least, it seems altogether sensible that if one were to institute a wealth tax at all, its scope should be as comprehensive as possible. In other words, the taxpayer should be taxed on the total value of all his assets, wherever situated; however, the broader the coverage the more difficult it would be to prevent evasion by under-reporting. Assets like cash, gold, art, jewelry and some intangibles which are generally in unregistered form are extremely difficult to discover. This problem could be alleviated by exempting from the wealth tax all household and personal effects, jewelry, works of art, and collections. Of course, this would encourage avoidance of the tax. It would also destroy the rationale that the tax encouraged investment. Even without such an exemption, a wealth tax necessarily discriminates against real property owners whose net wealth is easily identified in favor of those whose wealth is unable to be traced.

It has been suggested that this problem is not insurmountable, provided that the government has access to all insurance records of individuals who would normally insure their valuables. Notwithstanding the administrative nightmare caused by monitoring insurance policies, tax avoiders would respond to this policing method by simply not buying insurance. It is likely that no effective wealth tax could be administered without the adoption of a far more circumscribed system of property registration and property transfer, prospects which many would find unsettling.

D. Valuation of Assets

As previously mentioned, any tax which attempts to take into account all accrued but unrealized changes in the value of assets and liabilities might not be desirable even if it were feasible. The argument against its feasibility has been stated as follows:

> To take account of unrealized gains and losses would require the detailed listing of taxpayers' assets and liabilities and annual valuations. The lists would be long, and for many items market quotations would not be readily available. Considerable difficulty is encountered in valuing certain securities and many business properties for purposes of the estate tax, even though these valuations need to be made only once for each of a relatively small number of taxpayers. Most experts agree that annual appraisals would not be feasible under the income tax. Even if valuations were made somewhat less frequently, the accrual treatment seems impractical despite some offsetting gains in the form of simplification or elimination of certain complex features of the present income tax.[114]

An annual wealth tax would compound the aforementioned difficulties insofar as it contemplates an assessed valuation for *all* assets on an annual basis, not merely those upon which gain has accrued. This means ascertaining representative market values for all forms of property. It has been pointed out that the task is not difficult wherever there is a large and continuous market in the rights or commodities involved, as there are in most stocks and bonds. Where, however, there are few or no market transactions the valuation problem is particularly acute. Furthermore, nonliquid assets such as partnerships, farms, buildings, real estate, oil wells and other mineral rights, and closely held business enterprises also present valuation problems.

"Fair market value" has been defined as "that amount which one ready and willing but not compelled to buy would pay to another ready and willing but not compelled to sell the property." The application of this principle for wealth tax purposes is desirable because any higher value might be regarded as unfair while any lower value might create a "locked-in" effect. Even where the fair market value of property is easily ascertained, there may be a big difference between the price at which a taxpayer can purchase an asset and that at which he can sell the very same asset. Thus a value for wealth tax purposes, if it is set at the upper range of what the asset would cost, could be unfair.

A number of solutions have been proposed to handle valuation problems. * * *

Whichever method is chosen, there is a real danger that certain wealth holders will be forced to sell their assets to pay the tax. Clearly, it would be undesirable to compel farmers, whose agricultural land has been rising steadily in price, to liquidate in whole or in part their principal asset in order to satisfy the tax. This problem would be felt similarly in a business where a sole proprietor places a substantial portion of his assets as well as accumulated profits into the venture, only to be confronted with the wealth tax assessment.

---

[114]   R. GOODE, [THE INDIVIDUAL INCOME TAX 28 (rev. ed. 1976)]. For a contrary view, see Thurow, *supra* note 70, at 421. Thurow declares that the administrative difficulties of wealth tax are illusory and that tax lawyers and tax economists are to blame for having scared away the public.

* * *

VII. ECONOMIC ASPECTS OF A WEALTH TAX

The practical effects of a wealth tax on economic behavior are unpredictable because they generally encompass but a small part of the economy as a whole and because economic behavior is influenced by many more considerations than a particular form of taxation. Numerous economic benefits are claimed for the net wealth tax relative to its effects upon investment and economic development generally. An important asserted benefit is that since the tax will not impinge upon the incremental gain from investment or expansion but rather upon the total accumulation of an individual, there should be a disincentive to avoid earning income; that is, past and future effort will be taxed regardless of yield, so the assets might as well be directed towards meeting the tax payments. In addition, as mentioned earlier, there may be a tendency to push investments out of cash, gold, and low income securities and into higher-yield investments, presumably contributing to economic growth and efficiency. No economic benefits, however, are seriously asserted for a wealth tax when the combination of wealth and income tax levies approaches or exceeds 100% of net income. * * * [A] tax on 3% of net worth * * * would be the equivalent of a 60% tax on income derived from net wealth on which the yield is 5%. Depending on an individual's tax bracket, the yield on his assets, and the source of that yield, the prospect of certain individuals being unable to meet reasonable consumption requirements from disposable net income becomes very real. This would not be as serious if the tax were designed to reduce higher marginal rates of taxation on both income and investments. * * *

Whether or not there are investment incentives caused by the introduction of a wealth tax, even when it is substituted for a higher rate of income tax of equal yield, is a highly complex and debatable question. * * * It is safe to say only that any reward resulting from risk-taking will increase wealth tax liability only in the event that it is added to net worth.

The effect of a wealth tax on savings appears to be much easier to assess because the tax falls directly on all accumulations as such. The opportunity to add to future consumption through saving would seem to be restricted among the affected taxpayers, with no likelihood that the incidence of the tax can be shifted. On the other hand, it has been found that large wealth tends to be associated with individuals whose marginal propensity to save is very high and who would be likely to save any increment in income or assets if they were able to do so. Additionally, the psychological effect of a wealth tax spread over the entire amount rather than an income tax concentrated on the fruits of additional savings may not prove negative after all. Whether or not a potential decline in aggregate saving would condemn a wealth tax depends to a great extent on government savings and prevailing employment conditions. Thus, this question too remains unanswered.

VIII. CONCLUSION

Individuals who advocate a redistribution of wealth in America often are so irresistibly drawn to any proposal which has as its purpose the economic leveling of the wealthiest group of individuals, that they are either unmindful or unconcerned about the inherent problems which will ensue. * * *

* * *

NOTE

Which of Isaacs' concerns—administrative problems or adverse economic consequences—is the more serious obstacle to enacting a wealth tax? For further discussion of the administrative problems of a wealth tax, see G.S.A. Wheatcroft, *The Administrative Problems of a Wealth Tax*, 1963 BRITISH TAX REV. 410.

Gilbert Paul Verbit, *Taxing Wealth: Recent Proposals from the United States, France, and the United Kingdom*, 60 B.U. L. REV. 1 (1980)*

I. INTRODUCTION

In his Mortimer Hess Memorial Lecture * * *,[1] Professor George Cooper stated as his goal the convincing of his audience to "take seriously" the idea of a wealth tax, a tax on "the net value of a person's assets, imposed periodically." Although the idea of a wealth tax is hardly novel, Professor Cooper's address is the first time that the concept has been presented in so prestigious an American forum by so distinguished a speaker.[2] Wealth taxation has also received renewed attention in France and the United Kingdom. Within the past few years both the French and British governments have commissioned studies to determine the advisability of some form of wealth tax for their respective countries.[3] Is it, then, an idea whose time has come?

Rather than undertake an exhaustive, independent analysis of an annual wealth tax, this article contrasts Professor Cooper's guardedly optimistic support for such a tax with the essential reasoning and differing conclusions of the European studies. Many of the problems and proposed responses that comprise the wealth tax debates in the United States, Britain and France are sufficiently common to warrant comparison. * * *

* * *

III. THE FRENCH ALTERNATIVE

A. Evolution of Wealth Taxation

* * * [A] commission of three experts—popularly known as the three Sages— * * * reported its conclusions on December 30, 1978 * * * .

* * *

---

*   Volume 60:1 (1980) (pp. 1-45), The Boston University Law Review. Reprinted with permission. © 1980 by Gilbert Paul Verbit and the Trustees of Boston University. Forum of original publication. Boston University bears no responsibility for any errors which have occurred in reprinting or editing.

1   Cooper, *Taking Wealth Taxation Seriously*, 34 REC. ASS'N B. CITY N.Y. 24, 24-25 (1979).

2   The proposal was previously made by Ramsey Clark, a candidate in the 1976 primary race for the Democratic nomination for the United States Senate election in New York. *See* Isaacs, *Do We Want a Wealth Tax in America?*, 32 U. MIAMI L. REV. 23 (1977).

3   *See* REPORT OF A COMMITTEE CHAIRED BY PROFESSOR J. E. MEADE, THE STRUCTURE AND REFORM OF DIRECT TAXATION (1978) [*hereinafter* cited as MEADE]; RAPPORT DE LA COMMISSION D'UN PRÉLÈVEMENT SUR LES FORTUNES: RAPPORT (1979) [*hereinafter* cited as RAPPORT].

In light of (a) the heavy burden of direct and indirect taxes borne by French white and blue collar workers, (b) the persistent disparity in the distribution of personally-held wealth in France, and (c) the government policy to break up family control of important sectors of the economy, the Commission concluded that an increased tax burden on the wealthy was both economically and morally justified. Unlike Professor Cooper, however, the Commission was unwilling to recommend an annual wealth tax as the means to impose that justifiable burden.

The three Sages rejected an annual wealth tax on several grounds. First, France already has a wealth tax in the form of an annual real estate tax (*impôt foncier*), which reaches a high proportion of personally-held wealth. * * *

The second reason for the Commission's rejection of an annual wealth tax flowed from its mandated examination of wealth taxes in other European countries. Unlike Professor Cooper, who saw these existent taxes as empirical support for an annual wealth tax, the Commission viewed that same experience as militating against such a tax. * * *

* * *

From its examination of existing annual wealth tax systems, the Commission concluded that these taxes are retained primarily to compensate for the lack of a capital gains tax. * * * Moreover, the Commission found that there was a fairly clear correlation between countries that have a wealth tax and those which have a weak system of transfer and real property taxes. * * *

The three Sages identified as the third principal reason for their rejection of an annual wealth tax the difficult problems which would arise in implementing the tax. For example, unlike Professor Cooper, who characterized an annual wealth tax rate of 1% as very low, the Sages recognized that this rate may be too high, at least in France. Consider the fact that the net yield of agricultural land in France is approximately 2%. An annual wealth tax of 1% would thus reduce farm income by 50%. Residential rental property was also estimated to yield about 2% and would thus similarly suffer under an annual wealth tax of 1%.

Although the Sages, like Professor Cooper, perceived the valuation question as central to the wealth tax debate, they did not share his perception of it as "an opportunity." Instead, the Commission feared that an annual wealth tax would serve to penalize holdings of quoted shares as opposed to unquoted shares, and thus deter privately held companies from going public at a time the government was seeking to enlarge the French equity market. Moreover, although Professor Cooper believed the world can learn from the positive West German experience with the valuation problem, the Commission thought otherwise. It found that the West German solution to the real property valuation problem was largely to ignore it. * * * The three Sages concluded that the base for the West German wealth tax was in general valued at a level much below reality.

The Commission also criticized the projected cost of administering the wealth tax. They estimated that the French equivalent of the IRS would have to hire at least 1000 new agents, primarily from the highest level of the civil service, to enforce and collect the tax. The cost of administering the new tax was projected at 130 million francs—close to 10% of the anticipated revenue. Since administration of the income tax requires only about 1 to 2% of anticipated revenue, the Sages concluded that the government might be better advised to recruit 1000 new agents to improve enforcement of the income tax, thereby reducing tax fraud and increasing revenues.

Nor was the Commission impressed by the argument that the net wealth tax would supplement the income tax. They observed in the *Rapport* that unrealized capital gains, to the extent they are in the form of appreciation in the value of real property, are already taxed under the local property tax. As for other assets which yield no taxable income—for example, gold, works of art, jewelry—these are unlikely to be declared for wealth taxation. Finally, the Sages were not convinced that a wealth tax would uncover information which would lead to better enforcement of the income tax. * * *

The Commission's recommendation against adoption of an annual wealth tax did not entail a rejection of other means to increase the "fiscal pressure" on the wealthy. Citing the English aphorism that "a good tax is an old tax," the Sages proposed a reform of the oldest of French taxes—the inheritance tax. In reaching this conclusion, the Commission began from a premise endorsed by Professor Cooper, that the focal point of tax reform should be not wealth in general but inherited wealth. Given this premise, an annual wealth tax cuts too broadly in its failure to distinguish between inherited wealth and wealth accrued from savings. According to the Sages, a properly defined transfer tax would generate the same fiscal pressure on wealth as that which would be accomplished by an annual wealth tax. * * *

* * *

IV. THE BRITISH ALTERNATIVE

* * *

As so far described, an accessions tax leaves unanswered the primary objection to transfer taxes which an annual wealth tax is designed to overcome—the problem of periodicity. In contrast to an annually imposed wealth tax, an accessions tax imposes liability only at the time of receipt. * * * [A]s the Meade Committee recognized, the effective tax rate on gratuitous transfers would vary considerably in individual cases depending on the length of time between transfers. Differing time gaps between transfers result in differing effective rates of inheritance tax, whereas an annual wealth tax would be levied at a uniform rate regardless of how long or short the period between transfers.

The Meade Committee combined this advantage of an annual wealth tax with an accessions tax to produce a progressive annual wealth accessions tax (PAWAT). To understand how the PAWAT would work, begin with the concept of an accessions tax. The rate for an accessions tax depends upon the amount of the gift or bequest plus the amount of gifts and bequests already received. PAWAT adds another variable to the rate—the age of the donee. At the time the donee receives a transfer, he would pay a tax representing a lump-sum advance payment of an annual wealth tax to age 85. If the donee transfers that property by gift or bequest he would deduct the amount of the transfer from his total of gifts received. Moreover, if the latter transfer occurs before the original donee reaches age 85, he is entitled to a rebate on that portion of the prepaid tax which reflects annual payments for the period between the date of the latter transfer and the date the donee would reach age 85. The Meade Committee offered the following illustration of how a PAWAT would work. Assume that A, age 60, inherits $1,000,000 in 1977. A has not received previously any gifts or bequests. To calculate the tax liability we refer to the following table:

Cumulative Transfers Received	Rate of Equivalent Annual Wealth Tax	Amount of Equivalent Annual Wealth Tax
$ 50,000	0%	$ 0.
next $ 50,000	0.5%	$ 250
next $ 400,000	1.0%	$ 4,000
next $ 500,000	1.5%	$ 7,500
next $ 1,000,000	2.0%	$ 20,000

According to the table, the receipt of $1,000,000 would subject the donee to a nominal annual wealth tax of $11,750. The PAWAT payable would be the present value of cumulative annual payments of $11,750 paid from age 60 until the donee reaches age 85. According to the table of annuity multipliers (discounted at 3%) presented in the *Meade Report*, the proper multiplier to be applied is 17.41, and therefore the total tax payable would be $204,568. Assume the next transaction occurs in 1982 when *A*, now age 65, receives a second inheritance of $1,000,000. *A* now would pay a PAWAT of $20,000 x 14.88 = $297,600. In 1992, at age 75, *A* makes a gift of $500,000. *A* is giving away 25% of his wealth which would have been subjected to the PAWAT. He is thus entitled to a rebate on the portion of prepaid annual wealth tax covering 25% of his taxed wealth for the period between his present age and age 85. His nominal annual wealth tax bill would be $31,750, 25% of which is $7,938. The annuity factor for the ten years between the donor's age at the time of this gift and age 85 is 8.53. Thus, *A* would be entitled to a PAWAT rebate of $67,711.

Assume that in the same year, *A* dies at age 75. Note that at this point his PAWAT total, the total amount on which tax has been paid, would be $1,500,000. This amount bears no necessary relation, however, to the amount of wealth *A* actually leaves since he could have spent his entire inheritance or, conversely, could have greatly enhanced it. Because *A* has died at age 75, his estate is entitled to a rebate on that portion of the PAWAT which reflects annual payments between age 75 and age 85. However, a rebate is due only to the extent *A* passes on to his heirs property on which he already had paid the tax. Assume *A* leaves to his heirs property worth $500,000, an amount less than *A*'s PAWAT total. We know that *A*'s rebate on $500,000 would be 13.5%, and thus the rebate would be $67,711. However, unlike the gift situation, the heirs will receive the $500,000 bequest plus the rebate. Because the rebate is itself property on which the PAWAT has been paid, it also must be treated as a transfer entitling *A*'s estate to a rebate. Therefore, the bequest of $500,000 must be grossed up by the rebate rate of 13.5%, which equals $578,000. If instead *A* leaves property worth $4,000,000, his estate would only be entitled to a rebate on that portion of his estate which, when grossed up, equals *A*'s PAWAT total. In *A*'s case, $1,298,000 would be the amount of property on which a PAWAT refund could be obtained because that amount grossed up at the rebate rate of 13.5% equals the PAWAT total of $1,500,000.

To reiterate, PAWAT is the equivalent of an annual tax on inherited property, a synthesis of what have heretofore been considered two mutually exclusive alternatives. Certain features of PAWAT, however, may dull some of its lustre. First, PAWAT continues to subject to tax wealth which may have been consumed or squandered by the wealth holder. Only by giving the surcharged wealth away during his lifetime, or bequeathing it at his death, may a recipient of gratuitous transfers stop the running of the PAWAT. The second drawback is that although the system creates an incentive to promptly pass on inherited wealth to persons with little inherited property, the system works as a disincentive for the transfer of saved wealth insofar as no rebate attaches to its transfer. Finally, PAWAT's administration is complicated by the fact that each transfer involves two calculations—one by the donor to compute his rebate and one by the donee to determine his PAWAT liability.

Two of these three objections can be met by adoption of a linear annual wealth accessions tax (LAWAT), a simplified version of PAWAT. Simplification is gained at the price of eliminating the accessions tax feature, i.e., by no longer taking into account the total of gratuitous transfers already received by a transferee. Assuming acceptance of this modification, the system would be designed so that each recipient of a gratuitous transfer would pay upon receipt a tax equal to the present value of an annual wealth tax for a certain future period—for example, "up to the time of the donee's 85th birthday." When a donor gratuitously transfers property, whether saved or inherited, the donee pays a tax only for the period from the donor's 85th birthday to the date when the donee would reach age 85. Under a LAWAT system there would be no rebate and the only tax due from the transferee could be easily determined from a table. Moreover, the absence of the accessions feature, and concomitant lack of distinction between saved and inherited wealth, minimizes the disincentive to transfer saved wealth characteristic of a PAWAT.

These advantages of a LAWAT over a PAWAT are purchased at a heavy price—the loss of a PAWAT's progressivity. According to the *Meade Report*, progressivity may be restored to the system by combining a LAWAT with an annual wealth tax. An annual wealth tax has the singular advantage of encouraging the wealth holder to disperse his wealth among persons of little wealth as quickly as possible. An accessions tax creates no such incentive.

As already discussed, however, adoption of an annual wealth tax carries with it a heavy burden of administrative and compliance costs. The Meade Committee recognized that "for such a severe and basic instrument of taxation to be acceptable it would have to be reliable, fair, and immune against extensive evasion and avoidance." Yet to achieve such immunity may be impossible where the rewards for avoidance and evasion are so high and the means so readily accessible. And the Committee itself cited some of the substantial barriers to ensuring the fairness of the tax. For example, the full value of owner-occupied housing would have to be included in the base of a fair wealth tax. More importantly, the Committee concluded that a fair wealth tax would have to include in its base the present value of future pension rights—a form of wealth excluded from the tax base in all Organization of Economic Cooperation and Development countries which have an annual wealth tax. Not only would inclusion of pension rights present formidable valuation problems, but it would also greatly expand the category of those persons considered rich. * * *

As a final example, consider Professor Meade's earlier criticism of the annual wealth tax concept on the ground that fairness would require that the base include the capitalized value of education and training. He reasoned that the direct costs of, and earnings in, acquiring a skill are a capital investment leading to higher personal income, at least part of which is really a return on this capital investment. * * *

The Meade Committee sought to resolve these problems of fairness with a simple answer— a very high threshold for the annual wealth tax so that it would affect only the "largest fortunes." Apparently satisfied with this resolution, the Committee recommended the adoption of either (1) a combination of an annual wealth tax and a LAWAT, or (2) a PAWAT. Although a PAWAT would leave saved wealth untaxed, and thus offer no incentive to give away saved property before death, it would create more of an incentive for "saving, enterprise and capital development" precisely because it focuses solely on inherited wealth. Thus, the choice between the alternative recommendations finally turns on whether as a policy matter one prefers to exempt wealth accumulated out of savings. If so, a PAWAT would be the choice.

V. OBSERVATIONS

My observations begin with this question of whether the tax system should distinguish between saved and inherited wealth. Professor Kaldor left us uninformed as to the source of his maharajah's wealth because such a distinction was irrelevant to his objective—illustrating the additional taxable capacity conferred by all wealth. If the existence of unreached taxable capacity alone justifies taxing wealth it makes no difference whether that wealth is inherited or acquired through hard labor and savings.

To tax wealth of all kinds is to increase the cost of holding wealth. Such a tax benefits society to the extent that it forces the liquidation of the maharajah's jewelry cache and generally compels him to convert his assets into more productive forms. But it also has the negative effect of discouraging saving because the dollar earned and saved would be subject to the wealth tax, whereas the dollar earned and consumed would not. Thus, by increasing the cost of saving, the tax would encourage consumption at the expense of saving. The resultant disequilibrium between savings and consumption can be corrected by increasing the cost of consumption through a countervailing tax on expenditures. Lester Thurow has suggested that an expenditure tax must accompany an annual wealth tax to prevent those subject to the wealth tax from frivolously squandering their fortunes.[222]

There are two principal approaches to a tax on expenditures. The more common method indirectly taxes purchases by means of a sales tax or value added tax. Presumably, such taxes could be imposed at a rate sufficiently high to discourage increased consumption by the wealthy, effectively offsetting the incentives to consume created by the wealth tax. However, these indirect expenditure taxes tend in fact to apply to a very broad range of goods and services; the cost of increasing the price of consumption items for the rich would be to increase the price for everyone. The rich, being rich, would be less discouraged from increased consumption than would the large majority of the population for whom the higher level of indirect taxation might create an absolute barrier to a wide range of consumer goods. The obvious solution of limiting the increase in indirect taxes to "luxury" goods simply would not work.

The alternative method for discouraging consumption and encouraging savings requires a more radical change in our present system of direct taxation—substitution of an expenditure tax for the income tax. At present the income tax, because it taxes income whatever the disposition of that income, discourages saving. Replacing it with a system whereby all income is received free of tax and only expenditures are taxed would introduce a strong incentive to save. * * * In addition, the substituted expenditure tax would greatly simplify the tax structure, obviating the need to distinguish between ordinary income and capital gains, and eliminating the myriad of rules governing the income taxation of trusts and their beneficiaries. Treatment of gifts and bequests as expenditures would even further simplify the present tax laws and regulations. For many of these reasons the Meade Committee favored substituting an expenditures tax for the income tax, and suggested that, if attempted, the reform "might command a wide consensus of political approval."

Regardless of its theoretical appeal and political feasibility, an expenditures tax addresses only one of the problems posed by an annual wealth tax—the disincentive to saving. Substantial obstacles to a fair and effective wealth tax remain, most importantly the problems of valuation and rate determination. As already discussed, none of the countries which at present have an annual wealth tax have adequately resolved the problem of valuation. The recent discussion of wealth taxation in France, however, has generated a number of simple, but likely effective methods. The proposals range from making the declared value of an asset for tax purposes the compensation which would be paid if the asset were taken under eminent domain, to giving the government an option to purchase listed assets at declared value, to the public posting of listed property and its declared value and giving the public the right to purchase the property at its declared value. It would be difficult to find more effective incentives to the declaration of property at its "true" value.

Determination of the rate at which the wealth tax should be imposed turns on a question left open by the taxable capacity rationale: Do we want to use the annual wealth tax as a means of reducing the size of the fortunes which form its base? Or, in Professor Cooper's terms, do we prefer a capital-directed or income-directed wealth tax? To the extent that the rate of taxation exceeds the rate of income generated by an asset, the tax is capital-directed. If we were to adopt a capital-directed tax, it would be the first of its kind. The wealth taxes which exist in Denmark, Finland, Sweden, the Netherlands, and Norway include a ceiling on the total amount of income tax and wealth tax which can be imposed, expressed as a percentage of income. But if the tax is imposed at a rate less than the rate of income generated, it is the equivalent of a surcharge on unearned income. Why not then just take the simpler step of surcharging unearned

---

[222]   Thurow, [*Net Worth Taxes*, 25 NAT. TAX J. 417, 422 (1972)].

income directly? According to wealth tax advocates, this would exclude the maharajah's wealth, putting us right back at step one.

We could, however, * * * impute income to the maharajah's treasure trove. Consider the example in which A and B each has $100,000 to invest. A buys a painting while B invests in a mutual fund yielding an income of $5,000 per annum. Having defined income as "a group of services or satisfactions emanating from capital," [one might] argue that A has an imputed income of $5,000 because by not investing in the mutual fund A showed that his ownership of the painting is worth at least $5,000 per year to him.

Of course, in practice it would be far more difficult to establish the proper imputed rate of return for A's painting. That may be the reason that the concept is usually illustrated by owner-occupied housing, an asset for which it is not difficult to calculate an imputed income. Even if the problem of accurate calculation can be surmounted, however, additional obstacles remain. The application of an annual wealth tax to nonincome producing assets, which has the effect of imputing an income to them, would depress the value of those assets below what it would be in the absence of the tax. Thus, if policymakers are to avoid a homeowners revolt they would have to adopt a threshold sufficiently high to exonerate most privately-owned homes. Moreover, the negative effect on the value of nonincome producing assets would not be uniform because some valuable assets, such as jewelry and postage stamps, are easily concealed from the tax authorities. Taken together, these factors militate against the extension of a surcharge on unearned income to include imputed unearned income as an alternative to an income based wealth tax.

To this point I have sought to identify some of the structural difficulties in the implementation of a satisfactory annual wealth tax. But the principal problem with an annual wealth tax is not one of tax design but one of tax reform. Tax reform essentially means moving from the status quo to a desired alternative, and inevitably involves a gamble. The change is warranted "only if the expected gain through increased efficiency and improved distribution outweighs the utility loss imposed by a gamble." Part of the utility loss of an annual wealth tax would be its direct impact in lowering the market price of assets within the tax base. Another part of that loss is caused by the inefficient precautionary behavior of individuals for whom the change would create uncertainty about possible future adverse changes in the tax law. * * *

* * *

Historically high inflation has intensified the anxiety over capital taxation. Without indexation in a time of high inflation, to tax capital gains is to tax wealth. Moreover, the primary weapon used to combat inflation—monetary policy emphasizing the power of central bank interest rates—has had a depressing effect on the value of traditional sources of personal wealth such as real estate and listed securities. Politically, inflation has the effect of undermining support for taxation of the wealthy by increasing the number of persons included in that group. Choosing a feasible threshold for a wealth tax is difficult enough. Inflation compounds the problem by lowering the effective threshold on an almost monthly basis.

Weighed against these disutilities is the additional taxable capacity to be tapped by a wealth tax. But if taxable capacity is the ultimate justification for an annual wealth tax, the European experience lends no weight to the argument that reaching that capacity will open a significant source of public finance. * * * No government has yet attempted to tap the taxable capacity of wealth as a significant independent source of revenue.

Rather than confront the difficulties in design and disutilities in reform posed by an annual tax on all wealth, the French and British commissions recommended that their governments concentrate on reforming the taxation of gratuitous transfers. * * * Both the Sages and the Meade Committee recognized that for the reform to succeed it must reach only for the taxable capacity conferred by that portion of capital which is gratuitously transferred. Given this, what must be determined is the most effective method to reach that taxable capacity.

The optimal tax design would appear to be Professor Meade's PAWAT, which combines the revenue features of an annual wealth tax, applied only to unearned wealth, with the administrative convenience of a transfer tax. The primary objection to the proposal is to its complexity. In the universe of present transfer tax law, however, such criticism seems disingenuous. There are far too few provisions of the Internal Revenue Code that appear uncomplicated to the novice, or even the expert. To the extent that the criticism holds merit, it goes to the theory of the PAWAT rather than its administration. Because the PAWAT combines the variables of the donor's and donee's ages, and the amount of prior gratuitous transfers received by the donee, it is bound to be a complicated exercise. But the taxpayer would not need to solve this complex equation. Instead, he could simply refer to a rate schedule to determine his liability for a given transfer. * * *

* * * By separating the formulae for calculating the PAWAT from the results of the formulae as presented to the taxpayer in the form of tables, the system's underlying complexity can easily be defused.

Like our experience with that hardy perennial, the expenditure tax, prior unsuccessful advocacy of an accessions tax that takes into account the unearned wealth and ages of the transferor and the transferee does not augur well for adoption of the PAWAT in the United States. During World War II Professor William Vickrey recommended adoption of such a tax as a new source of revenue to finance the war effort.[244] His formulae were as complicated as those of the Meade Committee, yet they too could be reduced to a table. * * *

* * *

Without forsaking the idea of a wealth tax, Professor Cooper proposed as a less controversial alternative a tax somewhat similar to the PAWAT. He recommended that we drop the present system of transfer taxation in favor of an annual tax on gratuitously transferred property. His proposal is simpler than the PAWAT in that it does not factor in the respective ages of the transferor and the transferee. But it is more complicated in that it involves all the administrative problems of an annually collected tax avoided by the PAWAT. Professor Cooper did not discuss the Meade Committee's refinement of discounting this stream of anticipated annual payments to their present value, thereby enabling the tax to be paid in one transaction. He did recognize, however, that the tax may present tracing problems. In response, he argued that so long as the transferred property is in the hands of the recipient there really is no tracing problem, and when it is sold we could "simply take the dollar value received as a substitute in the tax base." Presumably, if the property were disposed of in some other fashion, or consumed, the tax would no longer apply. This may be an advantage over the PAWAT prepayment provision, which would effectively continue to levy a tax on gratuitously transferred wealth until it either is given away or the present holder reaches age 85. This advantage, however, would be more than outweighed by the administrative convenience of the PAWAT single prepayment. Moreover, the PAWAT single payment format tracks our present system of transfer taxation and thus would be less likely to trigger the opposition's cry of unfamiliarity.

* * *

---

[244] W. VICKREY, AGENDA FOR PROGRESSIVE TAXATION 215 (1947) * * * .

VI. CONCLUSION

From among these various proposals, the PAWAT emerges as the best opportunity for reform of the transfer tax system in the United States. It synthesizes the most desirable feature of an annual tax on wealth with the familiar form and focus of a tax on gratuitous transfers. The single payment format avoids the administrative problems of an annual wealth tax yet preserves the major advantage of that tax—the elimination of variance in effective rates. Although incorporation of an accessions feature would be a radical step for the American tax system, its novelty is muted by the familiar form of a transfer tax which leaves undisturbed earned wealth. * * *

NOTE

In a later article, Verbit noted that "[d]espite my best advice, the French National Assembly enacted an annual tax on individual net wealth * * * [effective] January 1, 1982[, which] was repealed on July 11, 1986. A new annual tax on individual net wealth * * * came into effect on January 1, 1989 and remains in effect." Gilbert P. Verbit, *France Tries a Wealth Tax*, 12 U. PA. J. INT'L BUS. L. 181, 181 (1991). Verbit concludes that the jury is still out with respect to the new French wealth tax:

> As the French experiment with an annual tax on net wealth continues, it is premature to draw up a final statement on its successes and failures. To date it seems to have generated no surprises for those familiar with the issues associated with such taxes. On the positive side, it has generated tax revenues from sources that have previously gone untaxed. It has also provided valuable information for the verification of other tax liabilities, particularly the income tax. On the other hand, * * * the compliance costs are high. * * * Moreover, the cost of preparing what is the equivalent in the United States of an estate tax return every year is quite substantial. The compliance costs of the wealth tax may be such that its principal beneficiaries are the tax advisors who must file. * * *

Id. at 217.

E.   A Bequeathing Power Succession Tax

Fifty years ago, William Vickrey proposed a "bequeathing power succession tax."

WILLIAM VICKREY, AGENDA FOR PROGRESSIVE TAXATION (1947)*

THE BEQUEATHING POWER SUCCESSION TAX

* * *

Fundamental Requirements

* * * [I]t would be desirable to set up the succession tax structure in such a way that the tax burden would be exactly the same on the transfer of a given sum from one individual to another regardless of the number of steps or the channels through which the transfer is effected, and as nearly as may be regardless of the time of the transfer. * * * [I]t appears possible to devise a tax which very closely achieves this result, and to reduce it to a form in which the computations required of the taxpayer should not prove unduly burdensome, even though the rationale of the computations and the derivation of the tables upon which they are based may be fairly abstruse.[a]

The Notion of Bequeathing Power

In order to examine the principles on which such a tax might be constructed, consider a given estate as it is handed down, either directly or through various intermediaries, assuming that each holder of the estate keeps it intact, neither withdrawing funds from the estate either as interest or as capital, nor adding to the estate out of his own resources. An estate is thus kept intact if interest earnings are added back to the estate, while transfer taxes payable as the estate passes from hand to hand and income taxes attributable to the interest earned by the estate are paid out of the estate itself. An intermediate holder who keeps an estate intact in this sense and then passes it on to others is then neither better nor worse off as a result of having thus held the estate.

Let us suppose that if testator A has an estate valued at a and bequeaths the entire estate to F, the net estate remaining to F after the payment of transfer taxes will be f. We may say then that the estate a in A's hands represents the power to bestow a net estate of f on F. Now if A transfers the estate to some intermediary B instead of directly to F, then the net estate b remaining in B's hands after paying the tax on this transfer must be just sufficient, if our condition is to be satisfied, for B in turn to be able to bestow a net estate of f on F, otherwise the tax burden on a transfer from A to F directly would differ from the burden imposed when the transfer is made through B as an intermediary. We may say, then, that the bequeathing power of the net estate b in B's hands is the same as the bequeathing power of the net estate a in A's hands. Indeed if A were to transfer the estate to any other person C, D, or E instead of to B, the net estates c, d, or e that they would thus obtain after payment of transfer taxes must represent in their respective hands this same bequeathing power, if the condition that the tax burden be independent of the channel is to be fulfilled. Thus as long as a given estate is maintained intact,

---

[a]   The reader is warned of difficult reading ahead. The concepts presented in the following pages are entirely new and markedly different from those involved in any form of taxation heretofore attempted. * * * Yet the new concepts are believed to be significant enough amply to reward the careful reader.

it must always represent the same bequeathing power, even though the payment of taxes out of the estate as it passes from hand to hand leaves varying net amounts in the hands of different holders.

Now if we know the size of the estate that corresponds to a given amount of bequeathing power in the hands of different holders, the tax to be paid on the transfer of the estate from one holder to another can be determined; in fact the tax will be the difference between the net estates corresponding to the given bequeathing power. Thus in the above example, the tax on the transfer from A to B is simply $(a - b)$, the tax on the transfer from B to F is $(b - f)$, and so on. In order to put such a tax into operation, all that is necessary is to assign some arbitrary numerical value to a given bequeathing power, and to set up some relation between the size of the net estate and the bequeathing power that it represents in the hands of different holders.

Behavior of the Bequeathing Power Function

In order to imply the payment of a suitable tax as the estate is passed on from one hand to another and from one generation to the next, the relation between bequeathing power and the corresponding net estate may be made to depend on the date of birth of the holder. If a given estate is kept intact, the bequeathing power that it represents will remain unchanged as the estate is passed from one hand to another, but the tax due on successive transfers will be reflected in the decrease in the size of the net estate corresponding to this fixed bequeathing power as the estate is passed from older to younger holders. A given bequeathing power, regardless of the person in whom it is vested, will always represent a power of that person to bestow a net estate of a given fixed size on another given individual. However, the exercise of a given bequeathing power by conferring the corresponding gross gift or bequest (inclusive of the transfer tax) on different beneficiaries will incur different taxes and thus confer different estates (net after tax). In general, the younger the beneficiary the larger the tax incurred and the smaller the net estate conferred by the exercise of a given amount of bequeathing power. This differentiation is in the same general direction as that produced by graduating the inheritance tax by age differences.

A transfer which involves a given decrease in the bequeathing power of the donor will produce an equal increase in the bequeathing power of the recipient: one can in this sense say that bequeathing power is in general transferred undiminished from donor to recipient, even though a tax is levied and the estate becomes smaller.

Bequeathing Power Illustrated

For example, the following table could be taken as showing the relation between the net inherited estate and the corresponding bequeathing power for individuals of different ages for transfers effected in the year 1950:

Table 2

Abstract of Bequeathing Power Table for 1950

Holder of estate:	A	B	C	D	E	F
Date of birth:	1860	1880	1900	1910	1920	1940
Age in 1950:	90	70	50	40	30	10

Bequeathing Power (Thousands of units)	Net Inherited Estate (Thousands of dollars)					
0	0	0	0	0	0	0
2,000	1,053	706	429	323	238	123
4,000	1,657	1,052	611	451	328	161
6,000	2,135	1,320	751	545	388	187
8,000	2,542	1,550	858	619	438	208
10,000	2,911	1,748	952	682	480	226
12,000	3,252	1,920	1,036	729	518	242

Thus if *B* has an inherited[c] estate of $1,748,000, this estate would carry with it a bequeathing power of 10 million units, according to the above table. Similarly, 10 million bequeathing power units correspond to a net estate of $952,000 in *C*'s hands, and accordingly if *B* bestows his entire inherited estate upon *C*, *C* will receive, net after taxes, an estate of $952,000, and the tax payable on this transfer is therefore $1,748,000 − $952,000, or $796,000. Similarly, if the estate were bestowed by *B* upon *F*, *F* would receive a net estate of $226,000, and the tax on the transfer would be $1,522,000. But 10 million units of bequeathing power, no matter in whose hands they are vested, always represent the power to bestow $226,000 upon *F*; accordingly, if *C* were to get the estate from *B* and then turn around and transfer it to *F*, the tax on this second transfer would be $726,000 (952 − 226 = 726), and the total tax on the two transfers would be the same as though *B* had transferred the estate directly to *F*. With this method of determining the tax, it is easy to see that no matter how many intermediate hands the estate passes through, if the entire net estate is eventually bestowed upon *F* the net estate that *F* receives will be the same, and the total tax burden will be the same. The bequeathing power is transmitted unchanged, and since when this bequeathing power is finally vested in *F* it always produces the same net estate, whatever the route it has taken and whatever the number of intervening transfers, the tax must perforce be the same.

Taxes on transfers of parts of estates are computed in a corresponding manner. If for example *C*, having a net estate of $952,000, wishes to bestow only $187,000 on *F*, this will require the exercise of 6 million units of bequeathing power; *C* therefore retains 4 million units of bequeathing power, which permits him to retain $611,000 out of the estate; the tax on this transfer will then be $154,000 (952 − 187 − 611 = 154). If *C* then transfers this remaining estate to *D*, *D* will get $451,000 and the tax will be $160,000 (611 − 451 = 160); and if *D* then transfers this estate to *F*, the additional 4 million units of bequeathing power will raise *F*'s net estate from $187,000 to $226,000 and the tax on this last transaction will be $412,000 (451 + 187 − 226 = 412). Again the total tax payable on these successive transfers is the same as on the direct transfer of the entire estate from *B* to *F* (796 + 154 + 160 + 412 = 1,522).

---

[c]   For the time being discussion is limited to estates that have been received by inheritance from previous donors; estates that are built up out of the earnings of the present holder require separate treatment as will be explained below * * * .

Residual Bequeathing Power

If C should not pass the remaining $611,000 on to some beneficiary, but consumes this part of the estate himself, then in effect C will have used up the remaining bequeathing power by such consumption and having no property will be unable to make further gifts. Similarly, if he first consumes the $611,000, the remaining $341,000 will represent a bequeathing power available for making transfers of only 6 million units, instead of the 10 million units he received from B. Transfers of part of an estate take bequeathing power from the top of the scale of graduation, while consumption takes bequeathing power from the bottom of the scale of graduation; in this way if an individual's resources are gone before the gifts and bequests made by him have exhausted the bequeathing power transferred to him along with previous gifts and bequests received, then this leftover bequeathing power is that which he has absorbed himself through consumption of part of the bequests left to him.

Generated Bequeathing Power

We also have the opposite case, where an individual consumes less than the income he obtains from his own activities, and so has an estate to pass on to heirs that is greater than the amounts that he has inherited, together with the interest that has been earned on these inheritances. In such cases, the inherited bequeathing power will be exhausted before he has disposed of his entire fortune. After the gifts and bequests made by an individual have used up his inherited bequeathing power, further gifts and bequests will be coming from his own savings. We can set up another relation between the amount of such savings and the bequeathing power they represent: one possible relation is merely to use the same table for the relation between bequeathing power and inherited wealth as for the relation between bequeathing power and saved wealth. Thus if in addition to his inheritance, C saves $429,000 out of his earnings, we can assign to this savings a bequeathing power of 2 million units, which raises the total available bequeathing power to 12 million units. If C bestows his entire estate, both that inherited and that accumulated from his own savings, upon F, F will then receive $242,000, and the tax will be $1,139,000 ($429 + 952 - 242 = 1,139$).

The Time Factor

The above examples have for simplicity assumed that all the transfers take place at substantially the same time. Actually transfers will take place at different times, and to some extent the donor may have a choice as to the time at which he will make the transfer. It may be considered desirable that as long as the current holder of an estate consumes no part of it, but accumulates the interest and passes the estate on intact (except for taxes) with accumulated interest to his successor, the tax burden should not be affected by any change in the time at which the transfer takes place. This can be done readily enough by making the estate that corresponds to a given bequeathing power in the hands of a given individual increase with the passage of time, at compound interest. For example, if we assume interest to be 4%, the relation between bequeathing power and net estate in 1960, 10 years later, would be as follows:

Table 3

Abstract of Bequeathing Power Table for 1960

Holder of estate:	A	B	C	D	E	F
Date of birth:	1860	1880	1900	1910	1920	1940
Age in 1960:	100	80	60	50	40	20

Bequeathing Power (Thousands of units)	Net Inherited Estate (Thousands of dollars)					
2,000	1,558	1,045	635	478	352	182
4,000	2,452	1,557	904	667	485	243
6,000	3,160	1,954	1,111	807	574	277
8,000	3,762	2,294	1,270	916	648	308
10,000	4,308	2,687	1,409	1,009	710	334
12,000	4,813	2,846	1,533	1,094	766	358

Each estate is 1.48 times as large as 10 years previously. Thus if *C*, instead of passing the $952,000 estate on immediately to *F*, had kept it for 10 years, accumulating the interest, it would amount to $1,409,000. This estate would still represent a bequeathing power of 10 million units, but 10 million units now, in 1960, represent the power to bestow an estate of $334,000 on *F*. Accordingly, if the transfer is made in 1960 instead of 1950, *F* will get $334,000, which is what he could have obtained had he received the $226,000 in 1950 and accumulated the interest earned on this estate for the 10 years. The tax payable in 1960 is $1,075,000, which if discounted at 4% back to 1950 has the same present value as the $726,000 tax that would have been paid had the transfer taken place in 1950. Thus the burden is not affected by the time at which the transfer takes place.

* * *

Starting at Zero Bequeathing Power

To put such a scheme of taxation into effect, all that is necessary is to provide some means whereby the taxpayer can compute the bequeathing power corresponding to a given net estate. It is not actually necessary to value all the assets of the taxpayer each time that a transfer is made, but only the assets involved in the transfer; a comprehensive valuation is necessary only on the death of the taxpayer, just as at present. Taxes on gifts inter vivos can be computed as though the wealth of each party were no greater than that revealed by the current transfer and those in which the taxpayers have previously been involved. In effect, each taxpayer can be considered to start with a bequeathing power of zero. Each time he receives a gift or bequest, a corresponding addition is made to his inherited bequeathing power, and each time a gift is made, a corresponding subtraction is made from this inherited bequeathing power. When the inherited bequeathing power is exhausted by such subtractions, any further gifts and bequests will necessarily be out of his own savings and will produce an addition to his generated bequeathing power.

A taxpayer may indeed have savings and hence generated bequeathing power in excess of the amount so revealed, but it is not necessary to take it into account until it is disclosed by the making of further gifts and bequests. Similarly if a taxpayer has consumed part of his inheritance he will no longer be able to exercise the full bequeathing power indicated by the inheritance, but again this need not be taken into account until revealed by the small size of his estate.

Generated bequeathing power can be thought of as the negative counterpart of inherited bequeathing power, in that the gifts a taxpayer makes diminish his inherited bequeathing power until it is reduced to zero, after which they act to increase the amount of generated bequeathing power revealed. Similarly, if a person is on the generated bequeathing power side of the scale, the receipt of gifts or bequests offsets the gifts that he previously has made and reduces his rating on that side of the scale and moves him back toward the inherited bequeathing power side. A taxpayer who is currently on the inherited side of the scale has inherited to date more than he has distributed, whereas the taxpayer on the generated side has to date distributed more than he has inherited.

Upon the death of the taxpayer, the distribution of his estate will not in general reduce the final bequeathing power rating of the taxpayer to zero. The net value of his estate may be more or less than the net estate corresponding to the amount of inherited bequeathing power not yet exercised. If the estate is found to be less, then the final bequeathing power rating produced by the distribution of the estate will be on the positive or inherited wealth side, and will indicate that the taxpayer has consumed part of his inheritance or the income therefrom, and has thus reduced the amount of bequeathing power in circulation by using some of it for his own consumption. If, on the other hand, the estate is found to be greater than that indicated by the bequeathing power immediately before death, distribution of the estate will bring the bequeathing power rating to the negative or generated side of the scale, indicating that the taxpayer has consumed less than the income that he has himself produced during his lifetime, and accordingly has made a net addition to the total bequeathing power in circulation.

In effect, inherited bequeathing power is recognized as soon as it accrues through the receipt of gifts or bequests, and is cancelled as it is used; generated bequeathing power is recognized only as it is exercised and only after inherited bequeathing power has been exhausted.

Type of Tables Required

The actual computation of the bequeathing power from the net inherited wealth and vice versa can conceivably be done in a number of ways, as for example by a formula. But in practice the easiest method is probably to provide the taxpayer with sets of tables which will permit him to ascertain readily the amount of inherited wealth w corresponding to a given bequeathing power P at a given time t and for a taxpayer with a given birth date b, and conversely to compute P when w, t, and b are known. Tables will be needed both for the relation between net inherited wealth and net inherited bequeathing power (positive values of P and w) and for the relation between generated bequeathing power and net distributed wealth (negative values of P and w).

The taxpayer need not of course be concerned with the details of the way in which the tables are set up, any more than he is concerned with the methods of deriving the present surtax tables or the withholding schedules. Of course, for his general guidance in determining how to distribute his estate (as contrasted with the channels through which it is to be distributed to the ultimate recipients, differences in which will no longer affect the tax burden) the taxpayer should be made familiar with the general properties of the tax, for example, the fact that the ultimate total tax burden will be the same regardless of how a given distribution of an estate is effected, or the fact that the larger the number of beneficiaries and the older they are the smaller will be the tax on the distribution of a given estate. But at any one time, taxpayers will be concerned with only one value of t, so that during the year the only tables necessary to use are a set of tables giving the bequeathing power P in terms of the wealth w and age of the taxpayer b, and conversely giving w in terms of P and b for the current year. A new set of tables would be used each year, but only one set at a time.

* * *

Procedure for Computing Tax

With such tables set up, the computation of the tax on a given transfer would proceed as follows: Donor and recipient would both carry forward from a previous return their respective *P*'s (or bequeathing power ratings) as of after the previous transfer, which will be the same as those as of before the present transfer. From the table they would both compute their respective corresponding initial *w*'s. If the donor has decided to give a certain amount gross of tax, he will then deduct this gross gift from his initial *w* to get his new *w* as of after the transaction. By again referring to the tables he obtains the new *P* corresponding to this new *w*. The amount by which this new *P* is less than the old is the amount of bequeathing power to be exercised in favor of the recipient and transferred to him. This reduction in the *P* of the donor is added to the initial *P* of the recipient to get the final *P* of the recipient, and from this new *P* the tables will again give the recipient's new *w*. The excess of this new *w* over the recipient's old *w* will then be the amount he is entitled to receive net after tax, and the difference between this net gift and the gross amount surrendered by the donor is the tax to be paid.

Where it is desired to give a net amount free of tax, the computation is merely done in the reverse order. Adding the net gift to the recipient's old *w* gives his new *w*, from which the tables give his new *P*. The excess of this new *P* over the old *P* is the amount of bequeathing power required to make such a gift, and is accordingly the amount by which the old *P* of the donor must be reduced to obtain his new *P*. Entering the tables with this new *P*, the new *w* of the donor is obtained, and subtracting this from the old *w* gives the gross cost of the gift. Subtracting the net amount of the gift from this gross gift determines the tax to be paid.

This method of computing the tax can be applied to cases involving generated bequeathing power as well as inherited bequeathing power. All that is necessary is to treat generated bequeathing power as having a negative sign, and likewise to treat the corresponding *w*'s as having a negative sign. That is, if a positive *w* indicates that to date there has been an excess of inheritances and gifts received over gifts made, a negative *w* will logically enough indicate that to date the individual has distributed more than he has received. Similarly, positive values of *P* which will correspond to positive values of *w* will indicate that the individual has so far used [less than his inherited bequeathing power] in making gifts, and conversely a negative *P*, corresponding to negative values of *w* indicates that an individual, by making gifts in excess of his inherited wealth and hence out of his own savings, has passed on to others bequeathing power in excess of that which he has inherited. If we do this the algebraic signs will automatically take care of the combining of inherited wealth with personally saved wealth, and of combining inherited bequeathing power with generated bequeathing power.

For example, if *B* in Table 2 * * * has an inherited bequeathing power of 2 million units carried forward, while *D* has an inherited bequeathing power of 4 million units carried forward, and *B* wishes to give $231,000 to *D* free of tax, the computation would be made as follows: *B*'s initial *w* is found from the table to be $706,000 (inherited), and *D*'s initial *w* is similarly found from the table to be $451,000 (also inherited). Adding the proposed net gift, *D*'s final *w* will be $682,000 (inherited) which from the table is found to require raising *D*'s inherited bequeathing power to 10 million units, an increase of 6 million. Deducting this 6 million units from *B*'s initial 2 million units gives *B*'s final bequeathing power as –4 million units (generated). If we assume that the same table is to be used on both sides of the scale, this –4 million units corresponds to a final *w* of –$1,052,000. Subtracting this algebraically from the initial *w* of $706,000 gives $1,758,000 as the gross cost of the gift, and deducting the net gift gives $1,527,000 as the tax payable. That *B* ends up with a negative *P* indicates that part of the gift must come out of *B*'s own savings, the amount of wealth inherited by *B* being insufficient to make such a gift.

It should be noted that, while the P of any given individual stays constant during the periods between transfers, the w's do not stay constant but vary as a result of the accumulation of interest. They therefore cannot be carried forward from one return to the next, but are most conveniently computed anew from the P's. * * *

* * *

NOTE

Vickrey's proposal has been hailed by theorists because it specifies a progressive tax which depends primarily on age differences between transferors and recipients, without regard to the number of intermediate transfers. *See* CARL S. SHOUP, FEDERAL ESTATE AND GIFT TAXES 102 (1966) (describing proposal as "the only fairly loophole-proof formula that has yet been devised to assure transfer taxation once a generation"). Gilbert P. Verbit characterizes Vickrey's proposal as "an accessions tax system" because it "correlat[es] the tax on the transfer directly with the age difference between the donor and the ultimate recipient" and taxes legacies to the recipient "on a cumulative basis, i.e., at the marginal rate for the total lifetime gifts and inheritances *received* by the legatee." Gilbert Paul Verbit, *Annals of Tax Reform: The Generation-Skipping Transfer*, 25 UCLA L. REV. 700, 703 (1978). Does this self-adjusting feature make Vickrey's proposal more attractive than other proposals discussed in this Part? Why do you suppose a bequeathing power succession tax has received so little attention from subsequent reformers?